W9-BZU-054

Rick Steves

SCOTLAND

Rick Steves with Cameron Hewitt

CONTENTS

Welcome to Rick Steves' Europe

Travel is intensified living—maximum thrills per minute and one of the last great sources of legal adventure. Travel is freedom. It's recess, and we need it.

I discovered a passion for European travel as a teen and have been sharing it ever since—through my tours, public television and radio shows, and travel guidebooks. Over the years, I've taught millions of travelers how to best enjoy Europe's blockbuster sights—and experience "Back Door" discoveries that most tourists miss.

This book offers a balanced mix of Scotland's rich cultural heritage and the rugged beauty of its countryside. It's selective: Rather than listing every island, I recommend only the best. And it's in-depth: My self-guided city walks and driving tours provide insight into the country's vibrant history and today's living, breathing culture.

I advocate traveling simply and smartly. Take advantage of my money- and time-saving tips on sightseeing, transportation, and more. Try local, characteristic alternatives to expensive hotels and restaurants. In many ways, spending more money only builds a thicker wall between you and what you traveled so far to see.

We visit Scotland to experience it—to become temporary locals. Thoughtful travel engages us with the world, as we learn to appreciate other cultures and new ways to measure quality of life.

Judging by the positive feedback I receive from readers, this book will help you enjoy a fun, affordable, and rewarding vacation—whether it's your first trip or your tenth.

Happy travels!

Rick Steves

SCOTLAND

Rugged, colorful, and feisty, Scotland stands apart. From its stony architecture to its unmanicured landscape to the laid-back nature of its people—and their peculiar fondness for haggis—this little land packs a big punch. A proud identity unites the sparsely populated country, all the way from the southern Lowlands, which border England just north of Hadrian's Wall, up to the Norwegian latitudes of the rocky Highlands and remote coastal islands.

Scotland is one of three countries, along with England and Wales, that make up Great Britain. Add Northern Ireland, and you've got the United Kingdom (UK). Scotland is not a sovereign state (it shares the monarchy with the rest of the UK), but it is a "nation" in that it has its own traditions, ethnic identity, languages, and football league. To some extent, it even has its own government.

In modern times, Scotland has enjoyed its greatest measure of political autonomy in centuries—the Scottish parliament convened in 1999 for the first time in almost 300 years. Though its powers are limited (most major decisions are still made in London), the Scottish people are enjoying increased self-governance. The question of total independence from the UK remains a pivotal issue in Scottish politics.

Scotland even has its own currency...sort of. Scotland uses the same coins as England, Wales, and Northern Ireland but prints its own bills, featuring Scottish rather than English people and landmarks. Fortunately for visitors, all UK currency works throughout the UK.

Building-size murals enliven Glasgow's streets; Arthur's Seat hovers over Edinburgh's old town.

Across Scotland, fortunes were long tied to the sea; leading cities are all located along firths (estuaries), where major rivers connect to ocean waters. Outside the main cities, Scotland's sights are subtle, but the misty glens, brooding castles, wind-swept moors, peaty whisky, and warm culture are plenty engaging. The northern Highlands feature a wild, undulating terrain, punctuated by lochs (lakes) and fringed by sea lochs (inlets) and islands. The southern Lowlands are relatively flat and urbanized.

The geologic fault line that divides the Highlands from the Lowlands also divides Scotland culturally. Historically, the country had two distinct identities: refined Lowlanders in the southern flatlands, and rougher Highlanders in the northern wilderness. After the 16th-century Scottish Reformation, the Lowlanders embraced Protestantism, while most Highlanders stuck to Catholicism.

Today, the Lowlands are dominated by rival cities: bustling Edinburgh, on the east coast, and friendly Glasgow, on the west. Edinburgh, the capital, teems with history and is rich in culture. It's been home to esteemed writers (Robert Burns, Robert Louis Stevenson, Sir Walter Scott) and hosts a huge international arts festival every August. Glasgow, once gloomy and industrial, is now a hip, laid-back center of art, music, and architecture. Other Lowlands highlights include the town of

The Kilt

The kilt, Scotland's national dress, is intimately tied to the country's history. It originated in the 1500s as a multipurpose robe, toga, tent, poncho, and ground cloth. A wearer would lay a length of fabric (roughly 2 x 6 yards) on the ground, scrunch it up into pleats, then wrap it around the waist and belt it. Extra fabric was thrown over the shoulder or tucked into the belt, creating both a rakish sash and a rucksack-like pouch.

The colors and patterns of the first kilts depended on who wove them and what dyes were available in a locale (colors were muted, unlike later kilts). Because members of one clan tended to live in the same area, they often wore similar patterns—but they weren't specifically designed to represent a single clan.

The kilt became standard Highlands dress and a patriotic statement during conflicts with England. After the tragic-for-Scotland Battle of Culloden in 1746, the victorious English dismantled the Scottish clan system. Wearing the kilt, speaking Gaelic, and playing the bagpipes were all outlawed.

In 1782, kilts were permitted again, but by then the tradition had faded, and many Scots no longer wanted to wear one. Then, in 1822 King George IV visited Edinburgh (the first royal visit in 200 years). In a not-so-subtle assertion of his authority over Scotland, he wore a kilt. That bit of pageantry charmed Scottish noblemen, and the kilt was in vogue once more.

Custom kilt shops offer colorful tartans; King George IV on his 1822 trip to Edinburgh

During the king's visit, Sir Walter Scott organized a Highland festival that reinvented and romanticized the image of traditional Scottish culture, giving it a newfound respectability. The brightly colored "clan ▶▶▶

▶▶▶ tartans" you'll see in Scottish souvenir shops got their start at this time, as fabric salesmen hastily designed and assigned patterns to particular clans to capitalize on the newfound enthusiasm for kilts.

A generation later, Queen Victoria enhanced the cachet of the kilt even more. She loved Scotland and wallpapered her palace at Balmoral with tartan patterns and wore dresses made from tartan fabric. Since then, tartanry has been embraced as if it were historic. (By the way, Scots use these key terms differently than Americans do: "Tartan" is the pattern itself, while "plaid" is the piece of cloth worn over the shoulder with a kilt.)

If shopping for a kilt, consider where you'll wear it. Unless you want just a casual kilt for festivals and pubs, the rule of thumb is to get the best you can afford, since it never goes out of style. You'll choose a tartan and fabric weight (a heavier weight is considered higher quality, hangs well, and is easier to press). The kilt should sit high on the waist a couple of inches above the hip bone.

Kilt-related gear includes the kilt pin, worn on the front fringed side of the kilt; kilt hose (socks) and flashes (sock garters, with a decorative ribbon that peeks from the sock cuff); the sporran, the leather pouch worn around the waist; and the *sgian dubh* ("black knife"), the short blade worn in the top of the sock. Traditional shoes worn with kilts are ghillie brogues, with laces wrapped around the ankles and tied in front. ◼

You'll still find traditional dress in today's Scotland; the art of custom kiltmaking; standard kilt accessories include the leather pouch, worn at the waist, and the sgian dubh *knife, tucked into a sock.*

Stirling with its grand castle, and the university town and golf mecca of St. Andrews.

In contrast, the Highlands are rugged and remote. Once the home of rival clans, this region is now the domain of nature lovers. Here you'll experience what many think of as traditional Scotland: weathered bluffs, countryside castles, whisky distilleries, deep lochs, heather-strewn moors, and lush green mountains (called Munros). Throughout the summer, towns host traditional Highland Games, where travelers can enjoy a full dose of Scottish culture in a day. To the tune of bagpipes, locals compete in contests of intricate Highland dancing and feats of strength from stone lifting to caber tossing (log throwing).

While the Highlands' most touristed city is modern Inverness, the region's beauty is best experienced in the countryside, in smaller towns like Oban and on the islands. Those who really want to get off the beaten path head up the mountainous west coast to Britain's northeastern tip (at John O'Groats), then ferry to the Orkney Islands.

At these northern latitudes, cold and drizzly weather isn't uncommon—even in midsummer. The blazing sun can quickly give way to dark clouds and howling wind. Your B&B host will warn you to prepare for "four seasons in one day."

Even in "English-speaking" Scotland, you may encounter a language barrier. The lovely, lilting Scottish brogue may take a while to understand. You may also hear an impenetrable dialect of Scottish English that many linguists consider to be

Whisky tasting at Talisker Distillery; historic Urquhart Castle perched on the shores of Loch Ness

Scotland's loveable cow, the hairy coo; clinking glasses in one of Scotland's fine pubs

a separate language, called "Scots" (you already know several Scots words: lad, lassie, wee, bonnie, glen, loch, and aye). And about one percent of the population, particularly in the Highlands, speaks the ancient Celtic language of Gaelic (pronounced "gallic").

Travelers of Scottish descent enjoy coming "home" to Scotland. If you're Scottish, your surname will tell you which clan your ancestors likely belonged to. The prefix "Mac" (or "Mc") means "son of"—so "MacDonald" means the same thing as "Donaldson." Tourist shops everywhere can help you track down the distinctive plaid pattern of your clan's tartan.

Rural Scotland offers more natural beauty than tourist attractions, and you'll encounter engaging friendliness everywhere. Whether toasting with beer, whisky, or Irn-Bru (Scotland's favorite soft drink), you'll enjoy meeting the Scottish people. It's easy to fall in love with the irrepressible spirit and beautiful landscape of this faraway corner of Britain.

Scotland's Top Destinations

This bonnie wee country offers plenty to see. This overview sorts its top destinations by location—Lowlands or Highlands—and ranks them into must-see sights (to help you prioritize) and worth-it sights (if you have extra time or special interests). I've also suggested a minimum number of days to allow per destination.

NORTHERN SCOTLAND

50 Kilometers

50 Miles

ISLE OF SKYE

INVERNESS & LOCH NESS

EASTERN SCOTLAND

GLENCOE & FORT WILLIAM

OBAN & THE INNER HEBRIDES

STIRLING & NEARBY

North Sea

ST. ANDREWS

GLASGOW

EDINBURGH

Irish Sea

SCOTLAND

PLACES COVERED IN THIS BOOK

▲▲▲ Must See
▲▲ Try Hard to See
▲ Worthwhile

ENGLAND

THE LOWLANDS

Southern Scotland's vibrant cities and excellent museums provide a superb introduction to Scottish culture and history.

▲▲▲Edinburgh (allow 2-3 days)

Tucked amid bluffs, Scotland's delightful capital boasts world-class museums and lively culture. The attraction-studded Royal Mile, lined with medieval buildings, connects a grand castle at one end with a stately palace at the other. The city's exuberance is enjoyable year-round and nonstop during August's festivals.

▲▲Glasgow (2 days)

Glasgow, once a mighty ship-building center, is now rejuvenated, funky, and fun, offering warm hospitality, great food and nightlife, top-notch museums, and a treasure trove of Art Nouveau architecture, courtesy of Charles Rennie MacKintosh.

▲▲St. Andrews (half-day)

This coastal town hosts Scotland's top university and the world's most famous golf course. With a medieval old town, cathedral ruins, sandy beaches, and a student vibe, St. Andrews attracts visitors of all ages, whether they prefer tee time, teatime, or a fun time. Dundee (with fine museums) and the East Neuk's seaside villages are nearby.

▲Stirling & Nearby (1 day)

Stirling proudly showcases the home of the Stuart kings, Stirling Castle, overlooking a historic plain where three pivotal battles were fought. Falkirk, to the south, has the Kelpies (a gigantic sculpture of horse heads) and a working Ferris wheel for boats. To the north are Doune Castle and the wooded glens known as the Trossachs.

Lively locals at the Edinburgh Festival; teeing off in St. Andrews; giant Kelpies sculptures near Falkirk; Glasgow's Art Nouveau

Finding serenity on the Isle of Iona; Inverness footbridge spanning the River Ness; sheepdogs running the show at a Highlands sheep farm; hiking amid the blooms in Glencoe

THE HIGHLANDS

Northern Scotland's scenic beauty shines in the Highlands, bordered by quaint ports and islands, and dotted with castles, distilleries, historic battlefields, and sweeping loch and mountain vistas.

▲▲Oban & the Inner Hebrides (1 day)
The handy home base of Oban hosts a fine distillery tour and boat excursions. This charming "gateway to the isles" is the jumping-off point for day trips by ferry to the islands of the Inner Hebrides: hilly Mull, spiritual Iona, and small Staffa, populated by puffins in summer.

▲Glencoe & Fort William (1 day)
The stirring "Weeping Glen" of Glencoe offers some of the Highlands' saddest clan history and best mountain scenery, with hikes ranging from easy to strenuous. And all roads pass through the transit-hub town of Fort William, leading to the historic Road to the Isles (to the Isle of Skye and more).

▲▲Inverness & Loch Ness (1 day)
Considered the capital of the Highlands, modern Inverness is a springboard to nearby sights, including Culloden Battlefield (where Bonnie Prince Charlie was defeated), Loch Ness (famous for monster spotting), the ruins of medieval Urquhart Castle, and the tranquil Caledonian Canal.

▲Eastern Scotland (2 days)
Appealing sights between Inverness and Edinburgh include Pitlochry (a town known for whisky and hill walking), an early Iron Age crannog site on Loch Tay, sheepdog shows, the distilleries of Speyside, the Queen's retreat at Balmoral Castle, and cliff-topping Dunnottar Castle.

▲▲Isle of Skye (1 day)

The dramatically scenic island—the best of the Inner Hebrides—offers a concentrated dose of the Highlands, featuring craggy Cuillin Hills, the jagged Trotternish Peninsula, castles galore, a distillery, dynamic clan history, and the colorful harbor town of Portree.

▲Northern Scotland (2-4 days)

This remote, less-touristed region includes Wester Ross (the mountainous west coast, with winding, narrow roads), the beachy north coast, and the intriguing Orkney Islands—with Scotland's best prehistoric sites, evocative Old Norse history, and a naval harbor with a fascinating wartime past.

Barrel makers at the Speyside Cooperage; the old Sligachan Bridge, Isle of Skye; Neolithic settlement at Skara Brae, Orkney Islands

Planning Your Trip

To plan your trip, you'll need to design your itinerary—choosing where and when to go, how you'll travel, and how many days to spend at each destination. For my best general advice on sightseeing, accommodations, restaurants, and more, see the Practicalities chapter.

DESIGNING AN ITINERARY

As you read this book and learn your options...

Choose your top destinations.

My recommended itinerary (on the next page) gives you an idea of how much you can reasonably see in 14 days, but you can adapt it to fit your own interests and time frame.

Edinburgh and, on a smaller scale, Glasgow offer the most art, architecture, history, and nightlife.

Nature lovers add extra time in the Highlands for hiking in Glencoe and on the Isle of Skye. For fun, fit in a Highland Game or the Leault sheepdog demonstration (near Inverness). Golfers make a pilgrimage to St. Andrews.

Whisky aficionados savor Speyside and Pitlochry (though most any town offers tastings). Prehistorians prioritize Kilmartin Glen (near Oban), the Crannog Centre (Loch Tay), Clava Cairns (near Inverness), and the Orkney Islands.

Those interested in Scotland's industrial heritage check out the Caledonian Canal, Falkirk Wheel, and museums in Dundee.

If you're crazy for castles, tour Edinburgh, Dunvegan (Isle of Skye), and Stirling. (There are many more; see "Scottish Castles at a Glance" in the Past & Present chapter for a list.)

Scotland's Best Two-Week Trip by Car

Taking geographic proximity into account, I've organized my recommended sightseeing priorities into a doable two-week itinerary. Except for the two city stops at the outset, you'll travel by car.

Day	Plan	Sleep in
1	Arrive in Edinburgh	Edinburgh
2	Edinburgh	Edinburgh
3	Edinburgh	Edinburgh
4	More time in Edinburgh, then train to Glasgow	Glasgow
5	Glasgow	Glasgow
6	Pick up car; drive to Oban	Oban
7	Side trip to Mull and Iona	Oban
8	Drive through Glencoe this morning, then to Isle of Skye	Isle of Skye
9	Isle of Skye	Isle of Skye
10	Drive along Caledonian Canal and Loch Ness to Inverness	Inverness
11	Inverness and side trip to Culloden and other sights	Inverness
12	Head south, enjoying your choice of sights in Eastern Scotland or St. Andrews	Pitlochry, Ballater, or St. Andrews
13	More Eastern Scotland or St. Andrews sightseeing; spend evening in Stirling	Stirling
14	Stirling Castle and nearby sights	Stirling
15	Drive to Edinburgh for your flight home	

Without a Car: While this two-week itinerary is designed to be done by car, most connections can be made by bus, with a few modifications: You may want to rent a car for your day on Skye; consider a package tour for Highland side-tripping from Inverness; and at the end, go from Inverness straight to Stirling (skipping Eastern Scotland sights, which are out of the way by public transit).

Notes: If cities aren't your thing, you can see more of the countryside by skipping Glasgow, or by doing it at the end, as a day trip from Stirling or Edinburgh.

With more time, there are many ways to slow down and linger in the Highlands. Stretch out your visit by adding an overnight in Glencoe (more time for hiking) and/or Wester Ross (more scenery). If you loop around the north of Scotland, consider a two-night trip to the Orkney Islands (see the Scottish Highlands chapter for more details).

Boats ferry you to Scotland's many islands; if you're looking for a bagpipe, you can buy one here.

Castle ruins set in the scenic Highlands can be stunning, though photographers will be happy wherever they go.

Decide when to go.

While Scotland never quite feels crowded, it can get busy. Most tourists visit between mid-May and mid-September. In most of Scotland, July and August offer the best weather and busiest schedule of tourist fun—and consequently jam-packed B&Bs and restaurants. Edinburgh is especially swamped throughout August, the city's festival season. Any town is busy during its Highland Games.

Travel from April to mid-May and mid-September to mid-October is easier. Those times tend to have fewer tourists, a full range of sights, and better room availability (and prices). In the off-season, castles and historic sites may be closed, but cities welcome visitors any time of year.

Temperatures below 32°F cause headlines, and days that break 80°F—while more frequent in recent years—are still rare in Scotland. While sunshine may be uncommon, summer daylight hours are very long (6:30-22:30). Any season can have rainy spells. For weather specifics, see the climate chart in the appendix.

Trip Costs Per Person

Run a reality check on your dream trip. You'll have major transportation costs in addition to daily expenses.

Flight: A round-trip flight from the US to Edinburgh costs about $900-1,500, depending on where you fly from and when.

Transportation: For a two-week trip, allow $250 per person for public transportation (train and bus tickets). A short flight can be cheaper than the train.

Car Rental: Allow roughly $250 per week, not including tolls, gas, parking, and insurance.

AVERAGE DAILY EXPENSES PER PERSON

$160
Applies to cities, figure on less for towns

Lodging
Based on two people splitting the cost of a $140 double room (includes breakfast)
★★★★★
$70

Meals
$15 for lunch and $35 for dinner
$50

City Transit
Buses or trams
$10

Sights and Entertainment
This daily average works for most people.
$30

Budget Tips

To cut your daily expenses, take advantage of the deals you'll find throughout Scotland and mentioned in this book.

The Historic Scotland Explorer Pass can save some money if you visit the castles in both Edinburgh and Stirling, or are also going to the Orkney Islands. Throughout Scotland, prioritize the sights you most want to see, and seek out free sights and experiences (people-watching counts).

Some businesses—especially hotels and walking-tour companies—offer discounts to my readers (look for the RS% symbol in the listings in this book).

Book your rooms directly ▶▶▶

Rick Steves Scotland

▶▶▶ with the hotel. Some hotels offer a discount if you pay in cash and/or stay three or more nights (check online or ask). Rooms cost less in early spring and late fall. And even seniors can sleep cheap in hostels (some have double rooms) for about $30 per person. Or check Airbnb-type sites for deals.

It's no hardship to eat cheap in Scotland. You can get tasty, inexpensive meals at bakeries, cafeterias, sandwich shops, pubs, cheap chain restaurants, and takeaway spots. Cultivate the art of picnicking in atmospheric settings.

When you splurge, choose an experience you'll always remember, such as a fancy dinner, a scenic bus tour, or a flight to the Orkney Islands. Minimize souvenir shopping; focus instead on collecting wonderful memories. ◼

Try the catch of the day; observe puffins on the Isle of Staffa; sip tea at Glasgow's famous Art Nouveau tearoom.

Connect the dots.

Link your destinations into a logical route. Determine which cities you'll fly into and out of. Begin your search for transatlantic flights at Kayak.com.

Decide if you'll travel by car or public transportation, or a combination. For Scotland, a combination works well: Connect the big cities by train, then rent a car for the Highlands.

If relying on public transportation, you'll generally use trains in the Lowlands and a mix of buses and trains in the hilly Highlands. To reach scattered regional sights from a major city, consider the efficiency of a minibus excursion. With more time, everything is doable without a car.

To determine approximate travel times between destinations, study the driving map in the Practicalities chapter or check Google maps; visit NationalRail.co.uk for train schedules. Compare the cost of a long train ride with a budget flight; check Skyscanner.com for intra-European flights.

Write out a day-by-day itinerary.

Figure out how many destinations you can comfortably fit in your time frame. Don't overdo it—few travelers wish they'd hurried more. Allow enough days per stop (see estimates in "Scotland's Top Destinations," earlier). Minimize one-night stands. It can be worth taking a late-afternoon drive or train ride to settle into a town for two consecutive nights—and gain a full day for sightseeing. Include sufficient time for transportation, whether you travel by car, train, or bus, it'll take you a half-day to get between most destinations.

Staying in a home base (like Inverness or Oban) and making day trips can be more time-efficient than changing locations and hotels.

Take sight closures into account. Avoid visiting a town on the one day a week its must-see sights are closed. Check if any holidays or festivals fall during your trip—these attract crowds and can close sights (for the latest, visit Scotland's tourist website, www.visitscotland.com).

Give yourself some slack. Every trip, and every traveler, needs downtime for doing laundry, picnic shopping, people-watching, and so on. Pace yourself. Assume you will return.

BEFORE YOU GO

You'll have a smoother trip if you tackle a few things ahead of time. For more information on these topics, see the Practicalities chapter (and RickSteves.com, for helpful travel tips and talks).

Make sure your travel documents are valid. If your passport is due to expire within six months of your ticketed date of return, you need to renew it. Allow up to six weeks to renew or get a passport (www.travel.state.gov).

Arrange your transportation. Book your international flights. Figure out your transportation options within Scotland: It's worth thinking about renting a car, buying train tickets online in advance, getting a rail pass, or booking a cheap flight. (You can wing it once you're there, but it may cost more.)

Book rooms well in advance, especially if your trip falls during peak season or any major holidays or festivals. Those visiting Edinburgh in August or the Isle of Skye in high season should book especially early.

Make reservations or buy tickets in advance for major sights. Tickets to Edinburgh's Military Tattoo (Aug) sell out early—book as far ahead as possible. If you'll be in Edinburgh at festival time (most of Aug), check the schedule for theater and music, and if there's something you just have to see, consider buying tickets ahead of time. To golf at St. Andrews' famous Old Course, you'll need to reserve the previous fall, or put your name in for the "ballot" two days before.

Hire guides in advance. Popular guides can get booked up. If you want a specific guide, reserve by email as far ahead as possible—especially for Edinburgh and Glasgow.

Consider travel insurance. Compare the cost of the insurance to the cost of your potential loss. Check whether your existing insurance (health, homeowners, or renters) covers you and your possessions overseas.

Call your bank. Alert your bank that you'll be using your debit and credit cards in Europe. Ask about transaction fees, and get the PIN number for your credit card. You don't need to bring pounds for your trip; you can withdraw pounds from cash machines in Scotland.

Use your smartphone smartly. Sign up for an international service plan to reduce your costs, or rely on Wi-Fi in Europe instead. Download any apps you'll want on the road, such as maps, translators, transit schedules, and Rick Steves Audio Europe (see sidebar).

Rip up this book! Turn chapters into mini guidebooks: Break the book's spine and use a utility knife to slice apart

Rooms are plentiful if you book ahead; buy tickets in advance to avoid lines at Edinburgh Castle; learning how to drive on the left gives you freedom and flexibility.

chapters, keeping gummy edges intact. Reinforce the chapter spines with clear, wide tape; use a heavy-duty stapler; or make or buy a cheap cover (see Travel Store at www.ricksteves.com), swapping out chapters as you travel.

Pack light. You'll walk with your luggage more than you think. I travel for weeks with a single carry-on bag and a day-pack. Use the packing checklist in the appendix as a guide.

Rick's Free Video Clips and Audio Tours

Travel smarter with these free, fun resources:

Rick Steves Classroom Europe, a powerful tool for teachers, is also useful for travelers. This video library contains over 400 three- to five-minute clips excerpted from my public television series. Enjoy these videos as you sort through options for your trip and to better un-derstand what you'll see in Europe. Just enter a topic (city name, historical event, etc.) into the search bar for a list of everything I've filmed on a subject. Check it out at Classroom.RickSteves.com.

Rick Steves Audio Europe, a free app, makes it easy to down-load my audio tours and listen to them offline as you travel. For Scotland, this includes my Edinburgh Royal Mile Walk (look for the 🎧). The app also offers in-sightful travel interviews from my public radio show with experts from Europe and around the globe. Find it in your app store or at RickSteves.com/AudioEurope.

Travel Smart

If you have a positive attitude, equip yourself with good information (this book), and expect to travel smart, you will.

Read—and reread—this book. To have an "A" trip, be an "A" student. Note opening hours of sights, closed days, crowd-beating tips, and whether reservations are required or advisable. Check the latest at RickSteves.com/update.

Be your own tour guide. As you travel, get up-to-date info on sights, reserve tickets and tours, reconfirm hotels and travel arrangements, and check transit connections. Visit local tourist information offices (TIs). Upon arrival in a new town, lay the groundwork for a smooth departure; confirm the train, bus, or road you'll take when you leave.

Outsmart thieves. Pickpockets abound in crowded places where tourists congregate. Treat commotions as smokescreens for theft. Keep your cash, credit cards, and passport secure in a money belt tucked under your clothes; carry only a day's spending money in your front pocket. Don't set valuable items down on counters or café tabletops, where they can be quickly stolen or easily forgotten.

Minimize potential loss. Keep expensive gear to a minimum. Bring photocopies or take photos of important documents (passport and cards) to aid in replacement if they're lost or stolen. Back up photos and files frequently.

Guard your time and energy. Taking a taxi can be a good value if it saves you a long wait for a cheap bus or an exhausting walk across town. To avoid long lines, follow my crowd-beating tips, such as making advance reservations, or sightseeing early or late.

Be flexible. Even if you have a well-planned itinerary, expect changes, strikes, closures, sore feet, bad weather, and so on. Your Plan B could turn out to be even better.

Connect with the culture. Interacting with locals carbonates your experience. Enjoy the friendliness of the Scottish people. You speak the language—use it! Ask questions; most locals are happy to point you in their idea of the right direction. Set up your own quest for the best hike, castle, or whisky. When an opportunity pops up, make it a habit to say "yes."

Scotland...here you come!

EDINBURGH

Edinburgh is the historical, cultural, and political capital of Scotland. For nearly a thousand years, Scotland's kings, parliaments, writers, thinkers, and bankers have called Edinburgh home. Today, it remains Scotland's most sophisticated city.

Edinburgh (ED'n-burah—only tourists pronounce it like "Pittsburgh") is Scotland's showpiece and one of Europe's most entertaining cities. It's a place of stunning vistas—nestled among craggy bluffs and studded with a prickly skyline of spires, towers, domes, and steeples. Proud statues of famous Scots dot the urban landscape. The buildings are a harmonious yellow-gray, all built from the same local sandstone.

Culturally, Edinburgh has always been the place where Lowland culture (urban and English) met Highland style (rustic and Gaelic). Tourists will find no end of traditional Scottish clichés: whisky tastings, kilt shops, bagpipe-playing buskers, and gimmicky tours featuring Scotland's bloody history and ghost stories.

Edinburgh is two cities in one. The Old Town stretches along the Royal Mile, from the grand castle on top to the palace on the bottom. Along this colorful labyrinth of cobbled streets and narrow lanes, medieval skyscrapers stand shoulder to shoulder, hiding peaceful courtyards.

A few hundred yards north of the Old Town lies the New Town. It's a magnificent planned neighborhood (from the 1700s). Here, you'll enjoy upscale shops, broad boulevards, straight streets, square squares, circular circuses, and Georgian mansions decked out in Greek-style columns and statues.

Just to the west of the New Town, the West End is a prestigious and quieter neighborhood boasting more Georgian architecture, cobbled lanes, fine dining options, and a variety of concert and theater venues.

Today's Edinburgh is big in banking, scientific research, and scholarship at its four universities. Since 1999, when Scotland regained a measure of self-rule, Edinburgh reassumed its place as home of the Scottish Parliament. The city hums with life. Students and professionals pack the pubs and art galleries. It's especially lively in August, when the Edinburgh Festival takes over the town. Historic, monumental, fun, and well organized, Edinburgh is a tourist's delight.

PLANNING YOUR TIME

While the major sights can be seen in a day, I'd give Edinburgh two days and three nights.

Day 1: Tour the castle, then take my self-guided Royal Mile walk, stopping in at St. Giles' Cathedral and whichever shops and museums interest you. At the bottom of the Mile, consider visiting the Scottish Parliament, the Palace of Holyroodhouse, or both. If the weather's good and the trail is open, you could hike back to your B&B along the Salisbury Crags.

Day 2: Visit the National Museum of Scotland. After lunch, stroll through the Scottish National Gallery. Then follow my self-guided walk through the New Town, visiting the Scottish National Portrait Gallery and the Georgian House—or squeeze in a quick tour of the good ship *Britannia* (check last entry time before you head out).

Evenings: Options include various "haunted Edinburgh" walks, the literary pub crawl, or live music in pubs. Sadly, full-blown traditional folk performances are just about extinct, surviving only in excruciatingly schmaltzy variety shows put on for tour-bus groups. Perhaps the most authentic evening out is just settling down in a pub to sample the whisky and local beers while meeting the locals...and attempting to understand them through their thick Scottish accents.

Orientation to Edinburgh

A VERBAL MAP

With 500,000 people (835,000 in the metro area), Edinburgh is Scotland's second-biggest city (after Glasgow). But the tourist's Edinburgh is compact: Old Town, New Town, West End, and the B&B area south of the city center.

Edinburgh's **Old Town** stretches across a ridgeline slung between two bluffs. From west to east, this "Royal Mile" runs from the Castle Rock—which is visible from anywhere—to the base of the 822-foot extinct volcano called Arthur's Seat. For visitors, this east-west axis is the center of the action. Just south of the Royal Mile are the university and the National Museum of Scotland; farther to the south is a handy B&B neighborhood that lines up along **Dalkeith Road** and **Mayfield Gardens.** North of the Royal Mile ridge is the **New Town,** a neighborhood of grid-planned streets and elegant Georgian buildings, and the **West End,** near Charlotte Square—a posh, quiet neighborhood that's still close to the sightseeing action.

In the center of it all—in a drained lake bed between the Old and New Towns—sit the Princes Street Gardens park and Waverley Bridge, where you'll find the Waverley train station, Waverley Mall, bus info office (starting point for most city bus tours), Scottish National Gallery, and a covered dance-and-music pavilion.

TOURIST INFORMATION

The TI, branded "iCentre," is on the Royal Mile across from St. Giles' Cathedral (Mon-Sat 9:00-17:00, Sun from 10:00, June daily until 18:00, July-Aug daily until 19:00, 249 High Street, tel. 0131/473-3868, www.visitscotland.com). The staff is scattered at various tables with laptops on and ready to help.

For more information than what's included in the TI's free map, buy the excellent *Collins Discovering Edinburgh* map (which comes with opinionated commentary and locates almost every major sight). If you're interested in evening music, ask for the comprehensive entertainment listing, *The List.* Also consider buying Historic Scotland's Explorer Pass, which can save you some money if you visit the castles at both Edinburgh and Stirling, or are also visiting the Orkney Islands (for details, see page 465).

ARRIVAL IN EDINBURGH

By Train: Most long-distance trains arrive at **Waverley Station** in the city center. For groceries to go, M&S Simply Food, near track 2, is economic and efficient (daily 7:00-22:00, Thu-Fri until 23:00, Sun from 8:00). Taxis line up outside, on Princes Street or Waverley Bridge. To catch a city bus, exit the train station via Princes Street and ride up several escalators (Waverley Mall is on your left). City buses #14, #30, and #33 stop around the corner to your right, along North Bridge, and are handy if you're staying in my recommended B&B neighborhood south of town. Those staying at one

EDINBURGH

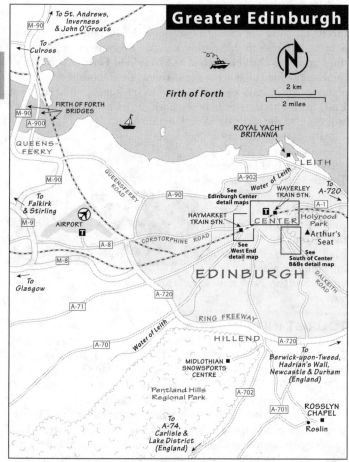

of my recommended West End accommodations might consider taking the train directly to **Haymarket Station** (rather than Waverley). For more specifics on linking to my recommended hotel neighborhoods, see the "Sleeping in Edinburgh" section, later.

By Bus: Scottish Citylink, Megabus, and National Express buses use the bus station (with luggage lockers) in the New Town, two blocks north of the train station on St. Andrew Square.

By Car: No matter where you're coming from, avoid needless driving in the city by taking advantage of Edinburgh's bypass road, A-720. To conveniently reach my recommended B&Bs, circle the city on the A-720 (direction: Edinburgh South), until the last roundabout, named *Sheriffhall*. Exit the roundabout at the first left *(A-7 Edinburgh)*. From here it's four miles to the B&B neighborhood. After a while, the A-7 becomes Dalkeith Road. If you see the huge Royal Commonwealth Pool, you've gone a couple of blocks too far.

By Plane: Edinburgh's airport is eight miles west of down-town—about a 30-minute tram or taxi ride. For information, see "Edinburgh Connections," at the end of this chapter.

HELPFUL HINTS

Festivals: August is a crowded, popular month to visit Edinburgh thanks to the multiple festivals hosted here, including the official Edinburgh International Festival, the Fringe Festival, and the Military Tattoo. Book ahead for hotels, events, and restaurant dinners if you'll be visiting in August, and expect to pay significantly more for your room. Many museums and shops have extended hours in August. For more festival details, see page 513.

Wi-Fi: The city-wide network **EdiFreeWiFi** is free and unlimited in the city center. Just enter your basic information where prompted, and connect.

Baggage Storage: At the train station, a luggage storage office is near platform 2 (£7.50/3 hours, daily 7:00-23:00). Cheaper lockers are at the bus station on St. Andrew Square, just two blocks north of the train station (£8/12 hours, daily 4:30-24:00). Apps like Stasher can also help you find convenient baggage storage locations around big cities like Edinburgh.

Laundry: The **Ace Cleaning Centre** launderette is located near my recommended B&Bs south of town. You can pay for full-service laundry (drop off in the morning for same-day service) or stay and do it yourself. For a small extra fee, they'll collect your laundry from your B&B and drop it off the next day (Mon-Fri 8:00-19:30, Sat 9:00-17:00, Sun 10:00-16:00, along bus route to city center at 13 South Clerk Street, opposite Queens Hall, tel. 0131/667-0549). In the West End, **Johnsons the Cleaners** will do your laundry (no hotel or B&B drop-off, Mon-Fri 9:30-18:00, Sat until 17:00, closed Sun, 5 Drumsheugh Place, tel. 0131/225-8077).

Bike Rental and Tours: The laid-back crew at **Cycle Scotland** happily recommends good bike routes with your rental (prices starting at £20/3 hours or £30/day, electric bikes available for extra fee, daily 10:00-18:00, may be closed in winter, just off Royal Mile at 29 Blackfriars Street, tel. 0131/556-5560, mobile 0779-688-6899, www.cyclescotland.co.uk, Peter). They also run guided three-hour bike tours daily at 11:00 (and sometimes at 15:00) that start on the Royal Mile and ride through Holyrood Park, Arthur's Seat, Duddingston Village, Doctor Neil's (Secret) Garden, and along the Innocent railway path (£45/person, extra fee for e-bike, book ahead).

EDINBURGH

EDINBURGH

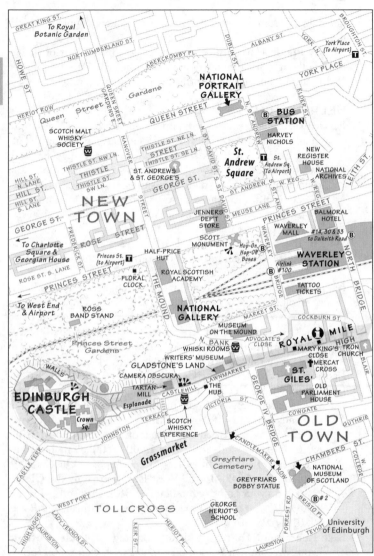

Car Rental: These places have offices both in the town center and at the airport: **Avis** (24 East London Street, tel. 0344-544-6059, airport tel. 0344-544-6004), **Europcar** (Waverley Station, near platform 2, tel. 0371-384-3453, airport tel. 0371-384-3406), **Hertz** (10 Picardy Place, tel. 0843-309-3026, airport tel. 0843-309-3025), and **Budget** (24 East London Street, tel. 0344-544-9064, airport tel. 0344-544-4605). Some downtown offices close or have reduced hours on Sunday, but the airport locations tend to be open daily. If you plan to rent a

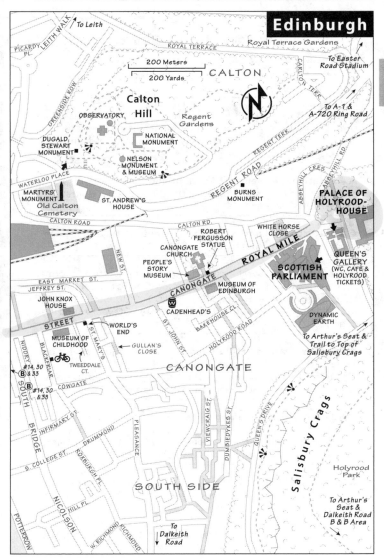

car, pick it up on your way out of Edinburgh—you won't need it in town.

Dress for the Weather: Weather blows in and out—bring your sweater and be prepared for rain.

GETTING AROUND EDINBURGH

By Bus: Many of Edinburgh's sights are within walking distance of one another, but buses come in handy—especially if you're staying at a B&B south of the city center (use buses #14, #30, or #33).

EDINBURGH

Edinburgh at a Glance

▲▲▲**Royal Mile** Historic road—good for walking—stretching from the castle down to the palace, lined with museums, pubs, and shops. See page 41.

Apr 1 - 30th   Castle hours 9:30 - 6:00 pm

▲▲▲**Edinburgh Castle** Iconic hilltop fort and royal residence complete with crown jewels, Romanesque chapel, memorial, and fine military museum. **Hours:** Daily 9:30-18:00, Oct-March until 17:00. See page 62.

▲▲▲**National Museum of Scotland** Intriguing, well-displayed artifacts from prehistoric times to the 20th century. **Hours:** Daily 10:00-17:00. See page 86.

▲▲**Gladstone's Land** Seventeenth-century Royal Mile merchant's residence. **Hours:** Daily 11:00-16:30. See page 75.

▲▲**St. Giles' Cathedral** Preaching grounds of Scottish Reformer John Knox, with spectacular organ, Neo-Gothic chapel, and distinctive crown spire. **Hours:** Mon-Fri 9:00-19:00, Sat until 17:00; Nov-March Mon-Sat 9:00-17:00; Sun 13:00-17:00 year-round. See page 75.

▲▲**Scottish Parliament Building** Striking headquarters for parliament, which returned to Scotland in 1999. **Hours:** Mon-Sat 10:00-17:00, longer hours Tue-Thu when parliament is in session (Sept-June), closed Sun year-round. See page 82.

▲▲**Palace of Holyroodhouse** The Queen's splendid official residence in Scotland, with lavish rooms, 12th-century abbey, and gallery with rotating exhibits. **Hours:** Daily 9:30-18:00, Nov-March until 16:30, closed during royal visits. See page 83.

▲▲**Scottish National Gallery** Choice sampling of European masters and Scotland's finest. **Hours:** Fri-Wed 10:00-17:00, Aug until 18:00; Thu 10:00-19:00 year-round. See page 91.

▲▲**Scottish National Portrait Gallery** Beautifully displayed Who's Who of Scottish history. **Hours:** Daily 10:00-17:00. See page 92.

▲▲**Georgian House** Intimate peek at upper-crust life in the late 1700s. **Hours:** Daily 10:00-17:00, March and Nov 11:00-16:00, closed Dec-Feb. See page 95.

▲▲**Royal Yacht** *Britannia* The Queen's former floating palace, with a history of distinguished passengers, a 15-minute trip out of town. **Hours:** Daily 9:30-16:30, Oct until 16:00, Nov-March 10:00-15:30. See page 96.

▲**Camera Obscura** Five floors of illusions, holograms, and gags, topped with the best view of the Royal Mile. **Hours:** Daily 9:00-21:00, Sat until 22:00, shorter hours off-season. See page 74.

▲**Scotch Whisky Experience** Gimmicky but fun and educational introduction to Scotland's most famous beverage. **Hours:** Generally daily 10:00-18:30. See page 74.

▲**Writers' Museum at Lady Stair's House** Aristocrat's house, built in 1622, filled with artifacts from Robert Burns, Robert Louis Stevenson, and Sir Walter Scott. **Hours:** Daily 10:00-17:00. See page 75.

▲**The Real Mary King's Close** Underground street and houses last occupied in the 17th century, viewable by guided tour. **Hours:** Daily generally 9:00-21:45, Oct-April until 17:00 (these are last tour times). See page 79.

▲**Museum of Childhood** Five stories of nostalgic fun. **Hours:** Daily 10:00-17:00. See page 79.

▲**John Knox House** Medieval home with exhibits on the life of Scotland's great Protestant reformer. **Hours:** Mon-Sat 10:00-18:00, closed Sun except in July-Aug. See page 80.

▲**People's Story Museum** Everyday life from the 18th to 20th century. **Hours:** Daily 10:00-17:00. See page 81.

▲**Museum of Edinburgh** Historic mementos, from the original National Covenant inscribed on animal skin to early golf balls. **Hours:** Daily 10:00-17:00. See page 82.

▲**Queen's Gallery** Intimate museum with treasures from the royal art collection. **Hours:** Daily 9:30-18:00, Nov-March until 16:30. See page 85.

 ▲**Rosslyn Chapel** Small 15th-century church chock-full of intriguing carvings a short drive outside of Edinburgh. **Hours:** Mon-Sat 9:30-17:00, June-Aug until 18:00, Sun 12:00-16:45 year-round. See page 97.

Double-decker buses come with fine views upstairs. It's easy once you get the hang of it: Buses come by frequently and have free, fast Wi-Fi on board. The only hassle is that you must pay with exact change (£1.70/ride). As you board, tell your driver where you're going (or just say "single ticket") and drop your change into the box. The £4 all-day pass pays for itself in three rides and frees you from worrying about change. You can also use a payment app on your smartphone, such as ApplePay or Google Pay, to pay for your bus fare when you board. (For a day pass, tap the sensor each time you ride. If you ride three or more times, you'll be charged £4 at the end of the day.)

You can pick up a route map at the TI, in the train station, or at the transit office at the Old Town end of Waverley Bridge (tel. 0131/555-6363, www.lothianbuses.com).

By Tram: Edinburgh's single tram line (also £1.70/ride, buy at ticket machine before boarding, credit card or exact change) is designed more for locals than tourists. It's most useful for reaching the airport (£6 one-way; see "Edinburgh Connections" at the end of this chapter) or getting from my recommended West End hotels to Princes Street and St. Andrew Square, near the Waverley train station.

By Taxi or Uber: The 1,300 taxis cruising Edinburgh's streets are easy to flag down (a ride between downtown and the B&B neighborhood costs about £7; rates go up after 18:00 and on weekends). They can turn on a dime, so hail them in either direction. Uber also works very well here and is substantially cheaper than taxis (with quick pickups and most rides in town averaging £5-6).

Tours in Edinburgh

Royal Mile Walking Tours

Walking tours are an Edinburgh specialty; you'll see groups trailing entertaining guides all over town. Below I've listed good all-purpose walks; for **literary pub crawls** and **ghost tours,** see "Nightlife in Edinburgh" on page 110.

Edinburgh Tour Guides offers a good historical walk (without all the ghosts and goblins). Their Royal Mile tour is a gentle three-hour downhill stroll from the top of the Mile to the palace (£25; daily at 9:30 and 19:00—evening tour is only two hours; meet outside Gladstone's Land, near the top of the Royal Mile—see map on page 43, must reserve ahead, mobile 0785-888-0072, www.edinburghtourguides.com, info@edinburghtourguides.com). Their other offerings include *Outlander*-themed Edinburgh walks and day tours.

Mercat Tours offers a 1.5-hour "Secrets of the Royal Mile" walk that's more entertaining than intellectual (£14; £30 includes optional, 45-minute guided Edinburgh Castle visit; daily at 10:00 and 13:00, leaves from Mercat Cross on the Royal Mile, tel. 0131/225-5445, www.mercattours.com). The guides, who enjoy making a short story long, ignore the big sights and take you behind the scenes with piles of barely historical gossip, bully-pulpit Scottish pride, and fun but forgettable trivia. They also offer other tours, such as ghost walks, tours of 18th-century underground vaults on the southern slope of the Royal Mile, and *Outlander* sights (see their website for a rundown).

Sandemans New Edinburgh runs "free" tours multiple times a day; you won't pay upfront, but the guide will expect a tip (check schedule online, 2-3 hours, meet in front of Frankie & Benny's by Tron Kirk on High Street, www.neweuropetours.eu).

The **Voluntary Guides Association** offers free two-hour walks, but only during the Edinburgh Festival. You don't need a reservation—just show up (check website for times, generally depart from City Chambers across from St. Giles' Cathedral on the Royal Mile, www.edinburghfestivalguides.org). You can also hire their guides (for a small fee) for private tours outside of festival time.

Blue Badge Local Guides

The following guides charge similar prices and offer half-day and full-day tours: **Jean Blair** (a delightful teacher and guide, £230/day without car, £450/day with car, mobile 0798-957-0287, www.travelthroughscotland.com, scotguide7@gmail.com); **Sergio La Spina** (an Argentinean who adopted Edinburgh as his hometown more than 20 years ago, £250/day, tel. 0131/664-1731, mobile 0797-330-6579, www.vivaescocia.com, sergiolaspina@aol.com); **Ken Hanley** (who wears his kilt as if pants don't exist, £130/half-day, £250/day, extra charge if he uses his car—seats up to six, tel. 0131/666-1944, mobile 0771-034-2044, www.small-world-tours.co.uk, kennethhanley@me.com); **Liz Everett** (walking tours only—no car; £175/half-day, £265/day, mobile 0782-168-3837, liz.everett@live.co.uk); and **Maggie McLeod** (another top-notch guide, £175/half-day walking tour, £660 day trips with car to farther-flung destinations, mobile 0775-151-6776, www.scotlandandmore.com, margaret.mcleod@live.co.uk).

Hop-On, Hop-Off Bus Tours

The following one-hour hop-on, hop-off bus tour routes, all run by the same company, circle the town center, stopping at the major sights. **Edinburgh Tour** (green buses) focuses on the city center, with live guides (stay on for the entire 75-minute loop if you like your guide). **City Sightseeing** (red buses, focuses on Old Town) has recorded commentary, as does the **Majestic Tour** (blue-and-yellow buses, goes to the port of Leith and includes a stop at the *Britannia*

and Royal Botanic Garden). You can pay for just one tour (£16/24 hours), but most people pay a few pounds more for a ticket covering all buses (£24/48 hours). It's a great convenience to be able to hop on any bus that goes by with the same ticket (buses run April-Oct roughly 9:00-19:00, shorter hours off-season; about every 10 minutes, buy tickets on board, tel. 0131/220-0770, www.edinburghtour.com). On sunny days the buses go topless. As is generally the case with such tours, there's patter the entire time but almost nothing of real importance other than identifying what you're driving by and a few random factoids (the live guides are little better than the recorded spiels).

The **Royal Edinburgh Ticket** costs £57 and covers 48 hours of unlimited travel on all three hop-on, hop-off buses, as well as admission at Edinburgh Castle, the Palace of Holyroodhouse, and *Britannia* (www.royaledinburghticket.co.uk). This is a good deal if you plan to use the buses and see all three sights. As you'll already have your ticket, you save time too, skipping ticket lines at the included sights.

The **3 Bridges Tour** combines a hop-on, hop-off bus to South Queensferry with a boat tour on the Firth of Forth (£25, 3 hours total).

Day Trips from Edinburgh

Many companies run a variety of day trips to regional sights, as well as multiday and themed itineraries. (Several of the local guides listed earlier have cars, too.)

The most popular tour is the all-day **Highlands trip,** which gives those with limited time a chance to experience the wonders of Scotland's wild and legend-soaked Highlands in a single long day (about £50, roughly 8:00-20:00). Itineraries vary but you'll generally visit/pass through the Trossachs, Rannoch Moor, Glencoe, Fort William, Fort Augustus on Loch Ness (some tours offer an optional boat ride), and Pitlochry. To save time, look for a tour that gives you a short glimpse of Loch Ness rather than driving its entire length or doing a boat trip. (Once you've seen a little of it, you've seen it all.) Also popular are all-day tours of locations from the *Outlander* novels and TV series (about £50, roughly 8:00-20:00); for more about *Outlander* sights, see page 518.

Larger outfits, typically using bigger buses, include **Timberbush Tours** (tel. 0131/226-6066, www.timberbush-tours.co.uk), **Gray Line** (tel. 0131/555-5558, www.graylinescotland.

com), **Highland Experience** (tel. 0131/226-1414, www.highlandexperience.com), **Highland Explorer** (tel. 0131/558-3738, www.highlandexplorertours.com), and **Scotline** (tel. 0131/557-0162, www.scotlinetours.co.uk). Other companies pride themselves on keeping group sizes small, with 16-seat minibuses; these include **Rabbie's** (tel. 0131/226-3133, www.rabbies.com) and **Heart of Scotland Tours: The Wee Red Bus** (RS%—10 percent Rick Steves discount on full-price day tours, mention when booking, does not apply to overnight tours or senior/student rates; may cancel off-season if too few sign up—leave a contact number; tel. 0131/228-2888, www.heartofscotlandtours.co.uk, run by Nick Roche).

For young backpackers, **Haggis Adventures** runs day tours plus overnight trips of up to 10 days (tel. 0131/557-9393, www.haggisadventures.com).

At **Discreet Scotland,** Matthew Wight and his partners specialize in tours of greater Edinburgh and Scotland in spacious SUVs—good for families (£380/2 people, 8 hours, mobile 0798-941-6990, www.discreetscotland.com).

Walks in Edinburgh

I've outlined two walks in Edinburgh: along the Royal Mile, and through the New Town. Many of the sights we'll pass on these walks are described in more detail later, under "Sights in Edinburgh."

THE ROYAL MILE

The Royal Mile is one of Europe's most interesting historic walks—it's worth ▲▲▲. The following self-guided stroll is also available as a free 🎧 downloadable Rick Steves audio tour.

This 1.5-hour walk covers the Royal Mile's landmarks, but skips the many museums and indoor sights along the way (these are described in walking order under "Sights in Edinburgh" on page 74). Doing this walk as an orientation upon arrival in the morning or evening allows you to focus on the past without having to dodge crowds. You can return later to stroll the same walk during the much livelier business hours when shops, museums, and the cathedral are all open.

Another option is to review the sight descriptions beforehand, plan your walk around their open hours, and pop into those that interest you as you pass them. Several of the sights you'll pass on this walk are free to enter, including the Writers' Museum, St. Giles' Cathedral, Old Parliament House, People's Story Museum, Museum of Edinburgh, and Scottish parliament building.

Overview

Start at Edinburgh Castle at the top and amble down to the Palace of Holyroodhouse. The street itself changes names—Castlehill, Lawnmarket, High Street, and Canongate—but it's a straight, downhill shot totaling just over one mile. And nearly every step is packed with shops, cafés, and lanes leading to tiny squares.

The city of Edinburgh was born on the rock at the top, where the castle stands today. Celtic tribes (and maybe the Romans) once occupied this site. As the town grew, it spilled downhill along the sloping ridge that became the Royal Mile. Because this strip of land is so narrow, there was no place to build but up. So in medieval times, it was densely packed with multistory "tenements"—large edifices under one roof that housed a number of tenants.

As you walk, you'll be tracing the growth of the city—its birth atop Castle Hill, its Old Town heyday in the 1600s, its expansion in the 1700s into the Georgian New Town (leaving the old quarter an overcrowded, disease-ridden Victorian slum), and on to the 21st century at the modern Scottish parliament building (2004).

Most of the Royal Mile feels like one long Scottish shopping mall, selling all manner of kitschy souvenirs (known locally as "tartan tat"), shortbread, and whisky. But the streets are also packed

Royal Mile Walk

DUGALD
STEWART
MONUMENT
To
Leith

NATIONAL
MONUMENT

NELSON
MONUMENT
& MUSEUM

WATERLOO PLACE

MARTYRS'
MONUMENT
Old Calton
Cemetery

ST. ANDREW'S
HOUSE

CALTON ROAD

REGENT ROAD

BURNS
MONUMENT

ABBEYHILL CRES.

ABBEYHILL

PALACE OF
HOLYROOD-
HOUSE

WALK ENDS

CALTON RD.

NEW ST.

EAST MARKET ST.

JEFFREY ST.

JOHN KNOX
HOUSE

PUBS

STREET

NIDDRY

BLACKFRIARS

#14, 30
& 33

#14, 30
& 33

SOUTH

BRIDGE

S. COLLEGE ST.

To Dalkeith
Road

ROBERT
FERGUSSON
STATUE

CANONGATE
CHURCH

PEOPLE'S
STORY
MUSEUM

WORLD'S
END

MUSEUM OF
CHILDHOOD

TWEEDDALE
CT.

COWGATE

INFIRMARY ST.

DRUMMOND

ROXBURGH PL.

CADENHEAD'S

CANONGATE

MUSEUM OF
EDINBURGH

ST. JOHN ST.

BAKEHOUSE CL.

ST. MARY'S

GULLAN'S
CLOSE

CLARINDA'S

ROYAL MILE

WHITE HORSE
CLOSE

SCOTTISH
PARLIAMENT

HOLYROOD ROAD

CANONGATE

N

QUEEN'S
GALLERY
(WC, CAFE &
HOLYROOD
TICKETS)

DYNAMIC
EARTH

To Arthur's Seat &
Trail to Top of
Salisbury Crags

200 Meters

200 Yards

① Edinburgh Castle
② Castlehill
③ Lawnmarket
④ Bank/High Streets
   Intersection
⑤ St. Giles' Cathedral
⑥ More of High Street

⑦ John Knox House
⑧ The World's End
⑨ Canongate
⑩ Scottish Parliament
   Building
⑪ Palace of Holyroodhouse

with history, and if you push past the postcard racks into one of the many side alleys, you can still find a few surviving rough edges of

the old city. Despite the drizzle, be sure to look up—spires, carvings, and towering Gothic "skyscrapers" give this city its unique urban identity.

As you stroll this mostly traffic-free tourist strip, you'll weave between big military-style barriers designed to frustrate terrorists, and navigate a can-can of low-grade souvenir shops and eateries, tourists with rolling suitcases, and cruise groups following their guides' umbrellas. Along the way, you'll be entertained by buskers, perused by pickpockets, hit up by beggars, and tempted by street merchants. Oh, and as it's quite haunted, you may feel the presence of a few ghosts.

• *We'll start at the castle esplanade, the big parking lot at the entrance to...*

EDINBURGH

❶ Edinburgh Castle

Edinburgh was born on the bluff—a big rock—where the castle now stands. Since before recorded history, people have lived on this strategic, easily defended perch.

The **castle** is an imposing symbol of Scottish independence (for a self-guided tour of Edinburgh Castle, see page 63.) Its esplanade—built as a military parade ground (1816)—is now the site of the annual Military Tattoo. This spectacular massing of regimental bands fills the square nightly for most of August. Fans watch from temporary bleacher seats to see kilt-wearing dancers and bagpipers marching against the spectacular backdrop of the castle. TV crews broadcast the spectacle to all corners of the globe.

When the bleachers aren't up, there are fine views in both directions from the esplanade. Facing north, you'll see the body of water called the Firth of Forth, and Fife beyond that. (The Firth of Forth is the estuary where the River Forth flows into the North Sea.) Still facing north, find the lacy spire of the Scott Monument and two Neoclassical buildings housing art galleries. Beyond them, the stately buildings of Edinburgh's New Town  rise. Panning to the right, find the Nelson Monument and some faux Greek ruins atop Calton Hill (see page 101).

The city's many bluffs, crags, and ridges were built up by volcanoes, then carved down by glaciers—a city formed in "fire and ice," as the locals say. So, during the Ice Age, as a river of glaciers swept in from the west (behind today's castle), it ran into the super-hard volcanic basalt of Castle Rock and flowed around it, cutting valleys on either side and leaving a tail that became the Royal Mile you're about to walk.

At the bottom of the esplanade, where the square hits the road, look left to find a plaque on the wall above the tiny **witches' well** (now a planter). This memorializes 300 women who were accused of witchcraft and burned here. Below was the Nor' Loch, the swampy lake where those accused of witchcraft (mostly women) were bound and dropped into the lake. If they sank and drowned, they were innocent. If they floated, they were guilty, and were burned here in front of the castle, providing the city folk a nice afternoon out. The plaque shows two witches: one good and one bad. Tickle the serpent's snout to sympathize with the witches. (I just made that up.)

• *Start walking down the bustling Royal Mile. The first block is a street called...*

EDINBURGH

❷ Castlehill

The big, squat, tank-like building immediately on your left was once the Old Town's reservoir. While it once held 1.5 million gallons of

water, today it's filled with the touristy **Tartan Weaving Mill** (open daily 9:00-17:30), a massive complex of four floors selling every kind of Scottish cliché. At the bottom level (a long way down) is a floor of big looms and weavers sometimes at work.

The black-and-white tower ahead on the left has entertained visitors since the 1850s with its **camera obscura,** a darkened room where a mirror and a series of lenses capture live images of the city surroundings outside. (Giggle at the funny mirrors as you walk fatly by.) Across the street, filling the old Castlehill Primary School, is a gimmicky-if-intoxicating whisky-sampling exhibit called the **Scotch Whisky Experience** (a.k.a. "Malt Disney"). Both are described later, under "Sights in Edinburgh."

• *Just ahead, in front of the church with the tall, lacy spire, is the old market square known as...*

❸ Lawnmarket

During the Royal Mile's heyday, in the 1600s, this intersection was bigger and served as a market for fabric (especially "lawn," a linen-like cloth). The market would fill this space with hustle, bustle, and lots of commerce. The round white hump in the middle of the roundabout is all that remains of the official weighing beam called the Butter Tron—where all goods sold were weighed for honesty and tax purposes.

Towering above Lawnmarket, with the highest spire in the city, is the former Tolbooth Church.

This impressive Neo-Gothic structure (1844) is now home to **the Hub,** Edinburgh's festival-ticket and information center. This is a handy stop for its WC, café, and free Wi-Fi, and for information on Edinburgh's many festivals: The world-famous Edinburgh Festival fills the month of August with cultural action, while other August festivals feature classical music, traditional and fringe theater (especially comedy), art, books, and more.

In the 1600s, this—along with

the next stretch, called High Street—was the city's main street. At that time, Edinburgh was bursting with breweries, printing presses, and banks. Tens of thousands of citizens were squeezed into the narrow confines of the Old Town.

Here on this ridge, they built tenements (multiple-unit residences) similar to the more recent ones you see today. These tenements, rising 10 stories and more, were some of the tallest domestic buildings in Europe. The living arrangements shocked class-conscious English visitors to Edinburgh because the tenements were occupied by rich and poor alike—usually the poor in the cellars and attics, and the rich in the middle floors.

• *Continue a half-block down the Mile.*

Gladstone's Land (at #477b, on the left), a surviving original tenement, was acquired by a wealthy merchant in 1617. Stand in front of the building and look up at this centuries-old skyscraper. This design was standard for its time: a shop or shops on the ground floor, with columns and an arcade, and residences on the floors above. Because window glass was expensive, the lower halves of window openings were made of cheaper wood, which swung out like shutters for ventilation—and were convenient for tossing out garbage. Now a museum, Gladstone's Land is worth visiting for its intimate look at life here 400 years ago (see page 75).

Branching off the spine of the Royal Mile are a number of narrow alleyways that go by various local names. A "wynd" (rhymes with "kind") is a narrow, winding lane. A "pend" is an arched gateway. "Gate" is from an Old Norse word for street. And a "close" is a tiny alley between two buildings (originally with a door that "closed" at night). A "close" usually leads to a "court," or courtyard.

To explore one of these alleyways, head into Lady Stair's Close (on the left, 10 steps downhill from Gladstone's Land). This alley pops out in a small courtyard, where you'll find the **Writers' Museum** (described on page 75). It's free and well worth a visit for fans of Scotland's holy trinity of writers (Robert Burns, Sir Walter Scott, and Robert Louis Stevenson), but also for a glimpse of what a typical home might have looked like in the 1600s. Burns actually lived for a while in this neighborhood, in 1786, when he first arrived in Edinburgh.

Opposite Gladstone's Land (at #322), another close leads to **Riddle's Court.** Wander through here and imagine Edinburgh in the 17th and 18th centuries, when tourists came here to marvel at its skyscrapers. Some 40,000 people were jammed into the few blocks between here and the World's End pub (which we'll reach soon). Visualize the labyrinthine maze of the old city, with people scurrying through these back alleyways, buying and selling, and popping into taverns.

No city in Europe was as densely populated—or perhaps as

filthy. Without modern hygiene, it was a living hell of smoke, stench, and noise, with the constant threat of fire, collapse, and disease. The dirt streets were soiled with sewage from bedpans emptied out windows. By the 1700s, the Old Town was rife with poverty and disease. The smoky home fires rising from tenements and the infamous smell (or "reek" in Scottish) that wafted across the city gave it a nickname that sticks today: "Auld Reekie."

• *Return to the Royal Mile and continue down it a few steps to take in some sights at the...*

❹ Bank/High Streets Intersection

Several sights cluster here, where Lawnmarket changes its name to High Street and intersects with Bank Street and George IV Bridge.

Begin with **Deacon Brodie's Tavern.** Read the "Doctor Jekyll and Mr. Hyde" story of this pub's notorious namesake on  the wall facing Bank Street. Then, to see his spooky split personality, check out both sides of the hanging signpost. Brodie—a pillar of the community by day but a burglar by night—epitomizes the divided personality of 1700s Edinburgh. It was a rich, productive city—home to great philosophers and scientists, who actively contributed to the Enlightenment. Meanwhile, the Old Town was riddled with crime and squalor. The city was scandalized when a respected surgeon—driven by a passion for medical research and needing corpses—was accused of colluding with two lowlifes, named Burke and Hare, to acquire freshly murdered corpses for dissection. (In the next century, in the late 1800s, novelist Robert Louis Stevenson would capture the dichotomy of Edinburgh's rich-poor society in his *Strange Case of Dr. Jekyll and Mr. Hyde.*)

In the late 1700s, Edinburgh's upper class moved out of the Old Town into a planned community called the New Town (a quarter-mile north of here). Eventually, most tenements were torn down and replaced with newer Victorian buildings. You'll see some at this intersection.

Look left down Bank Street to the green-domed **Bank of Scotland.** This was the headquarters of the bank, which had practiced modern capitalist financing since 1695. The building now houses the Museum on the Mound, a free exhibit on banking history (see page 75), and is also the Scottish headquarters for Lloyds Banking Group—which swallowed up the Bank of Scotland after the financial crisis of 2008.

If you detour left down Bank Street toward the bank, you'll

find the recommended **Whiski Rooms Shop.** If you head in the opposite direction, down George IV Bridge, you'll reach the excellent **National Museum of Scotland,** the famous Greyfriars Bobby statue, photogenic Victoria Street, which leads to the pub-lined Grassmarket square (all described later in this chapter), and several recommended eateries. Victoria Street (to the left) is so dreamy, many Potterheads figure it must be the inspiration for J. K. Rowling's Diagon Alley.

Across the street (downhill) from Deacon Brodie's Tavern is a seated green statue of hometown boy **David Hume** (1711-1776)—one of the most influential thinkers not only of Scotland, but in all of Western philosophy. The atheistic Hume was one of the towering figures of the Scottish Enlightenment of the mid-1700s. Thinkers and scientists were using the scientific method to challenge and investigate everything, including religion. Hume questioned cause and effect in thought puzzles such as this: We can see that when one billiard ball strikes another, the second one moves, but how do we know the collision "caused" the movement? Notice his shiny toe: People on their way to trial (in the high court just behind the statue) or students on their way to exams (in the nearby university) rub it for good luck.

Follow David Hume's gaze to the opposite corner, where a **brass H** in the pavement marks the site of the last public execution in Edinburgh in 1864. Deacon Brodie himself would have been hung about here (in 1788, on gallows whose design he had helped to improve—smart guy).

• *From the brass H, continue down the Royal Mile, pausing just before the church square at a stone wellhead with the pyramid cap.*

All along the Royal Mile, **wellheads** like this (from 1835) provided townsfolk with water in the days before buildings had plumbing. These neighborhood wells were served by the reservoir up at the castle. Imagine long lines of people in need of water standing here, gossiping and sharing the news. Eventually buildings were retrofitted with water pipes—the ones you see running along building exteriors.

• *Ahead of you (past the Victorian statue of some duke), embedded in the cobblestones near the street, is a big heart.*

The **Heart of Midlothian** marks the spot of the city's 15th-century municipal building and jail. In times past, in a nearby open space, criminals were hanged, traitors were decapitated, and witches were burned. Citizens hated the rough justice doled out here.

Locals still spit on the heart in the pavement. Go ahead...do as the locals do—land one right in the heart of the heart. By the way, Edinburgh has two soccer teams—Heart of Midlothian (known as "Hearts") and Hibernian ("Hibs"). If you're a Hibs fan, spit again.

• *Make your way to the entrance of the church.*

EDINBURGH

❺ St. Giles' Cathedral

This is the flagship of the Church of Scotland (Scotland's largest denomination)—called the "Mother Church of Presbyterianism."

The interior serves as a kind of Scottish Westminster Abbey, filled with monuments, statues, plaques, and stained-glass windows dedicated to great Scots and moments in history.

A church has stood on this spot since 854, though this structure is an architectural hodgepodge, dating mostly from the 15th through 19th century. In the 16th century, St. Giles was a kind of national stage on which the drama of the Reformation was played out. The reformer John Knox (1514-1572) was the preacher here. His fiery sermons helped turn once-Catholic Edinburgh into a bastion of Protestantism. During the Scottish Reformation, St. Giles was transformed from a Catholic cathedral to a Presbyterian church. The spacious interior is well worth a visit (for a self-guided tour, see page 75).

• *Facing the church entrance, curl around its right side, into a parking lot.*

Sights Around St. Giles

The grand building across the parking lot from St. Giles is the **Old Parliament House.** Since the 13th century, the king had ruled a rubber-stamp parliament of nobles and bishops. But the Protestant Reformation promoted democracy, and the parliament gained real power. From the early 1600s until 1707, this building evolved to become the seat of a true parliament of elected officials. That came to an end in 1707, when Scotland signed an Act of Union, joining what's known today as the United Kingdom and giving up their right to self-rule. (More on that later in the walk.) If you're curious to peek inside, head through the door at #11 (described on page 79).

The great reformer **John Knox** is buried—with appropriate austerity—under parking lot spot #23. The statue among the cars shows King Charles II riding to a toga party back in 1685.

• *Continue through the parking lot, around the back end of the church.*

Every Scottish burgh (town licensed by the king to trade) had three standard features: a "tolbooth" (basically a Town Hall, with a courthouse, meeting room, and jail); a "tron" (official weighing scale); and a "mercat" (or market) cross. The **mercat cross** standing just behind St. Giles' Cathedral has a slender column decorated with a unicorn holding a flag with the cross of St. Andrew. Royal proclamations have been read at this mercat cross since the 14th century. In 1952, a town crier heralded the news that Britain had a new queen—three days after the actual event (traditionally the time it took for a horse to speed here from London). Today, Mercat Cross is the meeting point for many of Edinburgh's walking tours—both historic and ghostly.

• *Circle around to the street side of the church.*

The statue to **Adam Smith** honors the Edinburgh author of the pioneering *Wealth of Nations* (1776), in which he laid out the economics of free-market capitalism. Smith theorized that an "invisible hand" wisely guides the unregulated free market. Stand in front of Smith and imagine the intellectual energy of Edinburgh in the mid-1700s, when it was Europe's most enlightened city. Adam Smith was right in the center of it. He and David Hume were good friends. James Boswell, the famed biographer of Samuel Johnson, took classes from Smith. James Watt, inventor of the steam engine, was another proud Scotsman of the age. With great intellectuals like these, Edinburgh helped create the modern world. The poet Robert Burns, geologist James Hutton (who's considered the father of modern geology), and the publishers of the first *Encyclopedia Britannica* all lived in Edinburgh. Steeped in the inquisitive mindset of the Enlightenment, they applied cool rationality and a secular approach to their respective fields.

• *Head on down the Royal Mile.*

❻ More of High Street

Continuing down this stretch of the Royal Mile, which is traffic-free most of the day (notice the bollards that raise and lower for permitted traffic), you'll see the Fringe Festival office (at #180), street musicians, and another wellhead (with horse "sippies," dating from 1675).

Notice those **three red boxes.** In the 20th century, people used these to make telephonic calls to each other. (Imagine that!) These cast-iron booths were produced in Scotland for all of Britain. As phone booths are decommissioned, some are finding new use as tiny shops and ATMs, and even showing up in residential neighborhoods as nostalgic garden decorations.

At the next intersection, on the left, is **Cockburn Street** (pronounced "COE-burn"), with a reputation for its eclectic independent shops and string of trendy bars and eateries. In the Middle Ages, only tiny lanes (like Fleshmarket Close just uphill) interrupted the long line of Royal Mile buildings. Cockburn Street was cut through High Street's dense wall of medieval skyscrapers in the 1860s to give easy access to the Georgian New Town and the train station. Notice how the sliced buildings were thoughtfully capped with facades that fit the aesthetic look of the Royal Mile.

• *When you reach the Tron Church (with a fine 17th-century interior, currently housing historic exhibits and shops), you're at the intersection of* **North and South Bridge** *streets. These major streets lead left to Waverley Station and right to the Dalkeith Road B&Bs. Several handy bus lines run along here.*

This is the halfway point of this walk. Stand on the corner diagonally across from the church. Look up to the top of the Royal Mile at the Hub and its 240-foot spire. In front of that, take in the spire of St. Giles' Cathedral—inspired by the Scottish crown and the thistle, Scotland's national flower.

With its faux turret and made-up 16th-century charm, the **Radisson Blu Hotel** just across the street is entirely new construction (1990), but built to fit in. The city is protecting its historic look. The **Inn on the Mile** next door was once a fancy bank with a lavish interior. As modern banks are moving away from city centers, their sumptuous buildings are being converted into ornate pubs and restaurants.

In the next block downhill are three **characteristic pubs** (The Mitre, Royal Mile, and Whiski), side by side, that offer free folk music many evenings. On the facing buildings, notice the chimneys. Tenement buildings shared stairways and entries, but held individual apartments, each with its own chimney.

• *Go down High Street another block, passing near the Museum of Childhood (on the right, at #42, and worth a stop; see page 79).*

Directly across the street, just below another wellhead, is the...

❼ John Knox House

Remember that Knox was a towering figure in Edinburgh's history, converting Scotland to a Calvinist style of Protestantism. His religious bent was "Presbyterianism," in which parishes are governed by elected officials rather than appointed bishops. This more democratic brand of Christianity also spurred Scotland toward political democracy. If you're interested in Knox or the Reformation, this sight is worth a visit (see page 80). Full disclosure: It's not certain that Knox ever actually lived here. Attached to the Knox House is

the Scottish Storytelling Centre, where locals with the gift of gab perform regularly; check the posted schedule.
• *A few steps farther down High Street, at the intersection with St. Mary's and Jeffrey streets, you'll reach...*

❽ The World's End

For centuries, a wall stood here, marking the end of the burgh of Edinburgh. For residents within the protective walls of the city, this must have felt like the "world's end," indeed. You can even pop in for a pint at the recommended The World's End pub, to your right. The area beyond was called Canongate, a monastic community associated with Holyrood Abbey. At the intersection, find the brass bricks in the street that trace the gate (demolished in 1764). Look to the right down St. Mary's Street about 200 yards to see a surviving bit of that old wall, known as the **Flodden Wall.** In the 1513 Battle of Flodden, the Scottish king James IV made the disastrous decision to invade northern England. James and 10,000 of his Scotsmen were killed. Fearing a brutal English counterattack, Edinburgh scrambled to reinforce its broken-down city wall. To the left, down Jeffrey Street, you'll see Scotland's top tattoo parlor, and a supplier for a different kind of tattoo (the Scottish Regimental Store).

Look left down Jeffrey Street past the train tracks for a good view of the **Calton Cemetery** up on Calton Hill. The obelisk,  called Martyrs' Monument, remembers a group of 18th-century patriots exiled by London to Australia for their reform politics. The round building to the left is the grave of philosopher David Hume. Today, the main reason to go up Calton Hill is for the fine views (see page 101).
• *Continue down the Royal Mile— leaving old Edinburgh—as High Street changes names to...*

❾ Canongate

A couple hundred yards farther along (on the right at #172) you reach **Cadenhead's,** a serious whisky shop (see page 107). About 30 yards beyond that, you'll pass two worthwhile and free museums, the **People's Story Museum** (on the left, in the old tollhouse at #163) and the **Museum of Edinburgh** (on the right, at #142), with the entry to the characteristic Bakehouse Close next door (for more on all three, see pages 81 and 82). But our next stop is the church just across from the Museum of Edinburgh.

The 1688 **Canongate Kirk** (Church)—located not far from

EDINBURGH

the royal residence of Holyroodhouse—is where Queen Elizabeth II and her family worship whenever they're in town. (So don't sit in the front pew, marked with her crown.) The gilded emblem at the top of the roof, high above the door, has the antlers of a stag from the royal estate of Balmoral. One of the Queen's granddaughters got married here in 2011.

The church is open only when volunteers have signed up to welcome visitors. Chat them up and borrow the description of the place. Then step inside the lofty blue and red interior, renovated with royal money; the church is filled with light and the flags of various Scottish regiments. In the narthex, peruse the photos of royal family events here, and find the list of priests and ministers of this parish—it goes back to 1143 (with a clear break with the Reformation in 1561).

Outside, turn right as you leave the church and walk up into the graveyard. The large, gated grave (abutting the back of the People's Story Museum) is the affectionately tended tomb of **Adam Smith,** the father of capitalism. (Throw him a penny or two.)

The statue on the sidewalk in front of the church is of the poet **Robert Fergusson.** One of the first to write verse in the Scots language, he so inspired Robert Burns that Burns paid for Fergusson's tombstone in the Canongate churchyard and composed his epitaph.

Now look across the street at the **gabled house** next to the Museum of Edinburgh. Scan the facade to see shells put there in the 17th century to defend against the evil power of witches yet to be drowned.

• *Walk about 300 yards farther along (past the recommended **Clarinda's Tea Room**). In the distance you can see the Palace of Holyroodhouse (the end of this walk) and soon, on the right, you'll come to the modern Scottish parliament building.*

Just opposite the parliament building is **White Horse Close** (on the left, in the white arcade that juts into the sidewalk). Step into this 17th-century courtyard. It was from here that the Edinburgh stagecoach left for Lon-

don. Eight days later, the horse-drawn carriage would pull into its destination: Scotland Yard. Note that bus #35 leaves in two directions from here—downhill for the Royal Yacht *Britannia,* and uphill along the Royal Mile (as far as South Bridge) and on to the National Museum of Scotland.

• *Now walk up around the corner to the flagpoles (flying the flags of Europe, Britain, and Scotland) in front of the...*

❿ Scottish Parliament Building

Finally, after centuries of history, we reach the 21st century. And finally, after three centuries of London rule, Scotland has a parliament building...in Scotland.

When Scotland united with England in 1707, its parliament was dissolved. But in 1999, the Scottish parliament was reestablished, and in 2004, it moved into this striking new home. Notice how the eco-friendly building, by the Catalan architect Enric Miralles, mixes wild angles, lots of light, bold windows, oak, and native stone into a startling complex. (People from Catalunya—another would-be breakaway nation—have an affinity for Scotland.) From the front of the parliament building, look in the distance at the rocky Salisbury Crags, with people hiking the traverse up to the dramatic next summit called Arthur's Seat. Now look at the building in relation to the craggy cliffs. The architect envisioned the building as if it were rising right from the base of Arthur's Seat, almost bursting from the rock.

Since it celebrates Scottish democracy, the architecture is not a statement of authority. There are no statues of old heroes. There's not even a grand entry. You feel like you're entering an office park. Given its neighborhood, the media often calls the Scottish Parliament "Holyrood" for short (similar to calling the US Congress "Capitol Hill"). For details on touring the building and seeing parliament in action, see page 82.

• *Across the street is the Queen's Gallery, where her majesty shares part of her amazing personal art collection in excellent revolving exhibits—each with a theme (see page 85). Finally, walk to the end of the road (Abbey Strand), and step up to the impressive wrought-iron gate of the Queen's palace. Look up at the stag with its holy cross, or "holy rood," on its forehead, and peer into the palace grounds. (The ticket office and palace entryway, a fine café, and a handy WC are just through the arch on the right.)*

EDINBURGH

⓫ Palace of Holyroodhouse

Since the 16th century, this palace has marked the end of the Royal Mile. An abbey—part of a 12th-century Augustinian mon-astery—originally stood in its place. While most of that old building is gone, you can see the surviving nave behind the palace on the left. According to one legend, it was named "holy rood" for a piece of the cross, brought here as a relic by Queen (and later

Saint) Margaret. (Another version of the story is that King David I, Margaret's son, saw the image of a cross upon a stag's head while hunting here and took it as a sign that he should build an abbey on the site.) Because Scotland's royalty preferred living at Holyrood-house to the blustery castle on the rock, the palace grew over time. If the Queen's not visiting, the palace welcomes visitors (get tickets in the Queen's Gallery; see page 85 for details).

• *Your walk—from the castle to the palace, with so much Scottish history packed in between—is complete. But if your appetite is whetted, don't worry, there's much more to see. Enjoy the rest of Edinburgh.*

NEW TOWN WALK: GEORGIAN EDINBURGH

Many visitors, mesmerized by the Royal Mile, never venture to the New Town. And that's a shame. With the city's finest Georgian architecture (from its 18th-century boom period), the New Town has a completely different character than the Old Town. This self-guided walk—worth ▲▲—gives you a quick orientation in about one hour.

• *Begin on Waverley Bridge, spanning the gully between the Old and New towns; to get there from the Royal Mile, just head down the curved Cockburn Street near the Tron Church (or cut down any of the "close" lanes opposite St. Giles Cathedral). Stand on the bridge overlooking the train tracks, facing the castle.*

❶ **View from Waverley Bridge:** From this vantage point, you can enjoy fine views of me-dieval Edinburgh, with its 10-story-plus "skyscrap-ers." It's easy to imagine how miserably crowded this area was, prompting the expansion of the city during the Georgian pe-riod. Pick out landmarks

EDINBURGH

New Town Walk: Georgian Edinburgh

200 Meters
200 Yards

1 View from Waverly Bridge
2 Princes Street Gardens
3 Scott Monument
4 Jenners Dep't Store
5 St. Andrew Square
6 George Street
7 St. Andrew's & St. George's Church
8 The Dome Restaurant
9 King George IV Statue
10 Thistle Street
11 William Pitt Statue
12 Rose Street
13 Charlotte Square
14 Georgian House

along the Royal Mile, most notably the open-work "thistle steeple" of St. Giles.

A big lake called the **Nor' Loch** once was to the north (nor') of the Old Town; now it's a valley between Edinburgh's two towns. The lake was drained around 1800 as part of the expansion. Before that, the lake was the town's water reservoir...and its sewer. Much has been written about the town's infamous stink. The town's nickname, "Auld Reekie," referred to both the smoke of its industry and the stench of its squalor.

The long-gone loch was also a handy place for drowning witches. With their thumbs tied to their ankles, they'd be lashed to dunking stools. Those who survived the ordeal were considered "aided by the devil" and burned as witches. If they died, they were innocent and given a good Christian burial. Edinburgh was Europe's witch-burning mecca—any perceived "sign," including a small birthmark, could condemn you. Scotland burned more witches per capita than any other country—17,000 souls between 1479 and 1722.

Visually trace the train tracks as they disappear into a tunnel below the **Scottish National Gallery** (with the best collection anywhere of Scottish paintings; you can visit it during this walk—see page 91). The two fine Neoclassical buildings of the National Gallery date from the 1840s and sit upon a mound that's called...**The Mound.** When the New Town was built, tons of rub-

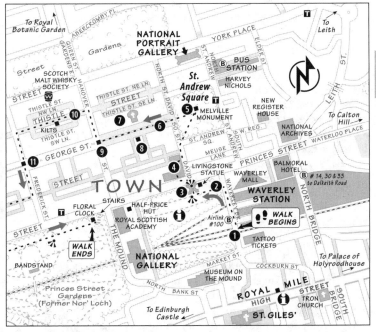

ble from the excavations were piled here (1781-1830), forming a dirt bridge that connected the new development with the Old Town to allay merchant concerns about being cut off from the future heart of the city.

Turning 180 degrees (and facing the ramps down into the train station), notice the huge, turreted building with the clock tower. (The clock is famously four minutes fast to help locals not miss their trains.) **The Balmoral** was one of the city's two grand hotels during its glory days (its opposite bookend, the **Waldorf Astoria Edinburgh,** sits at the far end of the former lakebed—near the end of this walk). Aristocrats arriving by train could use a hidden entrance to go from the platform directly up to their plush digs. (Today The Balmoral is known mostly as the place where J. K. Rowling completed the final Harry Potter book. She has a suite there that she uses when struggling with writer's block.)

• *Now walk across the bridge toward the New Town. Before the corner, enter the gated gardens on the left, and head toward the big, pointy monument. You're at the edge of...*

EDINBURGH

❷ **Princes Street Gardens:** This grassy park, filling the former lakebed, offers a wonderful escape from the bustle of the city. Once the private domain of the wealthy, it was opened to the public around 1870—not as a democratic gesture, but in hopes of increasing sales at the Princes Street department stores (Jenners is across the street). Join the office workers for a picnic lunch break.

• *Take a seat on the bench as encouraged by the Livingstone (Dr. Livingstone, I presume?) statue. (The Victorian explorer is well equipped with a guidebook but is hardly packing light—his lion skin doesn't even fit in his rucksack carry-on.)*

Look up at the towering...

❸ **Scott Monument:** Built in the early 1840s, this elaborate Neo-Gothic monument honors the great author Sir Walter Scott, one of Edinburgh's many illustrious sons.

When Scott died in 1832, it was said that "Scotland never owed so much to one man." Scott almost singlehandedly created the image of the Scotland we know. Just as the country was in danger of being assimilated into England, Scott celebrated traditional songs, legends, myths, architecture, and kilts, thereby reviving the Highland culture and cementing a national identity. And, as the father of the Romantic historical novel, he contributed to Western literature in general. Nicknamed "the Gothic Rocket," this 200-foot-tall monument shelters a marble statue of Scott and his favorite pet, Maida, a deerhound who was one of 30 canines this dog lover owned during his lifetime. Climbing the tight, stony spiral staircase of 220 steps earns you a peek at a tiny museum midway and a fine city view at the top (£8, open daily 10:00-17:00, Oct-March until 16:00; 30-minute tours depart on the half hour, last tour 30 minutes before closing; tel. 0131/529-4068).

• *Exit the park and head across busy Princes Street to the venerable...*

❹ **Jenners Department Store:** As you wait for the light to change, notice how statues of women support the building—just

as real women support the business. The arrival of new fashions here was such a big deal in the old days that they'd announce it by flying flags on the Nelson Monument atop Calton Hill (which you can see in the distance on the right).

Step inside and head upstairs into the grand, skylit atrium. The central space—filled with a towering tree at Christmas—is classic Industrial Age architecture. The Queen's coat of arms high above the clock indicates she shops here. But Jenners, like most department stores, is struggling in the age of online shopping.

• *Walk through the atrium, turn right, and exit onto South St. David Street. Turn left and follow this street uphill one block up to...*

❺ **St. Andrew Square:** This green space is dedicated to the patron saint of Scotland. In the early 19th century, there were no

shops around here—just fine residences; this was a private garden for the fancy people living here. Now open to the public, the square is a popular lunch hangout for workers. The Melville Monument honors a powermonger member of parliament who, for four decades (around 1800), was nicknamed the "uncrowned king of Scotland."

One block beyond the top of the park on Queen Street is the excellent **Scottish National Portrait Gallery,** which introduces you to all of the biggest names in Scottish history (described later, under "Sights in Edinburgh").

• *Follow the Melville Monument's gaze straight ahead out of the park. Cross the street and stand at the top of...*

❻ **George Street:** This is the main drag of Edinburgh's grid-planned New Town. Laid out in 1776, when King George III was busy putting down a revolution in a troublesome overseas colony, the New Town was a model of urban planning in its day. The architectural style is "Georgian"—British for "Neoclassical." And the street plan came with an unambiguous message: to celebrate the union of Scotland with England into the United Kingdom. (This was particularly important, since Scotland was just two decades removed from the failed Jacobite uprising of Bonnie Prince Charlie.)

If you look at a map, you'll see the politics in the street plan: St. Andrew Square (patron saint of Scotland) and Charlotte Square (George III's queen) bookend the New Town, with its three main streets named for the royal family of the time (George, Queen, and Princes). Thistle and Rose streets—which we'll see near the end of this walk—are named for the national flowers of Scotland and England.

The plan for the New Town was the masterstroke of the 23-year-old urban designer James Craig. George Street—20 feet wider than the others (so a four-horse carriage could make a U-turn)—was the main drag. Running down the high spine of the area, it afforded grand, unobstructed views. As you stroll down George Street, you'll notice that, with Craig's grid, grand cross streets come with fine Old Town and river views to the left and right, and monuments seem placed to accentuate the perspectives.

• *Halfway down the first block of George Street, on the right, is...*

❼ St. Andrew's and St. George's Church: Designed as part of the New Town plan in the 1780s, the church is a product of the Scottish Enlightenment. It has an elliptical plan (the first in Britain) so that all can focus on the pulpit. If it's open, step inside. The church conveys the idea that God is space, light, reason, and ordered beauty. A fine leaflet tells the story of the church, and a handy cafeteria downstairs serves cheap and cheery lunches.

❽ The Dome: Directly across the street from the church is another temple, this one devoted to money. This former bank building (now housing a recommended restaurant) has a pediment filled with figures demonstrating various ways to make money, which they do with all the nobility of classical gods. Consider scurrying across the street and ducking inside to view the stunning domed atrium.

❾ Statue of King George IV: Continue down George Street to the intersection with a statue commemorating the visit by George IV. Notice the particularly fine axis formed by this cross-street: The National Gallery lines up perfectly with the Royal Mile's skyscrapers and the former Tolbooth Church, creating a Gotham City collage.

• *By now you've gotten your New Town bearings. Feel free to stop this walk here: If you were to turn left and head down Hanover Street, in a block you'd run into the Scottish National Gallery; the street behind it curves back up to the Royal Mile.*

But to see more of the New Town—including the Georgian House, offering an insightful look inside one of these fine 18th-century homes—stick with me for a few more long blocks, zigzagging through side streets to see the various personalities that inhabit this rigid grid.

Turn right on Hanover Street; after just one (short) block, cross over and go left down...

❿ Thistle Street: Of the many streets in the New Town, this has perhaps the most vivid Scottish character. And that's fitting, as it's named after Scotland's national flower. At the beginning and end of the street, also notice that Craig's street plan included tranquil cul-de-sacs within the larger blocks. Thistle Street seems sleepy, but holds characteristic boutiques and good restaurants (see "Eating in Edinburgh," later). Halfway down the street on the left is a rare kiltmaking artisan in action: Howie Nicholsby's shop, **21st Century Kilts,** updates traditional Scottish menswear (though it's usually open by appointment only; for details see the listing on page 109).

• You'll soon reach Frederick Street. Turn left and head toward the...

⓫ Statue of William Pitt the Younger: Pitt was a prime minister under King George III during the French Revolution and the Napoleonic Wars. His father gave his name to the American city of Pittsburgh (which Scots pronounce as "Pitts-burrah"...I assume).

• For an interesting contrast, we'll continue down another side street. Pass the statue of Pitt (heading toward Edinburgh Castle), and turn right onto...

⓬ Rose Street: As a rose is to a thistle, and as England is to Scotland, so is brash, boisterous Rose Street to sedate, thoughtful Thistle Street. This stretch of Rose Street feels more commercialized, jammed with chain stores. The far end is packed with pubs and restaurants. As you walk, keep an eye out for the cobbled Tudor rose embedded in the brick sidewalk. When you cross the aptly named Castle Street, linger over the grand views to Edinburgh Castle. It's almost as if they planned it this way... just for the views.

• Popping out at the far end of Rose Street, across the street and to your right is...

⓭ Charlotte Square: The building of the New Town started cheap with St. Andrew Square, but finished well with this stately space. In 1791, the Edinburgh town council asked the prestigious Scottish architect Robert Adam to pump up the design for Charlotte Square. The council hoped that Adam's plan would answer criticism that the New Town buildings lacked innovation or ambition—and they got what they wanted. Adam's design, which raised the standard of New Town architecture to "international class," created Edinburgh's finest Georgian square. To this day, the fine garden filling the square is private, reserved for residents only.

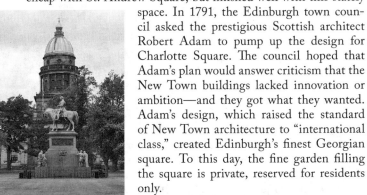

• Along the right side of Charlotte Square, at #7, you can visit the **⓮** *Georgian House, which gives you a great peek behind all of these harmonious Neoclassical facades (see page 95).*

When you're done touring the house, you can head back through the

New Town grid, perhaps taking some different streets than the way you came. If you're staying in the West End, you're just a few blocks away from your hotel. Or, for a restful return to our starting point, consider this...

Return Through Princes Street Gardens: From Charlotte Square, drop down to busy Princes Street (noticing the red building to the right—the grand Waldorf Astoria Hotel and twin sister of The Balmoral at the start of our walk). But rather than walking along the busy bus-and-tram-lined shopping drag, head into **Princes Street Gardens** (cross Princes Street and enter the gate on the left). With the castle looming overhead, you'll pass a playground, a fanciful Victorian fountain, more monuments to great Scots, war memorials, and a bandstand (which hosts Scottish country dancing—see page 112). Finally, you'll reach a staircase up to the Scottish National Gallery (though access from this entrance may be limited); and the oldest **floral clock** in the world—perhaps telling you it's time for a spot of tea.

• *Our walk is over. From here, you can tour the gallery; head up Bank Street just behind it to reach the Royal Mile; hop on a bus along Princes Street to your next stop (or B&B); or continue through another stretch of the Princes Street Gardens to the Scott Monument and our starting point.*

Sights in Edinburgh

▲▲▲EDINBURGH CASTLE

The fortified birthplace of the city 1,300 years ago, this imposing symbol of Edinburgh sits proudly on a rock high above the town. The home of Scotland's kings and queens for centuries, the castle has witnessed royal births, medieval pageantry, and bloody sieges. Today it's a complex of various buildings, the oldest dating from the 12th century, linked by cobbled roads that survive from its more recent use as a military garrison. The
castle—with expansive views, plenty of history, and the stunning crown jewels of Scotland—is a fascinating and multifaceted sight that deserves several hours of your time.

Cost and Hours: £20, daily 9:30-18:00, Oct-March until 17:00, last entry one hour before closing, tel. 0131/225-9846, www.edinburghcastle.scot.

Avoiding Lines: The castle is usually less crowded after 15:00 (cruise and bus-tour groups tend to come in the morning). To avoid ticket lines (worst in Aug), buy your ticket in advance online. You can print your ticket at home or pick it up at the black kiosk—with several nearby computer stations—just below the esplanade (facing the Tartan Weaving Mill) before joining the castle crowds. You can also pick up tickets at the machines just inside the castle entrance or at the visitor information desk a few steps uphill on the right.

You can skip the ticket line with a Historic Scotland Explorer Pass (see page 465 for details) or the Royal Edinburgh Ticket (see "Tours in Edinburgh," earlier).

Getting There: Simply walk up the Royal Mile (if arriving by bus from the B&B area south of the city, get off at South Bridge and huff up the Mile for about 15 minutes). Taxis get you closer, dropping you a block below the espla-nade at the Hub/Tolbooth Church.

Tours: Thirty-minute introducto-ry guided tours are free with admission (2-4/hour, depart from Argyle Battery, see clock for next departure; fewer off-season). The informative audioguide provides four hours of descriptions, including the National War Museum Scotland (£3.50, pick up inside Port-cullis Gate).

Eating: The **$ Redcoat Café**—just past the Argyle Battery—is a big, bright, efficient cafeteria with great views.

➔ Self-Guided Tour

❶ **Entry Gate:** Approaching from the esplanade, you're greeted by the two greatest Scottish heroes. Flanking the entryway are statues of the fierce warriors who battled English invaders, William Wal-lace (on the right) and Robert the Bruce (left). Between them is the Scottish motto, *Nemo me impune lacessit*—roughly, "No one messes with me and gets away with it."

Once inside, start winding your way uphill toward the main sights—the crown jewels and the Royal Palace—located near the summit. Since the castle was protected on three sides by sheer cliffs, the main defense had to be here at the entrance. During the castle's heyday in the 1500s, a 100-foot tower loomed overhead, facing the city.

• *Passing through the **portcullis gate**, you reach the...*

❷ **Argyle (Six-Gun) Battery, with View:** These front-load-ing, cast-iron cannons are from the Napoleonic era, around 1800, when the castle was still a force to be reckoned with.

From here, look north across the valley to the grid of the

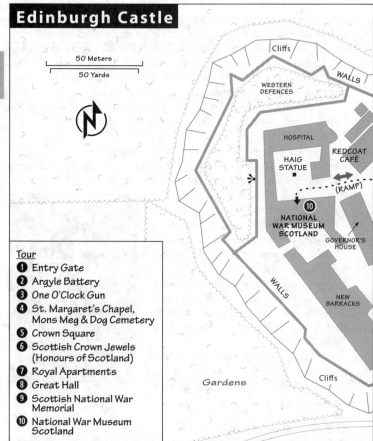

Edinburgh Castle

50 Meters
50 Yards

Cliffs

WESTERN
DEFENCES

WALLS

HOSPITAL

REDCOAT
CAFÉ

HAIG
STATUE

(RAMP)

⑩
NATIONAL
WAR MUSEUM
SCOTLAND

GOVERNOR'S
HOUSE

WALLS

NEW
BARRACKS

Gardens

Cliffs

Tour
1 Entry Gate
2 Argyle Battery
3 One O'Clock Gun
4 St. Margaret's Chapel, Mons Meg & Dog Cemetery
5 Crown Square
6 Scottish Crown Jewels (Honours of Scotland)
7 Royal Apartments
8 Great Hall
9 Scottish National War Memorial
10 National War Museum Scotland

New Town. The valley (directly below) sits where the Nor' Loch once was; this lake was drained and filled in when the New Town was built in the late 1700s, its swamps replaced with gardens. Later the land provided sites for the Greek-temple-esque Scottish National Gallery (above the train line tunnels), Waverley Station, and the tall, lacy Sir Walter Scott Memorial. Looking farther north, you can make out the port town of Leith (fac-

ing the island of Inchkeith), the Firth of Forth, and—in the far, far distance (to the extreme right)—the cone-like mountain of North Berwick Law, a former volcano.

Now look down. The sheer north precipice looks impregnable.

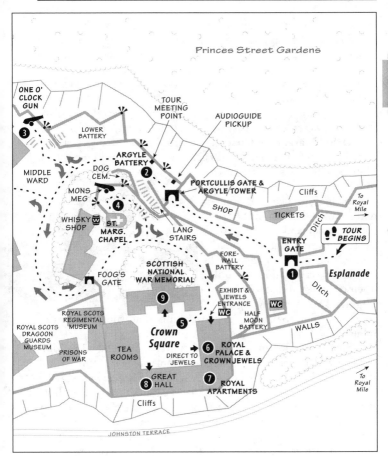

But on the night of March 14, 1314, 30 armed men silently scaled this rock face. They were loyal to Robert the Bruce and determined to recapture the castle, which had fallen into English hands. They caught the English by surprise, took the castle, and—three months later—Bruce defeated the English at the Battle of Bannockburn.

Looking back at the gate you just entered, the curved stairway to the right known as Lang Stairs leads steeply up to St. Margaret's Chapel and Crown Square—where we'll end up eventually. But we'll take a more gradual approach.

• *A little farther along, to the right of the Redcoat Café, is the...*

❸ **One O'Clock Gun:** Crowds gather for the 13:00 gun blast (which comes with a little military ceremony), a tradition that gives ships in the bay something to set their navigational devices by. Before the gun, sailors set their clocks with help from the Nelson Monument—that's the tall pillar in the distance on Calton Hill. The monument has a "time ball" affixed to the cross on top, which drops precisely at the top of the hour. But on foggy days, ships couldn't see the ball, so the cannon shot was instituted instead (1861). The tradition stuck, every day at 13:00. (Locals joke that the frugal Scots don't fire it at high noon, as that would cost 11 extra rounds a day.) For more information, there's a small exhibit just down the stairs.

• *Continue uphill, winding to the left and passing through **Foog's Gate**. At the very top of the hill, climb up the stairs on your left to reach...*

❹ St. Margaret's Chapel: This tiny stone chapel is Edinburgh's oldest building (around 1120) and sits atop its highest point (440 feet). It represents the birth of the city.

In 1057, Malcolm III murdered King Macbeth (of Shakespeare fame) and assumed the Scottish throne. Later, he married Princess Margaret, and the family settled atop this hill. Their marriage united Malcolm's Highland Scots with Margaret's Lowland Anglo-Saxons—the cultural mix that would define Edinburgh.

Step inside the tiny, unadorned church—a testament to Margaret's reputed piety. The elegant-yet-simple stone structure is Romanesque. The nave is wonderfully simple, with classic Norman zigzags decorating the round arch that separates the tiny nave from the sacristy. You'll see a facsimile of St. Margaret's 11th-century gospel book. The small (19th-century Victorian) stained-glass windows feature St. Margaret herself, St. Columba, St. Ninian (who brought Christianity to Scotland in AD 397), St. Andrew (Scotland's patron saint), and William Wallace (the defender of Scotland). These days, the place is popular for weddings. (As it seats only 20, it's particularly popular with parents funding the festivities.)

Margaret died at the castle in 1093, and her son King David I built this chapel in her honor (she was sainted in 1250). David expanded the castle and also founded Holyrood Abbey, across town. These two structures were soon linked by a Royal Mile of buildings, and Edinburgh was born.

Mons Meg, in front of the church, is a huge and once-upon-a-time frightening 15th-century siege cannon that fired 330-pound stones nearly two miles. Look at the huge granite cannon

EDINBURGH

balls and imagine. It was a gift from Philip the Good, duke of Burgundy, to his great-niece's husband King James II of Scotland.

Nearby, belly up to the banister and look down to find the **Dog Cemetery,** a tiny patch of grass with a sweet little line of doggie tombstones, marking the graves of soldiers' faithful canines-in-arms.

• *Continue on, curving downhill into...*

❺ Crown Square: This courtyard is the center of today's Royal Castle complex. Get oriented. You're surrounded by the crown

jewels, the Royal Palace (with its Great Hall), and the Scottish National War Memorial.

The castle has evolved over the centuries, and Crown Square is relatively "new." After the time of Malcolm and Margaret, the castle was greatly expanded by David II (1324-1371), complete with tall towers, a Great Hall, dungeon, cellars, and so on. This served as the grand royal residence for two centuries. Then, in 1571-1573, the Protestant citizens of Edinburgh laid siege to the castle and its Catholic/monarchist holdouts, eventually blasting an earlier castle to smithereens. The palace was rebuilt nearby—around what is today's Crown Square.

• *We'll tour the buildings around Crown Square. First up: the crown jewels. There are two entrances—both usually with a line. The one on Crown Square, only open in peak season, deposits you straight into the room with the crown jewels but usually comes with a longer line. The other entry, around the left side (near the WCs), takes you—at a shuffle—to the jewels the long way, through the interesting, Disney-esque "Honours of Scotland" exhibit, which tells the story of the crown jewels and how they survived the harrowing centuries, but lacks any actual artifacts.*

❻ Scottish Crown Jewels: For centuries, Scotland's monarchs were crowned in elaborate rituals involving three wondrous objects: a jewel-studded crown, scepter, and sword. These objects—along with the ceremonial Stone of Scone (pronounced "skoon")—are known as the "Honours of Scotland." Scotland's crown jewels may not be as impressive as England's, but locals treasure them as a symbol of Scottish nationalism. They're also older than England's; while Oliver Cromwell destroyed England's jewels, the Scots managed to hide theirs.

History of the Jewels: The Honours of Scotland exhibit that leads up to the Crown Room traces the evolution of the jewels, the ceremony, and the often-turbulent journey of this precious regalia. Here's the short version:

In 1306, Robert the Bruce was crowned with a "circlet of gold" in a ceremony at Scone—a town 40 miles north of Edin-burgh, which Scotland's earliest kings had claimed as their capital. Around 1500, King James IV added two new items to the coronation ceremony—a scepter (a gift from the pope) and a huge sword (a gift from another pope). In 1540, James V had the original crown augmented by an Edinburgh goldsmith, giving it the imperial-crown shape it has today.

These Honours were used to crown every monarch: nine-month-old Mary, Queen of Scots (she cried); her one-year-old son James VI (future king of England); and Charles I and II. But the days of divine-right rulers were numbered.

In 1649, the parliament had Charles I (king of both England and Scotland) beheaded. Soon Cromwell's rabid English antiroyalists were marching on Edinburgh. Quick! Legend says two women scooped up the crown and sword, hid them in their skirts, and buried them in a church far to the northeast until the coast was clear.

When the monarchy was restored, the regalia were used to crown Scotland's last king, Charles II (1660). Then, in 1707, the Treaty of Union with England ended Scotland's independence. The Honours came out for a ceremony to bless the treaty, and were then locked away in a strongbox in the castle. There they lay for over a century, until Sir Walter Scott—the writer and great champion of Scottish tradition—forced a detailed search of the castle in 1818. The box was found...and there the Honours were, perfectly preserved. Within a few years, they were put on display, as they have been ever since.

The crown's most recent official appearance was in 1999, when it was taken across town to the grand opening of the reinstated parliament, marking a new chapter in the Scottish nation. As it represents the monarchy, the crown is present whenever a new session of parliament opens. (And if Scotland ever secedes, you can be sure that crown will be in the front row.)

The Honours: Finally, you enter the Crown Room to see the regalia itself. The four-foot steel **sword** was made in Italy under orders of Pope Julius II (the man who also commissioned Michelangelo's Sistine Chapel and St. Peter's Basilica). The **scepter** is made of silver, covered with gold, and topped with a rock crystal and a pearl. The gem- and pearl-encrusted **crown** has an imperial arch

EDINBURGH

William Wallace (c. 1270-1305)

In 1286, Scotland's king died without an heir, plunging the prosperous country into a generation of chaos. As Scottish nobles bickered over naming a successor, the English King Edward I—nicknamed "Longshanks" because of his long legs—invaded and assumed power (1296). He placed a figurehead on the throne, forced Scottish nobles to sign a pledge of allegiance to England (the "Ragman's Roll"), moved the British parliament north to York, and took the highly symbolic Stone of Scone to London, where it would remain for centuries.

WILLIAM WALLACE.

A year later, the Scots rose up against Edward, led by William Wallace (popularized in the film *Braveheart*). A mix of history and legend portrays Wallace as the son of a poor-but-knightly family that refused to sign the Ragman's Roll. Exceptionally tall and strong, he learned Latin and French from two uncles, who were priests. In his teenage years, his father and older brother were killed by the English. Later, he killed an English sheriff to avenge the death of his wife, Marion. Wallace's rage inspired his fellow Scots to revolt.

In the summer of 1297, Wallace and his guerrillas scored a series of stunning victories over the English. On September 11, a well-equipped English army of 10,000 soldiers and 300 horsemen began crossing Stirling Bridge. Wallace's men attacked, and in the chaos, the bridge collapsed, splitting the English ranks in two. The ragtag Scots drove the confused English into the river. The Battle of Stirling Bridge was a rout, and Wallace was knighted and appointed guardian of Scotland.

All through the winter, King Edward's men chased Wallace, continually frustrated by the Scots' hit-and-run tactics. Finally, at the Battle of Falkirk (1298), they drew Wallace's men out onto the open battlefield. The English with their horses and archers easily destroyed the spear-carrying Scots. Wallace resigned in disgrace and went on the lam, while his successors negotiated truces with the English, finally surrendering unconditionally in 1304. Wallace alone held out.

In 1305, the English tracked him down and took him to London, where he was convicted of treason and mocked with a crown of oak leaves as the "king of outlaws." On August 23, they stripped him naked and dragged him to the execution site. There he was strangled to near death, castrated, and dismembered. His head was stuck on a spike atop London Bridge, while his body parts were sent on tour to spook would-be rebels. But Wallace's martyrdom only served to inspire his countrymen, and Robert the Bruce picked up the torch of independence (see page 73). Despite the *Braveheart* movie, Robert the Bruce, not Wallace, was considered the original "Braveheart." (For the full story, see page 204.)

topped with a cross. Legend says the band of gold in the center is the original crown that once adorned the head of Robert the Bruce.

The **Stone of Scone** (a.k.a. the "Stone of Destiny") sits plain and strong next to the jewels. It's a rough-hewn gray slab of sandstone, about 26 by 17 by 10 inches. As far back as the ninth century, Scotland's kings were crowned atop this stone, when it stood at the medieval capital of Scone. But in 1296, the invading army of Edward I of England carried the stone off to Westminster Abbey. For the next seven centuries, English (and subsequently British) kings and queens were crowned sitting on a coronation chair with the Stone of Scone tucked in a compartment underneath.

In 1950, four Scottish students broke into Westminster Abbey on Christmas Day and smuggled the stone back to Scotland in an act of foolhardy patriotism. But what could they do with it? After three months, they abandoned the stone, draped in Scotland's national flag. It was returned to Westminster Abbey, where (in 1953) Queen Elizabeth II was crowned atop it. In 1996, in recognition of increased Scottish autonomy, Elizabeth agreed to let the stone go home, on one condition: that it be returned to Westminster Abbey for all British coronations. Assuming Scotland remains in the United Kingdom, one day, the next monarch of the UK—Prince Charles is first in line—will sit atop this stone, re-enacting a coronation ritual that dates back a thousand years.

• *Exit the crown jewel display, heading down the stairs. But just before exiting into the courtyard, turn left through a door that leads into the...*

❼ **Royal Apartments:** Scottish royalty lived in the Royal Palace only when safety or protocol required it (they preferred the Palace of Holyroodhouse at the bottom of the Royal Mile). Here you can see several historic but unimpressive rooms. The first one, labeled **Queen Mary's Chamber,** is where Mary, Queen of Scots (1542-1587) gave birth to James VI of Scotland, who later became King James I of England. Nearby  **Laich Hall** (Lower Hall) was the dining room of the royal family.

• *Head back outside, across the square, to find the entry on the left to the...*

❽ **Great Hall:** Built by James IV to host the castle's official banquets and meetings, the Great Hall is still used for such purposes today. Most of the interior—its fireplace, carved walls, pikes, and armor—is Victorian. But the well-constructed wood ceiling is original. This hammer-beam roof (constructed like the hull of a ship) is self-supporting. The complex system of braces and arches distributes the weight of the roof outward to the walls,

EDINBURGH

so there's no need for supporting pillars or long cross beams. Before leaving, look for the tiny iron-barred window above the fireplace, on the right. This allowed the king to spy on his subjects while they partied.

• *Across the Crown Square courtyard is the...*

❾ **Scottish National War Memorial:** This commemorates the 149,000 Scottish soldiers lost in World War I, the 58,000 who

died in World War II, and the nearly 800 (and counting) lost in British battles since. Before entering, notice how the Art Deco facade (built in the 1920s with the historic stones of a church that once stood on this spot) fits perfectly with the surrounding buildings.

Inside, the main memorial is directly ahead, but you circulate counterclockwise. Since this structure was built after World War I, the scenes in the windows are from that war. Memorials honor regiments from each of the four branches of the British military with maroon remembrance books listing all the names of the fallen.

The main shrine, featuring a green Italian-marble memorial that contains the original WWI rolls of honor, sits on an exposed chunk of the castle rock. Above you, the archangel Michael is busy slaying a dragon. The bronze frieze accurately shows the attire of various wings of Scotland's military. The stained glass starts with Cain and Abel on the left and finishes with a celebration of peace on the right. To appreciate how important this place is, consider that Scottish soldiers died at twice the rate per capita of other British soldiers in World War I.

• *There are several other exhibits (including "Prisons of War," covering the lives of POWs held in the castle in 1781), memorials, and regimental museums in the castle. If you have seen enough, the Lang Stairs near St. Margaret's Chapel are a shortcut leading down to the Argyle Battery and the exit.*

*But there is one more important stop—the **National War Museum**. Backtrack down the hill toward the Redcoat Café (and the One O'Clock Gun). Just before the café head downhill to the left to the museum courtyard. (If you were in a horse-drawn carriage, you'd be thankful for the courtyard's cobblestone design—rough stones in the middle so your* *horse could get a grip, and smooth stones on the outside so your ride was even.) The statue in front of the museum is* **Field Marshall Sir Douglas Haig**—*the Scotsman who commanded the British Army through the WWI trench warfare of the Battle of the Somme and in Flanders Fields.*

🔟 **National War Museum Scotland:** This thoughtful museum covers four centuries of Scottish military history. Instead of the usual musty, dusty displays of endless armor, there's a compelling mix of videos, uniforms, weapons, medals, mementos, and eloquent excerpts from soldiers' letters. Your castle audioguide includes coverage of this museum, and the introductory video in the theater is worth watching.

Here you'll learn the story of how the fierce and courageous Scottish warrior changed from being a symbol of resistance against Britain to being a champion of that same empire. Along the way, these military men received many decorations for valor and did more than their share of dying in battle. But even when fighting alongside—rather than against—England, Scottish regiments still promoted their romantic, kilted-warrior image.

Queen Victoria fueled this ideal throughout the 19th century. She was infatuated with the Scottish Highlands and the culture's untamed, rustic mystique. Highland soldiers, especially officers, went to great personal expense to sport all their elaborate regalia, and the kilted men fought best to the tune of their beloved bagpipes. For centuries the stirring drone of bagpipes accompanied Highland soldiers into battle—raising their spirits and announcing to the enemy that they were about to meet a fierce and mighty foe.

This museum shows the human side of war as well as the cleverness of government-sponsored ad campaigns that kept the lads enlisting. Two centuries of recruiting posters make the same pitch that still works today: a hefty signing bonus, steady pay, and job security with the promise of a manly and adventurous life—all spiked with a mix of pride and patriotism.

Leaving the castle complex, you're surrounded by cannons that no longer fire, stony walls that tell an amazing story, dramatic views of this grand city, and the clatter of tourists (rather than soldiers) on cobbles. Consider for a moment all the bloody history and valiant struggles, along with British power and Scottish pride, that have shaped the city over which you are perched.

Robert the Bruce (1274-1329)

In 1314, Robert the Bruce's men attacked Edinburgh's Royal Castle, recapturing it from the English. It was just one of many intense battles between the oppressive English and the plucky Scots during the Wars of Independence.

In this era, Scotland had to overcome not only its English foes but also its own divisiveness—and no one was more divided than Robert the Bruce. As earl of Carrick, he was born with blood ties to England and a long-standing family claim to the Scottish throne.

When England's King Edward I ("Longshanks") conquered Scotland in 1296, the Bruce family welcomed it, hoping Edward would defeat their rivals and put Bruce's father on the throne. They dutifully signed the "Ragman's Roll" of allegiance—and then Edward chose someone else as king.

Twentysomething Robert the Bruce (the "the" comes from his original family name of "de Bruce") then joined William Wallace's revolt against the English. As legend has it, he was the one who knighted Wallace after the victory at Stirling Bridge. When Wallace fell from favor, Bruce became a guardian of Scotland (caretaker ruler in the absence of a king) and continued fighting the English. But when Edward's armies again got the upper hand in 1302, Robert—along with Scotland's other nobles—diplomatically surrendered and again pledged loyalty.

In 1306, Robert the Bruce murdered his chief rival and boldly claimed to be king of Scotland. Few nobles supported him. Edward crushed the revolt and kidnapped Bruce's wife, the Church excommunicated him, and Bruce went into hiding on a distant North Sea island. He was now the king of nothing. Legend says he gained inspiration by watching a spider patiently build its web.

The following year, Bruce returned to Scotland and wove alliances with both nobles and the Church, slowly gaining acceptance as Scotland's king by a populace chafing under English rule. On June 24, 1314, he decisively defeated the English (now led by Edward's weak son, Edward II) at the Battle of Bannockburn. After a generation of turmoil (1286-1314), England was finally driven from Scotland, and the country was united under Robert I, king of Scotland.

As king, Robert the Bruce's priority was to stabilize the monarchy and establish clear lines of succession. His descendants would rule Scotland for the next 400 years, and even today, Bruce blood runs through the veins of Queen Elizabeth II, Prince Charles, Princes William and Harry, and wee George, Charlotte, Louis, and Archie.

EDINBURGH

SIGHTS ON AND NEAR THE ROYAL MILE
▲Camera Obscura
A big deal when it was built in 1853, this observatory topped with a mirror reflected images onto a disc before the wide eyes of peo-

ple who had never seen a photograph or a captured image. Today, you can climb 100 steps for an entertaining 20-minute demonstration (3/hour). At the top, enjoy the best view anywhere of the Royal Mile. This sight is a goofy and entertaining break from all the heavy history and culture of the city's standard sights—it's just flat-out fun. You'll work your way down through five floors of illusions, holograms, and entertaining gags.

Cost and Hours: £16, book online one day in advance in peak season to skip the ticket line; open daily 9:00-21:00, Sat until 22:00, shorter hours off-season; tel. 0131/226-3709, www.camera-obscura.co.uk.

▲The Scotch Whisky Experience
This attraction seems designed to distill money out of your pocket. The 50-minute experience consists of a "Malt Disney" whisky-

barrel ride through the pro-duction process followed by an explanation and movie about Scotland's five main whisky regions. Though gimmicky, it does succeed in providing an entertaining yet informative ori-entation to the creation of Scot-tish firewater (things get pretty psychedelic when you hit the yeast stage). Your ticket also includes sampling a wee dram and the chance to stand amid the world's largest Scotch whisky collection (almost 3,500 bottles). At the end, you'll find yourself in the bar, with a fascinating wall of unusually shaped whisky bottles. Serious connoisseurs should stick with the more substantial shops in town, but this place can be worthwhile for beginners.

Cost and Hours: £16 "silver tour" includes one sample, £28 "gold tour" includes five samples—one from each main region, gen-erally daily 10:00-18:30, last "silver tour" at 17:00, tel. 0131/220-0441, www.scotchwhiskyexperience.co.uk.

▲▲Gladstone's Land

This is a typical 16th- to 17th-century merchant's "land," or tenement building. These multistory structures—in which merchants ran their shops on the ground floor and lived upstairs—were typical of the time (the word "tenement" didn't have the slum connotation then that it has today). At six stories, this one was still just half the height of the tallest "skyscrapers."

Gladstone's Land comes complete with an almost-lived-in, furnished interior and 400-year-old Renaissance painted ceiling. You'll explore five rooms, each with a docent posted to answer your questions. Keep this place in mind as you stroll the rest of the Mile, imagining other houses as if they still looked like this on the inside. (For a comparison of life in the Old Town versus the New Town, also visit the Georgian House, described later.)

Cost and Hours: £7, daily 11:00-16:30, tel. 0131/226-5856, www.nts.org.uk/Visit/Gladstones-Land.

▲Writers' Museum at Lady Stair's House

This aristocrat's house, built in 1622, is filled with well-described manuscripts and knickknacks of Scotland's three greatest literary figures: Robert Burns, Robert Louis Stevenson, and Sir Walter Scott. If you'd like to see Scott's pipe and Burns' snuffboxes, you'll love this little museum. You'll wind up steep staircases through a maze of rooms as you peruse first editions and keepsakes of these celebrated writers. Edinburgh's high society gathered in homes like this in the 1780s to hear the great poet Robbie Burns read his work—it's meant to be read aloud rather than to oneself.

Cost and Hours: Free, daily 10:00-17:00, tel. 0131/529-4901, www.edinburghmuseums.org.uk.

Museum on the Mound

Located in the basement of the grand Bank of Scotland building, this exhibit tells the story of the bank, which was founded in 1695 (making it only a year younger than the Bank of England) and claims to be the longest operating bank in the world. Featuring lots of artifacts and displays on cash production, safe technology, and bank robberies, this museum (with a case holding £1 million in cash) makes banking almost interesting. It's worth popping in if you have extra time or find the subject appealing.

Cost and Hours: Free, Tue-Fri 10:00-17:00, Sat from 13:00, closed Sun-Mon, down Bank Street from the Royal Mile—follow the street around to the left and enter through the gate, tel. 0131/243-5464, www.museumonthemound.com.

▲▲St. Giles' Cathedral

This is Scotland's most important church. Its ornate spire—the Scottish crown steeple from 1495—is a proud part of Edinburgh's

skyline. The fascinating interior contains nearly 200 memorials honoring distinguished Scots through the ages.

Cost and Hours: Free, but consider the suggested £5 donation as a fair admission cost; Mon-Fri 9:00-19:00, Sat until 17:00; Nov-March Mon-Sat 9:00-17:00; Sun 13:00-17:00 year-round; info sheet-£1, guidebook-£6, tel. 0131/226-0677, www.stgilescathedral.org.uk.

Concerts: St. Giles' busy concert schedule includes free organ recitals and visiting choirs (frequent events at 13:30 and concerts Sun at 18:00; also sometimes Wed, Thu, or Fri at 20:00; see schedule or ask for *Music at St. Giles* pamphlet at welcome desk or gift shop).

⊘ Self-Guided Tour: Today's facade is 19th-century Neo-Gothic, but most of what you'll see inside is from the 14th and 15th centuries. Engage the cathedral guides in conversation; you'll be glad you did.

Just inside the entrance, turn around to see the modern stained-glass **❶ Robert Burns window,** which celebrates Scotland's favorite poet (see page 446). It was made in 1985 by the Icelandic artist Leifur Breidfjord. The green of the lower level symbolizes the natural world—God's creation. The middle zone with the circle shows the brotherhood of man—Burns was a great internationalist. The top is a rosy red sunburst of creativity, reminding Scots of Burns' famous line, "My love is like a red, red rose"—part of a song near and dear to every Scottish heart.

To the right of the Burns window is a fine **❷ Pre-Raphaelite window.** Like most in the church, it's a memorial to an important patron (in this case, John Marshall). From here stretches a great swath of war memorials.

As you walk along the north wall, find **❸ John Knox's statue** (standing like a six-foot-tall bronze chess piece). Look into his eyes for 10 seconds from 10 inches away, and think of the Reformation struggles of the 16th century. Knox, the great religious reformer and founder of austere Scottish Presbyterianism, first preached here in 1559. His insistence that every person should be able to

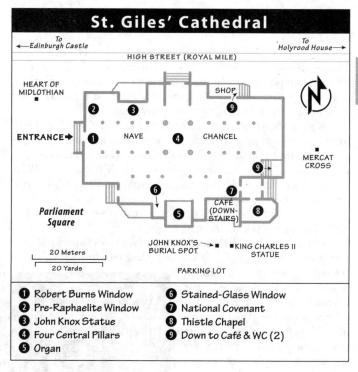

St. Giles' Cathedral

←—Edinburgh Castle
To

To
Holyrood House→

HIGH STREET (ROYAL MILE)

HEART OF
MIDLOTHIAN ■

SHOP

❷ ❸ ❾

ENTRANCE→ ❶ NAVE ❹ CHANCEL

■ MERCAT CROSS

❾

❻ ❼

Parliament Square

❺ CAFÉ (DOWN-STAIRS) ❽

JOHN KNOX'S → ■ BURIAL SPOT ■KING CHARLES II STATUE

20 Meters

20 Yards

PARKING LOT

❶ Robert Burns Window
❷ Pre-Raphaelite Window
❸ John Knox Statue
❹ Four Central Pillars
❺ Organ
❻ Stained-Glass Window
❼ National Covenant
❽ Thistle Chapel
❾ Down to Café & WC (2)

personally read the word of God—notice that he's pointing to a book—gave Scotland an educational system 300 years ahead of the rest of Europe (for more on Knox, see "The Scottish Reformation" on page 223). Thanks partly to Knox, it was Scottish minds that led the way in math, science, medicine, and engineering. Voltaire called Scotland "the intellectual capital of Europe."

Knox preached Calvinism. Consider that the Dutch and the Scots both embraced this creed of hard work, frugality, and strict ethics. This helps explain why the Scots are so different from the English (and why the Dutch and the Scots—both famous for their thriftiness and industriousness—are so much alike).

The oldest parts of the cathedral—the ❹ **four massive central pillars**—are Norman and date from the 12th century. They supported a mostly wooden superstructure that was lost when an invading English force burned it in 1385. The Scots rebuilt it bigger and better than ever, and in 1495 its famous crown spire was completed.

During the Reformation—when Knox preached here (1559-1572)—the place was simplified and whitewashed. Before this, when the emphasis was on holy services provided by priests, there were lots of little niches. With the new focus on sermons rather than rituals, the grand pulpit took center stage.

Knox preached against anything that separated you from God, including stained glass (considered the poor man's Bible, as illiterate Christians could learn from its pictures). Knox had the church's fancy medieval glass windows replaced with clear glass, but 19th-century Victorians took them out and installed the brilliantly colored ones you see today.

Cross over to the ❺ **organ** (1992, Austrian-built, one of Europe's finest) and take in its sheer might.

Immediately to the right of the organ is a tiny chapel for silence and prayer. The dramatic ❻ **stained-glass window** above shows the commotion that surrounded Knox when he preached. The bearded, fiery-eyed Knox had a huge impact on this community. Notice how there were no pews back then. The church was so packed, people even looked through clear windows from across the street. With his hand on the holy book, Knox seems to conduct divine electricity to the Scottish faithful.

In the corner to the far left of the organ, find a copy of the ❼ **National Covenant** (behind small curtains). It was signed in blood in 1638 by Scottish heroes who refused to compromise their religion for the king's. Most who signed were martyred (their monument is nearby in Grassmarket). You can see the original National Covenant in the Museum of Edinburgh, described later.

Head toward the east (back) end of the church, and turn right to see the Neo-Gothic ❽ **Thistle Chapel** (the volunteer guide is a wealth of information). The interior is filled with intricate wood carving. Built in two years (1910-1911), entirely with Scottish materials and labor, it is the private chapel of the Order of the Thistle, the only Scottish chivalric order. It's used several times a year for the knights to gather (and, if one dies, to inaugurate a new member). Scotland recognizes its leading citizens by bestowing a membership upon them. The Queen presides over the ritual from her fancy stall, marked by her Scottish coat of arms—a heraldic zoo of symbolism. Are there bagpipes in heaven? Find the tooting stone angel at the top of a window to the left of the altar, and the wooden one to the right of the doorway you came in.

❾ **Downstairs** you'll find handy public WCs and an inviting **$ café**—a good place for paupers to munch prayerfully—quick, quaint, and supporting the church (simple, light lunches, coffee and cakes; Mon-Sat 9:00-17:00, Sun from 11:00, in basement on back side of church, tel. 0131/225-5147).

Old Parliament House

This space housed the Scottish parliament until the Act of Union in 1707. The building now holds the Scottish Supreme Court, so you'll need to go through security as you enter. Peruse the grand hall, with its fine 1639 hammer-beam ceiling and stained glass. The biggest stained-glass window depicts the initiation of the first Scottish High Court in 1532. The building is busy with wigged and robed lawyers hard at work in the old library (peek through the door) or pacing the hall deep in discussion. The basement café is literally their supreme court's restaurant (open to public until 14:30).

Cost and Hours: Free, public welcome Mon-Fri 9:00-16:30, closed Sat-Sun, no photos, enter behind St. Giles' Cathedral at door #11; open-to-the-public trials are just across the street at the High Court—the doorman has the day's docket.

▲The Real Mary King's Close

For an unusual peek at Edinburgh's gritty, plague-ridden past, join a costumed performer on an hour-long trip through an excavated underground street and buildings on the northern slope of the Royal Mile. Tours cover the standard goofy, crowd-pleasing ghost stories, but also focus on authentic and historical insight into a part of town entombed by later construction. Book ahead (online up to the day before, or by phone or in person for a same-day booking).

Cost and Hours: £16.50, book at least one day in advance during peak season; tours leave every 15-30 minutes, daily generally 9:00-21:45, Oct-April until 17:00; these are last tour times, across from St. Giles at 2 Warriston's Close—but enter through door on High Street, tel. 0131/225-0672, www.realmarykingsclose.com.

▲Museum of Childhood

This five-story playground of historical toys and games is rich in nostalgia and history. Each well-signed gallery is as jovial as a Norman Rockwell painting, highlighting the delights and simplicity of childhood. The museum does a fair job of representing culturally relevant oddities, such as ancient Egyptian, Peruvian, and voodoo dolls, and displays early versions of toys it's probably best didn't make the final cut (such as a grim snake-centered precursor to the popular board game Chutes and Ladders).

Cost and Hours: Free, daily 10:00-17:00, 42 High Street.

EDINBURGH

Scotland's Literary Greats

Edinburgh was home to Scotland's three greatest literary figures, pictured above: Robert Burns (left), Robert Louis Stevenson (center), and Sir Walter Scott (right).

Robert Burns (1759-1796), known as "Rabbie" in Scotland and quite possibly the most famous and beloved Scot of all time, moved to Edinburgh after achieving overnight celebrity with his first volume of poetry (staying in a house on the spot where Deacon Brodie's Tavern now stands). Even though he wrote in the rough Scots dialect and dared to attack social rank, he was a favorite of Edinburgh's high society, who'd gather in fine homes to hear him recite his works. For more on Burns, see the sidebar on page 448.

One hundred years later, **Robert Louis Stevenson** (1850-1894) also stirred the Scottish soul with his pen. An avid traveler who always packed his notepad, Stevenson created settings that are vivid and filled with wonder. Traveling through Scotland, Europe, and around the world, he distilled his adventures into Romantic classics, including *Kidnapped* and *Treasure Island* (as well as *The Strange Case of Dr. Jekyll and Mr. Hyde*). Stevenson, who was married in San Francisco and spent his last years in the South Pacific, wrote, "Youth is the time to travel—both in mind and in body—to try the manners of different nations." He said, "I travel not to go anywhere...but to simply go." Travel was his inspiration and his success.

Sir Walter Scott (1771-1832) wrote the *Waverley* novels, including *Ivanhoe* and *Rob Roy*. He's considered the father of the

▲John Knox House

Intriguing for Reformation buffs, this fine medieval house dates back to 1470 and offers a well-explained look at the life of the great 16th-century reformer. Al-

though most contend he never actually lived here, preservationists called it "Knox's house" to save it from the wrecking ball in the 1840s. Regardless, the place has good information on Knox and his intellectual sparring partner, Mary, Queen of Scots. Imagine the Protestant firebrand John Knox and the devout Catholic Mary sitting face-to-face in old rooms like these, discussing the most intimate matters of their spiritual lives as they decided the course of Scotland's religious future. The sparsely furnished house contains some period furniture, an early 1600s hand-painted ceiling, information on the

EDINBURGH

Romantic historical novel. Through his writing, he generated a worldwide interest in Scotland, and reawakened his fellow countrymen's pride in their heritage. His novels helped revive interest in Highland culture—the Gaelic language, kilts, songs, legends, myths, the clan system—and created a national identity. An avid patriot, he wrote, "Every Scottish man has a pedigree. It is a national prerogative, as unalienable as his pride and his poverty." Scott is so revered in Edinburgh that his towering Neo-Gothic monument dominates the city center. With his favorite hound by his side, Sir Walter Scott overlooks the city that he inspired, and that inspired him.

The best way to learn about and experience these literary greats is to visit the Writers' Museum at Lady Stair's House (see page 75) and to take Edinburgh's Literary Pub Tour (see page 110).

While just three writers dominate your Edinburgh sightseeing, consider also the other great writers with Edinburgh connections: J. K. Rowling (who captures the "Gothic" spirit of Edinburgh with her Harry Potter series); current resident Ian Rankin (with his "tartan noir" novels); J. M. Barrie (who attended University of Edinburgh and later created Peter Pan); Sir Arthur Conan Doyle (who was born in Edinburgh, went to medical school here, and is best known for inventing Sherlock Holmes); and James Boswell (who lived 50 yards away from the Writers' Museum, in James Court, and is revered for his biography of Samuel Johnson).

house and its resident John Mossman (goldsmith to Mary, Queen of Scots), and exhibits on printing—an essential tool for early reformers.

Cost and Hours: £6, Mon-Sat 10:00-18:00, closed Sun except in July-Aug, 43 High Street, tel. 0131/556-9579, www. scottishstorytellingcentre.com.

▲People's Story Museum

This engaging exhibit, which occupies the Canongate Tolbooth (built in 1591), traces the working and social lives of ordinary people through the 18th, 19th, and 20th centuries. You'll see tools, products, and objects related to important Edinburgh trades (printing, brewing), a wartime kitchen, and a small theater on the top floor with a video.

Cost and Hours: Free, daily 10:00-17:00, 163 Canongate, tel. 0131/529-4057, www.edinburghmuseums.org.uk.

▲Museum of Edinburgh

Another old house full of old stuff, this one is worth a stop for a look at its early Edinburgh history (and its handy ground-floor WC). Be sure to see the original copy of the National Covenant—written in 1638 on animal skin. Scottish leaders signed this, refusing to adopt the king's religion—and were killed because of it. Exploring the rest of the collection, keep an eye out for Robert Louis Stevenson's antique golf ball, James Craig's architectural plans for the Georgian New Town, an interactive kids' area with dress-up clothes, a sprawling top-floor exhibit on Edinburgh-born Field Marshall Sir David Haig (who led the British Western Front efforts in World War I and later became Earl Haig), and locally made glass and ceramics.

Cost and Hours: Free, daily 10:00-17:00, 142 Canongate, tel. 0131/529-4143, www.edinburghmuseums.org.uk.

Nearby: Next to the museum is the entry to **Bakehouse Close,** a well-preserved 18th-century alleyway. It's worth a peek (and recognizable to fans of the *Outlander* TV series—the exterior of Jamie's print shop was filmed here).

▲▲Scottish Parliament Building

Scotland's parliament originated in 1293 and was dissolved when Scotland united with England in 1707. But after the Scottish

electorate and the British parliament gave their consent, in 1997 it was decided that there should again be "a Scottish parliament guided by justice, wisdom, integrity, and compassion." Formally reconvened by Queen Elizabeth in 1999 (note that, while she's "II" in England, she's only the first "QE" for the people of Scotland), the Scottish parliament now enjoys self-rule in many areas (except for matters of defense, foreign policy, immigration, and taxation). The current government, run by the Scottish Nationalist Party (SNP), is pushing for even more independence.

The innovative building, opened in 2004, brought together all the functions of the fledgling parliament in one complex. It's a people-oriented structure conceived by Catalan architect Enric Miralles. Signs are written in both English and Gaelic (the Scots' Celtic tongue).

For a peek at the building and a lesson in how the Scottish

parliament works, drop in, pass through security, and find the visitors' desk. You're welcome in the public parts of the building, including a small ground-floor exhibit on the parliament's history and function and, up the stairs, a viewing gallery overlooking the impressive Debating Chambers.

Cost and Hours: Free; Mon-Sat 10:00-17:00, Tue-Thu 9:00-18:00 when parliament is in session (Sept-June), closed Sun year-round. For a complete list of recess dates or to book tickets for debates, check their website or call their visitor services line, tel. 0131/348-5200, www.parliament.scot.

Tours: Proud locals offer worthwhile free hour-long tours covering history, architecture, parliamentary processes, and other topics. Tours generally run throughout the day Mon and Fri-Sat in session (Sept-June) and Mon-Sat in recess (July-Aug). While you can try dropping in, these tours can book up—it's best to book ahead online or over the phone.

Seeing Parliament in Session: The public can witness the Scottish parliament's hugely popular debates (usually Tue-Thu 14:00-18:00, but hours can vary). Book ahead online no more than seven days in advance, over the phone, or at the info desk. You're not required to stay the whole session.

You can also watch parliamentary committees in session (usually Tue-Thu mornings). Topics are published the Friday before (see business bulletin on website), and you must book ahead just as you would for debates.

On Thursdays from 11:40 to 12:45 the First Minister is on the hot seat and has to field questions from members across all parties (reserve ahead for this popular session over the phone a week in advance; spots book up quickly—call at 9:00 sharp on Thu for the following week). If you don't get tickets over the phone, show up at 10:00 and ask if you can get in—they sometimes have standby tickets.

▲▲Palace of Holyroodhouse

Built on the site of the abbey/monastery founded in 1128 by King David I, this palace was the true home, birthplace, and coronation spot of Scotland's Stuart kings in their heyday (James IV; Mary, Queen of Scots; and Charles I). It's particularly memorable as the site of some dramatic moments from the short reign of Mary, Queen of Scots—including the murder of her personal secretary,

David Rizzio, by agents of her jealous husband. Today, it's one of Queen Elizabeth II's official residences. She usually manages her Scottish affairs here during Holyrood Week, from late June to early July (and generally stays at Balmoral in August). Holyrood is open to the public outside of the Queen's visits. Touring the interior offers a more polished contrast to Edinburgh Castle, and is particularly worth considering if you don't plan to go to Balmoral. The one-way audioguide route leads you through the fine apart-

ments and tells some of the notable stories that played out here.

Cost: £15, includes quality one-hour audioguide; £20 combo-ticket includes the Queen's Gallery; £24.50 combo-ticket adds guided tour of palace gardens (April-Oct only); tickets sold in Queen's Gallery to the right of the castle entrance (see next listing).

Hours: Daily 9:30-18:00, Nov-March until 16:30, last entry 1.5 hours before closing, tel. 0131/556-5100, www.rct.uk. It's still a working palace, so it's closed when the Queen or other VIPs are in residence.

Eating: The **$$$ café** on the palace grounds, to the right of the palace entrance, has an inviting afternoon tea.

Visiting the Palace: The building, rich in history and decor, is filled with elegantly furnished Victorian rooms and a few darker, older rooms with glass cases of historic bits and Scottish pieces that locals find fascinating. Bring the palace to life with the audioguide. The tour route leads you into the grassy inner courtyard, then up to the royal apartments: dining rooms, *Downton Abbey*-style drawing rooms, and royal bedchambers. Along the way, you'll learn the story behind the 96 portraits of Scottish leaders (some real, others imaginary) that line the Great Gallery; why the king never slept in his official "state bed"; why the exiled Comte d'Artois took refuge in the palace; and how the current Queen puts her Scottish subjects at ease when she receives them here. Finally, you'll twist up a tight spiral staircase to the private chambers of Mary, Queen of Scots, where conspirators stormed in and stabbed her secretary 56 times.

After exiting the palace, you're free to stroll through the evocative **ruined abbey** (destroyed by the English during the time of Mary, Queen of Scots, in the 16th century) and the **palace gardens** (closed Nov-March except some weekends). Some 8,000 guests—including many honored ladies sporting fancy hats—gather here every July when the Queen hosts a magnificent tea party. (She gets help pouring.)

EDINBURGH

Nearby: Hikers, note that the wonderful trail up Arthur's Seat starts just across the street from the gardens (see page 99 for details). From the palace, face parliament, turn left, and head straight.

▲Queen's Gallery, Palace of Holyroodhouse

Over more than five centuries, the royal family has collected a wealth of art treasures. While the Queen keeps most of the royal

collection in her many private palaces, she shares an impressive sampling of it in this small museum, with themed exhibits changing about every six months. Though the gallery occupies just a few rooms, its displays can be exquisite.

Cost and Hours: £8 includes excellent audioguide, £20 combo-ticket includes Palace of Holyroodhouse, daily 9:30-18:00, Nov-March until 16:30, last entry one hour before closing, www.rct.uk. Buses #35 and #36 stop outside, saving you a walk to or from Princes Street/North Bridge.

Dynamic Earth

Located about a five-minute walk from the Palace of Holyroodhouse, this immense exhibit tells the story of our planet, filling several underground floors under a vast, white Gore-Tex tent. It's pitched, appropriately, at the base of the Salisbury Crags. The exhibit is designed for younger kids and does the same thing an American science exhibit would do—but with a charming Scottish accent. You'll learn about the Scottish geologists who pioneered the discipline, then step into a "time machine" to watch the years rewind, from cave dwellers to dinosaurs to the Big Bang. After viewing several short films on stars, tectonic plates, ice caps, and worldwide weather (in a "4-D" exhibit), you're free to wander past salty pools and a re-created rain forest.

Cost and Hours: £16, kids-£10, daily 10:00-17:30, July-Aug until 18:00, closed Mon-Tue Nov-Feb, last entry 1.5 hours before closing, on Holyrood Road, between the palace and mountain, tel. 0131/550-7800, www.dynamicearth.co.uk.

EDINBURGH

SIGHTS SOUTH OF THE ROYAL MILE
▲▲▲National Museum of Scotland

This huge museum has amassed more historic artifacts than every other place I've seen in Scotland combined. It's all wonderfully displayed, with fine descriptions offering a best-anywhere hike through the history of Scotland.

Cost and Hours: Free, daily 10:00-17:00; two long blocks south of St. Giles' Cathedral and the Royal Mile, on Chambers Street off George IV Bridge, tel. 0131/123-6789, www.nms.ac.uk.

Tours: Free one-hour general tours are offered daily at 11:00 and 13:00; themed tours at 15:00 (confirm tour schedule at info desk or on TV screens). The National Museum of Scotland Highlights app provides thin coverage of select items but is free and downloadable using their free Wi-Fi. Scattered interactive kiosks help navigate the stories behind important artifacts and figures.

Services: Bag check is on the ground floor (£1.50).

Eating: A **$$ brasserie** is on the ground floor near the information desks, and a **$ café** with coffee, tea, cakes, and snacks is on the level 3 balcony overlooking the Grand Gallery. On the museum's fifth floor, the dressy and upscale **$$$$ Tower restaurant** serves good food with a castle view (lunch/early-bird special, afternoon tea, three-course dinner specials; daily 10:00-22:00, Fri-Sat until 10:30—use Tower entry if eating after museum closes, reservations recommended, tel. 0131/225-3003, www.tower-restaurant. com). A number of good eating options are within a couple of blocks of the museum (see page 130).

Overview: The museum can be confusing to navigate, so pick up the map when you enter for a color-coded guide to each wing. The place gives you several museums in one, with each gallery rising vertically up several floors: the Natural World galleries (T. Rex skeletons and other animals), the Science and Technology galleries, and a fashion, art, and design exhibit. The World Cultures galleries feature clothing, tools, textiles, and artifacts from ancient Egypt, China, Japan, and the Pacific Islands. With time and interest, these are all worth a look.

We'll focus on yet another wing, the Scotland galleries, which sweep you through Scottish history covering Roman and Viking times, Edinburgh's witch-burning craze and clan massacres, the struggle for Scottish independence, the Industrial Revolution, and right up to Scotland in the 21st century.

EDINBURGH

⊃ Self-Guided Tour: Get oriented on level 1, in the impressive glass-roofed Grand Gallery right above the entrance hall. Just outside the Grand Gallery is the **millennium clock,** a 30-foot high clock with figures that move to a Bach concerto on the hour from 11:00 to 16:00. The clock has four parts (crypt, nave, belfry, and spire) and represents the turmoil of the 20th century, with a pietà at the top.

• *To reach the **Scottish history wing**, exit the Grand Gallery at the far right end, under the clock and past the statue of Scottish inventor James Watt.*

On the way, you'll pass through the science and technology wing. While walking through, on your left, look for **Dolly the sheep**—the world's first cloned mammal—born in Edinburgh and now stuffed and on display. Continue into Hawthornden Court (level 1, past the little snack bar), where our tour begins. (It's possible to detour downstairs from here to level -1 for

Scotland's prehistoric origins—geologic formation, Celts, Romans, Vikings.)

• *Enter the door marked...*

Kingdom of the Scots (c. 900s-late 1600s): From its very start, Scotland was determined to be free. You're greeted with proud quotes from what's been called the Scottish Declaration of Independence—the Declaration of Arbroath, a defiant letter written to the pope in 1320. As early as the ninth century, Scotland's patron saint, Andrew (see the small statue in the next room), had—according to legend—miraculously intervened to help the Picts and Scots of Scotland remain free by defeating the Angles of England. Andrew's X-shaped cross still decorates the Scottish flag today.

Enter the first room on your right, with imposing swords and other objects related to Scotland's most famous patriots—William Wallace and Robert the Bruce. Bruce's descendants, the Stuarts, went on to rule Scotland for the next 300 years. Eventually, James VI of Scotland (see his baby cradle) came to rule England as well (as King James I of England). In the middle of the room, a massive banner of the royal arms of Britain is adorned with the motto of James VI: "Blessed are the peacemakers."

In the next room, a big guillotine recalls the harsh justice meted out to criminals, witches, and "Covenanters" (17th-century political activists who opposed interference of the Stuart kings in affairs of the Presbyterian Church of Scotland). Look for the creepy mask of Covenanter Alexander Peden, who preached illegally in this disguise. Nearby, also check out the tomb (a copy) of Mary, Queen of Scots, the 16th-century Stuart monarch who opposed the Presbyterian Church of Scotland. Educated and raised in Renaissance France, Mary brought refinement to the

Scottish throne. After she was imprisoned and then executed by Elizabeth I of England in 1587, her supporters rallied each other by invoking her memory. Pendants and coins with her portrait stoked the irrepressible Scottish spirit (see display case next to tomb).

Browse the rest of level 1 to see everyday objects from that age: carved panels, cookware, and sculptures.

• *Backtrack to Hawthornden Court and head up to level 3.*

Scotland Transformed (1700s): You'll see artifacts related to Bonnie Prince Charlie and the Jacobite rebellions as well as items related to the Treaty of Union document, signed in 1707 by the Scottish parliament. This act voluntarily united Scotland with England under the single parliament of the United Kingdom. For some Scots, this move was an inevitable step in connecting to the wider world, but for others it symbolized the end of Scotland's existence.

Union with England brought stability and investment to Scotland. In this same era, the advances of the Industrial Revolution were making a big impact on Scottish life. Mechanized textile looms (on display) replaced hand craftsmanship. The huge Newcomen steam-engine water pump helped the mining industry to develop sites with tricky drainage. Nearby is a model of a coal mine (or "colliery"); coal-rich Scotland exploited this natural resource to fuel its textile factories.

How the parsimonious Scots financed these new, large-scale enterprises is explained in an exhibit on the Bank of Scotland. Powered by the Scottish work ethic and the new opportunities that came from the Industrial Revolution, the country came into relative prosperity. Education and medicine thrived. With the dawn of the modern age came leisure time, the concept of "healthful sports," and golf—a popular Scottish pastime. On display (near the back, in a small

EDINBURGH

corridor behind the machinery) are some early golf balls, which date from about 1820, made of leather and stuffed with feathers.

• *Leave this hall the way you came in, and journey up to level 5.*

Industry and Empire (1800s): Turn right and do a counter-clockwise spin around this floor to survey Scottish life in the 19th century. Industry had transformed the country. Highland farmers left their land to find work in Lowland factories and foundries. Modern inventions—the phonograph, the steam-powered train, the kitchen range—revolutionized everyday life. In Glasgow near the turn of the century, architect Charles Rennie Mackintosh helped to define Scottish Art Nouveau. Scotland was at the fore-front of literature (Robert Burns, Sir Walter Scott, Robert Louis Stevenson), science (Lord Kelvin, James Watt, Alexander Graham Bell...he was born here, anyway!), world exploration (John Kirk in Africa, Sir Alexander Mackenzie in Canada), and whisky production.

• *Climb the stairs to level 6.*

Scotland: A Changing Nation (1900s-present): Turn left and do a clockwise spin through this floor to bring the story to the present day. The two world wars decimated the population of this already wee nation. In addition, hundreds of thousands emigrated, especially to Canada (where one in eight Canadians has Scottish origins). Other exhibits include shipbuilding and the fishing indus-try; Scots in the world of entertainment (from folk singer Donovan to actor-comedian Billy Connolly); a look at the recent trend of devolution from the United Kingdom (1999 opening of Scotland's own parliament and the landmark 2014 referendum on Scottish independence); and a sports Hall of Fame (from tennis star Andy Murray to auto racers Jackie Stewart and Jim Clark).

• *Finish your visit on level 7, the rooftop.*

Garden Terrace: The well-described roof garden features grasses and heathers from every corner of Scotland and spectacular views of the city.

Greyfriars Bobby Statue and Greyfriars Cemetery

This famous **statue** of Edinburgh's fa-vorite dog is across the street from the National Museum of Scotland. Every business nearby, it seems, is named for this Victorian Skye terrier, who is re-puted to have slept upon his master's grave in Greyfriars Cemetery for 14 years. The story was immortalized in a 1960s Disney flick, but recent research suggests that 19th-century businessmen bribed a stray to hang out in the cemetery to attract sightseers. If it was a ruse, it still works.

Just behind Greyfriars Bobby is the entrance to his namesake **cemetery** (open until late). Stepping through the gate, you'll see the pink-marble grave of Bobby himself. (Rather than flowers, well-wishers bring sticks to remember Bobby.) The well-tended cemetery is an evocative place to stroll, and a nice escape from the city's bustle. Harry Potter fans could turn it into a scavenger hunt: J. K. Rowling sketched out her saga just around the corner at  The Elephant House café—and a few of the cemetery's weatherbeaten headstones bear familiar names, including McGonagall and Thomas Riddell. At the far end, past a stretch of the 16th-century Flodden Wall, peek through the black iron cemetery fence to see the frilly Gothic spires of posh George Heriot's School, said to have inspired Hogwarts. And just a few short blocks to the east is a street called...Potterrow.

The cemetery just feels made for ghost walks. It's said that the tombs with iron cages over them were designed so thieves couldn't break into the grave and steal bodies to sell to the medical school across the street (which always needed cadavers). Hmmm.

Grassmarket

Once Edinburgh's site for hangings (residents rented out their windows—above the wryly named "Last Drop" pub—for the view),  today Grassmarket is a people-friendly piazza. It was originally the city's garage, a depot for horses and cows (hence the name). It's rowdy here at night—a popular place for "hen dos" and "stag dos" (bachelorette and bachelor parties). In the early evening, the Literary Pub Tour departs from here (see "Nightlife in Edinburgh," later). Some good shopping streets branch off from Grassmarket: Picturesque Victoria Street, built in the Victorian Age, is lined with colorful little shops and eateries; angling off in the other direction, Candlemaker's Row has a few interesting artisan shops (and leads, in just a couple minutes' walk, up to Greyfriars Bobby and the National Museum; for more shopping tips in this area, see "Shopping in Edinburgh," later).

At the top of Grassmarket is the round monument to the "Covenanters." These strict 17th-century Scottish Protestants were killed for refusing to accept the king's Episcopalian prayer book. To this day, Scots celebrate their national church's emphatically democratic government. Rather than big-shot bishops (as in the Anglican or Roman Catholic Church), they have a low-key "moderator" who's elected each year.

MUSEUMS IN THE NEW TOWN
These sights are linked by my "New Town Walk" on page 55.

▲▲Scottish National Gallery
This delightful, small museum has Scotland's best collection of paintings—both European and Scottish. In a short visit, you can

admire well-described works by Old Masters (Raphael, Rembrandt, Rubens), Impressionists (Monet, Degas, Gauguin), and a few underrated Scottish painters. Although there are no iconic masterpieces, it's a surprisingly enjoyable collection that's truly world class. The museum is undergoing renovation until 2021, but it's still worthwhile.

Cost and Hours: Free; Fri-Wed 10:00-17:00, Aug until 18:00; Thu 10:00-19:00 year-round; café downstairs, The Mound (between Princes and Market streets), tel. 0131/624-6200, www.nationalgalleries.org.

Expect Changes: The museum is undergoing major renovation to increase the space of its Scottish collection and build a grand main entrance from Princes Street Gardens. As a result, some exhibits may be closed, and pieces may be relocated, on loan, or in storage. Ask one of the friendly tartan-sporting attendants or at the info desk downstairs (near the WCs and gallery shop) if you can't find a particular item.

Next Door: The skippable **Royal Scottish Academy** hosts temporary art exhibits and is connected to the Scottish National Gallery at the Gardens level (underneath the gallery) by the Weston Link building (same hours as gallery, fine café and restaurant).

Visiting the Museum: While it's tempting to give a painting-by-painting tour, the paintings on display here are always changing, there are few must-see masterpieces, and each painting is clearly labeled with a thoughtfully written description. It's easiest to simply wander through the collection. It's arranged chronologically, mostly on one floor with the more modern paintings (19th and early 20th century) upstairs.

The main-floor collection includes exquisite medieval altarpieces and works by the great masters (Botticelli, Raphael, Rubens, Rembrandt), as well as English artists (Gainsborough, Constable). Highlights of the more modern paintings (mostly upstairs) cover Celtic Revival, Pre-Raphaelites, Impressionists, and Post-Impressionists.

For the heart of the Scottish collection (on the main floor) look for the section labeled "Scottish, 1650-1850." But works by these homegrown artists are scattered throughout the museum:

Allan Ramsay, the son of the well-known poet of the same name, painted portraits of curly-wigged men of the Enlightenment era (the philosopher David Hume, King George III) as well as likenesses of his two wives. Ramsay's portrait of the duke of Argyll—founder of the Royal Bank of Scotland—appears on the front of notes printed by this bank.

Sir Henry Raeburn chronicled the next generation: Sir Walter Scott, the proud kilt-wearing Alastair MacDonell, and the ice-skating Reverend Robert Walker, minister of the Canongate Church.

Sir David Wilkie's forte was small-scale scenes of everyday life. *The Letter of Introduction* (1813) captures Wilkie's own experience of trying to impress skeptical art patrons in London; even the dog is sniffing the Scotsman out. *Distraining for Rent* (1815) shows the plight of a poor farmer about to lose his farm—a common occurrence during 19th-century industrialization.

William Dyce's *Francesca da Rimini* (1837) depicts star-crossed lovers—a young wife and her husband's kid brother—who can't help but indulge their passion. The husband later finds out and kills her; at the far left, you see his ominous hand.

William McTaggart's impressionistic landscape scenes from the late 1800s provide a glimpse of the unique light, powerful clouds, and natural wonder of the Highlands.

▲▲Scottish National Portrait Gallery

Put a face on Scotland's history by enjoying these portraits of famous Scots from the earliest times until today. From its Neo-Gothic facade to a grand entry hall highlighting Scottish history; to galleries showcasing the great Scots of each age, this impressive museum will fascinate anyone interested in Scottish culture. The gallery also hosts temporary exhibits highlighting the work of more contemporary Scots. Because of its purely Scottish focus, many travelers prefer this to the (pan-European) main branch of the National Gallery.

Cost and Hours: Free, daily 10:00-17:00, good cafeteria serving healthy meals, 1 Queen Street, tel. 0131/624-6490, www.nationalgalleries.org.

Visiting the Gallery: Start by studying the gallery map and the *What's On* quarterly, which gives you a rundown of special exhibits here (and at the National Gallery and Modern Art Gallery). While the entrance hall is stirring, its history frieze is better viewed from the balcony above (described later).

The meat of the collection is on the **top floor,** where Scottish history is illustrated by portraits and vividly described by information plaques next to each painting. With the 20th and 21st centuries, the chronological story spills down a level into Room 12 on the first floor. The rest of the gallery is devoted to special (and often very interesting) exhibits.

• *Start on the top floor, diving right into the thick of the struggle between Scotland and England over who should rule this land.*

Reformation to Revolution (Room 1): The collection starts with a portrait of **Mary, Queen of Scots** (1542-1587), her cross and rosary prominent. This controversial ruler set off two centuries of strife. Mary was born with both Stuart blood (the ruling family of Scotland) and the Tudor blood of England's monarchs (Queen Elizabeth I was her cousin). Catholic and French-educated, Mary felt alienated from her own increasingly Protestant homeland. Her tense conversations with the reformer John Knox must have been epic. Then came a series of scandals: She married unpopular Lord Darnley, then (possibly) cheated on him, causing Darnley

to (possibly) murder her lover, causing Mary to (possibly) murder Darnley, then (possibly) run off with another man, and (possibly) plot against Queen Elizabeth.

Amid all that drama, Mary was forced by her own people to relinquish her throne to her infant son, **James VI.** Find his portraits as a child and as a grown-up. James grew up to rule Scotland, and when Queen Elizabeth (the "virgin queen") died without an heir, he also became king of England (James I). But after a bitter civil war, James' son, **Charles I,** was arrested and executed in 1649: See the large *Execution of Charles I* painting, his blood-dripping head displayed to the crowd (in a section dedicated to his beheading and that tumultuous political time). His son, Charles II, restored the Stuarts to power. He was then succeeded by his Catholic brother James VII of Scotland (II of England), who was sent into exile in France. There the Stuarts stewed, planning a return to power, waiting for someone to lead them in what would come to be known as the Jacobite rebellions.

The Jacobite Cause (a few rooms later, in Room 4): One of the biggest paintings in the room is *The Baptism of Prince Charles Edward Stuart.* Born in 1720, this Stuart heir to the thrones of Great Britain and Ireland is better known to history as "Bonnie Prince Charlie." (See his bonnie features in various portraits nearby, as a child, young man, and grown man.) Charismatic Charles convinced France to invade Scotland and put him back on the throne there. In 1745, he entered Edinburgh in triumph. But he was defeated at the tide-turning Battle of Culloden (1746). The Stuart cause died forever, and Bonnie Prince Charlie went into exile, eventually dying drunk and wasted in Rome, far from the land he nearly ruled.

The Age of Improvement (Room 7): The faces portrayed here belonged to a new society whose hard work and public spirit achieved progress with a Scottish accent. Social equality and the Industrial Revolution "transformed" Scotland—you'll see portraits of the great poet Robert Burns, the son of a farmer (Burns was heralded as a "heaven-taught ploughman" when his poems were first published), and the man who perfected the steam engine, James Watt.

• *Check out the remaining galleries, then head back down to the first floor for a good look at the...*

Central Atrium (first floor): Great Scots! The atrium is decorated in a parade of late-19th-century Romantic Historicism. The **frieze** (below the bannister, working counterclockwise) is a visual encyclopedia, from an ax-wielding Stone Age man and a druid, to the early legendary monarchs (Macbeth), to warriors William Wallace and Robert the Bruce, to many kings (James I, II, III, and so on), to great thinkers, inventors, and

artists (Allan Ramsay, Flora MacDonald, David Hume, Adam Smith, James Boswell, James Watt), the three greatest Scottish writers (Robert Burns, Sir Walter Scott, Robert Louis Stevenson), and culminating with the historian Thomas Carlyle, who was the driving spirit (powered by the fortune of a local newspaper baron) behind creating this portrait gallery.

Around the first-floor mezzanine are large-scale **murals** depicting great events in Scottish history, including the landing of St. Margaret at Queensferry in 1068, the Battle of Stirling Bridge in 1297, the Battle of Bannockburn in 1314, and the marriage procession of James IV and Margaret Tudor through the streets of Edinburgh in 1503.

• *Also on this floor you'll find the...*

Modern Portrait Gallery: This space is dedicated to rotating art and photographs highlighting Scots who are making an impact in the world today, such as Annie Lennox, Alan Cumming, and physicist Peter Higgs (theorizer of the Higgs boson, the so-called God particle). Look for the *Three Oncologists,* a ghostly painting depicting the anxiety and terror of cancer and the dedication of those working so hard to conquer it.

▲▲Georgian House

This refurbished Neoclassical house, set on Charlotte Square, is a trip back to 1796. It recounts the era when a newly gentrified and well-educated Edin-

burgh was nicknamed the "Athens of the North." Begin on the second floor, where you'll watch a fascinating 16-minute video dramatizing the upstairs/ downstairs lifestyles of the aristocrats and servants who lived here. Try on some Georgian outfits, then head downstairs to tour period rooms and even peek into the fully stocked medicine cabinet. Info sheets are available in each room, along with volunteer guides who share stories and trivia, such as why Georgian bigwigs had to sit behind a screen while enjoying a fire. A walk down George Street after your visit here can be fun for the imagination.

Cost and Hours: £8, daily 10:00-17:00, March and Nov 11:00-16:00, closed Dec-Feb, last entry 45 minutes before closing; 7 Charlotte Square, tel. 0131/225-2160, www.nts.org.uk.

EDINBURGH

SIGHTS NEAR EDINBURGH
▲▲Royal Yacht *Britannia*

This much-revered vessel, which transported Britain's royal family for more than 40 years on 900 voyages (an average of once around the world per year) before being retired in 1997, is permanently moored in Edinburgh's port of Leith. Queen Elizabeth II said of the ship, "This is the only place I can truly relax." Today it's open to the curious public, who have access to its many decks—from engine rooms to drawing rooms—and offers a fascinating time-warp look into the late-20th-century lifestyles of the rich and royal. It's worth the 20-minute bus or taxi ride from the center; figure on spending about 2.5 hours total on the outing.

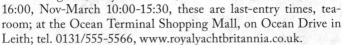

Cost and Hours: £16.50, includes 1.5-hour audioguide, daily 9:30-16:30, Oct until 16:00, Nov-March 10:00-15:30, these are last-entry times, tea-room; at the Ocean Terminal Shopping Mall, on Ocean Drive in Leith; tel. 0131/555-5566, www.royalyachtbritannia.co.uk.

Getting There: From central Edinburgh, catch Lothian bus #11 or #22 from Princes Street (just above Waverley Station), or #35 from the bottom of the Royal Mile (alongside the parliament building) to Ocean Terminal (last stop). From the B&B neighborhood, you can either bus to the city center and transfer to one of the buses above, or take bus #14 from Dalkeith Road to Mill Lane, then walk about 10 minutes. The Majestic Tour hop-on, hop-off bus stops here as well. If you're getting off the bus, go through the shopping center and take the escalator to level 2 (top floor).

Drivers can park free in the blue parking garage—park on level E (same floor as visitors center).

Visiting the Ship: First, explore the **museum,** filled with engrossing royal-family-afloat history. You'll see lots of family photos that evoke the fine times the Windsors enjoyed on the *Britannia,* as well as some nautical equipment and uniforms. Then, armed with your audioguide, you're welcome aboard.

This was the last in a line of royal yachts that stretches back to 1660. With all its royal functions, the ship required a crew of more than 200. Begin in the captain's bridge, which feels like it's been preserved from the day it was launched in 1953. Then head down a deck to see the officers' quarters, then the garage, where a Rolls Royce was hoisted aboard to use in places where the local transportation wasn't up to royal standards. The Veranda Deck at the back of the ship was the favorite place for outdoor entertain-

EDINBURGH

ment. Ronald Reagan, Boris Yeltsin, Bill Clinton, and Nelson Mandela all sipped champagne here. The Sun Lounge, just off the back Veranda Deck, was the Queen's favorite, with Burmese teak and the same phone system she was used to in Buckingham Palace. When she wasn't entertaining, the Queen liked it quiet. The crew wore sneakers, communicated in hand signals, and (at least near the Queen's quarters) had to be finished with all their work by 8:00 in the morning.

Take a peek into the adjoining his-and-hers bedrooms of the Queen and the Duke of Edinburgh (check out the spartan twin beds), and the honeymoon suite where Prince Charles and Lady Di began their wedded bliss.

Heading down another deck, walk through the officers' lounge (and learn about the rowdy games they played) and past the galleys (including custom cabine-try for the fine china and silver) on your way to the biggest room on the yacht, the state dining room. Now decorated with gifts given by the ship's many noteworthy guests, this space enabled the Queen to entertain a good-size  crowd. The drawing room, while rather simple (the Queen specifically requested "country house comfort"), was perfect for casual relaxing among royals. Princess Diana played the piano, which is bolted to the deck. Note the contrast to the decidedly less plush crew's quarters, mail room, sick bay, laundry, and engine room.

▲Rosslyn Chapel

This small but fascinating countryside church, about a 20-minute drive outside Edinburgh, is a riot of carved iconography. The patterned ceiling and walls have left scholars guessing about the symbolism for centuries.

Cost and Hours: £9, Mon-Sat 9:30-17:00, June-Aug until 18:00, Sun 12:00-16:45 year-round, located in Roslin Village, tel. 0131/440-2159, www.rosslynchapel.com.

Getting There: Ride Lothian bus #37 from Princes Street (stop PJ), North Bridge, or Newington Road in the B&B neighborhood (1-2/hour, 45 minutes). By car, take the A-701 to Penicuik/Peebles, and follow signs for *Roslin;* once you're in the village, you'll see signs for the chapel.

Background: After it was featured in the climax of Dan Brown's 2003 bestseller *The Da Vinci Code,* the number of visitors to Rosslyn Chapel more than quadrupled. But the chapel's allure existed well before the books, and will endure long after they move from bargain bin to landfill. Founded in 1446 as the private mausoleum of the St. Clair family—who wanted to be buried close to God—the church's interior is carved with a stunning mishmash of Christian, pagan, family, Templar, Masonic, and other symbolism. After the Scottish Reformation, Catholic churches like this fell into disrepair. But in the 18th and 19th centuries, Romantics such as Robert Burns and Sir Walter Scott discovered these evocative old ruins, putting Rosslyn Chapel back on the map. Even Queen Victoria visited, and gently suggested that the chapel be restored to its original state. Today, after more than a century of refits and refurbishments, the chapel transports visitors back to a distant and mysterious age.

Visiting the Chapel: From the ticket desk and visitors center, head to the chapel itself. Ask about docent lectures (usually at

the top of the hour—last talk at 17:00 in summer, 16:00 in winter). If you have time to kill, pick up the good laminated descriptions for a clockwise tour of the carvings. In the crypt—where the stonemasons worked—you can see faint architectural drawings engraved in the wall, used to help them plot out their master design.

Elsewhere, look for these fun details: In the corner to the left of the altar, find the angels playing instruments—including one with bagpipes. Nearby, you'll see a person dancing with a skeleton. This "dance of death" theme—common in the Middle Ages—is a reminder of mortality: We'll all die eventually, so we might as well whoop it up while we're here. On the other side of the nave are carvings of the seven deadly sins and the seven acts of mercy. One inscription reads: "Wine is strong. Kings are stronger. Women are stronger still. But truth conquers all."

Flanking the altar are two carved columns that come with a legend: The more standard-issue column, on the left, was executed by a master mason, who soon after (perhaps disappointed in his lack of originality) went on a sabbatical to gain inspiration. While he was gone, his ambitious apprentice carved the beautiful corkscrew-shaped column on the right. Upon returning, the master flew into an envious rage and murdered the apprentice with his carving hammer.

Scattered throughout the church, you'll also see the family's symbol, the "engrailed cross" (with serrated edges). Keep an eye out for the more than one hundred "green men"—chubby faces with leaves and vines growing out of their orifices, symbolizing nature. This paradise/Garden of Eden theme is enhanced by a smattering of exotic animals (monkey, elephant, camel, dragon, and a lion fighting a unicorn) and some exotic foliage: aloe vera, trillium, and corn. That last one (framing a window to the right of the altar) is a mystery: It was carved well before Columbus sailed the ocean blue, at a time when corn was unknown in Europe. Several theories have been suggested—some far-fetched (the father of the man who built the chapel explored the New World before Columbus), and others more plausible (the St. Clairs were of Norse descent, and the Vikings are known to have traveled to the Americas well before Columbus). Others simply say it's not corn at all—it's stalks of wheat. After all these centuries, Rosslyn Chapel's mysteries still inspire the imaginations of historians, novelists, and tourists alike.

Royal Botanic Garden

Britain's second-oldest botanical garden (after Oxford) was established in 1670 for medicinal herbs, and this 70-acre refuge is now one of Europe's best. A visitors center has temporary exhibits.

Cost and Hours: Gardens—free, greenhouse—£7, daily 10:00-18:00, Feb and Oct until 17:00, Nov-Jan until 16:00, greenhouse last entry one hour before closing, café and restaurant, a mile north of the city center at Inverleith Row, tel. 0131/248-2909, www.rbge.org.uk.

Getting There: It's a 10-minute bus ride from the city center: Take bus #8 from North Bridge, or #23 or #27 from George IV Bridge (near the National Museum) or The Mound. The Majestic Tour hop-on, hop-off bus also stops here.

Scottish National Gallery of Modern Art

This museum, set in a beautiful parkland, houses Scottish and international paintings and sculpture from 1900 to the present, including works by Matisse, Duchamp, Picasso, and Warhol. The grounds include a pleasant outdoor sculpture park and a café.

Cost and Hours: Free, daily 10:00-18:00, 75 Belford Road, tel. 0131/624-6200, www.nationalgalleries.org.

Getting There: It's about a 20-minute walk west from the city center. Or take the shuttle bus, which runs about hourly between this museum and the Scottish National Gallery (£1 donation requested, confirm times on website).

Experiences in Edinburgh

URBAN HIKES

▲▲Holyrood Park: Arthur's Seat and the Salisbury Crags

Rising up from the heart of Edinburgh, Holyrood Park is a lush green mountain squeezed between the parliament/Holyroodhouse (at the bottom of the Royal Mile) and my recommended B&B neighborhood. For an exhilarating hike, connect these two zones with a 30-minute walk along the Salisbury Crags—reddish cliffs with sweeping views over the city—but be aware that the crags occasionally close due to falling rocks. Or, for a more

serious climb, make the ascent to the summit of Arthur's Seat, the 822-foot-tall remains of an extinct volcano. You can run up like they did in *Chariots of Fire*, or just stroll. At the summit, you'll be rewarded with commanding views of the town and surroundings.

You can do this hike either from the bottom of the Royal Mile, or from the B&B neighborhood. A small road behind the bluff is accessible to taxis, so cheaters can ride halfway to the top. (Note that there are no facilities at the summit.)

From the Royal Mile: Begin in the parking lot below the Palace of Holyroodhouse. Facing the cliff, you'll see two trailheads. For the easier hike along the base of the **Salisbury Crags,** take the steps to the trail to the right. At the far end, you can descend into the Dalkeith Road area or continue steeply up the switchback trail to the Arthur's Seat summit. If you know you'll want to ascend **Arthur's Seat** from the start, take the wider path on the left from the Holyroodhouse parking lot (easier grade, through the abbey ruins and "Hunter's Bog").

From the B&B Neighborhood: If you're sleeping in this area, enjoy an early-morning or late-evening hike starting from

the other side (in June, the sun comes up early, and it stays light until nearly midnight). From the Commonwealth Pool, take Holyrood Park Road, bear left at the first roundabout, then turn right at the second roundabout (onto Queen's Drive). Soon you'll see the trailhead, and make your choice: Bear right up the steeper "Piper's Walk" to **Arthur's Seat** (about a 20-minute hike from here, up a steep switchback trail), or bear left for an easier ascent up the "Radial Road" to the **Salisbury Crags,** which you can follow—with great views over town—all the way up and over to Holyroodhouse Palace.

EDINBURGH

Duddingston Village and Dr. Neil's Garden

This low-key, 30-minute walk goes from the B&B neighborhood to Duddingston Village—a former village that got absorbed by the city but still retains its old, cobbled feel, local church, and great old-time pub, the recommended Sheep Heid Inn. Also here is Dr. Neil's Garden, a peaceful, free garden on a loch.

Walk behind the Commonwealth Pool along Holyrood Park Road. Before the roundabout, just after passing through the wall/gate, take the path to your right. This path runs alongside the Duddingston Low Road all the way to the village and garden. Ignore the road traffic and enjoy the views of Arthur's Seat, the golf course, and eventually, Duddingston Loch. When you reach the cobbled road, you're in Duddingston Village, with the church on your right and the Sheep Heid Inn a block down on your left. Another 100 feet down the main road is a gate labeled *"The Manse"* with the number 5—enter here for the garden.

Dr. Neil's Garden (also known as the Secret Garden) was started by doctors Nancy and Andrew Neil, who traveled throughout Europe in the 1960s gathering trees and plants. They brought them back here, planted them on this land, and tended to them with the help of their patients. Today it offers a quiet, secluded break from the city, where you can walk among flowers and trees and over quaint bridges, get inspired by quotes written on chalkboards, or sit on a bench overlooking the loch (free, daily 10:00-dusk, charming café, mobile 0784-918-7995, www.drneilsgarden.co.uk).

▲Calton Hill

For an easy walk for fine views over all of Edinburgh and beyond, head up to Calton Hill—the monument-studded bluff that rises from the eastern end of the New Town. From the Waverley Station area, simply head east on Princes Street (which becomes Waterloo Place).

About five minutes after passing North Bridge, watch on the right for the gated entrance to the **Old Calton Cemetery**—worth a quick walk-through for its stirring monuments to great Scots. The can't-miss-it round monument honors the philosopher David Hume; just next to that is a memorial topped by Abraham Lincoln, honoring Scottish-American troops who were killed in combat. The obelisk honors political martyrs.

The views from the cemetery are good, but for even better ones, head back out to the main road and continue a few more minutes on Waterloo Place. Across the street, steps lead up into **Calton Hill**. Explore the park, purchased by the city in 1724 and one of the first public parks in Britain. Informational plaques identify the key landmarks. At the summit of the hill is the giant, unfinished

replica of the Parthenon, honoring those lost in the Napoleonic Wars. Donations to finish
it never materialized, leaving it
with the nickname "Edinburgh's
Disgrace." Nearby, the old observatory holds an old telescope,
and the back of the hillside
boasts sweeping views over the
Firth of Forth and Edinburgh's

sprawl. Back toward the Old Town, the tallest tower (shaped like a
19th-century admiral's telescope) celebrates Admiral Horatio Nelson—the same honoree of the giant pillar on London's Trafalgar
Square. There's an interesting, free exhibit about Nelson at the base
of the tower. While you can pay to climb it for the view, it doesn't
gain you much. The best views are around the smaller, circular
Dugald Stewart Monument, with postcard panoramas overlooking
the spires of the Old Town and the New Town.

More Hikes

You can hike along the river (called the Water of Leith) through
Edinburgh. Locals favor the stretch between Roseburn and Dean
Village, but the 1.5-mile walk from Dean Village to the Royal Botanic Garden is also good. For more information on these and other
hikes, ask at the TI or your B&B.

WHISKY AND GIN TASTING
Whisky Tasting

One of the most accessible places to learn about whisky is at the
Scotch Whisky Experience on the Royal Mile, an expensive but
informative overview to whisky, including a tasting (see page 74).
To get more into sampling whisky, try one of the early-evening
tastings at the recommended **Cadenhead's Whisky Shop** (see page
107).

The **Scotch Malt Whisky Society,** in the New Town, is for
more serious whisky fans. It serves glasses from numbered bottles
of single malts from across Scotland and beyond. Each bottle—
pure from the cask and not blended—is only described and not
labeled. You read the description and make your choice...or enlist
the help of the bartender, who will probe you on what kind of flavor
profile you like. While this place's shrouded-in-mystery pretense
could get lost on novices, aficionados enjoy it (daily 11:00-23:00,
tastings listed on website, bar serves light dishes, on-site top-end
restaurant, 28 Queen Street, tel. 0131/220-2044, www.smws.com).

Gin Distillery Tours

The residents of Edinburgh drink more gin per person than any other city in the United Kingdom. The city is largely responsible for the recent renaissance of this drink, so it's only appropriate that you visit a gin distillery while in town. Two distilleries right in the heart of Edinburgh offer hour-long tours with colorful guides who discuss the history of gin, show you the stills involved in the production process, and ply you with libations. Both tours are popular and fill up; book ahead on their websites.

Pickering's is located in a former vet school and animal hospital at Summerhall, halfway between the Royal Mile and the B&B neighborhood. The bar and funky distillery have a cool, young, artsy vibe with skeletons and X-rays still hanging around. The mellow bar also serves cheap pub grub (£10 includes welcome gin and tonic, tour, and 3 samples; 5/day Thu-Sun, meet at the Royal Dick Bar in the central courtyard at 1 Summerhall—for location see the map on page 123, tel. 0131/290-2901, www.pickeringsgin.com).

Edinburgh Gin is a showroom (not a distillery) in the West End, near the Waldorf Astoria Hotel. Besides the basic tour, there's a connoisseur tour with more tastings and a gin-making tour (basic tour £10, 3/day daily, reserve ahead to guarantee a spot, 1A Rutland Place, enter off Shandwick Place next to the Ghille Dhu bar—for location see the map on page 120, tel. 0131/656-2810, www.edinburghgin.com). If you can't get on to one of their tours, visit their Heads & Tales bar to taste their gins (Tue-Sun 17:00-24:00, closed Mon).

LEISURE ACTIVITIES

Several enjoyable activities cluster near the B&B area around Dalkeith Road. For details, check their websites.

The **Royal Commonwealth Pool** is an indoor fitness and activity complex with a 50-meter pool, gym/fitness studio, and kids' soft play zone (daily, 21 Dalkeith Road—see map on page 123, tel. 0131/667-7211, www.edinburghleisure.co.uk).

The **Prestonfield Golf Club,** also an easy walk from the B&Bs, has golfers feeling like they're in a country estate (dress code, 6 Priestfield Road North—see map on page 123, general tel. 0131/667-9665, reservation tel. 0131/667-8597, www.prestonfieldgolf.co.uk).

At the **Midlothian Snowsports Centre** (a little south of town in Hillend; better for drivers), you can try skiing without any pesky snow. It feels like snow-skiing on a slushy day, even though you're schussing over matting misted with water. Four tubing runs offer fun even for nonskiers (£13/first hour, £6/hour after that, includes gear, generally Mon-Fri 9:30-21:00, Sat-Sun until 19:00,

EDINBURGH

shorter hours off-season, Biggar Road—see map on page 32, tel. 0131/445-4433, www.midlothian.gov.uk).

EDINBURGH'S FESTIVALS

Every summer, Edinburgh's annual festivals turn the city into a carnival of the arts. The season begins in June with the international film festival (www. edfilmfest.org.uk); then the jazz and blues festival in July (www. edinburghjazzfestival.com).

In August a riot of overlapping festivals known collectively as the **Edinburgh Festival** rages simultaneously—international, fringe, book, and art, as well as the Military Tattoo. There are enough music, dance, drama, and multicultural events to make even the most jaded traveler giddy with excitement. Every day is jammed with formal and spontaneous fun. Many city sights run on extended hours. It's a glorious time to be in Edinburgh...*if* you have (and can afford) a room.

If you'll be in town in August, book your room and tickets for major events (especially the Tattoo) as far ahead as you can lock in dates. Plan carefully to ensure you'll have time for festival activities as well as sightseeing. Check online to confirm dates; the best overall website is www.edinburghfestivalcity.com. Several publications—including the festival's official schedule, the *Edinburgh Festivals Guide Daily, The List, Fringe Program,* and *Daily Diary*—list and evaluate festival events. The *Scotsman* newspaper reviews every show.

The official, more formal **Edinburgh International Festival** is the original. Major events sell out well in advance (ticket office at the Hub, in the former Tolbooth Church near the top of the Royal Mile, tel. 0131/473-2000, www.hubtickets.co.uk or www. eif.co.uk).

The less formal **Fringe Festival,** featuring edgy comedy and theater, is huge—with 2,000 shows—and has eclipsed the original festival in popularity (ticket/info office just below St. Giles' Cathedral on the Royal Mile, 180 High Street, bookings tel. 0131/226-0000, www.edfringe.com). Tickets may be available at the door, and half-price tickets for some events are sold on the day of the show at the Half-Price Hut, located at The Mound, near the Scottish National Gallery.

The **Military Tattoo** is a massing of bands, drums, and bagpipes, with groups from all over the former British Empire and beyond. Displaying military finesse with a stirring lone-piper finale, this grand spectacle fills the castle esplanade (nightly during most of Aug except Sun, performances Mon-Fri at 21:00, Sat at 19:15 and 22:30, £25-90, booking starts in Dec, Fri-Sat shows sell out first, all seats generally sold out by early summer, some scattered same-day tickets may be available; office open Mon-Fri 10:00-16:30, closed Sat-Sun, during Tattoo open until show time and closed Sun; 1 Cockburn Street, behind Waverley Station, tel. 0131/225-1188, www.edintattoo.co.uk). Some performances are filmed by the BBC and later broadcast as a big national television special. This broadcast has become an annual ritual for the people of Britain.

Other **summer festivals** cover books (mid-late Aug, www. edbookfest.co.uk) and art (late July-Aug, www.edinburghartfestival. com). The **Festival of Politics** is held in October in the Scottish parliament building. It's a busy weekend of discussions and lectures on environmentalism, globalization, terrorism, gender, and other issues (www.festivalofpolitics.scot).

Shopping in Edinburgh

Edinburgh is bursting with Scottish clichés for sale: kilts, shortbread, whisky...if they can slap a tartan on it, they'll sell it. Locals dismiss the touristy trinket shops, which are most concentrated along the Royal Mile, as "tartan tat." Your challenge is finding something a wee bit more authentic. If you want to be sure you are taking home local merchandise, check if the label reads: "Made in Scotland." "Designed in Scotland" actually means "Made in China." Shops are usually open around 10:00-18:00 (later on Thu, shorter hours or closed on Sun). Tourist shops are open longer hours.

SHOPPING STREETS AND NEIGHBORHOODS

Near the Royal Mile: The Royal Mile is intensely touristy, mostly lined with interchangeable shops selling made-in-China souvenirs. I've listed a few worthwhile spots along here later, under "What to Shop For." But in general, the area near Grassmarket, an easy stroll from the top of the Royal Mile, offers more originality. **Victoria Street,** which climbs steeply downhill from the Royal Mile (near the Hub/Tolbooth Church) to Grassmarket, has a fine concentration of local chain shops, including I.J. Mellis Cheesemonger and Walker Slater for designer tweed, plus Calzeat (scarves, throws, and other textiles), a Harry Potter store, and more clothing and accessory shops. On **Grassmarket,** the Hawico shop sells top quality cashmere milled in southern Scotland. Exiting Grassmarket opposite Victoria Street, **Candlemaker Row** is more artisan, with boutiques selling hats (from dapper men's caps to outrageous

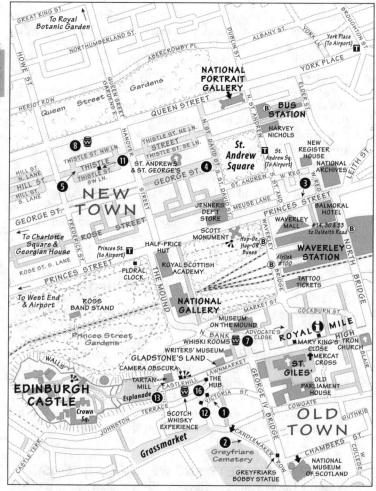

fascinators), jewelry, art, design items, and even fossils. The street winds a couple of blocks up toward the National Museum; Greyfriars Bobby awaits you at the top of the street.

In the New Town: For mass-market shopping, you'll find plenty of big chain stores along **Princes Street.** In addition to Marks & Spencer, H&M, Zara, Primark, and a glitzy Apple Store, you'll also see the granddaddy of Scottish department stores, Jenners (Mon-Wed 9:30-18:00, Thu-Sat until 17:00, Sun 11:00-18:00). Parallel to Princes Street, **George Street** has higher-end chain stores (including many from London, such as L.K. Bennett, Molton Brown, and Karen Millen). Just off St. Andrew Square is a branch of the high-end London department store Harvey Nichols.

For more local, artisan shopping, check out **Thistle Street,**

EDINBURGH

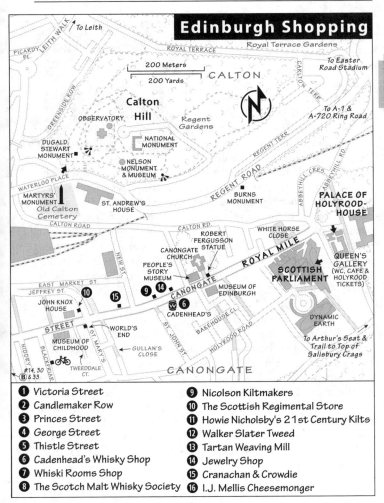

Edinburgh Shopping

1. Victoria Street
2. Candlemaker Row
3. Princes Street
4. George Street
5. Thistle Street
6. Cadenhead's Whisky Shop
7. Whiski Rooms Shop
8. The Scotch Malt Whisky Society
9. Nicolson Kiltmakers
10. The Scottish Regimental Store
11. Howie Nicholsby's 21st Century Kilts
12. Walker Slater Tweed
13. Tartan Weaving Mill
14. Jewelry Shop
15. Cranachan & Crowdie
16. I.J. Mellis Cheesemonger

lined with some fun eateries and a good collection of shops. You'll see some fun boutiques selling jewelry, shoes, and clothing. This is also the home of Howie Nicolsby's 21st Century Kilts (described later).

WHAT TO SHOP FOR
Whisky

You can order whisky in just about any bar in town, and whisky shops are a dime a dozen around the Royal Mile. But the places I've listed here distinguish themselves by their tradition and helpful staff. Before sampling or buying whisky, read all about Scotland's favorite spirit on page 484.

Cadenhead's Whisky Shop is not a tourist sight—don't expect

EDINBURGH

free samples or a hand-holding shopping experience. Founded in 1842, this firm prides itself on bottling good whisky straight from casks at the distilleries, without all the compromises that come with profitable mass production (coloring with sugar to fit the expected look, watering down to reduce the alcohol

tax, and so on). Those drinking from Cadenhead-bottled whiskies will enjoy the pure product as the distilleries' owners themselves do, not as the sorry public does. If you're serious about buying, the staff can explain the sometimes-complex whisky board and talk you through flavor profiles (prices start around £8.50 for about 3.5 ounces, open Mon-Sat 10:30-17:30, closed Sun, 172 Canongate, tel. 0131/556-5864, www.cadenhead.scot). They host hour-long whisky tastings—a hit with aficionados (£25, Mon-Fri at 17:45, 6 tastes, not designed for beginners).

Whiski Rooms Shop, just off the Royal Mile, comes with a knowledgeable, friendly staff that happily assists novices and experts alike to select the right bottle. Their adjacent bar usually has about 400 open bottles: Serious purchasers can get a sample. You can order a shareable flight in the bar, which comes with written information about each whisky you're sampling (variety of options starting around £25, available anytime the bar is open). Or you can opt for a guided tasting (£30 introductory tasting, £50 premium tasting, chocolate and cheese pairings also available; about one hour, reserve ahead; shop open daily 10:00-18:00, bar until 24:00, both open later in Aug, 4 North Bank Street, tel. 0131/225-1532, www.whiskirooms.co.uk).

Near the B&B Neighborhood: Perhaps the most accessible place to learn about local whiskies is conveniently located in the B&B area south of the city center. **Wood-Winters** has a passion both for traditional spirits and for the latest innovations in Edinburgh's booze scene. It's well stocked with 300 whiskies and gins (a trendy alternative to Scotch), as well as wines and local craft beers. Curious browsers can ask to sample a wee dram (Mon-Wed 10:00-19:00, Thu-Sat until 20:00, closed Sun, 91 Newington Road—for location, see the map on page 123, www.woodwinters.com, tel. 0131/667-2760).

Kilts and Other Traditional Scottish Gear

Many of the kilt outfitters you'll see along the Royal Mile are selling cheap knockoffs, made with printed rather than woven tartan material. If you want a serious kilt—or would enjoy window-shopping for one—try one of the places below. These have a few off-the-rack options, but to get a kilt in your specific tartan and size, they'll probably take your measurements, custom-make it, and ship it to you. For a good-quality outfit (kilt, jacket, and accessories), plan on spending about £1,000.

Nicolson Kiltmakers has a respect for tradition and quality. Owner Gordon enlists and trains local craftspeople who specialize in traditionally manufactured kilts and accessories. He prides himself on keeping the old ways alive (in the face of deeply

discounted "tartan tat") and actively cultivates the next generation of kiltmakers (Mon-Sat 9:30-17:30, Sun 12:00-16:00, 189 Canongate, tel. 0131/558-2887, www.nicolsonkiltmakers.com).

The Scottish Regimental Store, run by Nigel, is the official outfitter for military regiments. They sell top-of-the-line, formal kiltwear, as well as medals and pins that can be a more affordable souvenir (Mon-Fri 10:00-16:00, Sat until 17:00, closed Sun, 9 Jeffrey Street, tel. 0131/557-0249, www.scottishregimentalstore.co.uk).

Howie Nicholsby's 21st Century Kilts, in the New Town, brings this traditional craft into the present day. It's fun to peruse his photos of both kilted celebrities (he's dressed everyone from Sam Heughan to Vin Diesel) and wedding albums—which make you wish you were Scottish, engaged, and wealthy enough to hire Howie to outfit your bridal party (Howie asks that you make an appointment, though you're welcome to drop in if he happens to be there; closed Sun-Mon and Wed, 48 Thistle Street, send text to 0777-475-7222, www.21stcenturykilts.com, howie@21stcenturykilts.com).

Tweed

Several places around town sell the famous Harris Tweed, the authentic stuff hand woven on the Isle of Harris in the far west of Scotland. Harris Tweed is a protected name, so if the label says "Harris," you know it's the real thing. **Walker Slater** is the place to go for top-quality tweed at top prices. They have three locations on Victoria Street, just below the Royal Mile near Grassmarket:

menswear (at #16), womens-
wear (#44), and a sale shop (#5).
You'll find a rich interior and a
wide variety of gorgeous jackets,
scarves, bags, and more. This
place feels elegant and exclusive (Mon-Sat 10:00-18:00, Sun
11:00-17:00, www.walkerslater.
com). Harris Tweed is also available at the **Tartan Weaving
Mill** at the top of the Royal Mile (daily 9:00-17:30, 555 Castlehill,
tel. 0131/220-2477).

Jewelry

Jewelry with Celtic designs, mostly made from sterling silver, is a
popular and affordable souvenir. While you'll see it sold around
town, **Celtic Design** (156 Canongate) offers a quality and tasteful
selection.

Food and Treats

Cranachan & Crowdie is your one-stop shop for authentic Scottish goodies. They collect products (mostly edibles, some crafts)
from more than 300 small, independent producers all over Scotland. The selection goes well beyond the mass-produced clichés,
and American Beth and Scottish Fiona love to explain the story
behind each item. They also offer up Scottish gin samples upon
request (daily 11:00-18:00, on the Royal Mile at 263 Canongate,
tel. 0131/556-7194).

    I.J. Mellis Cheesemonger, tucked down Victoria Street just
off the top of the Royal Mile, stocks a wide variety of Scottish,
English, and international cheeses. They're as knowledgeable about
cheese as they are generous with samples (Mon-Sat 9:30-19:00,
Sun 11:00-18:00, 30A Victoria Street, tel. 0131/226-6215).

Nightlife in Edinburgh

▲▲Literary Pub Tour

This two-hour walk is interesting and a worthwhile way to spend
an evening—even if you can't stand "Auld Lang Syne." Think of it
as a walking theatrical performance, where you follow the witty di-
alogue of two actors as they debate the great literature of Scotland.
(You may ask yourself if this is high art or the creative re-creation of
fun-loving louts fueled by a passion for whisky.) You'll cover a lot of
ground, wandering from Grassmarket over the Old Town and New
Town, with stops in three to four pubs, as your guides share their
takes on Scotland's literary greats. The tour meets at the Beehive
Inn on Grassmarket (£16, just show up or book online and save £2,

drinks extra; May-Sept nightly at 19:30, April and Oct Thu-Sun, Jan-March Fri and Sun, Nov-Dec Fri only; 18 Grassmarket, tel. 0800-169-7410, www.edinburghliterarypubtour.co.uk).

EDINBURGH

▲Ghost Walks

A variety of companies lead spooky walks around town, providing an entertaining and affordable night out (offered nightly, most around 19:00 and 21:00, easy socializing for solo travelers). These two options are the most established.

Auld Reekie Tours offers a scary array of walks daily and nightly. Auld Reekie intertwines the grim and gory aspects of Scotland's history with the paranormal, witch covens, and pagan temples. They take groups into the "haunted vaults" under the old bridges "where it was so dark, so crowded, and so squalid that the people there knew each other not by how they looked, but by how they sounded, felt, and smelt." The guides are passionate, and the stories are genuinely spooky. Even if you don't believe in ghosts, you'll be entertained (£12-16, 1-1.5 hours, all tours leave from the modern Bank of Scotland building on the Royal Mile, opposite Deacon Brodie's Tavern, tel. 0131/557-4700, www.auldreekietours. com).

The theatrical **Cadies & Witchery Tours,** the most established outfit, offers two different 1.25-hour walks led by costumed actors: "Ghosts and Gore" (April-Aug only, in daylight and following a flatter route) and "Murder and Mystery" (year-round, after dark, hillier, more surprises and corny scares). The balance of historical context and slapstick humor makes these a fun pick for families (£10, includes book of stories, leaves from top of Royal Mile, outside the Witchery Restaurant, near castle esplanade, reservations required, tel. 0131/225-6745, www.witcherytours.com).

Scottish Folk Evenings

These Scottish variety shows include a traditional dinner with all the edible clichés, followed by a full slate of swirling kilts, blaring bagpipes, storytelling, and Scottish folk dancing. As these are designed for tour groups, you'll sit in a big music hall, served en masse before enjoying the stage show with an old-time emcee. If you like Lawrence Welk, you're in for a treat. But for most travelers, these are painfully cheesy. You can sometimes see the show without dinner for about two-thirds the price.

Taste of Scotland at Prestonfield House, filling a kind of circus tent in a luxurious estate near the Dalkeith Road B&Bs, offers its kitschy folk evening with or without dinner Sunday to Friday. For £55, you get the show with two drinks and a wad of haggis; £70 buys you the same, plus a three-course meal and a half-bottle of wine (dinner at 19:00, show from 20:00-22:00, April-Oct only). It's in the stables of "the handsomest house in Edinburgh," which is now home to the recommended Rhubarb Restaurant (Priest-field Road—see map on page 123, tel. 0131/225-7800, www. scottishshow.co.uk).

Spirit of Scotland Show is essentially the same experience but in the city center (£65 for dinner and show, dinner at 19:00, show from 20:00-21:30, next to the National Portrait Gallery at 5 Queen Street, tel. 0131/618-9899, https://spiritofscotlandshow.com).

The Princes Street Gardens Dancers perform a range of Scottish country dancing each summer at the Princes Street Gardens. The volunteer troupe demonstrates each dance, then invites spectators to give it a try (£5, June-July Mon 19:30-21:30, at Ross Bandstand in Princes Street Gardens—in the glen just below Edinburgh Castle, tel. 0131/228-8616, www.princesstreetgardensdancing.org. uk). The same group offers summer programs in other parts of town (see website for details).

Theater

Even outside festival time, Edinburgh is a fine place for lively and affordable theater and live music. Pick up *The List* for a complete rundown of what's on (free at TI; online at www.list.co.uk).

▲▲Live Music in Pubs

While traditional music venues have been eclipsed by beer-focused student bars, Edinburgh still has a few good pubs that can deliver a traditional folk-music fix. These days, many places that advertise "live music" offer only a solo singer/guitarist rather than a folk group. The monthly *Gig Guide* (free at TI, accommodations, and various pubs, www.gigguide.co.uk) lists several places each night that have live music, divided by genre (pop, rock, world, and folk). For locations, see the "Edinburgh City Center Eateries" map on page 127.

South of the Royal Mile: Tight, stuffy **Sandy Bell's** is a pub with live folk music nightly from 21:30 (near the National Museum of Scotland at 25 Forrest Road, tel. 0131/225-2751). There's no food, drinks are cheap, tables are small, and the vibe is local. They also have a few sessions earlier in the day (Sat at 14:00, Sun at 16:00, Mon at 17:30 is for beginners).

Captain's Bar is a crowded-but-cozy, music-focused pub with live sessions of folk and traditional music nightly around 21:00—see website for lineup (4 South College Street, https:// captainsedinburgh.webs.com).

The Royal Oak is another characteristic, snug place for a dose of folk and blues that feels like a friend's living room (just off South Bridge opposite Chambers Road at 1 Infirmary Street, tel. 0131/557-2976).

Grassmarket Neighborhood: This area below the castle bustles with live music and rowdy people spilling out of the pubs and into what was (once upon a time) a busy market square. While it used to be a mecca for Scottish folk music, today it's more youthful with a heavy-drinking, rowdy feel. It's fun to just wander through this area late at night and check out the scene. Thanks to the music and crowds, you'll know where to go...and where not to.

The Fiddlers Arms has a charming Grassmarket pub energy with live folk, pop, or rock, depending on the night (Thu-Sat from 21:00, at the far end of the square). Check out **Biddy Mulligans** or **White Hart Inn** (both on Grassmarket and both usually with a single Irish folk singer nightly). **Finnegans Wake,** on Victoria Street (which leads down to Grassmarket), is more of a down-and-dirty, classic rock bar with dancing. **The Bow Bar,** a couple doors away on Victoria Street, has no music but offers a hard-to-resist classic pub scene.

On the Royal Mile: Three characteristic pubs within a few steps of each other on High Street (opposite the Radisson Blu Hotel) offer a fun setting, classic pub architecture and ambience, and live music (generally just a single loud folk guitarist) for the cost of a beer: **Whiski Bar** (mostly trad and folk; nightly at 22:00), **Royal Mile** (classic pop; nightly at 22:00), and **Mitre Bar** (acoustic pop/rock with some trad; Fri-Sat at 22:00).

Just a block away (on South Bridge) is **Whistlebinkies Live Music Bar.** While they rarely do folk or Scottish trad, this is the most serious of the music pubs, with an actual stage and several acts nightly (schedule posted inside the door makes the genre clear; most nights music starts at 19:00 or 21:30, young crowd, fun energy, sticky floors, no cover, tel. 0131/557-5114). **No. 1 High Street** is an accessible little pub with a love of folk and traditional music (Wed-Thu from about 21:00, 1 High Street, tel. 0131/556-5758). **World's End,** across the street, also has music starting about 21:00 (trad on Thu, other genres Fri-Sat, 4 High Street, tel. 0131/556-3628).

In the New Town: All the beer drinkers seem to head for the pedestrianized, west end of Rose Street, famous for having the most pubs per square inch anywhere in Scotland—and plenty of live music.

Pubs near the B&B Neighborhood

The pubs in the B&B area don't typically have live music, but some are fun evening hangouts (for locations, see the "B&Bs & Restaurants South of the City Center" map, page 123). **Leslie's Bar,** sitting between a working-class and an upper-class neighborhood, has two sides. Originally, the gang (men) would go in on the right to gather around the great hardwood bar, glittering with a century of *Cheers* ambience. Meanwhile, the more delicate folks (women) would slip in on the left, with its discreet doors, plush snugs (cozy

EDINBURGH

private booths), and ornate ordering windows. Since 1896, this Victorian classic has been appreciated for both its real ales and its huge selection of fine whiskies (listed on a lengthy menu). Dive into the whisky mosh pit on the right, and let them show you how whisky can become "a very good friend" (daily 11:00-24:00, 49 Ratcliffe Terrace, tel. 0131/667-7205).

Other good pubs in this area include **The Old Bell** (uphill from Leslie's, popular and cozy, with big TV screens) and **The Salisbury Arms** (bigger, more sprawling, feels upscale); both are described later, under "Eating in Edinburgh."

Sleeping in Edinburgh

I've recommended accommodations in three areas: the city center, the West End, and a quieter neighborhood south of town.

To stay in the city center, you'll select from large hotels and mostly impersonal guesthouses. The West End (just a few blocks from the New Town, spanning from Haymarket to Charlotte Square) offers a few comfortable and more intimate hotels and guesthouses. These places provide a calm retreat in a central location.

For the classic B&B experience (friendly hosts and great cooked breakfasts), look south of town near Dalkeith Road or Mayfield Gardens. From either area, it's a long walk to the city center (about 30 minutes) or a quick bus or taxi/Uber ride. While the B&Bs here are not cheap (generally **$$**), they're less expensive than staying at a downtown hotel.

Note that during the Festival in August, prices skyrocket and most places do not accept bookings for one- or even two-night stays. If coming in August, book far in advance. Conventions, rugby matches, school holidays, and weekends can make finding a room tough at other times of year, too. In winter, when demand is light, some B&Bs close, and prices at all accommodations get soft.

I rank accommodations from **$** budget to **$$$$** splurge. For the best deal, contact smaller places directly by phone or email. When you book direct, the owner avoids a commission and may be able to offer a discount. For some travelers, short-term Airbnb-type rentals can be a good alternative to hotels; search for places in my recommended hotel and B&B neighborhoods. For more details on reservations, short-term rentals, and more, see the "Sleeping" section in the Practicalities chapter.

HOTELS IN THE CITY CENTER

These places are mostly characterless, but they're close to the sight-seeing action and Edinburgh's excellent restaurant and pub scene. Prices are very high in peak season and drop substantially in off-season (a good time to shop around). In each case, I'd skip the institutional breakfast and eat out. You'll generally pay about £10 a day to park near these hotels.

EDINBURGH

$$$$ The Inn Place, part of a small chain, fills the former headquarters of The *Scotsman* newspaper—a few steep steps below the Royal Mile—with 48 classy, minimalist rooms ("bunk rooms" for 6-8 people, best deals on weekdays, breakfast extra, elevator serves some rooms, 20 Cockburn Street, tel. 0131/526-3780, www.theinnplaceedinburgh.co.uk, reception@theinnplaceedinburgh.co.uk).

$$$$ The Inn on the Mile is your trendy, central option, filling a renovated old bank building right in the heart of the Royal Mile (at North Bridge/South Bridge). The nine bright and stylish rooms are an afterthought to the busy upmarket pub, which is where you'll check in. If you don't mind some noise (from the pub and the busy street) and climbing lots of stairs, it's a handy home base (breakfast extra, complimentary drink, 82 High Street, tel. 0131/556-9940, www.theinnonthemile.co.uk, info@theinnonthemile.co.uk).

$$$$ Grassmarket Hotel's 42 rooms are quirky and fun, from the Dandy comic-book wallpaper to the giant wall map of Edinburgh equipped with planning-your-visit magnets. The hotel is in a great location right on Grassmarket overlooking the Covenanters Memorial and above Biddy Mulligans Bar (family rooms, two-night minimum on some weekends, elevator serves half the rooms, 94 Grassmarket, tel. 0131/220-2299, www.grassmarkethotel.co.uk).

$$$ The Place Hotel, sister of the Inn Place listed earlier, has a fine New Town location 10 minutes north of the train station. It occupies three grand Georgian townhouses, with no elevator and long flights of stairs leading up to the 47 contemporary, no-frills rooms. Their outdoor terrace with retractable roof and heaters is a popular place to unwind (save money with a smaller city double, 34 York Place, tel. 0131/556-7575, www.yorkplace-edinburgh.co.uk, frontdesk@yorkplace-edinburgh.co.uk).

$$ Ten Hill Place Hotel is a seven-minute walk from the Royal Mile, down a quiet courtyard. It's run in conjunction with the 500-year-old Royal College of Surgeons and profits go toward funding student education. Its 129 rooms are classy, and some have views of the Salisbury Crags (family rooms, breakfast extra, elevator, 10 Hill Place, tel. 0131/662-2080, www.tenhillplace.com, reservations@tenhillplace.com).

$$ Motel One Edinburgh Royal, part of a stylish German budget-hotel chain, is between the train station and the Royal Mile; it feels upscale and trendy for its price range (208 rooms, pay more for a park view or less for a windowless "basic" room with

EDINBURGH

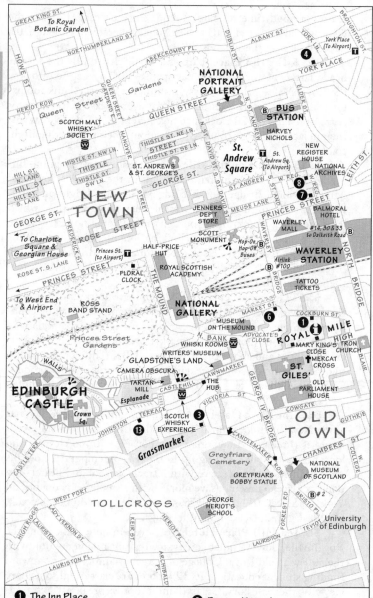

1 The Inn Place
2 The Inn on the Mile
3 Grassmarket Hotel
4 The Place Hotel
5 Ten Hill Place Hotel
6 Motel One Edinburgh Royal
7 Motel One Edinburgh Princes
8 Baxter Hostel
9 To Edinburgh Central Youth Hostel
10 SafeStay Edinburgh Hostel
11 High Street Hostel
12 Royal Mile Backpackers Hostel
13 Castle Rock Hostel

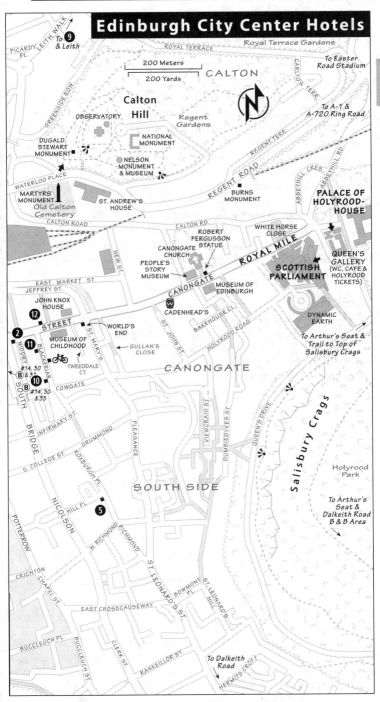

Edinburgh City Center Hotels

PICARDY PL.

LEITH WALK

To 9 & Leith

GREENSIDE ROW

ROYAL TERRACE

Royal Terrace Gardens

CALTON

Calton Hill

Regent Gardens

To Easter Road Stadium

CARLTON TERR.

To A-1 & A-720 Ring Road

OBSERVATORY

DUGALD STEWART MONUMENT

NATIONAL MONUMENT

NELSON MONUMENT & MUSEUM

REGENT TERR.

REGENT ROAD

ABBEYHILL CRES.

ABBEYHILL RD.

WATERLOO PLACE

MARTYRS' MONUMENT

Old Calton Cemetery

ST. ANDREW'S HOUSE

CALTON ROAD

BURNS MONUMENT

REGENT ROAD

PALACE OF HOLYROOD-HOUSE

CALTON RD.

ROBERT FERGUSSON STATUE

WHITE HORSE CLOSE

ROYAL MILE

CANONGATE CHURCH

PEOPLE'S STORY MUSEUM

CANONGATE

MUSEUM OF EDINBURGH

SCOTTISH PARLIAMENT

QUEEN'S GALLERY (WC, CAFE & HOLYROOD TICKETS)

EAST MARKET ST.

JEFFREY ST.

NEW ST.

CADENHEAD'S

BAKEHOUSE CL.

HOLYROOD ROAD

DYNAMIC EARTH

JOHN KNOX HOUSE

STREET

WORLD'S END

ST. MARY'S

ST. JOHN ST.

To Arthur's Seat & Trail to Top of Salisbury Crags

MUSEUM OF CHILDHOOD

GULLAN'S CLOSE

NIDDRY ST.

BLACKFRIARS

#14, 30 & 33

TWEEDDALE CT.

CANONGATE

#14, 30 & 33

COWGATE

SOUTH BRIDGE

INFIRMARY ST.

DRUMMOND ST.

PLEASANCE

VIEWCRAIG ST.

DUMBIEDYKES ST.

QUEEN'S DRIVE

Salisbury Crags

S. COLLEGE ST.

ROXBURGH PL.

NICOLSON

HILL PL.

SOUTH SIDE

Holyrood Park

To Arthur's Seat & Dalkeith Road B & B Area

POTTERROW

CRICHTON

CHAPEL ST.

W. RICHMOND

RICHMOND

ST.

BOWMONT PL.

ST. LEONARD'S ST.

ST. LEONARD'S

HILL PL.

EAST CROSSCAUSEWAY

BUCCLEUCH PL.

BUCCLEUCH ST.

CLERK ST.

KANKEILLOR ST.

To Dalkeith Road

HERMITS CROFT

200 Meters

200 Yards

skylight, breakfast extra, elevator, 18 Market Street, tel. 0131/220-0730, www.motel-one.com, edinburgh-royal@motel-one.com).

$$ Motel One Edinburgh Princes is a good deal for its location, with 140 rooms, some with nice views of Waverley Station and the Old Town. The rooms are cookie cutter, but the sprawling ballroom-like lounge offers great views (family rooms, reception on first floor, breakfast extra, elevator, 10 Princes Street, enter around the corner on West Register Street, www.motel-one.com, edinburgh-princes@motel-one.com).

Chain Hotels in the Center: Besides my recommendations above, you'll find a number of cookie-cutter chain hotels close to the Royal Mile, including **Jurys Inn** (43 Jeffrey Street), **Ibis Hotel** (two convenient branches: near the Tron Church and another around the corner along the busy South Bridge), **Holiday Inn Express** (two locations: just off the Royal Mile at 300 Cowgate and one in the New Town), and **Travelodge Central** (just below the Royal Mile at 33 St. Mary's Street; additional locations in the New Town).

HOSTELS

¢ **Baxter Hostel** is an appealing boutique hostel. Occupying one floor of a Georgian townhouse (up several long, winding flights of stairs and below two more hostels), it has tons of ambience: tartan wallpaper, wood paneling, stone walls, decorative tile floors, and a beautifully restored kitchen/lounge that you'd want in your own house. Space is tight—hallways are snug, and five dorms (42 beds) share one bathroom. Another room, with four beds, has its own en-suite bathroom (includes scrambled-egg breakfast; small fee for towel, travel adapters, and locks; 5 West Register Street, tel. 0131/503-1001, www.thebaxterhostel.com, thehost@thebaxterhostel.com).

¢ **Edinburgh Central Youth Hostel** rents 251 beds in 72 rooms accommodating three to six people (all with private bathrooms and lockers). Guests can eat cheaply in the cafeteria, or cook for the cost of groceries in the members' kitchen (private rooms available, pay laundry, 15-minute downhill walk from Waverley Station—head down Leith Walk, pass through two roundabouts, hostel is on your left—or take Lothian bus #22 or #25 to Elm Rowe, 9 Haddington Place off Leith Walk, tel. 0131/524-2090, www.hostellingscotland.org.uk, central@hostellingscotland.org.uk).

¢ **SafeStay Edinburgh,** just off the Royal Mile, rents 272 bunks in pleasing purple-accented rooms. Dorm rooms have 4 to 12 beds, and there are also a few private singles and twin rooms (all rooms have private bathrooms). Bar 50 in the basement has an inviting lounge. Half of the rooms function as a university dorm during the school year, becoming available just in time for the tourists (breakfast extra, kitchen, laundry, free daily walking tour, 50 Blackfriars Street, tel. 0131/524-1989, www.safestay.com, reservations-edi@safestay.com).

¢ **Cheap and Scruffy Bohemian Hostels in the Center:** These three sister hostels—popular crash pads for young, hip backpackers—are beautifully located in the noisy center (some locations also have private rooms, www.macbackpackers.com): **High Street Hostel** (150 beds, 8 Blackfriars Street, just off High Street/Royal Mile, tel. 0131/557-3984); **Royal Mile Backpackers** (38 beds, 105 High Street, tel. 0131/557-6120); and **Castle Rock Hostel** (300 beds, just below the castle and above the pubs, 15 Johnston Terrace, tel. 0131/225-9666).

THE WEST END

The area just west of the New Town and Charlotte Square is a quiet, classy, residential area of stately Georgian buildings. Hotels here can be pricey and ostentatious, catering mostly to business travelers. But my recommendations are central and offer character and hospitality. Though these places aren't as intimate as my recommended B&Bs south of town, the West End is convenient to most sightseeing. It's an easy 10- to 15-minute walk to bustling Princes Street.

To get here from the train station, take the Airlink #100 from Waverley Bridge to Shandwick Place, or take the train to Haymarket Station (depending on your hotel—confirm in advance). Coming from Princes Street, take the tram to the West End stop.

$$$$ B+B Edinburgh is a boutique hotel with 27 comfortable rooms (some with city views). It's situated on quiet Rothesay Terrace, where you'll feel like a diplomat retreating to your private suite (RS%, family rooms, elevator, 3 Rothesay Terrace, tel. 0131/225-5084, www.bb-edinburgh.com, info@bb-edinburgh.com).

$$$ Angels Share Hotel is an elegant and inviting place with a proud Scottish heritage. Each of its tidy, stylish 31 rooms is named after a contemporary Scottish figure (his or her portrait hangs above your bed). The attached bar is glitzy, with live music on weekends. The hotel is just off Shandwick Place, the artery of the West End (RS%, breakfast extra, 11 Hope Street, tel. 0131/247-7007, www.angelssharehotel.com, reception@angelssharehotel.com).

$$$ St. Valery Guest House is on a quiet street in a perfect line of Georgian buildings close to the Haymarket train station. Its 12 simple but well-maintained rooms (a couple with peaceful garden views) have frilly old-fashioned decor with nice modern touches. It's near the Haymarket tram stop and bus routes #26,

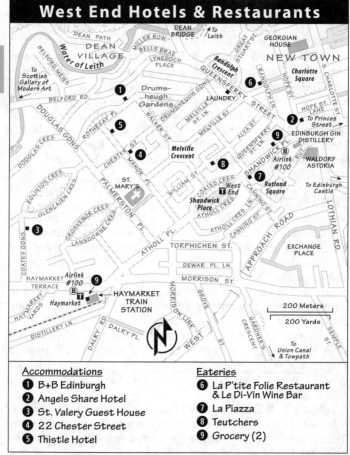

West End Hotels & Restaurants

Accommodations
1. B+B Edinburgh
2. Angels Share Hotel
3. St. Valery Guest House
4. 22 Chester Street
5. Thistle Hotel

Eateries
6. La P'tite Folie Restaurant & Le Di-Vin Wine Bar
7. La Piazza
8. Teuchters
9. Grocery (2)

#31, and Airlink #100 (family rooms, breakfast included, no elevator, 36 Coates Gardens, tel. 0131/337-1893, www.stvalery.co.uk, info@stvalery.co.uk, Agnes and Solveiga).

$$ 22 Chester Street offers a mix of Georgian charm and Ikea comfort, renting five smartly appointed rooms near St. Mary's Cathedral. The lounge is an elegant and cozy place to unwind. Two rooms have private bathrooms down the hall, and a couple rooms are below street level but get plenty of light (RS%, family rooms, no breakfast but lounge has stocked fridge and microwave, street parking only, 22 Chester Street, mobile 0795-755-8658, https://22 chesterstreetedinburgh.co.uk, marypremiercru@gmail.com, owner Mary and manager Lukasz).

$$ Thistle Hotel is your no-frills budget option (albeit still expensive) in this otherwise fancy neighborhood. The 16 rooms are basic but functional, and many bathrooms are remodeled (and others need to be). Two rooms have castle views (RS%, family rooms, breakfast extra, no elevator, 59 Manor Place, tel. 0131/225-6144, www.edinburghthistlehotel.com, enquiries@edinburghthislehotel.com, Gregory).

B&Bs SOUTH OF THE CITY CENTER

A B&B generally provides more warmth and lower prices. At these not-quite-interchangeable places, character is provided by the personality quirks of the hosts and sometimes the decor. In general, cash is preferred and can lead to discounted rates. Book direct—you will pay a much higher rate through a booking website.

Near the B&Bs, you'll find plenty of fine eateries and some good, classic pubs. A few places have their own private parking; others offer access to easy, free street parking (ask when booking—or better yet, don't rent a car for your time in Edinburgh). The nearest launderette is Ace Cleaning Centre (see page 33).

Taxi or Uber fare between the city center and these B&Bs is about £7. If taking the bus from the B&Bs into the city, hop off at the South Bridge stop for the Royal Mile (see below—and "Getting Around Edinburgh," earlier—for more bus specifics).

Near Dalkeith Road

Most of my B&Bs near Dalkeith Road are located south of the Royal Commonwealth Pool. This comfortable, safe neighborhood is a ten-minute bus ride from the Royal Mile.

To get here from the train station, catch the bus around the corner on North Bridge: Exit the station onto Princes Street, turn right, continue around the corner onto North Bridge, cross the street, and walk up the bridge to the bus stop (lines #14, #30, or #33). About 10 minutes into the ride, after following South Clerk Street for a while, the bus makes a left turn onto East Preston Street, then a right onto Dalkeith Road. Depending on where you're staying, you'll get off at the first stop (Commonwealth Pool) or second stop (Marchhall Place) after the turn—confirm specifics with your B&B.

$$ Gil Dun Guest House, with eight rooms—some contemporary, others more traditional—is on a quiet cul-de-sac just off Dalkeith Road. It's comfortable, pleasant, and managed with care by Gerry and Bill; Maggie helps out occasionally (family rooms, two-night minimum in summer preferred, limited off-street

EDINBURGH

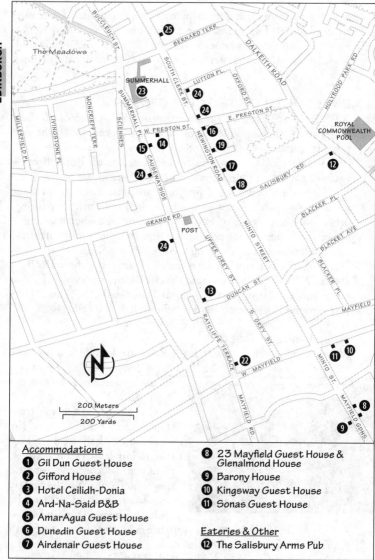

<u>Accommodations</u>
1 Gil Dun Guest House
2 Gifford House
3 Hotel Ceilidh-Donia
4 Ard-Na-Said B&B
5 AmarAgua Guest House
6 Dunedin Guest House
7 Airdenair Guest House

8 23 Mayfield Guest House & Glenalmond House
9 Barony House
10 Kingsway Guest House
11 Sonas Guest House

<u>Eateries & Other</u>
12 The Salisbury Arms Pub

parking, 9 Spence Street, tel. 0131/667-1368, www.gildun.co.uk, gildun.edin@btinternet.com).

$$ Gifford House, on busy Dalkeith Road, is a bright, flowery retreat with six peaceful, colorful rooms (some with ornate cornices and views of Arthur's Seat) and compact, modern bathrooms (RS%, family rooms, cash preferred, street parking, 103 Dalkeith Road, tel. 0131/667-4688, www.giffordhouseedinburgh.com, giffordhouse@btinternet.com, Melanie, David, and Margaret).

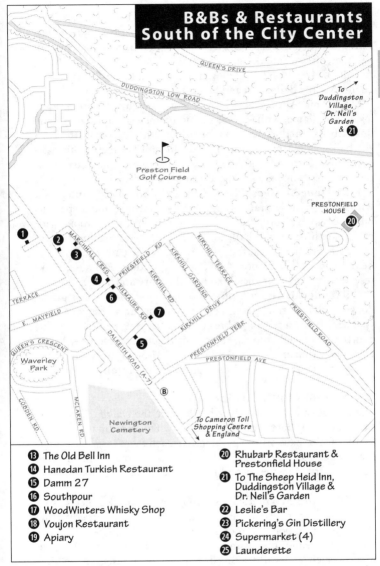

B&Bs & Restaurants South of the City Center

- ⑬ The Old Bell Inn
- ⑭ Hanedan Turkish Restaurant
- ⑮ Damm 27
- ⑯ Southpour
- ⑰ WoodWinters Whisky Shop
- ⑱ Voujon Restaurant
- ⑲ Apiary
- ⑳ Rhubarb Restaurant & Prestonfield House
- ㉑ To The Sheep Heid Inn, Duddingston Village & Dr. Neil's Garden
- ㉒ Leslie's Bar
- ㉓ Pickering's Gin Distillery
- ㉔ Supermarket (4)
- ㉕ Launderette

$$ Hotel Ceilidh-Donia is bigger (17 rooms) and more hotel-like than other nearby B&Bs, with a bar and a small reception area, but managers Kevin and Susan and their staff provide guesthouse warmth. The back deck is a pleasant place to relax on a warm day (family room, 2-night minimum on peak-season weekends, 14 Marchhall Crescent, tel. 0131/667-2743, www.hotelceilidh-donia.co.uk, reservations@hotelceilidh-donia.co.uk).

$$ Ard-Na-Said B&B, in an elegant 1875 Victorian house,

has seven bright, spacious rooms with modern bathrooms, including one ground-floor room with a pleasant patio and two with Ard-Na-Said (Arthur's Seat) views (2-night minimum preferred in summer, off-street parking, 5 Priestfield Road, tel. 0131/283-6524, mobile 0747-660-6202, www.ardnasaid.co.uk, info@ardnasaid.co.uk, Audrey Ballantine and her son Steven).

$$ AmarAgua Guest House is an inviting Victorian home away from home, with six welcoming rooms—a couple with four-poster beds—and eager hosts (one double has private bath down the hall, 2-night minimum, no kids under 12, street parking, 10 Kilmaurs Terrace, tel. 0131/667-6775, www.amaragua.co.uk, reservations@amaragua.co.uk, Lucia and Kuan).

$$ Dunedin Guest House (dun-EE-din) is bright and plush, with seven well-decorated rooms, a skylit atrium, and a spacious breakfast room/lounge with TV (family rooms, one room with private bath down the hall, includes continental breakfast, extra charge for cooked breakfast, limited off-street parking, 8 Priestfield Road, tel. 0131/668-4438, www.dunedinguesthouse.co.uk, reservations@dunedinguesthouse.co.uk, Mary and Tony).

$ Airdenair Guest House is a hands-off, bare-bones guesthouse, with no formal host greeting (you'll get an access code to let yourself in) and a self-serve breakfast buffet. But the price is right, and the five simple rooms—some with older bathrooms—do the trick (29 Kilmaurs Road, mobile 0781-731-3035, www.airdenair.co.uk, contact@airdenair-edinburgh.co.uk, Duncan).

On or near Mayfield Gardens

These places are just a couple of blocks from the Dalkeith Road options, along the busy Newington Road (which turns in to Mayfield Gardens). All have private parking. To reach them from the center, hop on bus #3, #7, #8, #29, #31, #37, or #49. Note: Some of these buses depart from the second bus stop, a bit farther along North Bridge.

$$$ At 23 Mayfield Guest House, Ross and Kathleen (with their wee helpers Ethan and Alfie) rent seven splurge-worthy, thoughtfully appointed rooms complete with high-tech bathrooms (rain showers and motion-sensor light-up mirrors). Little extras—such as locally sourced gourmet breakfasts, an inviting guest lounge outfitted with leather-bound Sir Arthur Conan Doyle books, an "honesty bar," and classic black-and-white movie screenings—make you feel like royalty (RS% with cash, family room, 2-night minimum preferred in summer, 23 Mayfield Gardens, tel. 0131/667-5806, www.23mayfield.co.uk, info@23mayfield.co.uk). They also rent an apartment.

$$$ Glenalmond House, run by Jimmy and Fiona Mackie, has nine smart rooms, two with garden patios (RS% with cash, discounts for longer stays, family room, no kids under 5, 25 May-field Gardens, tel. 0131/668-2392, www.glenalmondhouse.com, enquiries@glenalmondhouse.com).

$$ Barony House, the best value of all these places, is run with infectious enthusiasm by Aussies Paul and Susan. Their seven elegant doubles are lovingly decorated by Susan, who's made the beautiful friezes and fabric headboards (she also bakes welcome pastries for guests). Two of the rooms are next door, in a former servants' quarters, now a peaceful retreat with access to a shared kitchen (3-night minimum preferred in summer, no kids under 9, 20 Mayfield Gardens, tel. 0131/662-9938, www.baronyhouse. co.uk, booknow@baronyhouse.co.uk).

$$ Kingsway Guest House, with seven bright and stylish rooms, is owned by conscientious, delightful Gary and Lizzie, who have thought of all the little touches, such as a DVD library and in-room Internet radios, and offer good advice on neighborhood eats (RS% with cash, family rooms, one room with private bath down the hall, off-street parking, 5 East Mayfield, tel. 0131/667-5029, www.edinburgh-guesthouse.com, booking@kingswayguesthouse. com).

$$ Sonas Guest House is nothing fancy—just a simple, easy-going place with nine rooms, six of which have bathtubs (family room, 3 East Mayfield, tel. 0131/667-2781, www.sonasguesthouse. com, info@sonasguesthouse.com, Irene and Dennis).

Eating in Edinburgh

Edinburgh, with a strong economy and more tourism than ever, is thriving with dining options. Tourists clog the famous stretches where bottom-feeding eateries make easy money. But if you walk just a few blocks away from the chain restaurants and tacky strips, you'll find a different world. Things are very competitive, and you'll find even high-end places offer lunch and early dinner specials. Reservations are essential in August and on weekends, and a good idea anytime. Here are some favorites of mine, designed to fill the tank economically at lunch time or give you a great experience for dinner. With the ease and economy of Uber and the bus system, don't be too tied to your hotel or B&B neighborhood for dinner.

THE OLD TOWN

I prefer spots within a few minutes' walk of the tourist zone—just far enough to offer better value and a more local atmosphere.

Just off the Royal Mile on George IV Bridge
$$$ Le Bistrot is the tour guides' favorite—a delightful café hid-ing just steps off of the Royal Mile in the same building as the

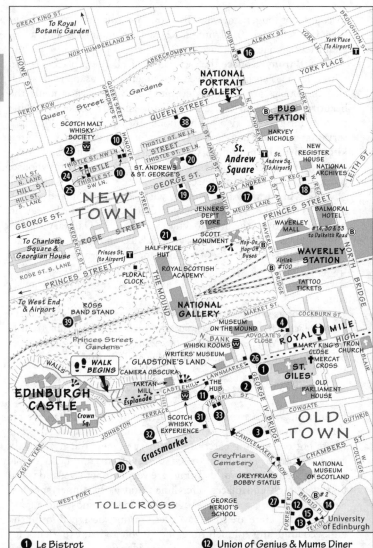

1 Le Bistrot
2 Ondine Seafood Restaurant
3 The Outsider
4 Devil's Advocate
5 Wedgwood Restaurant
6 David Bann Vegetarian Restaurant
7 Edinburgh Larder
8 Mimi's Little Bakehouse
9 Clarinda's Tea Room
10 Hendersons (3)
11 Oink (2)

12 Union of Genius & Mums Diner
13 Doctors Pub
14 Ting Thai Caravan
15 Ting Saboteur
16 The Magnum Restaurant and Bar
17 Dishoom Indian
18 Café Royal
19 The Dome Restaurant
20 St. Andrew's & St. George's Church Undercroft Café
21 Marks & Spencer Food Hall

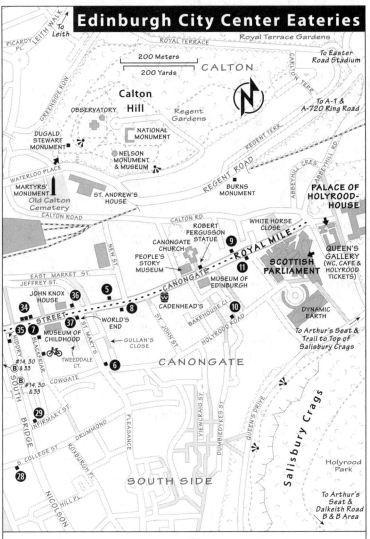

Edinburgh City Center Eateries

22 Sainsbury's
23 Le Café St. Honoré
24 The Bon Vivant
25 Fishers in the City

Pubs & Nightlife
26 Deacon Brodie's Tavern
27 Sandy Bell's Pub
28 Captain's Bar
29 The Royal Oak Pub

30 The Fiddlers Arms
31 Biddy Mulligans
32 White Hart Inn
33 Finnegans Wake & The Bow Bar
34 Whiski Bar, Royal Mile, Mitre Bar & Hewats on the Mile
35 Whistlebinkies Bar
36 No. 1 High Street Pub
37 The World's End Pub
38 Spirit of Scotland Show
39 Princes Street Gardens Dancers

French consulate (as if put here by the consulate to promote a love of French culture). Its glowy ambience, authentic French menu, and great prices make this a welcoming spot to have dinner before an evening stroll down the Royal Mile—when all the crowds have gone to the pubs. Try their soup or fish of the day (£16 fixed-price lunch, daily 9:00-22:00, 59 George IV Bridge, tel. 0131/225-4021, www.lebistrot.co.uk).

$$$$ Ondine Seafood Restaurant is a dressy, top-end restaurant with a smart clientele and a quality, sophisticated vibe; it's known for some of the best seafood in town (the menu is almost exclusively seafood). It's a block off the Royal Mile, upstairs in a modern building with a sleek dining room that overlooks the busy road, but feels a world apart. If you're looking for deals, oysters are £1 each at the bar during happy hour, and they serve an economical lunch menu until 18:30 (Mon-Sat 12:00-15:00 & 17:30-22:00, closed Sun, 2 George IV Bridge, tel. 0131/226-1888, www.ondinerestaurant.co.uk).

$$$ The Outsider has a thriving energy. It's a proudly independent bistro with a social (noisy) vibe filling its sleek, sprawling dining room. The menu features good-value, fresh, modern Scottish cuisine with daily specials "until sold out" scribbled on it. You feel like a winner eating here. Ask for a window table at the back for views of the castle floating above the rooftops (daily 12:00-23:00, lunch specials until 17:00, reservations smart, 15 George IV Bridge, tel. 0131/226-3131, www.theoutsiderrestaurant.com, Eddie and partners).

Along the Royal Mile, Downhill from St. Giles' Cathedral

Though the eateries along this most-crowded stretch of the city are invariably touristy, the scene is fun. Sprinkled in this list are some places a block or two off the main drag offering better values and maybe fewer tourists.

$$$ Hewats on the Mile, next to the recommended Whiski Bar, is an intimate refuge wedged among the shops on the Royal Mile. You'll step down into an atmospheric cavern with tartan accents and enjoy fine dining at reasonable prices for such a premium location. Its colorful Scottish-Mediterranean dishes are flavorful, and ingredients are local (Mon-Sat 17:00-22:00, Sun 18:00-21:00, reservations required, 123b High Street, tel. 0131/557-5732, www.hewatsedinburgh.com).

$$$ Devil's Advocate is a popular gastropub that hides down the narrow lane called Advocates Close, directly across the Royal Mile from St. Giles. With an old cellar setting—exposed stone and heavy beams—done up in modern style, it feels like a mix of old and new Edinburgh. Creative whisky cocktails kick off a menu that dares to be adventurous, but with a respect for Scottish tradition (daily 12:00-22:00, 9 Advocates Close, tel. 0131/225-4465).

$$$$ Wedgwood Restaurant is romantic, contemporary, chic, and as gourmet as possible with no pretense. Paul Wedgwood cooks while his wife Lisa serves with appetizing charm. The cuisine: creative, modern Scottish with an international twist. The pigeon-and-haggis starter is scrumptious, or consider their "Wee Tour of Scotland" tasting *menu* for £55. Paul and Lisa believe in making the meal the event of the evening—don't come here to eat and run (the table is yours). I like the ground level with the Royal Mile view and the busy kitchen ambience better than their basement seating (fine wine by the glass, daily 12:00-15:00 & 18:00-22:00, reservations smart, 267 Canongate on Royal Mile, tel. 0131/558-8737, www.wedgwoodtherestaurant.co.uk).

$$$ David Bann Vegetarian Restaurant is a worthwhile stop for well-heeled vegetarians in need of a break from traditional veggie grub. While vegetarian as can be, this place—with its candles and woody decor—doesn't have even a hint of hippie. It's upscale (it has a cocktail bar), sleek, minimalist, and stylish (gorgeously presented dishes), serious about quality, and organic. There's an enthusiastic local following—and decadent desserts (daily 12:00-22:00, vegan and gluten-free options, a long block off the Royal Mile at 56 St. Mary's Street, tel. 0131/556-5888, www.davidbann.co.uk).

Quick, Easy, and Cheap Breakfast and Lunch Options

$ Edinburgh Larder promises "a taste of the country" in the center of the city. They focus on high-quality, homestyle breakfast and lunches made from seasonal, local ingredients. The café, with table service, is a convivial space with rustic tables filled by local families. Their "Little Larder" sister outlet, next door, offers more of the same (Mon-Fri 8:00-16:00, Sat-Sun from 9:00, 15 Blackfriars Street, tel. 0131/556-6922).

$ Mimi's Little Bakehouse, a handy Royal Mile outpost of a prizewinning bakery, serves up baked goods—try the scones—and sandwiches in their cute and modern shop (daily 9:00-18:00, 250 Canongate, tel. 0131/556-6632).

$ Clarinda's Tea Room, near the bottom of the Royal Mile, is a charming time warp—a fine and tasty place to relax after touring the Mile or the Palace of Holyroodhouse. Stop in for a quiche, salad, or soup lunch. It's also great for sandwiches and tea and cake any time (Mon-Sat 9:00-16:30, Sun from 10:00, 69 Canongate, tel. 0131/557-1888).

$$ Hendersons is a bright and casual local chain with good vegetarian dishes to go or eat in (daily 9:00-17:00, 67 Holyrood Road—three minutes off Royal Mile near Scottish Parliament end, tel. 0131/557-1606).

$ Oink is handy for a cheap sandwich to go near the top (34 Victoria Street) or bottom (82 Canongate) of the Royal Mile. They carve from a freshly roasted pig each afternoon for sandwiches that come in "oink" or "grunter" sizes. Watch the pig shrink in the front window throughout the day (daily 11:00-18:00 or whenever they run out of meat, cash only, mobile 0777-196-8233).

Historic Pubs for Grub Along the Mile

To grab some forgettable pub grub in historic surroundings, consider one of these landmark pubs described on my self-guided walk. All serve basic pub meals for £10-20 (cheaper lunch deals) and serve food daily from about 12:00 to 21:00. Deacon Brodie's is the most touristy and famous. The others have better ambience and feature music at night (see "Live Music in Pubs" on page 112).

$$ Deacon Brodie's Tavern, at a dead-center location on the Royal Mile, has a sloppy pub on the ground floor with a sloppy restaurant upstairs (435 Lawnmarket).

$$ The Mitre Bar has a classic interior, and their menu includes good meat pies (131 High Street). The neighboring **$$$ Whiski Pub** and **$$ Royal Mile Pub** are also good options.

$$ The World's End Pub, farther down the Mile at Canongate, is a colorful old place dishing up hearty meals from a creative menu in a fun, dark, and noisy space (4 High Street).

Near the National Museum

These restaurants (all within about 100 yards of each other) are happily removed from the Royal Mile melee and skew to a youthful clientele with few tourists. After passing the Greyfriars Bobby statue and the National Museum, fork left onto Forrest Road. To get to the B&B neighborhood from here, take bus #2 from Bristo Place (across the street from Hotel du Vin).

$ Union of Genius is a creative soup kitchen with a strong identity. They cook up a selection of delicious soups with fun foodie twists each morning at their main location in Leith, then deliver them to this shop by bicycle (for environmental reasons). These are supplemented with good salads and fresh-baked breads. The "flight" comes with three small cups of soup and three types of bread. Line up at the counter, then either take your soup to go or sit in the cramped interior, with a couple of tables and counter seating (Mon-Fri 10:00-16:00, Sat from 12:00, closed Sun, 8 Forrest Road, tel. 0131/226-4436).

$$ Mums Diner, a kitschy Scottish diner, serves up comfort food just like mum used to make. The extensive menu offers huge portions of heavy, greasy Scottish/British standards—bangers (sausages), meat pies, burgers, and artery-clogging breakfasts (served until 12:00)—and vegetarian options. There's often a line out the door on weekends (Mon-Sat 9:00-22:00, Sun from 10:00, 4 Forrest Road, tel. 0131/260-9806).

$$ Doctors Pub is a big, inviting corner hangout with a wide-ranging menu of basic pub grub—along with an impressive array of gins, whiskies, and cask ales (kitchen open daily 12:00-14:00 & 18:00-21:00, 32 Forrest Road, where Forrest Road hits Teviot Place, tel. 0131/225-1819).

$$ Ting Thai Caravan, is a loud, industrial-mod eatery serving adventurous Thai street food (soups, noodles, and curries). It's a young, stark, and simple place with thumping music, communal tables, and great food (cash only, daily 11:30-22:00, Fri-Sat until 23:00, 8 Teviot Place, tel. 0131/225-9801).

$$ Ting Saboteur, just a few doors down from Ting Thai Caravan, serves Vietnamese and Southeast Asian cuisine in a slightly more casual (but equally hip), techy-chic space. The enticing menu of bao buns and creative bowls encourages a sense of adventure—consider ordering family-style (no reservations, daily 11:30-22:00, Fri-Sat until 23:00, 19 Teviot Place, tel. 0131/623-0384).

THE NEW TOWN

In the Georgian part of town, you'll find a bustling world of office workers, students, and pensioners doing their thing. These eateries are all within a 10-minute walk of Waverley Station.

Favorites on or near St. Andrew Square

$$$ The Magnum Restaurant and Bar is a relaxed, classy pub-gone-bistro serving beautifully presented Scottish dishes with smart service and no pretense. The appetizing menu is creative and inviting. A block beyond the tourist zone, it feels like a neighborhood favorite (£17-20 lunch specials, daily 12:00-14:30 & 17:30-22:00, 1 Albany Street, tel. 0131/557-4366).

$$ Dishoom is a sprawling, high-energy, Bombay Café phenom. The menu makes Indian food joyfully accessible (and affordable). You'll enjoy upscale South Asian cuisine in a bustling, dark, 1920s dining room on the second floor overlooking St. Andrew Square (I'd avoid the basement). It's a popular spot but no reservations are taken, so plan ahead (daily 12:00-23:00, 3A St. Andrew Square, tel. 0131/202-6406).

$$ Café Royal is a movie producer's dream pub—the perfect *fin de siècle* setting for a coffee, beer, or light meal. (In fact, parts of *Chariots of Fire* were filmed here.) Drop in, if only to admire the 1880 tiles featuring famous inventors. The menu is both traditional and modern with vegetarian dishes and lots of oysters (daily 12:00-22:00, 19 West Register Street, tel. 0131/556-1884, no reservations). The attached small, dressier **restaurant,** specializing in oysters, fish, and game—while stuffier and more expensive—is also good.

$$$$ The Dome Restaurant, filling what was a fancy bank, serves modern international cuisine around a classy bar and under the elegant 19th-century skylight dome. With soft jazz and chic, white-tablecloth ambience, it feels a world apart. Come here not for the food, but for the opulent atmosphere (lunch deals, early-bird special until 18:30, daily 12:00-23:00, reserve for dinner, open for a drink any time under the dome, 14 George Street, tel. 0131/624-8624, www. thedomeedinburgh.com).

$ St. Andrew's and St. George's Church Undercroft Café, in the basement of a fine old church, is the cheapest place in town for soup, sandwiches, quiche, or scones for lunch. Your tiny bill helps support the Church of Scotland (Mon-Fri 10:00-14:00, closed Sat-Sun, just off St. Andrew Square at 13 George Street, tel. 0131/225-3847). It's run by sweet volunteers who love to chat.

Supermarkets: Marks & Spencer Food Hall offers an assortment of tasty hot foods, prepared sandwiches, fresh bakery items, a wide selection of wines and beverages, and plastic utensils at the checkout queue. It's just a block from the Scott Monument and the picnic-perfect Princes Street Gardens (Mon-Sat 8:00-19:00, Thu until 20:00, Sun 11:00-18:00, Princes Street 54—separate stairway next to main M&S entrance leads directly to food hall, tel. 0131/225-2301). **Sainsbury's** supermarket, a block off Princes Street, also offers grab-and-go items (daily 7:00-22:00, on corner of Rose Street on St. Andrew Square, across the street from Jenners).

Hip Eateries on and near Thistle Street

Peaceful little Thistle Street has a cluster of enticing eateries. Browse the options, but tune into these favorites.

$$$ Le Café St. Honoré, tucked away like a secret bit of old Paris, is a charming place with friendly service and walls lined with wine bottles. It serves French-Scottish cuisine in tight, Old World, cut-glass elegance to a dressy crowd (three-course lunch and dinner specials, daily 12:00-14:00 & 17:30-22:00, reservations smart— I'd ask to sit upstairs rather than in the basement, 34 Northwest Thistle Street Lane, tel. 0131/226-2211, www.cafesthonore.com).

$$$ The Bon Vivant is woody, youthful, and candlelit, with a rotating menu of French/Scottish dishes, lots of champagne by the glass, and a companion wine shop next door. They have fun tapas plates and heartier dishes, served either in the bar up front or in the restaurant in back (daily 12:00-22:00, 55 Thistle Street, tel. 0131/225-3275, www.bonvivantedinburgh.co.uk).

$$$ Fishers in the City, a good place to dine on seafood, has an inviting menu and a fine value lunch and early-bird dinner menu (served daily until 18:00). The energy is lively, the clientele is smart, and the room is bright and airy with a simple elegance (daily 12:00-22:00, lots of nice wines by the glass, reservations smart, 58 Thistle Street, tel. 0131/225-5109, www.fishersrestaurants.co.uk).

$$ Hendersons Vegetarian has fed a generation of New Town vegetarians hearty cuisine and salads. Even carnivores love this place for its delectable salads, desserts, and smoothies. Their main restaurant, facing Hanover Street, is self-service by day but has table service after 17:00 (Mon-Sat 8:30-22:00, Sun 10:30-16:00, between Queen and George streets at 94 Hanover Street, tel. 0131/225-2131). Just around the corner on Thistle Street, **Hendersons Vegan** has a strictly vegan menu and feels a bit more casual (daily 12:00-21:30, tel. 0131/225-2605).

THE WEST END

In this posh neighborhood of high-end eateries, the following places have character, tasty food, and fair prices. For locations, see the map on page 120.

$$$ La P'tite Folie Restaurant occupies a beautiful, half-timbered Tudor house that once housed a Polish Catholic church. Its sophisticated, local clientele goes for flavorful specialties like steak and duck—all with a French flair (good-value two-course lunch, food served Mon-Thu 12:00-15:00 & 18:00-22:00, Fri-Sat until 23:00, closed Sun, reservations smart, 9 Randolph Place, tel. 0131/225-8678, www.laptitefolie.co.uk). Under the same roof, **$$ Le Di-Vin Wine Bar** is in the nave of the church, with an extensive wine list and nice cheese-and-meat boards (Mon-Sat 12:00-late, closed Sun, tel. 0131/538-1815).

$$$ La Piazza stands out among several Italian restaurants in this neighborhood. It's a welcoming place with solid pasta dishes, pizzas, and an Italian villa vibe. Pleasant terrace tables are out back (generally Mon-Sat 12:00-23:00, Sun 16:30-22:00, reservations strongly recommended, 97 Shandwick Place, tel. 0131/221-1150, www.lapiazzaedinburgh.com).

$$ Teutchers is a friendly joint on cute William Street, with a fun vibe and nice tables in a rustic space. The food is a cut above typical pub grub, and the downstairs restaurant serves Scottish specialties with local ingredients (daily 10:00-late, 26 William Street, tel. 0131/225-2973).

Supermarket: There's a handy **Sainsbury's** near my recommended West End accommodations (daily 6:00-23:00, 32 Shandwick Place). A **Marks & Spencer** is at the Haymarket train station (Mon-Fri 6:00-22:00, Sat 7:00-21:00, Sun from 9:00).

SOUTH OF THE CITY CENTER

These places are within a 10-minute walk of my recommended B&Bs. For locations, see the map on page 123. For a cozy drink after dinner, visit the recommended pubs in the area (see "Nightlife in Edinburgh," earlier). Except for the "memorable meals" places, I wouldn't eat here unless you're staying nearby.

Pub Grub

$$ The Salisbury Arms is a gastropub serving upscale, traditional classics with flair. While they have a bar area and a garden terrace, I'd dine in their elegant restaurant section. The menu ranges from burgers and salads to more sophisticated dishes (book ahead for restaurant, no reservations taken for pub, food served daily 12:00-22:00, across from the pool at 58 Dalkeith Road, tel. 0131/667-4518, www.thesalisburyarmsedinburgh.co.uk).

$$ The Old Bell Inn, with an old-time sports-bar ambience—fishing, golf, horses, lots of TVs—serves an extensive menu of pub meals with daily specials. This is a classic "snug pub"—all dark woods and brass beer taps, littered with evocative knickknacks (bar tables can be reserved, food served daily until 21:15, 233 Causewayside, tel. 0131/668-1573, www.oldbelledinburgh.co.uk).

Eateries Around Newington Road

$$ Hanedan serves fresh Turkish food at tiny tables in a cozy dining room. The lamb, fish, and vegetable dishes are all authentic and bursting with flavor, making this a welcome alternative to pub fare (Tue-Sun 12:00-15:00 & 17:30-late, closed Mon, 42 West Preston Street, tel. 0131/667-4242).

$$ Damm 27, tucked around the corner from Newington, is rustic-chic but unpretentious, with an appealing cocktail-and-wine list and attentive service. The menu features small plates, gourmet burgers, mussel pots, and good vegetarian and vegan options (daily 10:00-late, 27 Causewayside, tel. 0131/667-6693).

$$ Southpour is a nice place for a local beer, craft cocktail, or reliable meal from a menu of salads, sandwiches, meat dishes, and other comfort foods. The brick walls, wood beams, and giant windows give it a warm and open vibe (don't miss the specials board, daily 10:00-22:00, 1 Newington Road, tel. 0131/650-1100).

$$ Voujon Restaurant serves a fusion menu of Bengali and Indian cuisines. Vegetarians appreciate the expansive yet inexpensive offerings (daily 17:00-23:00, 107 Newington Road, tel. 0131/667-5046).

$$ Apiary has an inviting, casual interior and a hit-or-miss, eclectic menu that mingles various international flavors—they call it "local products with global spices" (early-bird specials, daily 10:00-15:00 & 17:30-21:00, 33 Newington Road, tel. 0131/668-4999).

Groceries: On the main streets near the restaurants you'll find **Sainsbury's Local** and **Co-op** (on South Clerk Road), and **Tesco Express** and another **Sainsbury's Local** one block over on Causewayside (all open late—until at least 22:00).

Memorable Meals Farther Out

$$$$ Rhubarb Restaurant specializes in Old World elegance. It's in "Edinburgh's most handsome house"—an over-the-top riot of antiques, velvet, tassels, and fringe. The plush dark-rhubarb color theme reminds visitors that this was the place where rhubarb was first popularized in Britain. It's a short taxi ride past the other recommended eateries behind Arthur's Seat, in a huge estate with big, shaggy Highland cattle enjoying their salads al fresco. At night, it's a candlelit wonder. Most spend a ton here. Reserve in advance and dress up if you can (daily 12:00-14:00 & 18:00-22:00, afternoon tea served daily 12:00-19:00, in Prestonfield House, Priestfield Road, tel. 0131/662-2303, www.prestonfield.com). For details on their schmaltzy Scottish folk evening, see "Nightlife in Edinburgh," earlier.

$$ The Sheep Heid Inn, Edinburgh's oldest and most inviting public house, is equally notable for its history, date-night appeal, and hearty portions of affordable, classy dishes. It's a short cab ride or pleasant 30-minute walk from the B&B neighborhood, but it's worth the effort to dine in this dreamy setting in the presence of past queens and kings—choose between the bar downstairs, dining room upstairs, or outside in the classic garden courtyard (food served Mon-Fri 12:00-21:00, Sat-Sun 12:00-21:30, 43 The Causeway, tel. 0131/661-7974, www.thesheepheidedinburgh.co.uk).

Edinburgh Connections

BY TRAIN OR BUS

From Edinburgh by Train to: Glasgow (7/hour, 50 minutes), **St. Andrews** (train to Leuchars, 2/hour, 1 hour, then 10-minute bus into St. Andrews), **Stirling** (2/hour, 45 minutes), **Pitlochry** (6/day direct, 2 hours, more with transfer), **Inverness** (6/day direct, 3.5 hours, more with transfer), **Oban** (roughly 6/day, 4.5 hours, change in Glasgow), **York** (3/hour, 2.5 hours), **London** (2/hour, 4.5 hours), **Durham** (2/hour direct, 2 hours, less frequent in winter), **Newcastle** (3/hour, 1.5 hours), **Keswick/Lake District** (8/day to Penrith—more via Carlisle, 1.5 hours, then 40-minute bus ride to Keswick), **Birmingham** (hourly, 5 hours, more with transfer), **Crewe** (every 2 hours, 3 hours), **Bristol,** near Bath (hourly, 6.5 hours), **Blackpool** (about every 2 hours, 3.5 hours, transfer in Preston). Train info: Tel. 0345-748-4950, www.nationalrail.co.uk.

By Citylink Bus: Direct buses go to **Glasgow** (#900, 4/hour, 1.5 hours), **Inverness** (express #G90, 2/day, 4 hours; or #M90, 2/day, 4 hours, more with transfer), **Pitlochry** (#M90, 3/day, 2.5 hours), **Stirling** (every 2 hours on #909, 1.5 hours). To reach other destinations in the Highlands—including **Oban, Fort William, Glencoe,** or **Portree** on the Isle of Skye—you'll have to transfer. It's usually fastest to take the train to Glasgow and change to a bus there. For details, see "Getting Around the Highlands" on page 254. For bus info, stop by the station or call Scottish Citylink (tel. 0871-266-3333, www.citylink.co.uk).

Additional long-distance routes may be operated by National Express (www.nationalexpress.com) or Megabus (www.megabus.com).

BY PLANE

Edinburgh Airport is located eight miles northwest of the center (code: EDI, tel. 0844-481-8989, www.edinburghairport.com). A **taxi** or **Uber** between the airport and city center costs about £30 (25 minutes to downtown, West End, or Dalkeith Road). The airport is also well connected to central Edinburgh by tram and bus. Just follow signs outside; the tram tracks are straight ahead, and the bus stop is to the right, along the main road in front of the terminal. **Trams** make several stops in town, including along Princes Street and at St. Andrew Square (£6, £8.50 round-trip, buy ticket from machine, runs every 5-10 minutes from early morning until 23:30, 35 minutes, www.edinburghtrams.com).

The Lothian **Airlink bus #100** drops you at Waverley Bridge (£4.50, £7.50 round-trip, runs every 10 minutes, 30 minutes, tel. 0131/555-6363, www.lothianbuses.com).

ROUTE TIPS FOR DRIVERS HEADING SOUTH

If you're linking by car to England, note that it's 100 miles south from Edinburgh to Hadrian's Wall; to Durham, it's another 50 miles.

To Hadrian's Wall: From Edinburgh, head south on Dalkeith Road (a handy Cameron Toll Shopping Center with a Sainsbury's grocery and cheap gas is off to your right as you head out of town; gas and parking behind store). Follow Dalkeith Road for about four miles (10 minutes) until you reach the *Sheriffhall* roundabout. Take the exit to A-68 (straight ahead). The A-68 road takes you to Hadrian's Wall in 2.5 hours. You'll pass Jedburgh and its abbey after one hour. (For one last shot of Scotland shopping, there's a bus tour's delight just before Jedburgh, with kilt makers, woolens, and a

EDINBURGH

sheepskin shop.) Across from Jedburgh's lovely abbey is a free park-ing lot, a good visitors center, and pay WCs. The England/Scotland border is a fun, quick stop (great view, ice cream, and tea caravan). Just after the turn for Colwell, turn right onto the A-6079, and roller-coaster four miles down to Low Brunton. Then turn right onto the B-6318, and stay on it by turning left at Chollerford, fol-lowing the Roman wall westward.

To Durham: If you're heading straight to Durham, you can take the scenic coastal route on the A-1 (a few more miles than the A-68, but similar time), which takes you near Holy Island and Bamburgh Castle.

GLASGOW

Glasgow (GLAZ-goh)—astride the River Clyde—is a surprising city. In its heyday, Glasgow was one of Europe's biggest cities and the second largest in Britain, right behind London. A century ago it had 1.2 million people, twice the size (and with twice the importance) of today. It was an industrial power-house producing 25 percent of the world's oceangoing ships. But in the mid-20th century, tough times hit Glasgow, giving it a rough edge and a run-down image.

At the city's low point during the Margaret Thatcher years (1980s), its leaders embarked on a systematic rejuvenation designed to again make Glasgow appealing to businesses, tourists...and locals. Today the city feels revitalized and goes out of its way to offer a warm welcome. Glaswegians (rhymes with "Norwegians") are some of the chattiest people in Scotland—and have the most entertaining (and impenetrable) accent.

Many travelers give Glasgow a miss, but that's a shame: I consider it Scotland's most underrated destination. Glasgow is a workaday Scottish city as well as a cosmopolitan destination, with

an unpretentious friendliness, an energetic and expanding dining and nightlife scene, top-notch museums (most of them free), and a unique flair for art and design. It's also a pilgrimage site for architecture buffs, thanks to a cityscape packed with Victorian facades, early-20th-century touches, and bold and glassy new

construction. Most beloved are the works by hometown boy Charles Rennie Mackintosh, the visionary—and now very trendy—architect who left his mark all over Glasgow at the turn of the 20th century.

Many more tourists visit Edinburgh, a short train trip away. But for a more complete look at urban Scotland, be sure to stop off in Glasgow. Edinburgh may have the royal aura, but Glasgow has down-to-earth appeal. In Glasgow, there's no upper-crust history, and no one puts on airs. In Edinburgh, people identify with the quality of the school they attended; in Glasgow, it's their soccer team allegiance. One Glaswegian told me, "The people of Glasgow have a better time at a funeral than the people of Edinburgh have at a wedding." Here, friendly locals do their best to introduce you to the fun-loving, laid-back Glaswegian way of life.

PLANNING YOUR TIME

While many visitors blitz Glasgow as a day trip from Edinburgh or Stirling (and a single day in Glasgow is certainly more exciting than a fourth day in Edinburgh), the city can easily fill two days of sightseeing.

On a quick visit, follow my "Get to Know Glasgow" self-guided walk, tying together the most important sights in the city's core. If your time is short, the interiors most worth considering are the Tenement House and the Kelvingrove Museum.

With additional time, your options open up. Follow my West End Walk to get a taste of Glasgow's appealing residential zone, which has some of the city's best restaurants as well as a number of worthwhile sights. Fans of Art Nouveau and Charles Rennie Mackintosh can lace together a busy day's worth of sightseeing (the TI has a brochure laying it out). At a minimum, those interested in Mackintosh should visit the Mackintosh House at the Hunterian Gallery (in the West End) and the Mackintosh exhibit at the Kelvingrove Museum.

Regardless of how long you're staying, consider the 1.5-hour hop-on, hop-off bus tour, which is convenient for getting the bigger picture and reaching three important sights away from the center (the Cathedral Precinct, the Riverside Museum, and the Kelvingrove Museum).

Day Trip from Edinburgh: For a full day, catch the 9:30 train to Glasgow (morning trains at least every 10 minutes; discount for

GLASGOW

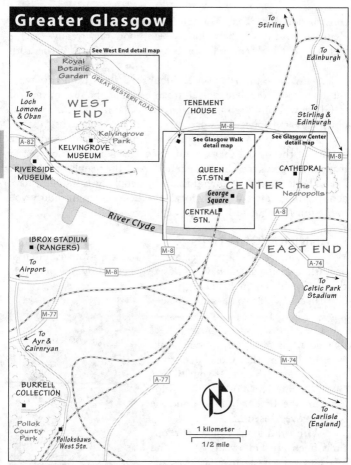

Greater Glasgow

To Stirling

To Edinburgh

See West End detail map

Royal Botanic Garden

GREAT WESTERN ROAD

To Loch Lomond & Oban

WEST END

TENEMENT HOUSE

M-8

To Stirling & Edinburgh

A-82

Kelvingrove Park

See Glasgow Walk detail map

See Glasgow Center detail map

M-8

KELVINGROVE MUSEUM

QUEEN ST.STN.

CATHEDRAL

CENTER

RIVERSIDE MUSEUM

George Square

The Necropolis

River Clyde

CENTRAL STN.

A-8

IBROX STADIUM (RANGERS)

M-8

EAST END

A-74

To Airport

M-8

To Celtic Park Stadium

M-77

To Ayr & Cairnryan

M-74

BURRELL COLLECTION

A-77

N

To Carlisle (England)

Pollok County Park

Pollokshaws West Stn.

1 kilometer

1/2 mile

same-day round-trip if traveling outside rush hours or on weekends); it arrives at Queen Street Train Station before 10:30. To fill your Glasgow hours smartly, I'd do the entire hop-on, hop-off bus tour circuit (1.5 hours), then follow my self-guided walk through downtown (finishing with the Tenement House). Next, check out the Kelvingrove Museum and have dinner nearby (in the Finnieston area). Catch a train that leaves around 21:00 to return to Edinburgh (evening trains depart every 10-20 minutes).

Orientation to Glasgow

Although it's often thought of as a "second city," Glasgow is actually Scotland's biggest (pop. 621,000, swelling to 1.2 million within Greater Glasgow—that's one out of every five Scots).

The tourist's Glasgow has two parts: the businesslike downtown (train stations, commercial zone, and main shopping drag) and the residential West End (B&Bs, restaurants, and nightlife). Both areas have good sights, and both are covered in this chapter by self-guided walks.

Glasgow's **downtown** is a tight grid of boxy office buildings and shopping malls, making it feel more like a midsized American city than a big Scottish one—like Cincinnati or Pittsburgh, but with shorter skyscrapers made of Victorian sandstone rather than glass and steel. The walkable city center has two main drags, both lined with shops and crawling with shoppers: Sauchiehall Street (pronounced "Sockyhall," running west to east) and Buchanan Street (running north to south). These two pedestrian malls—part of a shopping zone nicknamed the Style Mile—make a big zig and zag through the heart of town. The city is busy revamping both Sauchiehall and the third leg of the Style Mile, Argyle Street, in an effort to reduce car traffic and make the city more cycle- and pedestrian-friendly. You'll notice wide sidewalks and bike lanes (and very little parking).

The **West End** is a posh suburb, with big homes, upscale apartment buildings, and lots of green space. The area has three pockets of interest: near the Hillhead subway stop, with a lively restaurant scene and the Botanic Gardens; the University of Glasgow campus, with its stately buildings and fine museums; and, just downhill through a sprawling park, the area around the Kelvingrove Museum, with a lively nearby strip of trendy bars and restaurants (Finnieston).

TOURIST INFORMATION

The TI is on Buchanan Street, just across from Nelson Mandela Place and right behind the lower entrance to the Buchanan Street subway stop (good free Glasgow map; hours change seasonally but generally Mon-Sat 9:00-18:00, Sun 10:00-16:00; 156a Buchanan Street, www.visitscotland.com).

ARRIVAL IN GLASGOW

By Train: Glasgow, a major Scottish transportation hub, has two main train stations, which are just a few blocks apart in the heart of town: **Central Station** (with a grand, genteel interior under a vast steel-and-glass Industrial Age roof) and **Queen Street Station** (more functional, with better connections to Edinburgh—take the exit marked *Buchanan Street* to reach the main shopping drag). Both stations have pay WCs and baggage storage. If going between stations to change trains, you can walk five minutes or take the roundabout "RailLink" bus #398 (free with train ticket, otherwise

£1.20, 5/hour; also goes to the bus station). Either way, I'd allow at least 30 minutes to make a connection.

By Bus: Buchanan bus station is at Killermont Street, two blocks up the hill behind Queen Street Station (luggage lockers daily 6:00-23:00; travel center info desk daily 6:00-18:00; Citylink ticket office daily 9:00-17:00).

By Car: Glasgow's downtown streets are steep, mostly one-way, congested with buses and pedestrians, and a horrible place to drive. Ideally, do Glasgow without a car—for example, tour Edinburgh and Glasgow by public transit, then pick up your rental car on your way out of town. If you are stuck with a car in Glasgow, try to sleep in the West End, where driving and parking are easier (and use public transit or taxis as necessary). Parking downtown is a hassle: Metered street parking is expensive (£3/hour) and limited to two hours during the day; garages are even more expensive (figure £25/24 hours).

The M-8 motorway, which slices through downtown Glasgow, is the easiest way in and out of the city, and it connects well with other highways.

By Plane: For information on Glasgow's two airports, see "Glasgow Connections," at the end of this chapter.

HELPFUL HINTS

Safety: The city center, which is packed with ambitious career types during the day, can feel deserted at night. While the area between Argyle Street and the River Clyde has been cleaned up in recent years, parts can still feel sketchy. As in any big city, use common sense and don't wander alone down dark alleys. The Style Mile shopping drag, the Merchant City area (east of the train stations), and the West End all bustle with crowded restaurants well into the evening and feel well populated in the wee hours.

   If you've picked up a football (soccer) jersey or scarf as a souvenir, don't wear it in Glasgow; passions run very high, and most drunken brawls in town are between supporters of Glasgow's two rival soccer clubs: Celtic in green, and Rangers in blue and red. (For more on the soccer rivalry, see page 149.)

Sightseeing: Almost every sight in Glasgow is free, but most request £3-5 donations (www.glasgowlife.org.uk/museums). While these donations are not required, I like to consider what the experience was worth and decide if and how much to donate as I leave. (Voluntary donations are a nice option—but only work if people actually donate.)

Sunday Travel: Bus and train schedules are dramatically reduced on Sundays and in the off-season. (If you want to get to the Highlands by bus on a Sunday in winter, forget it.)

GLASGOW

Glasgow at a Glance

▲▲**Tenement House** Perfectly preserved 1930s-era middle-class row house offering a time-warp experience. **Hours:** Daily 10:00-17:00, Nov-Feb Sat-Mon 11:00-16:00, closed Tue-Fri. See page 163.

▲▲**Tennent's Brewery Tour** Scotland's biggest brewery, founded in 1740, offering hour-long tours of its 18-acre facility. **Hours:** Tours on the hour Mon-Sat 10:00-18:00, Sun 12:00-17:00. See page 167.

▲▲**Kelvingrove Art Gallery and Museum** Vast collection that includes the city's best Mackintosh works and paintings by the great masters. **Hours:** Mon-Thu and Sat 10:00-17:00, Fri and Sun from 11:00. See page 170.

▲▲**Riverside Museum** High-tech, kid-friendly museum along the River Clyde dedicated to all things transportation. **Hours:** Mon-Thu and Sat 10:00-17:00, Fri and Sun from 11:00. See page 171.

▲**National Piping Center** Small but insightful bagpipe museum, with historic instruments and pipers sometimes on hand for demos. **Hours:** Mon-Thu 9:00-19:00, Fri until 17:00, Sat until 15:00, closed Sun. See page 163.

▲**Glasgow Cathedral** Rare example of intact pre-Reformation Scottish cathedral. **Hours:** Mon-Sat 9:30-17:30, Sun 13:00-17:00; Oct-March Mon-Sat 10:00-16:00, Sun from 13:00. See page 165.

▲**St. Mungo Museum of Religious Life and Art** Secular, city-run museum promoting religious understanding and offering a great view from the top floor. **Hours:** Tue-Thu and Sat 10:00-17:00, Fri and Sun from 11:00, closed Mon. See page 166.

▲**Necropolis** Burial hill with grand tombstones of eminent Glaswegians from the city's Victorian glory days. **Hours:** Always open. See page 167.

▲**Hunterian Gallery and Mackintosh House** Two-for-one museum featuring works of Scottish artists and the reconstructed home of the country's greatest architect. **Hours:** Tue-Sat 10:00-17:00, Sun 11:00-16:00, closed Mon. See page 168.

▲**Hunterian Museum** Natural science museum housing everything from ancient Roman artifacts to animal oddities in a gorgeous university building. **Hours:** Tue-Sat 10:00-17:00, Sun 11:00-16:00, closed Mon. See page 169.

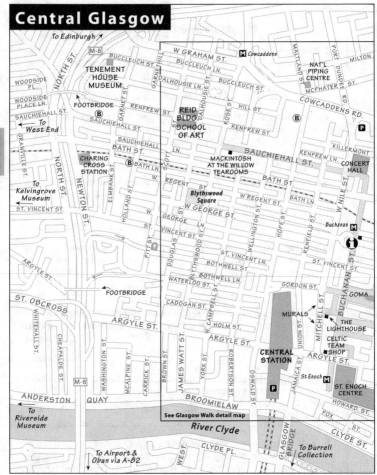

Central Glasgow

Laundry: Call to arrange **Majestic Launderette** to pick up and drop off at your B&B or hotel; they also have a launderette near the Kelvingrove Museum in the West End (self-serve or full service, Mon-Fri 8:00-18:00, Sat until 16:00, Sun 10:00-16:00, 1110 Argyle Street, see map on page 158, tel. 0141/334-3433).

GETTING AROUND GLASGOW

By City Bus: Most city-center routes are operated by First Bus Company (£1.65 or £2.40/ride depending on destination—ask driver when you board, £4.60 for all-day ticket, pay driver, exact change required or use contactless payment like ApplePay). Buses run every few minutes down Glasgow's main thoroughfares (such as Hope Street) to the downtown core (train stations). You can

GLASGOW

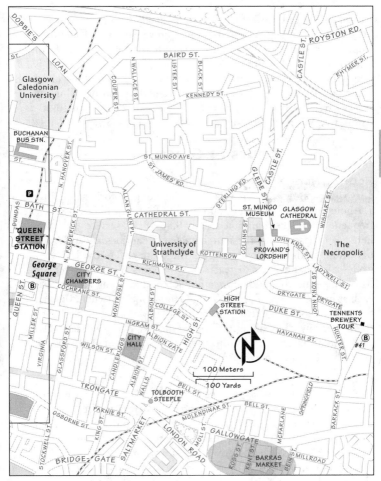

also get around the city via hop-on, hop-off bus (see "Tours in Glasgow," next).

By Taxi or Uber: Taxis are affordable, plentiful, and often come with nice, chatty cabbies (if your driver has an impenetrable Glaswegian accent, just smile and nod). Most taxi rides within the downtown area cost about £6; to the West End is about £8. Uber works particularly well in Glasgow and lets you make quick connections for about £5.

By Subway: Glasgow's cute and clean little single-line subway system, nicknamed The Clockwork Orange, makes a six-mile circle that has 15 stops. While simple today, when it opened in 1896 it was a wonder (it's the world's third-oldest subway system, after those in London and Budapest). Though the subway is useless for connecting city-center sightseeing (Buchanan Street and St.

Enoch are the only downtown stops), it's ideal for connecting to the West End for its sights (like the Kelvingrove Museum; Kelvinhall stop) and restaurants and nightlife (Hillhead stop). It's £1.75 for a single trip or £4.20 for an all-day ticket. The £3 Bramble card is reloadable and reduces your single-ride cost to £1.45, but is worthwhile only if you'll be in Glasgow for several days and/or riding the subway frequently (subway runs Mon-Sat 6:30-23:15, Sun 10:00-18:00, free Wi-Fi at each station,www.spt.co.uk/subway).

Tours in Glasgow

Hop-On, Hop-Off Bus
CitySightseeing connects Glasgow's far-flung historic sights in a 1.5-hour loop and lets you hop on and off as you like. Buses are frequent (every 10-20 minutes, daily 9:30-18:30, service ends earlier in off-season) and alternate between live guides and recorded narration (both are equally good). The route covers the city very well—it's a handy way to reach distant sights like the Riverside Museum—and the guide does a fine job of describing activities at each stop. While the first stop is on George Square (where you can buy your ticket from CitySightseeing staff), you can hop on and pay the driver anywhere along the route (one day-£16, two days-£17, cash only if buying ticket from driver, tel. 0141/204-0444, www. citysightseeingglasgow.co.uk).

Walking Tours
Walking Tours in Glasgow was started by Jenny and Liv, two University of Glasgow graduates who love their city. The city center tour starts in George Square and covers about 3 miles in 2.5 hours (daily at 10:30 and 14:00, off-season at 10:30 only); their street-art tour covers Glasgow's ever-growing mural scene (Fri-Sun at 14:00, off-season by request only). Ask about their West End tour (by request only; all tours £10, www.walkingtoursin.com, walkingtoursinglasgow@gmail.com).

Trainspotters may enjoy the guided, behind-the-scenes tours of **Central Station,** including a spooky, abandoned Victorian train platform (£13, book ahead, www.glasgowcentraltours.co.uk).

Local Guides
Joan Dobbie, a native Glaswegian and registered Scottish Tourist Guide, will give you the insider's take on Glasgow's sights (£155/half-day, £205/day, tours on foot or by public transit—no tours by car, tel. 01355/236-749, mobile 07773-555-151, joan.leo100@gmail.com).

Ann Stewart is a former high-school geography teacher turned Blue Badge guide who is excited to show you around Glasgow or take you on an excursion outside the city (£165/4 hours, £265/

8 hours, mobile 07716-358-997, www.comeseescotland.com, ann@
comeseescotland.com).

Highlands Day Trips

Most of the same companies that do Highlands side-trips from
Edinburgh also operate trips from Glasgow. If you'd like to spend
an efficient day away from the city, skim the descriptions and listings on page 40, and then check each company's website or browse
the brochures at the TI for details.

Glasgow Walks

These two self-guided walks introduce you to Glasgow's most interesting (and very different) neighborhoods: the downtown zone,
and the residential area and university sights of the West End.

GET TO KNOW GLASGOW
The Downtown Core

Glasgow isn't romantic, but it has an earthy charm, its people are
a joy to chat with, and architecture buffs love it. The more time
you spend here, the more you'll ap-
preciate the edgy, artsy vibe and the
quirky, fun-loving spirit. Be sure to
look up—above the chain restaurants
and mall stores—and you'll discover
a wealth of imaginative facades, complete with ornate friezes and expressive
sculptures. These buildings transport
you to the heady days around the turn
of the 20th century—when Victo-
rianism enthralled the rest of Britain, but Glasgow set its own course,
thanks largely to the artistic bravado

of Charles Rennie Mackintosh and his
Art Nouveau friends (the "Glasgow Boys"). This walking tour takes
about 1.5 hours (plus sightseeing stops along the way).

• *Start at the St. Enoch subway station, at the base of the pedestrian
shopping boulevard, Buchanan Street. (This is a short walk from Central Station, or a longer walk or quick cab ride from Queen Street Station.) Stand at the intersection of Argyle and Buchanan, where the
square hits the street (with your back to the glassy subway entry). Take a
moment to get oriented.*

❶ Argyle Street and Nearby

The grand pedestrian boulevard, Buchanan Street, leads uphill to
the Royal Concert Hall. This is the start of the "Style Mile"—the

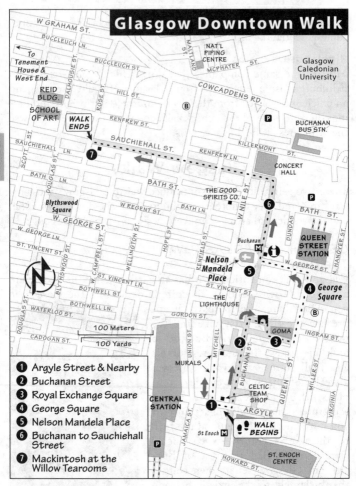

Glasgow Downtown Walk

1. Argyle Street & Nearby
2. Buchanan Street
3. Royal Exchange Square
4. George Square
5. Nelson Mandela Place
6. Buchanan to Sauchiehall Street
7. Mackintosh at the Willow Tearooms

nickname for a Z-shaped pedestrian zone made of three streets: Sauchiehall, Buchanan, and Argyle. While the city is always coming up with marketing slogans to goose its shopping metabolism, this district does have the top shops in town.

Look left (a long block away) to where Central Station (with its huge glass facade) makes a bridge over Argyle Street. This bridge was nicknamed "The Highlanders' Umbrella" from the days when poor Highlanders, who came to Glasgow to find work, would gather here to connect with their community.

Before heading up Buchanan Street, take a quick detour down Argyle to see a couple slices of Glasgow life. About halfway to the Highlanders' Umbrella, on the right, step into the extremely green sports store, the **Celtic Shop** (at #154).

GLASGOW

Green is the color of Glasgow's dominant (for now) soccer team. It's hard for outsiders to fathom the intensity of the rivalry between Glasgow's Celtic and Rangers teams. Celtic, founded by an Irish Catholic priest to raise money for poor Irish immigrants in the East End, is—naturally—green and favored by Catholics. (For reasons no one can explain, the Celtic team name is pronounced "sell-tic"—like it is in Boston; in all other cases, such as when referring to music, language, or culture, this word is pronounced "kell-tic.") Rangers, with team colors of the Union Jack (red, white, and blue), are more likely to be supported by Unionist and Protestant families. Wander into the shop (minimizing or hiding any red or blue you might be wearing). Check out the energy in the photos and shots of the stadium filled with 60,000 fans. You're in a world where red and blue don't exist. Upstairs, tucked in a back room, is a gallery with photos of the 1967 team, considered the best in club history.

Now head around the corner from the Celtic Shop and walk a few steps down the alley (Mitchell Street). While it's usually de-

serted and can seem a bit seedy, it should be safe...but look out for giant magnifying glasses and taxis held aloft by balloons. City officials have cleverly co-opted street artists by sanctioning huge, fun, and edgy **graffiti murals** like these. (You'll see even more if you side-trip down alleys along the Style Mile.) The girl with the magnifying glass was painted by graffiti artist Smug (see the girl's necklace). In the taxi painting, the driver is actually the artist and the license plate alludes to his tag name: Rogue-One. (By the way, there are no actual bricks on that wall.) Glasgow produces a free booklet, called City Center Mural Trail (also available at www.citycentremuraltrail.co.uk), which explains all this fun art around town. Some local companies offer tours of the murals (see "Tours in Glasgow," earlier).

• *Now return to the base of...*

❷ Buchanan Street

Buchanan Street has a friendly Ramblas-style vibe with an abundance of street musicians. As you stroll uphill, keep an eye out for a few big landmarks: Immediately on your left, **Frasers** (#45) is a vast and venerable department store, considered the "Harrods of Glasgow." The **Argyll Arcade** (#30, opposite Frasers), dating from 1827 with a proud red-sandstone facade, is the oldest arcade in town. It's filled mostly with jewelry and plenty of security guards.

Princes Square (at #48, just past Argyll Arcade) is a classic old building dressed with a modern steel peacock and foliage. Step inside to see the delightfully modernized Art Nouveau atrium.

Back on Buchanan Street, at your next left, peer down Mitchell Lane at **The Lighthouse.** This building was Charles Rennie Mack-

intosh's first public commission (built in 1895, when Mackintosh was in his late twenties). It was originally built to house the Glasgow Herald newspaper, but today the building hosts design exhibitions and a small exhibit on Mackintosh's contributions to Glasgow architecture (third floor). With the once-great Mackintosh-designed Glasgow School of Art gutted by a recent fire and years away from reopening, this is a good stop for a quick overview of his work. The Lighthouse's water tower (also designed by Mackintosh) has 135 spiral steps inside—consider climbing to the wraparound balcony for 360-degree views of the city (Mon-Sat 10:30-17:00, Sun from 12:00).

• *Just beyond Mitchell Lane, turn down the alley on the right, toward the large archway. This is Exchange Place. You'll pass the recommended Rogano restaurant on your right before emerging onto...*

❸ Royal Exchange Square

The centerpiece of this square—which marks the entrance to the shopping zone called Merchant City—is a stately, Neoclassical, bank-like building. This was once the **private mansion** of one of the tobacco lords, the super-rich businessmen who reigned here through the 1700s, stomping through the city with gold-tipped canes. During the port's heyday, these entrepreneurs helped Glasgow become Europe's sixth-biggest city—number two in the British Empire.

Today the mansion houses the **Glasgow Gallery of Modern Art,** nicknamed GoMA. Circle around the building to the main

entry (at the equestrian statue of the Duke of Wellington, often creatively decorated as Glasgow's favorite conehead), and step back to take in the full Neoclassical facade. On the pediment, notice the funky, mirrored mosaic celebrating the miracles of St. Mungo—an example of how Glasgow refuses to take itself too seriously. The temporary exhibits and installations inside GoMA are generally forgettable, but they occasionally show works by well-known artists such as Andy Warhol (free, £2 suggested donation, Mon-Wed and Sat 10:00-17:00, Thu until 20:00, Fri and Sun 11:00-17:00, www.glasgowlife.org.uk).

• *Facing the fanciful GoMA facade, turn right up Queen Street. Within a block, you'll reach...*

GLASGOW

➍ George Square

This square, the centerpiece of Glasgow, is filled with statues and lined with notable buildings, such as the Queen Street train station and the Glasgow City Chambers. (It's the big Neoclassical building standing like a secular church to the east; pop in to see its grand ground floor.) In front of the City Chambers stands a monument to Glaswegians killed fighting in

the World Wars. The square is decorated with a *Who's Who* of statues depicting great Glaswegians. Find James Watt (sitting in a chair; he perfected the steam engine that helped power Europe into the Industrial Age), as well as Scotland's two top literary figures: Robert Burns and Sir Walter Scott (capping the tallest pillar in the center). The twin equestrian statues are of Prince Albert and a skinny Queen Victoria—a rare image of her in her more svelte youth.

• *Just past skinny Vic and Robert Peel, turn left onto West George Street, and cross Buchanan Street to the tall church in the middle of...*

➎ Nelson Mandela Place

This first public space named for Nelson Mandela honors the man who, while still in prison, helped bring down apartheid in South Africa. The square was renamed in the 1980s while apartheid was still in place—and when the South African consulate was here. Subsequently, anyone sending the consulate a letter had to address it with the name of the man who embodied the anti-apartheid spirit: Mandela. (Glasgow, nicknamed Red Clyde Side

for its socialist politics and empathy for the working class, is quick to jump on progressive causes.)

The area around **St. George's Church** features some interesting bits of architectural detail. Facing the church's left side are the three circular friezes of the former **Stock Exchange** (with a Neo-Gothic facade, built in 1875). These idealized heads represent the industries that made Glasgow prosperous during its prime: building, engineering, and mining.

Around the back of the church, find the **Athenaeum,** the sandy-colored building at #8 (notice the low-profile label over the door). Now a law office, this was founded in 1847 as a school and city library during Glasgow's Golden Age. (Charles Dickens gave the building's inaugural address.) Like Edinburgh, Glasgow was at the forefront of the 18th-century Scottish Enlightenment, a celebration of education and intellectualism. The Scots were known for their extremely practical brand of humanism; all members of society, including the merchant and working classes, were expected to be well educated. Look above the door to find the symbolic statue of a reader sharing books with young children, an embodiment of this ideal.

• *Return to the big, pedestrianized Buchanan Street in front of the church. Head uphill (you'll pass the TI on your right).*

❻ Buchanan Street to Sauchiehall Street (More of the Style Mile)

A short distance uphill is the glass entry to Glasgow's subway. Soon after, on the right, you'll pass the Buchanan Galleries, an indoor mall that sprawls through several city blocks (filled with shopping temptations and offering a refuge in rainy weather).

Whisky Side Trip: For a fun education in whisky, take a little detour. At the Buchanan Galleries, head left down Bath Street a block and a half to #23, where stairs lead down on the left into **The Good Spirits Company** (note that as you cross West Nile Street you may first spot the Good Spirits beer-and-wine shop on the left—although tempting, continue down Bath Street to find the main whisky shop). This happy world of whisky is run by two young aficionados (Shane and Matthew) and their booze-geek staff. They welcome you to taste and learn (Mon-Wed and Sat 10:00-19:00, Thu until 20:00, Sun 12:00-17:00, tel. 0141/258-8427).

• *Returning to Buchanan Street, continue uphill to the top.*

At the top of Buchanan Street stands the **Glasgow Royal Concert Hall.** Its steps are a favorite perch where local office workers munch lunch and enjoy the street scene. The statue is of **Donald Dewar,** who served as Scotland's first-ever "First Minister" after the Scottish Parliament reconvened in 1999 (previously they'd been serving in London—as part of the British Parliament—since 1707).

• *From here, the Style Mile zags left, Buchanan Street becomes Sauchiehall Street, and the shopping gets cheaper and less elegant. While there's little of note to see, it's still an entertaining stroll. Walk a few blocks, passing "Pound Shops" (the equivalent of "dollar stores"), newspaper hawkers, beggars, buskers, souvenir shops, and a good bookstore. Enjoy the people-watching. Just before the end of the pedestrian zone, on the left side (at #217), is the...*

❼ Mackintosh at the Willow

This tearoom is in the old Willow Tea Rooms building, an Art Nouveau masterpiece designed by Charles Rennie Mackintosh. The original tearooms at this location were opened in 1903, and the restored version you see today is an exact replica of the original.

Tearooms were hugely popular during the industrial boom of the late 19th century. As Glasgow grew, more people moved to the suburbs, meaning that office workers couldn't easily return home for lunch. And during this age of Victorian morals, the temperance movement was trying to discourage the consumption of alcohol. Tearooms were designed to be an appealing alternative to eating in pubs.

Mackintosh made his living from design commissions, including multiple tearooms for businesswoman Kate Cranston. He took his theme for the café from the name of the street it's on—*saugh* is Scots for willow.

In the design of these tearooms, there was a meeting of the (very modern) minds. In addition to giving office workers an al-

ternative to pubs, Cranston also wanted a place where women could gather while unescorted— in a time when traveling solo could give a woman a less-than-desirable reputation. An ardent women's rights supporter, Cranston requested that the rooms be bathed in white, the suffragettes' signature color.

The **tearooms** recently underwent a several-year restoration and have reopened as the new Mackintosh at the Willow tearooms, with an interior that perfectly replicates Mackintosh's original de-

GLASGOW

Charles Rennie Mackintosh (1868-1928)

Charles Rennie Mackintosh brought an exuberant Art Nouveau influence to the architecture of his hometown. His designs challenged the city planners of this otherwise practical, working-class port city to create beauty in the buildings they commissioned.

As a student traveling in Italy, Mackintosh ignored the paintings inside museums and set up his easel to paint the exteriors of churches and buildings instead. He rejected the architectural traditions of ancient Greece and Rome. In Venice and Ravenna, he fell under the spell of Byzantine design, and in Siena he saw a unified, medieval city design he would try to import—but with a Scottish flavor and palette—to Glasgow.

When Mackintosh was at the Glasgow School of Art, the Industrial Age dominated life. Factories belched black soot as they burned coal and forged steel. Mackintosh and his artist friends drew inspiration from nature and created some of the first Art Nouveau buildings, paintings, drawings, and furniture. His first commission came in 1893, to design an extension to the Glasgow Herald building. More work followed, including the Glasgow School of Art (recently gutted by fire) and the Willow Tea Rooms (now the Mackintosh at the Willow).

A radical thinker, Mackintosh shared credit with his artist wife, Margaret MacDonald (who specialized in glass and metalwork). He once famously said, "I have the talent...Margaret has the genius." The two teamed up with another husband-and-wife duo—Herbert MacNair and Margaret's sister, Frances MacDonald—to define a new strain of Scottish Art Nouveau, called the "Glasgow Style." These influential couples were known as "the Glasgow Four."

signs and decor. You can have a meal or tea, visit the gift shop, or pay to browse the **exhibit** about the history of this place, the tradition of afternoon tea, and Mackintosh's work for Cranston (tearoom daily 9:00-17:45; exhibit-£5.50, daily 10:00-17:30, last entry at 16:00, earlier on Sun; tours available at 10:00 and 11:00). The upstairs Salon de Luxe **dining room** is only accessible by guided tour or by reserving a teatime in advance. It appears just as it did in Mackintosh's day, though most features (such as the chairs and the doors) are reproductions of the fragile originals.

You'll see two other "Willow Tea Rooms" locations around

Mackintosh's works show a strong Japanese influence, particularly in his use of black-and-white contrast to highlight the idealized forms of nature. He also drew inspiration from the Arts and Crafts movement, with an eye to simplicity, clean lines, respect for tradition, and an emphasis on precise craftsmanship over mass production. While some of his designs appear to be repeated, no two motifs are exactly alike—just as nothing is exactly the same in nature.

Mackintosh insisted on designing every element of his commissions—even the furniture, curtains, and cutlery. As a furniture and woodwork designer, Mackintosh preferred to use cheaper materials, then paint them with several thick coats, hiding seams and imperfections and making the piece feel carved rather than built. His projects often went past deadline and over budget, but resulted in unusually harmonious spaces.

Mackintosh inspired other artists, such as painter Gustav Klimt and Bauhaus founder Walter Gropius, but his vision was not appreciated in his own time as much as it is now; he died poor. Now, a century after Scotland's greatest architect set pencil to paper, his hometown is at last celebrating his unique vision.

In Glasgow, locals favor five main Mackintosh sights (listed in order of importance and all described in this chapter): The Mackintosh House (a reconstruction of his 1906 home filled with his actual furniture, on the University of Glasgow campus); the Kelvingrove Art Gallery (with a wonderful exhibit of his work along with the other three of the "Glasgow Boys"); the Mackintosh at the Willow tearooms (a building designed by Mackintosh and currently a functioning tearoom entirely furnished in his style); the Glasgow School of Art (currently closed to tourists), and The Lighthouse (Mackintosh's first public commission—a water tower and modern glass-and-metal building). For the mildly interested traveler, the easiest way to "experience" Mackintosh is to focus on the Kelvingrove Art Gallery exhibit and perhaps pop into the Mackintosh at the Willow tearooms.

town (on Buchanan Street and in the Watt Brothers store on Sauchiehall Street), but these are not associated with the original tearooms.

• *Our walk ends here. Two additional sights (described later) lie within a five-minute stroll (in different directions). The remarkably preserved* **Tenement House** *offers a fascinating glimpse into Glasgow lifestyles in the early 1900s. And the* **National Piping Centre** *goes beyond the clichés and provides a better appreciation for the history and musicality of Scotland's favorite instrument.*

GLASGOW

WEST END WALK

Glasgow's West End—just a quick subway, bus, or taxi ride from downtown—is the city's top residential neighborhood. The main drags are Byres Road, running north-south, and Great Western Road, running east-west. As in so many British cities, the western part of town—upwind of industrial pollution—was historically the most desirable. Today this area has great restaurants and nightlife, and fine accommodations.

This walk begins at the Hillhead subway stop, meanders through dining and residential zones, explores some grand old university buildings (and related museums), and ends with a wander through the park to the Kelvingrove Museum—Glasgow's top museum (to trace the route of this walk, see the "Glasgow's West End" map, later). Since this walk is most worthwhile as a scenic way to connect several important museums, it's best when they're open.

• *Start at the Hillhead subway station. Exiting the station, turn right and walk four short blocks up...*

Byres Road: A *byre* is a cowshed. So back when this was farmland outside the big city, cattle were housed along here. Today, Byres Road is a lively thoroughfare through this trendy district. A block before the big intersection, notice the **Waitrose** supermarket on the left. In Britain, this upscale grocery is a sure sign of a posh neighborhood.

Approaching the corner with Great Western Road, you'll see a church spire on the right. Dating from 1862, this church was converted into a restaurant and music venue called **Òran Mòr** (Gaelic for "The Great Music"). Step into the entryway to see the colorful murals (by Alasdair Gray, a respected Glaswegian artist and novelist). Consider a drink or meal in their pub (try some whisky—they have over 300 varieties). Also check what's on while you're in town, as this is a prime music and theater venue (take advantage of "a play, a pie, and a pint," described later under "Eating in Glasgow").

• *If the weather's good, cross Great Western Road and head into the...*

Glasgow Botanic Gardens: This inviting parkland is Glaswegians' favorite place to enjoy a break from the bustling city. And, like so many things in Glasgow, it's free. Locals brag about their many parks, claiming that—despite their industrial reputation—they have more green space per capita than any other city in Europe. And even the city's name comes from the Gaelic for "the dear green place."

Before going into the park, pause at the red-brick entrance

gate. On the gate on the left, look for Glasgow's quite-busy **city seal,** which honors St. Mungo, the near-legendary town founder. The jumble of symbols (a bird, a tree, a bell, and a salmon with a ring in its mouth) recalls Mungo's four key miracles. Ask any Glaswegian to tell you the tales of St. Mungo—they learn it all by heart. The city motto, "Let Glasgow Flourish," is apt—particularly given its recent rejuvenation following a long, crippling period of industrial rot. Glasgow's current renaissance was kicked off with an ambitious 1989 garden festival in a disused former shipyard. Now the city is one of Europe's trendiest success stories. Let Glasgow flourish, indeed.

Head into the park. If the sun's out, it'll be jammed with people enjoying some rare rays. Young lads wait all winter for the day when they can cry, "Sun's oot, taps aff!" and pull off their shirts to make the most of it.

In addition to the finely landscaped gardens, the park has two inviting greenhouse pavilions—both free and open to the public. The big white one on the right (from 1873; open 10:00-18:00, winter until 16:15) is the most elegant, with a classical statue welcoming you among the palm fronds (but beware the  killer plants, to the left as you enter). When the clouds roll in and the weather turns rotten—which is more the status quo—these warm, dry areas become quite popular.

When you're done in the park, head back out the way you came in. Back on the street, before crossing Great Western Road, go right a few steps to find the blue **police call box.** Once an icon of British life, these were little neighborhood mini offices where bobbies could store paperwork and equipment, use the telephone, and catch up with each other. These days, some of the call boxes are being repurposed as coffee shops, ice-cream stands, and time machines.

• *Cross back over Great Western Road and backtrack (past the Òran Mòr church/restaurant) one block down Byres Road. Turn left down Vinicombe Street (across from the Waitrose). Now we'll explore...*

Back-Streets West End: Peek inside the **Hillhead Bookclub**—a former cinema that's been converted into a hipster bar/ restaurant serving affordable food (described later, under "Eating in Glasgow"). A half-block after that, turn right (on poorly marked Cranworth Street) and walk along the row of red-sandstone **tenements.** While that word has negative connotations stateside, here a "tenement" is simply an apartment building. And judging from

GLASGOW

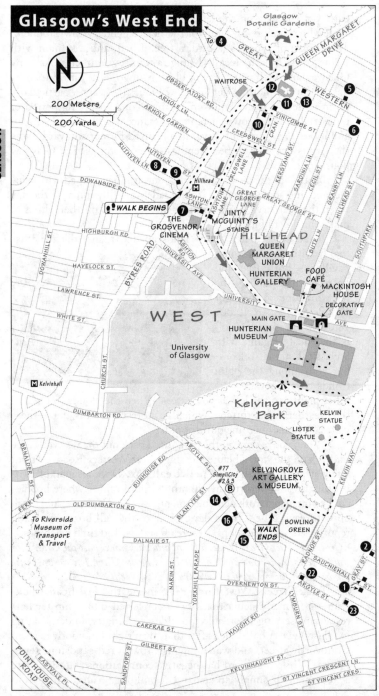

Glasgow's West End

Glasgow Botanic Gardens

QUEEN MARGARET DRIVE

GREAT

WESTERN

To ④

200 Meters
200 Yards

OBSERVATORY RD.

ARHOLE LN.

ARHOLE GARDEN

WAITROSE

⑫

⑪

⑬

⑤

RUTHVEN ST.

RUTHVEN LN.

CRAN. ST.

VINICOMBE ST.

CRESSWELL ST.

⑩

⑥

KERSLAND ST.

SARDINIA LN.

CECIL ST.

DOWANSIDE RD.

⑧ ⑨

CRESSWELL LANE

ASHTON LANE

GRANBY LN.

HILLHEAD ST.

Hillhead Ⓜ

WALK BEGINS

ASHTON LANE

GREAT GEORGE LANE

GREAT GEORGE ST.

BUTE LN.

SOUTHPARK

THE GROSVENOR CINEMA

⑦

JINTY MCGUINTY'S

HIGHBURGH RD.

DOWANHILL RD.

BYRES ROAD

ASHTON ROAD

STAIRS

HILLHEAD

HAVELOCK ST.

UNIVERSITY AVE.

QUEEN MARGARET UNION

LAWRENCE ST.

WHITE ST.

HUNTERIAN GALLERY

FOOD CAFÉ

MACKINTOSH HOUSE

UNIVERSITY

WEST

DECORATIVE GATE

MAIN GATE

AVE.

University of Glasgow

HUNTERIAN MUSEUM

CHURCH ST.

Ⓜ Kelvinhall

DUMBARTON RD.

Kelvingrove Park

KELVIN STATUE

LISTER STATUE

KELVIN WAY

BENALDER ST.

FERRY RD.

BUNHOUSE RD.

OLD DUMBARTON RD.

ARGYLE ST.

To Riverside Museum of Transport & Travel

#77 SimpliCity #2 & 3

Ⓑ

⑭

KELVINGROVE ART GALLERY & MUSEUM

DALNAIR ST.

BLANTYRE ST.

⑯

WALK ENDS

BOWLING GREEN

⑮

YORKHILL PARADE

②

NAKIN ST.

OVERNEWTON ST.

ARGYLE ST.

RADNOR ST.

GRAY ST.

㉒

①

CARFRAE ST.

GILBERT ST.

LYMBURN ST.

㉓

POINTHOUSE ROAD

EASTVALE PL.

SANDFORD ST.

KELVINHAUGHT ST.

ST. VINCENT CRESCENT LN.

ST. VINCENT CRES.

GLASGOW

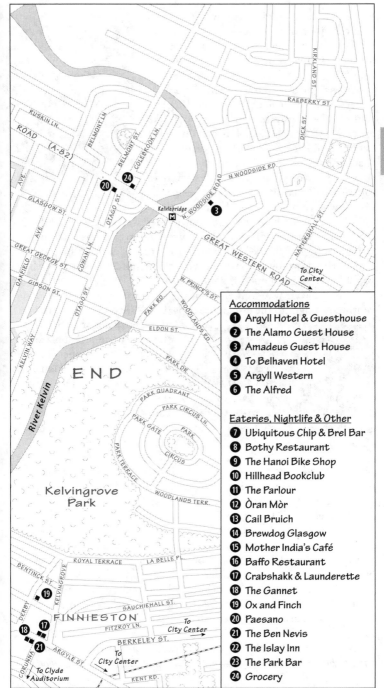

Accommodations

1 Argyll Hotel & Guesthouse
2 The Alamo Guest House
3 Amadeus Guest House
4 To Belhaven Hotel
5 Argyll Western
6 The Alfred

Eateries, Nightlife & Other

7 Ubiquitous Chip & Brel Bar
8 Bothy Restaurant
9 The Hanoi Bike Shop
10 Hillhead Bookclub
11 The Parlour
12 Òran Mòr
13 Cail Bruich
14 Brewdog Glasgow
15 Mother India's Café
16 Baffo Restaurant
17 Crabshakk & Launderette
18 The Gannet
19 Ox and Finch
20 Paesano
21 The Ben Nevis
22 The Islay Inn
23 The Park Bar
24 Grocery

GLASGOW

the grand size, bulging bay windows, and prime location of these, it's safe to say they're far from undesirable. Many are occupied by a single family, while others are subdivided into five or six rooms for students (the university is right around the corner). Across the street from this tenement row (at #12) is a **baths club**—a private swimming pool, like an exclusive health club. Historically, most people couldn't afford bathing facilities in their homes, so they came to central locations like this one to get clean every few days (or weeks). Today, it's the wealthy—not the poor—who come to places like this.

After the baths, turn right down Cresswell Street. A half-block down on the right, turn left down **Cresswell Lane**—an inviting, traffic-free, brick-lane shopping and dining zone. While the Style Mile downtown is packed with chain stores, this is where you'll find charming one-off boutiques.

Browse your way to the end of the lane, cross the street, and continue straight to the even more appealing **Ashton Lane,** strung

with fairy lights. Scout this street and pick a place to return for dinner tonight. Fancy a film? Halfway down the street on the right, the Grosvenor Cinema shows both blockbusters and art-house fare (see listing on page 175).

• *When you reach the end of the lane, take a very sharp left up the stairs (with the idyllic beer garden for Brel on your left). At the top of the stairs, turn right along the road. You're now walking through the modern part of the...*

University of Glasgow Campus: Founded in 1451, this is Scotland's second-oldest university (after St. Andrews). Its 28,000 students sprawl through the West End. Unlike the fancy "old university" buildings, this area is gloomy and concrete. The ugly, gray building on your left is the Queen Margaret Union, with a music venue that has hosted several big-name bands before they were famous—from Nirvana to Franz Ferdinand. (If you think Franz Ferdinand is an Austrian archduke rather than a Scottish alternative rock band...you've been out of college too long.)

• *Eventually you'll reach a wide cross street, University Avenue. Turn left up this street and walk two more blocks uphill. At the traffic light, the Hunterian Gallery and Mackintosh House are just up the hill on your left, and the Hunterian Museum is across the street on the right.*

Hunterian Gallery and Mackintosh House: First, stop in at the Hunterian Gallery to inquire about tours of the Mackintosh House. Ask if there's a wait, and if so, spend your time either in the adjacent gallery, the wonderful university cafeteria named Food (across the lane, cheap and cheery lunch), or the Hunterian Museum across the street. All three sights (the Mackintosh House, Hunterian Gallery, and Hunterian Museum) are important if you have the time and energy (all described later under "Sights in Glasgow" on page 168).

• *When you're done here, head for the Hunterian Museum in the university's big, old, main building across University Avenue. Instead of going through the main gate, go to the left end of the building facing the street to find a more interesting decorative gate.*

University of Glasgow Main Building: Take a good look at the gate, which is decorated with the names of illustrious alumni.

Pick out the great Scots you're familiar with: James Watt, King James II, Adam Smith, Lord Kelvin, William Hunter (the namesake of the university's museums), and Donald Dewar, a driving force behind devolution who became Scotland's first "First Minister" in 1999.

Go through the gate and face the main university building. Stretching to the left is Graduation Hall, where commencement takes place. Head straight into the building, ride the elevator to floor 4, and enjoy the **Hunterian Museum.**

After you visit the Hunterian Museum, find the grand staircase down (just off the main hall housing the Antonine Wall exhibit). You'll emerge into one of the twin quads enclosed by the enormous ensemble of university buildings. Veer right to find your way into the atmospheric, Neo-Gothic **cloisters** that support the wing separating the two quads. These are modeled

after the Gothic cloisters in the lower chapel of Glasgow Cathedral, across town. On the other side, you'll pop out into the adjoin-

GLASGOW

ing quad. Enjoy pretending you're a student for a few minutes, then head out the door at the bottom of the quad (to your left).

Leaving the university complex, head for the tall flagpole on a bluff overlooking a grand view. The turreted building just below is the Kelvingrove Museum, where this walk ends. (If you get turned around in the park, just head for those spires.)

• *From the flagpole, turn left and head to the end of the big building. Head down the stairs leading through the woods on your right (marked James Watt Building). When you reach the busy road, turn right along it for a few yards, then—as soon as you can—angle to the right back into the green space of...*

GLASGOW

Kelvingrove Park: Another of Glasgow's favorite parks, this originated in the Victorian period, when there was a renewed focus on trying to get people out into green spaces.  One of the first things you'll come to is a big statue of **Lord Kelvin** (1824-1907). Born William Thomson, he chose to take the name of the River Kelvin, which runs through Glasgow (and gives its name to many other things here, including the museum we're headed to). One of the most respected scientists of his time, Kelvin was a pioneer in the field of thermodynamics, and gave his name (or, actually, the river's) to a new, absolute unit of temperature measurement designed to replace Celsius and Fahrenheit.

Just past Kelvin, bear left at the statue of **Joseph Lister** (1827-1912, of "Listerine" fame—he pioneered the use of antiseptics to remove infection-causing germs from the surgical environment), and take the bridge across the River Kelvin. Once across the bridge, turn right toward the museum. You'll walk along a pleasant bowling green that was built for the Commonwealth Games that Glasgow hosted in 2014. They keep it free and open to anyone—hoping to create a popular interest in this very old and genteel sport (see page 171).

Now take some time to explore the Kelvingrove Museum, described on page 170.

• *When you're finished at the museum, exit out the back end, toward the busy road. Several recommended restaurants are ahead and to the left, in the Finnieston neighborhood (see page 184). Or, if you'd like to hop on the subway, just turn right along Argyle Street and walk five minutes to the Kelvinhall station.*

Sights in Glasgow

DOWNTOWN
▲▲Tenement House

Here's a chance to drop into a perfectly preserved 1930s-era middle-class residence. The National Trust for Scotland bought this otherwise ordinary row home, located in a residential neighborhood, because of the peculiar tendencies of Miss Agnes Toward (1886-1975). For five decades, she kept her home essentially unchanged. The kitchen calendar is still set for 1935, and canisters of licorice powder (a laxative) still sit on the bathroom shelf. It's a time-warp experience, where Glaswegian old-timers enjoy coming to reminisce about how they grew up.

Cost and Hours: £7.50, daily 10:00-17:00; Nov-Feb Sat-Mon 11:00-16:00, closed Tue-Fri; guidebook-£3, 145 Buccleuch Street (pronounced "ba-KLOO"), down from the top of Garnethill, tel. 0141/333-0183, www.nts.org.uk.

Visiting the House: Buy your ticket on the main floor, and poke around the little museum. You'll learn that in Glasgow, a  "tenement" isn't a slum—it's simply an apartment house. In fact, tenements like these were typical for every class except the richest. Then head upstairs to the apartment, which is staffed by caring volunteers. Ring the doorbell to be let in. Explore the four little rooms. Imagine a world without electricity (Miss Toward was a late adapter, making the leap to electricity only in 1960). Ask about the utility of the iron stove. Ponder the importance of that drawer full of coal and how that stove heated her entire world. Ask why the bed is in the kitchen. As you look through the rooms laced with Victorian trinkets—such as the ceramic dogs on the living room's fireplace mantle—consider how different they are from Mackintosh's stark, minimalist designs from the same period. Miss Toward's clothes and trinkets are switched up throughout the year to match the changing of the seasons.

▲National Piping Centre

If you consider bagpipes a tacky Scottish cliché, think again. At this small but insightful museum, you'll get a scholarly lesson in the proud and fascinating history of the bagpipe. For those with a healthy attention span for history or musical instruments—ideally both—it's fascinating. On Mondays, Thursdays, and Fridays at

12:00 and 14:00 (plus Saturdays at 12:00) a kilt-clad piper is on hand to perform, answer questions, and show you around the collection. He'll even give you a lesson on how to play. At other times, if it's quiet, ask the ticket-sellers to tell you more—some are bagpipe students at the music school across the street. The center also offers a shop, lessons, a restaurant, and accommodations.

Cost and Hours: £4.50, includes audioguide, Mon-Thu 9:00-19:00, Fri until 17:00, Sat until 15:00, closed Sun, 30 McPhater Street, tel. 0141/353-5551, www.thepipingcentre.co.uk.

Visiting the Museum: The collection is basically one big room packed with well-described exhibits, including several historic bag-

pipes. You'll learn that bagpipes from as far away as Italy, Spain, and Bohemia predated Scottish ones; that Lowlands bagpipes were traditionally bellows-blown rather than lung-powered; and why bagpipes started being used to inspire Scottish soldiers on the battlefield. You'll also learn about the tradition of bagpipe competitions around Scotland. The thoughtful, beautifully produced audioguide—which mixes knowledgeable commentary with sound bites of bagpipes being played and brief interviews with performers—feels like a 40-minute audio-documentary on the BBC. The 15-minute film shown at the end of the room sums up the collection helpfully. They also have chanters and a practice set of bagpipes in case you want to try your hand. The chanter fingering is easy if you play the recorder, but keeping the bag inflated is exhausting.

CATHEDRAL PRECINCT, WITH A HINT OF MEDIEVAL GLASGOW

Very little remains of medieval Glasgow, but a visit to the cathedral and the area around it—to the east of downtown—is a visit to the birthplace of the city (see the "Central Glasgow" map, earlier).

The first church was built here in the seventh century. Today's towering **cathedral** is mostly 13th-century—the only great Scottish church to survive the Reformation intact. Nearby, the **Provand's Lordship** is Glasgow's only secular building dating from the Middle Ages. The **St. Mungo Museum** of Religious Life and Art, built on the site of the old Bishop's Castle, is a unique exhibit covering the spectrum of religions. And the **Necropolis,** blanketing the hill behind the cathedral, provides an atmospheric walk through a world of stately Victorian tombstones. From there you can scan the city and look down on the brewery where Tennent's Lager (a longtime Glasgow favorite) has been made since 1885. And, if the spirit moves you, hike on down and tour the brewery (described later).

As you face the cathedral, the St. Mungo Museum is on your right (with handy public WCs), the Provand's Lordship is across the street from St. Mungo, and the Necropolis is behind the cathedral and to the right. The brewery is a 10-minute walk away.

Getting Here: To reach these sights from Buchanan Street, turn east on Bath Street, which soon becomes Cathedral Street, and walk about 15 minutes (or hop a bus along the main drag—try bus #38, or #57, confirm with driver that the bus stops at the cathedral). To head to the Kelvingrove Museum after your visit, from the cathedral, walk two blocks up Castle Street and catch bus #19 (on the cathedral side).

GLASGOW

▲Glasgow Cathedral

This blackened, Gothic cathedral is a rare example of an intact pre-Reformation Scottish cathedral. (It was once known as "the Pink

Church" for the tone of its stone, but with Industrial Age soot and modern pollution, it blackened. Cleaning would damage the integrity of the stone structure, so it was left black.) The zealous Reformation forces of John Knox ripped out the stained glass and ornate chapels of the Catholic age, but they left the church standing. The church is aching to tell its long and fascinating story and volunteers are standing by to do just that.

Cost and Hours: Free, £3 suggested donation; Mon-Sat 9:30-17:30, Sun 13:00-17:00; Oct-March Mon-Sat 10:00-16:00, Sun from 13:00; last entry to lower church 45 minutes before closing, request a free tour (Mon-Sat) or join one in progress, near junction of Castle and Cathedral Streets, tel. 0141/552-6891, www.historicenvironment.scot.

Visiting the Cathedral: Inside, look up to see the wooden barrel-vaulted ceiling, and take in the beautifully decorated section over the choir ("quire"). The choir screen is the only pre-Reformation screen surviving in Scotland. It divided the common people from the priests and big shots of the

day, who got to worship closer to the religious action. The cathedral's glass dates mostly from the 19th century. One window on the right side of the choir, celebrating the 14 trades of Glasgow (try to find them), dates from 1951. Left of that, a set of three windows tell the story of St. Mungo retrieving a ring from the mouth of a fish (it's a long story).

Step into the choir and enjoy the east end with the four evangelists presiding high above in stained glass. Two seats (with high backs, right of altar) are reserved for Queen Elizabeth II and her husband Prince Philip, the Duke of Edinburgh.

Move into the lower church (down stairs on right as you face the choir), where the central altar sits upon St. Mungo's tomb. Mungo was the seventh-century Scottish monk and mythical founder of Glasgow who established the first wooden church on this spot and gave Glasgow its name. Notice the ceiling bosses (decorative caps where the ribs come together) with their colorfully carved demons, dragons, and skulls.

Nearby: In front of the cathedral (near the street), you'll see an attention-grabbing statue of **David Livingstone** (1813-1873). Livingstone—the Scottish missionary/explorer/cartographer who discovered a huge waterfall in Africa and named it in honor of his queen, Victoria—was born eight miles from here.

▲St. Mungo Museum of Religious Life and Art

This secular, city-run museum, just in front of the cathedral, aims to promote religious understanding. Built in 1990 on the site of the old Bishop's Castle, it provides a handy summary of major and minor world religions, showing how each faith handles various rites of passage across the human life span: birth, puberty, marriage, death, and everything in between and after. Start with the 10-minute video overview on the first floor, and finish with a great view from the top floor of the cathedral and Necropolis. Ponder the Zen Buddhist garden out back as you leave.

Cost and Hours: Free, £3 suggested donation, Tue-Thu and Sat 10:00-17:00, Fri and Sun from 11:00, closed Mon, free WCs downstairs, cheap ground-floor café, 2 Castle Street, tel. 0141/276-1625, www.glasgowlife.org.uk/museums.

Nearby: To view a modern-day depiction of St. Mungo, walk two minutes down High Street from the museum to a building-sized mural by the artist Smug.

GLASGOW

Provand's Lordship

With low beams and medieval decor, this creaky home—suppos-edly the "oldest house in Glasgow"—is the only secular building surviving in Glasgow from the Middle Ages. On three floors it displays the *Lifestyles of the Rich and Famous*...circa 1471. First, sit down and watch the 10-minute video (ground floor). The interior, while sparse and stony, shows off a few pieces of furniture from the 16th, 17th, and 18th centuries. Out back, explore the St. Nicholas Garden, which was once part of a hospital that dispensed herbal remedies. The plaques in each section show the part of the body each plant is used to treat.

Cost and Hours: Free, small donation requested, Tue-Thu and Sat 10:00-17:00, Fri and Sun from 11:00, closed Mon, across the street from St. Mungo Museum at 3 Castle Street, tel. 0141/552-8819, www.glasgowlife.org.uk/museums.

▲Necropolis

From the cathedral, a lane leads over the "bridge of sighs" into the park filled with grand tombstones. Glasgow's huge burial hill has

a wistful, ramshackle appeal. A stroll among the tombstones of the eminent Glaswegians of the 19th century gives a glimpse of Victorian Glasgow and a feeling for the confidence and wealth of the second city of the British Empire in its glory days.

With the Industrial Age (in the early 1800s), Glasgow's pop-ulation tripled to 200,000. The existing churchyards were jammed and unhygienic. The city needed a beautiful place in which to bury its beautiful citizens, so this grand necropolis was established. Be-cause Presbyterians are more into simplicity, the statuary is simpler than in a Catholic cemetery. Wandering among the disintegrating memorials to once-important people, I thought about how, some-day, everyone's tombstone will fall over and no one will care.

The highest pillar in the graveyard is a memorial to John Knox. The Great Reformer (who's actually buried in Edinburgh) looks down at the cathedral he wanted to strip of all art, and even tear down. (The Glaswegians rallied to follow Knox, but saved the church.) If the cemetery's main black gates are closed, see if you can get in and out through a gate off the street to the right.

▲▲Tennent's Brewery Tour

Tennent's, founded in 1740, is now the biggest brewery in Scotland, spanning 18 acres. They give serious hour-long tours showing how they make "Scotland's favorite pint," and how they fill 750 kegs per hour and 2,000 cans per minute (you'll see more action Mon-Fri). It's hot and sweaty inside, with 100 steps to climb on your tour. When you're done (surrounded by "the Lager Lovelies"—cans from 1965 to 1993 that were decorated with cover girls), you'll enjoy a pint (£12.50, tours depart on the hour Mon-Sat 10:00-18:00, Sun 12:00-17:00; call or book online; 161 Duke Street, 0141/202-7145, www.tennentstours.com). To head back downtown, bus #41 stops in front of the brewery on Duke Street and goes to George Square.

If you're still thirsty after your tour, head around the corner to **Drygate Brewing,** with good pub food and a wider selection of craft beers (85 Drygate, see "Central Glasgow Hotels & Restaurants" map, later).

THE WEST END
These sights are linked by my "West End Walk" on page 156.

▲Hunterian Gallery and Mackintosh House
Here's a sightseeing twofer: an art gallery offering a good look at some Scottish artists relatively unknown outside their homeland, and the chance to explore the reconstructed home of Charles Rennie Mackintosh, decorated exactly the way he liked it. For Charles Rennie Mack fans—or anyone fascinated by the unique habitats of artists—it's well worth a visit.

Cost and Hours: Gallery— free, Tue-Sat 10:00-17:00, Sun 11:00-16:00, closed Mon, across University Avenue from the main university building, tel. 0141/330-4221, www.gla.ac.uk/hunterian; Mackintosh House—£6, same hours as gallery, last entry 45 minutes before closing. Only 12 people are allowed at a time, so there may be a short wait.

Visitor Information: First, check in at the reception desk to buy your ticket for the Mackintosh House and see if there's a wait to get in. You'll also need to check any bags (free lockers available). Spend your waiting time visiting the gallery, or, with a longer wait, head across the street to the Hunterian Museum (described later). If it's lunchtime, eat at **$ Food,** a cheap, healthy, fast, and modern student cafeteria across the lane from the museum that's open to the public. Inside the house, pick up the laminated guide as you enter.

Mackintosh House: In 1906, Mackintosh and his wife, Margaret MacDonald, moved into the end unit of a Victorian row house. Mackintosh gutted the place and redesigned it to his own liking—bathing the interior in his trademark style, a mix of curving, organic lines and rigid, proto-Art Deco functionalism. They moved out in 1914, and the house was demolished in the 1960s—but the university wisely documented the layout and carefully removed and preserved all of Mackintosh's original furnishings. In 1981, when respect for Mackintosh was on the rise, they built this replica house and reinstalled everything just as Mackintosh had designed it. You'll see the entryway, dining room, drawing room, and bedroom—each one offering glimpses into the minds of these great artists. You'll see original furniture and decorations by Mackintosh and MacDonald, providing insight into their creative process.

Hunterian Art Gallery: The adjacent gallery is manageable and worth exploring. Circling one floor, you'll enjoy thoughtfully described sections organized by theme. One highlight is the modern Scottish art, focusing on two groups: the "Glasgow Boys," who traveled to France to study during the waning days of Realism (1880s), and, a generation later, the Scottish Colourists, who found a completely different inspiration in circa-1910 France—bright, bold, with an almost Picasso-like exuberance. The gallery also has an extensive collection of portraits by American artist James Whistler—Whistler's wife was of Scottish descent, as was Whistler's mother. (Hey, that has a nice ring to it.) The painter always found great support in Scotland, and his heir donated his estate to the University of Glasgow. Another part of the gallery hosts temporary exhibits.

▲Hunterian Museum

The oldest public museum in Scotland was founded by William Hunter (1718-1783), a medical researcher. Today his natural science collection is housed in a huge and gorgeous space inside the university's showcase building. Everything is well presented and well explained. You'll see a perceptive exhibit on the Antonine Wall (the lesser-known cousin of Hadrian's Wall),  built in AD 142 to seal off the Picts from the Roman Empire. Ancient Roman artifacts on display include leather shoes, plumbing, weapons, and carved reliefs. The eclectic collection also includes musical instruments, a display on the Glasgow-built *Lusitania,* and a fine collection of fossils, including the aquatic dinosaur called plesiosaur (possibly a distant ancestor of the Loch Ness monster). But to some, most fascinating are the many morbid examples of deformities—two-headed animals, body parts in jars, and so on (main hall, left of Romans). Ever the curious medical researcher, Hunter collected these for study, and these intrigue, titillate, and nauseate visitors to this day.

Cost and Hours: Free, Tue-Sat 10:00-17:00, Sun 11:00-16:00, closed Mon, Gilbert Scott Building, University Avenue, tel. 0141/330-4221, www.gla.ac.uk/hunterian.

▲▲Kelvingrove Art Gallery and Museum

This "Scottish Smithsonian" displays everything from a stuffed elephant to paintings by the great masters and what, for me, is the city's best collection of work by Charles Rennie Mackintosh. The well-described contents are impressively displayed in a grand, 100-year-old, Spanish Baroque-style building. The Kelvingrove claims to be one of the most-visited museums in Britain—presumably because of all the field-trip groups you'll see

here. Watching all the excited Scottish kids—their imaginations ablaze—is as much fun as the collection itself.

Cost and Hours: Free, £5 suggested donation, Mon-Thu and Sat 10:00-17:00, Fri and Sun from 11:00, free tours at 11:00 and 14:30, Argyle Street, tel. 0141/276-9599, www.glasgowlife.org.uk/museums.

Getting There: My self-guided "West End Walk" leads you here from the Hillhead subway stop, or you can ride the subway to the Kelvinhall stop. When you exit, turn left and walk five minutes. Buses #2 and #3 run from Hope Street downtown to the museum. It's also on the hop-on, hop-off bus route. No matter how you arrive, just look for the huge, turreted red-brick building.

Organ Concerts: At the top of the main hall, the huge pipe organ booms with a daily 30-minute recital at 13:00 (15:00 on Sunday, 45 minutes).

Visiting the Museum: Built in 1901 to house the city collection, the museum is divided into two sections: Art ("Expression") and Natural ("Life"), each with two floors. The symmetrical floor plan can be confusing. Pick up a map and plan your strategy.

The "Expression" section, in the East Court, is marked by a commotion of heads—each with a different expression—raining down from the ceiling. This half of the museum focuses on artwork, including Dutch, Flemish, French, and Scottish Romanticism from the late 19th century. The exhibits on "Scottish Identity in Art" let you tour the country's scenic wonders and its history on canvas. The Mackintosh section, a highlight for many, demonstrates the Art Nouveau work of the "Glasgow Boys," including Charles Rennie Mackintosh. Upstairs, in the "south balcony," (above the "Glasgow Boys" section), you'll find the museum's most famous painting, Salvador Dalí's *Christ of St. John of the Cross,* which brought visitors to tears when it was first displayed here in the 1950s.

The "Life" section, in the West Court, features a menagerie of stuffed animals (including a giraffe, kangaroo, ostrich, and moose) with a WWII-era Spitfire fighter plane hovering overhead. Branching off are halls with exhibits ranging from Ancient Egypt to "Scotland's First People" to weaponry ("Conflict and Consequence").

Kelvingrove Lawn Bowling

For a fun and free activity surrounded by relaxed locals, try your hand at lawn bowling. There's a mission behind the perfectly manicured greens next to the Kelvingrove Museum (made beautiful to host the 2014 Commonwealth Games): Keep young people interested in the traditional sport. They'll provide balls (4 per person) and a court time. It's all free and tourists are welcome. While sunny weekends may be too busy, you'll always find a court on a cloudy weekday. It's a fine evening activity; you can bowl rain or shine (April-Sept Mon-Fri 9:00-21:00, Sat-Sun until 18:00, mobile 07920-048-945). Lawn bowling is a lot like *petanque* (popular in France); the object and scoring are the same. The balls are bigger and "biased" (lopsided on purpose to let experts throw curves). Let the attendant explain the rules if necessary. (They also rent tennis gear for the adjacent courts.) An efficient plan would be to end your sightseeing day at the huge Kelvingrove Museum (closes at 17:00), play an hour of "bowls," and have dinner a couple blocks away at a recommended Finnieston restaurant of your choice. You could cap your night with a beer and live music at a Gaelic pub.

AWAY FROM THE CENTER

For general locations, see the "Greater Glasgow" map near the beginning of this chapter.

▲▲Riverside Museum

Located along the River Clyde, this high-tech, kid-friendly museum dedicated to all things transportation-related is nostalgic and modern at the same time. Named the European museum of the year in 2013,

GLASGOW

visiting is a must for anyone interested in transportation and how it has shaped society.

Cost and Hours: Free, £5 suggested donation, Mon-Thu and Sat 10:00-17:00, Fri and Sun from 11:00, ground-floor café with £6-9 meals, upstairs coffee shop with basic drinks and snacks, 100 Pointhouse Place, tel. 0141/287-2720, www.glasgowlife.org.uk/museums.

Getting There: It's on the riverfront promenade, two miles west of the city center. Bus #100 runs between the museum and George Square (1-2/hour, operated by Garelochhead Coaches), or you can take a taxi (£7-8, 10-minute ride from downtown). The museum is also included on the hop-on, hop-off sightseeing bus route (described earlier, under "Tours in Glasgow").

Visiting the Museum: Most of the collection is strewn across one huge, wide-open floor. Upon entering, visit the info desk (to the

right as you enter, near the shop) to ask about today's free tours and activities—or just listen for announcements. Also pick up a map from the info desk, as the museum's open floor plan can feel a bit like a traffic jam at rush hour.

Diving in, explore the vast collection: stagecoaches, locomotives, double-decker trolleys, and an entire wall stacked with vintage automobiles and another with motorcycles. Learn about the opening of Glasgow's old-timey subway (Europe's third oldest). Explore the collections of old toys and prams, and watch a film about 1930s cinema. Stroll the re-creation of a circa-1900 main street, with video clips bringing each shop to life (there's one about a little girl who discovers her daddy was selling things to the pawn shop to pay the rent).

Don't miss the much-smaller upstairs section, with great views over the River Clyde (cross the footbridge over the trains), additional exhibits about ships built here in Glasgow (see the side-bar), and what may be the world's oldest bicycle. The description explains how two different inventors have tried to take credit for the bike—and both of them are Scottish.

Nearby: Be sure to head to the River Clyde directly behind the museum (just step out the back door). The *Glenlee,* one of five remaining tall ships built in

GLASGOW

When the Great Ships of the World Were "Clyde-Built"

Glasgow's River Clyde shipyards were the mightiest in the world, famed for building the largest moving man-made objects on earth. The shipyards, once 50 strong, have dwindled to just three. Yet a few giant cranes still stand to remind locals and visitors that from 1880 to 1950, a quarter of the world's ships were built here and "Clyde-built" meant reliability and quality. For 200 years, shipbuilding was Glasgow's top employer—as many as 100,000 workers at its peak, producing a new ship every two days. The glamorous Cunard ships were built here—from the *Lusitania* in 1906 (infamously sunk by a German U-boat in World War I, which almost brought the US into the war) to the *Queen Elizabeth II* in 1967. People still talk about the day when over 200,000 Glaswegians gathered for the launch, the Queen herself smashed the champagne bottle on the prow, and the magnificent ship slid into the harbor. To learn lots more about shipbuilding in Glasgow, visit the excellent Riverside Museum.

Glasgow in the 19th century (1896), invites visitors to come aboard (free, daily 10:00-17:00, Nov-Feb until 16:00, tel. 0141/357-3699, www.thetallship.com). Good exhibits illustrate what it was like to live and work aboard the ship. Explore the officers' living quarters, then head below deck to the café and more exhibits. Below that, the cargo hold has kids' activities and offers the chance to peek into the engine room. As you board, note the speedboat **river tour** that leaves from here each afternoon (£10, roughly hourly, 20 minutes).

Burrell Collection

This eclectic art collection of a wealthy local shipping magnate—which includes sculpture from Roman to Rodin, stained glass, tapestries, furniture, Asian and Islamic works, and halls of paintings starring Cézanne, Renoir, Degas, and a Rembrandt self-portrait—is closed for renovation until spring 2021 (three miles outside the city center in Pollok Country Park, tel. 0141/287-2550, www. glasgowlife.org.uk/museums).

Shopping in Glasgow

Downtown, the **"Style Mile"** has all the predictable chain stores, with a few Scottish souvenir stands mixed in. For more on this shopping area, see the start of my self-guided "Get to Know Glasgow" walk. The Glasgow Gallery of Modern Art (GoMA) has a quirky gift shop that many find enticing.

The West End also has some appealing shops. Many are concentrated on **Cresswell Lane** (covered in my self-guided West End Walk). Browsing here, you'll find an eclectic assortment of gifty shops, art galleries, design shops, hair salons, record stores, home-decor shops, and lots of vintage bric-a-brac. Be sure to poke into De Courcy's Arcade, a two-part warren of tiny offbeat shops.

Entertainment in Glasgow

Glasgow has a youthful vibe, and its nightlife scene is renowned. The city is full of live music acts and venues. Walking through the city center, you'll pass at least one club or bar on every block.

PUBS AND CLUBS

Downtown: Glasgow's central business and shopping district is pretty sleepy (and can be a little unsavory) after hours, but there are a few pockets of upbeat activity—each with its own personality. **Bath Street**'s bars and clubs are focused on young professionals as well as students; the recommended Pot Still is a perfect place to sample Scotch whisky (see "Eating in Glasgow," later). Nearby, **Sauchiehall Street** is younger, artsier, and more student-oriented. The recently revitalized **Merchant City** zone, stretching just east of the Buchanan Street shopping drag, has a slightly older crowd and a popular gay scene.

West End: You'll find fun bars and music venues in **Hillhead,** on Ashton Lane and surrounding streets. **Finnieston,** just below the Kelvingrove Museum, is packed with trendy bars and restaurants. But it also has an old-school selection of spit-and-sawdust Gaelic pubs, some of which have live music in the evenings (see next).

LIVE MUSIC

Glasgow has a great music scene, on its streets (talented buskers) and in its bars and clubs (including trad sessions). For the latest, *The Skinny* is Glasgow's information-packed alternative weekly (www.theskinny.co.uk). Or check out *The List* (www.list.co.uk) or the *Gig Guide* (www.gigguide.co.uk). All three are also available in print around town. Or check out what's going on at these bars:

Finnieston

The following pubs line up along Argyle Street. For locations, see the "Glasgow's West End" map on page 158.

The Ben Nevis hosts lively, toe-tapping sessions three times a week. It's a good scene—full of energy but crowded. Show up early to grab a seat in this tiny pub, or be ready to stand (Wed, Thu, and Sun at 21:00, no food service—just snacks, #1147).

The Islay Inn has bands twice weekly—some traditional,

some doing contemporary covers. On nonmusic nights you'll find televisions blasting sports (music Fri and Sat at 21:00, food available, #1256, at corner with Radnor).

At **The Park Bar,** you'll find live music several nights a week, including traditional Scottish bands and sessions on Thursdays (Thu-Sun around 21:00, food available, #1202).

Hillhead

For locations, see the "Glasgow's West End" map on page 158.

The **Òran Mòr** (a former church, www.oran-mor.co.uk) and **Hillhead Bookclub** (a former cinema, www.hillheadbookclub. co.uk) are popular live music venues (both recommended later, under "Eating in Glasgow").

Jinty McGuinty's has acoustic music every night, ranging from chart hits to Irish classics to soul and blues (daily at 21:30, 29 Ashton Lane).

Downtown

For locations, see the "Central Glasgow Hotels & Restaurants" map on page 178.

Twice weekly at **Babbity Bowster,** musicians take over a corner of this cute, simple, and bright pub (under a recommended B&B) for a trad session. The music, energy, and atmosphere are top-notch (Wed and Sat at 15:00, solid pub grub, 16 Blackfriars Street).

Sloans, hidden away through a muraled tunnel off Argyle Street, is a fun pub with outdoor tables filling an alley. They have live traditional music on Wednesdays (21:00) and *ceilidh* dancing instruction on Fridays (£10, starts at 20:30, book ahead, food available, 108 Argyle Street, www.sloansglasgow.com).

Waxy O'Connor's is a massive, almost Disneyesque, multilevel Irish bar featuring a maze of dark, atmospheric rooms, a tree climbing up a wall, and lots of live music (usually acoustic—check their website for days/times) and trad sessions on Sundays at 15:00 (food available until 22:00, 44 West George Street, www. waxyoconnors.co.uk).

MOVIES

The Grosvenor Cinema, right on Ashton Lane in the heart of the bustling West End restaurant scene, is an inviting movie theater, with cushy leather seats in two theaters showing films big and small (most movies £10) and lots of special events. Wine and beer are available at the theater, or you can order cocktails and warm food at the bar next door and have it delivered to your seat (21 Ashton Lane, tel. 0141/341-1234, http://grosvenorwestend.co.uk).

GLASGOW

Sleeping in Glasgow

For accommodations, choose between downtown (bustling by day, nearly deserted at night, close to main shopping zone and some major sights, very expensive parking and one-way streets that cause headaches for drivers) and the West End (neighborhoody, best variety of restaurants, easier parking, easy access to West End sights and parks but a bus or subway ride from the center and train station).

DOWNTOWN

These accommodations are scattered around the city center. For locations, see the "Central Glasgow Hotels & Restaurants" map. Glasgow also has all the predictable chains—**Ibis, Premier Inn, Travelodge, Novotel, Mercure, Jurys Inn,** and **EasyHotel.**

$$$ Pipers' Tryst has eight simple rooms enthusiastically done up in good tartan style above a restaurant in the National Piping Centre (described on page 163). It's in a grand, old former church building overlooking a busy intersection, across the street from the downtown business, shopping, and entertainment district. The location is handy, if not romantic, and it's practically a pilgrimage for fans of bagpipes (breakfast extra, 30 McPhater Street, tel. 0141/353-5551, www.thepipingcentre.co.uk, hotel@ thepipingcentre.co.uk).

$$$ Z Hotel, part of a small "compact luxury" chain, offers 104 sleek, stylish rooms (some are very small and don't have windows). It's impersonal but handy to Queen Street Station, just a few steps off George Square (breakfast extra, air-con, elevator, free wine-and-cheese buffet each afternoon, 36 North Frederick Street, tel. 0141/212-4550, www.thezhotels.com, glasgow@thezhotels. com).

$$ Grasshoppers is a cheerful, above-it-all retreat on the sixth floor of a building overlooking Central Station. The street-level entry is minimal, but popping out of the elevator, you know you've arrived. The 29 rooms are bright and welcoming (some with small "efficiency" bathrooms), the welcome is warm, and there's 24-hour access to fresh cupcakes, shortbread, and ice cream (free breakfast when you book direct, optional buffet dinner Mon-Wed, elevator, 87 Union Street, tel. 0141/222-2666, www.grasshoppersglasgow. com, info@grasshoppersglasgow.com).

$$ Motel One, part of a stylish German budget hotel chain, has a grand, modern lobby, 374 cookie-cutter rooms, and is conveniently located right next to Central Station (breakfast extra, corner of Oswald and Argyle streets at 78 Oswald Street, tel. 0141/468-0450, www.motel-one.com).

$ Babbity Bowster, named for a traditional Scottish dance, is a pub and restaurant renting five simple, mod rooms up top. It's located in the trendy Merchant City area on the eastern fringe of downtown, near several clubs and restaurants (lots of stairs and no elevator, 10-minute walk from either station, 16 Blackfriars Street, tel. 0141/552-5055, www.babbitybowster.com, info@babbitybowster.com). The ground-floor **$$** pub serves good grub (daily 12:00-23:00) and has twice-weekly sessions (see "Entertainment in Glasgow").

¢ The huge **Euro Hostel** is a well-run and well-located option for those on a tight budget (private rooms, family rooms, most rooms have en-suite bathrooms, some singles with shared bathrooms, very central on the River Clyde near Central Station, 318 Clyde Street, tel. 0845-539-9956, www.eurohostels.co.uk, glasgow@eurohostels.co.uk).

IN THE WEST END

For a more appealing neighborhood experience, bunk in the West End—the upper-middle-class neighborhood just a few subway stops (or a 15-minute, £8 taxi ride) from downtown. As this is also one of the city's best dining zones, you'll likely come here for dinner anyway—so why not sleep here? My favorites in this area are the Alamo and Amadeus, which have the most personality. For locations, see "Glasgow's West End" map, earlier.

Finnieston

These places are in an inviting residential area near the Kelvingrove Museum (not as handy to the subway, but easy by bus). They're close to the lively Argyle Street scene, with good restaurants and fun Gaelic pubs.

$$ Argyll Hotel and Guesthouse won't let you forget you're in Scotland. Each room, though simple, is accessorized with a different tartan and has info on the associated clan, while the halls are adorned with symbols of Scotland (bagpipes, thistle, local landmarks, etc.). The hotel has an elevator, breakfast room, and higher prices than the guesthouse (guesthouse customers must cross the street for breakfast and deal with stairs). Otherwise the rooms are comparable but a bit larger in the guesthouse (family rooms, save money by skipping breakfast, 973 Sauchiehall Street, tel. 0141/337-3313, www.argyllhotelglasgow.co.uk, info@argyllhotelglasgow.co.uk).

$ The Alamo Guest House, energetically run by Steve and Emma, faces the bowling green and tennis court. It has rich, lavish public spaces and 10 delicately decorated rooms with stylish bathrooms, including three luxury suites with bathtubs (family room, some rooms with bathroom down the hall, 2- or 3-night minimum

GLASGOW

Central Glasgow Hotels & Restaurants

GLASGOW

stay on weekends in peak season, 46 Gray Street, tel. 0141/339-2395, www.alamoguesthouse.com, info@alamoguesthouse.com).

Near Kelvinbridge
$$ Amadeus Guest House is a classy refuge just north of the large Kelvingrove Park, a 10-minute walk (or one subway stop) to the restaurants in the West End, and a 20-minute walk to the sights in the center. Its nine modern rooms are quiet and comfortable, with some artistic flourishes (411 North Woodside Road, tel. 0141/339-8257, www.amadeusguesthouse.co.uk, reservations@amadeusguesthouse.co.uk, Alex).

Hillhead
These places, overlooking the busy Great Western Road, are close

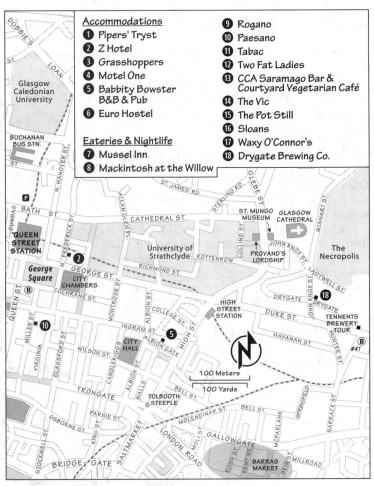

DOBBIE'S LOAN ST.

Glasgow Caledonian University

BUCHANAN BUS STN.

Accommodations
- 1 Pipers' Tryst
- 2 Z Hotel
- 3 Grasshoppers
- 4 Motel One
- 5 Babbity Bowster B&B & Pub
- 6 Euro Hostel

Eateries & Nightlife
- 7 Mussel Inn
- 8 Mackintosh at the Willow
- 9 Rogano
- 10 Paesano
- 11 Tabac
- 12 Two Fat Ladies
- 13 CCA Saramago Bar & Courtyard Vegetarian Café
- 14 The Vic
- 15 The Pot Still
- 16 Sloans
- 17 Waxy O'Connor's
- 18 Drygate Brewing Co.

ST. JAMES' RD.

GLEBE ST.

STERLING RD.

WISHART ST.

BATH ST.

DUNDAS ST.

ALLAN GLEN PL.

CATHEDRAL ST.

ST. MUNGO MUSEUM

GLASGOW CATHEDRAL

QUEEN STREET STATION

N. FREDERICK ST.

GEORGE ST.

University of Strathclyde

ROTTENROW

COLLINS ST.

JOHN KNOX ST.

PROVAND'S LORDSHIP

The Necropolis

George Square

CITY CHAMBERS

RICHMOND ST.

COCHRANE ST.

QUEEN ST.

MILLER ST.

N. HANOVER ST.

MONTROSE ST.

ALBION ST.

COLLEGE ST.

HIGH STREET STATION

DRYGATE

DRYGATE

LADYWELL ST.

JOHN KNOX ST.

TENNENTS BREWERY TOUR

#41

VIRGINIA

GLASSFORD ST.

WILSON ST.

CANDLERIGGS

CITY HALL

INGRAM ST.

ALBION GATE

HIGH ST.

DUKE ST.

HAVANAH ST.

HUNTER ST.

100 Meters
100 Yards

TRONGATE

ALBION ST.

HALLS

BELL ST.

BELL ST.

SPRINGFIELD

MCFARLANE

BARRACK ST.

TOLBOOTH STEEPLE

FARNIE ST.

KING ST.

OSBORNE ST.

SALTMARKET

MOLENDINAR ST.

LONDON ROAD

GALLOWGATE

MILLROAD

ROSS ST.

KENT ST.

MILLROAD

BARRAS MARKET

BRIDGE GATE

STOCKWELL ST.

to the Botanic Gardens and Hillhead restaurant scene but farther from the center (10-minute walk to Hillhead subway stop or catch bus to center from Great Western Road).

$$ Belhaven Hotel, a little farther out (about 10 minutes past Byres Road), has 18 sizeable, refurbished rooms in an elegant four-floor townhouse with a pretty, tiled atrium (huge family room, save money by skipping breakfast, bar in breakfast room serves drinks to guests, no elevator, 15 Belhaven Terrace, tel. 0141/339-3222, www.belhavenhotel.com, info@belhavenhotel.com).

$$ Argyll Western, with 17 sleek and tartaned Scottish-themed rooms, feels modern, efficient, and a bit impersonal (family rooms, breakfast included when you book direct, 6 Buckingham Terrace, tel. 0141/339-2339, www.argyllwestern.co.uk, info@

argyllwestern.co.uk, same family runs the Argyll Hotel, listed earlier).

$$ The Alfred, run by the landmark Òran Mòr restaurant/pub (located in the former church just up the street), is dark, creaky, and traditional. Some of the 14 rooms are newer and stylish, while others feel tired (family room, 1 Alfred Terrace, tel. 0141/357-3445, www.thealfredhotelglasgow.co.uk, alfred@thealfredhotelglasgow.co.uk).

Eating in Glasgow

DOWNTOWN

For locations, see the "Central Glasgow Hotel and Restaurants" map on page 178.

$$$ Mussel Inn offers light, good-value fish dinners and seafood plates in an airy, informal environment. The restaurant is a cooperative, owned and run by shellfish farmers. Their "kilo pot" of Scottish mussels is popular with locals and big enough to share ("lunchtime quickie" deals, daily specials, Mon-Fri 12:00-14:30 & 17:00-22:00, Sat 12:00-22:00, Sun from 12:30, 157 Hope Street, tel. 0141/572-1405).

$$ Mackintosh at the Willow, designed by Charles Rennie Mackintosh, serves breakfast, light lunches, and tea in several dining areas spread across three floors. Each room comes with a unique feel. If you want to have afternoon tea in the classy Salon de Luxe dining room upstairs, you must book ahead (daily 9:00-17:00, reservations smart any time, 217 Sauchiehall Street, tel. 0141/204-1903, www.mackintoshatthewillow.com).

$$ Rogano is a time-warp Glasgow institution that retains much of the same classy Art Deco interior it had when it opened in 1935. The restaurant has three distinct sections (all with varying but similar hours—roughly daily 12:00-22:00): **Rogano Bar** in front is an Art Deco diner with dressy outdoor seating and serves inexpensive soups, sandwiches, and simple dishes; **Rogano Restaurant,** a fancy and pricey dining room at the back of the main floor that smacks of the officers' mess on the *Queen Mary,* focuses on seafood, classic Scottish dishes, and afternoon tea (their early menu—until 19:00—is a good deal); and **Rogano Café,** a more casual yet still dressy bistro in the cellar, is filled with 1930s-Hollywood posters and offers a similar menu to the fancy restaurant, but cheaper (11 Exchange Place—just before giant Merchant City archway just off Buchanan Street, reservations smart, tel. 0141/248-4055, www.roganoglasgow. com).

$$ Paesano is the city's favorite pizza place, serving authentic and reasonably priced Neapolitan-style pizzas at jam-packed, convivial communal tables (Sun-Thu 12:00-22:30, Fri-Sat until 24:00, 94 Miller Street, tel. 0141/258-5565). There's a second location on Great Western Road, near my recommended West End accommodations.

$$ Tabac is a dark, mod, and artsy cocktail bar with spacious seating on a narrow lane just off Buchanan Street. They serve pizza, burgers, and big salads (daily 12:00-24:00, food served until 21:00, across from "The Lighthouse" at 10 Mitchell Lane, tel. 0141/572-1448).

$$$ Two Fat Ladies is a hardworking and dressy little place with a focus on food rather than atmosphere and a passion for white fish (lunch and early-bird fixed-price menu at 18:00 are great values, daily 12:00-14:30 & 17:00-22:00, 118 Blythswood Street, tel. 0141/847-0088).

$$ CCA Saramago Bar and Courtyard Vegetarian Café, located on the first floor of Glasgow's edgy contemporary art museum, charges art-student prices for its designer vegetarian and vegan food. An 18th-century facade, discovered when the site was excavated to build the gallery, looms over the atrium restaurant (food served daily 12:00-22:00, 350 Sauchiehall Street, tel. 0141/352-4920).

$ The Vic is a hipster student hangout within the Glasgow School of Art facilities (around the corner from the fire-damaged Mackintosh building). Face the modern Reid Building and hook around the left side to find the easy-to-miss entrance to this funky bar/café, with a menu of salads, burgers, sandwiches, and a few heartier main dishes (Mon-Sat 12:00-late, closed Sun; Aug Tue-Fri 10:00-18:00, closed Sat-Mon).

For Your Whisky: The Pot Still is an award-winning malt whisky bar dating from 1835 that's also proud of its meat pies. You'll see locals of all ages sitting in its leathery interior, watching football (soccer), and discussing their drinks. Give the friendly bartenders a little background on your beverage tastes, and they'll narrow down a good choice for you from their list of over 750 whiskies (daily 11:00-24:00, food served 12:00-17:00, 154 Hope Street, tel. 0141/333-0980, Frank has the long beard).

IN THE WEST END

This hip, lively residential neighborhood/university district is worth exploring, particularly in the evening. The restaurant scene focuses on two areas (at opposite ends of my West End Walk): near the Hillhead subway stop and, farther down, in the Finnieston neighborhood near the Kelvingrove Museum. For locations, see the "Glasgow's West End" map, earlier. It's smart to book ahead at any of these places—and for some, it's critical. For locations, see the map on page 158.

Near Hillhead

There's a fun concentration of restaurants on the streets that fan out from the Hillhead subway stop (£8 taxi ride from downtown).

If it's a balmy evening, several have convivial gardens designed to catch the evening sun. Before choosing a place, take a stroll and scout the Ashton Lane scene, which has the greatest variety of places (including Ubiquitous Chip and Brel Bar, recommended next). Tucked away on Ruthven Lane (opposite the subway station) are Bothy Restaurant and The Hanoi Bike Shop. And a couple blocks away (near the Botanic Gardens) are Hillhead Bookclub, The Parlour, Òran Mòr, and Cail Bruich.

$$$$ Ubiquitous Chip, aka "The Chip," is a beloved local landmark with a couple of inviting pubs and two great restaurant options. On the ground floor is their fine restaurant with beautifully presented contemporary Scottish dishes in a garden atrium. Their early-bird menu (order by 18:30) is a great value. Upstairs (looking down on the scene) is the less-formal, less-expensive, but still very nice brasserie (roughly Sun-Fri 12:00-22:00, Sat until 23:00, brasserie often open later, 12 Ashton Lane, tel. 0141/334-5007, www.ubiquitouschip.co.uk).

$$ Brel Bar is a fun-loving place with a happy garden and a menu with burgers, mussels, and quality bar food. On a nice evening, its backyard beer garden is hard to beat (daily 12:00-24:00, 37 Ashton Lane, tel. 0141/342-4966).

$$$ Bothy Restaurant is a romantic place offering tasty, traditional Scottish fare served by waiters in kilts. Sit outside in the inviting graveled alleyway or in the rustic-contemporary dining room (2- and 3-course dinner deals, Sun-Thu 12:00-21:00, Fri-Sat until 22:00, reservations recommended, down the lane opposite the subway station to 11 Ruthven Lane, tel. 0141/334-4040, www. bothyglasgow.co.uk).

$$ **The Hanoi Bike Shop,** a rare-in-Scotland Vietnamese "street food" restaurant, serves Asian tapas that are healthy and tasty, using local produce. With tight seating and friendly service, the place has a fun energy (daily 12:00-23:00, 8 Ruthven Lane, tel. 0141/334-7165).

$$ **Hillhead Bookclub** is a historic cinema building cleared out to make room for fun, good food, and lots of booze. It's a youthful and quirky art-school scene, with lots of beers on tap, creative cocktails, retro computer games, ping-pong, and theme evenings like "drag queen bingo" night. The menu features international-inspired dishes, from schnitzel to tacos to curry, plus the usual burgers and salads (daily 10:00-24:00, food served until 21:00, 17 Vinicombe Street, tel. 0141/576-1700).

$$ **The Parlour,** across from the Hillhead Bookclub, gets all the evening sun on its terrace seating. In bad weather, an open fire warms the spacious interior. It's young, fun, and pub-like, with tacos, burgers, and creative cocktails (daily 10:30-24:00, 28 Vinicombe Street, tel. 0141/560-8004).

$$ **Òran Mòr** fills a converted church from the 1860s with a classic pub. They offer basic pub grub either inside or on the front-porch beer garden—and have a good-value lunch deal ("a play, a pie, and a pint") for theater performances (daily 9:00-late, across from the Botanic Gardens at 731 Great Western Road, tel. 0141/357-6200).

$$$$ **Cail Bruich** serves award-winning classic Scottish dishes with an updated spin in an elegant and romantic setting. Reservations are smart (classy tasting menus for £60, lunch Wed-Sat 12:00-14:00, dinner Tue-Sat 18:00-21:00, closed Sun-Mon, 725 Great Western Road, tel. 0141/334-6265, www.cailbruich.co.uk).

Grocery: There's a **Co-op** supermarket between the Kelvinbridge subway stop and my recommended accommodations in the West End—handy for a quick grocery run on the walk back to your hotel (long hours daily, 470 Great Western Road).

Facing the Kelvingrove Museum

These three places are immediately across from the Kelvingrove Museum (which is likely to leave you hungry). They're more basic and less trendy than the Finnieston places (a few blocks away, listed next) that will leave you with better memories.

$$ **Brewdog Glasgow** is a beer-and-burgers joint. It's a great place to sample Scottish microbrews—from their own brewery in Aberdeen, as well as guest brews—in an industrial-mod setting reminiscent of American brewpubs (daily 12:00-24:00, 1397 Argyle Street, tel. 0141/334-7175).

$$ **Mother India's Café** is a busy joint with a line out the

GLASGOW

door on most nights (no reservations). It serves tasty Indian and is a good stop if you crave Scotland's national dish: "a good curry." The menu features small plates designed to enjoy family-style (about two plates per person makes a meal, Mon-Sat 12:00-22:30, Sun until 22:00, 1355 Argyle Street, tel. 0141/339-9145). They also run two nearby locations with the same name.

$ Baffo, a fun Italian place, serves up cheap pizzas and basic pastas. It's casual and buzzing with locals, and if you snag a window seat, you'll enjoy nice views of the Kelvingrove Museum (Sun-Thu 11:00–22:00, Fri-Sat 10:00-24:00, 1377 Argyle Street, tel. 0141/583-0000).

Trendy Finnieston Eateries on and near Argyle Street

This trendy neighborhood—with a hipster charm in this hipster city—stretches east from in front of the Kelvingrove Museum (a 10-minute walk from the Kelvinhall or Kelvinbridge subway stops). Each of these is likely to require a reservation. The Crab-shakk started things off here and today it anchors a strip of similarly funky foodie eateries.

$$$ Crabshakk, specializing in fresh, beautifully presented seafood, is a foodie favorite, with a very tight bar-and-mezzanine seating area and tables spilling out onto the sidewalk. It's casual but still respectable. If you can't reserve a table, ask to sit at the bar (daily 12:00-22:00, 1114 Argyle Street, tel. 0141/334-6127, www.crabshakk.com).

$$$$ The Gannet offers multicourse set menus of beautifully prepared Scottish ingredients with a modern spin. It's relaxed and stylish, but the owners/chefs are serious about the food (no à la carte, 4-course menu until 18:00, 6-course menu thereafter, open for lunch Thu-Sat 12:00-14:00, dinner Tue-Sat 17:00-21:30, Sun 13:00-15:00 & 17:30-21:00, closed Mon, 1155 Argyle Street, tel. 0141/204-2081, www.thegannetgla.com).

$$$ Ox and Finch is a trendy and bustling place with an open kitchen and an upscale, rustic, wood-meets-industrial atmosphere. They serve modern international cuisine in small, shareable portions (reservations strongly recommended, daily 12:00-22:00, 920 Sauchiehall Street, tel. 0141/339-8627, www.oxandfinch.com).

Glasgow Connections

Traveline Scotland's journey planner is linked to all of Scotland's train and bus schedule info. Go online (www.travelinescotland.com), call them at tel. 0871-200-2233, or use the individual websites listed below. If you're connecting with Edinburgh, note that the train is faster but the bus is cheaper.

BY TRAIN

Train info: Tel. 0345-748-4950, NationalRail.co.uk.

From Glasgow's Queen Street Station by Train to: Oban (6/day, fewer on Sun, 3 hours), **Fort William** (3/day, 4 hours), **Inverness** (4/day direct, 3 hours, more with change in Perth), **Edinburgh** (7/hour, 50 minutes), **Stirling** (3/hour, 45 minutes), **Pitlochry** (4/day direct, 1.5 hours, more with change in Perth).

From Glasgow's Central Station by Train to: Keswick in England's Lake District (train to Penrith, hourly, 1.5 hours; then bus to Keswick, 40 minutes), **Cairnryan** for ferry to Belfast (train to Ayr, 2/hour, 1 hour; then bus to Cairnryan, 1 hour), **Liverpool** (2/hour, 4 hours, change in Wigan or Preston), **Durham** (2/hour, 3 hours, may require change in Edinburgh), **York** (hourly, 4 hours, more with change in Edinburgh), **London** (2/hour, 5 hours direct).

BY BUS

Glasgow's Buchanan bus station is a hub for reaching the Highlands. If you're coming from Edinburgh, you can take the bus to Glasgow and transfer here. Or, for a speedier connection, zip to Glasgow on the train, then walk a few short blocks to the bus station. (Ideally, try to arrive at Glasgow's Queen Street Station, which is closer to the bus station.) For more details on these connections, see "Getting Around the Highlands" on page 254. Unless otherwise noted, connections below are on Citylink buses (tel. 0871-266-3333, www.citylink.co.uk).

From Glasgow by Bus to: Edinburgh (#900, 4/hour, 1.5 hours), **Oban** (#976 and #977; 5/day, 3 hours), **Fort William** (#914/#915/#916; 7-8/day direct, 3 hours), **Glencoe** (#914/#915/#916; 7-8/day, 2.5 hours), **Inverness** (express bus #G10, 5/day, 3 hours; 6/day direct on Megabus, 3.5 hours), **Portree** on the Isle of Skye (#915 and #916, 3/day, 7 hours), **Pitlochry** (#M10, 2/day direct, 2 hours; more with transfer in Perth), **Stirling** (#M8, hourly, 45 minutes).

BY PLANE

Glasgow International Airport: Located eight miles west of the city, this airport (code: GLA) has currency-exchange desks, a TI, luggage storage, and ATMs (www.glasgowairport.com). Taxis connect downtown to the airport for about £25. Your hotel can likely arrange a private taxi service for £15, or you can take Uber.

Bus #500 zips to central Glasgow (every 10 minutes, 5:00-23:00, £7.50 one-way, 25 minutes to both train stations and the bus station, catch at bus stop #1). Slow bus #77 goes to the West End, stopping at the Kelvingrove Museum and rolling along Argyle Street (departs every 30 minutes, £5 one-way, 50 minutes).

Prestwick Airport: A hub for Ryanair, this airport is 30 miles southwest of the city center (code: PIK, www.glasgowprestwick.com). The best connection is by train, which runs between the airport and Central Station (3/hour, 50 minutes, half-price with Ryanair ticket, trains also run to Edinburgh Waverley Station—about 2/hour, 2 hours). Stagecoach buses link the airport with Buchanan Bus Station (£10, 1-2/hour, 50 minutes, www.stagecoachbus.com).

ROUTE TIPS FOR DRIVERS

From England's Lake District to Glasgow: From Keswick, take the A-66 for 18 miles to the M-6 and speed north nonstop (via Penrith and Carlisle), crossing Hadrian's Wall into Scotland. The road becomes the M-74 just north of Carlisle. To slip through Glasgow quickly, leave the M-74 at Junction 4 onto the M-73, following signs to *M-8/Glasgow*. Leave the M-73 at Junction 2, exiting onto the M-8. Stay on the M-8 west through Glasgow, exit at Junction 30, cross Erskine Bridge, and turn left on the A-82, following signs to *Crianlarich* and *Loch Lomond*. (For a scenic drive through Glasgow, take exit 17 off the M-8 and stay on the A-82 toward Dumbarton.)

STIRLING & NEARBY

*Stirling • Wallace Monument • Bannockburn • Falkirk •
Culross • Doune • Loch Lomond & the Trossachs*

The historic city of Stirling is the crossroads of Scotland: Equidistant from Edinburgh and Glasgow (less than an hour from both), and rising above a plain where the Lowlands meet the Highlands, it's no surprise that Stirling has hosted many of the biggest names (and biggest battles) of Scottish history. Everyone from Mary, Queen of Scots to Bonnie Prince Charlie has passed through the gates of its stately, strategic castle.

From the cliff-capping ramparts of Stirling Castle, you can see where each of the three pivotal battles of Scotland's 13th- and 14th-century Wars of Independence took place: the Battle of Stirling Bridge, where against all odds, the courageous William Wallace defeated the English army; the Battle of Falkirk, where Wallace was toppled by a vengeful English king; and the Battle of Bannockburn, when—in the wake of Wallace's defeat—Robert the Bruce rallied to kick out the English once and for all (well, at least for a few generations). The Wallace Monument and Battle of Bannockburn Visitors Centre—on the outskirts of Stirling, in opposite directions—are practically pilgrimage sites for patriotic Scots.

Stirling itself is sleepy, but it's a good home base for a variety of side-trips. In Falkirk, take a spin in a fascinating Ferris wheel for boats, and ogle the gigantic horse heads called The Kelpies. Sitting on the nearby estuary known as the Firth of Forth—on the way to Edinburgh or St. Andrews—is the gorgeously preserved time-warp village of Culross. To the north, fans of Monty Python and *Outlander* flock to Doune Castle. And drivers seeking a quick and easy peek at the Highlands make a loop through the Trossachs and along the bonnie, bonnie banks of Loch Lomond.

STIRLING & NEARBY

Stirling Area

Crieff

Gleneagles

To Perth & Pitlochry

Strathyre

5 Kilometers
5 Miles

Muthill
Auchterarder
Braco

A-84

Loch Katrine
Brig o'Turk
Callander
Forth R.
DOUNE
DEANSTON
WALLACE MONUMENT
A-9
A-91

To Inveraray & Oban
Ben Lomond
The Trossachs
Drumvaich
Doune

Tarbet
Aberfoyle
Lake of Menteith
A-84
Stirling

Conic Hill
Buchlyvie
BANNOCKBURN
See Stirling detail map
M-9

Luss
Balmaha
A-82
Loch Lomond
THE KELPIES
Culross
M-80

Helensburgh
HILL HOUSE
Balloch
Forth & Clyde Canal
Bonnybridge
Falkirk
M-876
Bo'ness

Firth of Clyde
A-8
Dumbarton
Kirkintilloch
M-80
FALKIRK WHEEL
Cumbernauld
Union Canal
To Edinburgh

Clydebank
Bathgate

PLANNING YOUR TIME

You'll likely pass near Stirling at least once as you travel through Scotland. Skim this chapter to learn about your options and select the stops that interest you. If you can't fit it all in on a pass-through, spend the night. Just as Stirling was ideally situated for monarchs and armies of the past, it's handy for present-day visitors: It's much smaller, and arguably even more conveniently located, than Edinburgh or Glasgow, and it has a variety of good accommodations. You'd need a solid three days to see all the big sights within an hour's drive of Stirling—but most people are (and should be) more selective.

Stirling

Every Scot knows the city of Stirling (pop. 41,000) deep in their bones. This patriotic heart of Scotland is like Bunker Hill, Gettysburg, and the Alamo, all rolled into one. Stirling perches on a ridge overlooking Scotland's most history-drenched plain: a flat expanse—cut through by the twisting River Forth and the meandering stream called Bannockburn—that divides the Lowlands from the Highlands. And capping that ridge is Stirling's formidable castle, the seat of the final kings of Scotland.

From a traveler's perspective, Stirling is

a pleasant mini-Edinburgh, with a steep spine leading up to that grand castle. It's busy with tourists by day, but sleepy at night. The town, and its castle, may lack personality—but both are striking and strategic.

Orientation to Stirling

Stirling's old town is situated along a long, narrow, steep hill. At its base are the train and bus stations and a thriving commercial district; at its apex is the castle. The old town feels like a steeper, shorter, less touristy, and far less characteristic version of Edinburgh's Royal Mile.

Tourist Information: The TI is a five-minute walk below the castle, just inside the gates of the Old Town Jail (June-Sept Wed-Mon 9:30-17:00, Tue from 10:00; Oct-May daily from 10:00; St. Johns Street, tel. 01786/475-019, www.yourstirling.com).

Getting Around: While the sights within Stirling nestle together at the top of the town, the Wallace Monument and Battle of Bannockburn Visitors Centre are an easy taxi ride, longer bus ride, or short drive away. From July through mid-September, **hop-on, hop-off bus #1314** loops from the train station, bus station, and castle esplanade to the Wallace Monument visitors center (£4.90, every 40 minutes, daily 10:10-16:50, these are first and last departure times from the train station).

A tacky green **tourist train** shuttles people up and down the ridge to Stirling Castle. Unfortunately, it zips past the town's strollable streets and artisan shops. I'd skip the train and explore the town on your way up to the castle.

Sights in Stirling

▲▲STIRLING CASTLE

"He who holds Stirling, holds Scotland." These fateful words have been proven, more often than not, to be true. Stirling Castle's

prized position—perched on a volcanic crag overlooking a bridge over the River Forth, the primary passage between the Lowlands and the Highlands—has long been the key to Scotland. This castle was the preferred home of Scottish kings and queens in the Middle Ages; today it's one of the most historic—and most popular—castles in Scotland. While the compound is simple and its interiors are pretty empty and new-feeling, the castle still has plenty to offer: spectacular views over a gentle countryside, tales of the dynamic Stuart monarchs, and several exhibits that try to bring the place to life. April 1 ~30 same hours

Cost and Hours: £16, daily 9:30-18:00, Oct-March until 17:00, last entry 45 minutes before closing, Regimental Museum normally closes one hour before castle, good café, tel. 01786/450-000, www.stirlingcastle.scot.

Tours: The included 40-minute guided tour helps you get your bearings—both to the castle, and to Scottish history (generally on the hour 10:00-16:00, often on the half-hour too, departs from inside the main gate near the well). Docents posted throughout can tell you more, and you can rent a £3 audioguide.

Getting There: Stirling Castle sits at the very tip of a steep old town. Drivers should follow the *Stirling Castle* signs uphill through town to the esplanade and park at the £4 lot just outside the castle gate. Without a car, you can hike the 20-minute uphill route from the train or bus station to the castle, or take a taxi (about £5).

Background: The first real castle was built here in the 12th century by King David I. But Stirling Castle's glory days were in the 16th century, when it became the primary residence of the Stuart (often spelled "Stewart") monarchs, who turned it into a showpiece of Scotland—and a symbol of one-upmanship against England.

The 16th century was a busy time for royal intrigues here: James IV married the sister of England's King Henry VIII, thereby knitting together the royal families of Scotland (the Stuarts) and England (the Tudors). Later, James V further expanded the castle. Mary (who became the Queen of Scots) spent her early childhood at the castle before being raised in France. As queen and as a Catholic, she struggled against the rise of Protestantism in her realm. But when Mary's son, King James VI, was crowned King James I of England, he took his royal court with him away from Stirling to London—never to return.

During the Jacobite rebellions of the 18th century, the British military took over the castle—bulking it up and destroying its delicate beauty. Even after the Scottish threat had subsided, it remained a British garrison, home base of the Argyll and Sutherland regiments. (You'll notice the castle still flies the Union Jack of the United Kingdom.) Today, the fully restored Stirling Castle feels new but fairly empty—with almost no historic artifacts.

❍ Self-Guided Tour

Begin on the esplanade, just outside the castle entrance, with its grand views.

The Esplanade: The castle's esplanade, a military parade

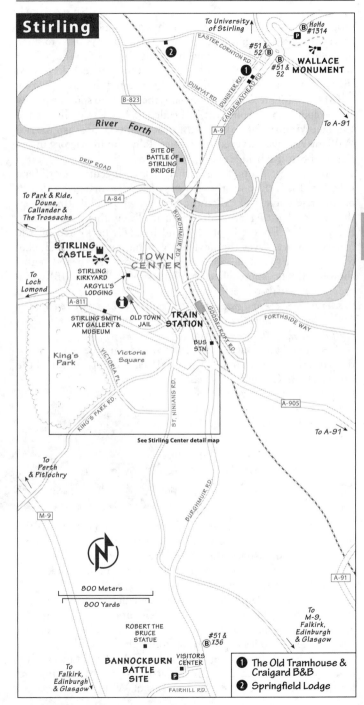

STIRLING & NEARBY

Stirling

To University of Stirling

EASTER CORNTON RD.

❷

#51 & 52 B

DUMYAT RD.

❶

CAUSEWAYHEAD RD.

DUNSTER RD.

B #51 & 52

B HoHo #1314 P

WALLACE MONUMENT

To A-91

B-823

River Forth

A-9

DRIP ROAD

SITE OF BATTLE OF STIRLING BRIDGE

To Park & Ride, Doune, Callander & The Trossachs

A-84

BURGHMUIR RD.

STIRLING CASTLE

TOWN CENTER

To Loch Lomond

STIRLING KIRKYARD

ARGYLL'S LODGING

A-811

❶

STIRLING SMITH ART GALLERY & MUSEUM

OLD TOWN JAIL

TRAIN STATION

GOOSECROFT RD.

FORTHSIDE WAY

King's Park

VICTORIA PL.

Victoria Square

BUS STN.

A-905

KING'S PARK RD.

ST. NINIANS RD.

To A-91

See Stirling Center detail map

To Perth & Pitlochry

M-9

BURGHMUIR RD.

A-91

N

800 Meters

800 Yards

To M-9, Falkirk, Edinburgh & Glasgow

ROBERT THE BRUCE STATUE

#51 & X36 B

BANNOCKBURN BATTLE SITE

VISITORS CENTER P

To Falkirk, Edinburgh & Glasgow

FAIRHILL RD.

❶ The Old Tramhouse & Craigard B&B

❷ Springfield Lodge

ground in the 19th century, is a tour-bus parking lot today. As you survey this site, remember that Stirling Castle bore witness to some of the most important moments in Scottish history. To the right as you face the castle, a statue of **King Robert the Bruce** looks toward the plain called Bannockburn, where he defeated the English army in 1314. Squint off to the horizon on Robert's left to spot the pointy stone monument capping the hill called Abbey Craig. This is the **Wallace Monument,** marking the spot where the Scottish warrior William Wallace surveyed the battlefield before his victory in the Battle of Stirling Bridge (1297).

These great Scots helped usher in several centuries of home rule. In 1315, Robert the Bruce's daughter married into an on-the-rise noble clan called the Stuarts, who had distinguished themselves fighting at Bannockburn. When their son Robert became King Robert II of Scotland in 1371, he kicked off the Stuart dynasty. Over the next few generations, their headquarters—Stirling Castle—flourished. The fortified grand entry showed all who approached that James IV (r. 1488-1513) was a great ruler with a powerful castle.

• *Head through the first gate into Guardroom Square, where you can buy your ticket, check tour times, and consider renting the audioguide. Then continue up through the inner gate.*

Gardens and Battlements: Once through the gate, follow the passage to the left into a delightful grassy courtyard called the **Queen Anne Garden.** This was the royal family's playground in the 1600s. Imagine doing a little lawn bowling with the queen here.

In the casemates lining the garden is the **Castle Exhibition.** Its "Come Face to Face with 1,000 Years of History" exhibit provides an entertaining and worthwhile introduction to the castle. You'll meet each of the people who left their mark here, from the first Stuart kings to William Wallace and Robert the Bruce. The video leaves you thinking that re-enactors of Jacobite struggles are even more spirited than our Civil War re-enactors.

Leave the garden the way you came and make a hairpin turn up the ramp (twice) to the top of the **battlements.** From up here, the castle's strategic position is evident: Defenders had a 360-degree view of enemy armies approaching from miles away. These battlements were built in 1710, long after the castle's Stuart glory days, in response to early rebellions by the Jacobites (from the Latin word for "James"). By this time, the successes of William Wallace and

Robert the Bruce were a distant memory; and through the 1707 Act of Union, Scotland had become welded to England. Bonnie Prince Charlie—descendant of those original Stuart "King Jameses" who built this castle—later staged a series of uprisings to try to reclaim the throne of Great Britain for the Stuart line, frightening England enough for it to further fortify the castle. And sure enough, Bonnie Prince Charlie found himself—ironically—laying siege to the fortress that his own ancestors had built: Facing the main gate (with its two round towers below the UK flag), notice the pockmarks from Jacobite cannonballs in 1746.

• *Now head back down the top ramp and pass through that main gate, into the...*

Outer Close: As you enter this courtyard, straight ahead is James IV's yellow **Great Hall.** To the left is his son **James V's royal**

palace, lined with finely carved Renaissance statues. In 1540, King James V, inspired by French Renaissance châteaux he'd seen, had the castle covered with about 200 statues and busts to "proclaim the peace, prosperity, and justice of his reign" and to validate his rule. Imagine the impression all these classical gods and goddesses made on visitors. The message: James' rule was a Golden Age for Scotland.

Guided tours of the castle depart from just to your right, near the well. Beyond that is the Grand Battery, with its cannons and rampart views and, underneath that, the Great Kitchens. We'll see both at the end of this tour.

• *Hike up the ramp between James V's palace and the Great Hall (under the crenellated sky bridge connecting them). You'll emerge into the...*

Inner Close: Standing at the center of Stirling Castle, you're surrounded by Scottish history. This courtyard was the core of the 12th-century castle. From here, additional buildings were added—each by a different monarch. Facing downhill, you'll see the Great Hall. To the left is the Chapel Royal—where Mary, Queen of Scots was crowned in 1543. Opposite that, to the right, is the royal palace (containing the Royal Apartments)—notice the "I5" monogram above the windows (for the king who built it: James, or Iacobus in Latin, V). Upstairs in this same palace is the Stirling Heads Gallery. And behind you is the Regimental Museum devoted to the Argyll and Sutherland Highlanders.

• *We'll visit each of these in turn. First, at the far-left end of the gallery with the coffee stand, step into...*

The Great Hall: This is the largest banqueting space ever built in Scotland. Dating from 1503, it was a grand setting for the great feasts and pagants of Scotland's Renaissance kings. One such party, to which all the crowned heads of Europe were invited, reportedly went on for three full days. This was also where kings and queens would hold court. The impressive hammer-beam roof is a modern reconstruction, modeled on the early-16th-century roof at Edinburgh Castle. It's made of 400 local oak trees, joined by wooden pegs. If you flipped it over, it would float.

• *At the far-right end of the hall, climb a few stairs and walk across the sky bridge into James V's palace. Here you can explore...*

The Royal Apartments: Six ground-floor apartments are colorfully done up as they might have looked in the mid-16th cen-

tury, when James V and his queen, Mary of Guise, lived here. Costumed performers play the role of palace attendants, happy to chat with you about medieval life as you explore. You'll begin in the King's Inner Hall, where he received guests. Notice the 60 colorfully painted oak medallions on the ceiling, carved with the faces of Scottish and European royalty and images from classical mythology. These are copies; you'll soon see the originals up close in the Stirling Heads Gallery.

Continue (left of the fireplace) into the other rooms: the King's Bedchamber, with a four-poster bed supporting a less-than-luxurious rope mattress; and then the Queen's Bedchamber, the Inner Hall, and the Outer Hall, offering a more vivid example of what these rich spaces would have looked like.

• *From the queen's apartments, you'll exit into the top corner of the Inner Close. Directly ahead and to your left, up the stairs, is the...*

Stirling Heads Gallery: This is, for me, the castle's highlight—a chance to see the originals of the elaborately carved and painted portrait medallions

that decorated the ceiling of the king's presence chamber. Each one is thoughtfully displayed and lovingly explained. Don't miss the video at the end of the hall.

• *If you were to leave this gallery through the intended exit, you'd wind up back down in the Queen Anne Garden. Instead, backtrack and exit the way you came in to return to the Inner Close, and visit the two remaining sights.*

The Chapel Royal: One of the first Protestant churches built in Scotland, the Chapel Royal was constructed in 1594 by James VI for the baptism of his first son, Prince Henry. The faint painted frieze high up survives from Charles I's coronation visit to Scotland in 1633. Clearly the holiness of the chapel ended in the 1800s when the army moved in.

Regimental Museum: At the top of the Inner Close, in the King's Old Building, is the excellent **Argyll and Sutherland Highlanders Museum** (www.argylls.co.uk). Another highlight of the castle, it's barely mentioned in castle promotional material because it's run by a different organization. With lots of tartans, tassels, and swords, it shows how the fighting spirit of Scotland was absorbed by Britain. The two regiments, established in the 1790s to defend Britain in the Napoleonic age and combined in the 1880s, have served with distinction in British military campaigns for more than two centuries. Their pride shows here in the building that has served as their headquarters since 1881. Look for exhibits on World War I, with accounts from the battlefield, and on World War II and conflicts in the Middle East to the present day.

• *When you're ready to move on, consider the following scenic route back to the castle exit.*

Rampart Walk to the Kitchen: The skinny lane between church and museum leads to the secluded Douglas Garden at the rock's highest point. Belly up to the ramparts for a commanding view, including the Wallace Monument. From here you can walk the ramparts downhill to the Grand Battery, with its cannon rampart back at the Outer Close. The Outer Close was the service zone, with a well and the kitchen (below the cannon rampart). The great banquets of James VI didn't happen all by themselves, as you'll appreciate when you explore the fine medieval kitchen exhibit (where mannequin cooks oversee medieval recipes); to find it, head down the ramp and look for the *Great Kitchens* sign. Also off the Outer Close are the **Palace Vaults,** with kid-themed exhibits where younger visitors can learn more about life as a musician, artist, or jester in the castle.

• *Your castle visit ends here. For a scenic route down into town, consider a detour through an old churchyard cemetery (described next).*

STIRLING & NEARBY

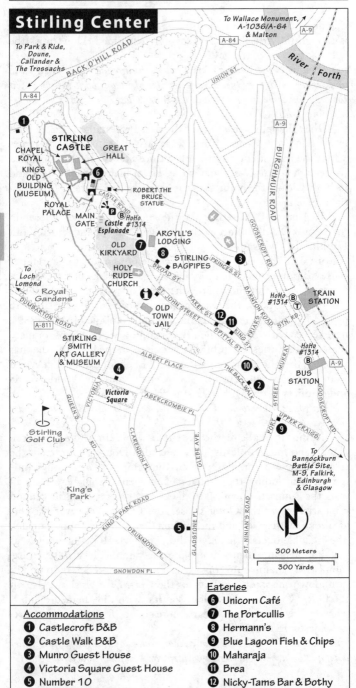

Stirling Center

To Wallace Monument,
A-1036/A-64
& Malton

A-84

A-9

River Forth

To Park & Ride,
Doune,
Callander &
The Trossachs

A-84

BACK O'HILL ROAD

UNION ST.

A-9

BURGHMUIR ROAD

STIRLING
CASTLE

GREAT
HALL

CHAPEL
ROYAL

KINGS
OLD
BUILDING
(MUSEUM)

❻

ROBERT THE
BRUCE
STATUE

CASTLE WYND

ROYAL
PALACE

MAIN
GATE

P

B HoHo
#1314

Castle
Esplanade

❼

ARGYLL'S
LODGING

GOOSECROFT RD.

To
Loch
Lomond

Royal
Gardens

OLD
KIRKYARD

❽

STIRLING
BAGPIPES

PRINCES ST.

❸

DUMBARTON ROAD

HOLY
RUDE
CHURCH

BROAD ST.

BAKER ST.

BARNTON ROAD

HoHo
#1314

B
T

TRAIN
STATION

A-811

ℹ

ST. JOHN STREET

OLD
TOWN
JAIL

❶❷

❶❶

FRIARS ST.

STN. RD.

STIRLING
SMITH
ART GALLERY
& MUSEUM

ALBERT PLACE

SPITTAL ST.

KING ST.

MURRAY

HoHo
#1314

B

A-9

❹

Victoria
Square

ABERCROMBIE PL.

THE BACK WALK

❶⓪

❷

PORT STREET

BUS
STATION

VICTORIA PL.

GOOSECROFT RD.

Stirling
Golf Club

QUEEN'S RD.

CLARENDON PL.

GLEBE AVE.

UPPER CRAIGS

❾

To
Bannockburn
Battle Site,
M-9, Falkirk,
Edinburgh
& Glasgow

King's
Park

KING'S PARK ROAD

DRUMMOND PL.

GLADSTONE PL.

❺

ST. NINIAN'S ROAD

N

300 Meters

SNOWDON PL.

300 Yards

Accommodations
❶ Castlecroft B&B
❷ Castle Walk B&B
❸ Munro Guest House
❹ Victoria Square Guest House
❺ Number 10

Eateries
❻ Unicorn Café
❼ The Portcullis
❽ Hermann's
❾ Blue Lagoon Fish & Chips
❶⓪ Maharaja
❶❶ Brea
❶❷ Nicky-Tams Bar & Bothy

MORE SIGHTS IN STIRLING

Old Kirkyard Stroll

Stirling has a particularly evocative old cemetery in the kirkyard (churchyard) just below the castle. For a soulful stroll, sneak down the stairs where the castle meets the esplanade parking lot (near the statue of the Scotsman fighting in the South African War). From here, you can wander through the tombstones—Celtic crosses, Victorian statues, and faded headstones—from  centuries gone by. The rocky crag in the middle of the graveyard is a fine viewpoint. Work your way over to the Church of the Holy Rude (well worth a visit, daily May-Sept 11:00-16:00), where you can re-enter the town. From here, Argyll's Lodging and the castle parking lot are to the left, and the Old Town Jail (also housing the TI) is just to the right.

Argyll's Lodging

Just below the castle esplanade is this 17th-century nobleman's fortified mansion. European aristocrats wanted to live near power—making this location, where the Earl of Argyll's family resided for about a century, prime real estate.

Cost and Hours: Although currently closed for renovations, Argyll's Lodging is usually included with your castle ticket. Check locally for details on whether it has reopened (generally daily 12:45-17:30, last entry once hour before closing).

▲Stirling Ghost Walk

David Kinnaird, a local actor/historian, gives haunted "Happy Hangman" walks through the old kirkyard cemetery at night. Meet at the TI (inside the gates of the Old Town Jail) for the 75-minute tour (£7.50, RS%—ask, July-Aug Tue-Sat at 20:30, Sept-June Fri-Sat at 20:00, tel. 01592/874-449, www.stirlingghostwalk.com). Just show up and pay him directly. David also offers historic walks (by request only), which tell the story of Stirling as you wander through town.

Old Town Jail

Stirling's jail was built during the Victorian Age, when the purpose of imprisonment was shifting from punishment to rehabilitation. While there's little to see today, theatrical 30-minute tours entertain families with a light and funny walk through one section of the jail. You'll end at the top of the tower for a Q&A with a commanding view of the surrounding countryside.

STIRLING & NEARBY

Cost and Hours: £7.50, July-early Sept only, tours every 30 minutes daily 10:15-17:15, last tour at 17:15, St. John Street, http://oldtownjail.co.uk/.

▲Stirling Bagpipes

This fun little shop, just a block below the castle on Broad Street, is worth a visit for those curious about bagpipes. Owner Alan refurbishes and repairs old bagpipes here, but also makes new ones from scratch, in a workshop on the premises. The pleasantly cluttered shop, which is a bit of a neighborhood hangout, is littered with bagpipe components—chanters, drones, bags, covers, and cords. If he's not too busy, Alan can answer your questions. He'll explain how the most expensive parts of the bagpipe are the "sticks"—the chanter and drones, carved from blackwood—while the bag and cover are cheaper and changeable. A serious set costs £700...beginners can consider a £50 starter kit that includes a practice chanter

(like a recorder) with a book of sheet music and a CD. Alan hopes to open a wee museum next door to show off his collection of historic bagpipes.

Cost and Hours: Free, Mon-Tue and Thu-Sat 10:00-18:00, closed Wed and Sun, 8 Broad Street, tel. 01786/448-886, www.stirlingbagpipes.com.

Nearby: On the wide street in front of the shop, look for Stirling's **mercat cross** ("market cross"). A standard feature of any medieval Scottish market town, this was the place where townsfolk would gather for the market, and where royal proclamations were read and executions took place. Today the commercial metabolism of this once-thriving street is at a low ebb. Locals joke that every 100 years, the shopping bustle moves one block farther down the road. These days, it's squeezed into the modern shopping mall between the old town and the river.

Stirling Smith Art Gallery and Museum

Tucked at the edge of the grid-planned, Victorian Age neighborhood just below the castle, this endearing and eclectic museum is a hodgepodge of artifacts from Stirling's past: art gallery (where you can meet historical figures with connections to this proud little town), pewter collection, local history exhibits, a steam-powered carriage, the mutton bone shard removed in the world's first documented tracheotomy (1853), and a 19th-century executioner's cloak and ax. The museum's prized piece is what they claim is the world's oldest surviving soccer ball—a 16th-century stitched-up pig's blad-

STIRLING & NEARBY

der that restorers found stuck in the rafters of Stirling Castle. The building is surrounded by a garden filled with public art.

Cost and Hours: Free, Tue-Sat 10:30-17:00, Sun from 14:00, closed Mon, Dumbarton Road, tel. 01786/471-917, www. smithartgalleryandmuseum.co.uk.

Sleeping in Stirling

IN AND NEAR THE TOWN CENTER

A variety of spots let you sleep in the shadow of Stirling Castle, in the town center, or a bit farther out.

Just Under the Castle

$$ Castlecroft B&B is well cared for by Laura, who keeps everything immaculate, bakes her own bread, and welcomes guests with tea/coffee and shortbread upon arrival. Just under the castle and overlooking a field with "hairy coos," it's a 10-minute walk down a scenic countryside path to the town center. Two of the five rooms come with their own patios, and anyone can make use of the peaceful living room and deck (Ballengeich Road, tel. 01786/474-933, mobile 0755/334-5497, www.castlecroft-uk.co.uk, castlecroft@gmail.com).

In the Town Center

$$ Castle Walk B&B, built into the old city walls, is a moderately priced option with antique touches in a convenient location. The eight rooms are pleasantly updated, but you'll still feel the authenticity of staying in the castle walls (two rooms with bathroom in hallway, family room, City Walls, Back Walk, tel. 07598/029-732, www.stirlingcastlewalk.co.uk, jackiecameron.uk@gmail.com, Jackie and Adrian).

$ Munro Guest House offers six simple but well-maintained rooms in a homey place in the center of town. One room is a single with private bathroom in the hall (family room, street parking, 14 Princes Street, tel. 01786/472-685, www.munroguesthouse.co.uk, munroguesthouse@gmail.com, Richard).

In the Victorian Town, South of the Castle

When Stirling expanded beyond its old walls during the Victorian Age, a modern, grid-planned town sprouted just to the south. Today, this posh-feeling area holds a few B&Bs that are within a (long) walk of Stirling's old town and castle. These places are in large, spacious homes with easy parking.

$$$$ Victoria Square has 10 plush rooms in a beautiful location facing a big, grassy park. While the prices are high, it's neat as a pin, and Kari and Phil keep things running smoothly. They also have a nice restaurant, The Orangery, in their elegant sunroom. It's about a 10-minute walk to the lower part of town, or 20 minutes up to the castle (no kids under 12, minifridges, 12 Victoria Square, tel. 01786/473-920, www.victoriasquare.scot, info@ victoriasquare.scot).

$$ Number 10 rents three nice, traditional rooms in a Scottish-feeling home with tartan carpets blanketing the halls and a lovely garden out back (no kids under 5, 10 Gladstone Place, tel. 01786/472-681, www.cameron-10.co.uk, cameron-10@tinyonline. co.uk, Carol and Donald Cameron).

ALONG AND NEAR CAUSEWAYHEAD ROAD, NORTH OF THE CASTLE

A number of moderately priced B&Bs and short-term rental apartments line Causewayhead Road, a busy thoroughfare that connects Stirling to the Wallace Monument. From here, it's a long walk into town (or the Wallace Monument), but the location is handy for drivers (each place has free parking). While this modern residential area lacks charm, it's convenient. For locations see the map on page 191.

$$ Craigard B&B has four small, modern, tidy, and proper rooms that offer good value and a shared breakfast table (40 Causewayhead Road, mobile 0778/728-8948, www.craigardstirling. co.uk, enquiries@craigardstirling.co.uk, Dee).

$$ Springfield Lodge sits at the back end of the residential zone that lines up along Causewayhead Road. It's across the street from farm fields, giving it a countryside feeling. The five neat rooms fill a spacious modern house. And owners Kim and Kevin can tell you where to find the local "hairy coos" (family room, no kids under 6, Easter Cornton Road, tel. 01786/474-332, mobile 0798/656-4340, www.springfieldlodgebandb.co.uk, springfieldlodgebandb@gmail.com).

$$ The Old Tramhouse is the frilliest of the bunch, offering two newly renovated self-catering apartments that sleep up to six people (2-night minimum, full kitchens, 42 Causewayhead Road, tel. 01786/449-774, mobile 0759-054-0604, www. theoldtramhouse.com, enquiries@theoldtramhouse.com, Alison Cowie). They also have two apartments for up to five people.

Eating in Stirling

Stirling isn't a place to go looking for high cuisine; eateries here tend to be barely satisfying but functional. All of these are open daily unless otherwise noted.

UP NEAR THE CASTLE

$$ Unicorn Café, tucked under the casemates inside the castle, is a decent cafeteria for lunch if touring the grounds (same hours as castle).

$$ The Portcullis, just below the castle esplanade, is a pub that aches with history, from its dark, wood-grained bar area to its stony courtyard. The food, like the setting, is old school. If the restaurant is full, you can eat at the bar (daily 11:30-15:00 & 17:30-20:30, tel. 01786/472-290).

$$$$ Hermann's, a block below the castle esplanade, is simple, spacious, and homey with a sunny conservatory out back. It serves a mix of Scottish and Austrian food—perfect when you've got a hankering for haggis, but your travel partner wants Wiener schnitzel (daily 12:00-14:30 & 18:00-late, top of Broad Street, tel. 01786/450-632, www.hermanns-restaurant.co.uk).

LOWER DOWN IN THE TOWN

Dumbarton Road, at the bottom of town, has a line of cheap eateries (Indian, Asian, cheap buffets) including **Blue Lagoon Fish & Chips** (11:00-23:00, at Port Street). Among a group of chain pubs and ethnic eateries (Thai and Italian), these three are within about a block of Stirling's clock tower near King Street in the old town center:

$$ Maharaja is popular for its "authentic Indian cuisine" served in a dressy dining room (Mon-Sat 12:00-14:30 & 17:00-22:30, Sun 13:00-15:00 & 17:00-22:00, 39 King Street, tel. 01786/470-728).

$$$ Brea, which means "love" in Gaelic, has a nice Scottish theme, from the menu to the decor to the pop music playing. It's unpretentious and popular for its modern and tasty dishes. Consider treating first courses like tapas and eating family-style (Tue-Thu 12:00-21:00, Fri-Mon until 21:30, 5 Baker Street, tel. 01786/446-277).

$$ Nicky-Tams Bar and Bothy is a fun little hangout with a somewhat gritty Irish-pub ambience, providing a great place to chat up a local and enjoy some good, basic pub grub. They serve meals from 12:00 to 20:00, then make way for drinking and, often, live music (29 Baker Street, tel. 01786/472-194).

Stirling Connections

From Stirling by Train to: Edinburgh (2/hour, 45 minutes), **Glasgow** (3/hour, 45 minutes), **Pitlochry** (5/day direct, 1 hour, more with transfer in Perth), **Inverness** (7/day direct, 3 hours, more with transfer in Perth). Train info: Tel. 0345-748-4950, NationalRail.co.uk.

By Bus to: **Glasgow** (hourly on #M8, 45 minutes), **Edinburgh** (every 2 hours on #909, 1.5 hours). Citylink: tel. 0871-266-3333, www.citylink.co.uk.

Near Stirling

The Wallace Monument and the Battle of Bannockburn Visitors Centre are just outside of town. Sights within side-trip distance include The Kelpies horse-head sculptures, the Falkirk Wheel boat "elevator," the stuck-in-time village of Culross, Doune Castle, and the Trossachs National Park.

JUST OUTSIDE STIRLING
▲Wallace Monument

Commemorating the Scottish hero better known to Americans as "Braveheart," this sandstone tower—built during a wave of Scottish nationalism in the mid-19th century—marks the Abbey Craig hill on the outskirts of Stirling. This is where, in 1297, William Wallace gathered forces and secured his victory against England's King Edward I at the Battle of Stirling Bridge. The victory was a huge boost to the Scottish cause, but England came back to beat the Scots the next year. (For more on Wallace, see page 69.)

Cost and Hours: £10.50; daily July-Aug 9:30-18:00, April-June and Sept-Oct until 17:00; Nov-Feb 10:00-16:00, March until 17:00; last entry 45 minutes before closing, café at visitors center, tel. 01786/472-140, www.nationalwallacemonument.com.

Getting There: The monument is two miles northeast of Stirling on the A-9, signposted from the city center. Bus #52 goes from the Stirling bus station to the roundabout below the monument, near the Co-op supermarket (£2.80, change given, 15-minute ride). From there, it's about a 15-minute hike up to the visitors center.

From July through mid-September, you can take the hop-on, hop-off bus #1314 (see "Orientation to Stirling," page 189) straight to the visitors center parking lot (£4.90, departs every 40 minutes, 15-30 minute ride depending on where you hop on).

Taxis cost about £8 one-way from Stirling. From the visitors center parking lot, you'll need to hike (a steep 15 minutes) or hop on the shuttle bus up the hill to the monument itself (free, departs every 10 minutes).

Visiting the Monument: Buy your ticket either at the visitors center below or the monument above. Then hike or ride the shuttle bus up to the monument's base. Gazing up, think about how this fanciful 19th-century structure, like so many around Europe in that age, was created and designed to evoke (and romanticize) earlier architectural styles—in this case, medieval Scottish castles. The crown-shaped top—reminiscent of St. Giles' Cathedral on the Royal Mile in Edinburgh—and the dynamic sculpture of William Wallace are patriotic to the max.

Climb the tight, stone spiral staircases (not for the claustrophobic) a total of 246 steps, stopping at each of the three levels to see museum displays. The first level, the Hall of Arms, tells the story of William Wallace and the Battle of Stirling Bridge and gives you the chance to ogle Wallace's five-foot-long broadsword. Second is the Hall of Heroes, adorned with busts of great Scots—suggesting the debt this nation owes to Wallace. But it's not all just hero worship: A thoughtful video presentation on the first level considers the role of Wallace in both Scottish and English history, and raises the point that one person's freedom fighter is another person's terrorist. The third level's exhibits are about the monument itself: why and how it was built.

Finally, you reach the top with stunning views over Stirling, its castle, the winding River Forth, and Stirling Bridge—a 500-year-old stone version that replaced the original wooden one. Looking out from the same vantage point as Wallace, imagine how the famous battle played out. But if you find yourself picturing *Braveheart*—with berserker Scots, their faces painted  blue, running across a field to take on the English cavalry—you have the wrong idea. While that portrayal was cinematically powerful, in reality the battle took place on a bridge in a narrow valley (see sidebar).

Battle of Bannockburn Visitors Centre and Monument

Just south of Stirling, this site commemorates what many Scots view as their nation's most significant military victory over the invading English: the Battle of Bannockburn, won by a Scottish army led by Robert the Bruce against England's King Edward II in 1314. The battle memorial is free and always open. The visitors center "Battle Game" is an interactive techy experience, with 3-D screens and a re-creation that basically reduces the battle to a video game.

Cost and Hours: Memorial—free, always open; Visitors Cen-

Debunking *Braveheart*

The 1995 multiple-Oscar-winner movie *Braveheart* informs many travelers' impressions of William Wallace and the battles near Stirling. But Mel Gibson's much-assailed Scottish accent may very well be the most authentic thing about the film.

In the 1297 Battle of Stirling Bridge, William Wallace and his ragtag Scottish forces hid out in the forest overlooking the bottleneck bridge, waiting until the perfect moment to ambush the English. Thanks to the tight quarters and the element of surprise, the Scots won an unlikely victory. *Braveheart* serves up an entirely different version of events: armies lining up across an open field, with blue-faced, kilted Highlanders charging at top speed toward heavily armored English troops. The filmmakers left out the bridge entirely, calling it simply "The Battle of Stirling." And the blue face paint? Never happened. A millennium before William Wallace, the ancient Romans did encounter war-painted fighters in Scotland, whom they called the Picts ("painted ones"). But painting faces in the late 13th century would be like WWII soldiers suiting up in chain mail.

Braveheart takes many other liberties with history. William Wallace was *not* the rugged-born Highlander depicted in the movie—he was born in Elderslie, next to Paisley, in the Lowlands. Wallace did *not* vengefully kill Andrew de Moray for deserting him at Falkirk (Moray fought valiantly by Wallace's side at Stirling, and died from battle wounds). Robert the Bruce did *not* betray Wallace to the English. And William Wallace most certainly did *not* impregnate the future King Edward II's French bride...who was 10 years old, not yet married to Edward, and still living in France at the time of Wallace's death.

Also, the modern concept of national "Freee-dooooom!" was essentially unknown during the divine-right Middle Ages. Wallace wasn't fighting for "democracy" or "liberty"; he simply wanted to trade one authoritarian, aristocratic ruler (from London) for another authoritarian, aristocratic ruler (from Scotland).

Even the film's title is a falsehood: No Scottish person ever referred to Wallace as "Braveheart," which was actually the nickname of one of the film's villains, Robert the Bruce. After Robert's death, his heart was taken (in a small casket) on a crusade to the Holy Land by his friend Sir James Douglas. During one battle, Douglas threw the heart at an oncoming army and shouted, "Lead on, brave heart, I will follow thee!" Gibson's title is a bit like naming a film about Abraham Lincoln *Old Hickory*.

Scottish people have mixed feelings about *Braveheart*. They appreciate the boost it gave to their underdog nation's profile—and to its tourist industry—juuust enough that they're willing to overlook the film's historical gaffes. For travelers, it can be enjoyable to watch *Braveheart* to prep for your trip...as entertainment. Then go to Stirling and get the real story. (For a fact-based account of Wallace's life, see page 69.)

tre and "Battle Game"—£11.50, daily 9:30-18:00, Oct-Feb 10:00-17:00, March until 17:30; 3-D experience lasts 75 minutes and runs every 45 minutes 10:00-16:00, off-season until 15:15 (these are last tour times); café, tel. 01786/812-664, www.battleofbannockburn.com. In summertime, the 3-D experience can sell out, so call or book online 2-3 days in advance.

Getting There: Bannockburn is two miles south of Stirling on the A-872, off the M-80/M-9.

For nondrivers, it's an easy bus ride from the Stirling bus station (bus #X36 or #51, 2/hour, 15 minutes, stop: Whins of Milton/Glasgow Road). You'll get off at the car rental stop on Glasgow Road, a two-minute walk from the Bannockburn visitors center. To get here from the Wallace Monument, take bus #51 from the roundabout below the monument (£2.80, direction: Cowie, 2/hour, 25 minutes). Or take bus #52 from the roundabout (hourly, 20 minutes), stop at the Stirling bus station, and switch to bus #X36.

Background: In simple terms, Robert the Bruce—who was first and foremost a politician—found himself out of political options after years of failed diplomatic attempts to make peace with the strong-arming English. William Wallace's execution left a vacuum in military leadership, and eventually Robert stepped in, waging a successful guerrilla campaign that came to a head as young Edward's army marched to Stirling. Although the Scots were greatly outnumbered, their strategy and use of terrain at Bannockburn—with its impossibly twisty stream presenting a natural barrier for the invading army—allowed them to soundly beat

the English and drive Edward out of Scotland...for the time being. (For more about Robert the Bruce, see page 73.)

The Battle Experience: Other than a small exhibit and weaponry room (free), there are no historic artifacts here—just the 3-D experience. First, you'll spend 30 minutes learning about the emerging battle from the perspective of both sides, and getting familiar with the characters and weaponry. Then, when your time arrives, you enter the "battle room" (the group gets divided into two sides—English and Scots), around a large, interactive 3-D map of the battleground. On screen, the "Battle Master" leads the group, but you get to move the troops and lead attacks. At the end, participants learn how the battle actually unfolded in 1314.

Monument and Statue of Robert the Bruce: Leaving the center, hike out into the field behind, where you can see a monument to those lost in the fight. Beyond that, on a plinth, stands an equestrian statue of Robert the Bruce.

FALKIRK

Two engaging landmarks sit just outside the town of Falkirk, 12 miles south of Stirling. Taken together, The Kelpies and the Falkirk Wheel offer a welcome change of pace from Scottish countryside kitsch. These flank Falkirk's otherwise unexciting town center, about a 5-mile, 20-minute drive apart. Driving between the two is a riddle of roundabouts. Think of it as fun: Carefully follow the brown signs and you'll eventually get there. (Ask for a flier illustrating directions between them at either site.)

▲The Kelpies

Unveiled in 2014 and standing over a hundred feet tall, these two giant steel horse heads quickly became a symbol of this town and region. They may seem whimsi-

cal, but they're rooted in a mix of mythology and real history: Kelpies are magical, waterborne, shape-shifting sprites of Scottish lore, who often took the form of a horse. And historically, horses—the ancestors of today's Budweiser Clydesdales— were used as beasts of burden to power Scotland's industrial output. These statues stand over old canals where hardworking horses towed heavily laden barges. But if you prefer, you can just forget all that and ogle the dramatic, energy-charged statues (particularly thrilling to Denver Broncos fans) that make for an entertaining photo op. A café nearby sells drinks and light meals, and a free visitors center shows how the heads were built. A 30-minute guided tour through the inside of one of the great beasts shows how they're supported by a sleek steel skeleton: 300 tons of steel apiece, sitting upon a foundation of 1,200 tons of steel-reinforced concrete, and gleaming with 990 steel panels.

Cost and Hours: Always open and free to view (£3 to park, £4 in July-Aug); visitors center open daily 9:30-17:00; tours-£7.50, daily every half hour 11:00-16:00 (but no 12:00 or 12:30 tours), fewer tours Oct-March, tel. 01324/590-600, www.thehelix.co.uk.

Getting There: The Kelpies are in a park called The Helix, just off the M-9 motorway—you'll spot them looming high over the motorway as if inviting you to exit. For a closer look, exit the M-9 for the A-905 (Falkirk/Grangemouth), then follow *Falkirk/A-904* and brown *Helix Park & Kelpies* signs.

▲▲Falkirk Wheel

At the opposite end of Falkirk stands this remarkable modern incarnation of Scottish technical know-how. You can watch the

beautiful, slow-motion contraption as it spins—like a nautical Ferris wheel—to efficiently shuttle ships between two canals separated by 80 vertical feet.

Cost and Hours: Wheel is free to view, visitors center open daily 10:00-17:30, park open until 20:00, shorter hours Nov-mid-March; cruises run about hourly and cost £13.50, call or go online to check schedule and book your seat, tel. 0870-050-0208, www. thefalkirkwheel.co.uk.

Getting There: Drivers can exit the M-876 motorway for *A-883/ Falkirk/Denny,* then follow brown *Falkirk Wheel* signs. Parking is free and a short walk from the wheel.

Without a car, the journey takes about 45-60 minutes from Stirling. It's a quick train ride from Stirling to Camelon or Falkirk Grahamston station, where you can take a cab (about £7) or ask locally for the best bus option.

Background: Scotland was a big player in the Industrial Revolution, thanks partly to its network of shipping canals (including the famous Caledonian Canal—see page 378). Using dozens of locks to lift barges up across Scotland's hilly spine, these canals were effective...but slow.

The 115-foot-tall Falkirk Wheel, opened in 2002, is a modern take on this classic engineering challenge: linking the Forth and Clyde Canal below with the aqueduct of the Union Canal, 80 feet above. Rather than using rising and lowering water through several locks, the wheel simply picks boats up and—ever so slowly—takes them where they need to go, like a giant waterborne elevator. In the 1930s, it took half a day to ascend or descend through 11 locks; now it takes only five minutes.

The Falkirk Wheel is the critical connection in the Millennium Link project, an ambitious £78 million initiative to restore the long-neglected Forth and Clyde and Union canals connecting Edinburgh and Glasgow. Today this 70-mile-long aquatic connection between Scotland's leading cities is a leisurely traffic jam of pleasure craft, and canalside communities have been rejuvenated.

Visiting the Wheel: Twice an hour, the wheel springs (silently) to life: Gates rise up to seal off each of the water-filled gondolas, and then the entire structure slowly rotates a half-turn to swap the positions of the lower and upper boats—each of which stays com-

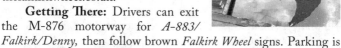

STIRLING & NEARBY

fortably upright. The towering structure is not only functional, but also beautiful: The wheel has an elegantly sweeping shape, with graceful cogs and pointed tips that slice into the water as they spin. It's strangely exciting to witness this.

The **visitors center** has a cafeteria (with a fine view of the wheel) and a shop, but no information about the wheel. The Falkirk **TI** is just steps away. The park around the canal is cluttered with trampolines, laser tag, and other family amusements.

Riding the Wheel: Each hour, a barge takes 96 people (listening to a recorded narration explaining everything) into the Falkirk Wheel for the slow and graceful ride. Once at the top, the barge cruises a bit of the canal. The slow-motion experience lasts about an hour.

CULROSS

This time warp of a village, sitting across the Firth of Forth from Edinburgh (about a 30-minute drive from Stirling), is a perfectly preserved artifact from the 17th and 18th centuries and worth ▲. If you're looking to let your pulse slow, stroll through a steep and sleepy village, and tour a creaky old manor house, Culross is your place. Filmmakers often use Culross to evoke Scottish villages of yore (most recently in *Outlander*). While not worth a  long detour, it's a workable stop for drivers connecting Edinburgh to either the Stirling area or St. Andrews (free parking lots flank the town center—an easy, 5-minute waterfront stroll away).

The story of Culross (which locals pronounce KOO-russ) is the story of Sir George Bruce, who, in the late 16th century, figured out a way to build coal mines beneath the waters of the Firth of Forth. The hardworking town flourished, Bruce built a fine mansion, and the town was granted coveted "royal burgh" status by the king. But several decades later, with Bruce's death and the flooding of the mines, the town's fortunes tumbled—halting its development and trapping it as if in amber for centuries. Rescued and rehabilitated by the National Trust for Scotland, today the entire village feels like one big open-air folk museum.

The main sightseeing attraction here is the misnamed **Culross "Palace,"** the big but creaky, half-timbered home of George Bruce (£10.50, April-Sept daily 10:00-17:00, Oct until 16:00, closed Nov-March, tel. 01383/880-359, www.nts.org.uk/culross). Buy your ticket at the office under the Town Hall's clock tower, pick up the included audioguide, then head a few doors down to the

ochre-colored palace. Following a 10-minute orientation film, you'll walk through several creaky floors to see how a small town's big shots lived four centuries ago. Docents in each room are happy to answer questions. You'll see the great hall, the "principal stranger's bedchamber" (guest room for VIPs), George Bruce's bedroom and stone strong room (where he stored precious—and flammable—financial documents), and the highlight, the painted chamber. The wood slats of its barrel-arched ceiling are painted with whimsical scenes illustrating Scottish virtues and pitfalls. You can also poke around the densely planted, lovingly tended garden out back.

A 45-minute **guided town walk** takes place for a small fee (April-Oct usually Mon-Sat at 14:00; check "Planning Your Visit" on palace website for current schedule).

The only other real sight, a steep hike up the cobbled lanes to the top of town, is the partially ruined **abbey.** While there are far more evocative ruins in Scotland, it's fun to poke into the stony, mysterious-feeling interior of this church. But the stroll up the town's cobbled streets past pastel houses, with their carefully tended flower boxes, is even better than the church itself.

BETWEEN STIRLING AND THE TROSSACHS

The village of Doune (pronounced "doon") is just a 15-minute drive north of Stirling. While there's not much to see in town, on its outskirts is a pair of attractions: a castle and a distillery. In the village of Doune itself, notice the town seal: a pair of crossed pistols. Aside from its castle and whisky, the town is known for its historic pistol factory. Locals speculate that the first shot of the American Revolution was fired with a Doune pistol.

Getting There: Bus #59 runs from Stirling to Doune and the distillery (just outside Doune). Drivers head to Doune, then follow castle signs on pretty back roads from there.

Doune Castle

Doune Castle is worth considering for its pop-culture connections: Most recently, Doune stands in for Castle Leoch in the TV series *Outlander*. But well before that, parts of *Monty Python and the Holy Grail* were filmed here. And, while the castle may underwhelm *Outlander* fans (only some exterior scenes were shot here), Python fans—and anyone who appreciates British comedy—will be tickled by the included audioguide, narrated by Python troupe member

STIRLING & NEARBY

Terry Jones (featuring sound clips from the film). The audioguide also has a few stops featuring Sam Heughan of *Outlander*. (If you're not into Python or *Outlander*, Scotland has better castles to visit.)

Cost and Hours: £9, daily April-Sept 9:30-17:30, Oct-March 10:00-16:00, tel. 01786/841-742.

Visiting the Castle: Buy your ticket and pick up the 45-min-ute audioguide, which explains that the castle's most important resident was not Claire Randall or the Knights Who Say Ni, but Robert Stewart, the Duke of Albany (1340-1420)—a man so influential he was called the "uncrowned king of Scotland." You'll see the cellars, ogle the empty-feeling courtyard, then

scramble through the two tall towers and the great hall that connects them. The castle rooms are almost entirely empty, but they're brought to life by the audioguide. You'll walk into the kitchen's ox-sized fireplace to peer up the gigantic chimney, and visit the guest room's privy to peer down the medieval toilet. You'll finish your visit at the top of the main tower, with 360-degree views that allow you to fart in just about anyone's general direction.

Deanston Distillery

This big, attractive red-brick industrial complex (formerly a cotton mill) sits facing the river just outside of Doune. While Deanston has long been respected for its fruity, slightly spicy Highland single-malt whisky, the 2012 movie *The Angels' Share*, filmed partly at this distillery, helped put it on the map. The complex boasts a slick visitors center that's open for tours. On the 50-minute visit, you'll see the equipment used to make the whisky and enjoy a sample. (For more on whisky and the distillation process, see page 484.) A bit more corporate-feeling than some of my favorite Scottish distilleries, Deanston has the advantage of being handy to Stirling.

Cost and Hours: £9-35 depending on number of tastings, tours depart at the top of each hour daily 10:00-16:00 (last tour), best to call ahead to reserve, tel. 01786/843-010, www.deanstonmalt.com.

LOCH LOMOND AND TROSSACHS NATIONAL PARK

Within about an hour's drive of half the population of Scotland is the country's most popular national park. Though it's a single park, it takes its name from two separate areas: The famous lake called Loch Lomond and, just to the east, the Trossachs—a hilly terrain that pleases hikers and joyriders. The Highland Boundary Fault—

the geologic line separating the flat Lowlands from the rugged Highlands—runs right through the middle of this area, and in several places you can actually see the terrain in transition.

To be honest, the charms of Loch Lomond and the Trossachs are subtle. Scottish scenery crescendos dramatically as you head north (at Glencoe, the Cairngorms, and the Isle of Skye, for starters). But this area's proximity to Stirling and Glasgow—and its many entertaining connections to Scottish history, literature, and folk culture—make it worth knowing about. For those on a quick visit to Scotland's Central Belt, Loch Lomond and the Trossachs offer a glimpse of "the Highlands in miniature."

Loch Lomond

Twenty-four miles long and speckled with islands, Loch Lomond

is Great Britain's biggest lake by surface area, and second in volume only to Loch Ness. Thanks largely to its easy proximity to Glasgow (about 15 miles away), this scenic lake is a favorite retreat for Scots as well as foreign tourists. The southernmost of the Munros, Ben Lomond (3,196 feet), looms over the eastern bank.

Loch Lomond's biggest claim to fame is its role in a beloved folk song: "Ye'll take the high road, and I'll take the low road, and I'll be in Scotland afore ye... For me and my true love will never meet again, on the bonnie, bonnie banks of Loch Lomond." As you'll now be humming that all day (you're welcome), here's one interpretation of the song's poignant meaning: Celtic culture believes that fairies return the souls of the deceased to their homeland through the soil. After the disastrous Scottish loss at the Battle of Culloden, Jacobite ringleaders were arrested and taken for trial in faraway London. In some cases, accused pairs were given a choice: One of you will die, and the other will live. The song is a bittersweet reassurance, sung from the condemned to the survivor, that the soon-to-be-deceased will take the spiritual "low road" back to his Scottish homeland—where his soul will be reunited with the living, who will return on the physical "high road" (over land).

Visiting Loch Lomond: There's not much to see, aside from some lochside scenery. You can get a fair dose simply driving by. People traveling from Glasgow toward Oban (or other points north) will get a good look at the loch's **west bank** as they follow the A-82 north (see "Glasgow to Oban Drive" on page 283).

To see the **east bank** of the lake, it's an easy detour from the

Trossachs loop described next, or from Glasgow. Take the A-811 west from Stirling, or the A-809 north from Glasgow, to the village of Drymen (DRIM-men). From here, carry on westward (along the B-837) to Balmaha. In this wide spot in the road, you'll find a visitors center with free geology and wildlife exhibits and advice about various hikes in the region. One easy and popular option is the ascent to Craigie Fort viewpoint (1 mile, 45 minutes round-trip), offering views over the southern part of the lake. For a more ambitious hike, you can follow part of the West Highland Way up to Conic Hill (2.5 miles, 3 hours round-trip).

▲Trossachs Drive

The hills-and-lochs terrain of the Trossachs, just northwest of Stirling (and due north of Glasgow), is a gently scenic, tourist-clogged corner of Highlands beauty. While the views here pale in comparison to more scenic areas farther north, this well-trod route is packed with interesting footnotes in Scottish history—from Rob Roy to Sir Walter Scott to the Beatles. The Trossachs makes for an easy, pretty spin close to Glasgow or Stirling, but can also be used as a slow-but-scenic connection to points in northern and eastern Scotland (see the options at the end of this drive). I've lightly narrated this loop in a clockwise order, coming from Stirling. But you can go in either direction, and begin or end wherever you like. I've focused on real history rather than silly legends...but sometimes the myths are hard to resist.

From Stirling to Aberfoyle: Leaving Stirling, head west on the A-84, then turn off to the left onto the A-873 (marked for *Thornhill;* watch for brown *Trossachs* signs). Carry on through Thornhill and then, in the village of Blairhoyle, turn left onto the A-81.

Soon you'll pass the **Lake of Menteith.** Many Scots are quick to point out that this is the only "lake" (as opposed to "loch") in all of Scotland, and have cooked up an explanation: Its namesake, Sir John Menteith, was a Scot who betrayed William Wallace, leading to his arrest and execution. To punish the traitor, "loch" became "lake." But, like most trumped-up Trossachs legends, this is bogus: The "lake" is likely derived from the Lowland Scots word *laich*— meaning simply "low place."

Continue along the A-81, then bear right onto the A-821 to **Aberfoyle.** Approaching the town, notice the landscape heaving up just beyond it—you can actually see where the Highland Boundary Fault marks the start of the Highlands. The town itself is attractive, if something of a tour-bus hell—with more parking lot than town. But it's a convenient place to take a break and grab picnic supplies. At the corner of the parking lot, the Scottish Wool Centre is a tacky tourist mall with a few free attractions out front that are worth a peek: sheep, noisy goats, birds of prey, and a fun

Rob Roy MacGregor (1671-1734)

The Trossachs region is Rob Roy country. This near-mythic Scottish folk hero was wounded fighting for the Jacobite cause, then became a trader of Highland cattle. He borrowed money from the Duke of Montrose (for whom the Duke's Pass is named), but when one of his men ran off with the cash, Rob Roy had to resort to stealing cattle and harassing the duke, who now called for his head. In his new life as a lovable Robin Hood-type rogue who stole from the rich and kept for himself, Rob Roy embodied the Scottish suspicion of authority. Immortalized in novels, verse, music, and film by everyone from Sir Walter Scott and William Wordsworth to Hector Berlioz and Liam Neeson, Rob Roy's reputation looms larger than his actual life. And today, visitors enjoy seeing his former stomping grounds, from Loch Katrine to his grave in Balquhidder.

little sheepdog demonstration, in which the clever dogs herd geese on a virtual "tour of Scotland." Across the parking lot, the TI has a small exhibit touting Aberfoyle's literary connections: Sir Walter Scott's *The Lady of the Lake* was inspired by nearby Loch Katrine (which we'll reach soon). This was also the home of Robert Kirk, who (in 1691) wrote *The Secret Commonwealth of Elves, Fauns, and Fairies*, which remains the definitive compendium of Scottish superstition. Soon after, Kirk died mysteriously in a forest glen supposedly inhabited by fairies. Locals love to share stories, theories, and superstitions about Kirk.

From Aberfoyle to Loch Katrine: Leaving Aberfoyle, carry on north along the A-821, following a twisty road called the **Duke's Pass.** This was built by the Duke of Montrose (the villain of the Rob Roy story) to access his mountain estates and to levy tolls. You'll wind your way up into a thickly forested hillscape; watch on the right for the turnoff for the Queen Elizabeth Forest Park visitors center. Here you can get maps and hiking advice, and peruse good exhibits on local geology and wildlife—including live cameras showing osprey nests. They share a parking lot with Go Ape, a popular zip-line and high-ropes course (best to book ahead, full course takes 2-3 hours, www.goape.co.uk).

As you crest the Duke's Pass, you'll get a small taste of the **Highland moor** terrain. For a good look at this landscape (and a parking lot with a handy viewpoint), pull off on the right at the start of the Three Lochs Forest Drive. You're surrounded by heather—the scrubby plant (with vibrant purple flowers in the late summer) that blankets much of the Highlands. The oldest pines around you are mostly Scotch (or "Scots") pines; more recently, these have been replaced by faster-growing pines that are better for harvesting.

Meanwhile, the deciduous trees (with red berries or white flowers, depending on the season) are rowan trees, also called "mountain ash." Superstitious Highlanders believe that rowans keep witches away and prevent fairies from switching out babies for change-lings. If you're bothered by the distant sight of wind farms from this viewpoint, you can commiserate with Donald Trump—before he became president he lobbied the Scottish government to outlaw these structures within sight of his Scottish golf courses.

Back on A-821, you'll start working your way downhill. On your right are glimpses of **Loch Drunkie.** Just ignore tour guides who tell you this was named for the practice of chugging and dumping illegal homebrew whisky here when the police showed up.

Farther down, you'll pass briefly along the banks of **Loch Achray.** Across the lake is the former Trossachs Hotel, which has hosted everyone from Queen Victoria to the Beatles. In the Fab Four's landmark 1964 tour around the UK, they'd do big shows in cities, then retreat to countryside getaways like this one.

At the end of Loch Achray, turn off on the left for **Loch Katrine.** Park in the big pay lot and stretch your legs. While this corner of the loch is nothing special, the scenery opens up if you follow its shore. You have several options: You can walk along the easy, paved lochside trail; you can pay for a boat trip (www.lochkatrine.com); or you can rent a bike (but be warned that the 14-mile path to the end of the lake gets increasingly hillier—consider taking a bike on the boat one way, and pedaling back; www.katrinewheelz.co.uk). Loch Katrine has various claims to fame. Sir Walter Scott's epic poem *The Lady of the Lake* was set here, and extols the beauties of this corner of the Trossachs. *Sir Walter Scott* is also the name of the steamship that does sight-seeing cruises around the loch; while steamships like this were once a common sight on Scottish lochs, this is the last one still in operation. At the boat dock, big displays explain how Loch Katrine was the home of Rob Roy (see sidebar). Loch Ka-

trine is also a primary water supply for Glasgow. In 1885, engineers harnessed the power of gravity to pipe the clean mountain waters into the big city. (Glaswegians of the time—accustomed to extremely polluted well water—were unimpressed. As one joke goes, a Glaswegian poured his first glass of water, eyed it suspiciously, and said, "It's got nae color, nae taste—nae good!") And finally, the US president's theme song also has a connection to this unassuming Scottish loch: "Hail to the Chief" came from a musical based on Scott's *Lady of the Lake*. In 1815, it was played to commemorate George Washington and to celebrate the end of the War of 1812, and the tradition stuck.

From Loch Katrine: When you're done at Loch Katrine, return to the main A-821 and head toward Callander. You'll go along the other bank of **Loch Achray** (and get a closer look at the former Trossachs Hotel—now a timeshare). Then you'll pass through **Brig O'Turk** (Gaelic for "Bridge of the Wild Boar") and drive along **Loch Venachar** before reaching a junction with the A-84. It's time to make your decision: Head north for more scenery and access to Loch Tay (Crannog Centre, Kenmore), Pitlochry, and other sights. Or head south for a speedy return to Stirling, by way of Callander and Doune Castle. Both options are outlined next.

To the North: If you head north on the A-84, you'll pass another pretty loch (Lubnaig), and soon after, you'll see the turnoff for **Balquhidder.** Fans of Rob Roy—or anyone named MacGregor—may want to take the two-mile detour (on single-track roads) to Balquhidder's humble stone church. In the kirkyard, look for the grave of the famous MacGregor clan chieftain. Rob Roy lived most of his life in these hills overlooking Loch Voil (visible in the distance). Back on the main A-84, carry on north (in Lochearnhead, it becomes the A-85); eventually you'll reach the junction with the A-827. From here, you can stick with the main A-85 all the way to **Oban.** Or you can turn right onto the A-827 (toward Killin) to reach the dramatic **Falls of Dochart,** which tumble through a tiny village, and then follow the north bank of Loch Tay to **Kenmore** and the **Crannog Centre;** farther along the A-827, you'll rejoin the main A-9 highway, which heads north to **Pitlochry** and several other attractions on the way up to **Inverness.** (For details on all of these sights, see the Eastern Scotland chapter.) Turning south on the A-9 zips you back toward Perth, then Stirling.

To the South: To complete our loop more directly, head south on the A-84. Just after you make the turn, watch on the left for **Trossachs Woollen Mill,** with a pair of "hairy coos" (shaggy Highland cattle) around back who love to pose for photos. Soon after, you'll pass through **Callander,** which feels like a very slightly less touristy version of Aberfoyle. Carrying on through town on the A-84, you'll pass through the village of Doune, where you can stop off for a tour of **Doune Castle** and/or the **Deanston Distillery** (both described earlier in this chapter). **Stirling** is just down the road.

ST. ANDREWS

St. Andrews • Dundee • Glamis Castle • The East Neuk

St. Andrews may be synonymous with golf, but there's much more to this charming town than its famous links. Dramatically situated at the edge of a sandy bay, St. Andrews is the home of Scotland's most important university—think of it as the Scottish Cambridge. And centuries ago, the town was the religious capital of the country.

In its long history, St. Andrews has seen two boom periods. First, in the early Middle Ages, the relics of St. Andrew made the town cathedral one of the most important pilgrimage sites in Christendom. The faithful flocked here from all over Europe, leaving the town with a medieval all-roads-lead-to-the-cathedral street plan that survives today. But after the Scottish Reformation, the cathedral rotted away and the town became a forgotten backwater. A new wave of visitors arrived in the mid-19th century, when a visionary mayor (with the on-the-nose surname Playfair) began to promote the town's connection with the newly in-vogue game of golf. Most buildings in town date from this Victorian era.

Today St. Andrews remains a popular spot for students, golf devotees (from amateurs to professional golfers to celebrities), and occasionally royal couple Will and Kate (college sweethearts, U. of St. A. class of '05). With vast sandy beaches, golfing opportunities for pros and novices alike, playgrounds of castle and cathedral ruins, and a fun-loving student vibe, St. Andrews is an appealing place to take a vacation from your busy vacation. It's also a handy home base for a variety of worthwhile side-trips: interesting museums in the big city of Dundee, the castle home of the late Queen Mother, and a string of relaxing fishing villages (the East Neuk).

PLANNING YOUR TIME

St. Andrews, hugging the east coast of Scotland, is a bit off the main tourist track. But it's well connected by train to Edinburgh (via bus from nearby Leuchars), making it a worthwhile day trip from the capital. Better yet, spend a night (or more, if you're a golfer) to enjoy this university town after dark.

If you're not here to golf, this is a good way to spend a day: Follow my self-guided walk, which connects the golf course, the university quad, the castle, and the cathedral. Dip into the Golf Museum, watch the golfers on the Old Course, and play a round at "the Himalayas" putting green. With more time, walk along the West Sands beach, take a spin by car or bus to the nearby East Neuk, or drive up to the museums in Dundee. Dundee and Glamis Castle are also fine stops for those connecting St. Andrews to points north.

Orientation to St. Andrews

St. Andrews (pop. 16,000, plus several thousand more students during term) is situated at the tip of a peninsula next to a broad bay. The town retains its old medieval street plan: Three main streets (North, Market, and South) converge at the cathedral, which overlooks the sea at the tip of town. The middle street—Market Street—has the TI and many handy shops and eateries. North of North Street, the seafront street called The Scores connects the cathedral with the golf scene, which huddles along the West Sands beach at the base of the old town. St. Andrews is compact: You can stroll across town—from the cathedral to the historic golf course—in about 15 minutes.

TOURIST INFORMATION

St. Andrews' helpful TI is on Market Street, about two blocks in front of the cathedral (Mon-Sat 9:00-17:00, July-Aug until 18:00, Sun 10:00-17:00, closed Sun in winter; 70 Market Street, tel. 01334/472-021, www.visitscotland.com).

ARRIVAL IN ST. ANDREWS

By Train and Bus: The nearest train station is in the village of Leuchars, five miles away. From there, a 10-minute bus ride takes you right into St. Andrews (bus #99, direction: St. Andrews, £3.30, buy ticket from driver, change given; buses meet most trains—see schedule at bus shelter; while waiting, read the historical info under the nearby flagpole). St. Andrews' bus station is near the base of Market Street—a short walk from most B&Bs and the TI. A taxi from Leuchars into St. Andrews costs about £14.

By Car: For a short stay, drivers can park anywhere along

ST. ANDREWS

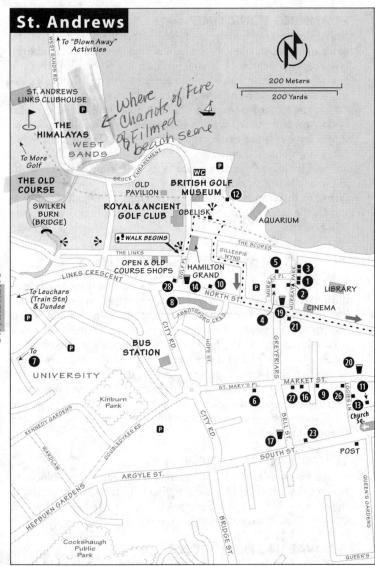

St. Andrews

To "Blown Away" Activities

WEST SANDS RD.

ST. ANDREWS LINKS CLUBHOUSE

THE HIMALAYAS

WEST SANDS

To More Golf

THE OLD COURSE

SWILKEN BURN (BRIDGE)

← Where Chariots of Fire ↙ Filmed beach scene

200 Meters
200 Yards

BRUCE EMBANKMENT

OLD PAVILION

BRITISH GOLF MUSEUM   WC   12

ROYAL & ANCIENT GOLF CLUB

OBELISK

AQUARIUM

THE LINKS

WALK BEGINS

LINKS CRESCENT

OPEN & OLD COURSE SHOPS

To Leuchars (Train Stn) & Dundee

GOLF PL.

HAMILTON GRAND

THE SCORES

GILLESPIE WYND

28   14   10
8

ABBOTSFORD CRES.

NORTH ST.

5
3
1
2

MURRAY PL.

MURRAY PARK

LIBRARY

CINEMA

4   19
21

CITY RD.

HOPE ST.

BUS STATION

UNIVERSITY

Kinburn Park

7

KENNEDY GARDENS

WARDLAW

DOUBLEDYKES RD.

ST. MARY'S PL.

6

MARKET ST.

27   16   9   26

GREYFRIARS

20

11
13
Church Sq.

LOGIE LN.

BELL ST.

17   23

SOUTH ST.

POST

QUEEN'S GARDENS

ARGYLE ST.

HEPBURN GARDENS

CITY RD.

BRIDGE ST.

Cockshaugh Public Park

QUEEN'S

streets in the town center (pay-and-display, coins only, 2-hour limit, monitored Mon-Sat 9:00-17:00, Sun from 13:00). For longer stays, you can park for free along certain streets near the center (such as the small lot near the B&B neighborhood around Murray Place, and along The Scores), or use one of the pay-and-display lots near the entrance to town. Parking near the Murray Place B&Bs tends to be full until 17:00—if so, pay for parking elsewhere, then

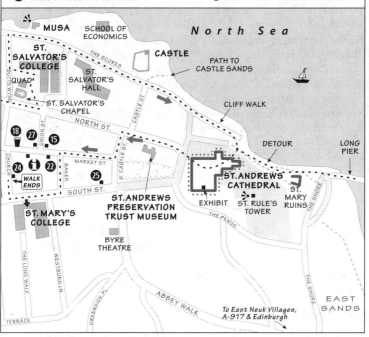

Accommodations

1. Glenderran Guest House & Cameron House
2. Hoppity House
3. Montague Guest House & Lorimer House
4. Shandon House
5. Doune Guest House
6. St. Andrews Tourist Hostel
7. Agnes Blackadder Hall
8. McIntosh Hall

Eateries & Other

9. Forgan's & Mitchell's
10. Playfair's
11. The Doll's House
12. The Seafood Ristorante
13. Little Italy
14. The Dunvegan Bar
15. Cromars Chippy
16. Tailend Chippy
17. Aikmans Pub
18. The Central Pub
19. Greyfriars Pub
20. The Keys Bar
21. Taste Coffee
22. Luvians Bottle Shop
23. I. J. Mellis Cheesemonger
24. Fisher and Donaldson
25. Jannettas Gelateria
26. Burns Candy Shop
27. Supermarket (2)
28. Auchterlonies Club Rental

ST. ANDREWS

after 17:00, move your car to a free spot near your guesthouse for the night.

HELPFUL HINTS

Golf Events: Every five years, St. Andrews is swamped with about 100,000 visitors when it hosts the British Open (officially called "The Open Championship"; the next one is the 150th in 2021). The town also fills up every year in early October for the

Alfred Dunhill Links Championship. Unless you're a golf pilgrim, avoid the town at these times (as room rates skyrocket).

School Term: The University of St. Andrews has two terms: spring semester ("Candlemas"), from mid-February through May; and fall semester ("Martinmas"), from mid-August until December. St. Andrews has a totally different vibe in the summer, when most students leave and are replaced by upper-crust golfers and tourists.

Sand Surfing and Adventure Activities: Nongolfers who want to stay busy while their travel partners play the Old Course may enjoy some of the adventure activities offered by **Blown Away**—including "land yachting" (zipping across the beach in wind-powered go-carts), kayaking, and paddle boarding. Brothers Guy and Jamie McKenzie set up shop at the northern tip of the West Sands beach (sporadic hours—call first, mobile 07784-121-125, www.blownaway.co.uk, ahoy@blownaway.co.uk).

Baggage Storage: The bus station has pay lockers.

Theater: The **Byre Theatre** regularly hosts concerts, shows, dance, and opera. Check their website or stop in to see what's on (tickets about £10-25, Abbey Street, tel. 01334/475-000, www.byretheatre.com).

Walking Tours: Richard Falconer, who has researched and written books on the history of the area—and its paranormal activity—gives 1.5-hour tours on golf, history, and ghosts (£12, tours at 17:30, 19:30, and 21:00, must book ahead, text 0746-296-3163 or visit https://standrewsghosttours.com).

St. Andrews Walk

This walk links all of St. Andrews' must-see sights and takes you down hidden medieval streets. Allow a couple of hours, or more if you detour for the sights along the way.

• *Start across from the Hamilton Grand (at the corner of Golf Place and The Links), overlooking the famous golf course.*

▲The Old Course

You're looking at the mecca of golf. The 18th hole of the world's first golf course is a few yards away, on your left.

The gray Neoclassical building to the right of the 18th hole is the clubhouse of the **Royal and Ancient Golf Club**—"R&A" for short. R&A is a private club with membership by invitation only; it was men-only until 2014, but now—finally!—women are also allowed to join. (In Scotland, men-only clubs lose tax benefits, which is quite costly, but they generally don't care about expenses because their membership is wealthy.) The **Old Course Shop** (to your left, across the street from the 18th hole, next to The Open—the oldest golf shop in the world) is a great spot to buy a souvenir for the golf lover back home. Even if you're not golfing, watch the action for a while. (Serious fans can walk around to the low-profile stone bridge across the creek called the Swilken Burn, with golf's single most iconic view: back over the 18th hole and the R&A Clubhouse.)

Overlooking the course at the base of the seaside street called The Scores is the big red-sandstone **Hamilton Grand,** an old hotel.

The hotel was turned into university dorms and then swanky apartments (rumor has it Samuel L. Jackson owns one). According to town legend, the Hamilton Grand was originally built to upstage the R&A Clubhouse by an American upset over being declined membership to the exclusive club.

Between Hamilton Grand and the beach is the low-profile but thoughtfully presented **British Golf Museum** (described later, under "Golfing in St. Andrews").

• *Now turn your back to the golf course and walk through the park toward the obelisk (along The Scores). Stop at the top of the bluff.*

Beach Viewpoint

The broad, two-mile-long sandy beach that stretches below the golf course to your left is the **West Sands.** It's a wonderful place for a relaxing and/or invigorating walk (beware the aggressive seagulls). Or do a slo-mo jog, humming the theme to *Chariots of Fire*—this is the beach on which the characters run in the movie's famous opening scene.

From the bluff, look at the **cliffs** on your right. The sea below was once called "Witches' Lake" because of all the women and men pushed off the cliff on suspicion of witchcraft.

The big obelisk is a **martyrs' monument,** commemorating all those who died for their Protestant beliefs during the Scottish Reformation. (We'll learn more about that chapter of St. Andrews history farther along this walk.)

The Victorian bandstand **gazebo** (between here and the Old Course) recalls the town's genteel heyday as a seaside resort, when the train line ran all the way to town.

• *Just opposite the obelisk, across The Scores and next to Alexander's Restaurant, walk down the tiny alley called...*

Gillespie Wynd

This winds through the back gardens of the city's stone houses.

Notice how the medieval platting gave each landowner a little bit of street front and a long back garden. St. Andrews' street plan typifies that of a medieval pilgrimage town: All main roads lead to the cathedral; only tiny lanes, hidden alleys, and twisting "wynds" (rhymes with "minds") such as this one connect the main east-west streets.

• *The wynd pops you out onto North Street. Head left, past the cinema toward the church tower with the red clock face, on the corner of North Street and Butts Wynd. For some reason, this street sign often goes missing.*

St. Salvator's College

The tower with the red clock marks the entrance to St. Salvator's College. If you're a student, be careful not to stand on the **"PH" initials** in the reddish cobbles in front of the gate. These mark the spot where St. Andrews alum and professor Patrick Hamilton—the Scottish Reformation's most famous martyr—was burned at the stake. According to student legend, as he suffered in the flames, Hamilton threatened that any students who stood on this spot would fail their exams.

Now enter the grounds by walking through the arch under the tower. (If the entrance is closed, you can go halfway down Butts Wynd and enter, or at least look, through the gate to the green square.) This grassy square, known to students as **Sally's Quad,** is the heart of the university. As most of the university's classrooms, offices, and libraries are spread out across the medieval town, this quad is the one focal point for student gatherings. It's where graduation is held every July, where the free-for-all food fight of Raisin Monday takes place in November (see sidebar on page 225), and where almost the entire student body gathered on the wedding day of their famous alumni couple Prince William and Kate Middleton for a celebration complete with military flybys.

On the outside wall of St. Salvator's Chapel, under the arcade, are **display cases** holding notices and university information; if you're here in spring, you might see students nervously clustered here, looking to see if they've passed their exams.

Go through the simple wooden door and into the **chapel.** Dating from 1450, this is the town's most beautiful medieval church. It's a Gothic gem, with a wooden ceiling, 19th-century stained glass, a glorious organ, and what's supposedly the pulpit of reformer John Knox.

The Scottish Reformation

It's easy to forget that during the 16th-century English Reformation—when King Henry VIII split with the Vatican and formed the Anglican Church (so he could get an officially recognized divorce)—Scotland was still its own independent nation. Like much of northern Europe, Scotland eventually chose a Protestant path, but it was more gradual and grassroots than Henry VIII's top-down, destroy-the-abbeys approach. While the English Reformation resulted in the Church of England (a.k.a. the Anglican Church, called "Episcopal" outside of England), with the monarch at its head, the Scottish Reformation created the Church of Scotland, which had groups of elected leaders (called "presbyteries" in church jargon).

One of the leaders of the Scottish Reformation was John Knox (1514-1572), who studied under the great Swiss reformer John Calvin. Returning to Scotland, Knox hopped from pulpit to pulpit, and his feverish sermons incited riots of "born-again" iconoclasts who dismantled or destroyed Catholic churches and abbeys (including St. Andrew's Cathedral). Knox's newly minted Church of Scotland gradually spread from the Lowlands to the Highlands. The southern and eastern part of Scotland, around St. Andrews—just across the North Sea from the Protestant countries of northern Europe—embraced the Church of Scotland long before the more remote and Catholic-oriented part of the country to the north and west. Today about 40 percent of Scots claim affiliation with the Church of Scotland, compared with 20 percent who are Catholic (still mostly in the western Highlands). Glasgow and western Scotland are more Catholic partly because of the Irish immigrants who settled there after fleeing the potato famine in the 1840s.

ST. ANDREWS

Stroll around Sally's Quad counterclockwise. On the east (far) side, stop to check out the crazy faces on the heads above the second-floor windows. Find the **university's shield** over the door marked *School 6.* The diamonds are from the coat of arms of the bishop who issued the first university charter in 1411; the crescent moon is a shout-out to Pope Benedict XIII, who gave the OK in 1413 to found the university (his given name was Peter de Luna); the lion is from the Scottish coat of arms; and the X-shaped cross is a stylized version of the Scottish flag (a.k.a. St. Andrew's Cross). On the next building to the left, facing the chapel, is St. Andrew himself (above the door of the building labeled *Lower & Upper College Halls*).

• *Exit the square and make your way back to Butts Wynd. Walk to the end; you're back at The Scores. Across the street and a few steps to the right is the...*

Museum of the University of St. Andrews (MUSA)

This free museum is worth a stop if it's open (as planned) following a major renovation. The new exhibit will be much bigger and the collection rearranged—pick up a map for the latest layout. Among the collection's highlights are medieval artifacts and a copy of the earliest-known map of the town, made in 1580—back when the town walls led directly to the countryside and the cathedral was intact. Notice that the street plan within the town walls has remained the same—but no golf course. Exhibits on student life explain the "silver arrow competition" (which determined the best archer on campus from year to year) and several of the traditions explained in the "Student Life in St. Andrews" sidebar. The museum also hosts scientific equipment, great books tied to the school, and an exhibit on the Scottish Reformation. For a great view of the West Sands, climb to the rooftop terrace.

Cost and Hours: Free; Mon-Sat 10:00-17:00, Sun 12:00-16:00, shorter hours and closed Mon-Wed in winter; 7 The Scores, tel. 01334/461-660, www.st-andrews.ac.uk/museums.

• *Leaving the museum, walk left toward the castle. The turreted stone buildings along here (including one fine example next door to the museum) are built in the Neo-Gothic Scottish Baronial style, and most are academic departments. About 100 yards farther along, the grand building on the right is St. Salvator's Hall, the most prestigious of the university residences and former dorm of Prince William.*

Just past St. Salvator's Hall on the left are the remains of...

St. Andrews Castle

Overlooking the sea, the castle is an evocative empty shell—another casualty of the Scottish Reformation. With a small museum and good descriptions, it offers a quick king-of-the-castle experience in a striking setting.

Cost and Hours: £9, includes audioguide; £12 combo-ticket includes cathedral exhibit; daily April-Sept 9:30-17:30, Oct-March 10:00-16:00, tel. 01334/477-196, www. historicenvironment.scot.

Visiting the Castle: Your visit starts with a colorful, kid-friendly exhibit about the history of the castle. Built by a bishop to entertain visiting diplomats in the late 12th century, the castle was home to the powerful bishops, archbishops, and cardinals of St. Andrews. In 1546, the cardinal burned a Protestant preacher at the stake in front of the castle. In retribution, Protestant reformers took the castle and killed the cardinal. In 1547, the French came to

Student Life in St. Andrews

St. Andrews is first and foremost a university town. Scotland's most prestigious university, founded in 1411, is the third-oldest in the English-speaking world after Oxford and Cambridge. While U. of St. A. is sometimes called "England's northernmost university" due to the high concentration of English students—as numerous as the Scottish ones—a quarter of the 6,000 undergrads and 1,000 grad students hail from overseas.

Some Scots resent the preponderance of upper-crust English students (disparagingly dubbed "Yahs" for the snooty way they say "yes"). However, these southerners pay the bills—they are on the hook for tuition, unlike Scots and most EU citizens. And no one seems to mind that the school's most famous graduates, Prince William and Kate Middleton (class of '05), are the definition of upper class. Soon after "Wills" started studying art history here, the number of female art history majors skyrocketed. (He later switched to geography.)

As with any venerable university, St. Andrews has its share of quirky customs. Most students own traditional red academic "gowns" (woolen robes) to wear on special occasions, such as graduation. In medieval times, however, they were the daily uniform—supposedly so students could be easily identified in brothels and pubs. (In a leap of faith, divinity students—apparently beyond temptation—wear black.) The way the robe is worn indicates the student's status: First-year students (called "bejants") wear them normally, on the shoulders; second-years ("semi-bejants") wear them slightly off the shoulders; third-years ("tertians") wear them off one shoulder (right for "scientists," left for "artists"); and fourth-years ("magistrands") wear them off both shoulders.

The best time to see these robes is during the Pier Walk on Sundays during the university term. After church services (around noon), gown-clad students parade out to the end of the lonesome pier beyond the cathedral ruins. The tradition dates so far back that no one's sure how it started (probably to bid farewell to a visiting dignitary). Today, students just enjoy being a part of the visual spectacle of a long line of red robes flapping in the North Sea wind.

Another age-old custom is a social-mentoring system in which underclass students choose an "academic family." On Raisin Monday, in mid-November, students give their upperclass "parents" treats—traditionally raisins, but these days more often indulgences like wine and lingerie. Then the "parents" dress up their "children" in outrageous costumes and parade them through town. The underclass students are obliged to carry around "receipts" for their gifts—written on unlikely or unwieldy objects like plastic dinosaurs, microwave ovens, or even refrigerators—and to sing the school song in Latin on demand. This oddball scenario invariably degenerates into a free-for-all food fight on Sally's Quad.

attack the castle on behalf of their Catholic ally, Mary, Queen of Scots. During the ensuing siege, a young Protestant refugee named John Knox was captured and sent to France to row on a galley ship. Eventually he traveled to Switzerland and met the Swiss Protestant ringleader, John Calvin. Knox brought Calvin's ideas back home and became Scotland's greatest reformer.

Next, head outside to explore. The audioguide explains the story of the castle and the siege, as told by several of the castle's historical figures. The most interesting parts are underground: the "bottle dungeon," where prisoners were sent, never to return (peer down into it in the Sea Tower—at the far left end of the complex facing the water); and the tight "mine" and even tighter "counter-mine" tunnels (follow the signs; crawling is required to reach it all—go in as far as your claustrophobia allows). This shows how the besieging pro-Catholic Scottish government of the day dug a mine to take (or "undermine") the castle—but was followed at every turn by the Protestant counter-miners.

Nearby: Just below the castle is a small beach called the **Castle Sands,** where university students take a traditional and chilly morning dip on May 1st. Supposedly, doing this May Day swim is the only way to reverse the curse of having stepped on Patrick Hamilton's initials (explained earlier).

• *Leaving the castle, turn left and continue along the bluff on The Scores, which soon becomes a pedestrian lane leading directly to the gate to the cathedral graveyard. For a quick detour, continue along the cliffside path, passing the ruins of St. Mary on the Rock, downhill to the pier where university students parade in their robes (see the "Student Life" sidebar). In nice weather, you'll enjoy views of the little harbor and (behind you) the cathedral and castle ruins. Otherwise, enter the graveyard to stand amid the tombstone-strewn ruins of...*

▲St. Andrews Cathedral

Between the Great Schism and the Reformation (roughly the 14th-16th centuries), St. Andrews was the ecclesiastical capital of Scotland—and this was its showpiece church. Today the site features the remains of the cathedral and cloister (with walls and spires pecked away by centuries of scavengers), a graveyard, and a small exhibit and climbable tower.

Cost and Hours: Cathedral ruins—free, exhibit and tower—£6, £12 combo-ticket includes castle; daily April-Sept 9:30-17:30, Oct-March 10:00-16:00; tel. 01334/472-563, www.historicenvironment.scot.

Background: It was the relics of the Apostle Andrew that first put this town on the map and gave it its name. There are numerous legends associated with the relics. According to one version, in the fourth century, St. Rule was directed in a dream to bring the relics northward from Constantinople. When the ship wrecked offshore from here, it was clear that this was a sacred place. Andrew's bones (an upper arm, a kneecap, some fingers, and a tooth) were kept on this site, and starting in 1160, the cathedral was built and pilgrims began to arrive. Since St. Andrew had a direct connection to Jesus, his relics were believed to possess special properties, making them worthy of pilgrimages on par with St. James' relics in Santiago de Compostela, Spain (of Camino de Santiago fame). St. Andrew became Scotland's patron saint; in fact, the white "X" on the blue Scottish flag evokes the diagonal cross on which St. Andrew was crucified (he chose this type of cross because he felt unworthy to die as Jesus had).

Visiting the Cathedral: You can stroll around the cathedral **ruins**—the best part of the complex—for free. First, walk

between the two ruined but still-towering ends of the church, which used to be the apse (at the sea end, where you entered) and the main entry (at the town end). Visually trace the gigantic footprint of the former church in the ground, including the bases of columns—like giant sawed-off tree trunks. Plaques identify where elements of the church once stood.

Looking at the one wall that's still standing, you can see the architectural changes that were made over the 150 years the cathedral was built—from the rounded, Romanesque windows at the front to the more highly decorated, pointed Gothic arches near the back. Try to imagine this church in its former majesty, when it played host to pilgrims from all over Europe.

The church wasn't destroyed all at once, like all those ruined abbeys in England (demolished in a huff by Henry VIII when he broke with the pope). Instead, because the Scottish Reformation was more gradual, this church was slowly picked apart over time. First just the decorations were removed from inside the cathedral. Then the roof was pulled down to make use of its lead. Without a roof, the cathedral fell further and further into disrepair, and was quarried by locals for its handy precut stones (which you'll still find in the walls of many old St. Andrews homes). The elements—a big storm in the 1270s and a fire in 1378—also contributed to the cathedral's demise.

The surrounding **graveyard,** dating from the post-Reformation Protestant era, is much more recent than the cathedral. In this golf-obsessed town, the game even infiltrates the cemeteries: Many

ST. ANDREWS

notable golfers from St. Andrews are buried here, including four-time British Open winner Young Tom "Tommy" Morris.

Go through the surviving wall into the former **cloister,** marked by a gigantic grassy square in the center. You can still see the cleats up on the wall, which once supported beams. Imagine the cloister back in its heyday, its passages filled with strolling monks.

At the end of the cloister is a small **exhibit** (entry fee required), with a relatively dull collection of old tombs and other carved-stone relics that have been unearthed on this site. Your ticket also includes entry to the surviving **tower of St. Rule's Church** (the rectangular tower beyond the cathedral ruins that was built to hold the precious relics of St. Andrew about a thousand years ago). If you feel like hiking up the 157 very claustrophobic steps for the view over St. Andrews' rooftops, it's worth the price. Up top, you can also look out to sea to find the pier where students traditionally parade in their robes (see the "Student Life" sidebar).

• *Leave the cathedral grounds on the town side of the cathedral. Angling right, head down North Street. Just ahead, on the left, is the adorable...*

▲St. Andrews Preservation Trust Museum and Garden

Filling a 17th-century fishing family's house that was protected from developers, this charming little museum is a time capsule of an earlier, simpler era. The house itself seems built for Smurfs, but it once housed 20 family members. The ground floor features replicas of a grocer's shop and a "chemist's" (pharmacy), using original fittings from actual stores. Upstairs are temporary exhibits. Out back is a tranquil garden (dedicated to the memory of a beloved professor) with "great-grandma's washhouse" featuring an exhibit about the history of soap and washing. Lovingly presented, this quaint, humble house provides a nice contrast to the big-money scene around the golf course at the other end of town.

Cost and Hours: Free but donation requested, generally open June-Sept daily 10:00-17:00 but depends on volunteer presence, closed off-season, 12 North Street, tel. 01334/477-629, https://standrewspreservationtrust.com.

• *From the museum, hang a left around the next corner to South Castle Street. Soon you'll reach...*

Market Street

As you approach the top of Market Street—one of the most atmospheric old streets in town—look left for the tiny white house with the cute curved staircase. What's that chase scene on the roof?

Now turn right down Market Street (which leads directly to the town's center, but we'll take a curvier route). Notice how the streets and even the buildings are smaller at this oldest end of town, as if the whole city is shrinking as the streets close in on the cathedral. Homeowners along Market Street are particularly proud of their address, and pooled their money to spiff up the cobbles and sidewalks.

Passing an antique bookstore on your right, take a left onto Baker Lane, a.k.a. Baxter Wynd. You'll pass a tiny and inviting public garden on your right before landing on South Street.

• *Turn right and head down South Street. After 50 yards, cross the street and enter a gate marked by a cute gray façade and a university insignia.*

St. Mary's College

This is the home of the university's School of Divinity (theology). If the gate's open, find the peaceful quad, with its gnarled tree that was purportedly planted by Mary, Queen of Scots. To get a feel of student life from centuries past, try poking your nose into one of the old classrooms.

• *Back on South Street, continue to your left. Some of the plainest buildings on this stretch of the street have the most interesting history—several of them were built to fund the Crusades. Turn right on Church Street. You can end this walk at charming Church Square—perhaps while enjoying a decadent pastry from the recommended Fisher and Donaldson bakery. Or if you continue a few more yards down Church Street, you'll spill onto Market Street and the heart of town.*

Golfing in St. Andrews

St. Andrews is the Cooperstown of golf. While St. Andrews lays claim to founding the sport (the first record of golf being played here was in 1553), nobody knows exactly where and when peo-

ple first hit a ball with a stick for fun. In the Middle Ages, St. Andrews traded with the Dutch; some historians believe they picked up a golf-like Dutch game played on ice and translated it to the bonnie rolling hills of Scotland's east coast. Since the grassy beachfront strip just outside St. Andrews was too poor to support crops, it was used for playing the game—and, centuries later, it still is. Why do golf courses have 18 holes? Because that's how many fit at the Old Course—golf's single most famous site.

The Old Course

The Old Course hosts the British Open every five years (next in 2021). At other times it's open to the public for golfing. The famous Royal and Ancient Golf Club (R&A) doesn't actually own the course, which is public and managed by the St. Andrews Links Trust. Drop by the St. Andrews Links Clubhouse, overlooking the beach near the Old Course (open long hours daily). They have a well-stocked shop, a restaurant, and a rooftop garden with nice views over the Old Course.

Old Course Tours: 75-minute guided tours visit the 1st, 17th, and 18th holes (£12.50, daily April-Sept at 11:00 and 14:00, mid-June-July also Sun at 15:30, March and Oct daily at 11:00, leaves from the St. Andrews Links Clubhouse, tel. 01334/466-666, www.standrews.com).

Teeing Off at the Old Course: Playing at golf's pinnacle course is pricey (£195/person, less off-season), but open to the public—subject to lottery drawings for tee times and reserved spots by club members. You can play the Old Course only if you have a handicap of 24 (men) or 36 (women and juniors) or better; bring along your certificate or card. If you don't know your handicap—or don't know what "handicap" means—you're not good enough to play here (they want to keep the game moving). If you play, you'll do nine holes out, then nine more back in—however, all but four share the same greens.

Reserving a Tee Time: To ensure a specific tee time at the Old Course, reserve a year ahead during a brief window between late August and early September (fill out form at www.standrews.com). Otherwise, some tee times are determined each day by a lottery called the "daily ballot." Enter your name on their website, in person, or by calling 01334/466-666 by 14:00 two days before (2 players minimum, 4 players max). Lottery results are posted online the same afternoon. Note that no advance reservations are taken on Saturdays or in September, and the courses are closed on Sundays—which is traditionally the day reserved for townspeople to stroll.

Singleton Strategies: Single golfers aren't eligible to reserve or ballot. If you're golfing solo, you could try to team up with someone (ask your B&B for tips). Otherwise, each day, a few single golfers fill out a two- or three-golfer group by showing up in person at the Old Pavilion (in front of the R&A Clubhouse). It's first-come, first-served, and a very long shot, so get there early. The starter generally arrives at 6:00, but die-hard golfers start lining up sev-

The Home of Golf

Bagpipes, haggis, and whisky are Scottish icons—but for golfers, Scotland is first and foremost the birthplace of the sport. Over 550 golf courses dot the landscape, from the Borders region in the south to John O'Groats in the north, offering pleasure and challenges for experts and duffers alike. While Mark Twain famously dismissed golf as a "good walk spoiled," a round can be a memorable part of a trip to Scotland.

While versions of golf existed in ancient times, the modern game was invented in Scotland in the 15th century and received the royal stamp of approval shortly afterward when King James IV picked up primitive clubs and whacked at a lopsided wooden ball. The Old Course at St. Andrews dates to 1553, but golf's golden age didn't take shape until the 19th century, when many courses were established and the sport was introduced to the US—by two Scotsmen. The first British Open (officially The Open Championship) was held in Prestwick, Scotland, in 1860 and winner Willie Park was awarded the red leather Challenge Belt, worth £25 (the 2019 winner took home almost $2 million).

While golf courses are as common as kilts in Scotland, the best are concentrated near Glasgow and Edinburgh. Besides St. Andrews—which for golf aficionados is the course of a lifetime—Scotland's other prestigious courses include Carnoustie (on the east coast), Royal Troon (near Glasgow), and Gleneagles (near Edinburgh). Famous venues are often pricey and crowded, so it's worth seeking out less-renowned courses where you're more likely to rub elbows with locals.

Popular courses require reservations well in advance—especially from May through September. Testing your skills on the Old Course at St. Andrews requires careful planning and some luck (see page 230). The majority of Scottish courses are private, but most welcome nonmembers on a limited basis. As in the US, greens fees vary widely depending on the time of year and the course's reputation. Costs for a round start at £20 at a public course and soar to nearly £200 at the Old Course—but that's still only half the cost of top courses in the US like Pebble Beach. (Use the excellent FergusonGolf.com website to help you do some homework).

Most Scottish courses are links courses, meaning they lie amidst treeless coastal dunes, putting you at the mercy of the elements. Lining up a putt while being buffeted by rain and sea spray in a howling gale is part of the experience. Good raingear is a must. But weather does change—often rapidly—and minutes after a downpour you may find yourself gazing at blue skies and wonderful views. Rain or shine, that 19th-hole meal and wee dram in the clubhouse are a welcome reward.

eral hours before or even camp out overnight (especially in peak season). Swing by the day before, when they should have a sense of how likely a spot is to open up and can recommend just how early to arrive.

Other Courses: Two of the seven St. Andrews Links courses are right next to the Old Course—the New Course and the Jubilee Course. And the modern cliff-top Castle Course is just outside the city. These are cheaper, and it's much easier to get a tee time (£85 for New and Jubilee, £120 for Castle Course, much less for others). It's usually possible to get a tee time for the same day or next day (if you want a guaranteed reservation, make it at least 2 weeks in advance). The Castle Course has great views overlooking the town, but even more wind to blow your ball around.

Club Rental: You can rent decent-quality clubs around town for about £35. The **Auchterlonies** shop has a good reputation (on Golf Place—a few doors down from the R&A Clubhouse, tel. 01334/473-253, www.auchterlonies.com); you can also rent clubs from the St. Andrews Links Clubhouse for a few pounds more.

▲The Himalayas

The St. Andrews Ladies' Putting Club, better known as "The Himalayas" (for its dramatically hilly terrain), is basically a very classy (but still relaxed) game

of minigolf. The course presents the perfect opportunity for nongolfers (female or male) to say they've played the links at St. Andrews—for about the cost of a Coke. It's remarkable how this cute little patch of undulating grass can present even more challenging obstacles than the tunnels, gates, and distractions of a miniature golf course back home. Flat shoes are required. You'll see it on the left as you walk toward the St. Andrews Links Clubhouse from the R&A Clubhouse.

Cost and Hours: £3 for 18 holes. The putting green is open to nonmembers (tourists like you) April-Sept Mon and Wed-Fri 10:30-18:30, Tue until 16:30, Sat until 18:00, Sun 12:00-18:30, closed in winter, tel. 01334/466-666, www.standrewsputtingclub.com.

British Golf Museum

This exhibit, which started as a small collection in the R&A Clubhouse across the street, is the best place in Britain to learn about the Scots' favorite sport. It's fascinating for golf lovers and an interesting overview for the casual tourist. The museum will close at the end of 2020 for a few months for a major renovation, and the layout is expected to change. During the renovation, the gift shop and upstairs café will stay open.

Cost and Hours: £8.50, Mon-Sat 9:30-17:00, Sun from 10:00; Nov-March daily 10:00-16:00; last entry 45 minutes before closing; café upstairs; Bruce Embankment—in the blocky modern building squatting behind the R&A Clubhouse by the Old Course, tel. 01334/460-046, www.britishgolfmuseum.co.uk.

Visiting the Museum: The compact, one-way exhibit takes about 45 minutes to explore and reverently presents a meticulous survey of the game's history. Start with the short film, then follow the counterclockwise route to learn about the evolution of golf—from the monarchs who loved and hated golf (including the king who outlawed it because it was distracting men from church and archery practice), to Tom Morris and Bobby Jones, all the way up to the "Golden Bear" and a randy Tiger. Along the way, you'll see plenty of old clubs, balls, medals, and trophies, and learn about how the earliest "feathery" balls and wooden clubs were made. Touchscreens invite you to learn more, and you'll also see a "hall of fame" with items donated by today's biggest golfers. Finally, you'll have a chance to dress up in some old-school golfing duds and try out some of that antique equipment for yourself.

Sleeping in St. Andrews

Owing partly to the high-roller golf tourists flowing through the town, St. Andrews' accommodations are quite expensive. During graduation week in June, hotels often require a four-night stay and book up quickly. All of the guesthouses I've listed are on the streets called Murray Park and Murray Place, between North Street and The Scores in the old town. If you need to find a room on the fly, look around in this same neighborhood, which has far more options than just the ones I've listed below.

$$$ Glenderran Guest House offers five plush rooms (including two true singles) and a few nice breakfast extras (no kids under 12, pay same-day laundry, 9 Murray Park, tel. 01334/477-951, www.glenderran.com, info@glenderran.com, Ray and Maggie).

$$ Hoppity House is a bright and contemporary place, with attention to detail and fun hosts Heather and Valerie, who are helpful and generous with travel tips. There's a lounge and kitchen for guest use and a storage closet for golf equipment. You may find a stuffed namesake bunny or two hiding out among its four impeccable rooms (fridges in rooms, 4 Murray Park, mobile 07967/044-801, www.hoppityhouse.co.uk, enquiries@hoppityhouse.co.uk).

$$ Cameron House has five clean and simple rooms around

a beautiful stained-glass atrium. Its common area feels like a re-furbished Victorian lounge (two-night minimum in summer, 11 Murray Park, tel. 01334/472-306, www.cameronhouse-sta.co.uk, info@cameronhouse-sta.co.uk, Donna).

$$ Montague Guest House has richly furnished public spaces—with a dark, cozy, leather-couch-filled lounge/break-fast room—and eight decently sized rooms with tartan accents (21 Murray Park, tel. 01334/479-287, www.montaguehouse.com, info@montaguehouse.com, Raj and Judith).

$$ Lorimer House has six comfortable, tastefully decorated rooms, including one on the ground floor. Some doubles are cheap-er and more compact than others (two-night minimum preferred, no kids under 12, 19 Murray Park, tel. 01334/476-599, www.lorimerhouse.com, info@lorimerhouse.com, Scott and Ashley).

$$ Shandon House is a refreshing and breezy seaside retreat with six bright and comfortable rooms. Two rooms have private bathrooms across the hall (2-night minimum preferred, 10 Mur-ray Place, tel. 1334/472-412, www.shandonhouse.co.uk, info@shandonhouse.co.uk, Liz and Stuart).

$$ Doune Guest House's seven rooms provide a more imper-sonal but fine place to stay in St. Andrews (breakfast extra, two-night minimum preferred in summer, single with private bath, 5 Murray Place, tel. 01334/475-195, www.dounehouse.com, info@dounehouse.com, Ilya).

¢ St. Andrews Tourist Hostel has 44 beds in colorful 5- to 8-bed rooms about a block from the base of Market Street. The high-ceilinged lounge is a comfy place for a break, and the friendly staff is happy to recommend their favorite pubs (kitchen, St. Mary's Place, tel. 01334/479-911, www.hostelsscotlandltd.com, info@hostelsstandrews.com).

UNIVERSITY ACCOMMODATIONS

In the summer (early June-Aug), some of the University of St. An-drews' student-housing buildings are tidied up and rented out to tourists. I've listed the most convenient options below (website for both: https://ace.st-andrews.ac.uk; pay when reserving). Both of these include breakfast and Wi-Fi. Because true single rooms are rare in St. Andrews' B&Bs, these dorms are a good option for solo travelers.

$ Agnes Blackadder Hall has double beds and private bath-rooms; it's more comfortable, but also more expensive and less central (family rooms, North Haugh, tel. 01334/467-000, agnes.blackadder@st-andrews.ac.uk).

$ McIntosh Hall is cheaper and more central, but it only has twin beds and shared bathrooms (Abbotsford Crescent, tel. 01334/467-035, mchall@st-andrews.ac.uk).

Eating in St. Andrews

RESTAURANTS

$$$ Forgan's, occupying a former golf club factory, is tempting and popular. It's done up country-kitschy, with high ceilings, cool lanterns, a fun energy, and a little taxidermy. It serves up refined Scottish dishes and offers a tempting steak selection (Mon-Fri 11:00-late—kitchen open 12:00-22:00, Sat-Sun 10:00-late—kitchen open 10:00-22:00, reservations strongly recommended, 110 Market Street, tel. 01334/466-973, www.forgans.co.uk). On Friday and Saturday nights after 22:30, they have live *ceilidh* (traditional Scottish) music, and everyone joins in the dancing; consider reserving a booth for a late dinner, then stick around for the show. They also have live acoustic music on Thursday evenings.

$$ Mitchell's, with a casual and rustic dining room, is a simpler alternative to the upscale restaurants in town. The menu features hearty salads, creative sandwiches, burgers, and "sharing boards," and you'll enjoy live music every Friday and Saturday night from 20:30. The attached deli serves up locally made meats, cheeses, and other organic products for takeaway (Mon-Thu 8:00-22:00, Fri-Sat 8:00-late, Sun 9:00-22:00, 110 Market Street, tel. 01334/466-970).

$$$ Playfair's, a restaurant and steakhouse downstairs in the Ardgowan Hotel between the B&B neighborhood and the Old Course, has a cozy/classy interior and outdoor seating at rustic tables set just below the busy street. Their bar next door (Pilmour) serves a similar menu (daily 12:00-late, off-season weekdays open for dinner only, 2 Playfair Terrace on North Street, tel. 01334/472-970).

$$$ The Doll's House serves dressed-up Scottish cuisine in a stone-and-wood interior or at tables on the square in front (daily 9:00-22:00, across from Holy Trinity Church at 3 Church Square, tel. 01334/477-422).

$$$$ The Seafood Ristorante, in a modern glassy building overlooking the beach near the Old Course, is like dining in an aquarium. They serve high-end Italian with a focus on seafood in a formal space with floor-to-ceiling windows providing unhindered views (minimum £20/person food order at dinner, daily 12:00-14:30 & 18:00-21:30, reservations a must on weekends and in summer, The Scores, tel. 01334/479-475, www.theseafoodrestaurant.com, dine@theseafoodristorante.com).

$$ Little Italy is a crowded Italian joint with all the clichés—red-and-white checkered tablecloths, replica Roman busts, a bit frenetic, and even a moped in the wall. But the food is authentically good and the menu is massive. It's the town favorite—make reservations (daily 12:30-22:30, 2 Logies Lane, tel. 01334/479-299, www.littleitaly.cc).

$$$ The Dunvegan Bar, part of the hotel of the same name and just around the corner from the Old Course, is on the 19th hole of St. Andrews. It serves overpriced, unexciting pub grub, but you're coming for the energetic atmosphere—and the walls (and ceiling) covered with golf memorabilia (daily 11:30-22:00, off-season until 21:00, 7 Pilmour Place, tel. 1334/473-105). Their simple **$$** restaurant, Claret Jug, is in the back, with a calmer ambience.

Fish-and-Chips: Two places battle for the "best chippy in town" crown. **$ Cromars** is a local favorite for takeaway fish-and-chips (and burgers). At the counter, you can order yours to go, or—in good weather—enjoy it at the sidewalk tables; farther in is a small **$$** sit-down restaurant with more choices (both open daily 11:00-22:00, at the corner of Union and Market, tel. 01334/475-555). **Tailend** also has a **$** takeaway counter up front (fish-and-chips) and a **$$** restaurant with a bigger selection in the back (daily 11:30-22:00, 130 Market Street, tel. 01334/474-070).

BEER, COFFEE, AND WHISKY

Pubs: There's no shortage in this college town. These aren't "gastropubs," but they all serve straightforward pub fare (all open long hours daily).

Aikmans, run by Barbara and Malcolm (two graduates from the university who couldn't bring themselves to leave), features a cozy wood-table ambience, a focus on ales, live music (usually Fri-Sat), and simple soups, sandwiches, and snacks (32 Bell Street, tel. 01334/477-425). **The Central,** right along Market Street, is a St. Andrews standby, with old lamps and lots of brass (77 Market Street, tel. 01334/478-296). **Greyfriars,** with forgettable food, is in a classy, modern hotel steps away from my recommended Murray Park B&Bs (129 North Street, tel. 01334/474-906). **The Keys Bar** is a lively pub in the middle of Market Street. It's a good time any night of the week (87 Market Street, tel. 0133/447-2414).

Coffee: $ Taste, a little café just across the street from the B&B neighborhood, has the best coffee in town and a laid-back ambience that feels like a big-city coffeehouse back home. It also serves cakes and light food (daily 7:00-18:00 in summer, open later when students are back, 148 North Street, tel. 01334/477-959).

Whisky: Luvians Bottle Shop—run by three brothers (Luigi, Vincenzo, and Antonio)—is a friendly place to talk, taste, and purchase whisky. Distilleries bottle unique single-cask vintages exclusively for this shop to celebrate the British Open every five years (ask about the 21-year-old Springbank they received in 2015 to commemorate the tournament). With nearly 50 bottles open for tastings, a map of Scotland's whisky regions, and helpful team members, this is a handy spot to learn about whisky. They also sell fine wines and a wide range of microbrews (Mon-Sat 10:00-22:00, Sun from 12:30, 66 Market Street, tel. 01334/477-752).

PICNIC FOOD AND SWEETS

Cheese: I.J. Mellis Cheesemonger, the excellent Edinburgh cheese shop with a delectable array of Scottish, English, and international cheeses, has a St. Andrews branch. On Friday and Saturday nights, the shop stays open late as a wine bar (Mon-Thu 9:00-19:00, Fri-Sat until 22:00, Sun 10:00-17:00, 149 South Street, tel. 01334/471-410).

Pastries: Fisher and Donaldson is beloved for its rich, affordable pastries and chocolates. Listen as the straw-hatted bakers chat with their regular customers, then try their Coffee Tower—like a giant cream puff filled with lightly coffee-flavored cream—or their number-one seller, the fudge doughnut (Mon-Sat 6:00-17:00, closed Sun, just around the corner from the TI at 13 Church Street, tel. 01334/472-201).

Gelato: You'll see many people walking around licking cones from **Jannettas Gelateria,** which has been around for more than a century. While waiting in line in the cute pastel parlor, ponder what you want from their range of 50-plus gelato flavors (daily 9:00-22:30, café, 31 South Street, tel. 01334/473-285). If you don't have time to wait in line, the less crowded **Burns** candy shop on Market Street scoops about a dozen flavors of Jannettas gelato (96 Market Street).

Supermarkets: You can stock up for a picnic at **Tesco** or **Sainsbury's Local** on Market Street.

St. Andrews Connections

Trains don't go into St. Andrews—instead, use the Leuchars station (5 miles from St. Andrews, connected by buses coordinated to meet most trains, 2-4/hour, see "Arrival in St. Andrews" at the beginning of this chapter). To head back to the train station, take any #99 bus (several variations of #99—A, B, D, etc.—work for this route; direction: Dundee), but confirm with the driver that it's going straight to Leuchars. Some routes make stops through town first (extending your travel time by 20-30 minutes).

From Leuchars by Train to: Edinburgh (1-2/hour, 1 hour), **Glasgow** (2/hour, 2 hours, transfer in Haymarket or Edinburgh Waverley), **Inverness** (roughly hourly, 3.5 hours, 2 changes). Trains run less frequently on Sundays. Train info: Tel. 0345-748-4950, www.nationalrail.co.uk. To reach **Dundee,** take bus #99 from St. Andrews bus station near the base of Market Street (every 10 minutes, 30 minutes).

Near St. Andrews

Two starkly different destinations are within a half-hour's drive of St. Andrews, in opposite directions. To the north is the up-and-coming city of Dundee, with three interesting museums; just beyond is Glamis Castle, the childhood home of Queen Elizabeth's late mother, known as the Queen Mother. And to the south is the charming string of seaside villages called the East Neuk. Either one makes a good half-day side-trip, or you can squeeze them in on your way between St. Andrews and other destinations.

DUNDEE

The once-prosperous, then decrepit, and now steadily rejuvenating city of Dundee (Scotland's fourth-largest, with about 150,000 people) sits at the mouth of the River Tay. In its heyday, Dundee was known for the "Three J's": jute (turning the raw fiber into rope, burlap, and canvas), jam (importing that orange marmalade that's on every B&B breakfast table), and journalism (being the home of D. C. Thomson & Co., the respected publishing company responsible for the *Sunday Post*, and for creating many beloved Scottish cartoon characters).

Then, like many Industrial Age British boomtowns, Dundee fell on hard times in the 20th century. Today, thanks to some promising rejuvenation through the tech industry, Dundee is working to reinvent its downtown core and its waterfront (where a huge mess of construction recently became an £80-million branch of the Victoria and Albert Museum). But the city still has a ways to go, and for now it merits only a quick stop for its interesting museums.

Getting There: Drivers can take advantage of nearby parking for a strategic visit to one or more of Dundee's museums. The Discovery Point and V&A museums along the waterfront are well signed and easy to find. The Verdant Works Jute Museum is buried in a mostly deserted industrial area higher up in town (look for brown signs), but it's more reliably found by using GPS or an app. **Train** travelers find that Discovery Point is easy (it's right across the street from the train station), but the Verdant Works Jute Museum, just under a mile away, isn't well connected by public transit; walk or take a taxi from Discovery Point.

▲Discovery Point and the RRS *Discovery*

At the turn of the 20th century—long after the Age of Discovery—Antarctica was the world's last great mystery. With a fervor matched a half-century later in the Space Race, ambitious countries set out to learn more about the unexplored continent. This

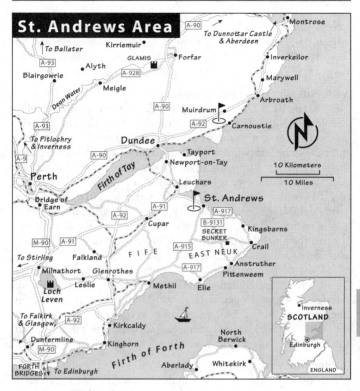

St. Andrews Area

To Ballater
Kirriemuir
GLAMIS
Forfar
A-90
To Dunnottar Castle & Aberdeen
Montrose
A-93
Alyth
Blairgowrie
A-928
Inverkeilor
Marywell
Meigle
Dean Water
Arbroath
A-90
Muirdrum
A-92
Carnoustie
To Pitlochry & Inverness
A-93
Dundee
A-90
Tayport
Newport-on-Tay
A-9
Perth
Firth of Tay
Leuchars
St. Andrews
A-91
A-917
Bridge of Earn
A-92
Cupar
B-9131
SECRET BUNKER
Kingsbarns
M-90
A-91
FIFE
A-915
EAST NEUK
Crail
To Stirling
Falkland
Milnathort
Glenrothes
A-917
Anstruther
Pittenweem
Leslie
Methil
Elie
Loch Leven
To Falkirk & Glasgow
A-92
Kirkcaldy
North Berwick
Dunfermline
M-90
Kinghorn
Firth of Forth
Aberlady
Whitekirk
FORTH BRIDGES
To Edinburgh

10 Kilometers
10 Miles

Inverness
SCOTLAND
Edinburgh
ENGLAND

ST. ANDREWS

museum tells the story of the Royal Research Ship (RRS) *Discovery*, which was built in Dundee and set sail for Antarctica in 1901. It was one of the most successful scientific expeditions of its time. This attraction, on Dundee's riverfront, has two parts: The **museum** shows how the *Discovery* was built and provisioned, and how the crew (led by Commander Robert Falcon Scott, who

died a decade later in a race to the South Pole) planned and perilously executed their icy journey; and the actual **ship,** restored to how it was in 1924, where you can walk across the decks and delve below to see the engine room, galley, sick bay, mess deck, and living quarters. The photographic darkroom, drawing table, and vials for scientific samples illustrate the ship's mission: opening up a new continent to human understanding.

Cost and Hours: £11.50, £18.25 combo-ticket with Verdant

Works Jute Museum; Mon-Sat 10:00-18:00, Sun from 11:00, off-season daily until 17:00, last entry one hour before closing; audioguide-£3, Riverside Drive, closest parking is next door at Discovery Car Park, tel. 01382/309-060, www.rrsdiscovery.com.

V&A Museum of Design Dundee

Next to the RRS *Discovery* along the River Tay is a new branch of London's eclectic Victoria and Albert Museum, this one focusing on Scottish design. It's worth a trip to the waterfront just to admire the dramatic building itself. Designed by renowned Japanese architect Kengo Kuma, its shape is meant to resemble a Scottish cliff face (and has already been featured prominently in an episode of HBO's show *Succession*). Since the museum's 2018 opening, rotating exhibits have ranged from video-game design to robotics to 1960s fashion. The museum's river-facing Tatha Bar and Kitchen is open for lunch, and offers those lingering later in town an opportunity for a drink or meal with a view.

Cost & Hours: Free but suggested donation, daily 10:00-17:00, 1 Riverside Esplanade, tel. 01382/411-611, www.vam.ac.uk/dundee; restaurant open daily 10:00-17:00, Thu-Sat also 18:00-late, kitchen until 20:45, reservations recommended for dinner; tel. 01382/411-633, www.vam.ac.uk/dundee/info/tatha-bar-and-kitchen.

▲Verdant Works Jute Museum

Hardworking, industrious Scotland has several fine museums about how things are made—and this is one of the best. Filling a former

jute-processing factory called Verdant Works, it's located in a gentrifying zone of brick factories. This museum explores every facet of the jute industry that put Dundee on the map. Especially worthwhile for those with a healthy interest in engineering, the well-presented museum accomplishes the remarkable task of making jute interesting even to those less mechanically inclined.

Cost and Hours: £11.50, £18.25 combo-ticket with Discovery Point, same hours as Discovery Point, West Henderson's Wynd, free parking lot in back, tel. 01382/309-060, www.verdantworks.com.

Background: Starting in the 1830s, Dundee businessmen—who came to be known as "jute barons"—developed a local industry around processing the fiber of a plant called jute, which could be used to make rope, burlap sacks, sails, canvases, carpeting, and even clothing. In an age before plastics, versatile jute was a prized material...and virtually all of the world's supply came through Dundee. Great Britain's nautical expansion further boosted the industry: Dundee-made materials sailed to every corner of the earth. Coinciding with the Highland Clearances and the decline of traditional rural lifestyles, the jute boom lured many floundering farmers and peasants into urban factories. By century's end, Dundee's population had tripled.

In Dundee, as in other Industrial Age cities, rapid changes created a sharply stratified society, with a tiny and obscenely wealthy upper class and a huge, desperately poor lower class. But before long, the jute industry fell victim to "outsourcing," a century before our time: By 1875, a jute factory opened in India (where the raw materials were harvested), and by 1900, more jute products were produced in Calcutta than in Dundee. The rise of plastics and other synthetic fibers in the 1970s drove the final nail into the industry's coffin; Dundee's last remaining jute factory closed in 1999.

Visiting the Museum: Start with the 15-minute *Juteopolis* film (which sets the stage for the museum and helps explain why you're spending your vacation learning about jute) or, if you catch it midway, keep going with your tour—you'll come to the theater again later in your visit.

Head across the courtyard to the Works Office and follow the one-way route through the exhibit. The highlight is the machine hall, where you'll see working (but much smaller) versions of the machinery used for each of the steps required to turn this tropical fiber into practical products. On some days, docents are standing by to explain more and demonstrate some of the century-old equipment.

Upstairs (access from outside, in the courtyard) is an exhibit about the social history of the city, showing different walks of life relating to the jute industry. The cavernous High Mill has more exhibits delving into different facets of the industry and a huge Boulton and Watt steam engine from 1801, still in working order.

Downtown Dundee

With a little time to spare, it's worth walking 10 minutes from Discovery Point to the town center. In front of the city's landmark Caird Hall concert venue (with the TI next door), you'll find a bustling, traffic-free people zone, with cafés, public tables, fountains, and a glitzy shopping mall. Find the life-sized statues of Desperate Dan and Minnie the Minx (Dundee-born cartoon characters who are as beloved among Scots as they are unknown to Americans). A quick walk here offers a peek into the Dundee of the future.

ST. ANDREWS

North of Dundee
▲Glamis Castle

A 20-minute drive north of Dundee (or 45 minutes north of St. Andrews) is the residence of the Earls of Strathmore—best known as the childhood-home castle of the Queen Mother (a.k.a. Elizabeth Bowes-Lyon, 1900-2002). Glamis (pronounced "glahms") is a proper castle inside and out: You'll drive down a grand, tree-lined driveway to a majestic palace bristling with turrets and filled with elaborately decorated rooms that drip with history and  blue-blood quirk. Coming here just seems the right way to pay respects to the Queen Mother, who gave birth to the longest-reigning monarch in British history and supported her husband, King George VI, as he rallied Britain through World War II (as depicted in *The King's Speech*). Their second daughter, Princess Margaret, was born right here at Glamis—the first royal baby born in Scotland in 300 years. The "Queen Mum" always had a deep affection for her home at Glamis and was often clad in a distinctive hue that she liked to call "Strathmore blue."

Cost and Hours: £15.50, daily 10:00-16:30 (last tour time), weekends-only Nov-early Dec, closed early Dec-Easter, tel. 01307/840-393, www.glamis-castle.co.uk.

Getting There: From Dundee, head north on the A-90 expressway (toward Aberdeen); the exit is well marked with brown *Glamis Castle* signs (also marked for *Kirriemuir*). From the exit, follow the A-928 seven miles to the castle.

Visiting the Castle: You can only visit the interior on a 50-minute guided tour. You'll see both grand state rooms and intimate quarters—including the private rooms of the Queen Mother, which her parents installed after she married the prince to ensure she'd keep coming home for visits. The tour is packed with fun insights into aristocratic eccentricities, from the paintings of one earl who simply adored his leather body armor (painted to resemble a sculpted Greek god), to a rare painting of Jesus wearing a hat. Glamis also loves to tout its title as the "most haunted castle in Scotland"—though the ghost tales your guide imparts are more silly than scary. (Even more suspect are boasts that Glamis inspired Shakespeare as the setting for *Macbeth*—a claim also made by Cawdor Castle.) After your tour, you can visit a few more exhibits and explore the grounds on your own—a handout suggests several walking routes.

THE EAST NEUK

On the lazy coastline meandering south from St. Andrews, the cute-as-a-pin East Neuk (pronounced "nook") is a collection of tidy fishing villages. While hardly earthshattering, the East Neuk is a pleasant detour if you've got the time. The villages of Crail and Pittenweem have their fans, but Anstruther is worth most of your attention. The East Neuk works best as a half-day side-trip  (by either car or bus) from St. Andrews, though drivers can use it as a scenic detour between Edinburgh and St. Andrews.

Getting There: It's an easy **drive** from St. Andrews. For the scenic route, follow the A-917 south of town along the coast, past Crail, on the way to Anstruther and Pittenweem. For a shortcut directly to Anstruther, take the B-9131 across the peninsula (or return that way after driving the longer coastal route there). **Buses** connect St. Andrews to the East Neuk: Bus #95 goes hourly from St. Andrews to Crail and Anstruther (50 minutes to Anstruther, catch bus at St. Andrews bus station or from Church Street, around the corner from the TI). The hourly #X60 bus goes directly to Anstruther, then on to Edinburgh (25 minutes to Anstruther, 2 hours more to Edinburgh). Bus info: Tel. 0871-200-2233, www.travelinescotland.com.

▲Anstruther

Stretched out along its harbor, colorful Anstruther (AN-stru-ther; pronounced ENT-ster by locals) is the centerpiece of the East Neuk. The main parking lot and bus stop are both right on the harbor. Anstruther's handy **TI,** which offers lots of useful information for the entire East Neuk area, is located next door to the town's main sight, the Scottish Fisheries Museum (open daily in summer, closed Nov-March, tel. 01333/311-073). Stroll the harborfront to the end, detouring inland around the little cove (or crossing the causeway at low tide) to reach some colorful old houses, including one encrusted with seashells.

Anstruther's **Scottish Fisheries Museum** is true to its slogan: "We are bigger than you think!" The endearingly hokey exhibit sprawls through several harborfront buildings, painstakingly tracing the history of Scottish seafaring from primitive dugout dinghies to modern vessels. You'll learn the story of Scotland's "Zulu" fishing boats and walk through vast boat-filled rooms. For a glimpse at humble fishing lifestyles, don't miss the Fisherman's Cottage, hiding upstairs from the courtyard (£9, open daily, tearoom, Harbourhead, tel. 01333/310-628, www.scotfishmuseum.org).

Eating in Anstruther: Anstruther's claim to fame is its fish-and-chips. Though there are several good chippies in town, the famous one is the **Anstruther Fish Bar,** facing the harbor just a block from the TI and Fisheries Museum (take out or dine in for a few pounds more, open long hours daily, 42 Shore Street, tel. 01333/310-518).

Scotland's Secret Bunker

Among the rolling farm fields between St. Andrews and the East Neuk, a blink-and-you'll-miss-it stone farmhouse conceals a sprawling network of secret corridors: 24,000 square feet, 100 feet under the ground, protected by 10-foot-thick reinforced concrete walls. The exhibit itself is overpriced and frustratingly hokey—a jumble of 1970s technology, scarcely explained other than by the melodramatic audioguide. But for those interested in the Royal Air Force and Cold War, simply exploring this space can be a powerful experience.

Cost and Hours: £13, daily 10:00-18:00, closed Nov-Feb, last entry one hour before closing, audioguide-£2, tel. 01333/310-301, www.secretbunker.co.uk.

Getting There: Head out of St. Andrews toward Crail, but just outside of town, turn off on the right toward *Dunino* and *Anstruther* (on the B-9131). Then follow brown *Secret Bunker* signs about six miles through farmland.

Visiting the Bunker: You'll climb down the stairs and hike through a long tunnel to explore a warren of Cold War-era control rooms, dormitories, and telecommunications centers, plus a chapel and the office of the Minister of State of Scotland (who would command the military in the event of an attack). Black-and-white films calmly explain to homeowners how to prepare for—and cope with—a nuclear attack.

The most striking part of the experience is watching the 46-minute BBC-produced film *The War Game,* a harrowing dramatization of what would happen in the event of a nuclear attack. Its "Keep Calm and Carry On," pull-no-punches straightforwardness is a haunting reminder of an age when global nuclear holocaust seemed not only possible, but likely. (Produced in 1965, the film was immediately branded too disturbing to broadcast, and was not shown on the BBC for 20 years.)

THE SCOTTISH HIGHLANDS

Filled with more natural and historical mystique than people, the Highlands are where Scottish dreams are set. Legends of Bonnie Prince Charlie linger around crumbling castles as tunes played by pipers in kilts swirl around tourists. Intrepid Munro baggers scale bald mountains, grizzled islanders man drizzly ferry crossings, and midges make life miserable (bring bug spray). The Highlands are the most mountainous, least inhabited, and—for many—most scenic and romantic part of Scotland.

The Highlands are covered with mountains, lochs, and glens, scarcely leaving a flat patch of land for building a big city. Geographically, the Highlands are defined by the Highland Boundary Fault, which slashes 130 miles diagonally through the middle of Scotland just north of the big cities of the more densely populated "Central Belt" (Glasgow and Edinburgh).

This geographic and cultural fault line is clearly visible on maps, and you can even see it in the actual landscape—especially around Loch Lomond and the Trossachs, where the transition from rolling Lowland hills to bald Highland mountains is almost too on-the-nose. Just beyond the fault, the Grampian Mountains curve across the middle of Scotland; beyond that, the Caledonian Canal links the east and west coasts (slicing diagonally through the Great Glen, another geologic fault, from Oban to Inverness), with even more mountains to the north.

Though the Highlands' many "hills" are technically too short to be called "mountains," they do a convincing imitation. (Just don't say that to a Scot.) Scotland has 282 hills over 3,000 feet. A list of these was first compiled in 1891 by Sir Hugh Munro, and to this day the Scots call their high hills "Munros." (Hills from 2,500-

Hiking the Highlands

Scotland is a hiker's paradise...as long as you bring rain gear. I've recommended a few hikes of varying degrees of difficulty throughout this book. Remember: Wear sturdy (ideally waterproof) shoes, and be prepared for any weather. For serious hikes, pick up good maps and get advice at local TIs or from a knowledgeable resident (such as your B&B host). A good resource for hiking route tips is WalkHighlands. co.uk.

For a more in-depth experience, consider one of Scotland's famous multiday walks. These are the most popular:

West Highland Way: 95 miles, 5-10 days, Milngavie to Fort William by way of Loch Lomond, Glencoe, and Rannoch Moor

Great Glen Way: 79 miles, 5-6 days, Fort William to Inverness along the Caledonian Canal, Fort Augustus, and Loch Ness

John Muir Way: 134 miles, 9-10 days, coast to coast through the Central Belt of Scotland, from Helensburgh to Dunbar via Falkirk, the Firth of Forth, and Edinburgh

3,000 feet are known as "Corbetts," and those from 2,000-2,500 are "Grahams.") Avid hikers—called "Munro baggers"—love to tick these mini mountains off their list. According to the Munro Society, more than 5,000 intrepid hikers can brag that they've climbed all of the Munros. (To get started, you'll find lots of good information at www.walkhighlands.co.uk/munros).

The Highlands occupy more than half of Scotland's area, but are populated by less than five percent of its people—a population density comparable to Russia's. Scotland's Hebrides Islands (among them Skye, Mull, Iona, and Staffa), while not, strictly speaking, in the Highlands, are often included simply because they share much of the same culture, clan history, and Celtic ties. (Orkney and Shetland, off the north coast of Scotland, are a world apart—they feel more Norwegian than Highlander.)

Inverness is the Highlands' de facto capital, and often claims to be the region's only city. (The east coast port city of Aberdeen—Scotland's third largest, and quadruple the size of Inverness—has its own Doric culture and dialect, and is usually considered its own animal.)

The Highlands are where you'll most likely see Gaelic—the old Celtic language that must legally accompany English on road signs. While few Highlanders actually speak Gaelic—and virtually no one speaks it as a first language—certain Gaelic words are used as a nod of respect to their heritage. *Fàilte* (welcome), *Slàinte mhath!* (cheers!—literally "good health"), and *tigh* (house—featured in many business names) are all common. If you're making friends in a Highland pub, ask your new mates to teach you some Gaelic words.

The Highlands are also the source of many Scottish superstitions, some of which persist in remote communities, where mischievous fairies and shape-shifting kelpies are still blamed for trouble. In the not-so-distant past, new parents feared that their newborn could be replaced by a devilish imposter called a changeling. Well into the 20th century, a midwife called a "howdie" would oversee key rituals: Before a birth, doors and windows would be unlocked and mirrors would be covered. And the day of the week a baby is born was charged with significance ("Monday's child is fair of face, Tuesday's child is full of grace...").

Many American superstitions and expressions originated in Scotland (such as "black sheep," based on the idea that a black sheep was terrible luck for the flock). Just as a baseball player might refuse to shave during a winning streak, many perfectly modern Highlanders carry a sprig of white heather for good luck at their wedding (and are careful not to cross two knives at the dinner table). And let's not even start with the Loch Ness monster...

In the summer, the Highlands swarm with tourists...and midges. These miniature mosquitoes—like "no-see-ums"—are bloodthirsty and determined. They can be an annoyance from late May through September, depending on the weather. Hot sun or a stiff breeze blows the tiny buggers away, but they thrive in damp, shady areas. Locals suggest blowing or brushing them off, rather than swatting them—since killing them only seems to attract more (likely because of the smell of fresh blood). Scots say, "If you kill one midge, a million more will come to his funeral." Even if you don't usually travel with bug spray, consider bringing or buying some for a summer visit. Locals recommend Avon's Skin So Soft, which is effective against midges, but less potent than DEET-based bug repellants.

Keep an eye out for another Scottish animal: shaggy Highland cattle called "hairy coos." They're big and have impressive horns, but are best known for their adorable hair falling into their eyes (the hair protects them from Scotland's troublesome insects and unpredictable weather). Hairy coos graze on sparse vegetation that other animals ignore, and, with a heavy coat (rather than fat) to keep them insulated, they produce a lean meat that resembles venison. (Highland cattle meat is not commonly eaten, and the relatively few hairy coos you'll see are kept around mostly as a national symbol.)

While the prickly, purple thistle is the official national flower, heather is the unofficial national shrub. This scrubby vegetation blankets much of the Highlands. It's usually a muddy reddish-brown color, but it bursts with purple flowers in late summer; the less common bell heather blooms in July. Heather is one of the few things that will grow in the inhospitable terrain of a moor, and it can be used to make dye, rope, thatch, and even beer (look for Fraoch Heather Ale).

Highlanders are an outdoorsy bunch. For a fun look at local athletics, check whether your trip coincides with one of the Highland Games that enliven Highland communities in summer (see the sidebar later in this chapter). And keep an eye out for the unique Highland sport of shinty: a brutal, fast-paced version of field hockey, played for keeps. Similar to Irish hurling, shinty is a full-contact sport that encourages tackling and fielding airborne balls, with players swinging their sticks (called camans) perilously through the air. The easiest place to see shinty is at Bught Park in Inverness (see page 351), but it's played across the Highlands.

PLANNING YOUR TIME

Here are three recommended Highland itineraries: two days, four days, or a full week or more. These plans assume you're driving, but can be done (with some modifications) by bus. Think about how many castles you really need to see: One or two is enough for most people. You can review your options in the "Scottish Castles at a Glance" sidebar on page 444.

Two- to Three-Day Highland Highlights Blitz

This ridiculously fast-paced option squeezes the maximum Highland experience out of a few short days, and assumes you're starting from Glasgow or Edinburgh.

Day 1: In the morning, head up to the Highlands. (If coming from Edinburgh, consider a stop at Stirling Castle en route.) Drive along Loch Lomond and pause for lunch in Inveraray. Try to get to

Oban in time for the day's last distillery tour (see page 262; smart to book ahead). Have dinner and spend the night in Oban.

Day 2: Get an early start from Oban and make a beeline for Glencoe, where you can visit the folk museum and enjoy a quick, scenic drive up the valley. Then drive to Fort William and follow the Caledonian Canal to Inverness, stopping at Fort Augustus to see the locks (and have a late lunch). Drive along Loch Ness to search for monsters, then wedge in a visit to the Culloden Battlefield (outside Inverness) in the late afternoon. Finally, make good time south on the A-9 back to Edinburgh (3 hours, arriving late).

Day 3: To extend this plan, take your time getting to Inverness on Day 2 and spend the night there. Follow my self-guided Inverness Walk either that evening or the next morning. Leaving Inverness, tour Culloden Battlefield, visit Clava Cairns, then head south, stopping off at any place that appeals: The best options near the A-9 are Pitlochry and the Scottish Crannog Centre on Loch Tay, or take the more rugged eastern route to see the Speyside whisky area, Balmoral Castle and Ballater village, and Cairngorms mountain scenery. Or, if this is your best chance to see Stirling Castle or the Falkirk sights (Falkirk Wheel, Kelpies sculptures), fit them in on your way south.

Six-Day Highlands and Islands Loop

While you'll see the Highlands on the above itinerary, you'll whiz past the sights in a misty blur. This more reasonably paced plan is for those who want to slow down a bit.

Day 1: Follow the plan for Day 1, above, sleeping in Oban (2 nights).

Day 2: Do an all-day island-hopping tour from Oban, with visits to Mull, Iona, and (if you choose) Staffa.

Day 3: From Oban, head up to Glencoe for its museum and valley views. Consider lingering for a (brief) hike. Then zip up to Fort William and take the "Road to the Isles" west (pausing in Glenfinnan to see its viaduct) to Mallaig. Take the ferry over the sea to Skye, then drive to Portree to sleep (2 nights).

Day 4: Spend today enjoying the Isle of Skye. In the morning, do the Trotternish Peninsula loop; in the afternoon, take your pick of options (Talisker Distillery, Dunvegan Castle, multiple hiking options).

Day 5: Leaving Portree, drive across the Skye Bridge for a photo-op pit stop at Eilean Donan Castle. The A-87 links you over to Loch Ness, which you'll follow to Inverness. If you get in early enough, consider touring Culloden Battlefield this evening. Sleep in Inverness (1 night).

Day 6: See the Day 3 options for my Highlands Highlights Blitz, earlier.

SCOTTISH HIGHLANDS

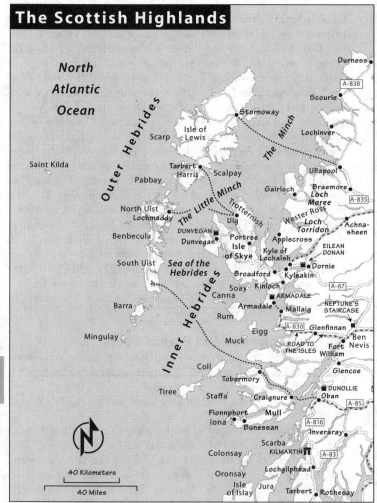

The Scottish Highlands

North Atlantic Ocean

Durness

A-838

Scourie

Lochinver

Stornoway

The Minch

Ullapool

Braemore

A-835

Isle of Lewis

Scarp

Tarbert

Harris

Scalpay

Gairloch

Loch Maree

Wester Ross

Loch Torridon

Achna-sheen

Saint Kilda

Outer Hebrides

Pabbay

The Little Minch

Trotternish

North Uist

Lochmaddy

Uig

Applecross

EILEAN DONAN

DUNVEGAN

Dunvegan

Portree

Isle of Skye

Kyle of Lochalsh

Dornie

Benbecula

Sea of the Hebrides

Broadford

Kyleakin

A-87

South Uist

Soay

Kinloch

ARMADALE

NEPTUNE'S STAIRCASE

Barra

Canna

Armadale

Mallaig

A-830 Glenfinnan

Rum

Ben Nevis

Mingulay

Muck

Eigg

ROAD TO THE ISLES

Fort William

Inner Hebrides

Glencoe

Coll

Tobermory

DUNOLLIE

Oban

Tiree

Staffa

Craignure

A-85

Fionnphort

Mull

Iona

Bunessan

A-816

Inveraray

Scarba

KILMARTIN

A-83

Colonsay

Lochgilphead

Oronsay

Isle of Islay

Jura

Tarbert

Rothesay

40 Kilometers

40 Miles

10-Day (or More) Highlands Explorer Extravaganza

Using the six-day Highlands and Islands Loop as a basis, pick and choose from these possible modifications (listed in order of where they'd fit into the itinerary):

• Add an overnight in **Glencoe** to make more time for hiking there.

• Leaving the Isle of Skye, drive north along **Wester Ross** (the scenic northwest coast). Go as far as Ullapool, then cut back down to Inverness, or...

• Take another day or two (after spending the night in Ullapool) to carry on northward through remote and rugged scenery

to Scotland's **north coast.** Drive east along the coast all the way to John O'Groats; then either take the ferry from Scrabster across to Orkney, or shoot back down to Inverness on the A-9 (about 3 hours).

• Visit **Orkney** (2-night minimum). This can fit into the above plan after John O'Groats. Or, to cut back on the remote driving, simply zip up on the A-9 from Inverness (about 3 hours)—or fly up from Inverness, Edinburgh, or Aberdeen.

• On the way south from Inverness, follow the **Speyside whisky trail,** cut through the **Cairngorms,** visit **Balmoral Castle,** and sleep in **Ballater.** Between Balmoral and Edinburgh, consider

Scottish Highland Games

Throughout the summer, Highland communities host traditional festivals of local sport and culture. These Highland Games (sometimes called Highland Gatherings) combine the best elements of a track meet and a county fair. They range from huge and glitzy (such as Braemar's world-famous games, which the Queen attends, or the Cowal Highland Gathering, Scotland's biggest) to humble and small-town. Some of the more modern games come with loud pop music and corporate sponsorship, but still manage to celebrate the Highland spirit.

Most Highland Games take place between mid-June and late August (usually on Saturdays, but occasionally on weekdays). The games are typically a one-day affair, kicking off around noon and winding down in the late afternoon. At smaller games, you'll pay a nominal admission fee (typically around £5-7). Events are rain or shine (so bring layers) and take place in a big park ringed by a running track, with the heavy events and Highland dancing stage at opposite ends of the infield. Surrounding the whole scene are junk-food stands, a few test-your-skill carnival games, and local charities raising funds by selling hamburgers, fried sausage sandwiches, baked goods, and bottles of beer and Irn-Bru. The emcee's running commentary is a delightful opportunity to just sit back and enjoy a lilting Scottish accent.

The day's events typically kick off with a **pipe band** parading through town—often led by the local clan chieftain—and ending with a lap around the field. Then the sporting events begin.

In the **heavy events**—or feats of Highland strength—brawny, kilted athletes test their ability to hurl various objects of awkward shapes and sizes as far as possible. In the weight throw, competitors spin like ballerinas before releasing a 28- or 56-pound ball on a chain. The hammer throw involves a similar technique with a 26-pound ball on a long stick, and the stone put (with a 20- to 25-pound ball) has been adopted in American sports as the shot put. In the "weight over the bar" event, Highlanders swing a 56-pound weight over a horizontal bar that begins at 10 feet high and ends at closer to 15 feet. (That's like tossing a 5-year-old child over a double-decker bus.) And, of course, there's the caber toss: Pick up a giant log (the caber), get a running start, and release it end-over-end with enough force to (ideally) make the caber flip all the way over and land at the 12 o'clock position. (Most competitors wind up closer to 6.)

Meanwhile, the **track events** run circles around the muscle: the 90-meter dash, the 1,600-meter, and so on. The hill race adds a Scottish spin: Combine a several-mile footrace with the ascent of a nearby summit. The hill racers begin with a lap in the stadium before disappearing for about an hour. Keep an eye on nearby hillsides to pick out their colorful jerseys bobbing up and down a distant peak. This custom supposedly began when an 11th-century king staged a competition to select his personal letter carrier. After about an hour—when you've forgotten all about them—the hill racers start trickling back into the stadium to cross the finish line.

The **Highland dancing** is a highlight. Accompanied by a lone piper, the dancers (in groups of two to four) toe their routines

with intense concentration. Dancers remain always on the balls of their feet, requiring excellent balance and stamina. While some men participate, most competitors are female—from wee lassies barely out of nappies, all the way to poised professionals. Common steps are the Highland fling (in which the goal is to keep the feet as close as possible to one spot), sword dances (in which the dancers step gingerly over crossed swords on the stage), and a variety of national dances.

Other events further enliven the festivities. The pipe band periodically assembles to play a few tunes, often while marching around the track (giving the runners a break). Larger games may have a massing of multiple pipe bands, or bagpipe and drumming competitions. You may also see re-enactments of medieval battles, herd-dog demonstrations, or dog shows (grooming and obedience). Haggis hurling—in which participants stand on a whisky barrel and attempt to throw a cooked haggis as far as possible—has caught on recently. And many small-town events end with the grand finale of a town-wide tug-of-war, during which everybody gets bruised, muddy, and hysterical.

If you're traveling to Scotland in the summer, check online schedules to see if you'll be near any Highland Games before locking in your itinerary. Rather than target the big, famous gatherings, I make a point of visiting the smaller clan games. A helpful website—listing dates for most but not all of the games around Scotland—is www.shga.co.uk. For many travelers to Scotland, attending a Highland Games can be a trip-capping highlight. And, of course, many communities in the US and Canada also host their own Highland Games.

visiting Glamis Castle (Queen Mum's childhood home), Dundee (great industrial museums), or Culross (scenic firthside village).

• Add an overnight wherever you'd like to linger; the best options are the **Isle of Skye** (to allow more island explorations) or **Inverness** (to fit in more side-trips).

GETTING AROUND THE HIGHLANDS

By Car: The Highlands are made for joyriding. There are a lot of miles, but they're scenic, the roads are good, and the traffic is light.

Drivers enjoy flexibility and plenty of tempting stopovers. Be careful about passing, but don't be too timid; otherwise, diesel fumes and large trucks might be your main memory of driving in Scotland. The farther north you go, the more away-from-it-all you'll feel, with few signs of civilization. Even on a sunny weekend, you can go miles without seeing another car. Don't wait too long to gas up—village gas stations are few and far between, and can close unexpectedly. Get used to single-lane roads: While you can make good time when they're empty (as they often are), stay alert, and slow down on blind corners—you never know when an oncoming car (or a road-blocking sheep) is just around the bend. If you do encounter an oncoming vehicle, the driver closest to a pullout is expected to use it—even if they have to back up. A little "thank-you" wave (or even just an index finger raised off the steering wheel) is the customary end to these encounters.

By Public Transportation: Glasgow is the gateway to this region (so you'll most likely have to transfer there if coming from Edinburgh). **Trains** zip from Glasgow to Fort William, Oban, and Kyle of Lochalsh in the west; and up to Stirling, Pitlochry, and Inverness in the east. For more remote destinations (such as Glencoe), the bus is better.

Most **buses** are operated by Scottish Citylink. In peak season—when these buses fill up—it's smart to buy tickets at least a day in advance: Book at Citylink.co.uk, call 0871-216-3333, or stop by a bus station or TI. Otherwise, you can pay the driver in cash when you board.

Glasgow's Buchanan Station is the main Lowlands hub for reaching Highlands destinations. From Edinburgh, it's best to transfer in Glasgow (fastest by train, also possible by bus)—though there are direct buses from Edinburgh to Inverness, where you can connect to Highlands buses. Once in the Highlands, Inverness and Fort William serve as the main bus hubs.

Note that bus frequency can be substantially reduced on Sundays and in the off-season (Oct-mid-May). Unless otherwise noted, I've listed bus information for summer weekdays. Always confirm schedules locally.

These buses are particularly useful for connecting the sights in this book:

Buses **#976** and **#977** connect Glasgow with Oban (5/day, 3 hours).

Buses **#914/#915/#916** go from Glasgow to Fort William, stopping at Glencoe (7-8/day, 2.5 hours to Glencoe, 3 hours total to Fort William). From Fort William, some of these buses continue all the way up to Portree on the Isle of Skye (3/day, 7 hours for the full run).

Bus **#918** goes from Oban to Fort William, stopping en route at Ballachulish near Glencoe (2/day, 1 hour to Ballachulish, 1.5 hours total to Fort William).

Bus **#N44** (operated by Shiel Bus) is a cheaper alternative for connecting Glencoe to Fort William (about 8/day, fewer Sat-Sun, www.shielbuses.co.uk).

Buses **#919** and **#920** connect Fort William with Inverness (6/day, 2 hours, fewer on Sun).

Buses **#M90** and **#G90** run from Edinburgh to Inverness (express #G90, 2/day, 3.5 hours; slower #M90, some stop in Pitlochry, 6/day, 4 hours).

Bus **#917** connects Inverness with Portree, on the Isle of Skye (3-4/day, 3 hours).

Bus **#G10** is an express connecting Inverness and Glasgow (5/day, 3 hours). National Express **#588** also goes direct (1/day, 4 hours, www.nationalexpress.com).

OBAN & THE INNER HEBRIDES

Oban • Isles of Mull, Iona & Staffa • Glasgow to Oban Drive

For a taste of Scotland's west coast, head to Oban, a port town that's equal parts endearing and functional. This busy little ferry and train terminus has no important sights, but makes up the difference in character, in scenery (with its low-impact panorama of overlapping islets and bobbing boats), and with one of Scotland's best distillery tours. But Oban is also convenient: It's midway between the Lowland cities (Glasgow and Edinburgh) and the Highland riches of the north (Glencoe, Isle of Skye). And it's the "gateway to the isles," with handy ferry service to the Hebrides Islands.

If time is tight and serious island-hopping is beyond the scope of your itinerary, Oban is ideally situated for a busy and memorable full-day side trip to three of the most worthwhile Inner Hebrides: big, rugged Mull; pristine little Iona, where buoyant clouds float over its historic abbey; and Staffa, a remote, grassy islet inhabited only by sea birds. (The best of the Inner Hebrides—the Isle of Skye—is covered in its own chapter.) Sit back, let someone else do the driving, and enjoy a tour of the Inner Hebrides.

This chapter also outlines the most scenic route between Glasgow and Oban (along the bonnie, bonnie banks of Loch Lomond and through the town of Inveraray, with its fine castle), with a detour through Kilmartin Glen, the prehistoric homeland of the Scottish people.

PLANNING YOUR TIME

If you're on a speedy blitz tour of Scotland, Oban is a strategic and pleasant place to spend the night. But you'll need two nights to enjoy Oban's main attraction: the side-trip to Mull, Iona, and Staffa. There are few actual sights in Oban itself, beyond the distillery tour, but—thanks to its manageable size, scenic waterfront setting, and great restaurants—the town is an enjoyable place to linger.

Oban

Oban (pronounced OH-bin) is a low-key resort. Its winding promenade is lined by gravel beaches, ice-cream stands, fish-and-chips joints, a tourable distillery, and a good choice of restaurants. Everything in Oban is close together, and the town seems eager to please its many visitors: Wool and tweed are perpetually on sale, and posters announce a variety of day tours to Scotland's  wild and wildlife-strewn western islands. When the rain clears, sun-starved Scots sit on benches along the Esplanade, leaning back to catch some rays. Wind, boats, gulls, layers of islands, and the promise of a wide-open Atlantic beyond give Oban a rugged charm.

Orientation to Oban

Oban, with about 10,000 people, is where the train system of Scotland meets the ferry system serving the Hebrides Islands. As "gateway to the isles," its center is not a square or market, but its harbor. Oban's business action, just a couple of streets deep, stretches along the harbor and its promenade.

TOURIST INFORMATION

Oban's TI, located at the North Pier, sells bus and ferry tickets and can help you sort through your island-hopping day-trip options (generally daily July-Aug 9:00-19:00, April-June until 17:30, Sept-March 10:00-17:00, 3 North Pier, tel. 01631/563-122, www. oban.org.uk).

HELPFUL HINTS

Bookstore: Overlooking the harborfront, Waterstones offers maps and a fine collection of books on Scotland (Mon-Sat 9:00-17:30, Sun 11:00-17:00, longer hours July-Aug, 12 George Street, tel. 0843/290-8529).

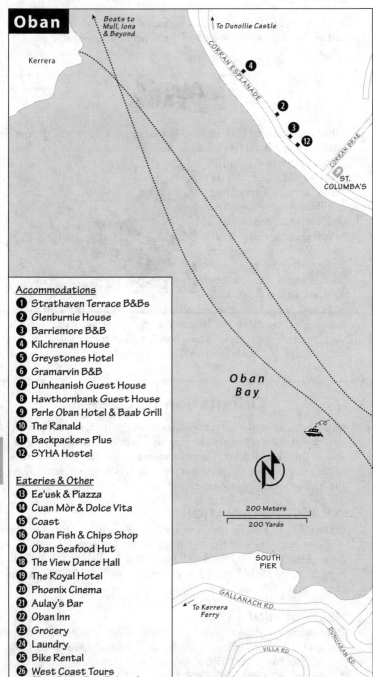

OBAN & INNER HEBRIDES

Oban

Kerrera

Boats to Mull, Iona & Beyond

To Dunollie Castle

CORRAN ESPLANADE

❹
❷
❸ ❿

CORRAN BRAE

ST. COLUMBA'S

Oban Bay

To Kerrera Ferry

SOUTH PIER

GALLANACH RD.

VILLA RD.

DUNUARAN RD.

200 Meters
200 Yards

Accommodations
1 Strathaven Terrace B&Bs
2 Glenburnie House
3 Barriemore B&B
4 Kilchrenan House
5 Greystones Hotel
6 Gramarvin B&B
7 Dunheanish Guest House
8 Hawthornbank Guest House
9 Perle Oban Hotel & Baab Grill
10 The Ranald
11 Backpackers Plus
12 SYHA Hostel

Eateries & Other
13 Ee'usk & Piazza
14 Cuan Mòr & Dolce Vita
15 Coast
16 Oban Fish & Chips Shop
17 Oban Seafood Hut
18 The View Dance Hall
19 The Royal Hotel
20 Phoenix Cinema
21 Aulay's Bar
22 Oban Inn
23 Grocery
24 Laundry
25 Bike Rental
26 West Coast Tours (Day Trips, Bus Tickets)

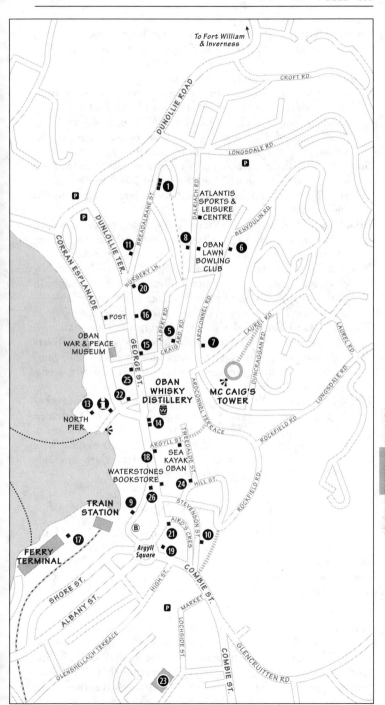

To Fort William & Inverness

CROFT RD.

DUNOLLIE ROAD

LONGSDALE RD.

P

BREADALBANE ST.

1

DALRIACH RD.

ATLANTIS SPORTS & LEISURE CENTRE

P

P

DUNOLLIE TER.

11

8

BENVOULIN RD.

CORRAN ESPLANADE

NURSERY LN.

20

OBAN LAWN BOWLING CLUB

6

POST

16

ALBERT RD.

ARDCONNEL RD.

LAUREL RD.

OBAN WAR & PEACE MUSEUM

GEORGE ST.

15

5

CRAIGARD RD.

7

LAUREL RD.

DUNCRAGGAN RD.

25

OBAN WHISKY DISTILLERY

ARDCONNEL TERRACE

MC CAIG'S TOWER

LONGSDALE RD.

13

22

14

ROCKFIELD RD.

NORTH PIER

ARGYLL ST.

TWEEDDALE ST.

ROCKFIELD RD.

18

SEA KAYAK OBAN

HILL ST.

24

WATERSTONES BOOKSTORE

26

STEVENSON ST.

ROCKFIELD RD.

TRAIN STATION

9

B

AIRD'S CRES.

21

10

17

19

Argyll Square

HIGH ST.

COMBIE ST.

FERRY TERMINAL

SHORE ST.

ALBANY ST.

P

MARKET ST.

LOCHSIDE ST.

GLENSHELLAGH TERRACE

23

COMBIE ST.

GLENCRUITTEN RD.

OBAN & INNER HEBRIDES

Baggage Storage: The train station has pay luggage lockers, but is open limited hours (Mon-Sat 5:00-20:30, Sun 10:45-18:00)—confirm the closing time before committing.

Laundry: You'll find **Oban Quality Laundry** tucked a block behind the main drag just off Stevenson Street (same-day drop-off service, no self-service, Mon-Tue and Thu-Fri 9:00-17:00, Wed and Sat 9:00-13:00, closed Sun, tel. 01631/563-554). The recommended **Backpackers Plus Hostel** (see "Sleeping in Oban") will also do laundry for nonguests.

Supermarket: The giant **Tesco** is a five-minute walk from the train station (Mon-Sat until 24:00, Sun until 20:00, walk through Argyll Square and look for entrance to large parking lot on right, Lochside Street).

Bike Rental: Get wheels at **Oban Cycles,** right on the main drag (£25/day, Tue-Sat 10:00-17:00, closed Sun-Mon, 87 George Street, tel. 01631/566-033, www.obancyclescotland.com).

Bus Station: The "station" is just a pullout, marked by a stubby clock tower, at the roundabout in front of the train station. In peak season, it's wise to book bus tickets the day before—either at the TI, or at the West Coast Tours office (see next).

Bus and Island Tour Tickets: A block from the train station in the bright-red building along the harbor, **West Coast Tours** sells bus- and island-tour tickets (Tue-Sat 6:30-17:30, Sun-Mon from 8:30, 17 George Street, tel. 01631/566-809, www. westcoasttours.co.uk).

Highland Games: Oban hosts its touristy Highland Games every August (www.obangames.com), and the more local-oriented Lorne Highland Games some years in June (www.lorne-highland-games.org.uk). Nearby Taynuilt, a 20-minute drive east, hosts their sweetly small-town Highland Games in mid-July (www.taynuilthighlandgames.com).

Tours from Oban

For the best day trip from Oban, tour the islands of Mull, Iona, and/or Staffa (offered daily Easter-Oct, described later)—or consider staying overnight on remote and beautiful Iona. With more time or other interests, consider one of many other options you'll see advertised.

Wildlife Tours

If you just want to go for a boat ride, the easiest option is the one-hour seal-watching tour (£10, various companies—look for signs at the harbor). But to really get a good look at Scottish coastal wildlife, several groups—including **Coastal Connection** (based in Oban, https://coastal-connection.co.uk) and **Sealife Adventures** and

SeaFari (based in nearby coastal towns, https://sealife-adventures. com and www.seafari.co.uk/oban)—run whale-watching tours that seek out rare minke whales, basking sharks, bottlenose dolphins, and porpoises. For an even more ambitious itinerary, the holy grail is Treshnish Island (out past Staffa), which brims with puffins, seals, and other sea critters. For multi-day cruising trips around the islands, try **St. Hilda Sea Adventures,** with their own small fleet of boats (www.sthildaseaadventures.co.uk).

Sea Kayak Tours

If the weather is good and you'd like to get out on the water under your own power, **Sea Kayak Oban** rents gear and offers classes and guided tours for novice and experienced kayakers. A full-day tour costs £90 including equipment (office at 6 Argyll Street, tel. 01631/565-310, www.seakayakoban.com).

Sights in Oban

▲The Burned-Out Sightseer's Visual Tour from the Pier

If the west-coast weather permits, get oriented to the town while taking a break: Head out to the North Pier, just past the TI, and find the benches that face back toward town (in front of the recommended Piazza restaurant). Take a seat and get to know Oban.

Scan the harborfront from left to right, surveying the mix of grand Victorian sandstone buildings and humbler modern storefronts. At the far-right end of town is the **ferry terminal** and—very likely—a huge ferry loading or unloading. Oban has always been on the way to somewhere, and today is no different. (A recent tourism slogan: Oban...it's closer than you think.) The townscape seems dominated by Caledonian-MacBrayne, Scotland's biggest ferry company. CalMac's 30 ships serve 24 destinations and transport over 4 million passengers a year. The town's port has long been a lifeline to the islands.

Hiding near the ferry terminal is the **train station.** With the arrival of the train in 1880, Oban became the unofficial capital of Scotland's west coast and a destination for tourists. Close by is the former Caledonian Hotel, the original terminus hotel (now the Perle Oban Hotel) that once served those train travelers.

Tourism aside, herring was the first big industry. A dozen boats still fish commercially—you'll see them tucked around the ferry terminal. The tourist board, in an attempt to entice tourists to linger longer, is trying to rebrand Oban as a "seafood capital" rather than just the "gateway to the isles." As the ocean's supply has become depleted, most local fish is farmed. There's still plenty of shellfish.

After fishing, big industries here historically included tobacco (imported from the American colonies), then whisky. At the left end of the embankment, find the building marked *The Oban Distillery*. It's rare to find a distillery in the middle of a town, but Oban grew up around this one. With the success of its whisky, the town enjoyed an invigorating confidence, optimism, and, in 1811, a royal charter. Touring Oban's distillery is the best activity in Oban.

Above the distillery, you can't miss the odd mini-Colosseum. This is **McCaig's Tower,** an employ-the-workers-and-build-me-a-fine-memorial project undertaken by an Oban tycoon in 1900. McCaig died before completing the structure, so his complete vision for it remains a mystery. This is an example of a "folly"—that uniquely British notion of an idiosyncratic structure erected by a colorful aristocrat. Building a folly was an in-your-face kind of extravagance many extremely wealthy people enjoyed even when surrounded by struggling working-class people (an urge that survives among some of the upper crust to this day). While the building itself is nothing to see up close, a 10-minute hike through a Victorian residential neighborhood leads you to a peaceful garden and a commanding view (nice at sunset).

Now turn and look out to sea, and imagine this: At the height of the Cold War, Oban played a critical role when the world's first two-way transatlantic telephone cable was laid from Gallanach Bay to Newfoundland in 1956—a milestone in global communication. This technology later provided the White House and the Kremlin with the "hotline" that was created after the Cuban Missile Crisis to avoid a nuclear conflagration.

▲▲Oban Whisky Distillery Tours

Founded in 1794, Oban Whisky Distillery produces more than 25,000 liters a week, and exports much of that to the US. Their exhibition (upstairs, free to all) gives a quick, whisky-centric history of Oban and Scotland.

The distillery offers serious and fragrant one-hour tours explaining the process from start to finish, with two smooth samples of their signature product: Oban whisky is moderately smoky ("peaty") and characterized by notes of sea salt, citrus, and honey. You'll also receive a whisky glass and a discount coupon for the shop. This is the handiest whisky tour you'll encounter—just a block off the harbor—and one of the best. Come 10 minutes before your tour starts to check out the exhibition upstairs. Then your guide will walk you through each step of the process: malting, mashing, fermentation, distillation, and maturation. Photos are not allowed inside. For details on the distilling process and tips on tasting whisky, see page 484.

Cost and Hours: Tours cost £12, are limited to 16 people and depart every 20 to 30 minutes. Tours fill up, so for the greatest choice of times, book in advance by phone or online. Or drop by in person—unless it's really a busy day, you should be able pay for a tour leaving in the next hour or so, then easily pass time in the town center. Generally open July-Sept Mon-Fri 9:30-19:30, Sat-Sun until 17:00; March-June and Oct-Nov daily 9:30-17:00; Dec-Feb daily 12:00-16:30; last tour 1.25 hours before closing, Stafford Street, tel. 01631/572-004, www.obanwhisky.com.

Serious Tasting: Connoisseurs can ask about their "exclusive tour," which adds a visit to the warehouse and four premium tastings in the manager's office (£75, 2 hours, likely July-Sept Mon-Fri at 16:00 only, reservation required).

Oban War & Peace Museum

Opened in 1995 on the 50th anniversary of Victory in Europe Day, this charming little museum focuses on Oban's experience during World War II. But it covers more than just war and peace. Photos show Oban through the years, and a 15-minute looped video gives a simple tour around the town and region. Volunteer staffers love to chat about the exhibit—or anything else on your mind (free; May-Oct Mon-Thu 10:00-18:00, Fri-Sun and off-season until 16:00; next to Regent Hotel on the promenade, tel. 01631/570-007, www.obanmuseum.org.uk).

Dunollie Castle and Museum

In a park just a mile up the coast, a ruined castle and an old house hold an intimate collection of clan family treasures. This spartan, stocky castle with 10-foot walls offers a commanding, windy view of the harbor—a strategic spot back in the days when transport was mainly by water. For more than a thousand years, clan chiefs ruled this region from this ancestral home of Clan MacDougall, but the castle was abandoned in 1746. The adjacent house, which dates from 1745, shows off the MacDougall clan's heritage with a handful of rooms filled with a humble yet fascinating trove of treasures. While the exhibit won't dazzle you, the family and clan pride in the display, their "willow garden," and the lovely walk from Oban make the visit fun.

To get there, head out of town along the harborfront promenade. At the war memorial (with inviting seaview benches), cross the street. A gate leads to a little lane, lined with historic and nature boards along the way to the castle.

Cost and Hours: £6, Mon-Sat 10:00-17:00, Sun from 13:00;

OBAN & INNER HEBRIDES

free tours given most days at 10:30 and 14:30, Sun 12:30 only; closed Nov-March, tel. 01631/570-550, www.dunollie.org.

ACTIVITIES IN OBAN

Atlantis Leisure Centre

This industrial-type sports center has a rock-climbing wall, tennis courts, indoor "soft play centre" (for kids under 5), and an indoor swimming pool with a big water slide. The outdoor playground is free and open all the time (pool only-£4.50, no rental towels or suits, fees for other activities; open Mon-Fri 6:30-21:00, Sat-Sun 9:00-18:00; on the north end of Dalriach Road, tel. 01631/566-800, www.atlantisleisure.co.uk).

Oban Lawn Bowling Club

The club has welcomed visitors since 1869. This elegant green is the scene of a wonderfully British spectacle of old men tiptoeing wishfully after their balls. It's fun to watch, and—if there's no match scheduled and the weather's dry—anyone can rent shoes and balls and actually play (£5/person; generally daily 10:00-12:00 & 14:00-16:00 or "however long the weather lasts"; just south of sports center on Dalriach Road, tel. 01631/570-808).

ISLANDS NEAR OBAN

The isles of Mull, Iona, and Staffa are farther out, require a full day to visit, and are described later in this chapter. For a quicker glimpse at the Inner Hebrides, consider these two options.

Isle of Kerrera

Functioning like a giant breakwater, the Isle of Kerrera (KEH-reh-rah) makes Oban possible. Just offshore from Oban, this stark but very green island offers a quick, easy opportunity to get that romantic island experience. While it has no proper roads, it offers nice hikes, a ruined castle, and a few sheep farms. It's also a fine place to bike (ask for advice at Oban Cycles; see "Helpful Hints," earlier). You may see the Kerrera ferry filled with sheep heading for Oban's livestock market.

Getting There: You have two options for reaching the island. A boat operated by the Oban Marina goes from **Oban's North Pier** to the Kerrera Marina in the northern part of the island (£5 round-trip, roughly every hour, book ahead at tel. 01631/565-333, www.obanmarina.com).

A ferry departs from **Gallanach** (two miles south of Oban) and goes to the middle of the island. This is the best option if you want to hike to Kerrera's castle (passengers only, £4.80 round-trip, bikes free, runs 10:30-12:30 & 14:00-18:00, none off-season, 5-minute ride, tel. 01475/650-397, www.calmac.co.uk). To reach

Gallanach, drive south, following the coast road past the ferry terminal (parking available).

Eating and Sleeping on Kerrera: With a laid-back patio,
$$ Waypoint Bar & Grill has a simple menu of steak, burgers,
and seafood; on a nice day the open-air waterside setting is unbeat-
able (late May-Sept Thu-Sun lunch 12:00-14:30, Tue-Sun dinner
17:30-21:00, bar opens at 17:00, closed Mon and in winter, reserva-
tions highly recommended, tel. 01631/565-333, www.obanmarina.
com). For lodging, your only option is the **$ Kerrera Bunkhouse,**
a refurbished 18th-century stable that can sleep up to seven people
in a small, cozy space (1 double and 5 single bunks, 2-night mini-
mum, includes bedding but not towels, open Easter-Oct but must
book ahead, kitchen, tel. 01631/566-367, www.kerrerabunkhouse.
co.uk, info@kerrerabunkhouse.co.uk, Martin and Aideen). They
also run a tea garden that serves meals (daily 10:30-16:30, closed
Oct-Easter).

Isle of Seil

Enjoy a drive, a walk, some solitude, and the sea. Drive 12 miles
south of Oban on the A-816 to the B-844 to the Isle of Seil (pro-
nounced "seal"), connected to the mainland by a bridge (which,
locals like to brag, "crosses the Atlantic"...well, maybe a small part
of it).

Just over the bridge on the Isle of Seil is a pub called **Tigh-an-
Truish** ("House of Trousers"). After the Jacobite rebellions, a new
law forbade the wearing of kilts on the mainland. Highlanders on
the island used this pub to change from kilts to trousers before they
made the crossing. The pub serves great meals and good seafood
dishes to those either in kilts or pants (pub generally open daily—
call ahead, tel. 01852/300-242).

Seven miles across the island, on a tiny second island and fac-
ing the open Atlantic, is **Easdale,** a historic, touristy, windblown
little slate-mining town with a small folk museum (shuttle ferry
goes the 300 yards). Wildlife/nature tours plus tours to Iona and
Staffa also run from Easdale (www.seafari.co.uk).

Nightlife in Oban

Little Oban has a few options for entertaining its many visitors;
check ObanWhatsOn.co.uk. Fun low-key activities may include
open-mike, disco, or quiz theme nights in pubs; occasional Scot-
tish folk shows; coffee meetings; and—if you're lucky—duck races.
On Wednesday nights, the Oban Pipe Band plays in the square by
the train station. Here are a few other ways to entertain yourself
while in town.

Music and Group Dancing: On many summer nights, you

OBAN & INNER HEBRIDES

can climb the stairs to **The View,** a sprawling venue on the main drag for music and dancing. There's *ceilidh* (KAY-lee) dancing a couple of times per week, where you can learn some group dances to music performed by a folk band (including, usually, a piper). These group dances are a lot of fun—wallflowers and bad dancers are warmly welcomed, and the staff is happy to give you pointers (£9, May-Sept Mon & Thu at 21:00, sometimes also Sat). They also host concerts by folk and traditional bands (check website for schedule, 34 George Street, tel. 01631/569-599, www.obanview.com).

Traditional Music: Various pubs and hotels in town have live traditional music in the summer; the TI compiles these into its Oban Music Trail map—ask your B&B host or at the TI for the latest. **The Royal Hotel,** just above the train station on Argyll Square, is one popular venue.

Cinema: True to its name, **The Phoenix Cinema** closed down but then was saved by the community. It's now volunteer-run and booming (140 George Street, tel. 01631/562-905, www.obanphoenix.com).

Characteristic Pubs: With decor that shows off Oban's maritime heritage, **Aulay's Bar** has two sides, each with a different personality (I like the right-hand side). Having a drink here invariably comes with a good "blether" (conversation), and the gang is mostly local (daily 11:00-24:00, 8 Airds Crescent, just around the corner from the train station and ferry terminal). The **Oban Inn,** right on the harborfront, is also a fun and memorable place for a pint and possibly live music.

Sleeping in Oban

Oban's B&Bs offer a much better value than its hotels.

ON STRATHAVEN TERRACE

The following B&Bs line up on a quiet, flowery street that's nicely located two blocks off the harbor, three blocks from the center, and a 10-minute walk from the train station. Rooms here are compact and don't have views, but the location can't be beat.

By car, as you enter town from the north, turn left immediately after King's Knoll Hotel, and take your first right onto Breadalbane Street. ("Strathaven Terrace" is actually just the name for this row of houses on Breadalbane Street.) The alley behind the buildings has tight, free parking for all of these places.

$$ Rose Villa Guest House has five crisp and cheery rooms (at #5, tel. 01631/566-874, www.rosevillaoban.co.uk, info@rosevillaoban.co.uk, Stuart and Jacqueline).

$ Raniven Guest House has five simple, tastefully decorated rooms and gracious, fun-loving hosts Moyra and Stuart (cash only, 2-night minimum in summer, continental breakfast, at #1, tel. 01631/562-713, www.ranivenoban.com, bookings@ranivenoban.com).

$ Sandvilla B&B rents five pleasant, polished rooms (2-night minimum in summer, at #4, tel. 01631/564-483, www.holidayoban.co.uk, sandvilla@holidayoban.co.uk, Josephine and Robert).

ALONG THE ESPLANADE

These are a 10-minute walk from the center along the Corran Esplanade, which stretches north of town above a cobble beach. Rooms here are generally spacious and many have beautiful bay views. Walking from town, you'll reach them in this order: Kilchrenan, Glenburnie, and Barriemore.

$$$ Glenburnie House, a stately Victorian home, has an elegant breakfast room overlooking the bay. Its 12 spacious, comfortable, classy rooms feel like plush living rooms. There's a nice lounge and a tiny sunroom with a stuffed "hairy coo" head (closed mid-Nov-March, tel. 01631/562-089, www.glenburnie.co.uk, stay@glenburnie.co.uk, Graeme).

$$$ Barriemore B&B, at the very end of Oban's grand waterfront Esplanade, is a welcome refuge after a day of exploration. Its 14 well-appointed rooms come with robes, sherry, etc. It has a nice front patio, spacious breakfast room, and glassed-in sun porch with a view of the water (family suite, closed Nov-March, tel. 01631/566-356, www.barriemore.co.uk, info@barriemore.co.uk, Jan and Mark).

$$ Kilchrenan House, the turreted former retreat of a textile magnate, has 15 large rooms, most with bay views. The stunning rooms #5, #9, and #15 are worth the few extra pounds, while the "standard" rooms in the newer annex are a good value (2-night minimum for some rooms, welcome drink of whisky or sherry, different "breakfast special" every day, family rooms, closed Oct-March, tel. 01631/562-663, www.kilchrenanhouse.co.uk, info@kilchrenanhouse.co.uk, Colin and Frances).

ABOVE THE TOWN CENTER

These places perch on the hill above the main waterfront zone—a short (but uphill) walk from all of the action. Many rooms come with views, and are priced accordingly.

$$$$ Greystones is an enticing splurge. It fills a big, stately,

OBAN & INNER HEBRIDES

turreted mansion at the top of town with five spacious rooms that mix Victorian charm and sleek gray-and-white minimalism. Built as the private home for the director of Kimberley Diamond Mine, it later became a maternity hospital, and today Cathy and John run it as a stylish and restful retreat. The lounge and breakfast room offer stunning views over Oban and the offshore isles (closed Nov-mid-Feb, 1-3 Dalriach Road, tel. 01631/562-423, www.greystonesoban. co.uk, stay@greystonesoban.co.uk).

$$ Gramarvin B&B feels a little more homey and personal, with just two rooms and warm host Mary. Window seats in each room provide a lovely view over Oban, but be warned—the climb up from town and then up their stairs is steep (simple breakfast, cash only, 2-night minimum in summer preferred, on-street parking, Benvoulin Road, tel. 01631/564-622, www.gramarvin.co.uk, mary@gramarvin.co.uk, Mary and Joe).

$$ Dunheanish Guest House offers six pleasant rooms (two on the ground floor) and wide-open views from its perch above town, which you can enjoy from the front stone patio, breakfast room, and several guest rooms (lots of stairs, parking, Ardconnel Road, tel. 01631/566-556, www.dunheanish.com, info@ dunheanish.com, William and Linda).

$$ Hawthornbank Guest House fills a big Victorian sandstone house with seven traditional-feeling rooms. Half of the rooms face bay views, and the other half overlook the town's lawn-bowling green (2-night minimum in summer, Dalriach Road, tel. 01631/562-041, www.hawthornbank.co.uk, info@hawthornbank. co.uk).

IN THE TOWN CENTER

A number of hotels are in the center of town along or near the main drag—but you'll pay for the convenience.

$$$$ Perle Oban Hotel is your luxury boutique splurge. Right across from the harbor, it has 59 super-sleek rooms with calming sea-color walls, decorative bath-tile floors, and rain showers (suites, fancy restaurant, bar with light bites, pay parking nearby, Station Square, tel. 01631/700-301, www.perleoban.co.uk, stay@perleoban.co.uk).

$$$ The Ranald is a modern change of pace from the B&B scene. This narrow, 17-room, three-floor hotel has a budget-boutique vibe; they also rent eight studio apartments on the same street (family rooms, bar, no elevator, street parking, a block behind the Royal Hotel at 41 Stevenson Street, tel. 01631/562-887, https:// theranaldhotel.com, info@theranaldhotel.com).

HOSTELS

¢ **Backpackers Plus** is central, laid-back, and fun. It fills part of a renovated old church with a sprawling public living room and a staff generous with travel tips. Check out the walls as you go up to the reception desk—they're covered with graffiti messages from guests (10-minute walk from station, on Breadalbane Street, tel. 01631/567-189, www.backpackersplus.com, info@backpackersplus.com, Peter). They have two other locations nearby with private rooms.

¢ The official **SYHA hostel** is institutional but occupies a grand building on the waterfront Esplanade with smashing views of the harbor and islands from the lounges and dining rooms (all rooms en suite, private rooms available, also has family rooms and 8-bed apartment with kitchen, bike storage, tel. 01631/562-025, www.hostellingscotland.org.uk, oban@hostellingscotland.org.uk).

Eating in Oban

Oban brags that it is the "seafood capital of Scotland," and indeed its sit-down restaurants are surprisingly high quality for such a small town. For something more casual, consider a fish-and-chips joint.

SIT-DOWN RESTAURANTS

These fill up in summer, especially on weekends. To ensure getting a table, you'll want to book ahead. The first five are generally open daily from 12:00-15:00 and 17:30-21:00.

$$$ Ee'usk (Scottish Gaelic for "fish") is a popular, stylish seafood place on the waterfront. It has a casual-chic, yacht-clubby atmosphere, with a bright and glassy interior and sweeping views on three sides—fun for watching the ferries come and go. They sometimes offer an early-bird special until 18:45, and their seafood platters are a hit. Reservations are recommended (no kids under age 12 at dinner, North Pier, tel. 01631/565-666, www.eeusk.com, MacLeod family).

$$$ Cuan Mòr is a popular, casual restaurant that combines traditional Scottish food with modern flair—both in its crowd-pleasing cuisine and in its furnishings, made of wood, stone, and metal scavenged from the beaches of Scotland's west coast (brewery in back, 60 George Street, tel. 01631/565-078, www.cuanmor.co.uk). Its harborside tables on the sidewalk are popular when it's warm.

$$$ Coast proudly serves fresh local fish, meat, and veggies in a mod pine-and-candlelight atmosphere. As everything is cooked to order and presented with care by husband-and-wife team Richard and Nicola—who try to combine traditional Scottish elements in innovative new ways—this is no place to dine and dash (two- and three-course specials, closed Sun for lunch, 104 George Street, tel. 01631/569-900, www.coastoban.co.uk).

$$ Baab Grill brings a refreshing taste of the Eastern Mediterranean to Western Scotland. Besides the usual standbys (baba ghanoush, tabbouleh, moussaka) the menu includes some "fusion" dishes such as Scottish salmon in a tahini sauce (attached to the Perle Oban Hotel, no midday closure, Station Road, tel. 01631/707-130, www.baabgrill.co.uk).

$$ Piazza, next door to Ee'usk, is a casual, family-friendly place serving basic Italian dishes with a great harborfront location. They have some outdoor seats and big windows facing the sea (smart to reserve ahead July-Aug, tel. 01631/563-628, www.piazzaoban.com).

$$ Oban Fish and Chips Shop—run by Lewis, Sammy, and their family—serves praiseworthy haddock and mussels among other tasty options in a cheery cabana-like dining room. Consider venturing away from basic fish-and-chips into a world of more creative seafood dishes—like their tiny squat lobster. You can bring your own wine for no charge (daily, sit-down restaurant closes at 21:00, takeaway available later, 116 George Street, tel. 01631/569-828).

LUNCH

$ Oban Seafood Hut, in a green shack facing the ferry dock, is a finger-licking festival of cheap and fresh seafood. John and Marion regularly get fresh deliveries from local fishermen—this is the best spot to pick up a seafood sandwich or a snack. They sell smaller bites (such as cold sandwiches), as well as some bigger cold platters and a few hot dishes (outdoor seating only, daily from 10:00 until the boat unloads from Mull around 18:00).

$ Dolce Vita has a prime location on the main drag to sit outside when the sun shines. It does nice soups, sandwiches, and panini (daily 8:00-18:00, 62 George Street, tel. 01631/571-221).

Oban Connections

By Train: Trains link Oban to the nearest transportation hub in **Glasgow** (6/day, fewer on Sun, 3 hours); to get to **Edinburgh,** you'll transfer in Glasgow (roughly 6/day, 4.5 hours). To reach **Fort William** (a transit hub for the Highlands), you'll take the same Glasgow-bound train, but transfer in Crianlarich (3/day, 4 hours)—the direct bus is easier (see next). Oban's small train station has a ticket window and lockers (both open Mon-Sat 5:00-20:30, Sun 10:45-18:00). Train info: Tel. 0845-748-4950, NationalRail.co.uk.

By Bus: Bus #918 passes through Ballachulish—a half-mile from **Glencoe**—on its way to **Fort William** (2/day, 1 hour to Bal-lachulish, 1.5 hours total to Fort William). Take this bus to Fort William, then transfer to reach **Inverness** (4 hours) or **Portree** on the Isle of Skye (5 hours)—see page 308 for onward bus informa-tion. A different bus (#976 or #977) connects Oban with **Glasgow** (5/day, 3 hours), from where you can easily connect by bus or train to **Edinburgh** (figure 4.5 hours). Buses arrive and depart from a roundabout, marked by a stubby clock tower, just before the en-trance to the train station (tel. 0871-266-3333, www.citylink.co.uk). You can buy bus tickets at the West Coast shop near the bus stop, or at the TI across the harbor. Book in advance during peak times.

By Boat: Ferries fan out from Oban to the **southern Hebrides** (see information on the islands of Iona and Mull, later). Caledo-nian MacBrayne Ferry info: Tel. 0800-066-5000, CalMac.co.uk.

ROUTE TIPS FOR DRIVERS

From Glasgow to Oban via Loch Lomond and Inveraray: For details on this photogenic route from Glasgow to the coast, see the "Glasgow to Oban Drive" at the end of this chapter.

From Oban to Glencoe and Fort William: It's an easy one-hour drive from Oban to Glencoe. From Oban, follow the coastal A-828 toward Fort William. After about 20 miles—as you leave the village of Appin—you'll see the photogenic **Castle Stalker** ma-rooned on a lonely island (you can pull over at the Castle Stalker View Café for a good photo from just below its parking lot). At North Ballachulish, you'll reach a bridge spanning Loch Leven; rather than crossing the bridge, turn off and follow the A-82 into the Glencoe Valley for about 15 minutes. (For tips on the best views and hikes in Glencoe, see the next chapter.) After exploring the dramatic valley, make a U-turn and return through Glencoe village. To continue on to Fort William, backtrack to the bridge at North Ballachulish (great view from bridge) and cross it, following the A-82 north.

For a scenic shortcut directly back to Glasgow or Edinburgh, continue south on the A-82 after Glencoe via Rannoch Moor and Tyndrum. Crianlarich is where the road splits, and you'll either continue on the A-82 toward Loch Lomond and Glasgow or pick up the A-85 and follow signs for Stirling, then Edinburgh.

Isles of Mull, Iona, and Staffa

For the easiest one-day look at a good sample of the dramatic and historic Inner Hebrides (HEB-rid-eez) islands, take a tour from Oban to Mull, Iona, and Staffa. Though this trip is spectacular when it's sunny, it's worthwhile in any weather (but if rain or rough seas are expected, I'd skip the Staffa option). For an even more in-depth look at the Inner Hebrides, head north to Skye.

GETTING AROUND THE ISLANDS
Visiting Mull and Iona

To visit Mull and ultimately Iona, you'll take a huge ferry run by Caledonian MacBrayne (CalMac) from Oban to the town of Craignure on Mull (45 minutes). From there, you'll ride a bus or drive across Mull to its westernmost ferry terminal, called Fionnphort (1.25 hours), where you can catch the ferry to Iona (10 minutes) for several hours of free time. It's a long journey, but it's all incredibly scenic.

By Tour (Easiest): If you book a tour with **West Coast Tours,** all of the transportation is taken care of. The CalMac ferry leaves from the Oban pier daily at 9:50 (as schedule  can change from year to year, confirm times locally; board at least 20 minutes before departure). You can buy tickets online at www. westcoasttours.co.uk, from the West Coast Tours office, or from the Tour Shop Oban at the ferry building (tel. 01631/562-244, tourshop@calmac.co.uk). Book as far in advance as possible for July and August (tickets can sell out). When you book, you'll receive a strip of tickets—one for each leg; if you book online, you must go to the West Coast Tours office and collect the tickets in person (£39; April-Oct only, no tours Nov-March).

Tour Tips: The best inside seats on the **Oban-Mull ferry**—with the biggest windows—are in the sofa lounge on the "observation deck" (level 4) at the back end of the boat. (Follow signs for the toilets, and look for the big staircase to the top floor). The ferry has a fine cafeteria with hot meals and packaged sandwiches, a small snack bar on the top floor (hot drinks and basic sandwiches), and a bookshop. If it's a clear day, ask a local or a crew member to point out Ben Nevis, the tallest mountain in Britain. Five minutes before landing on Mull, you'll see the striking 13th-century Duart Castle on the left.

Walk-on passengers disembark from deck 3, across from the

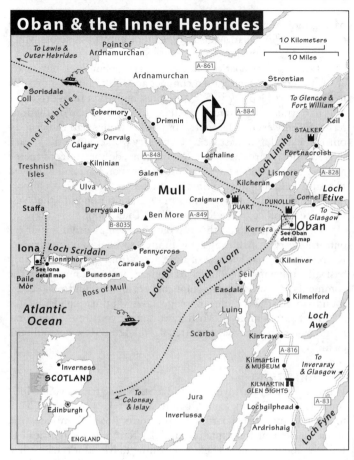

Oban & the Inner Hebrides

To Lewis & Outer Hebrides

Point of Ardnamurchan

10 Kilometers

10 Miles

Ardnamurchan

A-861

Strontian

Sorisdale

Coll

To Glencoe & Fort William

A-884

Keil

Tobermory

Drimnin

STALKER

Inner Hebrides

Dervaig

Calgary

A-848

Lochaline

Portnacroish

Loch Linnhe

Kilninian

Lismore

A-828

Treshnish Isles

Salen

Kilcheran

Loch Etive

Ulva

Mull

Craignure

DUNOLLIE

Connel

Staffa

Derryguaig

DUART

To Glasgow

▲ Ben More

A-849

Oban

See Oban detail map

B-8035

Kerrera

Iona Loch Scridain

Pennycross

Kilninver

Fionnphort

See Iona detail map

Carsaig

Firth of Lorn

Baile Mòr

Bunessan

Seil

Ross of Mull

Loch Buie

Easdale

Kilmelford

Atlantic Ocean

Luing

Loch Awe

Scarba

Kintraw

A-816

To Inveraray & Glasgow

Kilmartin & MUSEUM

Inverness

SCOTLAND

KILMARTIN GLEN SIGHTS

A-83

Jura

Lochgilphead

Loch Fyne

Edinburgh

To Colonsay & Islay

Inverlussa

Ardrishaig

ENGLAND

bookshop (port side). Upon arrival in Mull, find your **bus** for the entertaining and informative ride across the Isle of Mull. The right (driver's) side offers better sea views during the second half of the journey to Fionnphort, while the left side has fine views of Mull's rolling wilderness. The driver spends the entire ride chattering away about life on Mull, slowing to point out wildlife, and sharing adages like, "If there's no flowers on the gorse, snogging's gone out of fashion." These hardworking locals make historical trivia fascinating—or at least fun. At Fionnphort, you'll board a small, rocking **ferry to Iona.** You'll have about two hours to roam freely around the island before returning to Oban (arrives around 18:00).

By Public Transit: For an early start, fewer crowds, and more time on Iona (including spending the night—see "Sleeping and Eating on Iona"), or if you don't get a space on the tour described earlier, you can take the early ferry and public bus across Mull, paying individually per leg (Tue-Sat only; approximate round-trip prices: £7.40 for Oban-Mull ferry, £15 for public bus across Mull, £3.50 for Mull-Iona ferry).

Take the first boat of the day (departs about 7:30, buy ticket at Oban ferry terminal), then connect at Mull to bus #96 or #496 to Fionnphort (departs 8:25, 80 minutes, buy ticket from driver, no tour narration, no guarantee you'll get to sit), then hop on the Iona ferry (roughly every 30 minutes, buy ticket from small trailer ferry office; if closed, purchase ticket from ferry worker at the dock; cash or credit/debit cards accepted; leaving Iona, do the same, as there's no ferry office). You'll have about four hours on Iona and will need to return to Fionnphort in time for the bus back (15:15). It's important to confirm all of these times in Oban (just pop in to the West Coast Tours office or the ferry terminal Tour Shop).

By Car: You can do this trip on your own by driving your car onto the ferry to Mull. Space is limited so book way in advance. Keep in mind that because of tight ferry timings, you'll wind up basically following the tour buses anyway, but you'll miss all of the commentary. Note that no visitor cars are allowed on Iona (£27.50 round-trip for the car, plus passengers, www.calmac.co.uk).

By Taxi: Alan from **Mull Taxi** can get you around his home island, and also offers day trips (tel. 07760/426-351, www.mulltaxi.co.uk).

Visiting Staffa

With two extra hours, you can add a Staffa side trip to your Mull/Iona visit. You'll ferry from Oban to Mull, take a bus across Mull to Fionnphort, then board a **Staffa Tours** boat (35-minute trip, about an hour of free time on Staffa). From Staffa you'll head to Iona for about two hours before returning to Mull for the bus then ferry back to Oban. You can either depart Oban on the 9:50 ferry, arriving back to Oban around 20:05; or do the "early bird" tour, departing at 7:30 and returning at 18:00 (£35 for the Staffa portion, daily; book through West Coast Tours or Staffa Tours—mobile 07831-885-985, www.staffatours.com).

For a more relaxed schedule, **Staffa Trips** offers a guided tour with the same route as described above, but with more time on Staffa and Iona (£35, daily, depart Fionnphort at 10:30, tel. 01681/700-358, www.staffatrips.co.uk).

Turus Mara offers nature/wildlife tours to just Staffa or Staffa and the small island of Ulva, departing from Oban (book at Tour Shop at Oban ferry terminal or contact Turus Mara—tel. 01688/400-242, www.turusmara.com).

Mull

The Isle of Mull, the second largest of the Inner Hebrides (after Skye), has nearly 300 scenic miles of coastline and castles and a

3,169-foot-high mountain, one of Scotland's Munros. Called Ben More ("Big Mountain" in Gaelic), it was once much bigger. At 10,000 feet tall, it made up the entire island of Mull—until a volcano erupted. Things are calmer now, and, similarly, Mull has a noticeably laid-back population. My bus driver reported that there are no deaths from stress, and only a few from boredom.

With steep, fog-covered hillsides topped by cairns (piles of stones, sometimes indicating graves) and ancient stone circles, Mull has a gloomy, otherworldly charm. Bring plenty of rain protection and wear layers in case the sun peeks through the clouds. As my driver said, Mull is a place of cold, wet, windy winters and mild, wet, windy summers.

On the far side of Mull, the caravan of tour buses unloads at Fionnphort, a tiny ferry town. The ferry to the island of Iona takes about 200 walk-on passengers. Confirm the return time with your bus driver, then hustle to the dock to make the first trip over (otherwise, it's a 30-minute wait; on very busy days, those who dillydally may not fit on the first ferry). At the dock, there's a small ferry-passenger building with a meager snack bar and a pay WC; a more enticing seafood bar is across the street. After the 10-minute ride, you wash ashore on sleepy Iona (free WC on this side), and the ferry mobs that crowded you on the boat seem to disappear up the main road and into Iona's back lanes.

Iona

The tiny island of Iona, just 3 miles by 1.5 miles, is famous as the birthplace of Christianity in Scotland. If you're on the West Coast Tours bus trip from Oban outlined earlier, you'll have about two hours here on your own before you retrace your

OBAN & INNER HEBRIDES

steps (your bus driver will tell you which return ferry to take back to Mull).

A pristine quality of light and a thoughtful peace pervades the stark, (nearly) car-free island and its tiny community. With buoyant clouds bouncing playfully off distant bluffs, sparkling-white crescents of sand, and lone tourists camped thoughtfully atop huge rocks just looking out to sea, Iona is a place that's perfect for meditation. To experience Iona, it's important to get out and take a little hike; you can follow some or all of my self-guided walk outlined below. And you can easily climb a peak—nothing's higher than 300 feet above the sea.

Orientation to Iona

The ferry arrives at the island's only real village, Baile Mòr, with shops, a restaurant/pub, a few accommodations, and no bank (get cash back with a purchase at the grocery store). The only taxi based on Iona is **Iona Taxi** (mobile 07810-325-990, www.ionataxi.co.uk). Up the road from the ferry dock is a little **Spar** grocery with free island maps. Iona's official website (www.isle-of-iona.net) has good information about the island.

Iona Walk

Here's a basic self-guided route for exploring Iona on foot (since no private cars are permitted unless you're a resident or have a permit). With the standard two hours on Iona that a day trip allows, you will have time for a visit to the abbey (with a guided tour and/or audioguide) and then a light stroll; or do the entire walk described below, but skip the abbey (unless you have time for a quick visit on your way back).

Nunnery Ruins: From the ferry dock, head directly up the single paved road that passes through the village and up a small hill to visit one of Britain's best-preserved medieval nunneries (free).

Immediately after the nunnery, turn right on North Road. You'll curve up through the fields—passing the parish church.

Heritage Center: This little museum, tucked behind the church (watch for signs), is small but well done, with displays on local and natural history and a tiny tearoom (free but donation requested, closed Sun and in off-season, tel. 01681/700-576, www.ionaheritage.co.uk).

St. Oran's Chapel and Iona Abbey: Continue on North Road. After the road swings right, you'll soon see **St. Oran's Chapel,** in the graveyard of the Iona Abbey. This chapel is the oldest church building on the island. Inside you'll find a few grave slabs carved in the distinctive Iona School style, which was developed

History of Iona

St. Columba (521-597), an Irish scholar, soldier, priest, and founder of monasteries, got into a small war over the posses-

sion of an illegally copied psalm book. Victorious but sickened by the bloodshed, Columba left Ireland, vowing never to return. According to legend, the first bit of land out of sight of his homeland was Iona. He stopped here in 563 and established an abbey.

Columba's monastic community flourished, and Iona became the center of Celtic Christianity. Missionaries from Iona spread the gospel throughout Scotland and northern England, while scholarly monks established Iona as a center of art and learning. The Book of Kells—perhaps the finest piece of manuscript art from early medieval Europe—was probably made on Iona in the eighth century. The island was so important that it was the legendary burial place for ancient Scottish clan chieftains and kings (including Macbeth, of Shakespeare fame) and even some Scandinavian monarchs.

Slowly, the importance of Iona ebbed. Vikings massacred 68 monks in 806. Fearing more raids, the monks evacuated most of Iona's treasures to Ireland (including the Book of Kells, which is now in Dublin). Much later, with the Reformation, the abbey was abandoned, and most of its finely carved crosses were destroyed. In the 17th century, locals used the abbey only as a handy quarry for other building projects.

Iona's population peaked at about 500 in the 1830s. In the 1840s, a potato famine hit, and in the 1850s, a third of the islanders emigrated to Canada or Australia. By 1900, the population was down to 210, and today it's only around 200.

But in our generation, a new religious community has given the abbey fresh life. The Iona Community is an ecumenical gathering of men and women who seek new ways of living the Gospel in today's world, with a focus on worship, peace and justice issues, and reconciliation (http://iona.org.uk).

OBAN & INNER HEBRIDES

by local stone-carvers in the 14th century. On these tall, skinny headstones, look for the depictions of medieval warrior aristocrats with huge swords. Many more of these carvings have been moved to the abbey, where you can see them in its cloister and museum.

It's free to see the graveyard and chapel; the ▲ **Iona Abbey** itself has an admission fee, but it's worth the cost just to sit in the stillness of its lovely, peaceful interior courtyard (£9, tel. 01681/700-512, www.historicenvironment.scot—search for "Iona Abbey").

The abbey marks the site of Christianity's arrival in Scotland. You'll see Celtic crosses, the original shrine of St. Columba, a big church slathered with medieval carvings, a tranquil cloister, and an excellent museum with surviving fragments of this site's fascinating layers of history. While the

present abbey, nunnery, and graveyard go back to the 13th century, much of what you'll see was rebuilt in the 20th century. Be sure to read the "History of Iona" sidebar to prepare for your visit.

At the entrance building, pick up your included audioguide, and ask about the good 30-minute guided tours (4/day and worthwhile). Then head toward the church. You'll pass two faded **Celtic crosses** (and the base of a third); the originals are in the museum at the end of your visit. Some experts believe that Celtic crosses—with their distinctive shape so tied to Christianity on the British Isles—originated right here on Iona.

Facing the entrance to the church, you'll see the original **shrine to St. Columba** on your left—a magnet for pilgrims.

Head inside the **church.** It feels like an active church—with hymnals neatly stacked in the pews—because it is, thanks to the Iona community. While much of this space has been rebuilt, take a moment to look around. Plenty of original medieval stone carving (especially the capitals of many columns) still survives. To see a particularly striking example, stand near the pulpit in the middle of the church and look back to the entrance. Partway up the left span of the pointed arch framing the transept, look for the eternally screaming face. While interpretations vary, this may have been a reminder for the priest not to leave out the fire-and-brimstone parts of his message. Some of the newer features of the church—including the base of the baptismal font near the entrance, and the main altar—are carved from locally quarried Iona marble: white with green streaks. In the right/south transept is the tomb of George Campbell—the Eighth Duke of Argyll, who donated this property in 1900, allowing it to be restored.

When you're ready to continue, find the poorly marked door into the **cloister.** (As you face the altar, it's about halfway down the nave on the left, before the transept.) This space is filled with harmonious light,

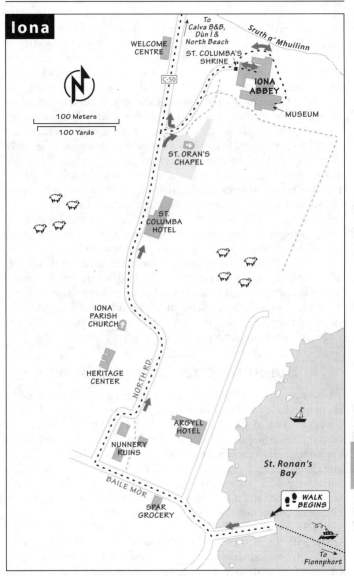

Iona

To Calva B&B, Dùn Ì & North Beach

Sruth a' Mhuilinn

WELCOME CENTRE

ST. COLUMBA'S SHRINE

C-50

IONA ABBEY

MUSEUM

100 Meters

100 Yards

ST. ORAN'S CHAPEL

ST. COLUMBA HOTEL

IONA PARISH CHURCH

NORTH RD.

HERITAGE CENTER

ARGYLL HOTEL

NUNNERY RUINS

St. Ronan's Bay

BAILE MÒR

WALK BEGINS

SPAR GROCERY

To Fionnphort

OBAN & INNER HEBRIDES

additional finely carved capitals (these are modern re-creations), and—displayed along the walls—several more of the tall, narrow tombstones like the ones displayed in St. Oran's Chapel. On these, look for a couple of favorite motifs: the long, intimidating sword (indicating a warrior of the Highland clans) and the ship with billowing sails (a powerful symbol of this seafaring culture).

Around the far side of the cloister is the shop. But before leaving, don't overlook the easy-to-miss **museum.** (To find it, head outside and walk around the left side of the abbey complex, toward the sea.) This modern, well-presented space exhibits a remarkable collection of original stonework from the abbey—including what's left of the three Celtic crosses out front—all eloquently described.

Iona Community's Welcome Centre: Just beyond and across the road from the abbey is the Iona Community's Welcome Centre (free WCs), which runs the abbey with Historic Scotland and hosts modern-day pilgrims who come here to experience the birthplace of Scottish Christianity. (If you're staying longer, you could attend a worship service at the abbey—check the schedule here; tel. 01681/700-404, www.iona.org.uk.) Its gift shop is packed with books on the island's important role in Christian history.

Views: A 10-minute walk on North Road past the welcome center brings you to the footpath for **Dùn Ì,** a steep but short climb with good views of the abbey looking back toward Mull.

North Beach: Returning to the main road, walk another 20-25 minutes to the end of the paved road, where you'll arrive at a gate leading through a sheep- and cow-strewn pasture to Iona's pristine white-sand beach. Dip your toes in the Atlantic and ponder what this Caribbean-like alcove is doing in Scotland. Be sure to allow at least 40 minutes to return to the ferry dock.

Sleeping and Eating on Iona

For a chance to really experience peaceful, idyllic Iona, spend a night or two (Scots bring their kids and stay on this tiny island for a week). To do so, you'll have to buy each leg of the ferry-bus-ferry (and return) trip separately (see "By Public Transit," earlier). These accommodations are listed roughly in the order you'll reach them as you climb the main road from the ferry dock. The first two hotels listed have **$$$** restaurants that are open to the public for lunch, tea, and dinner and closed in winter. For more accommodation options, see Isle-of-Iona.net/accommodation.

$$$ Argyll Hotel, built in 1867, proudly overlooks the waterfront, with 17 cottage-like rooms and pleasingly creaky hallways lined with bookshelves. Of the two hotels, this one feels classier (reserve far in advance for summer, comfortable lounge and sunroom, tel. 01681/700-334, www.argyllhoteliona.co.uk, reception@ argyllhoteliona.co.uk).

$$$ St. Columba Hotel, a bit higher up in town and situated in the middle of a peaceful garden with picnic tables, has 27 institutional rooms and spacious lodge-like common spaces—such as a big, cushy seaview lounge (closed Nov-March, next door to abbey on road up from dock, tel. 01681/700-304, www.stcolumba-hotel. co.uk, info@stcolumba-hotel.co.uk).

$$ Calva B&B, a five-minute walk past the abbey, has three spacious rooms (second house on left past the abbey, look for sign in window and gnomes on porch, tel. 01681/700-340; friendly Janetta and Ken).

Staffa

Those more interested in nature than in church history will enjoy the trip to the wildly scenic Isle of Staffa. Completely uninhabited (except for seabirds), Staffa is a knob of rock draped with a vibrant green carpet of turf. Remote and quiet, it feels like a Hebrides nature preserve.

Most day trips give you an hour on Staffa—barely enough time to see its two claims to fame: The basalt columns of Fingal's Cave, and (in summer) a colony of puffins. To squeeze in both, be ready to hop off the boat and climb the staircase. Partway up to the left, you can walk around to the cave (about 7 minutes). Or continue up to the top, then turn right and walk across the spine of the grassy island (about 10-15 minutes) to the cove where the puffins gather. Be sure to get clear instructions from your captain on how and where to best watch the puffins. It's worth doing right.

▲▲Fingal's Cave
Staffa's shore is covered with bizarre, mostly hexagonal basalt columns that stick up at various heights. It's as if the earth were offering God his choice of thousands of six-sided cigarettes. (The island's name likely came from the Old Norse word for "stave"—the building timbers these columns resemble.) This is the other end of Northern Ireland's popular Giant's Causeway. You'll walk along the uneven surface of these columns, curling around the far side of the island, until you can actually step inside the gaping mouth of a cave—where floor-to-ceiling columns and crashing waves combine to create a powerful experience. Listening to the water and air

OBAN & INNER HEBRIDES

Puffins

The Atlantic puffin (Fratercula arctica) is an adorably stout, tuxedo-clad seabird with a too-big orange beak and beady black eyes. Puffins live most of their lives on the open Atlantic, coming to land only to breed. They fly north to Scotland between mid-May and early June, raise their brood, then take off again in August. Puffins mate for life and typically lay just one egg each year, which the male and female take turns caring for. A baby puffin is called—wait for it—a puffling.

To feed their pufflings, puffins plunge as deep as 200 feet below the sea's surface to catch sand eels, herring, and other small fish. Their compact bodies, stubby wings, oil-sealed plumage, and webbed feet are ideal for navigating underwater. Famously, puffins can stuff several small fish into their beaks at once, thanks to their agile tongues and uniquely hinged beaks. This evolutionary trick lets puffins stock up before returning to the nest.

Squat, tiny-winged puffins have a distinctive way of flying. To take off, they either beat their wings like crazy (on sea) or essentially hurl themselves off a cliff (on land). Once aloft, they beat their wings furiously—up to 400 times per minute—to stay airborne. Coming in for a smooth landing on a rocky cliff is a challenge (and highly entertaining to watch): They choose a spot, swoop in at top speed on prevailing currents, then flutter their wings madly to brake as they try to touch down. At the moment of truth, the puffin decides whether to attempt to stick the landing; more often than not, he bails out and does another big circle on the currents...and tries again...and again...and again.

flowing through this otherworldly space inspired Felix Mendelssohn to compose his overture, *The Hebrides*.

While you're ogling the cave, consider this: Geologists claim these unique formations were created by volcanic eruptions more than 60 million years ago. As the surface of the lava flow quickly cooled, it contracted and crystallized into columns (resembling the caked mud at the bottom of a dried-up lakebed, but with deeper cracks). As the rock later settled and eroded, the columns broke off into the many stair-like steps that now honeycomb Staffa.

Of course, in actuality, these formations resulted from a heated rivalry between a Scottish giant named Fingal, who lived on Staffa, and an Ulster warrior named Finn MacCool, who lived across the sea on Ireland's Antrim Coast. Knowing that the giant was coming to spy on him, Finn had his wife dress him as a sleeping infant. The giant, shocked at the infant's size, fled back to Scotland in terror of whomever had sired this giant baby. Breathing a sigh of relief, Finn tore off the baby clothes and prudently knocked down the bridge.

▲▲Puffin Watching

A large colony of Atlantic puffins settles on Staffa each spring and summer during mating season (generally early May through early August). The puffins tend to  scatter when the boat arrives. But after the boat pulls out and its passengers hike across the island, the very tame puffins' curiosity gets the better of them. First you'll see them flutter up from the offshore rocks, with their distinctive, bobbing flight. They'll zip and whirl around, and finally they'll start to land on the lip of the cove. Sit quietly, move slowly, and be patient, and soon they'll get close. (If any seagulls are nearby, shoo them away—puffins are undaunted by humans, who do them no harm, but they're terrified of predatory seagulls.)

In the waters around Staffa—on your way to and from the other islands—also keep an eye out for a variety of **marine life,** including seals, dolphins, porpoises, and the occasional minke whale, fin whale, or basking shark (a gigantic fish that hinges open its enormous jaw to drift-net plankton).

Glasgow to Oban Drive

The following drive outlines the best route from Glasgow to Oban, including the appealing town of Inveraray, with an optional stop at one of Scotland's most important prehistoric sites, Kilmartin Glen.

GLASGOW TO OBAN VIA INVERARAY

The drive from Glasgow (or Edinburgh) to Oban via Inveraray provides dreamy vistas and your first look at the dramatic landscapes of the Highlands, as well as historic sites and ample opportunity to stop for a picnic.

• *Leaving Glasgow on the A-82, you'll soon be driving along the west bank of...*

OBAN & INNER HEBRIDES

Loch Lomond

The first picnic turnout has the best views of this famous lake (described on page 210), benches, a park, and a playground. You're driving over an isthmus between Loch Lomond and a sea inlet. Halfway up the loch, you'll find the town of Tarbet—the Viking word for isthmus, a common name on Scottish maps. Imagine, a thousand years ago, Vikings dragging their ships across this narrow stretch of land to reach Loch Lomond.

• *At Tarbet, the road forks. The signs for Oban keep you on the direct route along A-82. For the scenic option that takes you past Loch Fyne to Inveraray (about 30 minutes longer to drive), keep left for the A-83 (toward Campbeltown).*

Highland Boundary Fault

You'll pass the village of **Arrochar,** then drive along the banks of Loch Long. The scenery crescendos as you pull away from the loch and twist up over the mountains and through a pine forest, getting your first glimpse of bald Highlands mountains—it's clear that you've just crossed the **Highland Boundary Fault.** Enjoy the waterfalls, and notice that the road signs are now in English as well as Gaelic. As you climb into more rugged territory—up the valley called Glen Croe—be mindful that the roads connecting the Lowlands with the Highlands (like the one down in the glen below) were originally a military project designed to facilitate government quelling of the Highland clans.

• *At the summit, watch for the large parking lot with picnic tables on your left (signed for Argyll Forest Park). Stretch your legs at what's aptly named...*

Rest-and-Be-Thankful Pass

The colorful name comes from the 19th century, when just reaching this summit was exhausting. At the top of the military road,

just past the last picnic table, there's actually a stone (dated 1814) put there by the military with that phrase.

As you drive on, enjoy the dramatic green hills. You may see little bits of hillside highlighted by sunbeams. Each of these is known as a "soot" (Sun's Out Over There). Look for soots as you drive farther north into the Highlands.

• *Continue twisting down the far side of the pass. You'll drive through Glen Kinglas and soon reach...*

Loch Fyne

This saltwater "sea loch" is famous for its shellfish (keep an eye out for oyster farms and seafood restaurants). In fact, Loch Fyne is the namesake of a popular UK restaurant chain with locations across the UK. **$$$$ Loch Fyne Oyster Bar and Deli,** in the big white building at the end of the loch, is the original. It's a famous stop for locals—an elegant seafood restaurant and oyster bar worth travel-ing for. If the restaurant is full, order from the bar menu (about the same as the restaurant) and grab more casual seating (open daily from 9:00, last order at 17:45, no reservations, tel. 01499/600-482, www.lochfyne.com). Even if you're not eating, it's fun to peruse their salty deli (tasty treats to go, picnic tables outside, good coffee).

• *Looping around Loch Fyne, you approach Inveraray. As you get close, keep an eye on the right (when crossing the bridge, have your camera ready) for the dramatic...*

▲Inveraray Castle

This residence of the Duke of Argyll comes with a dramatic, tur-reted exterior (one of Scotland's most striking) and an interior that feels spacious, neatly tended, and lived in. His-torically a stronghold of one of the more notorious branches of the Campbell clan, this castle is most appealing to those with Campbell connections or fans of *Downton Abbey*.

Cost and Hours: £12.50, daily 10:00-17:45, closed Nov-March, last entry 45 min-utes before closing, nice basement café, buy tickets at the car-park booth, tel. 01499/302-551, www.inveraray-castle.com.

Visiting the Castle: Roam from room to room, reading the laminated descriptions and asking questions of the gregarious do-cents. The highlight is the Armory Hall that fills the main atrium, where swords and rifles are painstakingly arrayed in starburst pat-terns. The rifles were actually used when the Campbells fought with the British at the Battle of Culloden in 1746.

Upstairs is a room with reminders of *Downton Abbey*. Pub-lic television fans may recognize this as "Duneagle Castle" (a.k.a. Uncle Shrimpy's pad) from one of the *Downton Abbey* Christmas specials—big photos of the Grantham and MacClare clans deco-rate the genteel rooms.

As with many such castles, the aristocratic clan still lives here (*private* signs mark rooms where the family resides). Another up-

OBAN & INNER HEBRIDES

The Irish Connection

The Romans called the people living in what is now Ireland the "Scoti" (meaning pirates). When the Scoti crossed the narrow Irish Sea and invaded the land of the Picts 1,500 years ago, that region became known as Scoti-land. Ireland and Scotland were never fully conquered by the Romans, and they retained similar clannish Celtic traits. Both share the same Gaelic branch of the linguistic tree.

On clear summer days, you can actually see Ireland—just 17 miles away—from the Scottish coastline. The closest bit to Scotland is the boomerang-shaped Rathlin Island, part of Northern Ireland. Rathlin is where Scottish leader Robert the Bruce retreated in 1307 after defeat at the hands of the English. Legend has it that he hid in a cave on the island, where he observed a spider patiently rebuilding its web each time a breeze knocked it down. Inspired by the spider's perseverance, Bruce gathered his Scottish forces once more and finally defeated the English at the decisive battle of Bannockburn (see page 73).

Flush with confidence from his victory, Robert the Bruce decided to open a second front against the English...in Ireland. In 1315, he sent his brother Edward over to enlist their Celtic Irish cousins in an effort to thwart the English. After securing Ireland, Edward hoped to move on and enlist the Welsh, thus cornering England with their pan-Celtic nation. But Edward's timing was bad: Ireland was in the midst of famine. His Scottish troops had to live off the land and began to take food and supplies from the starving Irish. Some of Ireland's crops may have been intentionally destroyed to keep it from being used as a colonial "breadbasket" to feed English troops. The Scots quickly wore out their welcome, and Edward the Bruce was eventually killed in battle near Dundalk in 1318.

It's interesting to imagine how things might be different today if Scotland and Ireland had been permanently welded together as a nation 700 years ago. You'll notice the strong Scottish influence in Northern Ireland when you ask a local a question and he answers, "Aye, a wee bit." And in Glasgow— near Scotland's west coast, closest to Ireland—an Ireland-like division between royalist Protestants and republican Catholics survives today in the form of soccer team allegiances. In big Scottish cities (like Glasgow and Edinburgh), you'll even see "orange parades" of protesters marching in solidarity with their Protestant Northern Irish cousins.

The Irish—always quick to defuse tension with humor—joke that the Scots are just Irish people who couldn't swim home.

stairs room is like an Argyll family scrapbook; for example, see photos of the duke playing elephant polo—the ultimate aristocratic sport. The kids attend school in England, but spend a few months here each year; in the winter, the castle is closed to the public and they have the run of the place. After touring the interior, do a loop through the finely manicured gardens

• *After visiting the castle, spend some time exploring...*

▲Inveraray Town

Nearly everybody stops at this lovely, seemingly made-for-tourists town on Loch Fyne. Browse the main street—lined with touristy shops and cafés all the way to the church at its top. As this is the geological and demographic border between the Highlands and the Lowlands, traditionally church services here were held in both Scots and Gaelic. Just before the church is Loch Fyne Whiskies with historic bottles on its ceiling.

There's free parking on the main street and plenty of pay-and-display parking near the pier (TI open daily, on Front Street, tel. 01499/302-063; public WCs at end of nearby pier).

The **Inveraray Jail** is the main site in town—an overpriced, corny, but mildly educational former jail converted into a museum. This "living 19th-century prison" includes a courtroom where mannequins argue the fate of the accused. Then you'll head outside and explore the various cells of the outer courtyard. The playful guards may lock you up for a photo op, while they explain how Scotland reformed its prison system in 1839—you'll see both "before" and "after" cells in this complex (£12.25, includes 75-minute audioguide, open daily, tel. 01499/302-381, www.inverarayjail.co.uk).

• *To continue directly to Oban from Inveraray (about an hour), leave town through the gate at the woolen mill and get on the A-819, which takes you through Glen Aray and along the aptly named Loch Awe. A left turn on the A-85 takes you into Oban.*

But if you have a healthy interest in prehistoric sites, you can go to Oban by way of Kilmartin Glen (adds about 45 minutes of driving). To get there from Inveraray, head straight up Inveraray's main street and get on the waterfront A-83 (marked for Campbeltown); after a half-hour, in Lochgilphead, turn right onto the A-816, which takes you through Kilmartin Glen and all the way up to Oban. (To avoid backtracking, be ready to stop at the prehistoric sites lining the A-816 between Lochgilphead and Kilmartin village.)

Kilmartin Glen

Except for the Orkney Islands, Scotland isn't as rich with prehistoric sites as South England is, but the ones in Kilmartin Glen, while faint, are some of Scotland's most accessible—and most

OBAN & INNER HEBRIDES

important. This wide valley, clearly imbued with spiritual and/or strategic power, contains reminders of several millennia worth of inhabitants. Today it's a playground for those who enjoy tromping through grassy fields while daydreaming about who moved these giant stones here so many centuries ago. This isn't worth a long detour, unless you're fascinated by prehistoric sites.

Four to five thousand years ago, Kilmartin Glen was inhabited by Neolithic people who left behind fragments of their giant, stony monuments. And 1,500 years ago, this was the seat of the kings of the Scoti, who migrated here from Ireland around AD 500, giving rise to Scotland's own branch of Celtic culture. From this grassy valley, the Scoti kings ruled their empire, called Dalriada (also sometimes written Dál Riata), which encompassed much of Scotland's west coast, the Inner Hebrides, and the northern part of Ireland. The Scoti spoke Gaelic and were Christian; as they overtook the rest of the Highlands—eventually absorbing their rival Picts—theirs became a dominant culture, which is still evident in pockets of present-day Scotland.  Today, Kilmartin Glen is scattered with burial cairns, standing stones, and a hill called Dunadd—the fortress of the Scoti kings.

Visiting Kilmartin Glen: Sites are scattered throughout the valley, including some key locations along or just off the A-816 south of Kilmartin village. If you're coming from Inveraray, you'll pass these *before* you reach the village and museum itself. Each one is explained by good informational signs.

Dunadd: This bulbous hill sits just west of the A-816, about four miles north of Lochgilphead and four miles south of Kilmartin village (watch for blue, low-profile *Dunadd Fort* signs). A fort had stood here since the time of Christ, but it was the Scoti kings—who made it their primary castle from the sixth to ninth centuries—that put Dunadd on the map. Park in the big lot at its base and hike through the faint outlines of terraces to the top, where you can enjoy sweeping views over all of Kilmartin Glen; this southern stretch is a marshland called "The Great Moss" (Moine Mhor). Look for carvings in the rock: early Celtic writing, the image of a boar, and a footprint (carved into a stone crisscrossed with fissures). This "footprint of fealty" (a replica) recalls the inauguration ceremony in which the king would place his foot into the footprint, symbolizing the marriage between the ruler and the land.

Dunchraigaig Cairn: About two miles farther north on the A-816, brown *Dunchraigaig* signs mark a parking lot where you can cross the road to the 4,000-year-old, 100-foot-in-diameter Dunchraigaig Cairn—the burial place for 10 Neolithic VIPs. Circle around to find the opening, where you can still crawl into a small recess. This is one of at least five such cairns that together created a mile-and-a-half-long "linear cemetery" up the middle of Kilmartin Glen.

From this cairn, you can walk five minutes to several more prehistoric structures: Follow signs through the gate, and walk to a farm field with **Ballymeanoch**—an avenue of two stone rows (with six surviving stones), a disheveled old cairn, and a stone circle.

Sites near Kilmartin Burn: About one more mile north on the A-816, just off the intersection with the B-8025 (toward *Tayvallich*), is the small Kilmartin Burn parking lot. From here, cross the stream to a field where the five **Nether Largie Standing Stones** have stood in a neat north-south line for 3,200 years. Were these stones designed as an astronomical observatory? Burial rituals or other religious ceremonies? Sporting events? Or just a handy place for sheep to scratch themselves? From here, you can hike the rest of the way through the field (about 10 minutes) to the **Nether Largie South Cairn** and the **Temple Wood Stone Circles** (which don't have their own parking). The larger, older of these circles dates to more than 5,000 years ago, and both were added onto and modified over the millennia.

Kilmartin Museum: To get the big picture, head for the Kilmartin Museum, in the center of Kilmartin village. The cute stone house has a ticket desk, bookshop, and café; the museum—with exhibits explaining this area's powerful history—fills the basement of the adjacent building (though a new home for the exhibit is in the works). The modest but modern museum features handy explanations, a few original artifacts, and lots of re-creations (£7, daily, closed Christmas-Feb, tel. 01546/510-278, www.kilmartin.org).

From the museum, you can look out across the fields to see **Glebe Cairn,** one of the five cairns of the "linear cemetery." Another one, the **Nether Largie North Cairn,** was reconstructed in the 1970s and can actually be entered (a half-mile south of the museum; ask for directions at museum).

Many more prehistoric sites fill Kilmartin Glen (more than 800 within a six-mile radius); the museum sells in-depth guidebooks for the curious, and can point you in the right direction for what you're interested in.

OBAN & INNER HEBRIDES

GLENCOE & FORT WILLIAM

Glencoe • Fort William • Road to the Isles

Scotland is a land of great natural wonders. And some of the most spectacular—and most accessible—are in the valley called Glencoe, just an hour north of Oban and on the way to Fort William, Loch Ness, Inverness, or the Isle of Skye. The evocative "Weeping Glen" of Glencoe aches with both history and natural beauty. Beyond that, Fort William anchors the southern end of the Caledonian Canal, offering a springboard to more Highlands scenery. This is where Britain's highest peak, Ben Nevis, keeps its head in the clouds, and where you'll find a valley made famous by a bonnie prince...and (later) by a steam train carrying a young wizard named Harry.

PLANNING YOUR TIME

On a quick visit, this area warrants just a few hours between Oban and either Inverness or Skye: Wander through Glencoe village, tour its modest museum, then drive up Glencoe valley for views before continuing north. But if you have only a day or two to linger in the Highlands, Glencoe is an ideal place to do it. Settle in for a night (or more) to make time for a more leisurely drive and to squeeze in a hike or two.

Beyond Glencoe, Fort William—a touristy and overrated transportation hub—is skippable, but can be a handy lunch stop. The Road to the Isles, stretching west from Fort William to the coast, isn't worth a detour on its own, but is very handy for those connecting to the Isle of Skye. Along the way, the only stop worth more than a quick photo is the village of Glenfinnan, with its powerful ties to Bonnie Prince Charlie and Jacobite history.

Glencoe

This valley is the essence of the wild, powerful, and stark beauty of the Highlands. Along with its scenery, Glencoe offers a good dose of bloody clan history: In 1692, government Red-coats (led by a local Camp-bell commander) came to the valley, and were shel-tered and fed for 12 days by the MacDonalds—whose leader had been late in swearing an oath to the British monarch. Then,

on the morning of February 13, the soldiers were ordered to rise up early and kill their sleeping hosts, violating the rules of High-land hospitality and earning the valley the nickname "The Weep-ing Glen." Thirty-eight men were killed outright; hundreds more fled through a blizzard, and some 40 additional villagers (mostly women and children) died from exposure. It's fitting that such an epic, dramatic incident—dubbed the Glencoe Massacre—should be set in this equally epic, dramatic valley, where the cliffsides seem to weep (with running streams) when it rains.

Aside from its tragic history, this place has captured the imaginations of both hikers and artists. Movies filmed here include everything from *Monty Python and the Holy Grail* to *Harry Potter and the Prisoner of Azkaban* and the James Bond film *Skyfall,* and Glencoe appears in the opening credits for the TV series *Outlander.* When filmmakers want a stunning, rugged backdrop; when hikers want a scenic challenge; and when Scots want to remember their hard-fought past...they all think of Glencoe.

Orientation to Glencoe

The valley of Glencoe is an easy side trip just off the main A-828/A-82 road between Oban and points north (such as Fort William and Inverness). If you're coming from the north, the signage can be tricky—at the roundabout south of Fort William, follow signs to *Crianlarich* and *A-82.* The most appealing town here is the sleepy one-street village of Glencoe, worth a stop for its folk mu-seum and its status as the gateway to the valley. The town's hub of activity is its grocery store, which has an ATM (daily 8:00-19:30). The slightly larger and more modern town of Ballachulish (a half-mile away) has more services, including a Co-op grocery store (daily 7:00-22:00).

In the loch just outside Glencoe (near Ballachulish), notice the

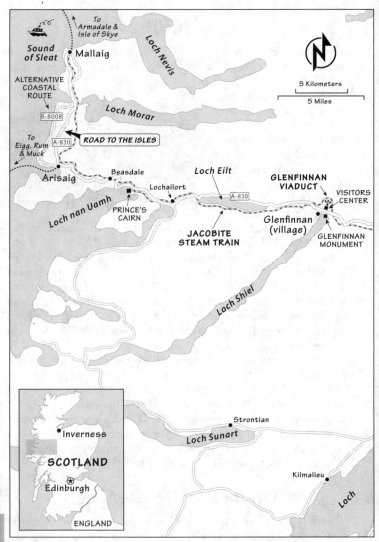

GLENCOE & FORT WILLIAM

burial island—where the souls of those who "take the low road" are piped home. (For an explanation of "Ye'll take the high road, and I'll take the low road," see page 211.) The next island was the Island of Discussion—where those in dispute went until they found agreement.

TOURIST INFORMATION

Your best source of information (especially for walks and hikes) is the **Glencoe Visitor Centre,** described later. The nearest **TI** is in the next town, Ballachulish (buried inside The Quarry Centre—

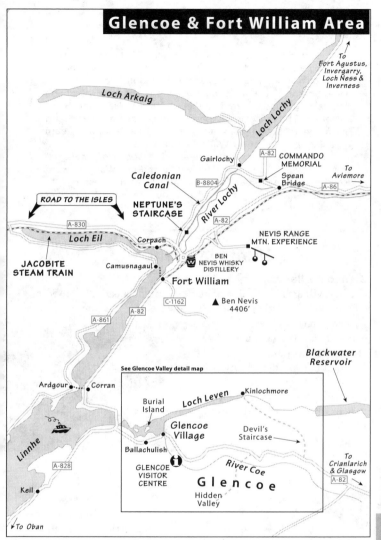

Glencoe & Fort William Area

a café/gift shop, daily 9:00-17:00, Nov-Easter 10:00-16:00, tel. 01855/811-866, www.glencoetourism.co.uk). For more information on the area, see www.discoverglencoe.com.

Bike Rental: At **Crank It Up Gear,** Davy rents road and mountain bikes, and can offer plenty of suggestions for where to pedal in the area (£15/half-day, £25/all day, just off the main street to the left near the start of town, 20 Lorn Drive, mobile 07746-860-023, www.glencoebikehire.com, book ahead).

Harry Potter Sights

Harry Potter's story is set in a magical, largely fictional Britain, but you can visit real locations used in the film series. Glencoe was the main location for outdoor filming in *The Prisoner of Azkaban* and *The Half-Blood Prince,* and many shots of the Hogwarts grounds were filmed in the Fort William and Glencoe areas. The Hogwarts Express that carries Harry, Ron, and Hermione to school runs along the actual Jacobite Steam Train line (between Fort William and Mallaig).

In *The Prisoner of Azkaban* and *The Goblet of Fire,* Loch Shiel, Loch Eilt, and Loch Morar (near Fort William) were stand-ins for the Great Lake. Steall Falls, at the base of Ben Nevis, is the locale for the Triwizard Tournament in *The Goblet of Fire.*

Sights in Glencoe

Glencoe Village

Glencoe village is just a line of houses sitting beneath the brooding mountains. The only real sight in town is the folk museum (described later). But walking the

main street gives a good glimpse of village Scotland. From the free parking lot at the entrance to town, go for a stroll. You'll pass a few little B&Bs renting two or three rooms, the stony Episcopal church, the folk museum, the town's grocery store, and the village hall.

At the far end of the village, on the left just before the bridge, a Celtic cross **WWI** memorial stands on a little hill. Even this wee

village lost 11 souls during that war—a reminder of Scotland's disproportionate contribution to Britain's war effort. You'll see memorials like this (usually either a Celtic cross or a soldier with bowed head) in virtually every town in Scotland.

If you were to cross the little bridge, you'd head up into Glencoe's wooded parklands, with some easy hikes (described later). But for one more landmark, turn right just before the bridge and walk about five minutes. Standing on a craggy bluff on your right is another memorial—this one to the **Glencoe Massacre,** which still haunts the memories of people here and throughout Scotland.

Glencoe Folk Museum

This gathering of thatched-roof, early-18th-century croft houses is a volunteer-run community effort. It's jammed with local history,

creating a huggable museum filled with humble exhibits gleaned from the town's old closets and attics. When one house was being rethatched, its owner found a cache of 200-year-old swords and pistols hidden there from the government Redcoats after the disastrous Battle of Culloden. You'll also see antique toys, boxes from old food products, sports paraphernalia, a cabinet of curiosities, evocative old black-and-white photos, and plenty of information on the MacDonald clan. Be sure to look for the museum's little door that leads out back, where additional, smaller buildings are filled with everyday items (furniture, farm tools, and so on) and exhibits on the Glencoe Massacre and a beloved Highland doctor (£3, Mon-Sat 10:00-16:30, closed Sun and Nov-March, tel. 01855/811-664, www.glencoemuseum.com). You can listen to an interview with the late Arthur Smith, a local historian, about the valley and its story in the "Scottish Highlands" program available on my Rick Steves Audio Europe app—for details, see page 26.

Glencoe Visitor Centre

This modern facility, a mile past Glencoe village up the A-82 into the dramatic valley, is designed to resemble a *clachan,* or traditional Highland settlement. The information desk inside the gift shop is your single best resource for advice (and maps or guidebooks) about local walks and hikes (several of which are outlined later in this chapter). At the back of the complex you'll find a viewpoint with a handy 3-D model of the hills for orientation; an easy woodland walk starts from here. There's also a small, rotating exhibit, generally covering the nature and mountaineering of the area, as well as a short film (topic changes yearly). Though worth a quick stop, the whole place can feel like an afterthought to its gift shop, through which you must enter and exit (free, parking-£4; daily 9:00-18:00, Nov-March 10:00-16:00; café, tel. 01855/811-307, http://www.nts. org.uk—search for "Glencoe").

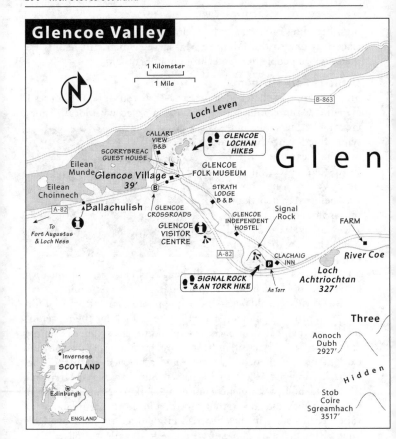

Glencoe Valley

Glencoe Valley

1 Kilometer
1 Mile

Loch Leven

B-863

G l e n

CALLART VIEW B&B

GLENCOE LOCHAN HIKES

SCORRYBREAC GUEST HOUSE

Eilean Munde

Glencoe Village 39'

GLENCOE FOLK MUSEUM

Eilean Choinnech

STRATH LODGE B&B

A-82 Ballachulish

GLENCOE CROSSROADS

GLENCOE INDEPENDENT HOSTEL

Signal Rock

FARM

To Fort Augustus & Loch Ness

GLENCOE VISITOR CENTRE

A-82

CLACHAIG INN

River Coe

SIGNAL ROCK & AN TORR HIKE

An Torr

Loch Achtriochtan 327'

Three

Aonoch Dubh 2927'

Hidden

Inverness

SCOTLAND

Edinburgh

ENGLAND

Stob Coire Sgreamhach 3517'

Glencoe Valley Drive

If you have a car, spend an hour or so following the A-82 through the valley, past the Glencoe Visitor Centre, up into the desolate moor beyond, and back again. You'll enjoy grand views, dramatic craggy hills, and, if you're lucky, a chance to hear a bagpiper in the wind: Roadside Highland buskers often set up here on good-weather summer weekends. (If you play the recorder—and the piper's not swarmed with other tourists—ask to finger a tune while he does the hard work.)

Here's a brief explanation of the route. Along the way, I've pointed out sometimes easy-to-miss trailheads, in case you're up for a hike (hikes described in the next section).

From Glencoe Village to the End of the Valley: Leaving Glencoe village on the A-82, it's just a mile to the **Glencoe Visitor Centre** (on the right, described earlier). Soon after, the road pulls

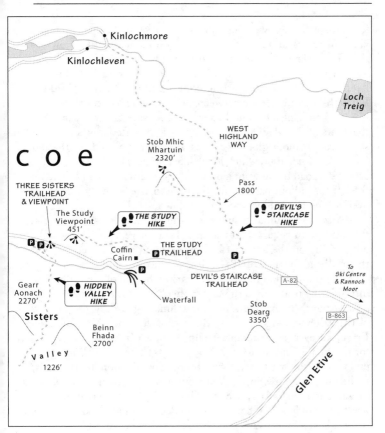

out of the forested hills and gives you unobstructed views of the U-shaped valley.

About a mile after the visitor center, on the left, is a parking lot for **Signal Rock and An Torr,** a popular place for low-impact forested hikes. Just beyond, also on the left, is a one-lane road leading to the recommended **Clachaig Inn,** a classic hikers' pub. The hillsides above the inn were the setting for Hagrid's hut in the third Harry Potter movie.

Continuing along the A-82, you'll hit a straight stretch, passing a lake (Loch Achtriochtan), and then a small farm, both on the right. After the farm, the valley narrows a bit as you cut through Glencoe Pass. On the right, you'll pass two small parking lots. Pull into the second one

for perhaps the best viewpoint of the entire valley, with point-blank views (directly ahead) of the steep ridge-like mountains known as the **Three Sisters.** Hike about 100 feet away from the pullout to your own private bluff to enjoy the view alone—it makes a big difference. This is also the starting point for the challenging **Hidden Valley hike,** which leads between the first and second sisters.

As you continue, you'll pass a raging waterfall in a canyon—the Tears of the MacDonalds—on the right. After another mile or so—through more glorious waterfall scenery—watch on the left for the **Coffin Cairn,** which looks like a stone igloo (parking is just across the road if you want a photo op). Just after the cairn, look on the left for pullout parking for the **hike to The Study,** a viewpoint overlooking the road you just drove down.

After this pullout, you'll hit a straightaway for about a mile, followed by an S-curve. At the end of the curve, look for the pullout parking on the left, just before the stand of pine trees. This is the trailhead for the **Devil's Staircase** hike, high into the hills.

Continuing past here, you're nearing the end of the valley. The intimidating peak called the Great Shepherd of Etive (Stob Dearg, on the right) looms like a dour watchman, guarding the far end of the valley. Soon you'll pass the turnoff (on the right) for **Glen Etive,** an even more remote-feeling valley. (This was the setting for the final scenes of *Skyfall.* Yes, this is where James Bond grew up.) Continuing past that, the last sign of civilization (on the right) is the Glencoe Ski Centre. And from here, the terrain flattens out as you enter the vast **Rannoch Moor**—50 bleak square miles of heather, boulders, and barely enough decent land to graze a sheep. Robert Louis Stevenson called it the "Highland Desert."

You could keep driving as far as you like—but the moor looks pretty much the same from here on out. Turn around and head back through Glencoe...it's scenery you'll hardly mind seeing twice.

Hiking in Glencoe

Glencoe is made for hiking. Many routes are not particularly well marked, so it's essential to get very specific instructions (from the rangers at the Glencoe Visitor Centre, or other knowledgeable locals) and equip yourself with a good map (the Ordnance Survey Explorer Map #384, sold at the center). I've suggested a few of the most enticing walks and hikes. These vary from easy, level strolls to challenging climbs. Either way, wear proper footwear (even the easy trails can get swamped in wet weather) and carry rain gear—you never know when a storm will blow in.

I've listed these roughly in order of how close they are to Glencoe village, and given a rough sense of difficulty for each. Some of them (including the first two) are more forested, but the ones

out in the open—which really let you feel immersed in the wonders of Glencoe—are even better.

While you can walk to the first two areas from Glencoe village, the rest are best for drivers. Some of these trailheads are tricky to find, which is why I've designed the driving commentary in the previous section to help you locate the hikes off the A-82.

Glencoe Lochan (Easy)

Perched on the forested hill above Glencoe village is an improbable slice of the Canadian Rockies. A century ago, this was the personal playground of Lord Strathcona, a local boy done good when he moved to Canada and eventually became a big Canadian Pacific Railway magnate. In 1894, he returned home with his Canadian wife and built the Glencoe House (which is now an exclusive, top-of-the-top hotel). His wife was homesick for the Rockies, so he had the grounds landscaped to represent the lakes, trees, and mountains of her home country. They even carved out a man-made lake (Glencoe Lochan), which looks like a piece of Canada tucked under a craggy Scottish backdrop. (She was still homesick—they eventually returned to Canada.)

Today, the house and immediate surroundings are closed to visitors, but the rest of the area is open for exploration. Head to the end of Glencoe village, cross the bridge, and continue straight up (following signs for *Glencoe Lochan*)—it's a 20-minute uphill walk, or 5-minute drive, from the village center. Once there, a helpful orientation panel in the parking lot suggests three different, color-coded, one-mile walking loops—mostly around that beautiful lake, which reflects the hillsides of Glencoe.

From this area, a good trail network called the **Orbital Recreational Track** follows the river through the forest up the valley, all the way to the Clachaig Inn (about 45 minutes one-way). This links you to the Signal Rock and An Torr areas (described next). Eventually they hope to extend this trail system across the valley and back to the Glencoe Visitor Centre, which would allow a handy loop hike around the valley floor.

Signal Rock and An Torr (Easy to Moderate)

This forested area has nicely tended trails and gives you a better chance of spotting wildlife than the more desolate hikes described later. To explore this area, park at the well-marked lot just off of the A-82 and go for a walk. A well-described panel at the trailhead narrates three options: easy yellow route to the Clachaig Inn;

GLENCOE & FORT WILLIAM

longer blue route to Signal Rock; and strenuous black route along the hillsides of An Torr. The Signal Rock route brings you to a panoramic point overlooking the valley—so named because a fire could be lit here to alert others in case of danger.

Hidden Valley (Challenging)

Three miles east of Glencoe village, this aptly named glen is tucked between two of the dramatic Three Sisters mountains. Also called the Lost Valley (Coire Gabhail in Gaelic), this was supposedly where the MacDonalds hid stolen cattle from their rivals, the Campbells (who later massacred them). This is the most challenging of the hikes I describe—it's strenuous and has stretches with uneven footing. Expect to scramble a bit over rocks, and to cross a river on stepping stones (which may be underwater after a heavy rain). As the rocks can be slippery when wet, skip this hike in bad weather. Figure about two-and-a-half to three hours round-trip (with an ascent of more than 1,000 feet).

Begin at the second parking lot at Glencoe Pass (on the right when coming from Glencoe), with views of the Three Sisters. You're aiming to head between the first and second Sisters (counting from the left). Hike down into the valley between the road and the mountains. Bear left, head down a metal staircase, and cross the bridge over the river. (Don't cross the bridge to the right of the parking lots—a common mistake.) Once across, you'll start the treacherous ascent up a narrow gorge. Some scrambling is required, and at one point a railing helps you find your way. The next tricky part is where you cross the river. You're looking for a pebbly beach and a large boulder; stepping stones lead across the river, and you'll see the path resume on the other side. But if the water level is high, the stones may be covered—though still passable with good shoes and steady footing. (Don't attempt to scramble over the treacherous slopes on the side of the river with the loose rocks called scree.) Once across the stepping stones, keep on the trail, hiking further up into the valley.

Much Easier Alternative: If you'd simply enjoy the feeling of walking deep in Glencoe valley—with peaks and waterfalls overhead—you can start down from the parking lot toward the Hidden Valley trail, and then simply stroll the old road along the valley floor as far as you want in either direction.

The Study (Easy to Moderate)

For a relatively easy, mostly level hike through the valley with a nice viewpoint at the end, consider walking to the flat rock called "The Study" and back. It takes about 45-60 minutes round-trip. The walk essentially parallels the main highway, but on the old road a bit higher up. You'll park just beyond the Three Sisters and the Coffin Cairn. From there, cut through the field of stone and marshy turf to the old road—basically two gravel tire ruts—and follow them to your left. You'll hike above the modern road, passing several modest waterfalls, until you reach a big, flat rock with stunning views of the Three Sisters and the valley be-

yond. (Fellow hikers have marked the spot with a pile of stones.)

The Devil's Staircase (Strenuous but Straightforward)

About eight miles east of Glencoe village, near the end of the valley, you can hike this brief stretch of the West Highland Way. It was built by General Wade, the British strategist who came to Scotland after the 1715 Jacobite rebellion to help secure government rule here. Designed to connect Glencoe valley to the lochside town of Kinlochmore, to the north, it's named for its challenging switchbacks. Most hikers simply ascend to the pass at the top (an 800-foot gain), then come back down to Glencoe. It's challenging, but easier to follow and with more comfortable footing than the Hidden Valley hike. Figure about 45-60 minutes up, and 30 minutes back down (add 45-60 minutes for the optional ascent to the summit of 2,320-foot Stob Mhic Mhartuin).

From the parking lot, a green sign points the way. It's a steep but straightforward hike up, on switchback trails, until you reach the pass—marked by a cairn (pile of stones). From here, you can return back down into the valley. Or, if you have stamina left, consider continuing higher—head up to the peak on the left, called **Stob Mhic Mhartuin.** The 30-40-minute hike to the top (an additional gain of 500 feet) earns you even grander views over the entire valley.

For an even longer hike, it's possible to carry on down the other side of the staircase to **Kinlochmore** (about 2 hours' descent)—but your car will still be in Glencoe village. Consider this plan: Leave your car in Glencoe. Take a taxi to the trailhead. Hike across to Kinlochmore. From there you can take the #N44 bus back to Glencoe and your car, though be aware that the bus only runs a few times midday (see "Glencoe Connections," later).

Sleeping in Glencoe

Glencoe is an extremely low-key place to spend the night between Oban or Glasgow and the northern destinations. You'll join two kinds of guests: one-nighters just passing through and outdoorsy types settling in for several days of hiking.

B&Bs IN GLENCOE VILLAGE
The following B&Bs are along or just off the main road through the middle of the village.

$$ Beechwood Cottage B&B is a shoes-off, slippers-on, whisky-honor-bar kind of place where Jackie rents three lovely rooms and Iain pursues his rock-garden dreams in the yard (look for the sign at the church on Main Street, tel. 01855/811-062, www.beechwoodcottage.scot, stay@beechwoodcottage.scot).

$$ Heatherlea B&B is at the far end of the village, with a relaxed atmosphere, hotel-meets-country-home rooms, and a serene grassy garden with berry bushes (harvested for homemade jam). Host Helen is a fun, outdoorsy type who opened a guesthouse because she "wanted to get out of the rat race" (3 rooms, sack lunches available, tel. 01855/811-519, mobile 07884/367-354, www.heatherleaglencoe.com, info@heatherleaglencoe.com).

OUTSIDE TOWN
These options are a bit outside town, with good proximity to both the village and the valley. Strath Lodge, Glencoe Independent Hostel, and Clachaig Inn are on the back road that runs through the forest parallel to the A-82 (best suited for drivers). Scorrybreac is on a hill above the village, and Callart View is along the flat road that winds past Loch Leven.

$$$ Strath Lodge, energetically run by Ann and Dan (who are generous with hiking tips and maps), brings a fresh perspective to Glencoe's sometimes-stodgy accommodations scene. Their four rooms, in a modern, light-filled, lodge-like home, are partway down the road to the Clachaig Inn (2-3 night minimum preferred, no kids under 16, tel. 01855/811-337, www.strathlodgeglencoe.com, stay@strathlodgeglencoe.com). Take the road up through the middle of Glencoe village, cross the bridge, and keep right following the river for a few minutes; it's on the right.

$$$ Clachaig Inn, which runs two popular pubs on site, also rents 23 rooms, all with private bath. It's a family-friendly place surrounded by a dramatic setting that works well for hikers seeking a comfy mountain inn (recommended pub, tel. 01855/811-252, 3 miles from Glencoe, www.clachaig.com, frontdesk@clachaig.com). Follow the directions for the Strath Lodge, and drive another three miles past the campgrounds and hostels—the Clachaig Inn is on the right.

$$ Glencoe Independent Hostel offers a few snazzy, self-contained "eco-cabins" with kitchenettes and cheap, basic dorm beds in a rehabbed crofter farm building. It's a good choice if you're looking for either a bargain-basement sleep or a private, self-catering option (2-night minimum for cabins, tel. 01855/811-906, www.glencoehostel.co.uk, info@glencoehostel.co.uk, energetic Keith). It's a few minutes farther up the road beyond Strath Lodge.

$$ Scorrybreac Guest House enjoys a secluded forest setting and privileged position next to the restored Glencoe House (now a luxury hotel). From here, walks around the Glencoe Lochan wooded lake park are easy, and it's about a 10-minute walk down into the village. Emma and Graham rent five homey rooms and serve a daily breakfast special that goes beyond the usual offerings (2-3 nights preferred in peak season, tel. 01855/811-354, www.scorrybreacglencoe.com, stay@scorrybreacglencoe.com). After crossing the bridge at the end of the village, head left up the hill and follow signs.

$ Callart View B&B offers four rooms, quilted-home comfort, and a peaceful spot overlooking Loch Leven, less than a mile outside the village and close to the wooded trails of Glencoe Lochan. You'll be spoiled by Lynn's homemade shortbread (family room, self-catering cottages, sack lunches available, tel. 01855/811-259, www.callart-view.co.uk, callartview@hotmail.com, Lynn and Geoff). Turn off from the main road for Glencoe village but instead of turning right into the village, keep left and drive less than a mile along the loch.

IN BALLACHULISH

$ St. Munda's Manse sounds rather grand—because Colin and Mary renovated a lovely old stone house that once belonged to the church down the road. Now they offer two bright rooms that manage to feel both modern and classic, in a quiet location above Ballachulish village (cash only, tel. 01855/811-966, www.bedandbreakfastglencoe.com, hello@stmundasmanse.com). See their website for driving directions.

$ Strathassynt Guest House sits in the center of Ballachulish, across from the recommended Laroch Bar & Bistro. Katya will make you pancakes for breakfast, and the six bedrooms are a good value (family rooms, closed Nov-Feb, tel. 01855/811-261, www.strathassynt.com, info@strathassynt.com, Neil and Katya).

Eating in Glencoe

Choices around Glencoe are slim—this isn't the place for fine dining. But the following options offer decent food a short walk or drive away. For evening fun, take a walk or ask your B&B host where to find music and dancing.

In Glencoe: The only real restaurant is **$$$ The Glencoe Gathering,** with a busy dining area and a large outdoor deck. The menu has a variety of seafood, burgers, and pasta. While the food is nothing special, it will fill you up after a day in the mountains (daily 8:30-22:00, at junction of A-82 and Glencoe village, tel. 01855/811-265).

The **$ Glencoe Café,** also in the village, is just right for soups and sandwiches, and Deirdre's homemade baked goods—especially the carrot loaf—are irresistible (soup-and-panini lunch combo, daily 10:00-17:00, last order at 16:15, Alan).

Near Glencoe: Set in a stunning valley a few miles from Glencoe village, **$$ Clachaig Inn** serves solid pub grub all day long to a clientele that's half locals and half tourists. This unpretentious and very popular social hub features billiards, live music, and a wide range of whiskies and hand-pulled ales. There are two areas, sharing the same menu: The Bidean Lounge feels a bit like an upscale ski lodge while the Boots Bar has a spit-and-sawdust, pub-around-an-open-fire atmosphere (open daily for lunch and dinner, music Sat from 21:00, Sun open-mike folk music, see hotel listing earlier for driving directions, tel. 01855/811-252, no reservations).

In Ballachulish: Aiming to bring some sophistication to this rugged corner of Scotland, **$$$ The Laroch Bar & Bistro** has both a low-key pub section and a proper restaurant sharing the same menu (Tue-Sat 12:00-15:00 & 18:00-21:00, closed Sun-Mon, tel. 01855/811-940, www.thelarochrestaurantandbar.co.uk). Drive three minutes from Glencoe into Ballachulish village, and you'll see it on the left. There's also a simple **$ fish-and-chips** joint next door (Fri-Sat 16:30-21:30, closed Sun-Thu).

Glencoe Connections

Buses don't actually drive down the main road through Glencoe village, but they stop nearby at a place called **"Glencoe Crossroads"** (a short walk into the village center). They also stop in the town of **Ballachulish,** which is just a half-mile away (or a £3 taxi ride). Tell the bus driver where you're going ("Glencoe village") and ask to be let off as close as possible.

Citylink buses #914/#915/#916 stop at Glencoe Crossroads and Ballachulish, heading north to **Fort William** (7-8/day, 30 minutes) or south to **Glasgow** (3 hours). Another option is Shiel bus #N44, which runs from either Glencoe Crossroads or Balla-chulish to **Fort William** (about 8/day, less Sat-Sun). From Bal-lachulish, you can take Citylink bus #918 to **Oban** (2/day, 1 hour).

To reach **Inverness** or **Portree** on the Isle of Skye, transfer in Fort William. To reach **Edinburgh,** transfer in Glasgow.

Bus info: Citylink tel. 0871-266-3333, Citylink.co.uk; Shiel Buses tel. 01967/431-272, ShielBuses.co.uk.

Fort William

Fort William—after Inverness, the second biggest town in the Highlands (pop. 10,000)—is Glencoe's opposite. While Glencoe is a humble one-street village, appealing to hikers and nature-lovers, Fort Wil-liam's glammed-up car-free main drag feels like one big Scottish shopping mall (with souvenir stands and outdoor stores touting perpetual "70 percent off" sales). The town is clogged  with a United Nations of tourists trying to get out of the rain. Big bus tours drive through Glencoe...but they sleep in Fort William.

While Glencoe touches the Scottish soul of the Highlands, Fort William was a steely and intimidating headquarters of the British counter-insurgency movement—in many ways designed to crush that same Highland spirit. After the English Civil War (early 1650s), Oliver Cromwell built a fort here to control his re-bellious Scottish subjects. This was beefed up (and named for King William III) in 1690. And following the Jacobite uprising in 1715, King George I dispatched General George Wade to coordinate and fortify the crown's Highland defenses against further Jaco-bite dissenters. Fort William was the first of a chain of intimidat-ing bastions (along with Fort Augustus on Loch Ness, and Fort George near Inverness) stretching the length of the Great Glen. But Fort William's namesake fortress is long gone, leaving pre-cious little tangible evidence (except a tiny bit of rampart in a park near the train station) to help today's visitors imagine its milita-ristic past.

With the opening of the Caledonian Canal in 1822, the first curious tourists arrived. Many more followed with the arrival of the train in 1894, and grand hotels were built. Today, sitting at the foot of Ben Nevis, the tallest peak in Britain, Fort William is considered the outdoors capital of the United Kingdom.

Orientation to Fort William

Given its strategic position—between Glencoe and Oban in the south, Inverness in the east, and the Isle of Skye in the west—you're likely to pass through Fort William at some point during your Highlands explorations. And, while "just passing through" is the perfect plan here, Fort William can provide a good opportunity to stock up on whatever you need (last supermarket before Inverness), grab lunch, and get any questions answered at the TI.

Arrival in Fort William: You'll find pay parking lots flanking the main pedestrian zone, High Street. The train and bus stations sit side by side just north of the old town center, where you'll find a handy pay parking lot.

Tourist Information: The TI is on the car-free main drag (daily July-Aug 9:30-18:30, Sept-June 9:00-18:00; 15 High Street, tel. 01397/701-801, FortWilliamTIC@visitscotland.com). Free public WCs are up the street, next to the parking lot.

Sights in Fort William

Fort William's High Street

Enjoy an hour-long stroll up and down the length of Fort William's main street for lots of Scottish clichés, great people watching, and a shop at #125 (near the south end) called Aye2Aye, which favors a new referendum on Scottish independence.

▲West Highland Museum

Fort William's only real sight is its humble but well-presented museum. It's a fine opportunity to escape the elements, and—if you take the time to linger over the many interesting exhibits—genuinely insightful about local history and Highland life.

Cost and Hours: Free, £3 suggested donation, Mon-Sat 10:00-17:00, and maybe Sun in high season; Nov-April until 16:00; closed Jan-Feb; midway down the main street on Cameron Square, tel. 01397/702-169, www.westhighlandmuseum.org.uk.

Visiting the Museum: Follow the suggested one-way route through exhibits on two floors. You'll begin by learning about the WWII green beret commandos, who were trained in secrecy near here (see "Commando Memorial" listing, later). Then you'll see the historic Governor's Room, decorated with the original paneling from the room in which the order for the Glencoe Massacre was signed. The ground floor also holds exhibits on natural history (lots of stuffed birds and other critters), mountaineering (old equipment), and archaeology (stone and metal tools).

Upstairs, you'll see a selection of old tartans and a salacious exhibit about Queen Victoria and John Brown (her Scottish servant... and, possibly, suitor). The Jacobite exhibit gives a concise timeline of that complicated history, from Charles I to Bonnie Prince Charlie, and displays a selection of items emblazoned with the prince's bonnie face—including a clandestine portrait that you can only see by looking in a cylindrical mirror. Finally, the Highland Life exhibit collects a hodgepodge of tools, musical instruments (some fine old harps that were later replaced by the much louder bagpipes as the battlefield instrument of choice), and other bric-a-brac.

NEAR FORT WILLIAM
Ben Nevis
From Fort William, take a peek at Britain's highest peak, Ben Nevis (4,406 feet). Thousands walk to its summit each year. On a clear day, you can admire it from a distance. Scotland's only mountain cable cars—at the **Nevis Range Mountain Experience**—can take you to a not-very-lofty 2,150-foot perch on the slopes of Aonach Mòr for a closer look (£19.50, 15-minute ride, generally open daily but closed in high winds and winter—call ahead, signposted on the A-82 north of Fort William, café at bottom and restaurant at top, tel. 01397/705-825, www.nevisrange.co.uk). The cable car also provides access to trails particularly popular with mountain bikers.

▲Commando Memorial
This powerful bronze ensemble of three stoic WWII commandos, standing in an evocative mountain setting, is one of Britain's most beloved war memorials. During World War II, Winston Churchill decided that Britain needed an elite military corps. He created the British Commandos, famous for wearing green berets (an accessory—and name—later borrowed by elite fighting forces in the US and other countries). The British Commandos trained in the Lochaber region near Fort William, in the windy shadow of Ben Nevis. Many later died in combat, and this memorial—built in 1952—remembers those fallen British heroes.

Nearby is the Garden of Remembrance, honoring British Commandos who died in more recent conflicts, from the Falkland Islands to Afghanistan. It's also a popular place to spread Scottish military ashes. Taken together, these sights are a touching reminder that the US is not alone in its distant wars. Every nation has its share of honored heroes willing to sacrifice for what they believe to be the greater good.

Getting There: The memorial is about nine miles outside of Fort William, on the way to Inverness (just outside Spean Bridge); see "Route Tips for Drivers" later in this section.

Sleeping and Eating in Fort William

Sleeping: The Hobbit-cute **$ Gowan Brae B&B** ("Hill of the Big Daisy") has an antique-filled dining room and three rooms with loch or garden views (one room has private bath down the hall, cash only, 2-night minimum July-Aug, on Union Road—a 5-minute walk up the hill above High Street, tel. 01397/704-399, www.gowanbrae.co.uk, gowan_brae@btinternet.com, Jim and Ann Clark).

Eating: These places are on traffic-free High Street, near the start of town. For lunch and picnics, try **$ Deli Craft,** with good, made-to-order deli sandwiches and other prepared foods (61 High Street, tel. 01397/698-100), or **$ Hot Roast Company,** which sells beef, turkey, ham, or pork sandwiches topped with some tasty extras, along with soup, salad, and coleslaw (127 High Street, tel. 01397/700-606).

For lunch or dinner, **$$ The Grog & Gruel** serves real ales, good pub grub, and Tex-Mex and Cajun dishes, with some unusual choices such as burgers made from boar and haggis or Highland venison. There's also a variety of "grog dogs" (66 High Street, tel. 01397/705-078).

Fort William Connections

Fort William is a major transit hub for the Highlands, so you'll likely change buses here at some point during your trip.

From Fort William by Bus to: Glencoe or **Ballachulish** (all Glasgow-bound buses—#914, #915, and #916; 8/day, 30 minutes; also Shiel bus #N44, hourly, fewer on Sun), **Oban** (bus #918, 2/day, 1.5 hours), **Portree** on the Isle of Skye (buses #914, #915, and #916, 3/day, 3 hours), **Inverness** (bus #919, 6/day, 2 hours, fewer on Sun), **Glasgow** (#914/#915/#916, 7-8/day direct, 3 hours). To reach **Edinburgh,** take the bus to Glasgow, then transfer to a train or bus (figure 5 hours total). Citylink: tel. 0871-266-3333, Citylink.co.uk; Shiel Bus: tel. 01397/700-700, ShielBuses.co.uk.

From Fort William by Train to: Glasgow (4/day, 4 hours), **Mallaig** and ferry to Isle of Skye (4/day, 1.5 hours). Also see the listing for the Jacobite Steam Train on page 312.

ROUTE TIPS FOR DRIVERS

From Fort William to Loch Ness and Inverness: Head north out of Fort William on the A-82. After about eight miles, in the village of Spean Bridge, take the left fork (staying on the A-82). About a mile later, on the left, keep an eye out for the **Commando Memorial** (described earlier and worth a quick stop). From here, the A-82 sweeps north and follows the Caledonian Canal, passing through **Fort Augustus** (a good lunch stop, with its worthwhile Caledonian Canal Centre), and then follows the north side of Loch Ness on its way to Inverness. Along the way, the A-82 passes **Urquhart Castle** and two **Loch Ness monster exhibits** in Drumnadrochit (described in the Inverness & Loch Ness chapter).

From Oban to Fort William via Glencoe: See page 271 in the Oban chapter.

From Fort William to the Isle of Skye: You have two options: Head west on the A-830 through **Glenfinnan,** then catch the ferry from Mallaig to Armadale on the Isle of Skye (this "Road to the Isles" area is described in the next section). Or, head north on the A-82 to Invergarry, and turn left (west) on the A-87, which you'll follow (past **Eilean Donan Castle**) to Kyle of Lochalsh and the **Skye Bridge** to the island. Consider using one route one way, and the other on the return trip.

The Road to the Isles

Between Fort William and the Isle of Skye lies a rugged landscape with close ties to the Jacobite rebellions. It was here that Bonnie Prince Charlie first set foot on Scottish soil in 1745, in his attempt to regain the British throne for his father. The village of Glenfinnan, about 30 minutes west of Fort William, is where he first raised the Stuart family standard— and an army of Highland-

ers. Farther west, the landscape grows even more rugged, offering offshore glimpses of the Hebrides. It's all tied together by a pretty, meandering road—laid out by the great Scottish civil engineer Thomas Telford—that's evocatively (and aptly) named "The Road to the Isles." While these sights aren't worth going out of your way to see, they're ideal for those heading to the Isle of Skye (via the

GLENCOE & FORT WILLIAM

Mallaig-Armadale ferry), or for those who'd enjoy taking the so-called "Harry Potter train" through a Hogwartian landscape.

If you're driving, be sure you allow enough time to make it to Mallaig at least 20 minutes before the Skye ferry departs (figure at least 90 minutes of driving time from Fort William to the ferry, not including stops). In summer it's smart to reserve a spot on the ferry the day before, either online or by phone. For more tips on the Mallaig-Armadale ferry, see "Getting to the Isle of Skye" on page 315.

Sights on the Road to the Isles

I've connected these sights with some commentary for those driving from Fort William to Mallaig for the Skye ferry. (If you're interest-ed in the Jacobite Steam Train instead, see the end of this chapter.) In addition to the sights at Glenfinnan, this route is graced with plenty of loch-and-mountain views and, near the end, passes along a beautiful stretch of coast with some fine sandy beaches.

• *From Fort William, head north on the A-82 (signed* Inverness *and* Mallaig*). At the big roundabout (where you'll see the tempting Ben Nevis Whisky Distillery with a visitors center), turn left onto the A-830 (marked for Mallaig and Glenfinnan). You'll pass a big sign listing the next Skye ferry departure. Just after, you'll cross a bridge; look up and to the right to see Neptune's Staircase. There's a park-like viewing zone on the right.*

Neptune's Staircase
This network of eight stair-step locks, designed by Thomas Tel-ford in the early 19th century, offers a handy look at the ingenious locks of the Caledonian Canal. For more on this remarkable engineering accomplishment—which combined natural lochs with man-made locks and canals to connect Scotland's east and west coasts—see the sidebar on page 378. Engineers might want to pull over just after the bridge (well marked) to stroll around  the locks for a closer look, but the rest of us can pretty much get the gist from the road.

• *Continue west on the A-830 for another 14 miles, much of it along Loch Eil. Soon you'll reach a big parking lot and visitors center at...*

▲Glenfinnan
In the summer of 1745, Bonnie Prince Charlie—grandson of James II of England, who was kicked off the British throne in 1688—

arrived at Glenfinnan...and waited. He had journeyed a long way to this point, sailing from France by way of the Scottish Isle of Eriskay, and finally making landfall at Loch nan Uamh (just west of here). For the first time in his life, he set foot on his ancestral homeland...the land he hoped that, with his help, his father would soon rule. But to reclaim the thrones of England and Scotland for the Stuart line, the fresh-faced, 24-year-old prince would need the support of the Highlanders. And here at Glenfinnan, he held his breath at the moment of truth. Would the Highland clans come to his aid?

As Charlie waited, gradually he began to hear the drone of bagpipes filtering through the forest. And then, the clan chiefs appeared: MacDonalds. Camerons. MacDonnells. McPhees. They had been holding back—watching and waiting, to make sure they weren't the only ones. Before long, the prince felt confident that he'd reached a clan quorum. And so, here at Glenfinnan, on August 19, 1745, Bonnie Prince Charlie raised his royal standard—officially kicking off the armed Jacobite rebellion that came to be known as "The '45." Two days later, Charlie and his 1,500 clansmen compatriots headed south to fight for control of Scotland. (Glenfinnan is also the place where Bonnie Prince Charlie retreated, just eight months later, after his crushing defeat at Culloden.)

Today Glenfinnan, which still echoes with history, is a wide spot in the road with a big visitors center and two landmarks: a monument to Bonnie Prince Charlie's raising of the standard, and a railroad viaduct made famous by the Hogwarts Express.

Visiting Glenfinnan: Start at the **visitors center** (free, £4 tickets for Glenfinnan Monument sold here, daily 9:00-19:00, Oct-March 10:00-16:00, café, WCs, tel. 01397/722-250, www.nts.org.uk). The small but enlightening **Jacobite Exhibit** inside the visitors center explains the story of Bonnie Prince Charlie and "The '45."

The **Glenfinnan Viaduct,** with 416 yards of raised track over 21 supporting arches, is visible from the parking lot. But it's worth hiking 10 minutes up the adjacent hill for much better views. Find the well-marked, steep switchback path behind the visitors center and huff on up. From the viewpoint, you'll enjoy sweeping (if distant) views of the viaduct in one direction, and the monument and banks of Loch Shiel in the other. You may even catch

GLENCOE & FORT WILLIAM

a glimpse of the Jacobite Steam Train chugging along (described below).

The **Glenfinnan Monument** sits across the road, between the visitors center and the loch. Capped with a stirring statue of a kilted "Unknown Highlander," it commemorates the Jacobites who perished in the 1745 uprising. (From here you can see back to the viaduct and the viewpoint above the visitors center.)

• *Carrying on west along the A-830, the scenery grows more rugged. Shortly you'll begin to catch glimpses of silver sand beaches at the heads of the rocky lochs. (If catching a ferry, figure 50 minutes' drive from Glenfinnan to Mallaig.)*

Fans of Bonnie Prince Charlie with a half-hour to spare should consider the next stop, 13 miles west of Glenfinnan. Just after the road passes under a railway viaduct, look for a small sign on the right. Park in the waterside pullout just beyond.

The Prince's Cairn

Perched above bonnie Loch nan Uamh, this cairn memorializes the spot from where Prince Charlie sailed for France after his failed uprising. (To find the cairn, from the pullout, hug the roadside guardrail and backtrack a hundred yards to the short trail.) The haystack-shaped cairn is made of local stone and marked by a memorial plaque. Imagine the day, September 20, 1746, when a French frigate spirited away the weary prince and his followers. He would never set foot in Scotland again.

• *Continuing west you'll soon reach the village of...*

Arisaig

While there's not much to see in this village, it has an interesting history. Gaelic for "safe place," Arisaig has provided shelter for many seafarers—including the real Long John Silver (Robert Louis Stevenson was inspired by tales from his father, who was an engineer who built lighthouses here). In the 20th century, remote Arisaig was a secret training ground for WWII-era spies. The "Special Operations Executive" prepared brave men and women here for clandestine operations in Nazi-occupied Europe.

• *Around Arisaig, signs for the* Alternative Coastal Route *direct you to the B-8008, which parallels the A-830 highway the rest of the way (7 miles) to Mallaig. If you've got ample time to kill, consider taking these back roads for a more scenic approach to the end of the road. Either way, you'll end up at* **Mallaig** *and the* **Skye Ferry.**

The Jacobite Steam Train

The West Highland Railway Line chugs 42 miles from Fort William west to the ferry port at Mallaig. This train (they don't actually call it the "Hogwarts Express") offers a small taste of the Harry Potter experience...but it may be a letdown for those who take this trip only for its wizarding connections. Although one of the steam engines and some of the coaches were used in the films, don't expect a Harry Potter theme ride. However, you can expect beautiful scenery. Along the way, the train stops for 20 minutes at Glenfinnan Station (just after the Glenfinnan Viaduct), and then gives you too much time (1.75 hours) to poke around the dull port town of Mallaig before heading back to Fort William.

Cost and Hours: £37.75; more for first class, purchase tickets far in advance. Trains make the roughly 2-hour round-trip twice daily (April-Sept, departs Fort Williams at 10:15 and 14:30, tel. 0844/850-3131, www.westcoastrailways.co.uk/jacobite). Pay lockers for storing luggage are at the Fort William train station (station open long hours daily).

Booking Tickets: You must book ahead online or by phone—you cannot buy tickets for this train at ticket offices. In summer, trips often sell out; booking months in advance is your best bet. A limited number of seats may be available each day on a first-come, first-served basis (cash only, buy from conductor at coach D). Rail passes are not accepted.

Cheaper Alternative: The 84-mile round-trip from Fort William takes the better part of a day to show you the same scenery twice. Modern "Sprinter" trains follow the same line and accept rail passes. Consider taking the steam train one-way to Mallaig, then speeding back on a regular train to avoid the long Mallaig layover and slow return ("Sprinter" train: £13.40 one-way between Fort William and Mallaig, 4/day, 1.5 hours, to ensure a seat in peak season book by 18:00 the day before, tel. 03457/484-950, www.nationalrail.co.uk).

Skye Connection: Note that you can use either the steam train or the Sprinter to reach the Isle of Skye: Take the train to Mallaig, walk onto the ferry to Armadale (on Skye), then catch a bus in Armadale to your destination on Skye (bus #52, www.stagecoachbus.com).

GLENCOE & FORT WILLIAM

ISLE OF SKYE

Portree • Touring the Isle of Skye

The rugged, remote-feeling Isle of Skye has a reputation for unpredictable weather ("Skye" comes from the Old Norse for "The Misty Isle"). But it also offers some of Scotland's best scenery, and it rarely fails to charm its many visitors. Narrow, twisty roads wind around Skye in the shadows of craggy, black, bald mountains, and the coastline is ruffled with peninsulas and sea lochs (inlets).

Skye is the largest of the Inner Hebrides, and Scotland's second-biggest island overall (over 600 square miles), but it's still manageable: You're never more than five miles from the sea. The island has only about 13,000 residents; roughly a quarter live in the main village, Portree. The mountain-like Cuillin Hills separate the northern part of the island (Portree, Trotternish, Dunvegan) from the south (Skye Bridge, Kyleakin, Sleat Peninsula).

Set up camp in Portree, Skye's charming, low-key tourism hub. Then dive into Skye's attractions. Drive around the appealing Trotternish Peninsula, enjoying Scotland's scenic beauty: sparsely populated rolling fields, stony homes, stark vistas of jagged rock formations, and the mysterious Outer Hebrides looming on the horizon. Go for a hike in (or near) the dramatic Cuillin Hills, sample a peaty dram of whisky, and walk across a desolate bluff to a lighthouse at the end of the world. Learn about the clan history of Skye, and visit your choice of clan castles: the MacLeods' base at Dunvegan, the MacDonalds' ruins near Armadale, and—nearby but not on Skye—the postcard-perfect Eilean Donan fortress, previously a Mackenzie stronghold but today held by the Macraes. Or just settle in, slow down, and enjoy island life.

The most useful TI is in Portree; shops in smaller towns (including Dunvegan) host more basic "information points." At nearly every pullout you'll find an info post giving background on that stop.

PLANNING YOUR TIME

With two weeks in Scotland, Skye merits two nights, allowing a full day to hit its highlights: Trotternish Peninsula loop, Dunvegan Castle, the Fairy Pools hike (or another hike in the Cuillin Hills), and the Talisker Distillery tour. Mountaineers need extra time for hiking and hillwalking. Because it takes time to reach, Skye is skippable if you only have a few days in Scotland—instead, focus on the more accessible Highlands sights (Oban and its nearby islands, and Glencoe).

Situated between Oban/Glencoe and Loch Ness/Inverness, Skye fits neatly into a Highlands itinerary. To avoid seeing the same scenery twice, it works well to drive the "Road to the Isles" from Fort William to Mallaig, then take the ferry to Skye; later, leave Skye via the Skye Bridge and follow the A-87 east toward Loch Ness and Inverness, stopping at Eilean Donan Castle en route, or vice versa. With more time, take the very long and scenic route north from Skye, up Wester Ross and across Scotland's north coast, then down to Inverness (see the Northern Scotland chapter).

GETTING TO THE ISLE OF SKYE

By Car: Your easiest bet is the slick, free **Skye Bridge** that crosses from Kyle of Lochalsh on the mainland to Kyleakin on Skye (for more on the bridge, see "South Skye" on page 344).

The island can also be reached by **car ferry.** The major ferry line connects the mainland town of Mallaig (west of Fort William along the "Road to the Isles"—see page 309) to Armadale on Skye (£16/car with 2 people, reservations required, April-late Oct 9/day each way, off-season very limited Sat-Sun connections, must check in at least 20 minutes before sailing or your place will be sold and you will not get on, can be canceled in rough weather, 30-minute trip, operated by Caledonian Mac-Brayne, tel. 01475/650-397, www.calmac.co.uk).

By Bus: Skye is connected to the outside world by Scottish Citylink buses (www.citylink.co.uk), which use Portree as their Skye hub. From Portree, buses connect to **Inverness** (bus #917, 2/day, 3 hours) and **Glasgow** (buses #915 and #916, 3/day, 7.5 hours,

Isle of Skye

To Harris

The Little Minch

To North Uist

DUNTULM
FORT
SKYE MUSEUM OF ISLAND LIFE
Kilmuir
Quiraing
Flodigarry
Staffin
KILT ROCK
The Fairy Glen
Lealt Gorge

Geary

Loch Snizort Beag

Uig
A-87
Trotternish Peninsula
A-855

The Old Man of Storr

Kensaleyre
TRAILHEAD

Skeabost
Borve

Sound of Raasay

Glendale
Colbost
2
DUNVEGAN
Dunvegan

Loch Dunvegan
A-850

Neist Point

LIGHTHOUSE
Duirinish Peninsula
Ramasaig
MacLeod's Tables

Portree
See Portree detail map
See Trotternish Peninsula detail map

Skye

DUN BEAG
Bracadale

Loch Bracadale

Carbost
A-863
Sconser
Sligachan
1
Glamaig

TALISKER DISTILLERY

FAIRY POOLS HIKE
Sgurr Alasdair
Glenbrittle
Bualintur
Loch Coruisk
Cuillin Hills
Bla Bheinn

Sea of the Hebrides

Elgol

Soay

Cuillin Sound

N

5 Kilometers
5 Miles

Canna

Kinloch

Rum

Askival

Sound of Rum

SCOTLAND
ENGLAND
WALES
London

Cleadale

Eigg

Galmisdale

Atlantic Ocean

ISLE OF SKYE

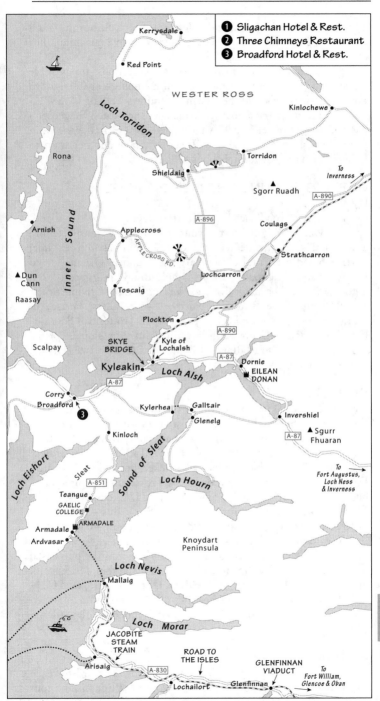

1 Sligachan Hotel & Rest.
2 Three Chimneys Restaurant
3 Broadford Hotel & Rest.

Kerrysdale

Red Point

WESTER ROSS

Loch Torridon

Kinlochewe

Rona

Torridon

Shieldaig

▲ Sgorr Ruadh

To
Inverness

A-890

Arnish

Applecross

A-896

Coulags

Strathcarron

▲ Dun
Cann

APPLECROSS RD.

Lochcarron

Inner Sound

Toscaig

Raasay

Plockton

A-890

Scalpay

SKYE
BRIDGE

Kyle of Lochalsh

A-87

Dornie
EILEAN
DONAN

Kyleakin

Loch Alsh

A-87

Corry
Broadford

A-87

Kylerhea

Galltair

Invershiel

3

Kinloch

Glenelg

▲ Sgurr
Fhuaran

Loch Eishort

Sleat

A-851

Sound of Sleat

Loch Hourn

A-87

To
Fort Augustus,
Loch Ness
& Inverness

Teangue

GAELIC
COLLEGE

ARMADALE

Armadale

Ardvasar

Knoydart
Peninsula

Loch Nevis

Mallaig

Loch Morar

JACOBITE
STEAM
TRAIN

ROAD TO
THE ISLES

GLENFINNAN
VIADUCT

To
Fort William,
Glencoe & Oban

Arisaig

A-830

Lochailort

Glenfinnan

ISLE OF SKYE

also stop at **Fort William** and **Glencoe**). For **Edinburgh,** you'll transfer in either Inverness or Glasgow (5/day, 8-9 hours total). For connections within the Isle of Skye, see later.

More complicated **train-plus-bus** connections are possible for the determined: Take the train from Edinburgh or Glasgow to Fort William; transfer to the "Sprinter" train to Mallaig (4/day, 1.5 hours); take the ferry across to Armadale; then catch Stagecoach bus #52 to Portree (1 hour). Alternatively, you can take the train from Edinburgh or Glasgow to Inverness, take another train to Kyle of Lochalsh, then catch a bus to Portree.

GETTING AROUND THE ISLE OF SKYE
By Car
Once on Skye, you'll need a car to thoroughly enjoy the island. (Even if you're doing the rest of your trip by public transportation, a car rental is worthwhile here to make maximum use of your time; Portree-based car-rental options are listed under "Orientation to Portree," later.) The roads here are simple and well signposted, but a good map can be helpful for exploring. Sample driving times: Kyleakin and Skye Bridge to Portree—45 minutes; Portree to Dunvegan—30 minutes; Portree to the tip of Trotternish Peninsula and back again—2 hours (more with sightseeing stops); Portree to Armadale/ferry to Mallaig—1 hour; Portree to Talisker Distillery—40 minutes.

By Public Bus
Getting around Skye can be frustrating by bus (slow and limited). Portree is the hub for bus traffic. Most buses within Skye are operated by Stagecoach (www.stagecoachbus.com; buy individual tickets or, for longer journeys, consider the £9.50 all-day Dayrider ticket or the £35.50 weeklong Megarider ticket; buy tickets onboard). From Portree, you can loop around the **Trotternish Peninsula** on bus #57A (counterclockwise route) or bus #57C (clockwise route; Mon-Sat 4/day in each direction, fewer Sun). Bus #56 connects Portree and **Dunvegan Castle** (2/day, none on Sun, 40 minutes).

The following Citylink connections are not covered by the Stagecoach Dayrider or Megarider tickets and must be purchased individually. From Portree to **Kyleakin,** take Citylink #915, #916, or #917 (7/day, 1 hour); to reach **Eilean Donan Castle,** take Citylink #915, #916, or #917 bus heading toward Fort William or Inverness (get off at Dornie and walk about 5 minutes, 7/day, 1 hour, www.citylink.co.uk).

By Tour
Several operations on the island take visitors to hard-to-reach spots. Figure about £50 per person to join an all-day island tour

(about 8 hours). Compare the offerings at the following companies, which use smaller 8- or 16-seat minibuses: **Skye Scenic Tours** (tel. 01478/617-006, www.skyescenictours.com), **Tour Skye** (tel. 01478/613-514, www.tourskye.com), and **SkyeBus** (tel. 01470/532-428, www.realscottishjourneys.com).

Portree-based **Michelle Rhodes** offers all-day guided drives around the island, tailored to your interests. Her specialty: clan battles, fairies, myths, and legends (£80/person, mobile 07833-073-951, tel. 01478/611-915, www.skyehistoryandheritagetours.co.uk, michellelorrainerhodes@gmail.com). Michelle also does walking tours around town (see "Helpful Hints" under "Orientation to Portree," later).

By Taxi

Don's Taxis is available for private rides (tel. 01478/613-100, https://donstaxis.vpweb.co.uk).

Portree

Skye's main attraction is its natural beauty, not its villages. But of those villages, the best home base is Portree (pore-TREE), Skye's largest settlement, trans-portation hub, and tour-ism center—ideally lo-cated for exploring Skye's quintessential sights on the Trotternish Peninsula loop drive.

Portree is nestled deep in its protective, pas-tel harbor; overlapping peninsulas just offshore guard it from battering west coast storms. Most of today's Portree dates from its early-19th-century boom time as a kelp-gathering and herring-fishing center.

As the most popular town on Scotland's most popular island, Portree is jammed with visitors in the summer. There are lots of ho-tels and B&Bs (which book up well in advance) and an abundance of good restaurants (the best of which merit reservations).

Orientation to Portree

Although Portree doesn't have any real sights, it does boast a gor-geous harbor area and—in the streets above—all of the necessary tourist services: a good TI, fine B&Bs, great restaurants, a gro-

ISLE OF SKYE

cery store, a launderette, and so on. The main business zone of this functional town of about 3,000 residents is in the tight grid of lanes on the bluff just above the harbor, anchored by Portree's tidy main square, Somerled Square. From here, buses fan out across the island and to the mainland. B&Bs line the roads leading out of town.

Tourist Information: Portree's helpful TI is a block off the main square (June-Aug Mon-Sat 9:00-18:00, Sun until 17:00; off-season Mon-Sat 9:30-16:30, closed Sun; just below Bridge Road, tel. 01478/612-992, www.visitscotland.com).

HELPFUL HINTS

WCs: Public WCs are across the street and down a block from the TI, across from the hostel.

Laundry: There's a **self-service launderette** below the Independent Hostel, just off the main square (usually 11:00-21:00, last load at 20:00, The Green, tel. 01478/613-737).

Bike Rental: The nearest place is **Skye Bike Shack,** about four miles outside of town (£30/day, reserve ahead in peak season, Tue-Sat 9:00-13:00, closed Sun-Mon, tel. 01470/532-375, www.skyebikeshack.com).

Car Rental: To make the most of your time on Skye, rent a car. Several options line up along the road to Dunvegan and charge around £40-60/day (most are closed Sun; smart to call several days ahead in peak season, but worth trying last-minute). The most user-friendly option is **M2 Motors,** which can pick you up at your B&B or the bus station (tel. 01478/613-344, www.m2-motors.co.uk). If they're booked up, try **Jansvans** (tel. 01478/612-087, www.jans.co.uk), **Highland Motors/ HM Hire** (based nearby in Borve but can pick up in Portree, tel. 01470/532-264, www.hm-hire.co.uk), or **Morrison** (tel. 01478/612-688, www.morrisoncarrental.com).

Parking: As you enter town, you'll see signs on the right directing you to a free parking lot below, at water level—after parking, just head up the stairs to the TI. You can also pay-and-display to park in the main town square (2-hour max, free after 18:00).

Town Walk: Michelle Rhodes leads guided one-hour town walks through Portree by request. While there's not a lot to say about the town, it's fun to have a local to explain things, and Michelle is a fine storyteller (£10/person, call or email to set a time, also offers driving tours; see contact information earlier, under "Getting Around the Isle of Skye").

Sights in Portree

There's not a turnstile in town, but Portree itself is fun to explore. Below I've described the village's three areas: the main square and "downtown," the harborfront, and the hill above the harbor.

Somerled Square and the Town Center

Get oriented to Portree on the broad **main square,** with its mercat cross, bus stops, parking lot, and highest concentration of public

benches. The square is named for Somerled (Old Norse for "Summer Wanderer"), the 12th-century ruler who kicked off the Mac-Donald clan dynasty and first united Scotland's western islands into the so-called Lordship of the Isles.

It seems every small Scottish town has both a mercat cross and a WWI memorial—and in Portree, they're combined into one. A **mercat cross** indicated the right for a town to host a market, and was the community gathering point for celebrations, public shamings, and executions. The **WWI memorial** is a reminder of the disproportionate loss of life that Scotland suffered in the Great War. In the case of wee Portree, a band of 28 Gaelic-speaking brothers went to war... and eight came back. (Ten were killed in a single night of fighting.)

Much of present-day Portree was the vision of Sir James Mac-Donald, who pushed to develop the town in the late 18th century. City leaders commissioned the impressive engineer Thomas Telford (famous for his many great canals, locks, and bridges) to help design the village's harbor and the roads connecting it to the rest of the island.

Wentworth Street, running from this square to the harbor, is the main shopping drag. Several English-sounding streets in Portree (Wentworth, Bosville, Douglas, Beaumont) are named for aristocratic families that the MacDonalds married into, helping to keep the clan financially afloat. Window-shop your way two blocks along Wentworth Street. Turn right on Bank Street. The **Royal Hotel,** built on the site of MacNab's Inn, is where Bonnie Prince Charlie bid farewell to Flora MacDonald following his crushing defeat at Culloden, then set sail, never again to return to Scotland.

Quay Street leads down the hill to...

▲▲Portree Harbor

Portree's most pleasant space (unless you've got food the seagulls want) is its harbor, where colorful homes look out over bobbing boats and the surrounding peninsulas. As one of the most protected natural harbors on the west coast, it's the reason that Portree emerged as Skye's leading town. Find a scenic perch at the corner of the harbor and take it all in.

While tourism is today's main industry, Portree first boomed in the mid-18th century thanks to kelp. Seaweed was gathered here, sun-dried, and burned in kilns to create an ashy-blue substance that was rich in soda, an essential ingredient in the production of glass and soap. But with the defeat of Napoleon at Waterloo, international sources of kelp opened up, causing this local industry to crash. This economic downturn coincided with a potato famine (similar to the one across the sea in Ireland), and by the mid-1800s, many locals were setting sail from this harbor to seek a better life in North America. But Portree soldiered on, bolstered by its prime location for fishing—especially for herring. By the early 20th century, a nationwide herring boom had again buoyed Portree's economy, with hundreds of fishing boats crowding its harbor.

Notice the stone building with the sealed-off door at the base of the stairs leading up into town. This was the former **ice house,** which was in operation until the 1970s. The winch at the peak of the building was used to haul big blocks of ice into an enormous subterranean cellar, to preserve Atlantic salmon throughout the summer.

Survey the harbor, enjoying the **pastel homes**—which come with lots of local gossip. Rumor has it that these used to be more uniform, until a proud gay couple decided to paint their house pink (it's now a recommended B&B). What used to be a blue-and-white house next door (now an all-blue hotel) belonged to a fan of the West Ham United soccer team. Soon the other homeowners followed suit, each choosing their own color. Speaking of bright colors, look for the traffic-cone-orange boat floating in the harbor. This belongs to the Royal National Lifeboat Institution (RNLI), Britain's charity-funded answer to the US Coast Guard.

You may notice the busy fish-and-chips joint, with its customers standing guardedly against the nearby walls and vicious seagulls perched on rooftops ready to swoop down at the first sight of battered cod.

Go for a stroll along the Telford-built pier. Along here, a couple of different companies offer 1.5-hour excursions out to the sea-eagle nests and around the bay (ask the captains at the port, or inquire at the TI). At the far end of the pier is a BP gas station with huge, underwater tanks for fueling visiting boats. When big cruise

Portree

PLAY FIELDS

To Uig, Dunvegan & Bike Rental

To Staffin, Portrush Peninsula & ⑬

HOME FARM RD.

WINDSOR CRES.

YORK DRIVE

MARTIN CRES.

To Scorrybreac Trail & ⑭

COOLIN DR.

STAFFIN RD.

KILSON CRES.

MILL RD.

STORRYHILL RD.

MANSE LN.

PARK RD.

PARK LN.

WENTWORTH ST.

DUNVEGAN

BRIDGE RD.

⑫

⑰

⑲

⑯

⑮

⑤

④

⑧ Somerled Square Ⓑ

⑦

⑨ THE GREEN

㉒

㉓

⑱

③

①

②

⑳

㉑

⑥

SCHOOL

VIEWFIELD RD.

SEAFIELD PL.

LISIGARRY COURT

BAYFIELD RD.

BANK ST.

BEAUMONT

QUAY ST.

ROYAL HOTEL

MEALE HOUSE

SKYE GATHERING HALL

P

P Main Parking Lot

P

PORTREE MEDICAL CENTRE

APOTHECARY TOWER

"The Lump"

HIGHLAND GATHERING BOWL

Harbor

BAYFIELD RD.

Loch Portree

N

200 Meters

200 Yards

⑨

⑩

⑪ To Slighachan & Kyle of Lochalsh

A-87

Accommodations
① Rosedale Hotel
② Pink Guest House
③ Marine House
④ The Portree Hotel & West Highland Bar
⑤ Ben Tianavaig
⑥ High Beech House
⑦ Youth Hostel
⑧ Independent Hostel & Launderette
⑨ Duirinish Guest House
⑩ Fishers Rock
⑪ To Greenacres Guest House & Aros Community Theatre
⑫ Easdale B&B

⑬ To Ballintoy B&B
⑭ To Fiona's B&B & Cullin Hills Hotel/Rest.

Eateries & Other
⑮ Scorrybreac
⑯ Dulse & Brose
⑰ The Isles Inn
⑱ Café Arriba & The Chippy
⑲ The Café
⑳ Sea Breezes
㉑ Harbour Fish & Chips
㉒ Fat Panda
㉓ Co-op Grocery & Relish
㉔ L'Incontro Pizza

ships are in port, they drop the hook and tender their passengers in to this pier.

Ascending "The Lump" (Hill Above the Harbor)

For a different perspective on Portree—and one that gets you away from the tourists—hike up the bluff at the south end of the harbor. From the Royal Hotel, head up Bank Street.

After a few steps, you'll spot the white **Meall House** on your left—supposedly Portree's oldest surviving home (c. 1800) and once the sheriff's office and jail. Today it's a center for the Gaelic cultural organization Fèisean nan Gàidheal, which celebrates the Celtic tongue that survives about as well here on Portree as anywhere in Scotland. Hiding behind the Meall House, along the harborview path, is the stepped-gable **Skye Gathering Hall** (from 1879). This is where Portree's upper crust throws big, fancy, invitation-only balls on the days before and after Skye's Highland Games. The rest of the year, it hosts cultural events and—on most days—a fun little market with a mix of crafts and flea-market-type items.

Back on Bank Street, continue uphill. Soon you'll approach the **Portree Medical Centre**—one of just two hospitals on the entire Isle of Skye. (Is it just me, or do those parking spots each come with a graveyard cross?)

Just before the hospital's parking lot, watch on the left for the uphill lane through the trees. Use this to hike on up to the top of the hill that locals call "The Lump" (or, for those with more local pride, "Fancy Hill"). Emerging into the clearing, you'll reach a huge, flat **bowl** that was blasted out of solid rock to hold 5,000 people during Skye's annual Highland Gathering. In addition to the typical Highland dancing, footraces, and feats of

strength, Skye's games have a unique event: From this spot, runners climb downhill, swim across Loch Portree, ascend the hill on the adjacent peninsula, then swim back again.

Walk left, toward the harbor, then head left again onto a path

leading away from the bowl; you'll run into the crenellated **apothecary tower.** It was built in 1834, not as a castle fortification but to alert approaching sailors that a pharmacist was open for business in Portree. This tower was literally blown over by gale-force winds in a 1991 storm, but has since been rebuilt. It's usually open if you'd like to climb to the top for views over the harbor and the region—on a clear day, you can see all the way to the Old Man of Storr (see page 333).

(see page 333).

Walks and Hikes near Portree

The Portree TI can offer advice about hikes in the area; if either of the below options interests you, get details there before you head out.

Scorrybreac Path: This popular choice doesn't require a car. To get to the trailhead—three-quarters of a mile from Somerled Square—walk north out of Portree on Mill Road, veer right onto Scorrybreac Road when you're just leaving town (following the sign for *Budhmor*), then follow the coastline to the start of the hiking trail, marked by signs. From here, you'll walk along the base of a bluff with fine views back on Portree's colorful harborfront. The loop back into town takes about an hour.

Old Man of Storr: Drivers can tackle the more ambitious hike up to this rocky formation. You'll drive about 15 minutes north of town (following the start of my Trotternish Peninsula Driving Tour) and park at the Old Man of Storr trailhead. Green trail signs lead you through a gate and up along a well-trod gravel path through a felled woodland. Once you've reached the top of the first bluff, take the right fork, and continue all the way up to the pinnacle. Plan on about two hours round-trip. (If you don't mind a longer drive, a better hike is at **The Quiraing**—see page 335.)

Nightlife in Portree

Portree goes to bed pretty early, but in high season a couple venues offer live music most evenings. The **West Highland Bar,** attached to the recommended Portree Hotel, has music nearly nightly. The **Isles Inn** (one of my recommended restaurants) hosts bands several nights a week in summer from 21:30. Also check what's on at the **Aros Community Theatre**, which alternates music, movies, and the occasional comedy performance (Viewfield Road, tel. 01478/613-750, https://aroscommunitytheatre.co.uk).

Sleeping in Portree

Portree is crowded with hikers and tourists in July and August: Book your room well in advance. You may need to check with several places. If you're late to the game, you might have better luck with a hotel, Airbnb, or one of the B&Bs lacking websites (of the ones I list, these include Marine House, Fiona's B&B, and Easdale B&B). Spring and fall (March-June and Sept-Oct) are also busy, but a bit more manageable (and cheaper).

If looking last minute, try the Facebook group "Skye Rooms," where hotels, B&Bs, and short-term apartments with late cancellations and random openings list their availability for the next day.

Travelers looking for accommodations can also post their desired dates.

ON THE HARBOR

$$$ Rosedale Hotel fills three former fishermen's houses with mazelike hallways and 23 rooms (some modern, some more traditional). With-it Neil runs the hotel with the help of his family, including his mom, who cooks (family room and a few small, no-view, cheaper doubles available; no elevator and lots of stairs; restaurant and bar, parking lot down the road; Beaumont Crescent, tel. 01478/613-131, www.rosedalehotelskye.co.uk, reservations@rosedalehotelskye.co.uk).

$$ Pink Guest House, run by the Portree Hotel, has 11 bright, spacious rooms (8 with sea views) on the harbor. The rates include a full Scottish breakfast (large family rooms, Quay Street, tel. 01478/612-263, www.pinkguesthouse.co.uk, info@pinkguesthouse.co.uk).

$$ Marine House, a cozy, welcoming, delightful time warp run by sweet Skye native Fiona Stephenson, has three simple, homey rooms (two with a private bathroom down the hall) and fabulous views of the harbor. Breakfast is conversational, as you'll eat with the other guests at one big table (cash only, reserved parking right on harbor, 2 Beaumont Crescent, tel. 01478/611-557, mobile 07512/921-230, stephensonfiona@yahoo.com).

UP IN TOWN

$$$$ The Portree Hotel is your functional, impersonal town-center accommodation (right on the main square), with 26 small but modern rooms on three floors and no elevator (family rooms, bar/restaurant, no parking—must use public lots, tel. 01478/612-511, www.theportreehotel.com, contact@theportreehotel.com).

$$ Ben Tianavaig, on the road through town overlooking the harbor, offers three fresh and airy rooms (all with views). Charlotte and Bill are generous with travel tips, offer a breakfast special of the day, and foster a shoes-off tidiness (2-night minimum required, cash only, street parking out front, closed Nov-March; 5 Bosville Terrace, tel. 01478/612-152, www.ben-tianavaig.co.uk, info@ben-tianavaig.co.uk).

$$ High Beech House wows guests with stupendous views from its breakfast room, overlooking the whole bay around Portree. Its two cozy rooms are a short walk up the hill above town, still central but with a peaceful and secluded vibe (2-night minimum preferred, street parking, Coolin Drive, tel. 07767/216-205, www.highbeechhouse.co.uk, info@highbeechhouse.co.uk, Jonathan and Pauline).

ISLE OF SKYE

¢ **Portree Youth Hostel,** run by Hostelling Scotland (SYHA), is a modern-feeling, institutional, cinderblock-and-metal building with 50 beds in 16 rooms (private and family rooms available, continental breakfast extra, kitchen, laundry, tel. 01478/612-231, www. hostellingscotland.org.uk, portree@hostellingscotland.org.uk).

¢ **Portree Independent Hostel,** in the unmissable yellow building just off the main square, has 60 beds and equally bold colors inside (one twin room and several 4-person rooms, no breakfast, kitchen, laundry, tel. 01478/613-737, www.hostelskye.co.uk, skyehostel@yahoo.co.uk).

JUST OUTSIDE TOWN
South of Portree, off Viewfield Road

Viewfield Road, stretching south from Portree toward the Aros Centre, is B&B central. All offer convenient parking and are within walking distance of town (figure 10-15 minutes). Some are on smaller side lanes that stretch down toward the water, but all are well marked from the main road.

$$ Duirinish Guest House feels homey, modern, and tidy. With four rooms, it sits across the main road from the water (only a few obstructed sea views) but comes with a spacious guest lounge and a warm welcome (two-night minimum, closed Nov-March, tel. 01478/613-728, www.duirinish-bandb-skye.com, ruth.n.prior@ hotmail.co.uk, Ruth and Allan).

$$ Fishers Rock, a serene waterfront retreat with a glassy, contemporary, light-filled view breakfast room, has a soothing energy and three rooms (2-night minimum, closed in winter, tel. 01478/612-122, www.fishersrock.com, fishersrock@btinternet. com, Heather).

$$ Greenacres Guest House feels estate-like and a bit more formal, with fine china on the table, fountain and manicured hedges in the garden, and a glassed-in sunroom with views. The four rooms have different color schemes and styles, and some feature Ewen's handmade headboards, built from wood recycled from an old school (cash only, closed Oct-Easter, one of the farthest houses from town on Viewfield Road, about a 20-minute walk, tel. 01478/612-605, https://greenacres-skye.co.uk, greenacreskye@aol. com, Marie and Ewen).

$ Easdale B&B is an old-school place with two rooms, a bright breakfast room with nice views, and a large, traditional lounge set just above the busy main road; it's a bit closer to town than the places listed above (cash only, no kids, closed Oct-March, Bridge Road, tel. 01478/613-244—call to reserve; spunky, plain-spoken, and happily computer-free Chrissie).

ISLE OF SKYE

North of Portree

$$ Ballintoy Bed and Breakfast, set back from the road and surrounded by a large field, has three immaculate ground-floor rooms accessorized with fun pops of color and artwork (family room, 2-night minimum preferred, includes continental breakfast, 15-minute walk from town on Staffin Road, tel. 01478/611-719, www.ballintoy-skye.co.uk, ballintoyskye@gmail.com, Gillian and Gavin).

$ Fiona's B&B is what B&Bs used to be like: snug, not fancy, but with a generous helping of Highlands hospitality thanks to friendly renegade Fiona. The four simple rooms have a shared WC and showers and are about a 10-minute walk from the center (cash only, a block from the big Cuillin Hills Hotel at Coolin Hills Gardens, no email or website so just call to make a reservation, tel. 01478/612-833).

BETWEEN PORTREE AND KYLEAKIN

$$$$ Sligachan Hotel (pronounced SLIG-a-hin), perched at a crossroads in the scenic middle of nowhere (yet handy for road-tripping sightseers) is a compound of sleeping and eating options that is a local institution and a haven for hikers. The hotel's 22 rooms are comfortable, if a bit dated and simple for the price, while the nearby campground and bunkhouse offer a budget alternative. The setting—surrounded by the mighty Cuillin Hills—is remarkably scenic (closed Dec-Feb, on the A-87 between Kyleakin and Portree in Sligachan, hotel and campground tel. 01478/650-204, bunkhouse tel. 01478/650-458, www.sligachan.co.uk, reservations@sligachan.co.uk). For location, see the map on page 316.

Eating in Portree

Note that Portree's eateries tend to close early (21:00 or 22:00), and the popular places can merit reservations any evening in the high season.

UP IN TOWN

$$$$ Scorrybreac is Portree's best splurge, offering a delightful array of well-presented international dishes that draw from local ingredients and traditions. The cozy, modern, unpretentious dining room with eight tables fills up quickly, so reservations are a must (set multicourse menus only, Tue-Sat 17:00-21:00, closed Sun-Mon, 7 Bosville Terrace, tel. 01478/612-069, www.scorrybreac.com).

$$$ Dulse & Brose is refined but unpretentious, with wooden bookshelves along the wall and old wooden benches (comfier than they sound). It offers a small menu of well-executed fish, beef, fowl, and veggie dishes, mostly using Scottish ingredients (daily 12:00-14:30 & 18:00-21:00, Bosville Terrace, tel. 01478/612-846, http://bosvillehotel.co.uk).

$$ The Isles Inn is a happening place, popular with hikers, with two halves serving the same menu—a brighter high-energy dining area and the darker pub—or you can sit at the bar. Offering a fun energy and warm service, they dish up simple, honest food one notch above pub grub. They have popular burgers, and their big slabs of salmon or haddock are served with fresh vegetables. While other places get stuffy, this has nice, fresh air circulation (daily 12:00-15:00 & 17:00-21:30, no reservations after 19:00, tel. 01478/612-129, facing the main square, Somerled Square).

$$ Café Arriba is a fun and welcoming space offering refreshingly eclectic flavors in this small Scottish town. With a menu that includes local specialties, burgers, and Italian, this youthful, colorful, easygoing eatery's hit-or-miss cuisine is worth trying. Drop in to see what's on the blackboard menu today (lots of vegetarian options, daily 8:00-17:00, Quay Brae, tel. 01478/611-830).

$$ The Café, a few steps off the main square, is a busy, popular hometown diner serving good crank-'em-out food to an appreciative local crowd. It's family-friendly, with a good selection of burgers and fish-and-chips (daily 9:00-15:30 & 17:30-21:00, Wentworth Street, tel. 01478/612-553). Their homemade ice cream from the stand in front is a nice way to finish your meal.

DINING BY THE WATER

Portree's little harbor has a scattering of good eateries but none have actual waterfront seating. My hunch: It's because of the mean seagulls that hang out here.

$$$ Sea Breezes is a basic, salty, no-nonsense eatery, with plain decor and a seafood-focused menu (daily 12:30-14:00 & 17:30-21:30 in summer, shorter hours off-season, closed Nov-Easter, tel. 01478/612-016).

$$$ Cuillin Hills Hotel Restaurant is in a big, classy old-world hotel set above the water. It has a peaceful and formal dining room, a commanding view, delightful service, and tasty food. It's quiet when in-town places are jammed—but reservations are still smart. It's a peaceful 15-minute walk north of town following the harbor (daily 12:00-14:00 & 18:00-21:30, Coolin Hills Gardens, tel. 01478/612-003, www.cuillinhills-hotel-skye.co.uk).

ISLE OF SKYE

EATING CHEAPER

Fish-and-Chips: Portree has two chippies: **$ The Harbour Fish & Chips Shop** is delightfully located on the charming harbor with good fish that's cheap and in big portions (daily 11:00-21:00, later in summer). The downside: Aggressive seagulls drive diners up against the wall. It's funny to watch. For a more relaxing meal, **$ The Chippy** sells very basic fish-and-chips and burgers, just up the harbor lane (on Bank Street) with peaceful-if-grungy tables and no seagulls.

Takeaway in Town: The **Fat Panda** Asian restaurant on Bayfield Road is satisfying, the **Co-op** grocery (daily 8:00-23:00) has a small selection of sandwiches and other prepared foods, and **Relish** is a deli serving good, fresh sandwiches (eat in or to go, end of Wentworth Street). **L'Incontro** is Portree's favorite place for pizza (Tue-Sun 10:30-21:00, closed Mon, The Green).

EATING ELSEWHERE ON THE ISLE OF SKYE

In addition to the following two destination restaurants, I've described some eateries in and near Kyleakin—where Skye meets the mainland—on page 344.

In Sligachan: The **Sligachan Hotel** (described earlier) is a grand and rustic old hotel in an extremely scenic setting, nestled in the Cuillin Hills. Its Harta Restaurant offers "casual dining with fine food" and a big and sloppy bar. Popular with campers and hikers, it's also family-friendly, with a zip-line for kids in the playground. The Seumas Bar has a Scotsman-pleasing range of whiskies. Choose between the lovely **$$$** dining room (nightly 18:30-21:00) and the big, open-feeling **$$** pub serving microbrews and mountaineer-pleasing grub (long hours daily, food served until 21:30, pub closed Oct-Feb; on the A-87 between Kyleakin and Portree in Sligachan, tel. 01478/650-204).

In Colbost, near Dunvegan: About a 15-minute drive west of Dunvegan (about 45 minutes each way from Portree), the **$$$$ Three Chimneys Restaurant** is out on a deserted road with just sheep for neighbors. This place is known throughout Scotland as a magnet for foodies. Its 16 tables fill an old three-chimney croft house, with a stone-and-timbers decor that artfully melds old and new—a perfect complement to the modern Scottish cuisine. It's cozy, classy, candlelit, and a bit dressy (do your best), but not stuffy. Reservations are essential (set multicourse menus only: £42 or £65 for lunch, £69 or £98 for dinner; daily 12:00-13:15 & 18:30-21:00, shorter hours off-season; tel. 01470/511-258, www.threechimneys. co.uk). They also rent six swanky, pricey **$$$$** suites next door.

Touring the Isle of Skye

There is a well-trodden tourist path around Skye, and it's clearly the most memorable way for someone with a car to spend the day. The three big sights are the Trotternish Peninsula (to the north of Portree), with its memorable Skye Museum of Island Life; Dunvegan Castle (to the east); and Talisker Distillery (to the south).

Planning Your Time: It's possible—but rushed—to see all three in one day. (The challenge: The Skye Museum of Island Life closes at 17:00.) Start with the first distillery tour at 10:00, tour the castle, and circle the peninsula to get to the museum by about 16:30. This will rush the wonderful natural sights along the peninsula, but it might be worth it if time is short and you want to experience it all.

While you could drive directly from Dunvegan Castle to the Skye Museum of Island Life and then tour the Trotternish Peninsula in a clockwise direction, it's far more scenic to drive it in a counterclockwise route as proposed here. Summer days are long, and the light can be wonderful in the early evening for the scenic west coast of the Trotternish Peninsula. Another option is to skip the distillery, do the castle first, and then take a leisurely tour of the peninsula. With two days, you can do it all at a more comfortable pace.

TROTTERNISH PENINSULA LOOP DRIVE

This inviting peninsula north of Portree is packed with windswept castaway views, unique geological formations, a few offbeat sights, and some of Scotland's most dramatic scenery. The following loop tour starts and ends in Portree, circling the peninsula counterclockwise (see the "Trotternish Peninsula" map). Along the way, you'll explore a gaggle of old-fashioned stone homes, learn about Skye's ancient farming lifestyles, and pay homage at the grave of

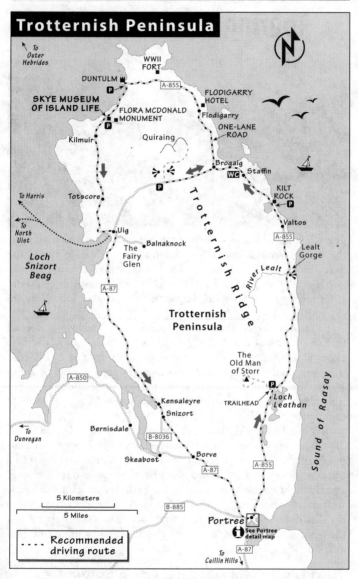

Trotternish Peninsula

To Outer Hebrides

WWII FORT

DUNTULM

SKYE MUSEUM OF ISLAND LIFE

FLORA MCDONALD MONUMENT

Kilmuir

Quiraing

A-855

FLODIGARRY HOTEL

Flodigarry

ONE-LANE ROAD

Brogaig

Staffin

WC

KILT ROCK

To Harris

Totscore

To North Uist

Uig

The Fairy Glen

Balnaknock

A-87

Loch Snizort Beag

Trotternish Ridge

River Lealt

Valtos

A-855

Lealt Gorge

Trotternish Peninsula

The Old Man of Storr

TRAILHEAD

Loch Leathan

A-850

Kensaleyre

Snizort

Bernisdale

B-8036

Skeabost

Borve

A-87

Sound of Raasay

To Dunvegan

5 Kilometers

5 Miles

B-885

Portree

See Portree detail map

To Cuillin Hills

A-87

.... Recommended driving route

a brave woman who rescued a bonnie prince. In good weather, a spin around Trotternish is the best activity Skye offers and is worth ▲▲▲.

Planning Your Drive: With minimal stops, this self-guided drive takes about two hours—but it deserves the better part of a day. Note that during several stretches, you'll be driving on a paved one-lane road; use the occasional "passing places" to pull over and allow oncoming traffic or faster cars to go by.

• *Head north of Portree on the A-855, following signs for* Staffin. *About three miles out of town, you'll begin to enjoy some impressive views of the Trotternish Ridge. You'll be passing peat bogs and may notice stretches where peat has been cut from the fields by the roadside. As you pass the small loch on your right, straight ahead is the distinctive rock tower called the...*

Old Man of Storr

This 160-foot-tall tapered slab of basalt stands proudly apart from the rest of the Storr (as the mountain is called). The unusual landscape of the Trotternish Peninsula is due to massive landslides (the largest in Britain). This block slid down the cliff about 6,500 years ago and landed on its end, where it has slowly been whittled by weather into a pinnacle. An icon of Skye, the Old Man of Storr has been featured in many films—from *Flash Gordon* to *Prometheus.* The lochs on your right supply drinking water for the town of Portree and have been linked together to spin the turbines at a nearby hydroelectric plant that once provided all of Skye's electricity.

If you'd like to tackle the two-hour hike to the Old Man, there's a pay parking lot directly below the formation (pay with coins or card; for details on the hike, see "Walks and Hikes near Portree," earlier).

• *After passing the Old Man, enjoy the scenery on your right, overlooking nearby islands and the mainland.*

As you drive, you'll notice that Skye seems to have more sheep than people. During the Highland Clearances of the early 19th century, many human residents were forced to move off the island to make room for more livestock. The people who remain are some of the most ardently Gaelic Scots in Scotland. While only about one percent of all Scottish people speak Gaelic (pronounced "gal-lic"), one-third of Skye residents are fluent. A generation ago, it was illegal to teach Gaelic in schools; today, Skye offers its residents the opportunity to enroll in Gaelic-only education, from primary school to college. (Sabhal Mòr Ostaig, on Skye's Sleat Peninsula, is the world's only college with courses taught entirely in Scottish Gaelic; see page 347).

• *About four miles after the Old Man parking lot, you'll pass a sign for the* River Lealt. *Immediately after, the turnoff on the right is an optional stop at the...*

Lealt Gorge

Where the River Lealt tumbles toward the sea, it carves out a long and scenic gorge. To stretch your legs, you can walk about five minutes along the lip of the gorge to reach a viewpoint overlooking a protected, pebbly cove and some dramatic rock formations. The formations on the left, which look like stacked rocks, are the opposite: They've been weathered by centuries of battering storms, which have peeled back any vegetation and ground the

stones to their smooth state. Peering down to the beach, you'll see a smokestack and some other ruins of a plant that once processed diatomite—a crumbly, clay-like substance made from algae fossils, which has hundreds of industrial uses. This factory, which closed in 1960, is a reminder of a time when tourism wasn't the island's main source of income. When this was functioning, no roads connected this point to Portree, so the factory's waterfront location made it possible to ship the diatomite far and wide.

• *Continue along the road. Just after the village of Valtos (about 2 miles after the Lealt Gorge viewpoint), you'll reach a loch (left), next to a parking lot (right). Park at the well-marked Kilt Rock viewpoint to check out...*

▲Kilt Rock

So named because of its resemblance to a Scotsman's tartan, this 200-foot-tall sea cliff has a layer of volcanic rock with vertical lava

columns that look like pleats (known as columnar jointing), sitting atop a layer of horizontal sedimentary rock. The dramatic formations in the opposite direction are just as amazing.

• *Continuing north, as you approach the village of **Staffin**, you'll begin to see interesting rock formations high on the hill to your left.*

Staffin's name, like that of the isle of Staffa, comes from Old Norse and means "the place of staves or pillars"—both boast dramatic basalt rock pillars. If you need a public WC, partway through town, watch on the left for the Staffin Community Hall (marked *Talla Stafainn,* sharing a building with a grocer). Or for a coffee or lunch break, you could visit (on the right) the Columba 1400 Centre, a Christian-run retreat for struggling teens from big cities. They run a nice cafeteria and shop to support their work (Mon-Sat 10:00-20:00, closed Sun, tel. 01478/611-400).

• *Just after you leave Staffin, watch for signs on the left to turn off and head up to the quintessential Isle of Skye viewpoint—a rock formation called...*

▲▲The Quiraing

You'll get fine views of this jagged northern end of the Trotternish Ridge as you drive up. Landslides caused the dramatic scenery in this area, and each rock formation has a name, such as "The Needle" or "The Prison."

At the summit of this road, you'll reach a parking area (which gets very busy in high season). Even a short walk to a nearby bluff—

to get away from the cars and alone with the wind and the island wonder—is rewarding. And there are several exciting longer hikes from here for a closer look at the formations. If you've got the time, energy, and weather for an unforgettable hike, here's your chance. You can follow the trail toward the bluff, and at the fork, decide to stay level (to the base of the formations) or veer off to the left and switch back up (to the top of the plateau). Both paths are faintly visible from the parking area. Once up top, your reward is a view of the secluded green plateau called "The Table," another landslide block, which isn't visible from the road.

• *You could continue on this road all the way to Uig, at the other end of the peninsula. But it's more interesting to backtrack, then turn left onto the main road (A-855, now a one-lane road), to reach the...*

Tip of Trotternish

A few miles north, after the village of Flodigarry, you'll pass the **Flodigarry Hotel,** with a cottage on the premises that was once home to Bonnie Prince Charlie's protector, Flora MacDonald (the cottage is now part of the hotel and not open to the public).

Soon after, at the top of a ridge ahead, you'll see the remains of an old **fort** from World War II, when the Atlantic was monitored for U-boats from this position.

Farther down the road, at the tip of the peninsula, you'll pass (on the right) the crumbling remains of another fort, this one much

ISLE OF SKYE

older: **Duntulm Castle** (free, roadside parking, 5-minute walk from road), which was the first stronghold on Skye of the influential MacDonald clan. It was from here that the MacDonalds fought many fierce battles against Clan MacLeod (for more on these clan battles, see "The Feuding Clans of Skye" sidebar later in this chapter). The castle was abandoned around 1730 for Armadale Castle on the southern end of Skye. While the castle ruins are fenced off, travelers venture in at their own risk. In the distance beyond, you can see the **Outer Hebrides**—the most rugged, remote, and Gaelic part of Scotland.

• *A mile after the castle, watch for the turnoff on the left to the excellent...*

▲▲Skye Museum of Island Life

This fine little stand of seven thatched stone huts, organized into a family-run museum, explains how a typical Skye family lived a century and a half ago.

Cost and Hours: £3, Mon-Sat 9:30-17:00, closed Sun and Oct-Easter, tel. 01470/552-206, www.skyemuseum.co.uk, run by Margaret, Hector, and Dinah. Though there are ample posted explanations, the £1 guidebook is worth buying.

Visiting the Museum: The three huts closest to the sea are original (more than 200 years old). Most interesting is The Old Croft House, which was the residence of the Graham family until 1957. Inside you'll find three rooms: kitchen (with peat-burning fire), parents' "master bedroom," and a bedroom for the 10 kids. Nearby, The Old Barn displays farm implements, and the Ceilidh House (a gathering place for the entire community) contains dense but very informative displays about crofting (the traditional tenant-farmer lifestyle on Skye), the Gaelic language, Flora MacDonald, and old tales from the area.

The four other huts, reconstructed here, house exhibits about weaving, the village smithy, and more. As you explore, admire the smart architecture of these humble but deceptively well-planned structures. Rocks hanging from the roof keep the thatch from blowing away, and the streamlined shape of the structure embedded in the ground encourages strong winds to deflect around the hut rather than hit it head-on.

• *After touring the museum, head out to the very end of the small road that leads past the parking lot, to a lonesome cemetery. Let yourself in through the gate to reach the tallest Celtic cross at the far end, which is the...*

ISLE OF SKYE

Monument to Flora MacDonald

This fine old cemetery, with mossy and evocative old tombs to ponder, features a tall cross dedicated to the local heroine who rescued the beloved Jacobite hero Bonnie Prince Charlie at his darkest hour. (After the original was chipped away by 19th-century souvenir seekers, this more modern replacement was placed here.) After his loss at Culloden, and with a hefty price on his head, Charlie retreated to the Outer Hebrides. But the Hanover dynasty, which controlled the islands, was closing in. Flora MacDonald rescued the prince, disguised him as her Irish maid, Betty Burke, and sailed him to safety on Skye. (Charlie pulled off the ruse thanks to

his soft, feminine features—hence the nickname "Bonnie," which means "beautiful" or "handsome.")

His flight inspired a popular Scottish folk song, "The Skye Boat Song": "Speed bonnie boat like a bird on the wing, / Onward, the sailors cry. / Carry the lad that's born to be king / Over the sea to Skye." You may recognize the tune as the theme to the television show *Outlander* (with lyrics adapted from a Robert Louis Stevenson poem).

• *Return to the main road and proceed about six miles around the peninsula. Soon after what was once a loch (now a giant depression), you'll drop down over the town of Uig ("OO-eeg"), the departure point for ferries to the Outer Hebrides (North Uist and Harris islands, 3/day) and a handy spot for services (cafés, a gas station, pottery shop, brewery, and WC).*

Continue past Uig, climbing the hill across the bay. To take a brief detour to enjoy some hidden scenery, consider a visit to the Fairy Glen. To find it, just after passing the big Uig Hotel, take a very hard left, marked for Sheadar and Balnaknock. Follow this one-lane road about a mile through the countryside. You'll emerge into an otherworldly little valley. Wind through the valley to just past the tiny lake and park below the towering Fairy Castle rock.

▲The Fairy Glen

Whether or not you believe in fairies, it's easy to imagine why locals claim that they live here. With evocatively undulating terrain—ruffled, conical hills called "fairy towers" reflected in glassy ponds, rising up from an otherwise flat and dull countryside—it's a magical place. There's little to see on a quick drive-by, but hikers enjoy exploring these hills, discovering little caves, weathered stone fences, and delightful views. As you explore, keep an eye out for "Skye landmines" (sheep droppings). Hardy hikers enjoy clambering 10 minutes up to the top of the tallest rock tower, the "Fairy Castle." (By the way, the sheep are actually fairies until a human enters the valley.)

• *Head back the way you came and continue uphill on the main road (A-87), with views down over Uig's port. Looking back at Uig, you can see a good example of Skye's traditional farming system—crofting.*

Traditionally, arable land on the island was divided into plots. If you look across to the hills above Uig, you can see strips of demarcated land running up from the water—these are crofts. Crofts were generally owned by landlords (mostly English aristocrats or Scottish clan chiefs, and later the Scottish government) and rented to tenant farmers. The crofters lived and worked under very difficult conditions and were lucky if they

could produce enough potatoes and livestock to feed their families. Historically, rights to farm the croft were passed down from father to eldest son over generations, but always under the auspices of a wealthy landlord.

• *But you live in a more affluent and equitable world, and more Scottish memories await to be created here on Skye. From here, you can continue along the main road, A-87, south toward Portree (and possibly continue from there to the Cuillin Hills). Or you can take the shortcut road just after Kensaleyre (B-8036) and head west on the A-850 to Dunvegan and its castle. All of your Skye options are described in the following pages.*

NORTHWEST SKYE
▲▲Dunvegan Castle

Perched on a rock overlooking a sea loch, Dunvegan Castle is the residence of the MacLeod (pronounced "McCloud") clan. One of Skye's preeminent clans, the MacLeods often clashed with their traditional rivals, the Mac-Donalds, whose castle is on the southern tip of the island (see "The Feuding Clans of Skye" sidebar, later). The MacLeods claim that Dunvegan is the oldest continuously inhabited castle in Scotland. The current clan

chief, Hugh Magnus MacLeod, is a film producer who divides his time between London and the castle, where his noble efforts are aimed at preserving Dunvegan for future generations. Worth ▲▲▲ to people named MacLeod, the castle offers an interesting look at Scotland's antiquated clan system, provides insight into rural Scottish aristocratic lifestyles, and has fine gardens that are a delight to explore. Dunvegan feels rustic and a bit worse for wear compared to some of the more famous Scottish castles closer to civilization.

Cost and Hours: £14, daily 10:00-17:30, closed mid-Oct-April, café in parking lot, tel. 01470/521-206, www.dunvegancastle.com.

Getting There: It's near the small town of Dunvegan in the northwestern part of the island, well signposted from the A-850 (free parking). From Portree, bus #56 takes you right to the castle's parking lot.

Visiting the Castle: Follow the one-way route through the castle, borrowing laminated descriptions in each room—and don't hesitate to ask the helpful docents if you have any questions. You'll start upstairs and then make your way to the ground floor with its unforgettable exhibit on the people of St. Kilda.

Up the main staircase and left down the main hallway, you'll reach the **bedroom.** On the elegant canopy bed, look for the clan's seal and motto, carved into the headboard. The words "Hold Fast," which you'll see displayed throughout the castle, recall an incident where a MacLeod chieftain saved a man from being gored by a bull by literally taking the bull by the horns and wrestling it to the ground.

Beyond the bedroom, you'll ogle several more rooms, including the **dining room.** Here and throughout the castle, portraits of clan chieftains and the MacLeod family seem to be constantly looking down on you. The library's shelves are crammed with rich, leather-bound books.

Then you're routed back across the top of the stairs to the right wing, with the most interesting rooms. The 14th-century **drawing room** is the oldest part of the castle—it served as the great hall of the medieval fortress. But today it's a far cry from its gloomy, stony, Gothic-vaulted original state. In the 18th century, a clan chief's new bride requested that it be brightened up and modernized, so they added a drop ceiling and painted plaster walls. The only clue to its original bulkiness is how thick the walls are (notice that the window bays are nine feet thick). In the drawing room, look for the tattered silk remains of the Fairy Flag, a mysterious swatch with about a dozen different legends attached to it (explained by the handout).

Leaving the drawing room, notice the entrance to the

ISLE OF SKYE

dungeon—a holdover from that stout medieval fortress. Squeeze inside the dungeon and peer down into the deep pit. (Hey, is that a MacDonald rotting down there?)

At the end of this wing is the **north room,** a mini museum of the clan's most prestigious artifacts. In the display case in the corner, find Rory Mor's Horn—made from a horn of the subdued bull that gave the clan its motto. Traditionally, this horn would be filled with nearly a half-gallon of claret (Bordeaux wine), which a potential heir had to drink in one gulp to prove himself fit for the role. Other artifacts include bagpipes and several relics related to Bonnie Prince Charlie (including his vest). In the center glass case, next to a lock of Charlie's hair, is a portrait of Flora MacDonald and some items that belonged to her.

From here a staircase leads to the ground floor, where you'll find some important exhibits in more utilitarian rooms. A glass case holds the Claymore Sword—one of two surviving swords made of extremely heavy Scottish iron rather than steel. Dating from the late 15th or early 16th century, this unique weapon is the bazooka of swords—designed not for dexterous fencing, but for one big kill-'em-all swing.

The MacLeods owned the rugged and remote St. Kilda islands (40 miles into the Atlantic, the most distant bit of the British Isles). They collected rent from the hardscrabble St. Kilda community of 100 or so (who were finally evacuated in 1930). The artifacts and dramatic photos of this community are a highlight of the castle visit. And, finally, you can watch a 12-minute video about the castle and the MacLeods, solemnly narrated by the 29th chief of the clan.

Between the castle and the parking lot are five acres of plush **gardens** to stroll through while pondering the fading clan system. Circling down to the sea loch, you'll enjoy grand views back up to the castle (and see a dock selling 30-minute boat rides on Loch Dunvegan to visit a seal colony on a nearby island-£9.50). Higher up and tucked away are some of the finer, hidden parts of the gardens: the walled garden, the woodland walk up  to the water garden (with a thundering waterfall and a gurgling stream), and the wide-open round garden.

The flaunting of inherited wealth and influence in some English castles rubs me the wrong way. But here, seeing the rough edges of a Scottish clan chief's castle, I had the opposite feeling: sympathy and compassion for a proud way of life that's dissolving with the rising tide of modernity. You have to admire the way they "hold fast" to this antiquated system (in the same way the Gaelic tongue is kept on life support). Paying admission here feels more like donating to charity than padding the pockets of a wealthy family. In fact, watered-down MacLeods and MacDonalds from America, eager to reconnect with their Scottish roots, help keep the Scottish clan system alive.

The Giant Angus MacAskill Museum

This oddball museum fills a humble roadside barn in the town of Dunvegan. Peter Angus MacAskill (whose son, Danny, is a You-Tube star for his extreme mountain biking on Skye) is happy to tell the story of "The Giant"—all seven feet nine inches of him—who teamed up with Tom Thumb to travel around the US in the circus and make Barnum and Bailey lots of money until he died in 1863 (£2, daily 10:00-18:00, closed off-season).

▲Dun Beag Fort

If driving between Talisker distillery and Dunvegan on A-863, you'll pass Skye's best-preserved Iron Age fort or "broch." This

2,000-year-old round stone tower caps a hill a 10-minute walk above its parking lot (just north of the village of Struan). The walk rewards you with an unforgettable chance to be alone in an ancient stone structure with a com-manding view. With all the stones scattered around Dun Beag, you can imagine it standing four times as tall—perhaps with three wood-framed floors inside protecting an entire community with their animals in times of threat—back before Julius Caesar sailed to Britannia.

▲Neist Point and Lighthouse

To get a truly edge-of-the-world feeling, consider an adventure on the back lanes of the Duirinish Peninsula, west of Dunvegan. This trip is best for hardy drivers looking to explore the most re-mote corner of Skye and undertake a moderately strenuous hike to a lighthouse. Although it looks close on the map, give this trip 30 minutes each way from Dunvegan, plus at least 30 minutes to hike from the parking lot to the lighthouse (with a steep uphill return). After hiking around the cliff, the lighthouse springs into view, with the Outer Hebrides beyond.

Getting There: Head west from Dunvegan, following signs for *Glendale.* You'll cross a moor, then twist around the Dunvegan sea loch, before heading overland and passing through rugged,

ISLE OF SKYE

desolate hamlets that seem like the setting for a BBC sitcom about backwater Britain. After passing through Glendale, carefully track *Neist Point* signs until you reach an end-of-the-road parking lot.

Eating: It's efficient and fun to combine this trek with lunch or dinner at the pricey, recommended **Three Chimneys Restaurant,** on the road to Neist Point at Colbost (reservations essential; see page 330).

WESTERN SKYE
▲▲Talisker Distillery

Talisker, a Skye institution, has been distilling here since 1830 and takes its tours seriously. This venerable whisky distillery is situated at the base of a hill with 14 springs, and at the edge of a sea loch—making it easier to ship ingredients in and whisky out. On summer days, the distillery swarms with visitors: You'll sniff both peated and unpeated grains; see the big mash tuns, washbacks, and stills; and sample a wee dram at the end. Island whisky tends to be smokier than mainland whisky due to the amount of peat smoke used during malting. Talisker workers describe theirs as "medium smoky," with peppery, floral, and vanilla notes.

Cost and Hours: £10 one-hour tour with tasting and a £5 voucher toward a bottle; daily 10:00-16:30, last tour one hour before closing; tours roughly every 30 minutes in summer, roughly hourly off-season; on the loch in Carbost village, tel. 01478/614-308, www.malts.com. Book online or call for a reservation (and plan on a 40-minute drive from Portree). Or, skip the tour and visit their tasting bar to select your own samples.

Nearby: Note that the **Fairy Pools Hike**—an easy walk that includes some of the best Cuillin views on the island—starts from near Talisker Distillery (see page 343).

CENTRAL SKYE
▲▲Cuillin Hills

These dramatic, rocky "hills" (which look more like mountains to me) stretch along the southern coast of the island, dominating Skye's landscape. Unusually craggy and alpine for Scotland, the Cuillin ("cool-in") seem to rise directly from the deep. You'll see them from just about anywhere on the southern two-thirds of the island, but no roads actually take you through the heart of the Cuillin—that's reserved for hikers and climbers, who love this area. To get the best views with a car, consider these options.

Sligachan: The road from the Skye Bridge to Portree is the easiest way to appreciate the Cuillin (you'll almost certainly drive along here at some point during your visit). These mountains are all that's left of a long-vanished volcano. As you approach, you'll see that there are three separate ranges (from right to left): red, gray, and black. The steep and challenging Black Cuillin is the most popular for serious climbers; the granite Red Cuillin ridge is more rounded.

The crossroads of Sligachan has an old triple-arched stone Telford bridge—one of Skye's iconic views—and a landmark hotel (see "Between Portree and Kyleakin" on page 328). The village is nestled at the foothills of the Cuillin, and is a popular launch pad for mountain fun. The 2,500-foot-tall cone-shaped hill looming over Sligachan, named Glamaig ("Greedy Lady"), is the site of an annual 4.5-mile hill race in July: Speed hikers begin at the door of the Sligachan Hotel, race to the summit, run around a bagpiper, and scramble back down to the hotel. The record: 44 minutes (30 minutes up, 13 minutes down, 1 minute dancing a jig up top). A Gurkha from Nepal did it in near record time...barefoot. The Sligachan Hotel feels like a virtual mountaineering museum with great old photos and artifacts throughout its ground floor (especially behind the reception desk). You're welcome to browse around.

Fairy Pools Hike: Perhaps the best easy way to get some Cuillin views—and a sturdy but manageable hike—is to follow the popular trail to the Fairy Pools. This is relatively near Talisker Distillery (in the southwestern part of the island).

To reach the hike from the A-863 between Sligachan and Dunvegan, follow signs to *Carbost*. Just before reaching the village of Carbost, watch for signs and a turn-off on the left to *Glenbrittle*. Follow this one-track road through the rolling hills, getting closer and closer to the Cuillin peaks. The well-marked *Fairy Pools* turnoff will be on your right. Parking here, you can easily follow the well-tended trail down across the field and toward the rounded peaks. (While signs suggest a 9.5-mile, 4- to 5-hour loop, most people simply hike 30 minutes to the pools and back; it's mostly level.)

Very soon you'll reach a gurgling river, which you'll follow toward its source in the mountains. Because the path is entirely through open fields, you enjoy scenery the entire time (and you can't get lost). Soon the river begins to pool at the base of each waterfall, creating a series of picturesque pools. Although footing can be treacherous, many hikers climb down across the rocks to swim and sunbathe. This is a fun place to linger (bring a picnic, if not a swimsuit). As I overheard one visitor say, "Despite the fact that it's so cold, it's so invitin'!"

Elgol: For the best view of the Cuillin, locals swear by the drive from Broadford (on the Portree-Kyleakin road) to Elgol, at the tip of a small peninsula that faces the Black Cuillin head-on. While it's just 12 miles as the crow flies from Sligachan, give it a half-hour each way to drive to the tip (mostly on single-track roads). For even more scenery, take a boat excursion from Elgol into Loch Coruisk, a sea loch surrounded by the Cuillin (April-Oct, departures several times a day, fewer Sun and off-season, generally 3 hours round-trip including 1.5 hours free time on the shore of the loch).

SOUTH SKYE
Kyleakin

Kyleakin (kih-LAH-kin), the last town in Skye before the Skye Bridge, used to be a big tourist hub...until the bridge connecting

it to the mainland enabled easier travel to Portree and other areas deeper in the island. Today this unassuming little village, with a ruined castle (Castle Moil), a cluster of lonesome fishing boats, and a forgotten ferry slip, is worth a quick look but little more.

Eating in Broadford: Up the road in Broadford is the Broadford Hotel, part of an upscale Skye hotel chain (Torrin Road at junction with Elgol, tel. 01471/822-204, www.broadfordhotel.co.uk). Its **$$$$ restaurant** is attempting to bring classy cuisine to this small town in a nice contemporary setting with harbor views (daily 12:00-14:00 & 17:00-21:00). The hotel's **$$ Gabbro Bar** is a relaxed pub-grub bistro. It was at this hotel that a secret elixir—supposedly once concocted for Bonnie Prince Charlie—was re-created by hotelier James Ross after finding the recipe in his father's belongings. Now known as Drambuie, the popular liqueur—which caught on in the 19th century—is made with Scotch whisky, heather honey, and spices. With its wide variety of Drambuie drinks, the Broadford's **Spinaker Lounge** is the place to try it.

Skye Bridge

Connecting Kyleakin on Skye with Kyle of Lochalsh on the mainland, the Skye Bridge was Europe's most expensive toll bridge per foot when it opened to great controversy in 1995 amid concerns that it would damage B&B business in the towns it connects, and disrupt native otter habitat. Here's the Skye natives' take on things: A generation ago, Lowlanders (city folk) began selling their urban homes and buying cheap property on Skye. Natives had grown to enjoy the slow-paced lifestyle that came with living life according to the whim of the ferry, but these new transplants found their commute into civilization too frustrating by boat. They demanded a bridge be built. Finally a deal was struck to privately fund the bridge, but the toll wasn't established before construction began. So when the bridge opened—and the ferry line it replaced closed— locals were shocked to be charged upward of £5 per car each way to go to the mainland. A few years ago, the bridge was bought by the Scottish government, the fare was abolished, and the Skye natives were somewhat appeased. There's no denying that the bridge has been a boon for Skye tourism, making a quick visit to the island possible without having to wait for a ferry.

SKYE'S SLEAT PENINSULA
Clan Donald Center and Armadale Castle
Facing the sea just outside Armadale is the ruined castle of Clan Donald, also known as the MacDonalds (Mac/Mc = "son of"), at

one time the most powerful clan in the Scottish Highlands and Hebrides. Today it is the "spiritual home of clan Donald," a sprawling site with woodland walks, a ruined castle, and a clan history museum.

Armadale Castle—more of a mansion than a fortress—was built in 1790, during the relatively peaceful, post-Jacobite age when life at the MacDonalds' traditional home, Duntulm Castle at the tip of the Trotternish Peninsula, had become too rugged and inconvenient. Today the Armadale Castle ruins (which you can view, but not enter) anchor a sprawling visitors center that celebrates the MacDonald way of life. You'll explore its manicured gardens, ogle the castle ruins, and visit the Museum of the Isles. This modern, well-presented museum tells the history of Scotland and Skye through the lens of its most influential clan (only a few artifacts but good descriptions, includes 1.5-hour audioguide). While fascinating for people named MacDonald, it's pricey and not worth a long detour for anyone else. But because it's right along the main road near the Armadale-Mallaig ferry, it can be an enjoyable place to kill some time while waiting for your ferry. At the parking lot is a big shop and café with free WCs.

ISLE OF SKYE

The Feuding Clans of Skye

Skye is one of the best places to get a taste of Scotland's colorful, violent history of clan clashes. As the largest of the Inner Hebrides Islands, with easy nautical connections to Scotland's west coast and much of northern Ireland, it's logical that Skye was home to two powerful rival clans: the MacDonalds and the MacLeods.

The MacDonalds (a.k.a. **"Clan Donald"**), with their base at Duntulm Castle, were the dominant clan of the Hebrides. In the 12th century, the MacDonalds' ancestral ruler Somerled first unified the disparate islands and western Highlands into a "Lordship of the Isles" that lasted for centuries. Throughout this period, they struggled to maintain control against rival clans—starting with the MacLeods.

Clan MacLeod, with its castle at Dunvegan, controlled the western half of Skye. Another branch of the MacLeods was based on the Isle of Lewis, holding down the fort in the Outer Hebrides. The MacLeods' ancestor, Olav the Black, had been defeated by Somerled, pulling their territory in to the Lordship of the Isles. But over the centuries, the MacLeods frequently challenged the authority of the MacDonalds, clashing in countless minor skirmishes as well as major clan battles in 1411, 1480, and 1578.

Adding to the volatile mix was **Clan Mackenzie,** which controlled much of the northern Highlands from their base at Eilean Donan Castle. The Mackenzies waged battle against the MacDonalds in 1491 and again in 1497.

The epic 1578 clash featured a series of grievous offenses. First, the MacLeods invaded the MacDonald-controlled Isle of Eigg, and, upon finding the islanders huddled in a cave for protection, set a roaring fire at the mouth of the cave—killing virtually the entire population. In retaliation, the MacDonalds barred the door of a church on the MacLeod-controlled Isle of Uist and burned all of the worshippers alive. In the ensuing battle, the furious MacLeods massacred the MacDonalds and buried the dead on a turf dike—earning the conflict the name "Battle of the Spoiling Dike."

The final clan battle on Skye began with a strategic marriage designed to broker a peace between the warring clans. Donald MacDonald married Margaret MacLeod, following a tradition called a "handfast," in which the groom was allowed a "trial period" of one year and one day with his new bride. After Margaret injured her eye, Donald decided to "return" her. Adding insult to injury, he sent her back to Dunvegan Castle on a one-eyed horse, led by a one-eyed man with a one-eyed dog. And so began two years of brutal warfare between the clans (the War of the One-Eyed Woman). In 1601, the Battle of Coire Na Creiche decimated both sides, but the MacDonalds emerged victorious. It would be the last of the great clan battles between the MacDonalds and the MacLeods, and it's said to be the final battle fought in Scotland using only medieval weapons (swords and arrows), not guns.

Cost and Hours: £8.75, April-Oct daily 9:30-17:30, Nov and March 10:00-15:00, closed in winter, 2 minutes north of the Armadale ferry landing, tel. 01471/844-305, www.armadalecastle.com.

Nearby: Heading north on the A-851 from the Clan Donald Centre, keep an eye out for **Sabhal Mòr Ostaig** (a big complex of white buildings on the point). Skye is very proud to host this college, with coursework taught entirely in Scottish Gaelic. Named "the big barn" after its origins, its mission is to further the Gaelic language (spoken today by about 60,000 people).

ON THE MAINLAND, NEAR THE ISLE OF SKYE
▲Eilean Donan Castle

This postcard-perfect castle, watching over a sea loch from its island perch, is scenically (and conveniently) situated on the road between the Isle of Skye and Loch Ness. While the photo op is worth ▲▲, the interior—with cozy rooms—is worth only a peek and closer to ▲. Eilean Donan (EYE-lan DOHN-an) might be Scotland's most photogenic countryside castle (chances are good it's on that Scotland postcard you bought during your trip). Strategically situated at

the confluence of three sea lochs, this was the stronghold of the Mackenzies— a powerful clan that was, like the MacLeods at Dunvegan, a serious rival to the mighty MacDonalds (see sidebar). Though it looks ancient, the current castle is actually less than a century old. The original castle on this site (dating from 800 years ago) was destroyed in battle in 1719, then rebuilt between 1912 and 1932 by the Macrae family as their residence. (The Macraes became bodyguards to the Mackenzies in the 14th century and later took over from their bosses as holders of the castle.)

Cost and Hours: £10, includes audioguide, good guidebook-£6; daily 10:00-17:00, July-Aug from 9:00, may open a few days a week Nov-Feb—call ahead; no backpacks, café, tel. 01599/555-202, www.eileandonancastle.com.

Getting There: It's not actually on the Isle of Skye, but it's quite close, in the mainland town of Dornie. Follow the A-87 about 15 minutes east of Skye Bridge, through Kyle of Lochalsh and toward Loch Ness and Inverness. The castle is on the right side of the road, just after a long bridge. Buses that run between Portree and Inverness stop at Dornie, a short walk from the castle (#917, 4/day, 1.5 hours from Portree).

Visiting the Castle: Buy tickets at the visitors center, then walk across the bridge and into the castle complex, and make your way into the big, blocky keep. You'll begin with some audiovisual introductory exhibits (left of main castle entry), then work through the historic rooms. While the castle is a footnote on a Scottish scale, the exhibits work hard to make its story engaging. Docents posted throughout can tell you more. First you'll see the claustrophobic, vaulted Billeting Room (where soldiers had their barracks), then head upstairs to the inviting Banqueting Room, with grand portraits of the honorable John Macrae-Gilstrap and his wife (who spearheaded the modern rebuilding of the castle). This room comes to life when you get a docent to explain the paintings and artifacts here. After the renovation, this was a sort of living room. Another flight of stairs takes you to the circa-1930 bedrooms, which feel more cozy and accessible than those in many other castles—and do a great job of evoking the lifestyles of the aristocrats who built the current version of Eilean Donan as their personal castle playset. Downstairs is a cute kitchen exhibit, with mannequins preparing a meal. Finally, you'll head through a few more humble exhibits (on old guns, bagpipes, and flags) to the exit.

INVERNESS & LOCH NESS

Inverness • Culloden Battlefield • Clava Cairns • Cawdor Castle • Loch Ness • Urquhart Castle

Inverness, the Highlands' de facto capital, is an almost-unavoidable stop on the Scottish tourist circuit. It's a pleasant town and an ideal springboard for some of the country's most famous sights. Hear the music of the Highlands in Inverness and the echo of muskets at Culloden, where government troops drove Bonnie Prince Charlie into exile and conquered his Jacobite supporters. Ponder the mysteries of Scotland's murky prehistoric past at Clava Cairns, and enjoy a peek at Highland aristocratic life at Cawdor Castle. Just to the southwest of Inverness, explore the locks and lochs of the Caledonian Canal while playing hide-and-seek with the Loch Ness monster.

PLANNING YOUR TIME

Though it has little in the way of sights, Inverness does have a workaday charm and is a handy spot to spend a night or two between other Highland destinations. With two nights, you can find a full day's worth of sightseeing nearby.

With a car, the day trips around Inverness are easy. Without a car, you can get to Inverness by train (better from Edinburgh, Stirling, Glasgow, or Pitlochry) or by bus (better from Skye, Oban, and Glencoe), then side-trip to Loch Ness, Culloden, and other nearby sights by public bus or with a package tour.

Note that Loch Ness is between Inverness and Oban, Glencoe, and the Isle of Skye. If you're heading to or from one of those places, it makes sense to see Loch Ness en route, rather than as a side trip from Inverness.

INVERNESS & LOCH NESS

Inverness

Inverness is situated on the River Ness at the base of a castle (now used as a courthouse, but with a public viewpoint). Inverness'

charm is its normalcy—it's a nice, midsize Scottish city that gives you a palatable taste of the "urban" Highlands and a contrast to cutesy tourist towns. It has a disheveled, ruddy-cheeked grittiness and is well located for enjoying the surrounding country-side sights. Check out the bustling, pedestrianized downtown, or meander the picnic-friendly riverside paths and islands—best at sunset, when the light hits the castle and couples hold hands while strolling along the water and over its footbridges.

Orientation to Inverness

Inverness, with about 70,000 people, is one of the fastest-growing cities in Scotland. Marked by its castle, Inverness clusters along the River Ness. The TI is on High Street, an appealing pedestrian shopping zone a few blocks away from the river; nearby are the train and bus stations. Most of my recommended B&Bs huddle atop a gentle hill behind the castle (a 10-minute uphill walk from the city center).

TOURIST INFORMATION
At the TI, you can pick up the self-guided *City Centre Trail* walking-tour leaflet and the *What's On* weekly events sheet (June-Sept Mon-Sat 9:00-19:00, shorter hours on Sun and off-season, 36 High Street, tel. 01463/252-401, www.visitscotland.com and www.visitinvernesslochness.com).

HELPFUL HINTS
Charity Shops: Inverness is home to several pop-up charity shops. Occupying vacant rental spaces, these are staffed by volunteers who are happy to talk about their philanthropy. You can pick

up a memorable knickknack, adjust your wardrobe for the weather, and learn about local causes.

Festivals and Events: The summer is busy with special events; book far ahead during these times: Etape Loch Ness bike race (early June), Highland Games (late July), Belladrum Tartan Heart Festival (music, early Aug), Black Isle farm show (early Aug), and Loch Ness Marathon (late Sept).

In summer (June-Sept), the TI can let you know whether a *ceilidh* (traditional dance and music) is scheduled at City Hall.

For a real Highland treat, catch a **shinty match** (a combination of field hockey, hurling, and American football—but without pads). Inverness Shinty Club plays at Bught Park, along Ness Walk. The TI or your B&B can tell you if there are any matches on, or check www.invernessshinty.com.

Bookstore: Located in a converted church built in 1649, **Leakey's Bookshop** is the place to browse through teetering towers of old books and vintage maps (Mon-Sat 10:00-17:30, closed Sun, Church Street, tel. 01463/239-947, Charles Leakey).

Baggage Storage: The train station has lockers (Mon-Sat 6:40-20:30, Sun from 10:40), or you can leave your bag at the bus station's ticket desk (small fee, daily until 17:30).

Laundry: Head to the west end of the Ness Bridge to find **New City Launderette** (self-service or same-day full-service, Mon-Fri 8:00-20:00, Sat until 18:00, Sun 10:00-16:00, last load one hour before closing, 17 Young Street, tel. 01463/242-507). **Thirty Degrees Laundry** on Church Street is another option (full-service only, drop off before 10:00 for same-day service, Mon-Sat 8:30-17:30, closed Sun, a few blocks beyond Victorian Market at 84 Church Street, tel. 01463/710-380).

Tours in Inverness

IN TOWN

Skip the City Sightseeing hop-on, hop-off bus tour (this format doesn't work in Inverness).

Walking Tours

Walk Inverness offers 1.5-hour walking tours departing from the TI several nights a week in summer at 18:00 and some Saturdays at 11:00. You'll learn about the history of Inverness, its castle, Victorian Market, and Old High Church, with a few *Outlander* landmarks thrown in for good measure (£10, www.walkinverness.com/tours, Cath Findlay). They also organize private tours—see website for details.

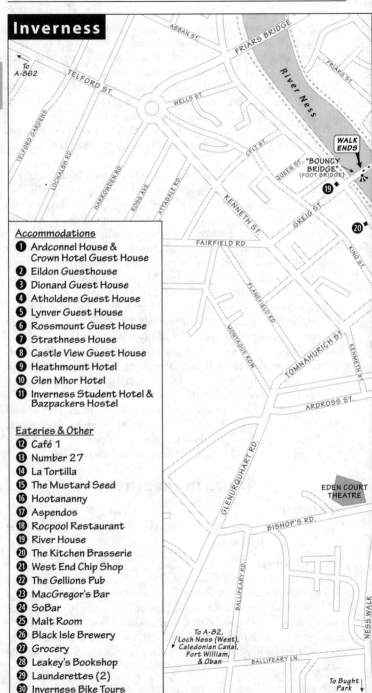

Inverness

Accommodations

1 Ardconnel House & Crown Hotel Guest House
2 Eildon Guesthouse
3 Dionard Guest House
4 Atholdene Guest House
5 Lynver Guest House
6 Rossmount Guest House
7 Strathness House
8 Castle View Guest House
9 Heathmount Hotel
10 Glen Mhor Hotel
11 Inverness Student Hotel & Bazpackers Hostel

Eateries & Other

12 Café 1
13 Number 27
14 La Tortilla
15 The Mustard Seed
16 Hootananny
17 Aspendos
18 Rocpool Restaurant
19 River House
20 The Kitchen Brasserie
21 West End Chip Shop
22 The Gellions Pub
23 MacGregor's Bar
24 SoBar
25 Malt Room
26 Black Isle Brewery
27 Grocery
28 Leakey's Bookshop
29 Launderettes (2)
30 Inverness Bike Tours

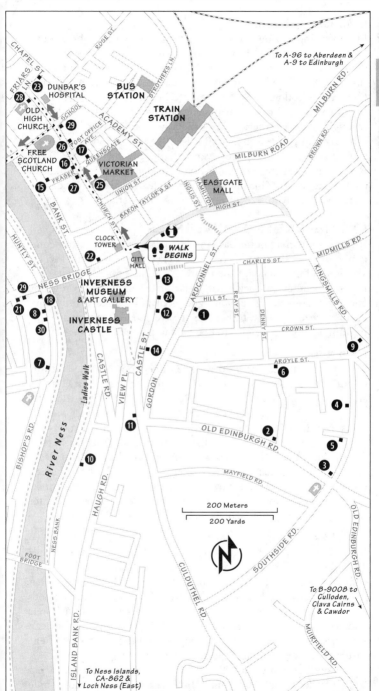

Inverness Bike Tours

Hardworking Alison leads small groups on two-hour bike tours. Her six-mile route is nearly all on traffic-free paths along canals and lochs outside of the city and comes with light guiding along the way. You'll pedal through Ness Island, stop at the Botanical Gardens, ride along the Caledonian Canal with its system of locks (you may even catch a boat passing through the locks), and cycle through a nature preserve (£21, generally no kids under 14, 10-person max; daily in season at 10:00, 13:00, and 15:45; best to book a spot in advance online, goes even in light rain, meet at the Prime Restaurant, near the west end of Ness Bridge at 5 Ness Walk, call or text mobile 07443-866-619, www.invernessbiketours.co.uk). Arrive a bit early to size up your bike and helmet.

EXCURSIONS FROM INVERNESS

Inverness is a great home base for day trips. A variety of tour companies offer excursions—details and tickets are available at the TI. While the big sellers are the many Loch Ness tours (because the monster is on every bucket list), I far prefer an all-day trip to the Isle of Skye—which gives you a good look at Loch Ness and Urquhart Castle along the way. For Isle of Skye and Orkney Island tours in summer, it's a good idea to book about a week in advance.

Loch Ness

The famous lake is just a 20-minute drive from Inverness. Tours often include a short boat ride, a visit to Urquhart Castle, and a stop at the Loch Ness monster exhibits. The lake is not particularly scenic, the castle is just a shell, and the monster is mostly a promotional gimmick. Still, if you have no car, this can be the most efficient way to check this off your list. **Jacobite Tours** focuses on trips that include Loch Ness, from a one-hour basic boat ride to a seven-hour extravaganza. Their four-hour "Sensation" tour includes a guided bus tour with live narration, a half-hour Loch Ness cruise, and visits to Urquhart Castle and the Loch Ness exhibits (£35, for more options see www.jacobite.co.uk, tel. 01463/233-999).

Isle of Skye

Several companies do good day tours to the Isle of Skye. They travel 110 miles (a 2.5-hour drive) to the heart of Skye (Portree). With about six hours of driving, and one hour for lunch in Portree, that leaves two or three hours for a handful of quick and scenic photo stops. All travel along Loch Ness so you can see Urquhart Castle and try for a monster sighting. And all stop for a view of Eilean Donan Castle. The longer rides loop around the Trotternish Peninsula. Websites explain the exact itineraries.

Wow Scotland's ambitious 12-hour itinerary goes in a big bus. They depart at 8:30 from the Inverness bus station and include short but smart and adequate stops all along the way (£79, nearly daily June-Aug, fewer departures in April-May and Sept, none Oct-March, tel. 01808/511-773, www.wowscotlandtours.com). I'd pay the extra for the £99 front row.

Highland Experience Tours runs another, shorter Isle of Skye itinerary in 24-seat buses (daily April-Oct, less off-season, 10 hours) but doesn't make it as far north as the Trotternish Peninsula (£55, tel. 0131-285-3314, www.highlandexperience.com). They offer a variety of other daylong tours, including to the far north with John O'Groats, or a trip to Royal Deeside and the Speyside Whisky Trail.

Happy Tours Scotland organizes daily minibus tours on a 10-hour joy ride (getting all the way to Quiraing) with top-notch guides (£80, 8 people per minibus, daily at 8:20, leaves from 7 Ness Walk at Columba Hotel, mobile 07828-154-683, book at www. happy-tours.biz, Cameron). They also offer Loch Ness and *Out-lander* itineraries, a Speyside whisky tour, and private minibus tours.

Rabbie's Small Group Tours does 12-hour trips to Skye in its 16-seater buses for £22 nearly daily from Inverness (www.rabbies. com). Their busy list of other tours cover Culloden and Clava Cairns, Cairngorms National Park, and Speyside.

Iona Highland Tours takes eight people on several different Isle of Skye itineraries, including one that allows hiking time at the Fairy Pools (£70, 9 hours, tel. 01463/250-457, www. ionahighlandtours.com).

By Train Then Tour: To avoid a long bus ride or skip the sights along the way to Skye, take the train from Inverness to Kyle of Lochalsh, where a Skye-based tour company will pick you up and take you around. Try **Skye Tours** (tel. 01471/822-716, www.skye-tours. co.uk) or **Tour Skye** (tel. 01478/613-514, www.tourskye.com). The train leaves Inverness before 9:00 and arrives around 11:30; the return train is around 17:15 (covered by BritRail Pass).

The Orkney Islands

For a very ambitious itinerary, John O'Groats Ferries offers an all-day tour that departs Inverness at 7:15, drives you up to John O'Groats to catch the 40-minute passenger ferry, then a second bus takes you on a whistle-stop tour of Orkney's main attractions (with an hour in the town of Kirkwall) before returning you to Inverness by 21:00. While it's a long day, it's an efficient use of your time if you're determined to see Orkney (£76, daily June-Aug only, tel. 01955/611-353, www.jogferry.co.uk).

Inverness Walk

Although humble Inverness is best as a jumping-off point for exploring the countryside, spare an hour or two for the town's fun history and quirky charm with this short self-guided walk (walk route shown on map earlier in this chapter).

• Start at the clock tower.

Clock Tower: Notice the **Gaelic language** on directional and street signs all around you. While nobody speaks Gaelic as a first language (and only about 60,000 Scottish people speak it fluently), this old Celtic language symbolizes the strength of Scottish Highland culture.

The clock tower looming 130 feet above you is all that remains of a tollbooth building erected in 1791. This is the highest spire in town, and for generations was a collection point for local taxes. Here, four streets—Church, Castle, Bridge, and High—come together, integrating God, defense, and trade—everything necessary for a fine city.

About 800 years ago, a castle was built on the bluff overhead and the town of Inverness coalesced right about here. For centuries, this backwater town's economy was based on cottage industries. Artisans who made things also sold them. In 1854, the train arrived, injecting energy and money from Edinburgh and Glasgow, and the Victorian boom hit. With the Industrial Age came wholesalers, distributors, mass production, and affluence. Much of the city was built during this era, in Neo-Gothic style—over-the-top and fanciful, like the City Hall (from 1882, kitty-corner to the clock tower). With the Victorian Age also came tourism.

Look for the **Bible quotes** chiseled into the facade of the building across the street from the City Hall. A civic leader, tired of his council members being drunkards, edited these Bible verses for maximum impact, especially the bottom two.

Hiding just up the hill (behind the eyesore concrete home of the Inverness Museum and Art Gallery) is **Inverness Castle,** where there is a small exhibition (with plans for a bigger museum) and a chance to climb to the top of the tower (£5). It's worth hiking up to the castle at some point during your visit to enjoy some of the best views of Inverness and its river. The castle has served as a courthouse in modern times, but it doesn't see a lot of action. In the last few decades, there have been only two murders to prosecute. As

locals like to say, "no guns, no problems." While hunters can own a gun, gun ownership in Scotland is complicated and tightly regulated.
• *Walk a few steps away from the river (toward McDonald's)...*

Mercat Cross and Old Town Center: Standing in front of the City Hall (known here as the "Town House") is a well-worn mercat cross, which designated the market in centuries past. This is where the townspeople gathered to hear important proclamations, share news, watch hangings, gossip, and so on. The scant remains of a prehistoric stone at the base of the cross are what's left of Inverness' "Stone of Destiny." According to tradition, whenever someone moved away from Inverness, they'd take a tiny bit of home with them in the form of a chip of this stone—so it's been chipped and pecked almost to oblivion.

The yellow **Caledonian** building faces McDonald's at the base of High Street. (Caledonia was the ancient Roman name for Scotland.) It was built in 1847, complete with Corinthian columns and a Greek-style pediment, as the leading bank in town, back when banks were designed to hold the money of the rich and powerful... and intimidate working blokes. Notice how nicely pedestrianized High Street welcomes people and seagulls...but not cars.
• *Next we'll head up Church Street, which begins between the clock tower and The Caledonian.*

Church Street: The street art you'll trip over at the start of Church Street is called *Earthquake*— a reminder of the quake that hit Inverness in 1816. As the slabs explain, the town's motto is "Open Heartedness, Insight, and Perseverance."

Stroll down Church Street. Look up above the modern storefronts to see centuries-old facades, more interesting than the town's regrettable post-WWII architecture. **Union Street** (the second corner on the right)—stately, symmetrical, and Neoclassical—was the fanciest street in the Highlands when it was built in the 19th century. Its buildings had indoor toilets. That was big news.

Midway down the next block of Church Street (on the right), an alley marked by an ugly white canopy leads to the **Victorian Market.** Venturing down the alley, you'll pass **The Malt Room** (a small and friendly whisky bar eager to teach you to appreciate Scotland's national tipple; see "Nightlife in Inverness") and **The Old Market Bar** (a dive bar worth a peek). Stepping into the Victorian Market, you'll find a gallery of shops under an iron-and-glass domed roof dating from 1876. The first section seems abandoned, but delve deeper to find some more active areas, where local shops mix with tacky "tartan tat" souvenir stands. If you're seriously into bagpipes, look for **Cabar Fèidh,** where American expat Brian sells CDs and sheet music, and repairs and maintains the precious instruments of local musicians.

Go back out of the market the way you came in and continue down Church Street. At the next corner you come to **Hootananny,** famous locally for its live music (pop in to see what's on tonight). Just past that is **Abertarff House,** the oldest house in Inverness. It was the talk of the town in 1593 for its "turnpike" (spiral staircase) connecting the floors.

Continue about a block farther along Church Street. The lane on the left leads to the **"Bouncy Bridge"** (where we'll finish this walk). Opposite that lane (on the right) is **Dunbar's Hospital,** with four-foot-thick walls. In 1668, Alexander Dunbar was a wealthy landowner who built this as a poor folks' home. Try reading the auld script in his coat of arms above the door.

A few steps farther up Church Street, walk through the iron gate on the left and into the churchyard (we're focusing on the shorter church on the right—ignore the bigger one on the left). Looking at the WWI and WWII memorials on the church's wall, it's clear which war hit Scotland harder. While no one famous is buried here, many tombstones go back to the 1700s. Dodging rabbits, head for the bluff overlooking the river and turn around to see...

Old High Church: There are a lot of churches in Inverness (46 Protestant, 2 Catholic, 2 Gaelic-language, and one offering a Mass in Polish), but these days, most are used for other purposes. This one, dating from the 11th century, is the most historic (but is generally closed). It was built on what was likely the site of a pagan holy ground. Early Christians called upon St. Michael to take the fire out of pagan spirits, so it only made

sense that the first Christians would build their church here and dedicate the spot as St. Michael's Mount.

In the sixth century, the Irish evangelist monk St. Columba brought Christianity to northern England, the Scottish islands (at Iona), and the Scottish Highlands (in Inverness). He stood here amongst the pagans and preached to King Brude and the Picts.

Study the bell tower from the 1600s. The small door to nowhere (one floor up) indicates that back before the castle offered protection, this tower was the place of last refuge for townsfolk under attack. They'd gather inside and pull up the ladder. Every night at 20:00, the bell in the tower rings 100 times. It has rung like this since 1730 to remind townsfolk that it's dangerous to be out after dinner.

This church became a prison for Jacobites after the Battle of Culloden; many of the prisoners were executed in the churchyard. (Look for marks where bullets hit the tower wall).

• *From here, you can circle back to the lane leading to the "Bouncy Bridge" and then hike out onto the pedestrian bridge. Or you can just survey the countryside from this bluff.*

The River Ness: Emptying out of Loch Ness and flowing seven miles to the sea (a mile from here), this is one of the shortest rivers in the country. While it's shallow (you can almost walk across it), there are plenty of fish in it. A 64-pound salmon was once pulled out of the river right here. In the 19th century, Inverness was smaller, with open fields across the river. Then, with the Victorian boom, the suspension footbridge (a.k.a. "Bouncy Bridge") was built in 1881 to connect new construction across the river with the town.

• *Your tour is over. Inverness is yours to explore.*

Sights in Inverness

Inverness Museum and Art Gallery

This free, likable town museum is worth poking around on a rainy day to get a taste of Inverness and the Highlands. The ground-floor exhibits on geology and archaeology peel back the layers of Highland history: Bronze and Iron ages, Picts (including some carved stones), Scots, Vikings, and Normans. Upstairs you'll find the "social history" exhibit (everything from Scottish nationalism to hunting and fishing) and temporary art exhibits.

Cost and Hours: Free, April-Oct Tue-Sat 10:00-17:00, shorter hours off-season, closed Sun-Mon year-round, cheap café, in the ugly modern building on the way up to the castle, tel. 01349/781-730, more info under the visitor attractions tab at www.highlifehighland.com.

Inverness Castle

Aside from nice views from the front lawn, a small exhibition, and a tower climb with a commanding city vista (£5), most of this Inverness landmark is not open to the public. A wooden fortress that stood on this spot was replaced by a stone structure in the 15th century. In 1715, that castle was named Fort George to assert English control over the area. In 1745, it was destroyed by Bonnie Prince Charlie's Jacobite army and remained a ruin until the 1830s, when the present castle was built. Now town leaders are discussing plans to build a new museum here, linking the two castle towers with a large exhibit space, but no timetable has been set. The statue outside (from 1899) depicts Flora MacDonald, who helped Bonnie Prince Charlie escape from the English (see page 337).

River Walks

As with most European cities, where there's a river, there's a walk. Inverness, with both the River Ness and the Caledonian Canal, does not disappoint. Consider an early-morning stroll along the Ness Bank to capture the castle at sunrise, or a post-dinner jaunt to Bught Park for a local shinty match. The path is lit at night. The forested islands in the middle of the River Ness—about a 10-minute walk south of the center—are a popular escape from the otherwise busy city.

Here's a good plan for your Inverness riverside constitutional: From the Ness Bridge, head along the riverbank under the castle (along the path called "Ladies Walk"). As you work your way up the river, you'll see the architecturally bold Eden Court Theatre (across the river), pass a white pedestrian bridge, see a WWI memorial, and peek into the gardens of several fine old Victorian sandstone riverfront homes. Nearing the tree-covered islands, watch for flyfishers in hip waders on the pebbly banks. Reaching the first, skinny little island, take the bridge with the wavy, wrought-iron railing and head down the path along the middle of the island. Notice that this is part of the Great Glen Way, a footpath that stretches from here all the way to Fort William (79 miles). Enjoy this little nature break, with gurgling rapids—and, possibly, a few midges. Reaching the bigger bridge, cross it and enjoy strolling through tall forests. Continue upriver. After two more green-railinged bridges, traverse yet another island, and find one last white-iron bridge that takes you across to the opposite bank. You'll pop out at the corner of Bught Park, the site of shinty practices and games—are any going on today?

From here, you can simply head back into town on this bank. If you'd like to explore more, near Bught Park you'll find minigolf, a skate park, the Highland Archive building, the free Botanic Gardens (daily 10:00-17:00, until 16:00 Nov-March), and the huge Active Inverness leisure center, loaded with amusements including a swimming pool with adventure slides, a climbing wall, a sauna and steam area, and a gym (www.invernessleisure.co.uk).

Continuing west from these leisure areas, you'll soon hit the Caledonian Canal; to the south, this parallels the River Ness, and to the north it empties into Beauly Firth, then Moray Firth and the North Sea. From the Tomnahurich Bridge, paths on either bank allow you to walk along the Great Glen Way until you're ready to turn around. It takes about an hour to circle around from the center of Inverness all the way to Clachnaharry, where the river meets Beauly Firth.

Nightlife in Inverness

Scottish Folk Music

While you can find traditional folk-music sessions in pubs and hotel bars anywhere in town, two places are well established as *the* music pubs. Neither charges a cover for the music, unless a bigger-name band is playing.

The Gellions has live folk and Scottish music nightly (from 21:30 or sometimes earlier). Very local and a bit rough, it has local ales on tap and brags it's the oldest bar in town (14 Bridge Street, tel. 01463/233-648, www.gellions.co.uk).

Hootananny is an energetic place with several floors of live rock, blues, or folk music, and drinking fun nightly. It's rock (upstairs) and reel (ground floor). Music in the main bar (ground floor) usually begins about 21:30 (traditional music sessions Sun-Wed, trad bands on weekends; also a daytime session on Sat afternoon at 14:30). On Friday and Saturday nights only, upstairs is the Mad Hatter's nightclub, complete with a cocktail bar (67 Church Street, tel. 01463/233-651, www.hootananyinverness.co.uk).

MacGregor's Bar is run by Bruce MacGregor, a founding member of the Scottish group Blazin' Fiddles, and his wife Jo. Their passion for local music (with several music evenings each week) is matched by good food, good local beers on tap, and a fun local crowd. From spring through fall, they also offer a twice-weekly whisky tasting (£35, Mon and Thu at 19:00) along with traditional Scottish music and stories (a few blocks past the pedestrian bridge at 113 Academy Street, tel. 01463/719-629, www.macgregorsbars.com).

Billiards and Darts

SoBar is a sprawling pub with dart boards (free), pool tables (£7.50 per hour), a museum's worth of sports memorabilia, and the biggest TV screens in town (popular on big game nights). It's a fine place to hang out and meet locals if you'd rather not have live music (just across from the castle at 55 Castle Street, tel. 01463/572-542).

Whisky Tastings and Brew Pubs

For a whisky education, or just a fine cocktail, drop in to the intimate **Malt Room,** with 250 different whiskies ranging from £4 to £115. The whisky-plus-chocolate flight makes for a fun nightcap (just off Church Street in the alley leading to the Victorian Market, 34 Church Street, tel. 01463/221-888, Matt).

At the **Black Isle Brewery,** you can sample their local organic beers and ciders. Choose from 26 beers on tap (including some non-Black Isle brews), all listed on the TV screens over the bar (wood-fired pizzas, 68 Church Street, tel. 01463/229-920).

MacGregor's Bar (listed earlier) also offers whisky tastings and beer flights.

Sleeping in Inverness

B&Bs NEAR THE TOWN CENTER

These B&Bs are popular; book ahead for June through August (and during the peak times listed in "Helpful Hints," earlier), and be aware that some require a two-night minimum during busy times. The places I list are a 10-15-minute walk from the train station and town center. To get to the B&Bs, either catch a taxi (£5) or walk: From the train and bus stations, go left on Academy Street. At the first stoplight (the second if you're coming from the bus station), veer right onto Inglis Street in the pedestrian zone. Go up the Market Brae steps. At the top, turn right onto Ardconnel Street.

On or near Ardconnel Street

Find these two above Castle Street (with several recommended restaurants).

$$ Ardconnel House is a classic, traditional place offering a nice, large guest lounge, along with six spacious and comfortable rooms (family room, two-night minimum preferred in summer, no children under 10, 21 Ardconnel Street, tel. 01463/418-242, www. ardconnel-inverness.co.uk, ardconnel@gmail.com, Graeme and Audrey).

$$ Crown Hotel Guest House isn't quite as cute and homey as some, and it has a few dated elements, but its seven rooms (five en suite, two with separate but private bathrooms) are pleasant and a solid value (family room, 19 Ardconnel Street, tel. 01463/231-135, www.crownhotel-inverness.co.uk, crownhotelguesthouse@gmail.com, Munawar and Asia).

Around Old Edinburgh Road and Southside Road

These places are just a couple of minutes farther out from Castle Street and the places on Ardconnel.

$$ Eildon Guesthouse offers five tranquil rooms with spacious baths. The cute-as-a-button 1890s brick home is centrally located yet exudes countryside warmth and serenity from the moment you open the gate (family rooms, 2-night minimum in summer, no kids under 10, in-room fridges, parking, 29 Old Edinburgh Road, tel. 01463/231-969, www.eildonguesthouse.co.uk, eildonguesthouse@yahoo.co.uk, Jacqueline).

$$ Dionard Guest House, wrapped in a fine hedged-in garden, has cheerful common spaces, six lovely rooms, some fun stag art, and lively hosts Gail and Anne—best friends turned business partners (family suite, in-room fridges, they'll do guest laundry for free, parking, 39 Old Edinburgh Road, tel. 01463/233-557, www.dionardguesthouse.co.uk, enquiries@dionardguesthouse.co.uk).

$$ Atholdene Guest House, run by amiable Gillian and Andrew, welcomes many return visitors—maybe they come back for the homemade scones? Most of its nine rooms are on the smaller side but comfortable, and classical music in the morning makes for a civilized breakfast (2-night minimum in summer, guests must be 18 or older, parking, 20 Southside Road, tel. 01463/233-565, www.atholdene.com, info@atholdene.com).

$$ Lynver Guest House will make you feel spoiled, with two large, boutique-y rooms (all with sitting areas), a backyard stone patio that catches the sun, and veggie and fish options at breakfast (2-night minimum preferred in summer, no kids under 10, in-room fridges, 30 Southside Road, tel. 01463/242-906, www.lynver.co.uk, info@lynver.co.uk, Michelle and Brian).

$$ Rossmount Guest House feels like home, with its curl-up-on-the-couch lounge space, unfussy rooms (five in all), and friendly hosts (2-night minimum in summer, Argyle Street, tel. 01463/229-749, www.rossmount.co.uk, mail@rossmount.co.uk, Ruth and Robert).

B&Bs ACROSS THE RIVER

$$$ Strathness House has a prime spot on the river a block from Ness Bridge. Formerly a hotel, it's a bigger place, with 12 rooms and a large ground-floor lounge, but comes with the same intimate touches of a guesthouse. They cater to all diets at breakfast, including vegan, gluten-free, halal, and kosher (family room for 3, no kids under 5, street or off-site parking, 4 Ardross Terrace, tel. 01463/232-765, www.strathnesshouse.co.uk, info@strathnesshouse.com, Joan and Javed).

$$ Castle View Guest House sits right along the River Ness at the Ness Bridge—and, true to its name, it owns smashing views of the castle. Its five big and comfy rooms (some with views) are colorfully furnished, and the delightful place is lovingly run by Eleanor (2A Ness Walk, tel. 01463/241-443, www.castleviewguesthouseinverness.com, enquiries@castleviewguesthouseinverness.com).

HOTELS

Inverness has a number of big chain hotels. These tend to charge a lot when Inverness is busy but are worth a look if the B&Bs are full or if it's outside the main tourist season. Options include the Inverness Palace Hotel & Spa (a Best Western fancy splurge right on the river with a pool and gym), Premier Inn (River Ness location), and Mercure. Or try these more local options.

$$$$ Heathmount Hotel's understated facade hides a chic retreat for comfort-seeking travelers. Its eight elegant rooms come with unique decoration, parking, and fancy extras (family room, no elevator, restaurant, Kingsmill Road, tel. 01463/235-877, www.heathmounthotel.com, info@heathounthotel.com).

$$$ Glen Mhor Hotel, with 122 rooms, sprawls across several buildings right along the river. The location can't be beat, even if the staff and rooms lack a personal touch (restaurant, Ness Bank, tel. 01463/234-308, www.glen-mhor.com, enquiries@glen-mhor.com).

HOSTELS

For funky and cheap dorm beds near the center and the recommended Castle Street restaurants, consider these friendly side-by-side hostels, geared toward younger travelers. They're about a 12-minute walk from the train station.

¢ Bazpackers Hostel, a stone's throw from the castle, has a quieter, more private feel for a hostel with dorm beds arranged in pods (private rooms with shared bath available, reception open 7:30-23:00, pay laundry service, 4 Culduthel Road, tel. 01463/717-663, www.bazpackershostel.co.uk, info@bazpackershostel.co.uk). They also rent a small apartment nearby (sleeps up to 4).

¢ Inverness Student Hotel has brightly colored rooms and a laid-back lounge with a bay window overlooking the River Ness. The knowledgeable, friendly staff welcomes any traveler over 18. Dorms are a bit grungy, but each bunk has its own playful name (breakfast extra, free tea and coffee, pay laundry service, kitchen, 8 Culduthel Road, tel. 01463/236-556, www.invernessstudenthotel.com, inverness@scotlandstophostels.com).

Eating in Inverness

In high season, Inverness' top restaurants (including many of those recommended below) can fill up quickly—reservations are wise.

BY THE CASTLE

The first three eateries line Castle Street, facing the back of the castle.

$$$ Café 1 serves up high-quality modern Scottish and international cuisine with trendy, chic bistro flair. Fresh meat from their farm adds to an appealing menu (lunch and early-bird dinner specials until 18:30, open Mon-Fri 12:00-14:30 & 17:00-21:30, Sat from 12:30 and 17:30, closed Sun, 75 Castle Street, tel. 01463/226-200, www.cafe1.net).

$$ Number 27 has a straightforward, crowd-pleasing menu that offers something for everyone—burgers, pastas, and more. The food is surprisingly elegant for this price range (daily 12:00-21:00, generous portions, local ales on tap, 27 Castle Street, tel. 01463/241-999).

$$ La Tortilla has Spanish tapas, including spicy king prawns (the house specialty), plus a vegan menu. It's an appealing, colorfully tiled, and vivacious dining option that feels like Spain. With the tapas format, three family-style dishes make about one meal (daily 12:00-22:00, 99 Castle Street, tel. 01463/709-809).

IN THE TOWN CENTER

$$$$ The Mustard Seed serves Scottish food with a modern twist in an old church with a river view. It's a lively place with nice outdoor tables over the river when sunny (early specials before 19:00, daily 12:00-15:00 & 17:30-22:00, reservations smart, on the corner of Bank and Fraser Streets, 16 Fraser Street, tel. 01463/220-220, www.mustardseedrestaurant.co.uk).

$$ Hootananny is a spacious pub with a hardwood-and-candlelight vibe and a fun menu with Scottish pub grub (food served Mon-Sat 12:00-15:00 & 17:00-20:30, dinner-only on Sun). The kitchen closes early to make way for the live music scene that takes over each night after 21:30 (see "Nightlife in Inverness," earlier).

$$ Aspendos serves up freshly prepared, delicious Turkish dishes in a spacious, dressy, and exuberantly decorated dining room (daily 12:00-22:00, 26 Queensgate, tel. 01463/711-950).

Picnic: There's a **Co-op** market with plenty of cheap picnic grub at 59 Church Street (daily until 22:00).

ACROSS THE RIVER

$$$$ Rocpool Restaurant is a hit with locals, good for a splurge, and perhaps the best place in town. Owner/chef Steven Devlin serves creative modern European food to a smart clientele in a sleek, contemporary dining room (early-bird weekday special until 18:45, open Mon-Sat 12:00-14:30 & 17:45-22:00, closed Sun, reservations essential; across Ness Bridge at 1 Ness Walk, tel. 01463/717-274, www.rocpoolrestaurant.com).

$$$$ River House, a classy, sophisticated, but unstuffy place, is the brainchild of Cornishman Alfie—who prides himself on melding the seafood know-how of both Cornwall and Scotland with Venetian-style *cicchetti* small plates (Mon-Sat 15:00-21:30, closed Mon off-season and Sun year-round, reservations smart, 1 Greig Street, tel. 01463/222-033, www.riverhouseinverness.co.uk).

$$$ The Kitchen Brasserie is a modern building overlooking the river, popular for their homemade comfort food—pizza, pasta, and burgers (early-bird special until 19:00, daily 12:00-15:00 & 17:00-22:00, 15 Huntly Street, tel. 01463/259-119, www.kitchenrestaurant.co.uk).

Fish-and-Chips: Consider the **$ West End** chippy for a nicely presented sit-down meal or to go (daily 12:00-14:00 & 16:30-22:00, closed Sun at lunch, a block over Ness Bridge on Young Street, tel. 01463/232-884).

Inverness Connections

From Inverness by Train to: Pitlochry (nearly hourly, 1.5 hours), **Stirling** (7/day direct, 3 hours, more with transfer in Perth), **Kyle of Lochalsh** near Isle of Skye (4/day, 2.5 hours), **Edinburgh** (nearly hourly, 3.5 hours, some with change in Perth), **Glasgow** (4/day direct, 3 hours, more with change in Perth), **Thurso** (for ferries to Orkney; 4/day, 4 hours). The Caledonian Sleeper provides overnight service to **London** (www.sleeper.scot). Train info: tel. 0345-748-4950, NationalRail.co.uk.

By Bus: Inverness has a handy direct bus to **Portree** on the Isle of Skye (bus #917, 2/day, 3 hours), but for other destinations in western Scotland, you'll first head for **Fort William** (buses #919 or #920, 6/day, 2 hours, fewer on Sun). For connections onward to **Oban** (figure 4 hours total) or **Glencoe** (3 hours total), see "Fort William Connections" on page 308. Inverness is also connected by direct bus to **Edinburgh** (express bus #G90, 2/day, 4 hours or #M90, 2/day, 4 hours, more with transfer) and **Glasgow** (express bus #G10, 5/day, 3 hours; 6/day direct on Megabus, 3.5 hours). Bus info: Citylink.co.uk.

Tickets are sold in advance online, by phone at tel. 0871-266-3333, or in person at the Inverness bus station (daily 7:45-18:15, baggage storage, 2 blocks from train station on Margaret Street, tel. 01463/233-371).

INVERNESS & LOCH NESS

ROUTE TIPS FOR DRIVERS

Inverness to Edinburgh (160 miles, 3.25 hours minimum): Leaving Inverness, follow signs to the A-9 (south, toward Perth). If you haven't seen Culloden Battlefield yet, it's an easy detour: Just as you leave Inverness, head four miles east off the A-9 on the B-9006. Back on the A-9, it's a wonderfully speedy, scenic drive (A-9, M-90, A-90) all the way to Edinburgh. If you have time, consider stopping en route in Pitlochry (just off the A-9; see the Eastern Scotland chapter).

Inverness to Portree, Isle of Skye (110 miles, 2.5 hours): The drive from Inverness to Skye is pretty but much less so than the valley of Glencoe or the Isle of Skye itself. You'll drive along boring Loch Ness and then follow signs to Portree and Skye on A-87 along Loch Cluanie (a loch tamed by a dam built to generate hydroelectric power). This valley was once a "drovers' route" for the cattle drive from the islands to the market—home of the original Scottish cowboys.

Inverness to Fort William (65 miles, 1.5 hours): This city, southwest of Inverness via the A-82, is a good gateway to Oban and Glencoe. See page 309.

Near Inverness

Inverness puts you in the heart of the Highlands, within easy striking distance of several famous and worthwhile sights: Commune with the Scottish soul at historic Culloden Battlefield, where British history reached a turning point. Wonder at three mysterious Neolithic cairns, which remind visitors that Scotland's story goes back thousands of years. And enjoy a homey country castle at Cawdor. Loch Ness—with its elusive monster—is another popular and easy day trip.

In addition to the sights in this section, note that the Speyside Whisky Trail, the Leault Working Sheepdogs farm show, and the Highland Folk Museum are also within side-tripping distance of Inverness (see the Eastern Scotland chapter).

CULLODEN BATTLEFIELD

Jacobite troops under Bonnie Prince Charlie were defeated at Culloden by supporters of the Hanover dynasty (King George II's family) in 1746. Sort of the "Scottish Alamo," this last major land battle fought on British soil spelled the end of Jacobite resistance and the beginning of the clan chiefs' fall from power. Wandering the desolate, solemn battlefield at Culloden (kuh-LAW-dehn), you sense that something terrible occurred here. Locals still bring white roses and speak of "The '45" (as Bonnie Prince Charlie's entire campaign is called) as if it just happened. Engaging even if you're not interested in military history, the battlefield at Culloden and its high-tech visitors center together are worth ▲▲▲.

Orientation to Culloden

Cost and Hours: £11, £5 guidebook; daily 9:00-18:00, June-Aug until 19:00, Nov-Feb 10:00-16:00; café, tel. 01463/796-090, http://www.nts.org/uk/culloden.

Tours: The included audioguide leads you through both the exhibition and the battlefield. There are several free tours daily along with costumed events (see schedule posted at entry).

Getting There: It's a 15-minute drive east of Inverness. Follow signs to *Aberdeen*, then *Culloden Moor*—the B-9006 takes you right there (well-signed on the right-hand side). Parking is £2 (pay with coins outside or with your admission inside). Public buses leave from Inverness' Queensgate Street and drop you off in front of the entrance (£5 round-trip, bus #5, roughly hourly, 40 minutes, ask at TI for route/schedule updates). A taxi costs around £15 one-way.

Length of This Tour: Allow 2 hours.

Background

The Battle of Culloden (April 16, 1746) marks the steep decline of the Scottish Highland clans and the start of years of cruel repression of Highland culture by the British. It was the culmination of a year's worth of battles, and at the center of it all was the charismatic, enigmatic Bonnie Prince Charlie (1720-1788).

Though usually depicted as a battle of the Scottish versus the English, in truth Culloden was a civil war between two opposing dynasties: Stuart (Charlie) and Hanover (George). However, as the history has faded into lore, the battle has come to be remembered as a Scottish-versus-English standoff—or, in the parlance of the Scots, the Highlanders versus the Strangers.

Charles Edward Stuart, from his first breath, was raised with a single purpose—to restore his family to the British throne. His grandfather was King James II (VII of Scotland), deposed in 1688 by the English Parliament for his tyranny and pro-Catholic bias. The Stuarts remained in exile in France and Italy, until 1745, when young Charlie crossed the Channel from France to retake the throne in the name of his father. He landed on the west coast of Scotland and rallied support for the Jacobite cause. Though Charles was not Scottish-born, he was the rightful heir directly down the line from Mary, Queen of Scots—and why so many Scots joined the rebellion out of resentment at being ruled by a "foreign" king (King George II, who was born in Germany, couldn't even speak English).

Bagpipes droned, and "Bonnie" (handsome) Charlie led an army of 2,000 tartan-wearing, Gaelic-speaking Highlanders across Scotland, seizing Edinburgh. They picked up other supporters of the Stuarts from the Lowlands and from England. Now 6,000 strong, they marched south toward London—quickly advancing as far as Derby, just 125 miles from the capital—and King George II made plans to flee the country. But anticipated support for the Jacobites failed to materialize in the numbers they were hoping for (both in England and from France). The Jacobites had so far been victorious in their battles against the Hanoverian government forces, but the odds now turned against them. Charles retreated to the Scottish Highlands, where many of his men knew the terrain and might gain an advantage when outnumbered. The English government troops followed closely on his heels.

Against the advice of his best military strategist, Charles' army faced the Hanoverian forces at Culloden Moor on flat, barren terrain that was unsuited to the Highlanders' guerrilla tactics. The Jacobites—many of them brandishing only broadswords, targes (wooden shields covered in leather and studs), and dirks (long daggers)—were mowed down by King George's cannons  and horsemen. In less than an hour, the government forces routed the Jacobite army, but that was just the start. They spent the next weeks methodically hunting down ringleaders and sympathizers (and many others in the Highlands who had nothing to do with the battle), ruthlessly killing, imprisoning, and banishing thousands.

Charles fled with a £30,000 price on his head (an equivalent of millions of today's pounds). He escaped to the Isle of Skye, hidden by a woman named Flora MacDonald (her grave is on the Isle of Skye, and her statue is outside Inverness Castle). Flora dressed Charles in women's clothes and passed him off as her maid. Later, Flora was arrested and thrown in the Tower of London before being released and treated like a celebrity.

Charles escaped to France. He spent the rest of his life wandering Europe trying to drum up support to retake the throne. He drifted through short-lived romantic affairs and alcohol, and died in obscurity, without an heir, in Rome.

The Battle of Culloden was the end of 60 years of Jacobite rebellions, the last major battle fought on British soil, and the final stand of the Highlanders. From then on, clan chiefs were deposed; kilts, tartans, and bagpipes were outlawed; and farmers were cleared off their ancestral land, replaced by more-profitable sheep. Scottish culture would never fully recover from the events of the campaign called "The '45."

❷ Self-Guided Tour

Your tour takes you through two sections: the exhibit and the actual battlefield.

The Exhibit

As you pass the ticket desk, note the **family tree:** Bonnie Prince Charlie ("Charles Edward Stuart") and George II were distant cousins. Then the exhibit's shadowy-figure **touchscreens** connect you with historical figures who give you details from both the Hanoverian and Jacobite perspectives. A **map** shows the other power struggles happening in and around Europe, putting this fight for political control of Britain in a wider context. This battle was no small regional skirmish, but rather a key part of a larger struggle between Britain and its neighbors, primarily France, for control over trade and colonial power. In the display case are **medals** from the early 1700s, made by both sides as propaganda.

From here, your path through this building is cleverly designed to echo the course of the Jacobite army. Your short march (with lots of historic artifacts) gets under way as Char-  lie sails from France to Scotland, then fina-gles the support of Highland clan chiefs. As he heads south with his army to take London, you, too, are walking south. Along the way, maps show the movement of troops, and wall panels cover the buildup to the attack, as seen from both sides. Note the clever division of information: To the left and in red is the story of the "government" (a.k.a. Hanoverians/Whigs/English, led by the Duke of Cumberland); to the right, in blue, is the Jacobites' perspective (Prince Charlie and his Highlander/French supporters).

But you, like Charlie, don't make it to London—in the dark room at the end, you can hear Jacobite commanders arguing over whether to retreat back to Scotland. Pessimistic about their chances of receiving more French support, they decide to U-turn, and so do you. Heading back up north, you'll get some insight into some of the strategizing that went on behind the scenes.

By the time you reach the end of the hall, it's the night before the battle. Round another bend into a dark passage, and listen to the voices of the anxious troops. While the English slept soundly in their tents (recovering from celebrating the Duke's 25th birthday), the scrappy and exhausted Jacobite Highlanders struggled through the night to reach the battlefield (abandoning their plan of a surprise night attack at Nairn and instead retreating back toward Inverness).

At last the two sides meet. As you wait outside the theater for the next showing, study the chart depicting how the forces were arranged on the battlefield.  Once inside the theater, you'll soon be surrounded by the views and sounds of a windswept moor. An impressive four-minute **360° movie** projects the re-enacted battle with you right in the center of the action. The movie drives home just how outmatched the Jacobites were.

The last room has **period weapons,** including ammunition and artifacts found on the battlefield, as well as **historical depictions** of the battle. You'll also find a section describing the detective work required to piece together the story from historical evidence. Be sure to tour the **aftermath corridor,** which talks about the nearly genocidal years following the battle and the cultural wake of this event to this day. Be sure to examine the **huge map,** with narration explaining the combat you've just experienced while giving you a bird's-eye view of the field through which you're about to roam.

The Battlefield

Leaving the visitors center, survey the battlefield (which you'll tour with the help of your audioguide). In the foreground is a cottage used as a makeshift hospital during the conflict. Red flags show the front line of the government army (8,000 troops). This is where most of the hand-to-hand fighting took place. The blue flags in the distance are where the Jacobite army (5,500 troops) lined up.

As you explore the battlefield, notice how uneven and boggy the ground is in parts, and imagine trying to run across this hummocky terrain with all your gear, toward almost-certain death.

The old stone memorial cairn, erected in 1881, commemorates the roughly 1,500 Jacobites buried in this field. It's known as the Graves of the Clans. As you wander the battlefield, following the audioguide, you'll pass by other **mass graves,** marked by small

headstones, and ponder how entire clans fought, died, and were buried here. *Outlander* fans often leave flowers at the Fraser clan headstone.

Near the visitor center, the restored stone-and-turf **Leanach Cottage** predates Culloden and may have been used as a field hospital during the battle. A small exhibit inside explains plans to preserve Culloden for future generations.

Heading back to the parking lot, notice the wall of **protruding bricks**. Each represents a soldier who died. The handful of Hanoverian casualties are on the left (about 50); the rest of the long wall's raised bricks represent the multitude of dead Jacobites.

CLAVA CAIRNS

Scotland is littered with reminders of prehistoric peoples—especially in Orkney and along the coast of the Moray Firth—but the Clava Cairns, worth ▲ for a quick visit, are among the best-preserved, most interesting, and easiest to reach. You'll find them nestled in the countryside just beyond Culloden Battlefield.

Cost and Hours: Free, always open; just after passing Culloden Battlefield on the B-9006 coming from Inverness, signs on the right point to *Clava Cairns*. Follow this twisty road a couple miles, over the "weak bridge" and to the free parking lot by the stones. Skip the cairns if you don't have a car.

Visiting the Cairns: These "Balnauran of Clava" are Neolithic burial chambers dating from 3,000 to 4,000 years ago. Although they appear to be just some giant piles of rocks in a sparsely forested clearing, a closer look will help you appreciate the prehistoric logic behind them. (The site is explained by a few information plaques.) There are three structures: a central "ring cairn" with an open space in the center but no access to it, flanked by two "passage cairns," which were once buried under turf-covered mounds. The entrance shaft in each passage cairn lines up with the setting sun at the winter solstice. Each cairn is surrounded by a stone circle, and the entire ensemble is framed by evocative trees—injecting this site with even more mystery.

Enjoy the site's many enigmas: Were the stone circles part of a celestial calendar system? Or did they symbolize guardians? Why were the clamshell-sized hollows carved into the stones fac-

ing the chambers? Was the soul of the deceased transported into the next life by the ray of sunlight on that brief moment that it filled the inner chamber? How many *Outlander* fans have taken selfies in front of the split standing stone (which inspired a similar stone in the novel)? No one knows.

CAWDOR CASTLE

Atmospheric, intimate, and worth ▲, this castle is still the residence of the Dowager (read: widow) Countess of Cawdor, a local

aristocratic branch of the Campbell family. While many associate the castle with Shakespeare's *Macbeth* (because "Cawdor" is mentioned more than a dozen times in the play), there is no actual connection with Shakespeare. *Macbeth* is set 300 years before the castle was even built. The castle is worth a visit simply because it's historic and beautiful in its own right—and because the woman who owns it flies a Buddhist flag from its tower. She is from Eastern Europe and was the Earl's second wife.

Cost and Hours: £12.50, includes audioguide, May-Sept daily 10:00-17:30, closed Oct-April, tel. 01667/404-401, www.cawdorcastle.com. The good £5.50 guidebook provides more detail on the family and the rooms. Storage is available for larger bags, which cannot be brought into the castle.

Getting There: It's on the B-9090, just off the A-96, about 15 miles east of Inverness (6 miles beyond Culloden and Clava Cairns). Public transportation to the castle is scant, but check at the TI for current options.

Visiting the Castle: You'll follow a one-way circuit around the castle with each room well-described with posted explanations written by the countess' late husband, the sixth Earl of Cawdor. His witty notes bring the castle to life and make you wish you'd known the old chap. Cawdor feels very lived-in because

it is. While the Dowager Countess moves out during the tourist season, for the rest of the year this is her home. You can imagine her stretching out in front of the fireplace with a good book. Notice her geraniums in every room.

The drawing room (for "withdrawing" after dinner) is lined with a family tree of portraits looking down. In the Tapestry Bedroom you'll see the actual marriage bed of Sir Hugh Campbell from 1662 and 17th-century tapestries warming the walls. In the Yellow Room, a flat-screen TV hides inside an 18th-century cabinet (ask a docent to show you). In the Tartan Passage, lined with modern paintings, find today's dowager—Lady Angelika—in a beautiful 1970 pastel portrait, staring at her late husband's predecessors. Notice how their eyes follow you creepily down the hall—but hers do not.

A spiral stone staircase near the end of the tour leads down to the castle's proud symbol: a holly tree dating from 1372. According to the beloved legend, a donkey leaned against this tree to mark the spot where the castle was to be built...and it was, around the tree.

The **gardens,** included with the castle ticket, are worth exploring, with some 18th-century linden trees and several surprising species (including sequoia and redwood). The hedge maze, crowned by a minotaur and surrounded by a laburnum arbor (dripping with yellow blossoms in spring), is not open to the public.

The nine-hole **golf course** on the castle grounds provides a quick and affordable way to have a Scottish golfing experience. The course is bigger than pitch-and-putt and fun even for non-golfers (£18.50/person with clubs). You're welcome to try the putting green for £4.

Nearby: The close but remote-feeling **village of Cawdor**—with a few houses, a village shop, and a tavern—is also worth a look if you've got time to kill.

Loch Ness

I'll admit it: I had my zoom lens out and my eyes on the water. The local tourist industry thrives on the legend of the Loch Ness monster. It's a thrilling thought, and there have been several seemingly reliable "sightings" (by monks, police officers, and sonar imaging). But even if you ignore the monster stories, the loch is impressive: 23 miles long, less than a mile wide, 754 feet deep, and containing more water than all of the freshwater bodies of England and Wales combined. It's essentially the vast chasm of a fault line, filled with water.

Getting There: The Loch Ness sights are a 20-minute drive southwest of Inverness. To drive the full length of Loch Ness takes about 45 minutes. Fort William-bound buses #919 and #920 make stops at Urquhart Castle and Drumnadrochit (8/day, 40 minutes).

Sights on Loch Ness

In July 1933, a couple swore they saw a giant sea monster shimmy across the road in front of their car by Loch Ness. Within days, ancient legends about giant monsters in the lake (dating as far back as the sixth century) were revived—and suddenly everyone was spotting "Nessie" poke its head above the waters of Loch Ness. Further sightings and photographic "evidence" have bolstered the claim that there's some-thing mysterious living in this unthinkably deep and murky lake. (Most sightings take place in the deepest part of the loch, near Urquhart Castle.) Most witnesses describe a water-bound dinosaur resembling the real, but extinct, plesiosaur. Others cling to the slightly more plausible theory of a gigantic eel. And skeptics figure the sightings can be explained by a combination of reflections, boat wakes, and mass hysteria. The most famous photo of the beast (dubbed the "Surgeon's Photo") was later discredited—the "monster's" head was actually attached to a toy submarine. But that hasn't stopped various cryptozoologists from seeking photographic, sonar, and other proof.

And that suits the thriving local tourist industry just fine. The Nessie commercialization is so tacky that there are two different monster exhibits within 100 yards of each other, both in the town of Drumnadrochit. Of the two competing sites, Nessieland is pretty cheesy while the Loch Ness Centre and Exhibition (described

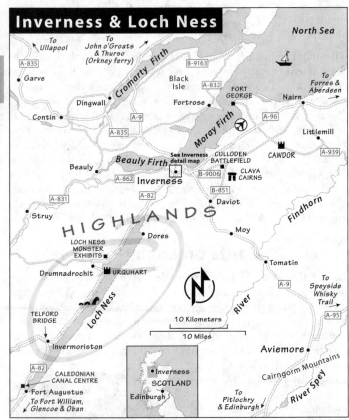

Inverness & Loch Ness

next) is surprisingly thoughtful. Each has a tour-bus parking lot and more square footage devoted to their kitschy shops than to the exhibits. While Nessieland is a tourist trap, the Loch Ness Centre may appease that small part of you that knows the *real* reason you wanted to see Loch Ness.

▲Loch Ness Centre & Exhibition

This attraction is better and more methodical than you might expect, and is worth visiting if you want to understand the geological and historical environment that bred the monster story. It's spearheaded by Adrian Shine, a naturalist fond of saying "I like mud," who has spent many years researching lake ecology and scientific phenomena. The exhibit has two parts: First you go through a series of rooms with videos and special effects, and then you enter a section on the history of the Great Glen and Loch Ness. The videos detail the various searches that have been conducted; refreshingly, they retain an air of healthy skepticism instead of breathless monster-chasing. You'll also see some artifacts related to the search, such as a hippo-foot ashtray used to fake monster footprints and the *Viperfish*—a harpoon-equipped submarine used in a 1969 Nessie expedition. And you'll learn how in 1952 record-seeker John Cobb died going 200 mph in his speedboat on the loch.

Cost and Hours: £8.45, RS%—ask, daily Easter-Oct 9:30-17:45, July-Aug until 18:45, Nov-Easter 10:00-16:15, last entry 45 minutes before closing, in the big stone mansion right on the main road to Inverness, tel. 01456/450-573, www.lochness.com.

▲Urquhart Castle

The ruins at Urquhart (UR-kurt), just up the loch from the Nessie exhibits, are gloriously situated with a view of virtually the entire lake but create a traffic jam of tourism on busy days.

The visitors center has a tiny exhibit with interesting castle artifacts and an eight-minute film taking you on a sweep through a thousand years of tumultuous history—from St. Columba's visit to the castle's final destruction in 1689. The castle itself, while dramatically situated and fun to climb through, is an empty shell. After its owners (who supported the crown) blew it up to keep the Jacobites from taking it, the largest me-  dieval castle in Scotland (and the most important in the Highlands) wasn't considered worth rebuilding or defending, and was abandoned. Well-placed, descriptive signs help you piece together this once-mighty fortress. As you walk toward the ruins, take a close look at the trebuchet (a working replica of one of the most destructive weapons of English King Edward I), and ponder how this giant catapult helped Edward grab almost every castle in the country away from the native Scots.

Cost and Hours: £12, guidebook-£5, daily April-May and Sept 9:30-18:00, June-Aug until 20:00, Oct until 17:00, shorter hours off-season, last entry 45 minutes before closing, café, tel. 01456/450-551, www.historicenvironment.scot. The parking lot can fill up in summer—either wait in the queue for a space, or park in the overflow lot. It's a 20-minute walk away, back toward Inverness.

Loch Ness Cruises

Cruises on Loch Ness are as popular as they are pointless. The lake is far from Scotland's prettiest—and the time-consuming boat trips show you little more than what you'll see from the road. As it seems that Loch Ness cruises are a mandatory part of every "High-

The Caledonian Canal

Two hundred million years ago, two tectonic plates collided, creating the landmass we know as Scotland and leaving a crevice of thin lakes slashing diagonally across the country. This Great Glen Fault, from Inverness to Oban, is easily visible on any map.

Scottish engineer Thomas Telford connected the lakes 200 years ago with a series of canals so ships could avoid the long trip around the north of the country. The Caledonian Canal runs 62 miles from Scotland's east to west coasts; 22 miles of it is man-made. Telford's great feat of engineering took 19 years to complete, opening in 1822 at a cost of one million pounds. But bad timing made the canal a disaster commercially. Napoleon's defeat in 1815 meant that ships could sail the open seas more freely. And by the time the canal opened, commercial ships were too big for its 15-foot depth. Just a couple of decades after the Caledonian Canal opened, trains made the canal almost useless...except for Romantic Age tourism.

From the time of Queen Victoria (who cruised the canal in 1873), the canal has been a popular tourist attraction. To this day the canal is a hit with vacationers, recreational boaters, and lock-keepers who compete for the best-kept lock.

The scenic drive from Inverness along the canal is entertaining, with Drumnadrochit (Nessie centers), Urquhart Castle, Fort Augustus (five locks), and Fort William (under Ben Nevis, with the eight-lock "Neptune's Staircase"). As you cross Scotland, you'll follow Telford's work—22 miles of canals and locks between three lochs, raising ships from sea level to 51 feet (Ness), 93 feet (Lochy), and 106 feet (Oich).

While Neptune's Staircase, a series of eight locks near Fort William, has been cleverly named to sound intriguing (see page 310), the best lock stop is midway, at Fort Augustus, where the canal hits the south end of Loch Ness. In Fort Augustus, the **Caledonian Canal Centre,** overlooking the canal just off the main road, gives a good rundown on Telford's work (see "Fort Augustus" at the end of this chapter). Stroll past several shops and eateries to the top for a fine view.

Seven miles north, in the town of **Invermoriston,** is another Telford structure: a stone bridge, dating from 1805, that spans the Morriston Falls as part of the original road. Look for a small parking lot just before the junction at A-82 and A-887, on your right as you drive from Fort Augustus. Cross the A-82 and walk three minutes back the way you came. The bridge, which took eight years to build and is still in use, is on your right.

lands Highlights" day tour, there are several options, leaving from the top, bottom, and middle of the loch. The basic one-hour loop costs around £15 and includes views of Urquhart Castle and lots of legends and romantic history (Jacobite is the dominant outfit of the many cruise companies, www.jacobite.co.uk). I'd rather spend my time and money at Fort Augustus or Urquhart Castle.

▲Fort Augustus

Perhaps the most idyllic stop along the Caledonian Canal is the little lochside town of Fort Augustus. It was founded in the 1700s—before there was a canal here—as part of a series of garrisons and military roads built by the English to quell the Highland clansmen, even as the Jacobites kept trying to take the throne in London. Before then, there were no developed roads in the Highlands—and without roads, it's hard to keep indigenous people down.

From 1725 to 1733, the English built 250 miles of hard roads and 40 bridges to open up the region; Fort Augustus was a central Highlands garrison at the southern tip of Loch Ness, designed to awe clansmen. It was named for William Augustus, Duke of Cumberland—notorious for his role in destroying the clan way of life in the Highlands. (When there's no media and no photographs to get in the way, ethnic cleansing has little effect on one's reputation.)

Fort Augustus makes for a delightful stop if you're driving through the area. Parking is easy. There are plenty of B&Bs, charming eateries, and an inviting park along the town's five locks. You can still see the capstans, surviving from the days when the locks were cranked open by hand.

The fine little **Caledonian Canal Centre** tells the story of the canal's construction (free, daily, tel. 01320/725-581). Also, consider the pleasant little canalside stroll out to the head of the loch.

Eating in Fort Augustus: You can eat reasonably at a string of $ eateries lining the same side of the canal. Consider **The Nourish Ness Community Café,** a good choice serving filled rolls and homemade soups; **The Lock Inn,** cozy and pub-like with great canalside tables, ideal if it's sunny; **The Bothy,** another pub with decent food; and the **Canalside Chip Shop** offering fish-and-chips to go (no seating, but plenty of nice spots on the canal). A small grocery store is at the gas station, next to the TI, which is a few steps from the canal just after crossing the River Oich (also housing the post office, a WC, and an ATM).

EASTERN SCOTLAND

Pitlochry • Between Inverness & Pitlochry • Loch Tay •
Speyside Whisky Trail • Balmoral Castle & Royal Deeside

Between Edinburgh and Inverness, the eastern expanse of Scotland bulges out into the North Sea. The main geological landmark is Cairngorms National Park, with gently rugged Highland scenery and great hiking terrain. If your time is limited, Scotland is more satisfying elsewhere. But this region is easily accessible—you'll likely pass through at some point—and has a lot to offer.

Those in a hurry should focus on the sights lined up along the A-9 highway between Inverness, Pitlochry, and St. Andrews. Pitlochry itself has a green-hills-and-sandstone charm, a warm welcome, and a pair of great distilleries linked by a nice hike, making it the region's best overnight stop. Nearby you'll find a fascinating trip back to prehistory (at the Scottish Crannog Centre on Loch Tay), a fun sheepdog show, and an open-air folk museum.

Other regional attractions offer an even better look at rural Scotland. They're especially convenient for those going slow between Inverness and St. Andrews, and may be worth detours depending on your interests. Whisky connoisseurs flock to Speyside, royalists visit Balmoral Castle and the nearby home-base village of Ballater, and ruined-castle fans head to Dunnottar.

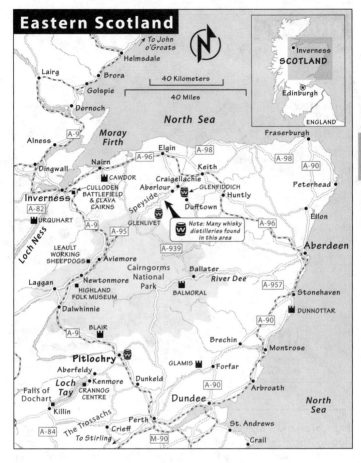

Eastern Scotland

To John o'Groats

Helmsdale

SCOTLAND

Inverness

Edinburgh

ENGLAND

Lairg

Brora

40 Kilometers

Golspie

40 Miles

Dornoch

North Sea

Alness

Moray Firth

Fraserburgh

A-9

Dingwall

Nairn

Elgin

A-98

A-98

CAWDOR

A-96

Keith

A-90

CULLODEN BATTLEFIELD & CLAVA CAIRNS

Craigellachie

Aberlour

GLENFIDDICH

Peterhead

Inverness

Speyside

Huntly

A-82

Dufftown

URQUHART

A-9

GLENLIVET

A-96

Ellon

Loch Ness

A-95

Note: Many whisky distilleries found in this area

Aberdeen

LEAULT WORKING SHEEPDOGS

A-939

Aviemore

Cairngorms National Park

Ballater

River Dee

A-957

Laggan

Newtonmore

HIGHLAND FOLK MUSEUM

BALMORAL

Stonehaven

Dalwhinnie

A-90

DUNNOTTAR

BLAIR

A-9

Brechin

Montrose

Pitlochry

GLAMIS

Forfar

Aberfeldy

Kenmore

Dunkeld

A-90

Loch Tay

CRANNOG CENTRE

Dundee

Arbroath

Falls of Dochart

North Sea

Killin

The Trossachs

Perth

St. Andrews

A-84

Crieff

To Stirling

M-90

Crail

EASTERN SCOTLAND

Pitlochry

This likable tourist town, famous for its whisky and its hillwalking (both beloved by Scots), makes an enjoyable overnight stop while exploring attractions along the busy A-9 highway. Just outside the craggy Highlands, Pitlochry is set amid pastoral rolling hills that offer plenty of forest hikes and riverside strolls. It seems that tourism is the town's only industry—with per-

EASTERN SCOTLAND

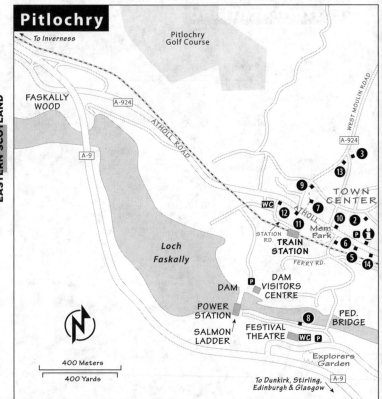

Pitlochry

To Inverness

Pitlochry
Golf Course

FASKALLY
WOOD

A-924

ATHOLL ROAD

A-9

WEST MOULIN ROAD

A-924

③

⑬

⑨

TOWN
CENTER

WC

⑦

⑫

ATHOLL

⑩ ②

⑪

Mem.
Park

P ℹ

STATION
RD.

TRAIN
STATION

⑥

FERRY RD.

⑤ ⑭

Loch
Faskally

DAM

P

DAM
VISITORS
CENTRE

POWER
STATION

PED.
BRIDGE

SALMON
LADDER

FESTIVAL
THEATRE

⑧

WC P

N

400 Meters

400 Yards

Explorers
Garden

To Dunkirk, Stirling,
Edinburgh & Glasgow

A-9

haps Scotland's highest concentration of woolens shops and out-door outfitters. (The name "Pitlochry" comes from the old Pictish word for "tourist trap.") But Pitlochry also has the feel of a real community. People here are friendly and bursting with town pride: They love to chat about everything from the high-quality local the-ater to the salmon ladder at the hydroelectric dam. It's also a restful place, where—after the last tour bus pulls out—you can feel your pulse slow as you listen to gurgling streams.

Orientation to Pitlochry

Plucky little Pitlochry (pop. 4,000) lines up along its tidy, tourist-minded main street, Atholl Road, which runs parallel to the River Tummel. The train station is on Station Road, off the main street. Its two distilleries are a walk—or short drive—out of town (see my self-guided whisky walk). Navigate by following the black direc-tional signs to Pitlochry's handful of sights.

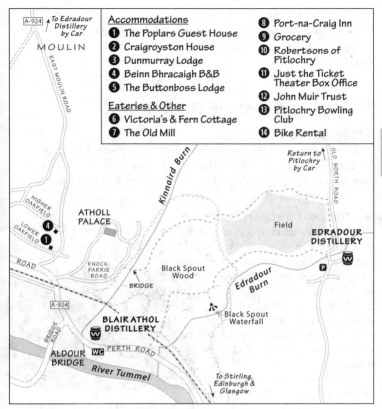

TOURIST INFORMATION

The helpful TI, at one end of town, sells maps for local hill walks and scenic drives. Their good *Pitlochry Path Network* brochure is handy (Mon-Sat 9:00-18:00, Sun 9:30-17:00, shorter hours and closed Sun Nov-March; 22 Atholl Road, tel. 01796/472-215, www. pitlochry.org).

HELPFUL HINTS

Special Events: In summer, a pipe band marches through town every Monday evening. From May through August, the salmon ladder at the dam comes to life (described later, under "Sights in Pitlochry"). Pitlochry's Highland Games are in early September (www.pitlochryhighlandgames.co.uk). And in October, over 80,000 people come to see the Enchanted Forest light-and-water show. Set to music, it illuminates Fas-kally Wood, just outside town (www.enchantedforest.org.uk).

Bike Rental: Across the street and a block from the TI (away from town), **Escape Route Bikes** rents a variety of bikes (£19/4

EASTERN SCOTLAND

hours, £27/24 hours, includes helmet and lock if you ask, Mon-Sat 9:00-17:30, Sun 10:00-17:00, 3 Atholl Road, tel. 01796/473-859, www.escape-route.co.uk).

Parking: Drivers who aren't spending the night can park in the large pay-and-display lot next to the TI, in the center of town.

Sights in Pitlochry

DISTILLERIES

Pitlochry's two distilleries can be linked by a relaxing two-hour hike (described later, under "Pitlochry Whisky Walk.") For background on types of whiskies, how whisky is made, and tasting it like a pro, see page 484.

▲▲Edradour Distillery

This cute distillery (pronounced ED-rah-dower)—the smallest historic distillery in Scotland (est. 1825)—takes pride in mak-

ing its whisky with a minimum of machinery, and maintains a proud emphasis on tradition. Small white-and-red buildings are nestled in a delightfully green Scottish hillside. ("Edradour"—also the name of the stream that gurgles through the complex—means "land between two rivers.") With its idyllic set-

ting and gregarious spirit, it's one of the most enjoyable distillery tours in Scotland. Unlike the bigger distilleries, they allow you to take photos of the equipment. If you like the whisky, buy some here and support the Pitlochry economy—this is one of the few independently owned distilleries left in Scotland.

Cost and Hours: £12 for a one-hour tour, departs 3/hour, April-Oct Mon-Sat 10:00-17:00; off-season Mon-Fri 10:00-16:00, closed Sat; closed Sun year-round, last tour departs one hour before closing, tel. 01796/472-095, www.edradour.com.

Getting There: Most come to the distillery by car—follow signs from the main (A-924) road, 2.5 miles into the countryside—but you can also get there on a peaceful hiking trail that you'll have all to yourself (follow my "Pitlochry Whisky Walk," later).

Visiting the Distillery: You'll watch a 10-minute orientation film, then enjoy a sit-down education while tasting two different drams. Then the guided tour proceeds through the facility: from the malt barn (where the barley is germinated and dried) to the still (where giant copper stills turn distiller's beer into whisky) to the warehouse (where 6,000 casks age in the darkness). Take a deep whiff of the rich aroma—you're smelling the so-called "angels' share," the tiny percentage of each cask that's lost to evaporation.

Blair Athol Distillery

This big, ivy-covered facility is conveniently located (about a half-mile from the town center) and more corporate-feeling, offering 45-minute tours with a wee taste at the end. I'd tour this only if you're a whisky completist, or if you lack the wheels or hiking stamina to reach Edradour.

Cost and Hours: £9.50, Easter-Oct tours depart roughly hourly daily 10:00-17:00, June-Sept until 18:30, last tour departs one hour before closing; shorter hours and fewer tours off-season; tel. 01796/482-003, www.malts.com—search for "Blair Athol."

Pitlochry Whisky Walk

A fun way to visit the distilleries is to hill-walk from downtown Pitlochry. The entire loop trip takes 2-3 hours, depending on how long you linger in the distilleries (at least an hour of walking each way). You'll see lush fern forests and a pretty decent waterfall. The walk is largely uphill on the way to the Edradour Distillery; wear good shoes, bring a rain jacket just in case, and be happy that you'll stroll easily downhill *after* you've had your whisky samples.

At the TI, pick up the *Pitlochry Path Network* brochure and follow along with its map. You'll be taking the **Edradour Walk** (marked on directional signs with yellow hiker icons; on the map it's a series of yellow dots). Leave the TI and head left along the busy A-924. The walk can be done in either direction, but I'll describe it counterclockwise.

Within 10 minutes, you'll walk under the railroad tracks and then come to **Blair Athol Distillery** on your left. If you're a whisky buff, stop in here. Otherwise, hold out for the much more atmospheric Edradour. You'll pass a few B&Bs and suburban homes, then a sign marked *Black Spout* on a lamppost. Just after this, you'll cross a bridge, then take the next left, walking under another stone rail overpass and away from the road. Following this path, you'll come to a clearing, and as the road gets steeper, you'll see signs directing you 50 yards off the main path to see the "Black Spout"—a wonderful waterfall well worth the few extra steps on your right.

At the top of the hill, you'll arrive in another clearing, where a narrow path hugs a huge field on your left. Low rolling hills surround you in all directions. It seems like there's not another person around for miles, with just the thistles to keep you company. From here it's an easy 20 minutes to the **Edradour Distillery.**

Leaving the distillery, to complete the loop, head right, following the paved road (Old North Road). In about 50 yards, a sign points left into the field. Take the small footpath that runs along the left side of the road. (If you see the driveway with stone lions on both sides, you've gone a few steps too far.) You'll walk parallel to the route you took getting to the distillery, hugging the far side of the same huge field. The trail then swoops back downhill through the forest, until you cross the footbridge and make a left. You'll soon reach Knockfarrie Road—take this downhill; you'll pass a B&B and hear traffic noises as you emerge from the forest. The trail leads back to the highway, with the TI a few blocks ahead on the right.

TOWN CENTER
Strolling the High Street

Pitlochry's main street is a pleasant place to wander and window-shop. As you stroll, consider this: The town exists thanks to the arrival of the train, which conveniently brought Romantic Age tourists from the big cities in the south to this lovely bit of Scotland. Queen Victoria herself visited three times in the 1860s, putting Pitlochry on the tourist map. The postcard-perfect Victorian sandstone architecture on the main street makes it clear that this was a delightful escape for city folks back in the 19th century.

Here are some things to look for, listed in order of how you'll reach them from the TI. Just past the recommended Victoria's restaurant, the **memorial park** with the Celtic cross honors men from the local parish whose lives were lost fighting in World War I—a reminder of Scotland's disproportionate sacrifices in that conflict. Throughout Scotland, even many tiny villages have similar monuments.

Ferry Road, next to the park, branches off under the rail bridge and leads to a footbridge that takes you to the other side of the river—home to Pitlochry's spunky Festival Theatre, as well as a power station with a salmon ladder (a fun excuse for a lazy walk—described later).

Pop into **Robertsons of Pitlochry** whisky shop, stocked with over 400 whiskies and other Scottish spirits. The collection is fun to peruse, and if you don't make it to one of Pitlochry's distilleries, ask Ewan for a wee dram here. You can book tastings of five drams in their bothy bar (£15, open Mon-Sat 10:00-18:00, Sun

11:00-17:00, tel. 01796/472-011, www.robertsonsofpitlochry.co.uk).

A few doors down, the **Love Your Sweets** shop, with a purple awning, stocks a staggering variety of uniquely Scottish candies in bulk. Step in to buy a mixed bag of some unusual flavors of hard candies, such as clove, rhubarb, or Irn-Bru. At the next little park on the right, a surging stream angles away from the main road and to the recommended Old Mill restaurant.

On the corner with Station Road is the headquarters of the **John Muir Trust.** John Muir (1838-1914) was born in Scotland, moved to the US when he was 10, and later helped establish the world's first national park system in his adopted country. Inside is a free tiny exhibit called Wild Space, with a feel-good nature video and a small art gallery. They also sell books, maps, and other conservation-themed souvenirs (Mon-Sat 10:00-17:00, Sun 11:00-16:30, shorter hours off-season and closed Wed year-round, tel. 01796/470-080, www.jmt.org).

Lawn Bowls
The **Pitlochry Bowling Club** lets outsiders rent shoes and balls and try their hand at the game (£3, generally Mon-Fri 10:00-12:00 & 14:00-16:00, 24 West Moulin Road, tel. 01796/473-459).

Pitlochry Golf Course
A 10-minute walk from the town center, the pleasant Pitlochry Golf Course and driving range offers a delightful way to spend an afternoon in Pitlochry, with views of the Tummel Valley (£42-50, short course available, open dawn until dusk, Golf Course Road, tel. 0179/472-792, www.pitlochrygolf.co.uk).

ACROSS THE RIVER
These sights lie along the largely undeveloped riverbank opposite Pitlochry's town center. While neither are knockouts, they're a fine excuse for a pretty stroll or drive. Walkers can reach this area easily in about 15 minutes: Head down Ferry Road (near the memorial park), cross the footbridge, and turn right.

Pitlochry Dam Visitors Centre and Salmon Ladder
Pitlochry's dam on the River Tummel provides a nice place to go for a stroll, and comes with a salmon ladder—a series of chambers that allow salmon to "step" their way upstream next to the dam (salmon generally run May-Aug).

The well-designed and family-friendly visitors center celebrates hydroelectric power in the Highlands. Its fine nine-minute video, "Power from the Glens," explains the epic vision of generating clean power from—and for—the Highlands. You can also walk all the way across the top of the dam, pausing to read informational plaques and to peer through windows into the hydroelectric plant (free, daily 9:30-17:00, https://pitlochrydam.com). Their cafeteria is delightful, with a nice river view. As you walk along the top of the dam, be sure to look back at the sleek, modern visitors center protruding from the trees.

Pitlochry Festival Theatre

This theater company rotates its productions, putting on a different play every few nights. Most are classics, with a few musicals and new shows mixed in (£15-35; plays generally run May-Oct Mon-Sat). The theater hosts concerts on Sunday evenings—usually tribute acts—and a variety of other performances in winter (purchase tickets online or by phone; in person at Just the Ticket, the company's box office in the town center—Tue-Sun 10:00-12:00 & 13:00-16:00, closed Mon, 89 Atholl Road; or at the theater on Port-na-Craig Road—same price, box office open daily 10:00-20:00, tel. 01796/484-626, www.pitlochryfestivaltheatre.com).

Nearby: Just above the theater's parking lot, the six-acre **Explorers Garden** features plants and wildflowers from around the world (£4, daily 10:00-17:00, closed Nov-March, last entry 45 minutes before closing, tel. 01796/484-626, www.explorersgarden.com).

Sleeping in Pitlochry

All of these have free parking.

$$ The Poplars Guest House, perched regally on a meticulously landscaped hill high above the main road, has been stylishly renovated by charming Jason and Nathalie. The huge home has a spacious lounge with views, and six rooms that combine modern comforts with a respect for tradition. Start the day off right with their whisky porridge (family room, closed in winter, at the end of Lower Oakfield at #27, tel. 01796/472-129, www.poplars-pitlochry.com, info@poplars-pitlochry.com).

$$ Craigroyston House, my sentimental favorite in Pitlochry, is a quaint, updated Victorian country house with eight large and luxe bedrooms. Their terraced yard is a great place to sip some wine or play croquet. Vaughan and Susan, originally from Orkney, are welcoming and generous (family rooms, no kids under 7, right above the TI parking lot at 2 Lower Oakfield, tel. 01796/472-053, www.craigroyston.co.uk, reservations@craigroyston.co.uk). Drivers can reach it on Lower Oakfield Road; walkers can hike up from the huge parking lot next to the TI on Atholl Road (find the small gate at the back of the lot).

$$ Dunmurray Lodge is a calming place to call home, with four springtime-colored rooms, and friendly hosts (family room, apartment, no kids under 5; breakfast includes gluten-free, vegetarian, and other options; 5-minute walk from town at 72 Bonnethill Road, mobile 0778-346-2625, www.dunmurray.co.uk, info@dunmurray.co.uk, Lorraine and Mike).

$$ Beinn Bhracaigh (pronounced "benny vrackie," meaning "speckled mountain") is a guesthouse with a hotel feel. The 13 rooms are modern and tasteful (each named after a different salmon river), and they have a sitting room where you can serve yourself at the well-stocked honesty bar. It sits high above the main road—still within a (longish, steep) walk, but easier by car. Most rooms come with fine views across the town center, the River Tummel, and valley beyond (minimum two-night stay in peak season and on weekends, room-only rates available, no kids under 8, no elevator, 14 Higher Oakfield, tel. 01796/470-355, www.beinnbhracaigh.com, info@beinnbhracaigh.com, James and Kirsty).

$ The Buttonboss Lodge has a less idyllic setting, right along the busy main road across from the TI (expect some traffic noise). But it's affordable and convenient for train travelers. The eight rooms, managed by Cristian, are straightforward and a bit old-fashioned (family suite with kitchenette and private entry, 25 Atholl Road, tel. 01796/472-065, mobile 0790-207-4309, www.buttonbosslodge.co.uk, info@buttonbosslodge.co.uk).

Eating in Pitlochry

Pitlochry may be small and touristy, but its restaurants offer quality local flavor. Several options line the main drag, including a couple of bakeries selling picnic supplies.

$$ Victoria's restaurant and coffee shop, a local favorite, feels like a dressed-up diner, serving up an eclectic menu of comfort food and gourmet dishes—including a hearty baked goat cheese salad (daily 10:00-21:00, patio seating, at corner of memorial park, 45 Atholl Road, tel. 01796/472-670).

$$$ Fern Cottage, just behind Victoria's, has a darker, cozy lodge ambience and a Mediterranean spin on their gourmet menu (patio tables, daily 12:00-16:00 & 17:00-21:00, Ferry Road, tel. 01796/473-840).

$$$ The Old Mill, tucked a block behind the main drag in an actual old mill, has good Scottish food, plus some pastas and salads. Sit in their popular, high-energy pub, calmer restaurant in back, or at

picnic tables outside (food served daily 12:00-15:00 & 17:00-21:00, tel. 01796/474-020).

$$$ Port-na-Craig Inn, on the river just downhill from the theater, is a fancier option catering to theatergoers. For a calmer experience, go at 20:00, after the show has started. In good weather, their outdoor patio makes a nice riverside hangout (soup-and-sandwich lunch specials, reservations smart, daily 11:00-21:00, tel. 01796/472-777, www.portnacraig.com).

Supermarket: A well-stocked **Co-op** grocery has everything for a healthy picnic (daily 6:00-23:00, West Moulin Road, tel. 01796/474-088).

Pitlochry Connections

The train station is open Monday to Saturday 8:00-18:30 and Sunday 10:30-18:00.

From Pitlochry by Train to: Inverness (nearly hourly, 1.5 hours), **Stirling** (5/day direct, 1 hour, more with transfer in Perth), **Edinburgh** (6/day direct, 2 hours, more with transfer), **Glasgow** (almost hourly, 4/day direct, 2 hours, some transfer in Perth). Train info: Tel. 0845-748-4950, www.nationalrail.co.uk.

By Bus to: Glasgow (2/day direct on Citylink #M10, 2 hours; more with change in Perth), **Edinburgh** (3/day on Citylink #M90, 2.5 hours).

Between Inverness and Pitlochry

The A-9 highway, connecting Inverness, Stirling, and Edinburgh, may be Scotland's most touristy road—and it's a scenic one, too. Heading south soon after leaving Inverness, the highway begins to skirt around the curved west edge of Cairngorms National Park, which it follows almost all the way to Pitlochry. These bald, heather-covered hills are what many people picture when they imagine Highland scenery.

As you follow the A-9, it seems every exit is stacked with brown "tourist attraction" signs. For the most part, the options along here are more convenient than good; they tend to pale in comparison to alternatives elsewhere in the country. But if your trip to Scotland isn't taking you beyond this Highland corridor, some of these may be worth a stop. I've listed them in the order you'll reach them traveling south from Inverness; the "Near Pitlochry" section, next, explores attractions just south of Pitlochry. For more remote sojourns, see "Whisky and Castles," later.

▲▲Leault Working Sheepdogs

Each afternoon, Neil Ross presents a 45-minute demonstration

of his well-trained sheepdogs. As Neil describes his work, he'll demonstrate why shepherds have used a crook for thousands of years, and explain why farmers get frustrated when "fancy people with numbers after their names" try to tell them how to manage their land. Then the dogs get to work: With shouts and whistles, each dog follows individual commands, demonstrating an impressive mastery over the sheep. (Watching in awe, you can't help but think: Sheepdogs are smart...and sheep are idiots.) After the presentation, you'll meet (and pet) the border collie stars of the show, and may have the chance to feed some lambs or to try your hand at shearing sheep. If they happen to have a litter of border collie puppies, even those who dislike dogs may find it hard to resist smuggling one home. The entire show is outdoors, so come prepared for all types of weather.

Cost and Hours: £7, £3.50 for kids, demonstration once per day, May-Oct Sun-Fri at 16:00, closed to the public at other times, no demonstrations Sat or Nov-April (Sat private bookings possible), no WC, tel. 01540/651-402, www.leaultworkingsheepdogs.co.uk.

Getting There: Heading south on A-9, exit at Aviemore, then follow B-9152 as it parallels A-9 south. Just past Kincraig, turn right at the *Leault* sign; you'll go under the A-9 to reach the farm. Traveling north on A-9, the unmarked farm turn-off is on your left about 1.5 miles after the A-9 becomes a divided highway. If you miss the turn-off, continue to Aviemore, then follow the instructions above.

▲Highland Folk Museum

Scotland doesn't have a top-notch open-air folk museum—but this is close enough. Just off the highway on the outskirts of Newtonmore, the museum features re-creations of traditional buildings from the surrounding area from the 1700s through the 1930s. The buildings are a bit spread out, and it's quiet outside of frequent "activity days" (check the schedule online).

Cost and Hours: Free but donations strongly encouraged, daily April-Aug 10:30-17:30, Sept-Oct 11:00-16:30, closed Nov-March, helpful £5 guidebook, tel. 01349/781-650, www.highlife-highland.com/highlandfolkmuseum.

Getting There: Exit the A-9 in Newtonmore, then follow brown signs for about five minutes through the village to the museum (free parking).

Visiting the Museum: The highlight of the museum is a circa-

EASTERN SCOTLAND

1700, thatched-roof Highland township called **Baile Gean,** a gathering of four primitive stone homes and three barns, each furnished as it would have been in the Jacobite era (it's a 15-minute walk from the entry—go to the right through a pine forest and up a small hill). Although built for the museum, the town-

ship was closely based on an actual settlement a few miles away that was populated until the 1830s. Costumed docents can explain traditional Highland lifestyles, and you'll likely see—and smell—a peat fire filling one of the homes with its rich smoke. (Because peat doesn't spit or spark, it was much safer to burn than wood—which was too valuable to feed fires anyway, as most tools were made of wood.) This area provided an ideal backdrop for some of the rural-life scenes in the TV production of *Outlander* (see sidebar on page 518).

With more time, visit the other structures in the rest of the open-air museum, such as the tweed shop; the schoolhouse, where you'll learn about early-20th-century classrooms; or the Lochan-hully House (look for the house with red eaves, past the playground), which depicts a 1950s Scottish home. At the far end of the complex you may see some hairy "coos."

▲Blair Castle

If you like Scottish history, aristocratic furnishings, and antlers, you'll like Blair Castle. It's a convenient stop for those zipping past on the A-9. In Gaelic, a "blàr" or "blair" is a flat bit of land surrounded by hills. And sure enough, this stately, white palace rises up from a broad clearing. A stout fortress during the Jacobite wars, it was later renovated and expanded as a mansion in the Scottish Baronial style.

The former residence of the Dukes of Atholl (a.k.a. Clan Murray) is now owned and run as a business by a trust. Filled with art, historic artifacts, and Clan Murray mementoes, it offers a fine look at 19th-century upper-crust life. Follow the self-guided, one-way route up the creaky "picture staircase" and try to spot the portrait of the cross-eyed forebear. Other highlights include the truly palatial main drawing room, where you can imagine the elite soirées that once took place,

EASTERN SCOTLAND

and the wood-paneled ballroom at the end, draped in tartan and bristling with antlers. In contrast, the WWI room recalls how the house was used as a hospital during that conflict.

If time allows, explore the grounds—especially the walled Hercules Garden, where rugged plantings surround a lily-padded pond, overlooked by a statue of Hercules (accessed via the trail near the parking lot).

Cost and Hours: £13, April-Oct daily 9:30-17:30, good cafeteria, closed Nov-March, last entry one hour before closing, tel. 01796/481-207, www.blair-castle.co.uk.

Getting There: From the town of Blair Atholl (just off of the A-9), drive down the long, tree-lined driveway to the free parking lot. From Pitlochry, you can take the more scenic B-8019/B-8079 instead of the A-9. Bus #87 runs from Pitlochry (5/day in summer, fewer off-season, 15 minutes, www.elizabethyulecoaches.co.uk).

Nearby: The **Atholl Country Life Museum** is a humble, volunteer-run museum literally across the street from the entrance to the Blair Castle grounds. A local teacher created these exhibits, filling an old school to show the other side of the social and economic coin. Chatting with the volunteers makes a visit extra fun (£4, May-Sept daily 13:30-17:00 plus July-Aug weekdays from 10:00, www.facebook.com/athollcountrylifemuseum).

Near Pitlochry

ON LOCH TAY

A 30-minute drive southwest of Pitlochry, Loch Tay is worth visiting mostly for its excellent Scottish Crannog Centre—the best place in Scotland to learn about early Iron Age life. You can also drive along Loch Tay (and past the thundering Falls of Dochart) to connect Pitlochry and the A-9 corridor with the Trossachs and Loch Lomond.

▲▲Scottish Crannog Centre

Across Scotland, archaeologists know that little round islands on the lochs are evidence of crannogs—circular houses on stilts, dating to 500 years before Christ. During the Iron Age, Scots built on the water because people traveled by boat, and because waterways were easily defended against rampaging ani-

mals (or people). Scientists have found evidence of 18 such crannogs on Loch Tay alone. One has been rebuilt, using mostly traditional methods, and now welcomes visitors. Guided by a passionate and well-versed expert, you'll spend an hour or two visiting the crannog and learning about how its residents lived.

Cost and Hours: £10, daily 10:00-17:30, closed Dec-Jan, well-marked just outside Kenmore on the south bank of Loch Tay, tel. 01887/830-583, http://www.crannog.co.uk.

Visiting the Museum: The highlight is the two-part tour, led by guides dressed in prehistoric garb. Join whichever group is going next.

One part of the tour takes you out across the rustic wooden bridge to the crannog itself, where you'll huddle under the thatched roof and learn about Iron Age architecture. Your guide explains how families of up to 20 people lived in just one crannog—along with their livestock—and paints a vivid picture of what life was like in those rugged times.

In the other part of the tour, guides demonstrate Iron Age "technology"—turning a lathe, grinding flour, spinning yarn, and even starting a fire using nothing but wood and string. You'll then have a hands-on opportunity to try the tools yourself—and realize how easy the guides made it look.

A modest exhibit just off the gift shop explains the history of crannogs, excavation efforts, and the building of this new one.

Kenmore

Located where Loch Tay empties into the River Tay, Kenmore is a sleepy, one-street, black-and-white village with a big hotel, a church, and a post office/general store. There's not much to do here, other than visit the nearby Scottish Crannog Centre, enjoy the Loch Tay scenery, and consider hiking through the woods to the Taymouth Castle (though the castle is usually closed to visitors). With its classic old hotel, Kenmore can be a handy home base for this area.

Sleeping and Eating in Kenmore: Dominating the village center, the **$$ Kenmore Hotel** feels like a classic Scottish country hotel—it claims to be the oldest inn in Scotland (dating from 1572). The 33 rooms are old-fashioned but cozy, and welcoming lounges, terraces, and other public spaces sprawl through the building. Look for the Robert Burns poem above the fireplace in one of the bars (elevator, The Square, Kenmore, tel. 01887/830-205, www. kenmorehotel.com, reception@kenmorehotel.com). The **$$$** pub, dining room, and various outdoor dining areas all share the same menu.

Falls of Dochart

At the far end of Loch Tay from Kenmore, in the village of Killin, the road passes on a stone bridge over a churning waterfall where the peat-brown waters of the River Dochart tumble dramatically into the loch. The romantic

bridge is busy with passing motorists enjoying a photo op; eateries and gift shops surround the scene. You can clamber down onto the flat stones for a closer look. From the bridge, notice the stone archway marking the burial ground of the Clan Macnab.

SOUTHEAST OF PITLOCHRY
▲Dunkeld

This charming wee town, just off the A-9, is worth a stretch-your-legs break. While the town center is pleasant—with flower boxes, cleverly named shops, folk music, and a growing foodie scene—its claim to fame is its partially ruined cathedral on the banks of the River Tay.

Pay-and-display parking is at both ends of town (the north end has a WC). The TI and cathedral are just down High Street from the main drag, Atholl Street.

The **Cathedral of St. Columba** was actually Scotland's leading church for a brief time in the ninth century, when that important saint's relics were being stored here during Viking raids. Later it blossomed into a

large cathedral complex in a secluded riverside setting. But it was devastated by the one-two punch of Reformation iconoclasts (who tore down most of the building) and Jacobites (who fought the Battle of Dunkeld near here). Duck inside to see the stony interior and its one-room museum (pick up the free info sheet or consider borrowing the good audioguide for a small donation). Outside, as you circle the entire complex, you'll discover that the current church is merely the choir of the original structure—a huge, ruined nave (currently undergoing restoration) stretches behind it.

The **$ Scottish Deli** is nice for a drop in, with soups, sandwiches, and salads (a few tables inside, corner of High Street and Atholl Street, tel. 01350/728-028).

Whisky and Castles

While the A-9 corridor is studded with touristy amusements, the region north and east of the Cairngorms (while hardly undiscovered) feels more rugged and lets you dig deeper into the countryside. In this area, I've focused on two river valleys with very different claims to fame. Speyside, curling along the top of the Cairngorms, is famous for its many distilleries. Royal Deeside, cutting through the middle of the Cairngorms, is the home of the Queen's country retreat at Balmoral and the neighboring village of Ballater. Overnighting in Ballater is an ideal way to linger in this region and sleep immersed in Cairngorms splendor.

Speyside Whisky Trail

Of the hundred or so distilleries in Scotland, half lie near the valley of the River Spey—a small area called Speyside. The ample waters of the river, along with generous peat deposits, have attracted distillers here for centuries. While I prefer some of the smaller, more intimate distillery tours elsewhere (including Oban Distillery in Oban, Talisker on the Isle of Skye, and Edradour near Pitlochry), Speyside is convenient to Inverness and practically a pilgrimage for aficionados. The distilleries here feel bigger and more corporate, but they also include some famous names (including the world's two best-selling brands of single malts, Glenfiddich and Glenlivet). And for whisky lovers, it's simply enjoyable to spend time in a region steeped in such reverence for your favorite drink.

PLANNING YOUR TIME

A quick car tour of Speyside takes about a half-day, and it's a scenic way to connect Inverness to Royal Deeside (it also works as a side-trip from Inverness). Whisky aficionados will have their own list of distilleries they want to hit. But, for the typical traveler, here is an easy plan for the day:

Enjoy the scenic drive to Aberlour, tour the Speyside Cooper-age, tour the Glenfiddich distillery, and finally have a short stop in Dufftown. All are within about five miles of each other. With an early start, you could easily do these stops and then drive down to Balmoral Castle to tour it and sleep nearby in Ballater.

Orientation to Speyside

The A-95, which parallels the River Spey, is the region's artery (to reach it, take the A-9 south from Inverness and turn off toward Grantown-on-Spey). Brown *Malt Whisky Trail* signs help connect the dots. While several distilleries lie along the main road, even more are a short side-trip away. Three humdrum villages form the nucleus of Speyside: Aberlour (the biggest), Craigellachie (a wide spot in the road), and Dufftown (with a clock tower and a good dose of stony charm).

Because public transit connections aren't ideal, Speyside works best for drivers—though if you're determined, you could take the train from Inverness to Elgin and catch the "whisky bus" from there (Stagecoach bus #36, stops in Craigellachie and Aberlour on the way to Dufftown, about hourly, none Sun).

A word of caution: In Scotland, DUI standards are very low (0.05 percent) and strictly enforced. Go easy on the tastings, or bring a designated driver. Distilleries are often happy to give drivers their dram "to go" so they can enjoy it safely later.

Sights in Speyside

I've listed these roughly west to east, as you'll reach them approaching Speyside on the A-95.

Aberlour

Officially named "Charlestown of Aberlour" for its founder, this attractive sandstone town lines up along the A-95. It's famous both for its namesake whisky distillery (www.aberlour.com) and as the home of Walkers Shortbread, which you'll see sold in red-tartan boxes all over Scotland (you can get some at the factory store in town, but no tours). **$$ The Mash Tun,** just off the main road (next to a welcoming little visitors center), is an atmospheric whisky bar that serves lunch and rents rooms upstairs (tel. 01340/881-771, www.mashtun-aberlour.com).

Craigellachie

The blink-and-you'll-miss-it village of Craigellachie (craig-ELL-a-kee) is home to the landmark **$$ Craigellachie Hotel.** This classic, grand old hotel, a handy home base for whisky pilgrims, is famous for its whisky bar—stocking more than 800 bottles (opens daily at 17:00, the receptionist may let you in for a peek at other times, 26 rooms, tel. 01340/881-204, www.craigellachiehotel.co.uk). Just past the hotel on the A-941, keep an eye out on the left for the picturesque **Craigellachie Bridge,** built by the great Scottish industrial architect Thomas Telford.

Note that the A-95 takes a sharp turn to the right in Craigellachie (just before the hotel), leading to the cooperage described next, and beyond that, to the Glenfiddich Distillery and Dufftown; the main road (past the hotel and the bridge) becomes A-941.

▲Speyside Cooperage

Perhaps the single biggest factor in defining whisky's unique flavor is the barrel it's aged in. At this busy workshop on the outskirts of Craigellachie, you can watch master coopers build or refurbish casks for distilleries throughout Scotland. The 14 coopers who work here—who must first complete a four-year apprenticeship to get the gig— are some of the last of a dying breed; while just about everything used to be transported in

barrels, today it's only booze. First you'll view an engaging 15-minute film, then you'll follow your guide up to an observation deck peering down over the factory floor. Oak timber is shaped into staves, which are gathered into metal hoops, then steamed to make them more pliable. Finally the inside is charred with a gas flame, creating a carbonized coating that helps give whisky its golden hue and flavor. Because the vast majority of casks used in Scotland are hand-me-downs from the US (where bourbon laws only allow one use per barrel), you're more likely to see reassembly of old casks (with new ends) rather than from-scratch creation of new ones. But the process is equally fascinating. Apart from observing the barrel-making, it's also interesting to see the intensity of the workers— who are paid by the piece.

Cost and Hours: £4, tours depart every 30 minutes, Mon-Fri 9:00-15:30, closed Sat-Sun, Dufftown Road, Craigellachie, tel. 01340/871-108, www.speysidecooperage.co.uk.

Glenfiddich Distillery

Before you enter Dufftown, keep an eye out on the left for the home of Scotland's top-selling single malt whisky. This sprawling but charming factory—with a name that means "Valley of the Deer" (hence the logo)—offers excellent tours and tastings. After a 15-minute promotional video, your kilted guide will walk you through the impressive plant, which includes a busy bottling hall. Your tour finishes with an extensive tasting session.

Cost and Hours: Basic £10 "Explorers" visit includes 1.5-hour tour and 4 tastings (departs every 30 minutes), more expensive options available, daily 9:30-16:00 (last tour), tel. 01340/822-373, www.glenfiddich.com.

Glenfiddich or Glenlivet? The two big distilleries of Speyside each offer £10-15 tours and tastings. Both tours are excellent, and they handle their crowds very well. I prefer Glenfiddich as it feels more historic and less corporate, and it's closer to other sights.

Dufftown

This charming, sleepy town has a characteristic crossroads street plan radiating from its clock-tower-topped main square. A few steps up Conval Street from the tower, the humble, one-room **Whisky Museum** doubles as the TI. You'll see a small selection of historical displays and tools from the whisky trade. Most importantly, you'll have a chance to chat with the

fun retirees who run the place (free, daily 10:00-16:00 in summer, tel. 01340/821-591). **The Whisky Shop,** directly behind the tower, is a serious place selling 650 different types of whisky (daily 10:00-18:00, closed Sun in winter, 1 Fife Street, tel. 01340/821-097, www.whiskyshopdufftown.com).

Glenlivet Distillery

Sitting five miles south of the A-95 (turn off at Bridge of Avon), or 13 miles southwest of Dufftown, this is one of the area's most famous and popular distilleries to tour. Their 75-minute tour spares you the gauzy video intro that comes with most tours and takes you right through the sprawling production facility—perched on a ridge overlooking Cairngorms National Park. The

tour finishes with three tastings. If you're not taking the tour, you're welcome to enjoy their history exhibit room. Note: This is just a short detour for those connecting Speyside to Ballater on the scenic route through the mountains (B-9008/A-939).

Cost and Hours: £12.50, daily mid-March-mid-Nov 9:30-18:00, tours depart every 30 minutes 10:00-16:30, closed in winter, head to the village of Glenlivet and follow signs from there, tel. 01340/821-720, www.theglenlivet.com.

Balmoral Castle and Royal Deeside

Royal Deeside—the forested valley of the River Dee—is two sights in one: the Scottish home of the British royal family, wrapped in some of the most gorgeous scenery of Cairngorms National Park. Driving through the park you'll see pockets of Scots pine (Scotland's national tree). While no longer widespread, these once blanketed the Scottish countryside. In fact, 2,000 years ago the Romans must have been impressed. They called this land "Caledonia Silva," meaning "wooded land." Driving on, closer to Balmoral, you'll enter a high, treeless moorland with lots of broom plants (what we'd call Scotch broom) and wild thistles (Scotland's national flower). As you drive, cresting hills to meet vast views, you can imagine royals out on the hunt. (In fact, you'll see tiny huts used by hunters to hide out while they await the stag of their dreams.) The only game you'll likely see is hairy cows and lots of roadkill—mostly rabbit. (Hare today...)

For those who enjoy exploring ruins and coastal scenery, it's worth a speedy detour to Dunnottar Castle on your way south from Ballater and Balmoral.

▲Balmoral Castle

The Queen stays at her 50,000-acre private estate, located within Cairngorms National Park, from August through early October.

But in the months leading up to Her Royal Highness' arrival, the grounds and the castle's ballroom are open to visitors. While royalists will enjoy this glimpse into the place where Liz, Chuck, Billy, and Katie unwind, cynics are disappointed that only one room (the ballroom) is open to the public. Some find the visit overrated and overpriced. Because this is a vacation palace (rather than a state residence), it lacks the sumptuous staterooms you'll see at Holyroodhouse in Edinburgh; this visit is about the grounds and the setting rather than the interior.

Cost and Hours: £12, includes audioguide, April-July daily 10:00-17:00, closed Aug-March, arrive at least an hour before closing, tel. 013397/42534, www.balmoralcastle.com.

Safaris: If you're caught up in the beauty of Balmoral, consider booking a ranger-led Land Rover safari through the grounds (£70, 3 hours, 2/day during the open season).

Background: Queen Victoria and Prince Albert purchased the Balmoral estate in 1848. The thickly forested hills all around reminded Albert of his Thuringian homeland, but Victoria adored it as well—calling it her "Highland paradise." Balmoral Castle was built in the Scottish Baronial style—a romantic, faux-antique look resembling turreted Scottish Renaissance castles from the 16th century—helping to further popularize that look. Ever since, each British monarch has enjoyed retreating to this sprawling property, designed for hunting (red deer) and fishing (salmon). The royal family was here in 1997 when news broke of Princess Diana's death. (Their initial decision not to return to London or to mourn publicly was highly criticized, as depicted in the film *The Queen*.) Today Balmoral has a huge staff, 80 miles of roads, a herd of Highland cattle, and a flock of Highland ponies (stout little miniature horses useful for hauling deer carcasses over the hills).

Visiting the Castle: From the parking lot (with a TI/gift shop, WCs, and the royal church across the street—described later),

walk across the River Dee to reach the ticket booth. From here, you can either hike 10 minutes to the palace, or hop on the free trolley.

Once at the stables, pick up your included audioguide and peruse a few exhibits, including an 8-minute orientation film. In the main exhibit, you'll see a video of the kilts-and-bagpipes welcome parade, plus a diorama of local wildlife, and lots and lots of historical photos of royals enjoying Balmoral—including about 60 years of royal family Christmas cards. Peek into the Queen's garage to see her custom Bentley.

Then follow your audioguide on a short loop through the grounds and gardens before arriving at the palace. (To cut to the chase, or if the weather is bad, you can shortcut from the exhibit directly to the palace and the one room open to the public.) As you walk through the produce and flower gardens, ponder the unenviable challenge of trying to time all of the flowers to bloom and the produce to ripen at the same time, coinciding with the royal family's arrival the first week of August (especially difficult given Scotland's notoriously uncooperative climate).

Finally you'll reach the single room in the palace open to the public: the palace ballroom. Display cases show off memorabilia (children's games played by royal tots, and a fully operational mini-Citroën that future kings and queens have enjoyed driving around). Near the exit, a touchscreen offers you a virtual glimpse at the tartaned private quarters that are off-limits to us commoners.

Nearby: For a free peek at another royal landmark, stop at **Crathie Kirk,** the small, stony, charming parish church where the royal family worships when they are at Balmoral, and where Queen Victoria's beloved servant John Brown is buried (small donation requested, daily 10:00-12:30 & 13:00-16:00, closed Nov-March). The church is just across the highway from the Balmoral parking lot.

The next town past Balmoral Castle (in the opposite direction from Ballater) is **Braemar** (bray-MAR). This tiny village hosts the most famous Highland Games in Scotland, as the Queen is almost always in attendance (first Sun in Sept, www.braemargathering. org). If you swing through town, you can take a look at its big games grandstand and its picturesque castle (not worth touring).

▲▲Ballater

Ballater (BAH-lah-tur) is the place where you'll feel as much royalist sentiment as anywhere in Scotland. For the people of Ballater

(many of whom work, either directly or indirectly, with Balmoral Castle), the Windsors are, simply, their neighbors. Royal connections aside, Ballater is a pleasant, unpretentious, extremely tidy little town. Just big enough to have all the essential tourist services—but neatly nestled in the wooded hills of the

Cairngorms, and a bit more "away from it all" than Pitlochry—Ballater is an ideal home base for those wanting to spend a night in this part of Scotland.

It was local springs—which bubbled up supposedly healing waters—that first put Ballater on the map. But there's no question the town is what it is today thanks to Queen Victoria and Prince Albert, who bought the nearby Balmoral Castle in 1848, then built a train station in Ballater to access it. Today, the town's best attraction may be its residents, who revel in telling tales of royal encounters. Prince Charles, who lives not at Balmoral but at Birkhall (not open to the public), has a particular affection for this part of the Cairngorms. He supports Ballater charities and has been known to show up unannounced at town events...and locals love him for it. ("Prince Charles is a really nice guy," one of them told me. "Not at all like the chap you see on TV.")

Sights in Ballater: The town's only real sight—the old **train station** built by Queen Victoria to more easily commute to her new summer home at Balmoral Castle—has been rebuilt after a fire in 2015. The station includes a TI, tearoom, library, and an exhibit of how Queen Victoria relied on trains to get to Balmoral.

The town is also fun for a wander. Facing the station are two stately sandstone buildings honoring the couple that put this little village on the map: the Prince Albert Hall and the Victoria Hall. Exploring the streets nearby, with their characteristic little shops, you'll notice several boasting the coveted seals announcing "By Appointment of her Majesty the Queen" or "By Appointment of H.R.H. the Prince of Wales"—meaning that they're authorized to sell their wares directly to the gang at Balmoral.

A block from the station—past the Balmoral Bar, with its turrets that echo its namesake castle—the unusually fine parish church is surrounded by an inviting green, with benches, flower gardens, and royal flourishes...like everything in Ballater.

Sleeping in Ballater: The town has several fine B&Bs; given the royal proximity and generally touristy nature of Ballater, prices are high...but so is quality.

$$ Osborne House is a big and cozy home, with spacious rooms, a walled garden, and delightful hosts Heather and Neil (4 Dundarroch Road, tel. 013397/55320, www.osbornehousebedandbreakfast.com, osbornehousebedandbreakfast@gmail.com). Just down the road past the Osborne House garden, look for the white fence surrounding the Victoria barracks—where soldiers tasked with guarding the Queen reside.

$$ Gordon Guest House, right in the center of town facing the historic train station, has five richly furnished rooms (Station Square, tel. 013397/55996, www.thegordonguesthouse.com, info@thegordonguesthouse.com, Martin and Amanda).

Eating in Ballater: If you're just passing through, consider grabbing lunch at **$ The Bothy,** an old-school café. Farther along the main street (toward Aberdeen), near the end of the strip of shops, **$$ Rocksalt & Snails** is a hipper choice. There's also a handy, long-hours **Co-op grocery store** facing the parish church, and nice tables on the green. For a more serious dinner, Ballater has two good Indian restaurants (both facing the green) and a few hotel restaurants and pubs. **$$$$ Rothesay Rooms Restaurant,** sponsored by Prince Charles as a charity project after the town suffered from devastating floods, has a good reputation (Wed-Thu 18:00-21:00, Thu-Sat 12:00-14:00 & 18:00-21:00, 3 Netherley Place near the church green, tel. 013397/53816, www.rothesay-rooms.co.uk). And **$$$ Clachan Grill,** serving modern Scottish cuisine, is about the most stylish and foodie place in town (Wed-Mon 17:00-21:00, closed Tue, tel. 013397/55999, look down a side lane near the bridge at 5 Bridge Square).

Dunnottar Castle

The mostly ruined and empty castle of Dunnottar (duh-NAW-tur) owns a privileged position: clinging to the top of a bulbous bluff, flanked by pebbly beaches and sur-rounded nearly 360 degrees by the North Sea. It's scenic and strategic. From the park-ing lot, you'll walk five minutes to a fork: To the right, you'll come to a ridge with a panoramic view of the castle's fine setting; to the left, you'll hike steeply down (almost all the way to the beach), then steeply back up, to the castle itself. Inside, there's not much to see. The only important thing that hap-pened here was the Battle for the Honours of Scotland, when the Scottish crown jewels were briefly hidden away in the castle from Oliver Cromwell's army, which laid siege to Dunnottar (unsuccessfully) for three days.
But don't worry too much about the history, or the scant posted descriptions—just explore the stately ruins while enjoying the pan-oramic views, sea spray, and cry of the gulls.

Cost and Hours: The photo-op view is free (and enough for many); entering the castle costs £7, daily 9:00-17:30, shorter hours Oct-March, tel. 01569/762-173, www.dunnottarcastle.co.uk.

Getting There: It's just off the busy A-90 expressway, which runs parallel to the coast between Aberdeen and Dundee; exit for Stonehaven, and you'll find Dunnottar well signed just to the south.

Nearby: Dunnottar sits just beyond **Stonehaven,** a pleasant, workaday seafront town that's a handy place to stretch your legs or grab some lunch (big pay parking lot right in the town center, ringed by eateries and grocery stores).

NORTHERN SCOTLAND

Wester Ross & the North Coast • Orkney Islands

Scotland's far north is its rugged and desolate "Big Sky Country"—with towering mountains, vast and moody moors, achingly desolate glens, and a jagged coastline peppered with silver-sand beaches. Far less discovered than the big destinations to the south, this is where you can escape the crowds and touristy "tartan tat" of the Edinburgh-Stirling-Oban-Inverness rut, and get a picturesque corner of Scotland all to yourself. Even on a sunny summer weekend, you may not pass another car for miles. It's just you and the Munro baggers. Beyond Orkney, there's no real "destination" in the north—it's all about the journey.

This chapter covers everything north of the Isle of Skye and Inverness: the scenic west coast (called Wester Ross); the sandy north coast; and the fascinating Orkney archipelago just offshore from Britain's northernmost point.

Fully exploring northern Scotland takes some serious time. The roads are narrow, twisty, and slow, and the pockets of civilization are few and far between. With two weeks or less in Scotland, this area doesn't make the cut (except maybe Orkney). But if you have time to linger, and you appreciate desolate scenery and an end-of-the-world feeling, the untrampled north is worth considering.

Even on a shorter visit, Orkney may be alluring for adventurous travelers seeking a contrast to the rest of Scotland. The islands' claims to fame—astonishing prehistoric sites, Old Norse (Norwegian) heritage, and recent history as a WWI and WWII naval base—combine to spur travelers' imaginations.

PLANNING YOUR TIME

For a scenic loop through this area, try this four-day plan. For some this may be a borderline-unreasonable amount of driving, on twisty, challenging, often one-lane roads (especially on days 1 and 2). Connecting Skye or Glencoe to Ullapool takes a full day. If you don't have someone to split the time behind the wheel, or if you want to really slow down, consider adding another overnight to trip to break up the trip.

Day 1 From the Isle of Skye, drive up the west coast (including the Applecross detour, if time permits), overnighting in Torridon or Ullapool.

Day 2 Continue the rest of the way up the west coast, then trace the north coast from west to east, catching the late-afternoon ferry to Orkney. Overnight in tidy Kirkwall (2 nights).

Day 3 Spend all day on Orkney.

Day 4 Finish up on Orkney and take the ferry back to the mainland; with enough time and interest, squeeze in a visit to John O'Groats before driving three hours back to Inverness (on the relatively speedy A-9).

Planning Tips: To reach Orkney most efficiently—without the slow-going west-coast scenery—consider zipping up on a flight (easy and frequent from Inverness, Edinburgh, or Aberdeen), or make good time on the A-9 highway from Inverness up to Thurso (figure 3 hours one-way) to catch the ferry.

It's possible (but very slow) to traverse this area by bus, but I'd skip it without a car. If you're flying to Orkney, consider renting a car for your time here.

Wester Ross & the North Coast

North of the Isle of Skye, Scotland's scenic Wester Ross coast (the western part of the region of Ross), is remote, sparsely populated, mountainous, and slashed with jagged "sea lochs." (That's "inlets" in American English, or "fjords" in Norwegian.) After seeing Wester Ross' towering peaks, you'll understand why

Northern Scotland

40 Kilometers

40 Miles

SCOTLAND

• Inverness

⊛ Edinburgh

ENGLAND

North Atlantic Ocean

Westray

Rousay

See Orkney Islands detail map

SKARA BRAE

Mainland

Stromness

Kirkwall

Hoy

Scapa Flow

Orkney Islands

Pentland Firth

Dunnet Head

Cape Wrath

Smoo Cave

Scabster

Gills

John o'Groats

Thurso

MEY

Durness

Kyle of Durness→

Loch Eriboll

A-838

A-836

Halkirk

Wick

Tongue

A-99

Scourie

Loch Glendhu

A-894

Kinbrace

A-9

The Minch

B-869

Kylesku

A-836

ARDVRECK

Lochinver

•Inchnadamph

Loch Assynt

A-835

Loch Shin

Lairg

Helmsdale

▲ Knockan Crag

INVEREWE GARDENS

Strathcanaird

Brora

Ardmare

Ullapool

Golspie

North Sea

Loch Broom

• Dornoch

Poolewe

A-832

Loch Maree

Braemore

Gairloch

A-835

Alness

Moray Firth

Elgin

W E S T E R   R O S S

Kinlochwe

Nairn

CAWDOR

Loch Torridon

Achnasheen

Dingwall

Speyside

Torridon

CULLODEN BATTLEFIELD

Applecross

A-890

APPLECROSS ROAD

Loch Carron

EILEAN DONAN

Inverness

CLAVA CAIRNS

A-95

Kyle

A-82

A-939

Kyleakin

Dornie

Loch Ness

URQUHART

A-9

Isle of Skye

A-87

Fort Augustus •

Aviemore

Ballater

Mallaig

CALEDONIAN CANAL

Laggan

Newtonmore

BALMORAL

A-830

George R.R. Martin named the primary setting of his *Game of Thrones* epic "Westeros."

The area is a big draw for travelers seeking stunning views without the crowds. For casual visitors, the views in Glencoe and on the Isle of Skye are much more accessible and just as good as what you'll find farther north. But diehards enjoy getting away from it all in Wester Ross.

Scotland's 100-mile-long north coast, which stretches from Cape Wrath in the northwest corner to John O'Groats in the northeast, is gently scenic, but less dramatic than Wester Ross. Views in this region are dominated by an alternating array of moors and rugged coastline. This is a good place to make up the long miles of Wester Ross.

Scenic Drives in the North

This section outlines three drives that, when combined, take you along this region's west and north coasts. The first Wester Ross leg (from Eilean Donan Castle to Ullapool) is the most scenic, with a fine variety of landscapes—but not many towns—along the way. The next Wester Ross leg gets you to Scotland's northwest corner and the town of Durness. The final leg sweeps you across the north coast, to John O'Groats.

If you want just a taste of this rugged landscape—without going farther north—you can drive the Wester Ross coastline almost as far as Ullapool, then turn off on the A-835 for a quick one-hour drive to Inverness.

In this region, roads are twisty and often only a single lane, so don't judge a drive by its mileage alone. Allow plenty of extra time.

EILEAN DONAN CASTLE TO ULLAPOOL

This long drive, worth ▲▲, connects the picture-perfect island castle of Eilean Donan to the humble fishing village of Ullapool, the logical halfway point up the coast. Figure about 130 miles and nearly a full day for this drive, plus another 20 slow-going miles if you take the Applecross detour (described below).

From the A-87, a few miles east of Kyle of Lochalsh (and the Skye Bridge), follow signs for the A-890 north toward *Lochcarron*. (Note that **Eilean Donan Castle** is just a couple of miles farther east from this turnoff; if coming from Skye, you could squeeze in a visit to that castle before backtracking to this turnoff; for castle details see page 347). From here on out, you can carefully track the brown *Wester Ross Coastal Trail* signs, which will keep you on track.

You'll follow the A-890 as it cuts across a hilly spine, then twists down and runs alongside **Loch Carron.** At the end of the loch, just after the village of Strathcarron, you'll reach a T-intersection that offers two choices. The faster route up to Ullapool—which skips much of the best scenery—takes you right on the A-890 (toward *Inverness*). But for the scenic route outlined here, instead turn left, following the A-896 (following signs for *Lochcarron*). From here, you'll follow the opposite bank of Loch Carron.

Applecross Detour: Soon after you pull away from the lochside, you'll cross over a high meadow and see a well-marked turnoff on the left for a super-scenic—but challenging—alternate route: the **Applecross Road,** over a pass called Bealach na Bà (Gaelic for "Pass of the Cattle"). Intimidating signs suggest a much more straightforward alternate route that keeps you on the

A-896 straight up to Loch Torridon (if doing this, skip down to the "Loch Torridon" section, later). But if you're relatively comfortable negotiating steep switchbacks, and have time to spare (adding about 20 miles to the total journey), this road is drivable. You'll twist up, up, up—hearing your engine struggle up gradients of up to 20 percent—and finally over, with rugged-moonscape views over peaks and lochs. From the summit (at 2,053 feet), the jagged mountains rising from the sea are the Cuillin Hills on the Isle of Skye. Finally, you'll corkscrew back down the other side, arriving at the humble seafront town of Applecross.

Once in **Applecross,** you could either return over the same pass to pick up the A-896 (slightly faster), or, for a meandering but very scenic route, carry on all the way around the northern headland of the peninsula. This provides you with further views of Raasay and Skye, through a deserted-feeling landscape on one-lane roads. Then, turning the corner at the top of the peninsula, you'll begin to drive above Loch Torridon, with some of the finest views on this drive.

Loch Torridon: Whether you take the Applecross detour or the direct route, you'll wind up at the stunning sea loch called **Loch Torridon**—hemmed in by thickly forested pine-covered hills, it resembles the Rockies. You'll pass through an idyllic fjord-side town, Shieldaig, then cross over a finger of land and plunge deeper into Upper Loch Torridon. Near the end of the loch,

keep an eye out for **The Torridon**—a luxurious lochfront grand hotel with gorgeous Victorian Age architecture, a café serving afternoon tea, and expensive rooms (www.thetorridon.com).

As you loop past the far end of the loch—with the option to turn off for the village of **Torridon** (which has a good youth hostel, www.hostellingscotland.org.uk)—the landscape has shifted dramatically, from pine-covered hills to a hauntingly desolate glen. You'll cut through this valley—bookended by towering peaks and popular with hikers—before reaching the town of Kinlochewe.

At Kinlochewe, take the A-832 west (following *Ullapool* signs from here on out), and soon you'll be tracing the bonnie, bonnie banks of **Loch Maree**—considered by many connoisseurs to be one of Scotland's finest lochs. You'll see campgrounds, nature areas, and scenic pullouts as you make good time on the speedy two-lane lochside road. (The best scenery is near the beginning, so don't put off that photo op.)

Nearing the end of Loch Maree, the road becomes single-track again as you twist up over another saddle of scrubby land. On the other side, you'll get glimpses of Gair Loch through the trees, before finally arriving at the little harbor of **Gairloch.** Just beyond the harbor, where the road straightens out as it follows the coast, keep an eye out (on the right) for the handy Gale Center. Run as a charity, it has WCs, a small café with treats baked by locals, a fine shop of books and crafts, and comfortable tables and couches for taking a break (www.galeactionforum.co.uk).

True to its name, Gair Loch ("Short Loch") doesn't last long, and soon you'll head up a hill (keep an eye out for the pullout on the left, offering fine views

over the village). The next village is Polewe, on **Loch Ewe.** Just after the village, on the left, is the **Inverewe Gardens.** These beautiful gardens, run by the National Trust for Scotland, were the pet project of Osgood Mackenzie, who in 1862 began transforming 50 acres of his lochside estate into a subtropical paradise. The warming Gulf Stream and—in some places—stout stone walls help make this oasis possible. If you have time and need to stretch your legs from all that shifting, spend an hour wandering its sprawling grounds. The walled garden, near the entrance, is a highlight, with each bed thoughtfully labeled (£12.50, daily, www.nts.org.uk).

Continuing on the A-832 toward Ullapool, you'll stay above Loch Ewe, then briefly pass above the open ocean. Soon you'll find yourself following **Little Loch Broom** (with imposing mountains on your right). At the end of that loch, you'll carry on straight and work your way past a lush strip of farmland at the apex of the loch. Soon you'll meet the big A-835 highway; turn left and take this speedy road the rest of the way into Ullapool. (Or you can turn right to zip on the A-835 all the way to Inverness—just an hour away.) Whew!

Ullapool

A gorgeously set, hardworking town of about 1,500 people, Ullapool (ulla-PEWL) is what passes for a metropolis in Wester Ross. Its most prominent feature is its big, efficient ferry dock, connecting the mainland with Stornoway on the Isle of Lewis (Scotland's biggest, in the Outer Hebrides). Facing the dock is a strip of cute little houses, today housing restaurants, shops,  B&Bs, and residences. Behind the waterfront, the town is only a few blocks deep—you can get the lay of the land in a few minutes' stroll. Curving around the back side of the town—along a big, grassy campground—is an inviting rocky beach, facing across the loch in one direction and out toward the open sea in the other.

Orientation to Ullapool: Ullapool has several handy services for travelers. An excellent **bookshop** is a block up, straight ahead from the ferry dock. Many services line Argyle Street, which runs parallel to the harbor one block up the hill: the **TI** is to the right, while a Bank of Scotland **ATM** and the **post office** are to the left. On this same street, the town runs a fine little **museum** with well-done exhibits about local history (closed Sun and Nov-March, www.ullapoolmuseum.co.uk). This street, nicknamed "Art-gyle Street," also has a smattering of local art **galleries.**

Sleeping in Ullapool: Several guesthouses line the harborfront Shore Street, including **$ Waterside House** (3 rooms, minimum two-night stay in peak season, https://waterside.uk.net) and the town's official **¢ youth hostel** (www.hostellingscotland.org.uk). A block up from the water on West Argyle Street, **$ West House** has three rooms and requires a two-night minimum stay (no breakfast, closed Oct-April, www.westhousebandb.co.uk).

Eating in Ullapool: The two most reliable places are the **$$ Ceilidh Place,** on West Argyle Street a block above the harbor (www.theceilidhplace.com); and **$$$ The Arch Inn,** facing the water a half-block from the ferry dock (www.thearchinn.co.uk).

Both have a nice pubby vibe as well as sit-down dining rooms with a focus on locally caught seafood. Both also rent rooms and frequently host live music. For a quick meal, two **$ chippies** (around the corner from each other, facing the ferry dock) keep the breakwater promenade busy with al fresco budget diners and happy seagulls.

ULLAPOOL TO THE NORTH COAST

This shorter drive, worth ▲, connects one quaint seaside town (Ullapool) to another (Durness—on the north coast) through rolling hills sprinkled with wee lochs and the dramatic landscape. Expect this drive (about 70 miles) to take another couple scenic hours, depending on your sightseeing stops.

Leaving Ullapool, follow signs that read simply *North (A-835)*. You'll pass through the cute little beachside village of **Ardmair,** then pull away from the coast.

About 15 minutes after leaving Ullapool, just after you exit the village of Strathcanaird and head uphill, watch on the left for a pullout with a handy orientation panel describing the panorama of **towering peaks** that line the road. It looks like a mossy Monument Valley. Enjoy the scenery for about four more miles—surrounded by lochs and gigantic peaks—and watch for the **Knockan Crag** visitors center, above you on the right, with exhibits on local geology, flora, and fauna and suggestions for area hikes (unmanned and open daily 24 hours, WCs, www.nnr.scot).

Continuing north along the A-835, you'll soon pass out of the region of Ross and Cromarty and enter Sutherland. At the T-intersection, turn left for *Kylesku* and *Lochinver* (on the A-837). From here on out, you can start following the *North & West Highlands Tourist Route;* you'll also see your first sign for John O'Groats at the northeastern corner of Scotland (152 miles away).

You'll roll through moors, surrounded on all sides by hills. Just after the barely-there village of Inchnadamph, keep an eye out on the left for the ruins of **Ardvrech Castle,** which sits in crumbled majesty upon its own little island in Loch Assynt, connected to the world by a narrow sandy spit. Just after these ruins, you'll have another choice: For the fastest route to the north coast, turn right to follow A-894 (toward *Kylesku* and *Durness*). If you have some time to spare, you could carry on straight to scenically follow Loch Assynt toward the sleepy fishing village of **Lochinver** (12 miles). After seeing the village, you could go back the way you came to the main road, or continue all the way around the little peninsula on the B-869, passing several appealing sandy beaches and villages.

Back on the main A-894, you'll pass through an almost lunar landscape, with peaks all around, finally emerging at the gorgeous, mountain-rimmed **Loch Glendhu,** which you'll cross on a stout modern bridge. From here, it's a serene landscape of rock, heather, and ferns, with occasional glimpses of the coast—such as at **Scourie,** with a particularly nice sandy beach. Finally (after the road becomes A-838—keep left at the fork, toward *Durness*), you'll head up, over, and through a vast and dramatic glen. At the end of the glen, you'll start to see sand below you on the left; this is **Kyle of Durness,** which goes on for miles. You'll see the turnoff for the ferry to Cape Wrath, then follow tidy stone walls the rest of the way into **Durness.**

NORTHERN SCOTLAND

THE NORTH COAST

This driving route takes you along the picturesque, remote north coast from west (Durness village) to east (the touristy town of John O'Groats). Allow at least 2.5 hours for this 90-mile drive (add more time for stops along the way).

Durness Town

This beachy village of cow meadows is delightfully perched on a bluff above sandy shores. This area has a different feel from Wester Ross—it's more manicured, with tidy farms hemmed in by neatly stacked stone walls. There's not much to see or do in the town, but there is a 24-hour gas station (gas up now—this is your last chance for a while...trust me) and a handy TI (by the big parking lot with the "Award Winning Beach," tel. 01971/509-005).

Head east out of the village on the A-838, watching for brown signs on your right to *Durness Village Hall*. Pull over here to stroll through the small **memorial garden for John Lennon,** who enjoyed his boyhood vacations in Durness.

Just after the village hall, on the left, pull over at **Smoo Cave** (free WCs in parking lot). Its goofy-sounding name comes from

the Old Norse *smúga,* for "cave." (Many places along the north coast—which had a strong Viking influence—have Norse rather than Gaelic or Anglo-Saxon place names.) It's free to hike down the well-marked stairs to a protected cove, where an underground river has carved a deep cave into the bluff. Walk inside the cave to get a free peek at the waterfall; for a longer visit, you can pay for a 20-minute boat trip and guided walk (unnecessary for most; sign up at the mouth of the cave).

Back on the road, soon after Smoo Cave, on the left, is the gorgeous **Ceannabeinne Beach** (Gaelic for "End of the Mountains"). Of the many Durness-area beaches, this is the locals' favorite.

Durness to Thurso

Heading east from the Durness area, you'll traverse many sparsely populated miles—long roads that cut in and out from the coast, with scrubby moorland and distant peaks on the other side. You'll emerge at the gigantic **Loch Eriboll,** which you'll circumnavigate—passing lamb farms and crumbling stone walls—to continue your way east. Leaving this fjord, you'll cut through some classic fjord scenery until you finally pop out at the scenic **Kyle of Tongue.** You'll cross over the big, modern bridge, then twist up through the village of Tongue and continue your way eastward (the A-838 becomes the A-836)—through more of the same scrubby moorland scenery. Make good time for the next 40 lonely miles. Notice how many place names along here use the term "strath"—a wide valley (as opposed to a narrower "glen"), such as where jagged mountains open up to the sea.

Finally—after going through little settlements like Bettyhill and Melvich—the moors begin to give way to working farms as you approach Thurso. The main population center of northern Scotland (pop. 8,000), Thurso is a functional transit hub with a charming old core. As you face out to sea, the heavily industrialized point on the left is **Scrabster,** with the easiest ferry crossing to Orkney (for details, see "Getting to Orkney," later).

Several sights near Thurso are worth the extra couple miles.

Dunnet Head: About eight miles east of Thurso (following brown *John O'Groats* signs on the A-836) is the village of Dunnet. If you have time for some rugged scenery, turn off here to drive the four miles (each way) to the Dunnet Head peninsula.

While John O'Groats is often dubbed "Britain's northernmost point," Dunnet Head pokes up just a bit farther. And, while it lacks the too-cute signpost marking distances to faraway landmarks, views from here are better than from John O'Groats. Out at the tip of Dunnet Head, a lonely lighthouse enjoys panoramic views across the Pentland Firth to Orkney, while a higher vantage point is just up the hill. Keep an eye out for seabirds, including puffins.

Mary-Ann's Cottage: In the village of Dunnet, between the main road and Dunnet Head, this little stone house explains traditional crofting lifestyles. It appears just as it was when 92-year-old Mary-Ann Calder moved out in 1990 (very limited hours).

Castle of Mey: About four miles east of Mary-Ann's Cottage (on the main A-836) is the Castle of Mey. The Queen Mother grew up at Glamis Castle (see page 242), but after her daughter became Queen Elizabeth II, she purchased and renovated this sprawling property as an escape from the bustle of royal life...and you couldn't get much farther from civilization than

this. For nearly 50 years, the Queen Mum stayed here for annual visits in August and October. Today it welcomes visitors to tour its homey interior and 30 acres of manicured gardens (closed Oct-April, www.castleofmey.org.uk).

From Mey, it's another six miles east to John O'Groats. About halfway there, in Gills Bay, is another ferry dock for cars heading to Orkney (see "Getting to Orkney," later).

John O'Groats

A total tourist trap that's somehow also genuinely stirring, John O'Groats marks the north-eastern corner of the Isle of Britain—bookending the country with Land's End, 874 miles to the southwest in Cornwall. People enjoy traversing the length of Britain by motorcycle, by bicycle, or even by foot (it takes about eight weeks

to trudge along the "E2E" trail—that's "End to End"). And upon arrival, whether they've walked for two months or just driven up for the day from Inverness, everyone wants to snap a "been there, done that" photo with the landmark signpost. Surrounding that is a huge parking lot, a souvenir stand masquerading as a TI, and lots of tacky "first and last" shops and restaurants. Orkney looms just off the coast.

Nearby: The real target of "End to End" pilgrims isn't the signpost, but the **Duncansby Head Lighthouse**—about two miles to the east, it's the actual northeasternmost point, with an even more end-of-the-world vibe. (By car, head away from the John O'Groats area on A-99, and watch for the Duncansby Head turnoff on the left, just past the Seaview Hotel.) If you have time for a hike, about a mile south of the lighthouse are the **Duncansby Stacks**—dramatic sea stacks rising up above a sandy beach.

The Orkney Islands

The Orkney Islands, perched just an hour's ferry ride north of the mainland, are uniquely remote, historic, and—for the right traveler—well worth the effort.

Crossing the 10-mile Pentland Firth separating Orkney from northern Scotland, you leave the Highlands behind and enter a new world. With no real tradition for clans, tartans, or bagpipes, Orkney feels not "Highlander" or even "Scottish," but Orcadian (as locals are called). Though Orkney was inhabited by Picts from the sixth century BC, during most of its formative history—from 875 all the way until 1468—it was a prized trading hub of the Norwegian realm, giving it a feel more Scandinavian than Celtic. The Vikings (who sailed from Norway, just 170 miles away) left their mark, both literally (runes carved into prehistoric stone monuments) and culturally: Many place names are derived from Old Norse, and the Orkney flag looks like the Norwegian flag with a few yellow accents.

There are other historic connections. In later times, Canada's Hudson's Bay Company recruited many Orcadians to staff its outposts. And given its status as the Royal Navy headquarters during both World Wars, Orkney remains one of the most pro-British corners of Scotland. In the 2014 independence referendum, Orkney cast the loudest "no" vote in the entire country (67 percent against).

Orkney's landscape is also a world apart: Aside from some dramatic sea cliffs hiding along its perimeter, the main island is mostly flat and bald, with few trees, the small town of Kirkwall, and lots of tidy farms with gently mooing cows. While the blustery weather (which can change several times a day) keeps the vegetation on the scrubby side, for extra greenery each town has a sheltered community garden run by volunteers. Orkney's fine sandy beaches seem always empty—as if lying on them will give you hypothermia. Sparsely populated, the islands have no traffic lights and most roads are single lane with "passing places" politely spaced as necessary.

Today's economy is based mostly on North Sea oil, renewable energy, and fishing. The boats you'll see are creel boats with nets and cages to collect crabs, lobsters, scallops, and oysters. Unless a cruise ship drops by, tourism seems to be secondary.

For the sightseer, Orkney has two draws unmatched elsewhere in Scotland: It has some of the finest prehistoric sites in northern Europe, left behind by an advanced Stone Age civilization that flourished here. And the harbor called Scapa Flow has fascinating remnants of its important military role during the World Wars—from intentional shipwrecks designed to seal off the harbor, to muscular Churchill-built barriers to finish the job a generation later.

Orientation to Orkney

Orkney (as the entire archipelago is called) is made up of 70 islands, with a total population of 24,500. The main island—with the primary town (Kirkwall) and ferry ports connecting Orkney to northern Scotland (Stromness and St. Margaret's Hope)—is called, confusingly, Mainland. (It just goes to show you: One man's island is another man's mainland.)

PLANNING YOUR TIME
Orkney merits at least two nights and one full day. Some people (especially WWII aficionados) spend days exploring Orkney, but I've focused on the main sights to see in a short visit—all on the biggest island.

NORTHERN SCOTLAND

NORTHERN SCOTLAND

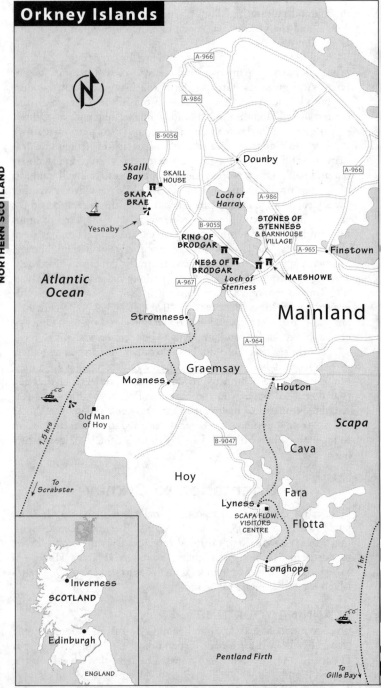

Orkney Islands

A-966

A-986

B-9056

• Dounby

Skaill Bay

SKAILL HOUSE

SKARA BRAE

A-966

Loch of Harray

A-986

Yesnaby

B-9055

STONES OF STENNESS & BARNHOUSE VILLAGE

A-965

• Finstown

RING OF BRODGAR

Atlantic Ocean

NESS OF BRODGAR

A-967

Loch of Stenness

MAESHOWE

Mainland

Stromness

A-964

Graemsay

Moaness

Houton

Scapa

Old Man of Hoy

Cava

1.5 hrs

B-9047

Hoy

Fara

To Scrabster

Lyness

SCAPA FLOW VISITORS CENTRE

Flotta

1 hr

Longhope

Inverness

SCOTLAND

Edinburgh

ENGLAND

Pentland Firth

To Gills Bay

NORTHERN SCOTLAND

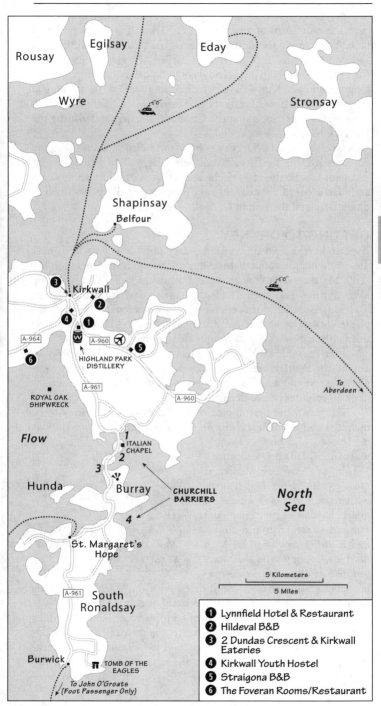

Rousay

Egilsay

Eday

Wyre

Stronsay

Shapinsay

Belfour

3 Kirkwall

2

4

1

A-964

W

A-960

HIGHLAND PARK DISTILLERY

5

6

A-961

A-960

To Aberdeen

ROYAL OAK SHIPWRECK

Flow

1 ITALIAN CHAPEL

2

3

Hunda

Burray

CHURCHILL BARRIERS

4

North Sea

St. Margaret's Hope

A-961

South Ronaldsay

5 Kilometers

5 Miles

Burwick

TOMB OF THE EAGLES

To John O'Groats (Foot Passenger Only)

1 Lynnfield Hotel & Restaurant
2 Hildeval B&B
3 2 Dundas Crescent & Kirkwall Eateries
4 Kirkwall Youth Hostel
5 Straigona B&B
6 The Foveran Rooms/Restaurant

The only town of any substance, Kirkwall is your best home base. You can see its sights in a few hours (a town stroll, the fine Orkney Museum, and its striking cathedral). From there, to see the best of Orkney in a single day, plan on driving about 70 miles, looping out from Kirkwall in two directions: Spend the morning at the prehistoric sites (Maeshowe and nearby sites, Skara Brae), and the afternoon driving along the Churchill Barriers and visiting the Italian Chapel.

Cruise Crowds: Orkney is Scotland's busiest cruise port; on days when ships are in port, normally sleepy destinations can be jammed. Check the cruise schedule at www.orkneyharbours.com and plan accordingly to avoid busy times at popular sights (such as Skara Brae and the Italian Chapel).

GETTING TO ORKNEY

By Car/Ferry: Two different car-ferry options depart from near Thurso, which is about a three-hour drive from Inverness (on the A-9); for the scenic longer route, you could loop all the way up Wester Ross, and then along the north coast from Durness to Thurso (see earlier in this chapter). The two companies land at opposite corners of Orkney, at Stromness and St. Margaret's Hope; from either, it's about a 30-minute drive to Kirkwall.

Plan on about £60 one-way for a car on the Northlink ferry, or £40 on the Pentland ferry, plus £20 per passenger. For either company, reserve online at least a day in advance; check in at the ferry dock 30 minutes before departure.

For most, the best choice is the **Scrabster-Stromness** ferry, operated by NorthLink (3/day in each direction in summer, 2/day off-season, 1.5-hour crossing, www.northlinkferries.co.uk). While it's a slightly longer crossing, it's also a bigger boat, with more services (including a good sit-down cafeteria—and famously tasty fish-and-chips), and it glides past the Old Man of Hoy, giving you an easy glimpse at one of Orkney's top

landmarks. This ferry is coordinated with bus #X99, connecting Scrabster to Inverness (www.stagecoachbus.com).

The **Gills Bay-St. Margaret's Hope** route is operated by Pentland Ferries; its main advantage is the proximity of Gills Bay to John O'Groats, making it easy to visit Britain's northeastern-most point on your way to or from the ferry—but Gills Bay is also that much farther from Inverness (3/day in each direction, one-hour crossing, www.pentlandferries.co.uk).

There's also a **passenger-only boat** directly from John O'Groats to Burwick, which connects conveniently to an onward bus to Kirkwall (3/day June-Aug, 2/day May and Sept, none Oct-April, 40-minute crossing, www.jogferry.co.uk). While this works for those leaving their car at John O'Groats for a quick Orkney day trip, it's more weather-dependent.

By Plane: Kirkwall's little airport has direct flights to Inverness, Edinburgh, Glasgow, and Aberdeen (www.flybe.com has good deals if you book ahead). Landing at the airport, you're four miles from Kirkwall; pick up a town map at the info desk. It's convenient to pick up a rental car at the airport. There are not many taxis, so without a car your best bet is the bus that runs every 30 minutes—just pay the driver (airport code: KOI, tel. 01856/872-421, www.hial.co.uk/kirkwall-airport).

By Tour from Inverness: The John O'Groats foot ferry operates a very long all-day tour from Inverness that includes bus and ferry transfers, and a guided tour around the main sights (£76, daily June-Aug only, www.jogferry.co.uk).

GETTING AROUND ORKNEY

While this chapter is designed for travelers with a car (or a driver/guide—see next), **public buses** do connect sights on Mainland (operated by Stagecoach, www.stagecoachbus.com). From Mainland, **ferries** fan out to outlying islets (www.orkneyferries.co.uk); the main ports are Kirkwall (for points north) and Houton (for Hoy). If taking a car on a ferry, it's always smart to book ahead.

Local Guide: Husband-and-wife team Kinlay and Kirsty run **Orkney Uncovered.** Energetic and passionate about sharing their adopted home with visitors, they'll show you both prehistoric and wartime highlights (everything in this chapter—which Kinlay helped research). They're also happy to tailor an itinerary to your interests and offer a special price for Rick Steves readers (RS%—£300 for a full-day, 9-hour tour in a comfy van, more for 5 or more people, multiday tours and cruise excursions possible, tel. 01856/878-822, www.orkneyuncovered.co.uk, enquiries@orkneyuncovered.co.uk).

Kirkwall

Kirkwall (pop. 9,000) is tidy and functional. Like the rest of the island, most of its buildings are more practical than pretty. But it has an entertaining and interesting old center and is a smart home base from which to explore the island. Whether sleeping here or not, you'll likely pass through at some point (to gas up, change buses, use the airport, or stock up on groceries).

Orientation to Kirkwall

Historic Kirkwall's shop-lined, pedestrian-only main drag leads from the cathedral down to the harbor, changing names several times as it curls through town.

It's a workaday strip, lined with a combination of humble local shops and places trying to be trendy. You'll pop out at the little harbor, where fishing boats bob and ferries fan out to the northern islets.

The handy **TI** is at the bus station (on West Castle Street, daily 9:00-18:00, Oct-March until 17:00, tel. 01856/872-856, www.orkney.com). They produce a handy "breakfast bulletin" with the day's events and tourist news. The bus station stores bags for free (but not overnight). If you don't have a car, **Craigies Taxi** is reliable and responds quickly to a call (tel. 01856/878-787).

You're likely to find live music somewhere most nights. The **Reel Coffee Shop,** next to the cathedral, is passionate about music and hosts folk and "trad" evenings with an inviting vibe (generally Wed, Thu, and Sat at 20:00). Among the local craft beers on tap, the most popular, a pale ale, is Scapa Special. (They say it goes down better than the German fleet.)

Sights in Kirkwall

▲St. Magnus Cathedral

This grand edifice, whose pointy steeple is visible from just about anywhere in town, is one of Scotland's most enjoyable churches to visit (free, Mon-Sat 9:00-18:00, Sun from 13:00). The building dates from the 12th century, back when this was part of the Parish of Trondheim, Norway. Built from vibrant red sandstone by many of the same stonemasons who worked on Durham's showpiece cathedral, St. Magnus is harmonious Romanesque

inside and out: stout columns and small, rounded windows and arches. Inside, it boasts a delightful array of engaging monuments, all well-described by the self-guided tour brochure: a bell from the *Royal Oak* battleship, sunk in Scapa Flow in 1939 (explained later); a reclining monument of arctic explorer John Rae, who appears to be enjoying a very satisfying eternal nap; the likely bones of St. Magnus (a beloved local saint); and many other characteristic flourishes. But the highlight is the gravestones that line the walls of the nave, each one carved with reminders of mortality: skull and crossbones, coffin, hourglass, and the shovel used by the undertaker. Read some of the poignant epitaphs: "She lived regarded and dyed regreted."

Nearby: The **Bishop and Earl's Palaces** (across the street) are a pair of once-grand, now-empty ruined buildings—for most, they're not worth the admission fee.

▲▲Orkney Museum

Just across the street from the cathedral, this museum packs the old parsonage with well-described exhibits covering virtually every dimension of history and life on the island. A visit here (to see the Stone Age, Iron Age, and Viking artifacts) can be good preparation before exploring the islands' archaeological sites. Poking around, you'll see a 1539 map showing how "Orcadia" was part of  Scandinavia, an exhibit about the crazy annual brawl called The Ba', and lots of century-old photos of traditional life (free, Mon-Sat 10:30-17:00, closed Sun, fine book shop, tel. 01856/873-535, www. orkney.gov.uk).

Mercat Cross

In front of the cathedral stands Kirkwall's mercat cross (market cross), which is the starting point for the annual event called The Ba'. Short for "ball," this is a no-holds-barred, citywide rugby match that takes place every Christmas and New Year's Day. Hundreds of Kirkwall's rough-and-tumble young lads team up based on neighborhood (the Uppies and the Doonies), and attempt to deliver the ball to the opposing team's goal by any means necessary. The only rule: There are no rules. While it's usually just one gigantic scrum pushing back and forth through the streets, other tactics are used (such as the recent controversy when one team simply tossed the ball in a car and drove it to the goal). Ask locals about their stories—or scars—from The Ba'.

▲Highland Park Distillery

Outside the town center is a sprawling stone facility that's been distilling whisky since 1789 (legally). They give 75-minute tours similar to other distilleries, but this is one of only six in all of Scotland that malts its own barley—you'll see the malting floor (where the barley is spread and stirred while germinating) and the peat-fired kilns. Guides love to explain how the distillery's well-regarded whiskies get their flavor from Orkney's unique composition of peat (composed mostly of

heather on this treeless island) and its high humidity (which minimizes alcohol "lost to the angels" during maturation). While the distillery is "silent" for much of July and August, its one-hour tour is good even if the workers are gone (£10, tours on the hour daily 10:00-16:00, Sun 12:00-16:00, fewer off-season, includes two tasty shots; on the edge of town to the south, toward the Scapa Flow WWII sites; tel. 01856/874-619, www.highlandparkwhisky.com).

Sleeping in Kirkwall

These accommodations are in or near Kirkwall. Orkney's B&Bs are not well-marked; get specific instructions from your host before you arrive.

In Kirkwall: $$$ Lynnfield Hotel rents 10 rooms that are a bit old-fashioned in decor, but with modern hotel amenities (on Holm Road/A-961, tel. 01856/872-505, www.lynnfield.co.uk). High up in town, consider **$$ Hildeval B&B,** in a modern home with five contemporary-style rooms (on East Road, tel. 01856/878-840, www.hildeval-orkney.co.uk). With a handy location just behind the cathedral, **$ 2 Dundas Crescent** has four old-fashioned rooms rented by welcoming Ruth, in a big old house that used to be a manse—a preacher's home (tel. 01856/874-805, www.twodundas.co.uk). And ¢ the **Kirkwall Youth Hostel** rents both dorm beds and private rooms (Old Scapa Road, 15-minute walk from center, tel. 01856/872-243, www.hostellingscotland.org.uk).

In the Countryside: Just past the airport, **$$ Straigona B&B,** about a five-minute drive outside of Kirkwall, has three rooms in a cozy modern home, run by helpful Julie and Mike (two-night minimum stay in summer, tel. 01856/861-328, www.straigona.co.uk). For more anonymity and grand views over Scapa Flow, the recommended restaurant **$$ The Foveran** has eight rooms, some with contemporary flourish and others more traditional (5 minutes from Kirkwall by car on the A-964, tel. 01856/872-389, www.thefoveran.com).

Eating in Kirkwall

The first two places are near the cathedral; the next two are on the harbor. The main pedestrian street connecting the harbor and cathedral is lined with other options. Hotels along the harbor are also a good bet for dinner.

$$ The Reel Coffee Shop is a music club, café, and pub popular for its light lunches (open daily 9:00-17:00, next to the cathedral). It reopens on many evenings to host live music (Wed, Thu, and Sat evenings from 20:00, 6 Broad Street, tel. 01856/871-000).

$$ Judith Glue Shop is a souvenir-and-craft shop across from the cathedral, with a cutesy café in the back (25 Broad Street, tel. 01856/874-225).

$ The Harbour Fry is the best place for fish-and-chips, with both eat-in and takeaway options (daily 12:00-21:00, half a block off the harbor at 3 Bridge Street, tel. 01856/873-170).

$$ Helgi's Pub, facing the harbor, serves quality food and is popular for its fun menu and burgers. Upstairs is boring, the ground floor is more fun, and you're welcome to sit at the bar if the tables are full. Reservations are smart for dinner (daily 12:00-14:00 & 17:00-21:00, 14 Harbor Street, tel. 01856/879-293, www.helgis.co.uk).

DESTINATION RESTAURANTS NEAR KIRKWALL

With talented chefs working hard to elevate Orcadian cuisine—using traditional local ingredients, but with international flourish, these are considered the best restaurants around.

$$$$ The Foveran, perched on a bluff with smashing views over Scapa Flow, has a cool, contemporary dining room with a wall of windows (dinner nightly May-Sept, weekends-only in winter, southwest of Kirkwall on the A-964, tel. 01856/872-389, www.thefoveran.com).

$$$$ Lynnfield Hotel, near the Highland Park Distillery on the way out of town, has a more traditional feel (open daily for lunch and dinner, reservations smart in the evening, on Holm Road/A-961, tel. 01856/872-505, www.lynnfield.co.uk).

Sights in Orkney

PREHISTORIC SITES

Orkney boasts an astonishing concentration of 5,000-year-old Neolithic monuments worth ▲▲▲—one of the best such collections in Great Britain (and that's saying something). And here on Orkney, there's also a unique Bronze and Iron Age overlay, during which Picts, and then Vikings, built their own monuments to complement the ones they inherited. The best of these sites are easily toured along a single stretch of road, as described below.

Background: Five thousand years ago—centuries before Stonehenge—Orkney had a bustling settlement with some 30,000 people (a population larger than today's). The climate, already milder than most of Scotland thanks to the Gulf Stream, was even warmer then, making this a desirable place to live. Orkney's prehistoric residents left behind structures from every walk of life: humble residential settlements (Skara Brae, Barnhouse Village), mysterious stone circles (Ring of Brodgar, Stenness Stones), more than 100 tombs (Maeshowe, Tomb of the Eagles), and what appears to be a sprawling ensemble of spiritual buildings (the Ness of Brodgar). And, this being the Stone Age, all of this was accomplished using tools made not of metal, but of stone and bone. Many more sites await excavation. (Any time you see a lump or a bump in a field, it's likely an ancient site—identified with the help of ground-penetrating radar—and protected by the government.) While you could spend days poring over all of Orkney's majestic prehistoric monuments, on a short visit focus on the following highlights. (Actual artifacts from these sites are on display only in the Orkney Museum in Kirkwall.)

Maeshowe

The finest chambered tomb north of the Alps, Maeshowe (mays-HOW) was built around 3500 BC. From the outside, it looks like yet another big mound. But inside, the burial chamber is remarkably intact. The only way to go inside is on a fascinating 30-minute tour. You'll squeeze through the entrance tunnel and emerge into a space designed for ancestor worship, surrounded by three smaller cells. At the winter solstice, the setting sun  shines through the entrance tunnel, illuminating the entrance to the main cell. How they managed to cut and transport gigantic slabs of sandstone, then assemble this dry-stone, corbeled pyramid—all in an age before metal tools—still puzzles present-day engineers. Adding to this place's mystique, in the 12th century, a band of Norsemen took shelter here for three days during a storm, and entertained themselves by carving runic messages into the walls—many of them still readable (£9, tours daily 10:00-16:00, tel. 01856/761-606, www.historicenvironment.scot/maeshowe). Reservations are required (book in person or online, but not by phone).

Prehistoric Sites near Maeshowe

A narrow spit of land just a few hundred yards from Maeshowe is lined with several stunning, free-to-visit, always-"open" Neolithic sites (from Maeshowe, head south on the A-965 and immediately turn right onto the B-9056, following *Bay of Skaill* signs). Along this road, you'll reach the following sites, in this order (watch for the brown signs). Conveniently, these line up on the way to Skara Brae.

Stones of Stenness: Three-and-a-half standing stones survive from an original 12 that formed a 100-foot-diameter ring. Dating from around 3000 BC, these are some of the oldest standing stones in Britain (a millennium older than Stonehenge).

Barnhouse Village: From the Stones of Stenness, a footpath continues through the field to the Barnhouse Village. Likely built around the same time as the Stones of Stenness, this was probably a residential area for the priests and custodians of the ceremonial monuments all around. Discovered in 1984, much of what you see today has been reconstructed—making this the least favorite site of archaeological purists. Still, it provides an illuminating contrast to Skara Brae (described later): While those Skara Brae homes were built underground, the ones at Barnhouse were thatched stone huts not unlike ones you still see around Great Britain today. The entire gathering was enclosed by a defensive wall.

Back on the road, just before the **causeway** between two lochs—saltwater on the left and freshwater on the right—two pillars flank the road (one intact, the other stubby). These formed a gateway of sorts to the important Neolithic structures just beyond.

Ness of Brodgar: On the left, look for a busy excavation site in action. The Ness of Brodgar offers an exciting opportunity to observe an actual archaeological dig in progress (discovered only in 2003). The work site you see covers only one-tenth of the entire complex, which was likely an ensemble of important ceremonial buildings...think of it as the "Orkney Vatican." The biggest foundation, nicknamed "the Cathedral," appears to have

been a focal point for pilgrimages. Don't be surprised if there's no action—due to limited funding, archaeologists are likely at work here only in July and August (at other times, it's carefully covered, with nothing to see). The archaeologists hope to raise enough funds to build a permanent visitors center. Free guided tours are sometimes available (July-Aug Mon-Fri at 11:00, 13:00, and 15:00, check www.nessofbrodgar.co.uk for details).

The Ring of Brodgat: Farther along on the left, look for stones capping a ridge above the road. The Ring of Brodgar is more than three times larger than the Stones of Stenness (and about 500 years newer). Of the original 60 or so stones—creating a circle as wide as a football field—25 still stand. The ring, which sits amidst a marshy moor, was surrounded by a henge (moat) that was 30 feet wide and 20 feet deep. Walking around the ring,

notice that some are carved with "graffiti"—names of visitors from the late 19th century to the early 20th century, as well as some faint Norse runes carved by a Viking named Bjorn around AD 1150 (park 300 yards away, across the road).

Skara Brae

At the far-eastern reaches of Mainland (about a 20-minute drive from Maeshowe), this remarkable site illustrates how some Neolithic people lived like rabbits in warrens—hunkered down in subterranean homes, connected by tunnels and lit only by whale-oil lamps. Uncovered by an 1850 windstorm, Skara Brae (meaning roughly "village under hills") has been meticulously excavated and is very well-presented.

Cost and Hours: £9, daily 9:30-17:30, shorter hours Oct-March, last entry 45 minutes before closing, café and WCs, http://www.historicenvironment.scot.

Visiting Skara Brae: Begin your visit in the small exhibition hall, where you'll watch a short film and see displays on Neolithic life. Then head out and walk inside a reconstructed home from Skara Brae—with a hearth, beds, storage area, and live-bait tanks dug into the floor. Finally, walk across a field to reach the site itself. Museum attendants stand by to answer any questions.

The oldest, standalone homes at Skara Brae were built around 3100 BC; a few centuries later, the complex was expanded and connected with tunnels. You'll walk on a grassy ridge just above the complex, peering down into 10 partially ruined homes and the tunnels that connect them. For safety, all of this was covered with turf, with only two or three entrances and exits. Because sandstone is a natural insulator, these spaces—while cramped and dank—would have been warm and cozy during the frequent battering storms. If you see a grate, squint down into the darkness: A

primitive sewer system, flushed by a rerouted stream, ran beneath all of the homes, functioning not too differently from modern sewers. And all of this was accomplished without the use of metal tools. They even created an ingenious system of giant stone slabs on pivots, allowing them to be opened and closed like modern doors.

Before leaving, look out over the nearby bay, and consider that this is only about one-third of the entire size of the original Skara Brae. What's now a beach was once a freshwater loch. But with the rising Atlantic, the water became unusable. About 800 years after it was built, the village was abandoned; since then, most of it has been lost to the sea. This area is called Skaill Bay, from the Old Norse *skål,* for "cheers!"—during Viking times, this was a popular place for revelry...but the revelers had no clue they were partying on top of a Neolithic village.

And now for something completely different: Your ticket to Skara Brae also includes the **Skaill House,** the sprawling stone mansion on the nearby hilltop. Here you can tour some lived-in rooms (c. 1950) and see a fascinating hodgepodge of items once important to a leading Orkney family. Some items illustrate Orkney's prime location for passing maritime trade: The dining room proudly displays Captain James Cook's dinner service—bartered by his crew on their return voyage after the captain was killed in Hawaii (Orkney was the first place they made landfall in the UK). You'll also see traditional Orkney chairs (with woven backs); in the library, an Old Norse "calendar"—a wooden stick that you could hold up to the horizon at sunset to determine the exact date;

a Redcoat's red coat from the Crimean War; a Spanish chest salvaged from a shipwreck; and some very "homely" (and supposedly haunted) bedrooms.

Nearby: About five miles south of Skara Brae, the sightseeing twofer of **Yesnaby** is worth a quick visit for drivers (watch for the turnoff on the B-9056). On a bluff overlooking the sea, you'll find an old antiaircraft artillery battery from World War II, and some of Orkney's most dramatic sea-cliff scenery.

SCAPA FLOW: WORLD WAR II SITES

For a quick and fascinating glimpse of Orkney's World War II locations, worth ▲▲▲, drive 10 minutes south from Kirkwall on the A-961 (leave town toward St. Mary's and St. Margaret's Hope, past the Highland Park Distillery)—to the natural harbor called Scapa Flow (see the sidebar). From the village of St. Mary's, you can cross over all four of the Churchill Barriers, with subtle reminders of war all around. The floor of Scapa Flow is littered with shipwrecks, and if you know where to look, you can still see many of them as you drive by.

Barrier #1 crosses from St. Mary's to the Isle of Burray. This narrow channel is where, in the early days of World War II, the German U-47 slipped between sunken ships to attack the *Royal Oak*—demonstrating the need to build these barriers. Notice that the Churchill Barriers have two levels: smaller quarried stone down below, and huge concrete blocks on top.

Just over the first barrier, perched on the little rise on the left, is Orkney's most fascinating wartime site: the **Italian Chapel** (£3, daily 9:00-18:30 in summer, shorter hours off-season). Italian POWs who were captured during the North African campaign

(and imprisoned here on Orkney to work on the Churchill Barriers) were granted permission to create a Catholic chapel to remind them of their homeland. While the front view is a pretty Baroque facade, if you circle around you'll see that the core of the structure is two prefab Nissen huts (similar to Quonset huts). Inside, you can see the remarkable craftsmanship of the artists who decorated the church. In 1943, Domenico Chiocchetti led the effort to create this house of worship, and personally painted the frescoes that adorn the interior. The ethereal *Madonna e Bambino* over the main altar is based on a small votive he had brought with him to

war. An experienced ironworker named Palumbi used scrap metal (much of it scavenged from sunken WWI ships) to create the gate and chandeliers, while others used whatever basic materials they could to finish the details. (Notice the elegant corkscrew base of the baptismal font near the entrance; it's actually a suspension spring coated in concrete.) These lovingly crafted details are a hope-filled symbol of the gentility and grace that can blossom even during brutal wartime. (And the British military is proud of this structure as an embodiment of Britain's wartime ethic of treating POWs with care and respect.) Spend some time examining the details—such as the stained-glass windows, which are painted rather than leaded. The chapel was completed in 1944, just two months before the men who built it were sent home. Chiocchetti returned for a visit in the 1960s, bringing with him the wood-carved Stations of the Cross that now hang in the nave.

Continuing south along the road, you'll cross over two more barriers in rapid succession. You'll see the masts and hulls of **shipwrecks** (on the left) scuttled here during World War I to block the harbor. As you cross over the bridges, notice that these are solid barriers, with no water circulation—in fact, the water level on each side of the barrier varies slightly, since the tide differs by an hour and a half.

At the far end of **Barrier #3,** on the left, watch for the huge wooden boxes on the beach. These were used in pre-barrier times (WWI) for boom floats, which supported nets designed to block German submarines.

After Barrier #3, as you climb the hill, watch for the pullout on the right with an orientation board. From this **viewpoint,** you can see three of the Churchill Barriers in one grand panorama.

Carrying on south, the next barrier isn't a Churchill Barrier

Scapa Flow: Britain's Remote Wartime Naval Base

Orkney's arc of scattered islands forms one of the world's largest natural harbors, called Scapa Flow (SKAH-pah flow). The Norsemen named this area *skalpai floi*—"scabbard water," where a sword was sheathed—suggesting that they used this area to store their warships when not in use. And in the 20th century, Scapa Flow was the main base for Britain's Royal Navy.

During World War I, to thwart U-boat attacks, dozens of old ships and fishing vessels were requisitioned and intentionally sunk to block the gaps between the islets that define Scapa Flow. You can still see many of these "block ships" breaking the surface today.

At the end of World War I, a fleet of 74 German battleships surrendered at Scapa Flow. On the morning of June 21, 1919—days before the Treaty of Versailles was formally enacted—the British admiral took most of his navy out on a "victory lap" patrol. Once they were gone, the German commander ordered his men to scuttle the entire fleet rather than turn the ships over. By the time the British returned five hours later, 52 German ships littered the bottom of the bay. The British opened fire on the remaining German ships, killing nine Germans—the final casualties of World War I. While most of the ships were later salvaged for scrap, to this day, German crockery washes up on Orkney beaches after a storm. Seven ships remain underwater, making this one of Europe's most popular scuba diving destinations.

at all—it's an ayre, a causeway that was built during the Viking period.

Finally you'll reach **Barrier #4**—hard to recognize because so much sand has accumulated on its east side (look for the giant breakwater blocks). Surveying the dunes along this barrier, notice the crooked concrete shed poking up—actually the top of a shipwreck. The far side of this sand dune is one of Orkney's best beaches—sheltered and scenic.

From here, the A-961 continues south past **St. Margaret's Hope** (where the ferry to Gills Bay departs) and all the way to Burwick, at the southern tip of South Ronaldsay. From here you can see the tip of Scotland. Nearby is the **Tomb of the Eagles,** a burial cairn similar to Maeshowe, but less accessible (time-consuming visit, www.tomboftheeagles.co.uk).

More WWII Sites: For those really interested in the World

Scapa Flow also played an important role in World War II. Even before Britain declared war on Germany, Luftwaffe reconnaissance flights had identified a gap in the sunken-ship barriers around the harbor. And on October 14, 1939—just weeks after war was declared—a Nazi U-47 slipped inside the harbor and torpedoed the HMS *Royal Oak,* killing 834 (including 110 seamen-in-training under the age of 15). To this day, the battleship—which had been fully loaded with fuel and ordnance—sits on the bottom of the bay, marked with a green warning buoy.

In April 1940, Luftwaffe planes flew from German-occupied Norway to bomb Orkney for three days straight in what's termed the "Battle of Orkney." But the islands were bulked up with heavy-duty gun batteries and other defenses, turning Orkney into a fortress. A sea of blimps called "barrage balloons"—designed to interfere with air attacks—clogged the air overhead. They even built a false fleet out of wood (also protected by barrage balloons) as a decoy for the Luftwaffe. The local population of 22,000 was joined by some 80,000 troops. Many surviving fragments from the Battle of Orkney can still be seen all over the island.

To ensure that no further surprises would sneak into the bay, First Lord of the Admiralty Winston Churchill visited here (just weeks before becoming prime minister) and hatched a plan to build sturdy barriers spanning the small distances between the islands south of Kirkwall. Throughout the wartime years, British workers and Italian prisoners of war labored to construct the "Churchill Barriers." The roads on top of the barriers opened just a few days after V-E Day, and today tourists use them to island-hop—and to learn about the dramatic history of Scapa Flow.

NORTHERN SCOTLAND

War II scene, consider a ferry trip out to the **Isle of Hoy;** the main settlement, Lyness, has the Scapa Flow Visitors Centre and cemetery (https://hoyorkney.com). Near Lyness alone are some 37 Luftwaffe crash sites. A tall hill, called Wee Fea, was hollowed out to hold 100,000 tons of fuel oil. Also on Hoy, you can hike seven miles round-trip to the iconic **Old Man of Hoy**—a 450-foot-high sea stack in front of Britain's tallest vertical sea cliffs. (Or you can see the same thing for free from the deck of the Stromness-Scrabster ferry.)

FERRY PORT TOWNS

With more time, check out these two towns with connections to northern Scotland. **Stromness** is Orkney's "second city," with 3,000 people. It's a stony 17th-century fishing town and worth a look. Equal parts fishing town and tourist depot, its traffic-free main drag has a certain salty charm. If driving, there's easy parking at the harbor. If catching the ferry to Scrabster, get here early to enjoy a stroll.

St. Margaret's Hope—named for a 13th-century Norwegian princess who was briefly Queen of Scots until she died en route to Orkney—is even smaller, with a charming seafront-village atmosphere. Ferries leave here for Gills Bay.

SCOTLAND: PAST & PRESENT

Rugged and remote, Scotland has had a particularly hard-fought history. Split by the Highland Boundary Fault, which separates the flatter, more Anglo-Saxon, more London-looking Lowlands in the south from the craggy, deeply Celtic Highlands in the north, the two halves have distinct cultural and topographic characters. Ringing the country are distant islands—Hebrides, Orkney, and Shetland—each bringing its own local customs, history, and traditions to the table. Since ancient times, the feisty people of Scotland, Highlanders and Lowlanders alike, have fought to preserve their region's unique identity. Scotland's rabble-rousing national motto is *Nemo me impune lacessit*—"No one provokes me with impunity." In Scotland, perhaps more than most places, legends of national heroes abound.

PREHISTORIC ORIGINS, ROMAN REBELLION, AND HIGHLAND CLANS

Scotland's first inhabitants were hunter-gatherers who came north as the Ice Age receded (7000 BC). In Neolithic times (4500-2000 BC), a new wave of farmer-herders arrived from the south. They left us stone circles and passage graves (funeral mounds with a burial chamber inside, reached by a passage). While few Neolithic structures survive in Scotland, Orkney—which flourished during this age—has some of the UK's best and oldest.

Also during the Stone Age, people began to settle on the waters of

Scotland's many lochs, building igloo-shaped fortified islands called crannogs. Made of wood and built upon timber pilings driven deep into the loch's floor, they were linked to the shore only by a removable wooden plank. Crannogs were at once well-protected and easy to access (in an age when most travel

was by boat), and they provided unobstructed views across the loch. Many circular "islands" you may notice in lochs today are likely grown-over, abandoned crannogs. (For more on crannogs, visit the excellent Crannog Centre on Loch Tay—see page 393.)

Around 500 BC, the Celts moved in from Europe, bringing Iron Age technology and the language that would develop into the Gaelic tongue. The Celts built hilltop forts, with large stone towers called brochs.

In AD 80, Roman legions—having already conquered England—marched north and established a camp near Edinburgh. They called today's Scotland "Caledonia" (a term you'll still see everywhere) and battled the fierce Celts, whom they dubbed Caledonii—or "Picts" ("painted"; for their war paint). But the Picts would not surrender. Eventually, the Romans decided they had expanded far enough—and Scotland just wasn't worth the effort. It was mountainous, wild, and dangerous—not just with Picts, but with predatory beasts such as bears, wolves, and lynx. The Romans sealed off Caledonia (and the pesky Picts) with two walls—the famous Hadrian's Wall (73 miles long and up to 20 feet high), running more or less along the modern-day border between Scotland and England, and the lesser-known Antonine Wall (from the Firth of Clyde to the Firth of Forth—essentially the "Central Belt" linking today's Glasgow and Edinburgh). From then on, while England was forever stamped with a Roman/European perspective, Scotland was set on a course that was isolated and Celtic.

Medieval Scotland was a stew of peoples: Picts in the northern Highlands, Anglo-Saxons (Germanic invaders) in the south, and the "Scoti" (Celtic cousins from Ireland) on the west coast. (While little survives from this time, you can still see faint remains of some of the Scoti's important sites in Kilmartin Glen near Oban.) The Scoti gradually overwhelmed and absorbed the Picts. In their kingdom of Alba (the Gaelic name for Scotland), they established Gaelic as the chief language and Christianity—brought from Ireland by St. Columba in the sixth century—as the dominant religion. Even at this early date, Scotland's geographical/ethnic boundary was already set: Gaelic/Celtic culture in the Highland north, English-friendly Anglo-Saxons in the Lowland south.

Vikings attacked from the north, and succeeded in capturing the northern islands, which remained Norse until the 15th century. (To this day, Orkney and Shetland have a Norwegian flavor and a heritage of Old Norse rune carvings and place names.) But much of the Scottish realm united under a Gaelic warlord named Kenneth MacAlpin. In 843, in his capital at Scone (50 miles north of Edinburgh), MacAlpin was crowned atop the Stone of Scone—making him the first king of Scots.

But this "Scotland" was a tiny and troubled land. In the 11th century (as Shakespeare later recalled it), King Duncan was murdered by one of his own men: Macbeth. King Macbeth was, in turn, killed by Duncan's son, Malcolm Canmore—the man who would establish Edinburgh and bring remote Scotland onto the stage of the wider world.

Meanwhile, in the remote reaches of the Highlands and the Hebrides, communities were based on the clan system: tribes of people sharing a stretch of land managed by a chieftain, who served as a kind of caretaker for the people and future generations. In Gaelic, *clann* means "children"; the clan system was the traditional Scottish way of passing along power—similar to England's dukes, barons, and counts. Although clan members took the chief's name in solidarity, they were not necessarily related by blood. The patrilineal clan system eventually became further subdivided into septs—alliances of families who pledged allegiance to the same chieftain.

Most Highlanders were crofters (small, self-subsistence farmers) who lived in humble huts with dirt floors, dry-stone walls, and peat fires with heavy smoke that escaped through thatched roofs. (For a glimpse of this lifestyle—which persisted well into the 18th century—visit the Highland Folk Museum near Pitlochry, or the Museum of Island Life on the Isle of Skye.) While it's not quite true that each clan had its own carefully designed

tartan pattern, clan members did tend to live in a single geographical area, where certain natural dyes and weavers predominated—so they likely dressed in (somewhat) similar colors. (For more on the kilt tradition, see page 7.)

Some clans were allies, either through intermarriage or through shared interests. Others were sworn enemies. One of the most famous rivalries was a three-way struggle between Clan Donald (or MacDonald), Clan Mackenzie, and Clan MacLeod, who clashed in several epic battles (see sidebar on page 346).

WILLIAM WALLACE, ROBERT THE BRUCE, AND MEDIEVAL INDEPENDENCE

When King Malcolm III married the English Princess Margaret in 1070, it united the culture of the Highland Scots with that of the Lowland Anglo-Saxons. Margaret was exceptionally pious, and she fostered the Christian faith as never before. Increasingly, Scotland became ruled from the southern Lowlands and influenced by its southern neighbor, England. As English settlers moved north, they built castles and abbeys. They also brought with them a new social order—a hierarchical government that went beyond the small social unit of the Highland clan.

But in the far reaches of Scotland, the clan system still flourished. Clan Donald, based on the Isle of Skye's Sleat Peninsula, controlled its own sprawling kingdom: In the 12th century, a great warrior named Somerled took control of the Lordship of the Isles, which included most of Scotland's west-coast islands, and penetrated deep into the Highlands and present-day Northern Ireland (Antrim). This fully independent maritime state lasted until 1493, when its territory was finally folded into the holdings of the Stuart kings. (To this day, the British heir apparent carries the title "Lord of the Isles.")

In 1286, the king of Scotland died without an heir. To settle the battle over succession, the Scots invited King Edward I of England ("Longshanks") to arbitrate. Edward seized the moment to assert his power over Scotland. He invaded, defeated the chosen successor, and stole the revered coronation stone—the Stone of Scone—taking it back to London (where it remained, almost untouched, until 1996).

Enraged, the Scots rallied around nobleman William Wallace (see page 69). He defeated the English at Stirling Bridge (1297) and was named the "guardian of Scotland." Wallace marched his army into England, plundered its north, then returned to Scotland—where he was defeated at the Battle of Falkirk in 1298. Disgraced, Wallace retreated to the Highlands and waged guerrilla warfare against the English until he was finally betrayed, arrested, and brutally executed in 1305.

The torch was passed to the earl of Carrick, Robert the Bruce (see page 73), who united Scotland's many clans and defeated the English at the tide-turning Battle of Bannockburn (1314). Bruce was crowned King Robert, and his heirs would rule Scotland for the next four centuries under the Stewart family name. (Later, when Mary, Queen of Scots moved to France, she changed the spelling to "Stuart" because the French alphabet of the time lacked the letter "w"—for simplicity, I've used that spelling throughout this book.) Scotland had secured its independence.

Over the next two centuries, Scotland's kings ruled from their castle in Stirling, gradually asserting central control over local clans and expanding the country's boundaries into the modern nation. But the Stuart monarchy was still weak, beleaguered with infighting over succession. Fortunately, England was kept at bay, plagued by its own troubles fighting the French (Hundred Years' War) and each other (Wars of the Roses). Scotland's long-standing "Auld Alliance" with the French existed mainly to support its independence from England.

MARY, QUEEN OF SCOTS; JOHN KNOX; AND THE PROTESTANT REFORMATION

Everything changed when Henry VIII became king of England, sparking a border war with Scotland. In the Battle of Flodden (1513), Scotland was utterly defeated. Soon Scotland faced an even greater enemy. As the Reformation crept into Scotland (c. 1540-1560), it split the country in two. The Highlands remained Catholic, rural, pro-monarchy, and pro-French. The Lowlands grew increasingly Protestant, urban, anti-monarchy, and pro-English.

When the Scottish King James V died in 1542, his six-day-old daughter Mary was named Queen of Scots (r. 1542-1567). Mary grew up staunchly Catholic and was educated in France, where she married the French crown prince in 1558. By the time the newly widowed Mary arrived back home (in 1561) to rule her native Scotland, the teenage queen found a hostile country in the throes of a Protestant Reformation (for the full story, see the sidebar on page 223).

The leader of the movement was John Knox (1514-1572), who grew up poor outside of Edinburgh. At a young age, he was at the forefront of the Reformation and a disciple of early reformer George Wishart, who was burned at the stake. Knox was arrested and exiled for two years; he spent much of this time among reformers in England, and with John Calvin in Geneva. Upon his return to Scotland (1559), he brought with him crates full of English bibles, which he used to spread both the Word of God and the English language. Knox went on an evangelical kick, preaching fire and brimstone throughout the Lowlands. He spread the message of Protestantism, wrote a Declaration of Independence-type manifesto called the "Confession of the Faith," and (with the help of some powerful supporters) outlawed Catholicism under punishment of prison or even death.

Mary, Queen of Scots' homecoming came just as Reformation fever was at its peak. Mary summoned Knox for a series of debates, where they hashed out their differences. While they ultimately agreed to disagree on the larger points, they did come to some compromises: Mary insisted on her personal right to say Mass in private, despite the national ban on the Catholic faith.

The Scots soon became disgusted with Mary's messy personal life, starting with her 1565 remarriage. The groom was her first cousin, Lord Darnley—an English-Scottish prince whose claim to both crowns had made him many enemies. Their marriage soured, and rumors flew that Mary was getting fresh with her secretary. The secretary was brutally murdered at Edinburgh's Palace of Holyroodhouse in front of a horrified Mary, and suspicion fell on Darnley. Then Darnley himself was found strangled in his Edinburgh home, while Mary fled the country with the prime suspect—the earl of Bothwell—soon to be Mary's third husband. Amid all of the drama, Mary gave birth to a son—whether Darnley's or the secretary's, no one knows—who would grow up to be king of both Scotland and England.

KING JAMES VI/I, KING CHARLES I, AND CIVIL WAR

Following an uprising in 1567, Mary was forced to abdicate in favor of her infant son, who became King James VI of Scotland. Raised a Protestant, James assumed official duties at age 17 (1584) and brought a tentative peace to religiously divided Scotland. (Meanwhile, Mary was arrested on suspicion of the murder of Darnley, charged with an unrelated plot against her cousin, Queen Elizabeth I of England, and eventually beheaded in 1587.)

In the 1592 Golden Act, Presbyterianism triumphed, and was made the rule of law. Scotland went forward as a predominantly

Typical Church Architecture

History comes to life when you visit a centuries-old church. Even if you wouldn't know your apse from a hole in the ground, learning a few simple terms will enrich your experience. Note that not every church has every feature, and a "cathedral" isn't a type of church architecture, but rather a designation for a church that's a governing center for a local bishop.

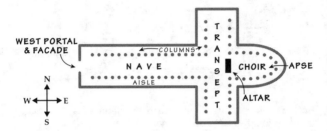

Aisles: The long, generally low-ceilinged arcades that flank the nave.

Altar: The raised area with a ceremonial table (often adorned with candles or a crucifix), where the priest prepares and serves the bread and wine for Communion.

Apse: The space beyond the altar, often bordered with small chapels.

Barrel Vault: A continuous round-arched ceiling that resembles an extended upside-down U.

Choir ("quire" in British English): A cozy area, often screened off, located within the church nave and near the high altar where services are sung in a more intimate setting.

Cloister: Covered hallways bordering a square or rectangular open-air courtyard, traditionally where monks and nuns got fresh air.

Facade: The front exterior of the church's main (west) entrance, usually highly decorated.

Groin Vault: An arched ceiling formed where two equal barrel vaults meet at right angles. Less common usage: term for a medieval jock strap.

Narthex: The area (portico or foyer) between the main entry and the nave.

Nave: The long, central section of the church (running west to east, from the entrance to the altar) where the congregation sits or stands through the service.

Transept: In a traditional cross-shaped floor plan, the transept is one of the two parts forming the "arms" of the cross. The transepts run north-south, perpendicularly crossing the east-west nave.

West Portal: The main entry to the church (on the west end, opposite the main altar).

Typical Castle Architecture

Castles were fortified residences for medieval nobles. Castles come in all shapes and sizes, but knowing a few general terms will help you understand them.

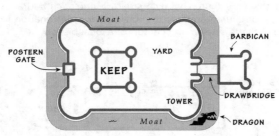

Barbican: A fortified gatehouse, sometimes a stand-alone building located outside the main walls.

Crenellation: A gap-toothed pattern of stones atop the parapet.

Drawbridge: A bridge that could be raised or lowered using counterweights or a chain and winch.

Great Hall: The largest room in the castle, serving as throne room, conference center, and dining hall.

Hoardings (or Gallery or Brattice): Wooden huts built onto the upper parts of the stone walls. They served as watch towers, living quarters, and fighting platforms.

The Keep (or Donjon): A high, strong stone tower in the center of the castle complex; the lord's home and refuge of last resort.

Loopholes (or Embrasures): Narrow wall slits through which soldiers could shoot arrows.

Machicolation: A stone ledge jutting out from the wall, with holes through which soldiers could drop rocks or boiling oil onto wall-scaling enemies below.

Moat: A ditch encircling the wall, often filled with water.

Motte-and-Bailey: A form of early English castle, with a small hilltop fort (motte) and an enclosed, fortified yard (bailey).

Parapet: Outer railing of the wall walk.

Portcullis: A heavy iron grille that could be lowered across the entrance.

Postern Gate: A small, unfortified side or rear entrance from which to launch attacks or escape.

Towers: Tall structures with crenellated tops or conical roofs serving as lookouts, chapels, living quarters, or dungeons.

Turret: A small lookout tower rising up from the top of the wall.

Wall Walk (or Allure): A pathway atop the wall where guards could patrol and where soldiers stood to fire at the enemy.

The Yard (or Bailey): An open courtyard inside the castle walls.

Protestant nation. But even among Protestants, there were religious divisions. Scottish Protestants were Presbyterians, members of the newly reorganized Church (or "Kirk") of Scotland. Presbyterianism (from the Greek word *prebuteros*, "elder") championed a self-governing congregation with leaders they elected themselves. This was in stark contrast to historic Catholic and Church of England hierarchies, led by a bishop (from the Greek *episkopos*) appointed by the king. The religious divide had political implications: Naturally, monarchs wanted to retain the politically powerful right to appoint bishops and rule congregations, while Presbyterians insisted on separation of kirk and state. Presbyterians also tended to be anti-king and pro-parliament.

In 1603, Queen Elizabeth I—England's "virgin queen"—died without an heir. Her distant cousin, Scotland's King James VI, was next in line for the English throne. Upon leaving Edinburgh and being crowned England's King James I in London (making him both King James VI and I), he united Scotland and England. The two nations have been tied together, however fitfully, ever since.

James' son Charles I (1600-1649) was born and crowned in Scotland, but otherwise spent most of his life in England. He continued his father's attempts to consolidate the many threads of Protestantism throughout his lands, favoring the English Episcopalian model. Charles I traveled to St. Giles' Cathedral in Edinburgh; appointed a bishop who, in turn, anointed him; and eventually introduced his own prayer book. This was a bridge too far for the Scots, who rioted and signed the National Covenant, proclaiming that the Scots had a special relationship with God that was outside the control of the crown. These "Covenanters" effectively declared their independence from the Church of England, and insisted that the Church of Scotland was under entirely Scottish control. A revolution was brewing.

The Covenanters went on military raids into northern England. King Charles attempted to quell the uprising with promises of reform, but became distracted by problems closer to home: Civil war broke out in England, pitting Charles (and the monarchy and Anglicanism) against Oliver Cromwell (with his supporters in parliament and the Puritans). Scotland was also divided. The Covenanters backed Cromwell, while many traditional Highlanders backed the king.

A Scottish army of 25,000 Covenanters invaded England,

Scottish Castles at a Glance

Scotland is a land of castles. But after seeing several, they start to blend together. To help you choose, here's a rundown of the defining characteristics of the castles listed in this book. These are listed roughly in order of worthiness.

▲▲▲**Edinburgh Castle** The granddaddy of them all, with good exhibits, historic chapels, royal apartments, the "Honours of Scotland" (crown jewels), a very big cannon, and lots of crowds. See page 62.

▲▲**Dunvegan Castle** (Isle of Skye) Remote, endearingly ragtag home of Clan MacLeod, with fine rugged gardens. See page 338.

▲▲**Palace of Holyroodhouse** (Edinburgh) Historic palace at the foot of the Royal Mile, with ties to Mary, Queen of Scots and still host to Queen Elizabeth II's annual Garden Party. See page 83.

▲▲**Stirling Castle** The historic home of Scotland's Stuart dynasty, with rebuilt rooms, fine exhibits, and a stunning and strategic location overlooking the site of many of Scotland's most important moments. See page 189.

▲**Balmoral Castle** (in eastern Scotland) The Queen's summer Highland home, with great Cairngorms scenery and fine gardens...but only one (ho-hum) room open to the public. See page 400.

▲**Blair Castle** (near Pitlochry, in eastern Scotland) Crenellated residence of Clan Murray, offering a glimpse of 19th-century aristocratic life. See page 392.

captured Charles I, and turned him over to Cromwell. On January 30, 1649, the English beheaded the king of Scotland.

ENGLAND'S ASCENDANCY AND THE ACT OF UNION

Left without a king, Scotland's landed gentry crowned Charles' son at Scone on January 1, 1651 (the last coronation at Scone). But Cromwell marched north and put a decisive end to any ideas of Scottish independence. It was clear that Scotland could never again be independent without the approval of England.

Charles II (1630-1685) escaped to France, where he spent the next nine years in exile. In 1660 he was invited back to London, and in 1661, the English parliament—suffering from Cromwell remorse—invited him to take the English throne. The monarchy

▲**Cawdor Castle** (near Inverness) Charming castle with personality and purported ties to Macbeth. See page 373.

▲**Eilean Donan Castle** (near Isle of Skye) One of Scotland's most scenically set castles, on an islet in a loch. See page 347.

▲**Glamis Castle** (north of Dundee) The Queen Mother's home castle, with a striking exterior and an enjoyably idiosyncratic interior. See page 242.

▲**Inveraray Castle** (near Oban) Classic castle exterior and a cozy interior used to film scenes from *Downton Abbey*. See page 285.

▲**Urquhart Castle** (on Loch Ness) Mostly ruined castle perched over Loch Ness. See page 377.

Armadale Castle (Isle of Skye) Ruined Clan Donald mansion with fine gardens and a museum of clan history—fascinating to Mac-Donalds, dull to most others. See page 345.

Doune Castle (near Stirling) Otherwise underwhelming castle with ties to Outlander and Monty Python, and an entertaining Terry Jones-narrated audioguide. See page 209.

Dunnottar Castle Ruins stunningly set on a huge, bald rock towering over Scotland's east coast. See page 404.

St. Andrews Castle Ruined shell overlooking the beach and offering an explanation of castle warfare techniques. See page 224.

was restored, with Charles II (a Stuart) ruling both England and Scotland.

But the two countries remained bitterly divided over religion. After Charles II died, his Catholic successor—James II (James VII of Scotland)—was ousted by England's parliament in a coup d'état (called the Glorious Revolution) and replaced by a Protestant noble from the Dutch House of Orange-Nassau and his English wife (King William III and Mary II).

In Scotland, the newly ascendant Lowland Protestants set about forcing Highland Catholics and Episcopalians to swear allegiance to the Protestant king. This culminated in the infamous Glencoe Massacre of 1692, where pro-William Protestants of the Campbell clan used the occasion as a pretext to slaughter their centuries-old enemy, the MacDonalds.

Robert Burns (1759–1796)

Robert Burns, Scotland's national poet, holds a unique place in the heart of the Scottish people—a heart that still beats loud and proud, thanks, in large part, to Burns himself.

Born on a farm in southwestern Scotland, Robbie (or "Rabbie," as Scots affectionately call him) was the oldest of seven children. His early years were full of backbreaking farm labor, which left him with a lifelong stoop. Though much was later made of his ascendance to literary acclaim from a rural, poverty-stricken upbringing, he was actually quite well educated (per Scottish tradition), equally as familiar with Latin and French as he was with hard work.

He started writing poetry at 15, but didn't have any published until age 28—to finance a voyage to the West Indies. When that first volume, *Poems, Chiefly in the Scottish Dialect,* became a sudden and overwhelming success, he reconsidered his emigration. Instead, he left his farm for Edinburgh, living just off the Royal Mile. He spent a year and a half in the city, schmoozing with literary elites, who celebrated this "heaven-taught" farmer from the hinterlands as Scotland's "ploughman poet."

His poetry, written primarily in the Scots dialect, drew on his substantial familiarity with both Scottish tradition and Western literature. By using the language of the common man to create works of beauty and sophistication, he found himself wildly popular among both rural folk and high society. Hearty poems such as "To a Mouse," "To a Louse," and "The Holy Fair" exalted the virtues of physical labor, romantic love, friendship, natural beauty, and drink—all of which he also pursued with vigor in real life. This further endeared him to most Scots, though considerably less so to Church fathers, who were particularly displeased with his love

At the same time as Scotland's king was being forced into exile, the world was changing in other ways. England, on the rise as a naval and colonial superpower, began encroaching on Scotland. Many Scots, particularly in the southern Lowlands, welcomed the English presence. These were people of Anglo-Saxon heritage, Calvinists and parliamentarians (who had like-minded counterparts in England), and traders and industrialists (who wanted to trade with wealthy England).

Due to a failed trading-post venture in Panama (the Darien Scheme), Scotland went bankrupt. Members of the Scottish parliament (some of whom were bribed) agreed to accept a bailout from life (of Burns' dozen children, nine were by his eventual wife, the others by various servants and barmaids).

After achieving fame and wealth, Burns never lost touch with the concerns of the Scottish people, championing such radical ideas as social equality and economic justice. Burns bravely and loudly supported the French and American revolutions, which inspired one of his most beloved poems, "A Man's a Man for A' That," and even an ode to George Washington—all while other writers were being shipped off to Australia for similar beliefs. While his social causes cost him some aristocratic friends, it cemented his popularity among the masses, and not just within Scotland (he became, and remains, especially beloved in Russia).

Intent on preserving Scotland's rich musical and lyrical traditions, Burns traveled the countryside collecting traditional Scottish ballads. If it weren't for Burns, we'd have to come up with a different song to sing on New Year's Eve—he's the one who found, reworked, and popularized "Auld Lang Syne." His championing of Scottish culture came at a critical time: England had recently and finally crushed Scotland's last hopes of independence, and the Highland clan system was nearing its end. Burns lent the Scots dialect a new prestige, and the scrappy Scottish people a reinvigorated identity. (The official Burns website, www.robertburns.org, features a full collection of his works.)

Burns died at 37 of a heart condition likely exacerbated by hard labor (all the carousing probably hadn't helped, either). By that time, his fortune was largely spent, but his celebrity was going strong—around 10,000 people attended his burial. Even the Church eventually overcame its disapproval, installing a window in his honor at St. Giles' Cathedral. In 2009, his nation voted Burns "Greatest Ever Scot" in a TV poll. And every January 25 (the poet's birthday), on Burns Night, Scots gather to recite his songs and poems, tuck into some haggis ("chieftain o' the puddin' race," according to Burns), and raise their whisky to friendship, and to Scotland.

England, which came with one major string attached: the Act of Union. So in 1707, Scotland's parliament (dominated by wealthy Lowlanders) voted itself out of existence, and the Scottish nation was officially joined with England, becoming part of "Great Britain." The independence of the Scottish nation—led by the Stuart family since the days of Robert the Bruce—was over.

JACOBITE RISINGS AND MASS EMIGRATIONS

Or was it? Many Scots, especially in the Highlands, clung loyally to their ousted King James II (VII of Scotland) and his successors. They were called Jacobites—after the Latin "Jacobus" for James—

and saw the Stuarts as their best hope to regain Scotland's independence. On the other side was the ascendant Protestant/urban faction, who supported the British government and monarch.

In the first of two Jacobite "risings," a coalition of traditionalists, Highland clans, and Catholics rallied around James II's son in 1715. But English troops easily routed them at the Battle of Sheriffmuir (10 miles north of Stirling), the grand hopes of "The '15" rebellion sputtered, and James Junior was sent scurrying back to his home-in-exile in France.

In 1745, a second rebellion was led by James II's grandson, known as "Bonnie Prince Charlie." That summer, the exiled Prince

Charles sailed across the sea from France and landed in Scotland near Glenfinnan, where he raised an army of Highlanders and set out to re-establish the Stuart monarchy. The terrified king put a price on Charles' bonnie head (the equivalent of £15 million today), but the outlaw prince succeeded in rallying many Scots to his cause. Within a few months, inspired by their charismatic leader, the Highlander forces had taken most of Scotland and even much of northern England. In their march toward London, they penetrated as far south as Derby—just 125 miles from the Tower of London. But the gains were ephemeral. Prince Charles' army was small (6,000 men) and disorganized; promised French support failed to materialize; and he had almost no popular support in the Lowlands, much less in England.

As better-equipped British troops advanced, Prince Charles pulled back to the Highlands. The two armies finally met in 1746 for one final, bloody conflict at Culloden Moor, just outside of Inverness, where Bonnie Prince Charlie's ragtag, kilted, bagpipe-bolstered army was routed and massacred. (For more on the prince and his defeat, see page 368.) Charles himself escaped the chaos, dressed as a female servant to sail "over the sea to Skye," and ultimately died in exile in Rome. To this day, patriotic Scots lament the crippling blow dealt to the rebellion they call "The '45."

After Charlie's defeat, the authorities (aristocratic landowners with government assistance) came down brutally on those who had supported the Jacobites, targeting the Highland clans and their traditional way of life. Kilt-wearing was forbidden, the feudal clan system was dismantled, homes were burned, and valuables were plundered. Clan chieftains who hadn't been exiled took over formerly communal lands and treated them as their own.

Landowners decided to make more efficient use of their land,

bringing about the so-called "Highland Clearances" (which esca-
lated following The '45, and peaked in the early 19th century). They
evicted their farming populations and transformed the agricultural
model from croft (subsistence farming of locally used crops) to mass
production (more profitable sheep). Many displaced farmers moved
to cities for factory work (as this coincided with the burgeoning
Industrial Revolution—see the next section). Many others sought
a better life in the New World.

From the mid- to late-19th century, an estimated two million
Scots emigrated, mostly to North America, Australia, and New
Zealand. Many bound for North America perished in the peril-
ous four-month Atlantic crossing, on vessels so rife with disease
they were nicknamed "coffin ships." Those who survived employed
their Scottish work ethic and industriousness to help build their
adopted nations (concentrated in places like Nova Scotia—"New
Scotland"). Some 15 percent of today's Canadians cite Scottish
heritage. In fact, the "Scottish" populations of both Canada and
the United States rival the population of Scotland.

Meanwhile, back home, Highland culture all but died out. It
was a bleak time for traditional life in Scotland.

SCOTTISH ENLIGHTENMENT, INDUSTRIAL REVOLUTION, AND HIGHLAND REVIVAL

Despite the difficult times in the Highlands, Lowlands Edinburgh thrived. In the last half of the 1700s, the city had become
one of Europe's (and the world's) most intellectual cities. Edinburgh benefited from a rich university tradition, a strong Protestant
work ethic, an educated middle class, connections with a powerful
England, and, simply, good genes. It was a city of secular, rational
thinkers who embraced the scientific method and empirical observation.

Scots of note from this period include philosopher David
Hume (who applied cool rationality and a scientific approach to
religion, morals, and philosophy); economist Adam Smith (who
wrote about division of labor and the free market in *The Wealth of
Nations*); James Watt (who developed better steam engines, propel-
ling Great Britain—and the world—into a busy Industrial Age);
and great names in virtually every discipline: geologist James Hutton, chemist Joseph Black, painter Allan Ramsay, and of course the
literary greats Robert Burns (see the sidebar) and Sir Walter Scott.
It's fitting that the *Encyclopedia Britannica*—the pre-Wikipedia authority on all things—was first published in Edinburgh in 1768.

As the Industrial Revolution dawned, Scotland became a
powerhouse: Textiles were woven in large factories, powered by
Watt's steam engine, which were fueled by Lanarkshire coal, then
exported on iron ships built in the Clyde shipyards. Scotland was

a global leader in pig iron exports and shipbuilding. Glasgow—an industrial center—overtook genteel Edinburgh as Scotland's biggest city. Dundee boomed, thanks to its skill for processing jute, which could be turned into rope, sacks, sails, and other essential items for a seafaring culture (for more, visit Dundee's interesting Jute Museum).

In the early 19th century, the Scottish civil engineer Thomas Telford (1757-1834)—nicknamed "The Colossus of Roads"—designed roadways, bridges, canals, and locks to tie together the remotest corners of Scotland, effectively shrinking the country for the modern era. (His masterpiece, the Caledonian Canal, is easy to see between Fort William and Inverness; see page 378.)

Meanwhile, just a few decades after the harsh post-Jacobite crackdown, Highland culture began to enjoy a renaissance. By the late 18th century, people were already romanticizing Bonnie Prince Charlie (further spurred by Sir Walter Scott's 1814 historical novel *Waverley*). In the Romantic Age of the 19th century, tartans, kilts, bagpipes, and other aspects of Highland culture made a big comeback. Queen Victoria and Prince Albert purchased Balmoral Castle (in the shadow of the Highlands' Cairngorm Mountains), rebuilding it in a fanciful interpretation of the Scottish Baronial style. This signaled not merely an acceptance, but a nostalgic embrace, of traditional Highland culture, just a century after it had been dismantled by the same monarchy.

This Scottish Baronial style, popularized by Sir Walter Scott, was a Romantic, Neo-Gothic celebration of medieval Highland castles. It features a stout sandstone structure with pointy turrets, fanciful finials, round towers, crenellated battlements, and narrow windows—based on Scotland's 16th-century tower houses, which were in turn based on the châteaux of France. In many ways, this is Scotland's signature architectural style:  You'll see it everywhere, from the urban streets of Glasgow, to castles on the remotest fringes of Scotland, to a fictional school for witchcraft and wizardry.

THE 20TH CENTURY: SCOTLAND AT WAR

By the 20th century, Scotland was the workhorse of Great Britain. And as bastion of the working class, there's little wonder that the government was typically controlled by the Labour Party. James Ramsay MacDonald was prime minister of the UK from 1929 until 1935.

Scotland was also the workhorse of the British military—never more so than during World War I, when Scottish lads were dispro-portionately massacred on the battle-fields of Europe. Scotland, with about one-tenth of the UK's population, had double the per-capita deaths of other parts of Britain. One out of every four Scottish soldiers never came home. Earl Haig of Edinburgh commanded British troops—victoriously—through some of the most gruesome trench warfare in history, at Flanders Fields in Belgium. As you travel around Scot-land, you'll find a WWI memorial in every tiny village—with unsettlingly long lists of local boys who sacrificed the utmost for Britain.

On most of these memorials, you'll find a little "addendum" plaque listing WWII deaths. While the Blitz was devastating to London and other English towns closer to the Continent (such as Coventry), the impact of World War II was felt less in the far-north reaches of Scotland—though Scapa Flow, a natural harbor surrounded by the Orkney Islands, was the remote headquarters of the British navy in both World Wars (see page 432).

SCOTLAND TODAY: DEVOLUTION AND SCOTTISH PRIDE

By the last decades of the 20th century, change was percolating in Scotland. Since the 1980s, the main topic of Scottish political debate has become "devolution": the push to "devolve" authority over Scottish affairs from London to Scotland proper. The gen-eral sea change in European culture over the last few generations of respecting smaller, underdog nations—even at the expense of big, historically dominant countries—has been felt here as much as anywhere.

For centuries—essentially ever since the crushed Jacobite up-risings—the notion of Scottish independence was rarely taken seri-ously. That began to change in the mid- to late-20th century. The independence-minded Scottish National Party (SNP), which had been founded as a fringe movement in 1934, won its first seat in the UK parliament in 1967. The discovery of North Sea oil in the late 1960s gave this often-overlooked corner of the United King-dom some serious economic clout, and with it, more political pull. Pro-independence factions gained traction with the slogan "It's Scotland's oil," proposing a windfall for Scots suffering through post-industrial rot and economic malaise.

Scotland Almanac

Official Name: Scotland.

Size: 30,400 square miles, about the size of South Carolina. The population is about 5.4 million.

Geography: Scotland's flatter southern portion is the Lowlands; the Highlands to the north are more wild and hilly. The country boasts over 6,000 miles of coastline and more than 790 islands (only about 130 are inhabited). Ben Nevis in western Scotland (at 4,406 feet) is Great Britain's highest peak.

Latitude and Longitude: 57°N and 4°W. The Shetland Islands are Scotland's northernmost point, at 60°N (similar to Anchorage, Alaska).

Biggest Cities: About three-quarters of Scotland's population lives along the nation's 75-mile-long "Central Belt." Glasgow near the west coast has 600,000 people, and Edinburgh on the east coast has 490,000.

Economy: The gross domestic product is about $218 billion, and the GDP per capita is $40,300. Natural resources remain important, but the Scottish service sector (including retail and financial services), renewable energy, and technology have become increasingly significant parts of its economy.

Scotland's main exports include food and drink, as well as chemicals and petroleum products. Scotch whisky comprises a quarter of all UK food and drink exports; exports to the US represent the biggest market for Scotch by value, though France is the biggest market by volume.

Government: Queen Elizabeth II officially heads the country—but for Scots she is simply Queen Elizabeth, not Queen Elizabeth II. (Scotland and England were separate monarchies when England had their first Elizabeth.) Nicola Sturgeon is Scotland's first minister.

Flag: The Saltire, with a diagonal, X-shaped white cross on a blue field, is meant to represent the crucifixion of Scotland's patron saint, the apostle Andrew.

Language: Scotland is primarily English-speaking, though about 1.5 million people also use the Scots "language," and about 60,000 speak Scottish Gaelic.

The Average Scot: The average Scottish person will live to age 79 and doesn't identify with an organized religion. He or she has free health care, gets 28 vacation days a year (about double the average American), lives within a five-minute walk of a park or green space, and spends time outdoors at least once a week.

British, Scottish, and English

Scotland and England have been tied together politically for more than 300 years, since the Act of Union in 1707. For a century and a half afterward, Scottish nationalists rioted for independence in Edinburgh's streets and led uprisings in the Highlands. In this controversial union, history is clearly seen through two very different filters.

If you tour a British-oriented sight, such as Edinburgh's National War Museum Scotland, you'll find things told in a "happy union" way, which ignores the long history of Scottish resistance—from the ancient Picts through the time of Robert the Bruce. The official line: In 1706-1707, it was clear to England and certain parties in Scotland (especially landowners from the Lowlands) that it was in their mutual interest to dissolve the Scottish government and fold it into the United Kingdom, to be ruled from London.

But talk to a cabbie or your B&B host, and you may get a different spin. Scottish independence is still a hot-button issue. Since 2007, the Scottish National Party (SNP) has owned the largest majority in the Scottish Parliament. During a landmark referendum in 2014, the Scots voted to remain part of the union—but many polls, right up until election day, suggested that things could easily have gone the other way.

The rift shows itself in sports, too. While the English may refer to a British team in international competition as "English," the Scots are careful to call it "British." If a Scottish athlete does well, the English call him "British." If he screws up... he's a clumsy Scot.

The SNP gained seats in the UK parliament and pushed for a 1979 referendum on devolution. The measure won with 52 percent of the vote, but turnout was too low to legitimize the result. Through the 1980s and most of the 1990s, anti-independence UK prime ministers Margaret Thatcher and John Major downplayed devolution talk. But the SNP and other agitators ensured that the idea never completely faded.

When Prime Minister Tony Blair took office in May 1997, his Labour government (mindful of Scotland's strong working-class roots and long-standing support for the Labour Party) was more open to the idea of devolution. And in a referendum in September 1997, three out of every four Scots voted "yes" to the statement, "I agree that there should be a Scottish parliament." In response, the UK parliament passed the Scotland Act 1998, creating a Scottish parliament that convened to much fanfare in Edinburgh on May 12, 1999 (with Donald Dewar becoming the first-ever First Minister of Scotland). For the first time since the Act of Union in 1707, Scotland had its own parliament. The Scottish Parliament building—with mind-bending architecture and an inviting garden—opened in 2004 across the street from the Queen's residence at the Palace of Holyroodhouse.

With devolution, Edinburgh once again has become the actual self-governing capital of Scotland. The Scotland Act 2012 further expanded the mandate of the Scottish parliament, and today, the list of "devolved" issues (under local Scottish control) includes education, the environment, health and social services, housing, and tourism. Other matters—including foreign policy, defense, energy policy, and social security—remain "reserved" for the central UK government.

Today the SNP is the most powerful party in Scotland, and the third-largest party in the UK (controlling the majority of Scotland's 59 seats in the House of Commons). Its leader, Nicola Sturgeon of Glasgow, is the public face of the SNP and has served as the nation's First Minister since 2014, giving voice to independence-minded Scots.

Today's supporters of Scottish independence take up ballots, not broadswords. In September 2014, the Scottish people went to the polls to vote on a simple question: "Should Scotland be an independent country?" Right up until the day of the referendum, many observers believed that Scotland was about to declare its independence. But in the end, a majority (55.3 percent) of Scots voted to remain part of the United Kingdom. But the referendum signaled to many in the greater UK that Scotland must be taken seriously.

In 2016, when Britain as a whole voted to "Brexit"—to leave the European Union—62 percent of Scots voted to remain with the EU. (It's likely that pro-EU Scotland would have voted for independence in 2014 had they known the UK would vote themselves out of the EU two years later, and Scotland's official government website states plainly, "Scotland voted to remain in the European Union.") Throughout the Brexit saga, Scottish officials have pressed their case that their nation's future lies with Europe.

On January 31, 2020, the UK officially left the European Union. But for Scotland, the question remains—as The Clash so elegantly put it—"Should I stay (in the UK) or should I go?" By the time you read this, there will likely be new wrinkles and complications.

NOTABLE SCOTS

Throughout Scotland's history, the country has been a center of both scientific and creative thought. The 18th-century age of Scottish Enlightenment in particular was a hotbed of intellectual progress—I've listed the greats of that era earlier in this chapter.

Famous artistic Scots include royal portraitist Henry Raeburn (known for his 1790s ice-skating minister, *The Reverend Robert*

Walker Skating on Duddingston Loch); sculptor Alexander Milne Calder (grandfather of the famous mobilist); 20th-century landscape painter William MacTaggart; and Scotland's greatest architect, Charles Rennie Mackintosh.

Scottish entertainers are everywhere, from the original James Bond (Sean Connery) and the young Obi-Wan Kenobi (Ewan McGregor), to two Dr. Whos (David Tennant and Peter Capaldi). Actors James McAvoy, Karen Gillan, Tilda Swinton, Craig Ferguson, Robert Carlyle, Robbie Coltrane, Kelly Macdonald, and Alan Cumming all hail from Scotland. The nation's pop music contributions have included Simple Minds, Annie Lennox, Belle and Sebastian, the Average White Band, and Franz Ferdinand, while sports stars of note include six-time Olympic gold-medal winning cyclist Chris Hoy, tennis player Andy Murray, and golfer Catriona Matthew. Jackie Stewart, nicknamed the "Flying Scot," was a top auto-racing champ for many years.

Robert Burns, Robert Louis Stevenson, and Sherlock Holmes creator Sir Arthur Conan Doyle all put Scotland on the world's literary map; in the 20th century, Muriel Spark *(The Prime of Miss Jean Brodie)* and Irvine Welsh *(Trainspotting)* wrote books that became hit films. On the scientific front, Peter Higgs was researching at the University of Edinburgh in the 1960s when he speculated on the existence of a subatomic "God particle" that might tie together many other theories on the structure of the universe.

Great people of Scottish descent fill American and Canadian history books, among them James Monroe, Washington Irving, Andrew Carnegie, Alexander Graham Bell, Jack Daniel, Ronald Reagan, Neil Armstrong, Hillary Clinton, Colin Powell, and Bill Gates. Whether it's as part of the United Kingdom, or as its own increasingly independent nation, it's clear that Scotland has had an outsized impact on the world.

PRACTICALITIES

This chapter covers the practical skills of European travel: how to get tourist information, pay for things, sightsee efficiently, find good-value accommodations, eat affordably but well, use technology wisely, and get between destinations smoothly. For more information on these topics, see RickSteves.com/travel-tips.

Tourist Information

Before your trip, start with the **Visit Scotland website,** which contains a wealth of information on destinations, activities, accommodations, and transport in Scotland (www.visitscotland.com).

In Scotland, a good first stop is generally the tourist information office (abbreviated **TI** in this book). Officially called Visit Scotland Information Centres, these are all operated by the national tourist board (look for the purple signs). They're found even in very small and remote places, where they're called "information points."

TIs are in business to help you enjoy spending money in their town, but even so, I still make a point to swing by to pick up a city map and get information on public transit, walking tours, special events, and nightlife. Anticipating a harried front-line staffer, prepare a list of questions and a proposed plan to double-check. Some TIs have information on the entire country or at least the region, so try to pick up maps and printed information for destinations you'll be visiting later in your trip.

Other Helpful Websites for Scotland: To learn more about destinations and sights around Scotland, see UndiscoveredScotland.co.uk. For hiking advice, see WalkHighlands.co.uk.

Travel Tips

Emergency and Medical Help: For any emergency service—ambulance, police, or fire—call **112 or 999** from a mobile phone or landline. Operators will deal with your request or route you to the right emergency service. If you get sick, do as the locals do and go to a pharmacy and see a "chemist" (pharmacist) for advice. Or ask at your hotel for help—they'll know of the nearest medical and emergency services.

ETIAS Registration: Beginning in 2021, US and Canadian citizens may be required to register online with the European Travel Information and Authorization System (ETIAS) before entering certain European countries (quick and easy process, $8 fee, valid 3 years). A useful private website with more details is SchengenVisaInfo.com/etias.

Theft or Loss: To replace a passport, you'll need to go in person to an embassy (see next). If your credit and debit cards disappear, cancel and replace them (see "Damage Control for Lost Cards," later). File a police report, either on the spot or within a day or two; you'll need it to submit an insurance claim for lost or stolen rail passes or electronics, and it can help with replacing your passport or credit and debit cards. For more information, see RickSteves.com/help.

US Consulate in Edinburgh: Tel. 0131/556-8315, no walk-in passport services; Mon-Fri 8:30-17:00, closed Sat-Sun—after-hours tel. 020/7499-9000; 3 Regent Terrace; https://uk.usembassy.gov/embassy-consulates/edinburgh.

Canadian Consulate in Edinburgh: Tel. 01250/870-831 (business hours); after hours call the High Commission of Canada in London at tel. 020/7004-6000, www.unitedkingdom.gc.ca.

PRACTICALITIES

Time Zones: Britain is five/eight hours ahead of the East/West Coasts of the US—and one hour earlier than most of continental Europe. The exceptions are the beginning and end of Daylight Saving Time: Europe "springs forward" the last Sunday in March (two weeks after most of North America), and "falls back" the last Sunday in October (one week before North America). For a handy time converter, use the world clock app on your phone or download one (see www.timeanddate.com/worldclock).

Business Hours: Most stores are open Monday through Saturday (roughly 9:00 or 10:00 to 17:00 or 18:00). In cities, some stores stay open later on Wednesday or Thursday (until 19:00 or 20:00). Sundays have the same pros and cons as they do for travelers in the US: Sightseeing attractions are generally open, many street markets are lively with shoppers, banks and many shops are closed, public transportation options are fewer (for example, no bus service to or from smaller towns), and there's no rush hour.

Watt's Up? Britain's electrical system is 220 volts, instead of North America's 110 volts. Most electronics (laptops, smartphones, cameras) and newer hair dryers convert automatically, so you won't need a converter, but you will need an adapter plug with three square prongs, sold inexpensively at travel stores in the US. Avoid bringing older appliances that don't automatically convert voltage; instead, buy a cheap replacement in Britain.

Discounts: Discounts (called "concessions" or "concs" in Britain) for sights are generally not listed in this book. However, seniors (age 65 and over), youths under 18, and students and teachers with proper identification cards (obtain from www.isic.org) can get discounts at many sights—always ask. Some discounts are available only for British citizens.

Money

Here's my basic strategy for using money in Europe:
- Upon arrival, head for a cash machine (ATM) at the airport and withdraw some local currency, using a debit card with low international transaction fees.
- In general, pay for bigger expenses with a credit card and use cash for smaller purchases. Use a debit card only for cash withdrawals.
- Keep your cash safe in a money belt.

PRACTICALITIES

Exchange Rate

1 British pound (£1) = about $1.30

Britain uses the pound sterling. The British pound (£), also called a "quid," is broken into 100 pence (p). Pence means "cents." You'll find coins ranging from 1p to £2 and bills from £5 to £50.

While the pound sterling is used throughout the UK, Scotland prints its own bills, which are decorated with Scottish landmarks and VIPs. These are interchangeable with British pound notes, which are widely circulated here. The coins are the same throughout the UK.

To convert prices from pounds to dollars, add about 30 percent: £20 = about $26, £50 = about $65. (Check www. oanda.com for the latest exchange rates.)

PLASTIC VERSUS CASH

Although credit cards are widely accepted in Europe, cash is sometimes the only way to pay for cheap food, taxis, tips, and local guides. Some businesses (especially smaller ones, such as B&Bs and mom-and-pop cafés and shops) may charge you extra for using a credit card—or might not accept credit cards at all. Having cash on hand helps you out of a jam if your card randomly doesn't work.

I use my credit card to book and pay for hotel reservations, to buy advance tickets for events or sights, and to cover most other expenses. It can also be smart to use plastic near the end of your trip, to avoid another visit to the ATM.

WHAT TO BRING

I pack the following and keep it all safe in my money belt.

Debit Card: Use this at ATMs to withdraw local cash.

Credit Card: Handy for bigger transactions (at hotels, shops, restaurants, travel agencies, car-rental agencies, and so on), payment machines, and online purchases.

Backup Card: Some travelers carry a third card (debit or credit; ideally from a different bank), in case one gets lost, demagnetized, eaten by a temperamental machine, or simply doesn't work.

Stash of Cash: I carry $100-200 in US dollars as a cash backup, which comes in handy in an emergency (such as when banks go on strike or if your ATM card gets eaten by the machine).

What NOT to Bring: Resist the urge to buy pounds before your trip or you'll pay the price in bad stateside exchange rates. Wait until you arrive to withdraw money. I've yet to see a European airport that didn't have plenty of ATMs.

PRACTICALITIES

460 Rick Steves Scotland

BEFORE YOU GO

Use this pre-trip checklist.

Know your cards. Debit cards from any major US bank will work in any standard European bank's ATM (ideally, use a debit card with a Visa or MasterCard logo). As for credit cards, Visa and MasterCard are universal, American Express is less common, and Discover is unknown in Europe.

Know your PIN. Make sure you know the numeric, four-digit PIN for all of your cards, both debit and credit. Request it if you don't have one, as it may be required for some purchases in Europe (see "Using Credit Cards," later), and allow time to receive the information by mail.

Report your travel dates. Let your bank know that you'll be using your debit and credit cards in Europe, and when and where you're headed.

Adjust your ATM withdrawal limit. Find out how much you can take out daily and ask for a higher daily withdrawal limit if you want to get more cash at once. Note that European ATMs will withdraw funds only from checking accounts; you're unlikely to have access to your savings account.

Ask about fees. For any purchase or withdrawal made with a card, you may be charged a currency conversion fee (1-3 percent) and/or a Visa or MasterCard international transaction fee (less than 1 percent). If you're getting a bad deal, consider getting a new debit or credit card. Reputable no-fee cards include those from Capital One, as well as Charles Schwab debit cards. Most credit unions and some airline loyalty cards have low or no international transaction fees.

IN EUROPE
Using Cash Machines

European cash machines work just like they do at home—except they spit out local currency instead of dollars, calculated at the day's standard bank-to-bank rate.

In most places, ATMs are easy to locate—in Britain ask for a "cashpoint." When possible, withdraw cash from a bank-run ATM located just outside that bank. Ideally, use the machine during the bank's opening hours, so you can go inside for help if your card is munched.

If your debit card doesn't work, try a lower amount—your request may have exceeded your withdrawal limit or the ATM's limit. If you still have a problem, try a different ATM or come back later—your bank's network may be temporarily down.

Avoid "independent" ATMs, such as Travelex, Euronet, Moneybox, Your Cash, Cardpoint, and Cashzone. These have high fees, can be less secure than a bank ATM, and may try to trick users with "dynamic currency conversion" (see below).

Exchanging Cash

Avoid exchanging money in Europe; it's a big rip-off. In a pinch you can always find exchange desks at major train stations or airports—convenient but with crummy rates. Anything over 5 percent for a transaction is piracy. Banks generally do not exchange money unless you have an account with them.

Using Credit Cards

Despite some differences between European and US cards, there's little to worry about: US credit cards generally work fine in Europe. I've been inconvenienced a few times by self-service payment machines that wouldn't accept my card, but it's never caused me serious trouble (I carry cash just in case).

European cards use chip-and-PIN technology; most chip cards issued in the US instead have a signature option. Some European card readers will accept your card as-is while others may generate a receipt for you to sign or prompt you to enter your PIN (so it's important to know the code for each of your cards). If a cashier is present, you should have no problems.

At self-service payment machines (transit-ticket kiosks, parking, etc.), results are mixed, as US cards may not work in some unattended transactions. If your card won't work, look for a cashier who can process your card manually—or pay in cash.

Drivers Beware: Be aware of potential problems using a US credit card to fill up at an unattended gas station, enter a parking garage, or exit a toll road. Always carry cash as a backup and be prepared to move on to the next gas station if necessary. When approaching a toll plaza, use the "cash" lane.

Dynamic Currency Conversion

If merchants offer to convert your purchase price into dollars (called dynamic currency conversion, or DCC), refuse this "service." You'll pay extra for the expensive convenience of seeing your charge in dollars. If an ATM offers to "lock in" or "guarantee" your conversion rate, choose "proceed without conversion." Other prompts might state, "You can be charged in dollars: Press YES for dollars, NO for pounds." Always choose the local currency.

Security Tips

Even in "Jollie Olde Britain," pickpockets target tourists. Keep your cash, credit cards, and passport secure in your money belt, and carry only a day's spending money in your front pocket or wallet.

Before inserting your card into an ATM, inspect the front. If anything looks crooked, loose, or damaged, it could be a sign of a card-skimming device. When entering your PIN, carefully block other people's view of the keypad.

Don't use a debit card for purchases. Because a debit card pulls funds directly from your bank account, potential charges incurred by a thief will stay on your account while the fraudulent use is investigated by your bank.

To access your accounts online while traveling, be sure to use a secure connection (see the "Tips on Internet Security" sidebar, later).

Damage Control for Lost Cards

If you lose your credit or debit card, report the loss immediately to the respective global customer-assistance centers. With a mobile phone, call these 24-hour US numbers: Visa (tel. +1 303/967-1096), MasterCard (tel. +1 636/722-7111), and American Express (tel. +1 336/393-1111). From a landline, you can call these US numbers collect by going through a local operator. European toll-free numbers can be found at the websites for Visa and MasterCard.

You'll need to provide the primary cardholder's identification-verification details (such as birth date, mother's maiden name, or Social Security number). You can generally receive a temporary card within two or three business days in Europe (see www.ricksteves.com/help for more).

If you report your loss within two days, you typically won't be responsible for unauthorized transactions on your account, although many banks charge a liability fee.

TIPPING

Tipping in Britain isn't as automatic and generous as it is in the US. For special service, tips are appreciated, but not expected. As in the US, the proper amount depends on your resources, tipping philosophy, and the circumstances, but some general guidelines apply.

Restaurants: If a service charge is included in the bill, it's not necessary to tip. Otherwise, it's appropriate to tip about 10-12 percent for good service. See page 478).

Taxis: For a typical ride, round up your fare a bit (maximum 10 percent; for instance, if the fare is £7.40, pay £8). If the cabbie hauls your bags and zips you to the airport to help you catch your flight, you might want to toss in a little more. But if you feel like you're being driven in circles or otherwise ripped off, skip the tip.

Services: In general, if someone in the tourism or service industry does a super job for you, a small tip of a pound or two is appropriate...but not required. If you're not sure whether (or how much) to tip, ask a local for advice.

GETTING A VAT REFUND

Wrapped into the purchase price of your British souvenirs is a value-added tax (VAT) of about 20 percent. You're entitled to get most of that tax back if you purchase more than £30 (about $40) worth of goods at a store that participates in the VAT-refund scheme (although individual stores can require that you spend more). Typically, you must ring up the minimum at a single retailer—you can't add up your purchases from various shops to reach the required amount. (If the store ships the goods to your US home, VAT is not assessed on your purchase.)

Getting your refund is straightforward...and worthwhile if you spend a significant amount on souvenirs.

Get the paperwork. Have the merchant completely fill out the necessary refund document (either an official VAT customs form, or the shop or refund company's own version of it). You'll have to present your passport. Get the paperwork done before you leave the shop to ensure you'll have everything you need (including your original sales receipt).

Get your stamp at the border or airport. Process your VAT document at your last stop in the European Union (such as at the airport) with the customs agent who deals with VAT refunds. Arrive an additional hour before you need to check in to allow time to find the customs office—and wait. Some customs desks are positioned before airport security; confirm the location before going through security.

It's best to keep your purchases in your carry-on. If your item (such as a knife) isn't allowed as carry-on, pack it in your checked bag and alert the check-in agent. You'll be sent (with your tagged bag) to a customs desk outside security; someone will examine your bag, stamp your paperwork, and put your bag on the belt. You're not supposed to use your purchased goods before you leave. If you show up at customs wearing your new kilt, officials might look the other way—or deny you a refund.

Collect your refund. You can claim your VAT refund from refund companies such as Global Blue or Planet with offices at major airports, ports, or border crossings (either before or after security, probably strategically located near a duty-free shop). These services (which extract a 4 percent fee) can refund your money in cash immediately or credit your card. Otherwise, mail the stamped refund documents to the address given by the shop where you made your purchase.

CUSTOMS FOR AMERICAN SHOPPERS

You can take home $800 worth of items per person duty-free, once every 31 days. Many processed and packaged foods are allowed, including vacuum-packed cheeses, dried herbs, jams, baked goods,

PRACTICALITIES

candy, chocolate, oil, vinegar, mustard, and honey. Fresh fruits and vegetables and most meats are not allowed, with exceptions for some canned items. As for alcohol, you can bring in one liter duty-free (it can be packed securely in your checked luggage, along with any other liquid-containing items).

To bring alcohol (or liquid-packed foods) in your carry-on bag on your flight home, buy it at a duty-free shop at the airport. You'll increase your odds of getting it onto a connecting flight if it's packaged in a "STEB"—a secure, tamper-evident bag. But stay away from liquids in opaque, ceramic, or metallic containers, which usually cannot be successfully screened (STEB or no STEB).

For details on allowable goods, customs rules, and duty rates, visit Help.cbp.gov.

Sightseeing

Sightseeing can be hard work. Use these tips to make your visits to Scotland's finest sights meaningful, fun, efficient, and painless.

MAPS AND NAVIGATION TOOLS

A good map is essential for efficient navigation while sightseeing. The maps in this book are concise and simple, designed to help you locate recommended destinations, sights, and local TIs, where you can pick up more in-depth maps. Maps with even more detail are sold at newsstands and bookstores. The *Rick Steves Britain, Ireland & London City Map* is useful for planning ($9, www.ricksteves.com).

You can also use a mapping app on your mobile device. Be aware that pulling up maps or looking up turn-by-turn walking directions on the fly requires a data connection: To use this feature, it's smart to get an international data plan. With Google Maps or City Maps 2Go, it's possible to download a map while online, then go offline and navigate without incurring data-roaming charges, though you can't search for an address or get real-time walking directions. A handful of other apps—including Apple Maps and Navmii—also allow you to use maps offline.

PLAN AHEAD

Set up an itinerary that allows you to fit in all your must-see sights. For a one-stop look at opening hours, see the "At a Glance" sidebars for Edinburgh (page 36), Glasgow (page 143), and Scottish castles (page 444). Most sights keep stable hours, but you can easily confirm the latest by checking with the TI or visiting museum websites.

Don't put off visiting a must-see sight—you never know when a place will close unexpectedly for a holiday, strike, or royal audience. Many museums are closed or have reduced hours at least a few days a year, especially on holidays such as Christmas, New Year's, and Bank Holiday Mondays in May and August. A list of holidays is in the appendix; check for possible closures during your trip. In summer, some sights may stay open late. In the off-season, hours may be shorter.

Going at the right time helps avoid crowds. This book offers tips on the best times to see specific sights. Try visiting popular sights very early or very late. Evening visits (when possible) are usually peaceful, with fewer crowds. Late morning is usually the worst time to visit a popular sight.

If you plan to hire a local guide, reserve ahead by email. Popular guides can get booked up.

Study up. To get the most out of the self-guided tours and sight descriptions in this book, read them before you visit.

RESERVATIONS AND ADVANCE TICKETS

Given how precious your vacation time is, I recommend getting reservations for any must-see sight that offers them (see page 24).

To deal with lines, many popular sights sell advance tickets that guarantee admission at a certain time of day, or that allow you to skip entry lines. Either way, it's worth giving up some spontaneity to book in advance. While hundreds of tourists sweat in long ticket-buying lines, those who've booked ahead can get in quicker. In some cases, getting a ticket in advance simply means buying your ticket earlier on the same day. But for other sights, you may need to book weeks or even months in advance. As soon as you're ready to commit to a certain date, book it.

The advance-purchase price is often less expensive than what you would pay on-site. And many museums offer convenient mobile ticketing. Simply buy your ticket online and send it to your phone, eliminating the need for a paper ticket.

SIGHTSEEING PASSES

Many sights in Scotland are managed by either Historic Scotland or the National Trust for Scotland. Each organization has a combo-deal that can save some money for busy sightseers.

Historic Scotland's Explorer Pass covers its 77 properties, including Edinburgh Castle, Stirling Castle, and several sights on Orkney (5-day pass-£35, 14-day pass-£45, www.historicenvironment.scot). This pass allows you to skip the ticket-buying lines at Edinburgh and Stirling castles.

Membership in the **National Trust** is best suited for garden-and-estate enthusiasts, ideally those traveling by car. It covers more than 350 historic houses, manors, and gardens throughout Great Britain, including 100 properties in Scotland. From the US, it's

PRACTICALITIES

easy to join online through the Royal Oak Foundation, the National Trust's American affiliate (one-year membership: single membership-$80, two-person membership-$125, family and student memberships, www.royal-oak.org). For more on National Trust properties, see www.nationaltrust.org.uk.

Factors to Consider: An advantage to these deals is that you'll feel free to dip into lesser sights without considering the cost of admission. But remember that your kids already get in free or cheaply at most places, and people over 60 get discounted prices at many sights. If you're traveling by car and can get to the remote sights, you're more likely to get your money's worth out of a pass or membership, especially during peak season (Easter-Oct), when all the sights are open.

AT SIGHTS

Here's what you can typically expect:

Entering: You may not be allowed to enter if you arrive too close to closing time. And guards start ushering people out well before the actual closing time, so don't save the best for last.

Many sights have a security check. Allow extra time for these lines. Some sights require you to check daypacks and coats. (If you'd rather not check your daypack, try carrying it tucked under your arm like a purse as you enter.)

At ticket desks, you may see references to "Gift Aid"—a tax-deduction scheme that benefits museums—but this only concerns UK taxpayers.

Photography: If the museum's photo policy isn't clearly posted, ask a guard. Generally, taking photos without a flash or tripod is allowed. Some sights ban selfie sticks; others ban photos altogether. Note that some whisky distilleries do not allow photos or photos with flash, supposedly because a spark from your camera could ignite the alcohol fumes.

Audioguides and Apps: Many sights rent audioguides with excellent recorded descriptions (about £5). If you bring your own earbuds, you can often enjoy better sound. If you don't mind being tethered to your travel partner, you'll save money by bringing a Y-jack and sharing one audioguide. Museums and sights often offer free apps that you can download to your mobile device (check their websites). ∩ I've produced a free, downloadable audio tour for my self-guided walk along Edinburgh's Royal Mile. For more on my audio tours, see page 26.

Guided tours are most likely to occur during peak season (either for free or a small fee—figure £5-10—and widely ranging in quality). Some sights also run short introductory videos featuring their highlights and history. These are generally well worth your time and a great place to start your visit.

Temporary Exhibits: Museums may show special exhibits in addition to their permanent collection. Some exhibits are included in the entry price, while others come at an extra cost (which you may have to pay even if you don't want to see the exhibit).

Expect Changes: Artwork can be on tour, on loan, out sick, or shifted at the whim of the curator. Pick up a floor plan as you enter, and ask museum staff if you can't find a particular item.

Services: Important sights and cathedrals usually have a reasonably priced on-site café or cafeteria (handy places to rejuvenate during a long visit). The WCs at sights are free and generally clean.

Before Leaving: At the gift shop, scan the postcard rack or thumb through a guidebook to be sure that you haven't overlooked something that you'd like to see. Every sight or museum offers more than what is covered in this book. Use the information I provide as an introduction—not the final word.

Sleeping

Extensive and opinionated listings of good-value rooms are a major feature of this book's Sleeping sections. Rather than list accommodations scattered throughout a town, I choose places in my favorite neighborhoods that are convenient to your sightseeing.

My recommendations run the gamut, from dorm beds to fancy rooms with all the comforts. I like places that are clean, central, relatively quiet at night, reasonably priced, friendly, small enough to have a hands-on owner or manager, and run with a respect for British traditions. I'm more impressed by a handy location and fun-loving philosophy than flat-screen TVs and a fancy gym. Most of my recommendations fall short of perfection. But if I can find a place with most of these features, it's a keeper.

Book your accommodations as soon as your itinerary is set, especially if you want to stay at one of my top listings or if you'll be traveling during busy times. See the appendix for a list of major holidays and festivals in Great Britain.

Some people make reservations as they travel, calling or emailing ahead a few days to a week before their arrival. If you're trying for a same-day reservation, it's best to call hotels at about 9:00 or 10:00, when the receptionist knows which rooms will be available. Some apps—such as HotelTonight.com—specialize in last-minute rooms, often at boutique or business-class hotels in big cities.

RATES AND DEALS

I've categorized my recommended accommodations based on price, indicated with a dollar-sign rating (see sidebar). The price ranges suggest an estimated cost for a one-night stay in high season in a standard double room with a private toilet and shower, and assume

PRACTICALITIES

Sleep Code

Hotels in this book are categorized according to the average price of a standard double room with breakfast in high season.

$$$$	**Splurge:**	Most rooms over £160
$$$	**Pricier:**	£120-160
$$	**Moderate:**	£80-120
$	**Budget:**	£40-80
¢	**Backpacker:**	Under £40
RS%	**Rick Steves discount**	

Unless otherwise noted, credit cards are accepted and free Wi-Fi is available. Comparison-shop by checking prices at several hotels (on each hotel's own website, on a booking site, or by email). For the best deal, *book directly with the hotel.* Ask for a discount if paying in cash; if the listing includes **RS%**, request a Rick Steves discount.

you're booking directly with the hotel (not through a booking site, which extracts a commission). Room prices can fluctuate significantly with demand and amenities (size, views, room class, and so on), but relative price categories remain constant.

In Scotland, small bed-and-breakfast places (B&Bs) generally provide the best value, though I also include some bigger hotels. Great Britain has a rating system for hotels and B&Bs. Its stars are supposed to imply quality, but I find they mean only that the place is paying dues to the tourist board. Rating systems often have little to do with value.

Room rates can be volatile at larger hotels that use "dynamic pricing" to set rates. Prices can skyrocket during festivals and conventions, while business hotels can have deep discounts on weekends, when demand plummets. Of the many hotels I recommend, it's difficult to say which will be the best value on a given day—until you do your homework.

Booking Direct: Once your dates are set, compare prices at several hotels. You can do this by checking Hotels.com or Booking.com, and hotel websites. Then book directly with the hotel itself. Contact small family-run hotels directly by phone or email. When you go direct, the owner avoids the commission paid to booking sites, thereby leaving enough wiggle room to offer you a discount, a nicer room, or a free breakfast (if it's not already included). If you prefer to book online or are considering a hotel chain, it's to your advantage to use the hotel's website. When establishing prices, confirm if the charge is per person or per room (if a price is too good to be true, it's probably per person).

Booking directly also increases the chances that the hotelier will be able to accommodate any special needs or requests (such as shifting your reservation). Going through a middleman makes it more difficult for the hotel to adjust your booking.

Getting a Discount: Some hotels extend a discount to those who pay cash or stay longer than three nights. And some accommodations offer a special discount for Rick Steves readers, indicated in this guidebook by the abbreviation **"RS%."** Discounts vary: Ask for details when you reserve. Generally, to qualify for this discount, you must book direct (not through a booking site), mention this book when you reserve, show this book upon arrival, and sometimes pay cash or stay a certain number of nights. In some cases, you may need to enter a discount code (which I've provided in the listing) in the booking form on the hotel's website. Rick Steves discounts apply to readers with either print or digital books. Understandably, discounts do not apply to promotional rates.

Staying in B&Bs and small hotels can save money over sleeping in big hotels. Chain hotels can be even cheaper, but they don't include breakfast. When comparing prices between chain hotels and B&Bs, remember you're getting two breakfasts (about a £25 value) for each double room at a B&B.

TYPES OF ACCOMMODATIONS
Hotels
In cities, you'll find big, Old World-elegant hotels with modern amenities, as well as familiar-feeling business-class and boutique hotels no different from what you might experience at home. But you'll also find hotels that are more uniquely European.

Outside of pricey big cities, you can expect to find good doubles for £80-120, including cooked breakfasts. Bigger cities, swanky B&Bs, and big hotels generally cost significantly more.

A "twin" room has two single beds; a "double" has one double bed. If you'll take either, let the hotel know, or you might be needlessly turned away. Some hotels can add an extra bed (for a small charge) to turn a double into a triple; some offer larger rooms for four or more people (I call these "family rooms" in the listings). If there's space for an extra cot, they'll cram it in for you. In general, a triple room is cheaper than the cost of a double and a single. Three or four people can economize by requesting one big room.

An "en suite" room has a bathroom (toilet and shower/tub) attached to the room; a room with a "private bathroom" can mean that the bathroom is all yours, but it's across the hall. If you want your own bathroom inside the room, request "en suite." If money's tight, ask about a room with a shared bathroom. You'll almost always have a sink in your room, and as more rooms go en suite, the hallway bathroom is shared with fewer guests.

Note that to be called a "hotel," a place technically must have

Using Online Services to Your Advantage

From booking services to user reviews, online businesses play a greater role in travelers' planning than ever before. Take advantage of their pluses—and be wise to their downsides.

Booking Sites

Booking websites such as Booking.com and Hotels.com offer one-stop shopping for hotels. While convenient for travelers, they present a real problem for independent, family-run hotels. Without a presence on these sites, small hotels become almost invisible. But to be listed, a hotel must pay a sizeable commission... and promise that its own website won't undercut the price on the booking-service site.

Here's the work-around: Use the big sites to research what's out there, then book directly with the hotel by email or phone, in which case hotel owners are free to give you whatever price they like. Ask for a room without the commission mark-up (or ask for a free breakfast if not included, or a free upgrade). If you do book online, be sure to use the hotel's website. The price will likely be the same as via a booking site, but your money goes to the hotel, not agency commissions.

As a savvy consumer, remember: When you book with an online booking service, you're adding a middleman who takes roughly 20 percent. To support small, family-run hotels whose world is more difficult than ever, book direct.

Short-Term Rental Sites

Rental juggernaut Airbnb (along with other short-term rental sites) allows travelers to rent rooms and apartments directly from locals, often providing more value than a cookie-cutter hotel. Airbnb fans appreciate feeling part of a real neighborhood and getting into a daily routine as "temporary Europeans." Depending on the host, Airbnb can provide an opportunity to get to know a

certain amenities, including a 24-hour reception (though this rule is loosely applied).

Modern Hotel Chains: Chain hotels—common in bigger cities all over Great Britain—can be a great value (£60-100, depending on location and season). These hotels are about as cozy as a Motel 6, but they come with private showers/WCs, elevators, good security, and often an attached restaurant. Branches are often located near the train station, on major highways, or outside the city center.

This option is especially worth considering for families, as kids often stay for free. While most of these hotels have 24-hour reception and elevators, breakfast and Wi-Fi generally cost extra, and

PRACTICALITIES

local person, while keeping the money spent on your accommodations in the community.

Critics view Airbnb as a threat to "traditional Europe," saying it creates unfair, unqualified competition for established guesthouse owners. In some places, the lucrative Airbnb market has forced traditional guesthouses out of business and is driving property values out of range for locals. Some cities have cracked down, requiring owners to occupy rental properties part of the year (and staging disruptive "inspections" that inconvenience guests).

As a lover of Europe, I share the worry of those who see residents nudged aside by tourists. But as an advocate for travelers, I appreciate the value and cultural intimacy Airbnb provides.

User Reviews

User-generated review sites and apps such as Yelp and TripAdvisor can give you a consensus of opinions about everything from hotels and restaurants to sights and nightlife. If you scan reviews of a restaurant or hotel and see several complaints about noise or a rotten location, you've gained insight that can help in your decision-making.

But as a guidebook writer, my sense is that there is a big difference between the uncurated information on a review site and the vetted listings in a guidebook. A user-generated review is based on the limited experience of one person, who stayed at just one hotel in a given city and ate at a few restaurants there. A guidebook is the work of a trained researcher who forms a well-developed basis for comparison by visiting many restaurants and hotels year after year.

Both types of information have their place, and in many ways, they're complementary. If something is well reviewed in a guidebook and it also gets good online reviews, it's likely a winner.

PRACTICALITIES

the service lacks a personal touch (at some, you'll check in at a self-service kiosk). When comparing your options, keep in mind that for about the same price, you can get a basic room at a B&B that has less predictable comfort but more funkiness and friendliness in a more enjoyable neighborhood.

Room rates change from day to day with volume and vary depending on how far ahead you book. The best deals generally must be prepaid a few weeks ahead and may not be refundable—read the fine print carefully.

The biggest chains are **Premier Inn** (www.premierinn.com) and **Travelodge** (www.travelodge.co.uk). Both have attractive deals for prepaid or advance bookings. Other chains operating in

PRACTICALITIES

Making Hotel Reservations

Reserve your rooms as soon as you've pinned down your travel dates. For busy national holidays, it's wise to reserve far in advance (see the appendix).

Requesting a Reservation: For family-run hotels, it's generally best to book your room directly via email or phone. For business-class and chain hotels, or if you'd rather book online, reserve directly through the hotel's official website (not a booking website).

Here's what the hotelier wants to know:
- Type(s) of rooms you want and size of your party
- Number of nights you'll stay
- Your arrival and departure dates, written European-style as day/month/year (for example, 18/06/21 or 18 June 2021)
- Special requests (such as en suite bathroom, cheapest room, twin beds vs. double bed, quiet room)
- Applicable discounts (such as a Rick Steves reader discount, cash discount, or promotional rate)

Confirming a Reservation: Most places will request a credit-card number to hold your room. If you're using an online reservation form, make sure it's secure by looking for the *https* or a lock icon at the top of your browser. If the hotel's website doesn't have a secure form where you can enter the number directly, it's best to share that confidential info via a phone call.

Canceling a Reservation: If you must cancel, it's courteous—and smart—to do so with as much notice as possible, especially for smaller family-run places. Cancellation policies can be strict; read

---

Britain include the Irish **Jurys Inn** (www.jurysinns.com) and the French-owned **Ibis** (www.ibishotel.com). Couples can consider **Holiday Inn Express,** which generally allow only two people per room. It's like a Holiday Inn lite, with cheaper prices and no restaurant (make sure Express is part of the name or you'll be paying more for a regular Holiday Inn, www.hiexpress.co.uk).

Arrival and Check-In: Hotels and B&Bs are sometimes located on the higher floors of a multipurpose building with a secured door. In that case, look for your hotel's name on the buttons by the main entrance. When you ring the bell, you'll be buzzed in.

Hotel elevators are common, though some older buildings still lack them. You may have to climb a flight of stairs to reach the elevator (if so, you can ask the front desk for help carrying your bags up). Elevators are typically very small—pack light, or you may need to send your bags up without you.

The EU requires that hotels collect your name, nationality, and ID number. When you check in, the receptionist will normally ask for your passport and may keep it for anywhere from a couple

From:	rick@ricksteves.com
Sent:	Today
To:	info@hotelcentral.com
Subject:	Reservation request for 19-22 July

Dear Hotel Central,

I would like to stay at your hotel. Please let me know if you have a room available and the price for:
• 2 people
• Double bed and en suite bathroom in a quiet room
• Arriving 19 July, departing 22 July (3 nights)

Thank you!
Rick Steves

the fine print before you book. Many discount deals require pre-payment, with no cancellation refunds.

Reconfirming a Reservation: Always call or email to reconfirm your room reservation a few days in advance. For B&Bs or very small hotels, I call again on my day of arrival to tell my host what time to expect me (especially important if arriving late—after 17:00).

Phoning: For tips on calling hotels overseas, see page 494.

minutes to a couple of hours. If you're not comfortable leaving your passport at the desk for a long time, ask when you can pick it up. Or, if you packed a color photocopy of your passport, you can generally leave that rather than the original.

If you're arriving in the morning, your room probably won't be ready. Check your bag safely at the hotel and dive right into sightseeing.

In Your Room: Most hotel rooms have a TV, telephone, and free Wi-Fi (although in old buildings with thick walls, the Wi-Fi signal might be available only in the lobby). Simpler places rarely have a room phone.

More pillows and blankets are usually in the closet or available on request. Towels and linens aren't always replaced every day.

Air-conditioning isn't a given (I've noted which of my listings have it), but most places have fans.

Electrical outlets may have switches that turn the current on or off; if your appliance isn't working, flip the switch at the outlet.

Breakfast and Meals: Your room cost usually includes a traditional full cooked breakfast (fry-up) or a lighter, healthier continental breakfast.

Checking Out: While it's customary to pay for your room upon departure, it can be a good idea to settle your bill the day before, when you're not in a hurry and while the manager's in.

Hotelier Help: Hoteliers can be a good source of advice. Most know their city well, and can assist you with everything from public transit and airport connections to finding a good restaurant, the nearest launderette, or a late-night pharmacy.

Hotel Hassles: Even at the best places, mechanical breakdowns occur: Sinks leak, hot water turns cold, toilets may gurgle or smell, the Wi-Fi goes out, or the air-conditioning dies when you need it most. Report your concerns clearly and calmly at the front desk.

If you find that night noise is a problem (if, for instance, your room is over a noisy pub or facing a busy street), ask for a quieter room in the back or on an upper floor. To guard against theft in your room, keep valuables out of sight. Some rooms come with a safe, and other hotels have safes at the front desk. I've never bothered using one and in a lifetime of travel, I've never had anything stolen from my room.

For more complicated problems, don't expect instant results. Above all, keep a positive attitude. Remember, you're on vacation. If your hotel is a disappointment, spend more time out enjoying the place you came to see.

B&Bs and Small Hotels

B&Bs and small hotels are generally family-run places with fewer amenities but more character than a conventional hotel. They range from large inns with 15-20 rooms to small homes renting out a spare bedroom. Places named "guesthouse" or "B&B" typically have eight or fewer rooms. The philosophy of the management determines the character of a place more than its size and amenities. I avoid places run as a business by absentee owners. My top listings are run by people who enjoy welcoming the world to their breakfast table.

Compared to hotels, B&Bs and guesthouses give you double the cultural intimacy for half the price. While you may lose some of the conveniences of a hotel— such as fancy lobbies, in-room phones, and frequent bedsheet changes—I happily make the tradeoff for the personal touches, whether it's joining my hosts for afternoon tea or relaxing by a

common fireplace at the end of the day. If you have a reasonable but limited budget, skip hotels and go the B&B way.

B&B proprietors are selective about the guests they invite in for the night. Many do not welcome children. If you'll be staying for more than one night, you are a "desirable." In popular weekend-getaway spots, you're unlikely to find a place to take you for Saturday night only. If my listings are full, ask for guidance. Mentioning this book can help. Owners usually work together and can call up an ally to land you a bed. Many B&B owners are also pet owners. If you're allergic, ask about resident pets when you reserve.

Rules and Etiquette: B&Bs and small hotels come with their own etiquette and quirks. Keep in mind that owners are at the whim of their guests—if you're getting up early, so are they; if you check in late, they'll wait up for you. Most B&Bs have set check-in times (usually in the late afternoon). If arriving outside that time, they will want to know when to expect you (call or email ahead). Most will let you check in earlier if the room is available (or they'll at least let you drop off your bag).

Most B&Bs and guesthouses serve a hearty cooked breakfast of eggs and much more (for details on breakfast, see the "Eating" section, later). Because the owner is often also the cook, breakfast hours are usually abbreviated. Typically the breakfast window lasts for 1-1.5 hours (make sure you know when it is before you turn in for the night). Some B&Bs ask you to fill in your breakfast order the night before. It's an unwritten rule that guests shouldn't show up at the very end of the breakfast period and expect a full cooked breakfast. If you do arrive late (or need to leave before breakfast is served), most establishments are happy to let you help yourself to cereal, fruit, juice, and coffee.

B&Bs and small hotels often come with thin walls and doors, and sometimes creaky floorboards, which can make for a noisy night. If you're a light sleeper, bring earplugs. And please be quiet in the halls and in your rooms at night...those of us getting up early will thank you for it.

Treat these lovingly maintained homes as you would a friend's house. Be careful maneuvering your bag up narrow staircases with fragile walls and banisters. And once in the room, use the luggage rack—putting bags on the bed can damage nice bedding.

In the Room: Most B&Bs offer "tea service" in the room—an electric kettle, cups, tea bags, coffee packets, and a pack of biscuits.

Your bedroom probably won't include a phone, but nearly every B&B has free Wi-Fi. However, the signal may not reach all rooms; you may need to sit in the lounge to access it.

You're likely to encounter unusual bathroom fixtures. The "pump toilet" has a flushing handle or button that doesn't kick in unless you push it just right: too hard or too soft, and it won't go.

(Be decisive but not ruthless.) Most B&B baths have an instant water heater. This looks like an electronic box under the shower-head with dials and buttons: One control adjusts the heat, while another turns the flow off and on (let the water run for a bit to moderate the temperature before you hop in). If the hot water doesn't work, you may need to flip a red switch (often located just outside the bathroom). If the shower looks mysterious, ask your B&B host for help...*before* you take off your clothes.

Paying: Many B&Bs take credit cards, but may add the card service fee to your bill (about 3 percent). If you do need to pay cash for your room, plan ahead to have enough on hand when you check out.

Short-Term Rentals

A short-term rental—whether an apartment (or "flat"), house, or room in a local's home—is an increasingly popular alternative, especially if you plan to settle in one location for several nights. For stays longer than a few days, you can usually find a rental that's comparable to—and cheaper than—a hotel room with similar amenities. Plus, you'll get a behind-the-scenes peek into how locals live.

Many places require a minimum night stay and have strict cancellation policies. And you're generally on your own: There's no hotel reception desk, breakfast, or daily cleaning service.

Finding Accommodations: Websites such as Airbnb, FlipKey, Booking.com, and the HomeAway family of sites (HomeAway, VRBO, and VacationRentals) let you browse a wide range of properties. Alternatively, rental agencies such as InterhomeUSA.com or RentaVilla.com, which list more carefully selected accommodations that might cost more, can provide more personalized service.

Before you commit, be clear on the location. I like to virtually "explore" the neighborhood using the Street View feature on Google Maps. Also consider the proximity to public transportation and how well-connected the property is with the rest of the city. Ask about amenities (elevator, air-conditioning, laundry, Wi-Fi, parking, etc.). Reviews from previous guests can help identify trouble spots.

Think about the kind of experience you want: Just a key and an affordable bed...or a chance to get to know a local? There are typically two kinds of hosts: those who want minimal interaction with their guests, and hosts who are friendly and may want to interact with you. Read the promotional text and online reviews to help shape your decision.

Confirming and Paying: Many places require you to pay the entire balance before your trip. It's easiest and safest to pay through the site where you found the listing. Be wary of owners who want to take your transaction offline; this gives you no recourse if things go awry. Never agree to wire money (a key indicator of a fraudulent transaction).

Apartments or Houses: If you're staying in one place for four or more nights, it's worth considering an apartment or rental house (shorter stays aren't worth the hassle of arranging key pickup, buying groceries, etc.). Apartment or house rentals can be especially cost-effective for groups and families. European apartments, like hotel rooms, tend to be small by US standards. But they often come with laundry machines and small, equipped kitchens, making it easier and cheaper to dine in.

Rooms in Private Homes: Renting a room in someone's home is a good option for those traveling alone, as you're more likely to find true single rooms—with just one single bed, and a price to match. These can range from air-mattress-in-living-room basic to plush-B&B-suite posh. Some places allow you to book for a single night; if staying for several nights, you can buy groceries just as you would in a rental house. While you can't expect your host to also be your tour guide—or even to provide you with much info— some may be interested in getting to know the travelers who come through their home.

Other Options: Swapping homes with a local works for people with an appealing place to offer (don't assume where you live is not interesting to Europeans). Good places to start are HomeExchange.com and LoveHomeSwap.com. To sleep for free, Couchsurfing.com is a vagabond's alternative to Airbnb. It lists millions of outgoing members, who host fellow "surfers" in their homes.

Hostels

Scotland has hostels of all shapes and sizes. Choose yours selectively. Hostels can be historic castles or depressing tenements, serene and comfy or overrun by noisy school groups.

A hostel provides cheap beds in dorms where you sleep alongside strangers for about £20-30 per night. Travelers of any age are welcome if they don't mind dorm-style accommodations and meeting other travelers. Most hostels offer kitchen facilities, guest computers, Wi-Fi, and a self-service laundry. Hostels almost always provide bedding, but the towel's up to you (though you can usually rent one for a small fee). Family and private rooms are often available.

Independent hostels tend to be easygoing, colorful, and informal (no membership required; www.hostelworld.com). You may pay slightly less by booking directly with the hostel. A few chains have multiple locations around Scotland, including **MacBack-**

PRACTICALITIES

packers (www.scotlandstophostels.com); others are listed on the **Scottish Independent Hostels** website, with a fun variety of well-established places (www.hostel-scotland.co.uk).

Official hostels are part of Hostelling International (HI) and share an online booking site (www.hihostels.com). In Scotland, these official hostels are run by the Scottish Youth Hostel Association (SYHA, also known as Hostelling Scotland, www.hostellingscotland.org.uk). HI hostels typically require that you be a member or pay extra per night.

Eating

These days, the stereotype of "bad food in Britain" is woefully dated. Britain has caught up with the foodie revolution—in fact, they're right there, leading the vanguard—and I find it's easy to eat very well here.

British cooking has embraced international influences and local, seasonal ingredients, making "modern British" food quite delicious. While some dreary pub food still exists, you'll generally find the cuisine scene here innovative and delicious (but expensive). Basic pubs are more likely to dish up homemade, creative dishes than microwaved pies, soggy fries, and mushy peas. Even traditional pub grub has gone upmarket, with gastropubs that serve locally sourced meats and fresh vegetables.

All of Britain is smoke-free. Expect restaurants and pubs to be nonsmoking indoors, with smokers occupying patios and doorways outside. You'll find the Brits eat at about the same time of day as Americans.

For listings in this guidebook, I look for restaurants that are convenient to your hotel and sightseeing. When restaurant-hunting, choose a spot filled with locals, not tourists. Venturing even a block or two off the main drag leads to higher-quality food for a better price.

Tipping: At pubs and places where you order at the counter, you don't have to tip. Regular customers ordering a round sometimes say, "Add one for yourself" as a tip for drinks ordered at the bar—but this isn't expected. At restaurants and fancy pubs with waitstaff, it's standard to tip about 10-12 percent; you can add a bit more for finer dining or extra-good service. Occasionally a service charge is added to your bill, in which case no additional tip is necessary—but this is rare in Scotland. Tip only what you think the

Restaurant Code

Eateries in this book are categorized according to the average cost of a typical main course. Drinks, desserts, and splurge items can raise the price considerably.

$$$$	**Splurge:** Most main courses over £20
$$$	**Pricier:** £15-20
$$	**Moderate:** £10-15
$	**Budget:** Under £10

In Great Britain, carryout fish-and-chips and other takeout food is **$**; a basic pub or sit-down eatery is **$$**; a gastropub or casual but more upscale restaurant is **$$$**; and a swanky splurge is **$$$$**.

service warrants (if it isn't already added to your bill), and be careful not to tip double.

RESTAURANT PRICING

I've categorized my recommended eateries based on the average price of a typical main course, indicated with a dollar-sign rating (see sidebar). Obviously, expensive specialties, fine wine, appetizers, and dessert can significantly increase your final bill.

The categories also indicate the personality of a place: **Budget** eateries include street food, takeaway, order-at-the-counter shops, basic cafeterias, and bakeries selling sandwiches. **Moderate** eateries are nice (but not fancy) sit-down restaurants, ideal for a straightforward, fill-the-tank meal. Most of my listings fall in this category—great for getting a good taste of the local cuisine at a reasonable price.

Pricier eateries are a notch up, with more attention paid to the setting, presentation, and (often inventive) cuisine. **Splurge** eateries are dress-up-for-a-special-occasion swanky—typically with an elegant setting, polished service, intricate cuisine, and an expansive (and expensive) wine list.

BREAKFAST (Fry-Up)

The traditional fry-up or full Scottish breakfast—generally included in the cost of your room—is famous as a hearty way to start the day. Also known as a "heart attack on a plate," your standard fry-up comes with your choice of eggs, Canadian-style bacon and/or sausage, a grilled tomato, sautéed mushrooms, baked beans, and often haggis, black pudding, or a dense potato scone. Toast comes in a rack (to cool quickly and crisply) with butter and marmalade. The meal is typically topped off with tea or coffee. At a B&B or hotel, it may start with juice and cereal or porridge. Many pro-

PRACTICALITIES

gressive B&B owners offer vegetarian, organic, gluten-free, or
other creative variations on the
traditional breakfast.

As much as the full breakfast fry-up is a traditional way
to start the morning, these days
most places serve a healthier
continental breakfast as well—
with a buffet of yogurt, cereal,
fruit, and pastries. At some hotels, the buffet may also include
hot items, such as eggs and sausage.

LUNCH AND DINNER ON A BUDGET

Even in pricey cities, plenty of inexpensive choices are available:
pub grub, daily lunch and early-bird dinner specials, global cuisine,
cafeterias, fast food, picnics, greasy-spoon cafés, cheap chain restaurants, and pizza. On menus, adding "supper" to an item means
it comes with fries (so "fish supper" is fish-and-chips).

I've found that portions are huge, and **sharing plates** is generally just fine. Ordering two drinks, a soup or side salad, and splitting a £10 meat pie can make a good, filling meal. If you're on a
limited budget, share a main course in a more expensive place for a
nicer eating experience.

Pub grub is the most atmospheric budget option. You'll usually get hearty lunches and dinners priced reasonably at £8-15 under
ancient timbers (see "Pubs," later). Gastropubs, with better food,
are more expensive.

Classier restaurants have some affordable deals. Lunch is
usually cheaper than dinner; a top-end, £30-for-dinner-type restaurant often serves the same quality two-course lunch deals for
about half the price.

Many restaurants have **early-bird** or **pre-theater specials** of
two or three courses, often for a significant savings. They are usually available only before 18:30 or 19:00 (and sometimes on weekdays only).

Global cuisine adds spice to Britain's food scene. Eating Indian, Bangladeshi, Chinese, or Thai is cheap (even cheaper if you do
takeout). Middle Eastern shops sell gyro sandwiches, falafel, and
shwarmas (grilled meat in pita bread). An Indian samosa (greasy,
flaky meat-and-vegetable turnover) costs about £2 and makes a
very cheap, if small, meal. (For more, see "Indian Cuisine," later.)
You'll find inexpensive, quick Asian options (often Chinese), such
as all-you-can-eat buffets and takeaway places serving up standard
dishes in to-go boxes.

Haggis and Other Traditional Scottish Dishes

Scotland's most unique dish, **haggis,** began as a peasant food. Waste-conscious cooks wrapped the heart, liver, and lungs of a sheep in its stomach lining, packed in some oats

and spices, and then boiled the lot to create a hearty, though barely palatable, meal. Traditionally served with "neeps and tatties" (turnips and potatoes), haggis was forever immortalized thanks to Robbie Burns' *Address to a Haggis.*

Today, haggis has been refined almost to the point of high cuisine. You're likely to find it on many menus, including at breakfast. You can dress it up with anything from a fine whisky cream sauce to your basic HP brown sauce. To appreciate this iconic Scottish dish, think of how it tastes—not what it's made of.

The king of Scottish **black puddings** (blood sausage) is made in the Hebrides Islands. Called Stornoway, it's so famous that the European Union has granted it protected status to prevent imitators from using its name. A mix of beef suet, oatmeal, onion, and blood, the sausage is usually served as part of a full Scottish breakfast, but it also appears on the menus of top-class restaurants.

Be on the lookout for other traditional Scottish taste treats. **Cullen skink,** Scotland's answer to chowder, is a hearty, creamy fish soup, often made with smoked haddock. A **bridie** (or Forfar bridie) is a savory meat pastry similar to a Cornish pasty, but generally lighter (no potatoes). A **Scotch pie**—small, double-crusted, and filled with minced meat, is a good picnic food; it's a common snack at soccer matches and outdoor events. **Crowdie** is a dairy spread that falls somewhere between cream cheese and cottage cheese.

And for dessert, **cranachan** is similar to a trifle, made with whipped cream, honey, fruit (usually raspberries), and whisky-soaked oats. Another popular dessert is the **Tipsy Laird,** served at "Burns Suppers" on January 25, the annual celebration of national poet Robert Burns. It's essentially the same as a trifle but with whisky or brandy and Scottish raspberries.

PRACTICALITIES

Fish-and-chips are a heavy, greasy, but tasty British classic. Every town has at least one "chippy" selling takeaway fish-and-chips in a cardboard box or (more traditionally) wrapped in paper for about £5-7. You can dip your fries in ketchup, American-style, or "go British" and drizzle the whole thing with malt vinegar and fresh lemon.

Most large **museums** (and many historic **churches**) have handy, moderately priced cafeterias with forgettably decent food.

Picnicking saves time and money. Fine park benches and polite pigeons abound in most towns and city neighborhoods. You can easily get prepared food to go. The modern chain eateries on nearly every corner often have simple seating but are designed for take-out. Bakeries serve a wonderful array of fresh sandwiches and pasties (savory meat pastries—sometimes called bridies in Scotland). Street markets, generally parked in pedestrian-friendly zones, are fun and colorful places to stock up for a picnic.

Open-air markets and supermarkets sell produce in small quantities. The corner grocery store has fruit, drinks, fresh bread, tasty British cheese, meat, and local specialties. Supermarkets often have good deli sections, even offering Indian dishes, and sometimes salad bars. Decent packaged sandwiches (£3-4) are sold everywhere. Munch a relaxed "meal on wheels" picnic during your open-top bus tour or river cruise to save 30 precious minutes for sightseeing.

PUBS

Pubs are a fundamental part of the British social scene, and whether you're a teetotaler or a beer guzzler, they should be a part of your travel here. "Pub" is short for "public house." It's an extended common room where, if you don't mind the stickiness, you can feel the local pulse. Smart travelers use pubs to eat, drink, get out of the rain, watch sporting events, and make new friends. Unfortunately, many city pubs have been afflicted

with an excess of brass, ferns, and video slot machines. The most traditional atmospheric pubs are in the countryside and in smaller towns.

It's interesting to consider the role pubs filled for Britain's working class in more modest times: For workers with humble domestic quarters and no money for a vacation, a beer at the corner pub was the closest they'd get to a comfortable living room, a place to entertain, and a getaway. And locals could meet people from far away in a pub—today, that's you!

Though hours vary, pubs generally serve beer daily from 11:00 to 23:00, though many are open later, particularly on Friday and Saturday. (Children are served food and soft drinks in pubs, but you must be 18 to order a beer.) As it nears closing time, you'll hear shouts of "last orders." Then comes the 10-minute warning bell. Finally, they'll call "Time!" to pick up your glass, finished or not, when the pub closes.

A cup of darts is free for the asking. People go to a public house to be social. They want to talk. Get vocal with a local. This is easiest at the bar, where people assume you're in the mood to talk (rather than at a table, where you're allowed a bit of privacy). The pub is the next best thing to having relatives in town. Cheers!

Pub Grub: For £8-15, you'll get a basic budget hot lunch or dinner in friendly surroundings. (For something more refined, try a **gastropub,** which serves higher-quality meals for £12-20.) The *Good Pub Guide* is an excellent resource (www.thegoodpubguide.co.uk). Pubs that are attached to restaurants, advertise their food, and are crowded with locals are more likely to have fresh food and a chef—and less likely to sell only lousy microwaved snacks.

Pubs generally serve traditional dishes, such as fish-and-chips, roast beef with Yorkshire pudding (batter-baked in the oven), and assorted meat pies, such as steak-and-kidney pie or shepherd's pie (stewed lamb topped with mashed potatoes) with cooked vegetables. Side dishes include salads, vegetables, and—invariably—"chips" (French fries). "Crisps" are potato chips. A "jacket potato" (baked potato stuffed with fillings of your choice) can almost be a meal in itself. A "ploughman's lunch" is a traditional British meal of bread, cheese, and sweet pickles. These days, you'll likely find more pasta, curried dishes, and quiche on the menu than traditional fare.

Meals are usually served from 12:00 to 14:00 and again from 18:00 to 20:00—with a break in the middle (rather than serving straight through the day). Since they make more money selling

Whisky 101

Whisky is high on the experience list of most visitors to Scotland—even for teetotalers. Whether at a distillery, a shop, or a pub, be sure to try a few drams. (From the Gaelic word for "drink," a dram isn't necessarily a fixed amount—it's simply a small slug.) While touring a distillery is a ▲▲▲ Scottish experience, many fine whisky shops (including Cadenhead's in Edinburgh) offer guided tastings and a chance to have a small bottle filled from the cask of your choice.

Types of Whisky

Scotch whiskies come in two broad types: **"single malt,"** meaning that the bottle comes from a single batch made by a single dis-

tiller; and **"blends,"** which master blenders mix and match from various whiskies into a perfect punch of booze.

While single malts get the most attention, blended whiskies represent 90 percent of all whisky sales. They tend to be light and mild—making them an easier way to tiptoe into the whisky scene. Overseen by a master blender (a prestigious job, like a "nose" in the French wine industry), a neutral base of grain whisky (usually made from corn or wheat) is merged with various single malts, and then aged in oak casks for just six months to a year of "marriage."

There are more than 100 distilleries in Scotland, each one proud of its unique qualities. The **Lowlands,** around Edinburgh, produce light and refreshing whiskies—more likely to be taken as an aperitif. Whiskies from the **Highlands** and **Islands** range from floral and sweet to smoky and robust. **Speyside,** southeast of Inverness, is home to half of all Scottish distilleries. Mellow and fruity, Speyside whiskies can be the most accessible for beginners. The **Isle of Islay** is just the opposite, specializing in the peatiest, smokiest whiskies—not for novices. Only a few producers remain to distill the smoky and pungent **Campbeltown** whiskies in the southwest Highlands, near Islay.

Making Whisky

Single-malt whisky has three ingredients: water, malted barley, and yeast. To malt (or germinate) the barley, it's spread out on a floor, watered, and periodically turned. In about a week, when the barley starts to sprout, it's dried in an oven. Some distilleries (especially on the islands) use peat in their kilns, giving their whisky a distinctive smoky flavor.

Once malted, the barley is milled into a fine grist that's mixed with hot water to create mash. A sugary solution called wort is extracted from the mash, then cooled and mixed with yeast. For three or four days, the wort fizzes and ferments in big "washback" tubs as the yeast turn sugar into alcohol.

To boost the alcohol content, the wash is then double-distilled in tall, copper stills. First, in the "wash still," the liquid is heated, to allow the alcohol to evaporate. Those gases are sent

through coiled tubes to condense them into a liquid called "low wines." That liquid flows through a second spirit still to create "spirit." No two stills are the same, and the copper in each brings about unique qualities in the spirit.

Distillers keep only the "heart" of the run; it has the most consistent alcohol levels and flavor profile. They snip off the "head" and "tail" (collectively called "feints") to be redistilled.

At the end of the distillation process, you have a concentrated, colorless liquid called "new make spirit"—but not yet "whisky." For that, the liquid must be aged for at least three years (more commonly eight or more years; the final product must register at least 40 percent alcohol by volume). This maturation typically takes place in casks made of American white oak, often recycled from the US. (American laws permit each cask to be used only once—but no such regulation exists in Scotland.) It's increasingly in vogue to use casks that have previously aged sherry, port, wine, or cognac, in order to infuse the whisky with faint echoes of those flavors.

During maturation, about 1 to 3 percent of the alcohol is lost to evaporation—what's poetically described as "the angel's share." For a long-aged whisky, it's more like the lion's share: A 25-year-old cask of whisky can end up being just over half full.

Finally, the aged whisky is bottled—or, in some cases, entire casks are sent to specialty stores.

Tasting Whisky

Tasting whisky is like tasting wine; you'll use all your senses. First, swirl the whisky in the glass and observe its color and "legs"—the trail left by the liquid as it runs back down the side of the glass (quick, thin legs indicate light, young whisky; slow, thick legs mean it's a heavier and older one). Then take a deep sniff—do you smell smoke and peat? And finally, taste it (sip!). What's the dominant first punch? The smooth middle? The "finish"? Swish it around and let your gums taste it, too. Adding a few drops of water is said to "open up the taste"—look for a little glass of water with a dropper standing by, and try tasting your whisky before and after.

A whisky's flavor is most influenced by three things: whether the malt is peat-smoked; the shape of the stills; and the composition of the casks. Even local climate can play a role; some island distilleries tout the salty notes of their whiskies, as the sea air permeates their casks.

beer, many pubs stop food service early in the evening—especially on weekends. There's generally no table service. Order at the bar, and then take a seat. Either they'll bring the food when it's ready or you'll pick it up at the bar. Pay at the bar (sometimes when you order, sometimes after you eat). It's not necessary to tip unless it's a place with full table service. Servings are hearty, and service is quick. A beer, cider, or dram of whisky adds another couple of pounds. Free tap water is always available. For details on ordering beer and other drinks, see the "Beverages" section, later.

GOOD CHAIN RESTAURANTS

I know—you're going to Britain to enjoy characteristic little hole-in-the-wall pubs, so mass-produced food is the furthest thing from your mind. But several excellent chains with branches across the UK offer long hours, reasonable prices, reliable quality, and a nice break from pub grub. My favorites are Pret and Eat. Expect to see these familiar names wherever you go:

$ Pret (a.k.a. Pret à Manger) is perhaps the most pervasive of these modern convenience eateries. Some are takeout only, and others have seating ranging from simple stools to restaurant-quality tables. The service is fast, the price is great, and the food is healthy and fresh. Their slogan: "Made today. Gone today. No 'sell-by' date, no nightlife."

$$ Côte Brasserie is a contemporary French chain serving good-value French cuisine in pleasant settings (early dinner specials).

$$ Byron Hamburgers, an upscale hamburger chain with hip interiors, is worth seeking out if you need a burger fix. While British burgers tend to be a bit overcooked by American standards, Byron's burgers are your best bet.

$$ Wagamama Noodle Bar, serving pan-Asian cuisine (udon noodles, fried rice, and curry dishes), is a noisy, organic slurpathon. Portions are huge and splittable. There's one in almost every mid-size city in Britain, usually located in sprawling halls filled with long shared tables and busy servers who scrawl your order on the placemat.

$$$ Loch Fyne Restaurant is a Scottish chain that raises its own oysters and mussels. Its branches offer an inviting, lively atmosphere with a fine fishy energy and no pretense (early-bird specials).

$ Marks & Spencer department stores have inviting deli sections with cheery sit-down eating (along with their popular sandwiches-to-go section). M&S food halls are also handy if you're renting a city flat and want to prepare your own meals.

$$ Franco Manca is a taverna-inspired pizzeria serving Neapolitan-style pies using organic ingredients and boasting typical

Italian charm. If you skip the pricey drinks, you can feast very cheaply here.

$$ Ask and **Pizza Express** serve quality pasta and pizza in a pleasant, sit-down atmosphere that's family-friendly.

$$ Yo! Sushi lets you pick your dish off a conveyor belt and pay according to the color of your plate.

Carry-Out Chains: While the following may have some seating, they're best as places to grab prepackaged food on the run.

Major supermarket chains have smaller, offshoot branches that specialize in sandwiches, salads, and other prepared foods to go. These can be a picnicker's dream come true. Some shops are stand-alone, while others are located inside a larger store. The most prevalent—and best—is **M&S Simply Food** (an offshoot of Marks & Spencer; there's one in every major train station). **Sainsbury's Local** grocery stores also offer decent prepared food; **Tesco Express** and **Tesco Metro** run a distant third.

Eat is a "cheap and cheery" chain providing office workers with good, healthful sandwiches, salads, and pastries to go.

INDIAN CUISINE

Eating Indian food is "going local" in cosmopolitan, multiethnic Britain. You'll find Indian restaurants in most cities, and even in small towns. Take the opportunity to sample food from Britain's former colony. Indian cuisine is as varied as the country itself. In general, it uses more exotic spices than British or American cuisine—some hot, some sweet. Indian food is very vegetarian-friendly, offering many meatless dishes.

For a simple meal that costs about £10-12, order one dish with rice and naan (Indian flatbread). Generally, one order is plenty for two people to share. Many Indian restaurants offer a fixed-price combination that offers more variety, and is simpler and cheaper than ordering à la carte. For about £20, you can make a mix-and-match platter out of several shareable dishes, including dal (simmered lentils) as a starter, one or two meat or vegetable dishes with sauce (for example, chicken curry, chicken *tikka masala* in a creamy tomato sauce, grilled fish tandoori, or chickpea *chana masala*), *raita* (a cooling yogurt that comes on the side—it helps extinguish your mouth if eating spicy dishes), rice, naan, and an Indian beer (wine and Indian food don't really mix) or spiced chai tea (usually served with milk). An easy way to taste a variety of dishes is to order a thali—a sampler plate of various specialties.

AFTERNOON TEA

While more of an English custom, afternoon tea is served in Scottish tearooms and generally includes a pot of tea, small finger foods (like sandwiches with the crusts cut off), homemade scones,

PRACTICALITIES

jam, and thick clotted cream. A lighter "cream tea" gets you tea and a scone or two. Tearooms, which often serve appealing light meals, are usually open for lunch and close at about 17:00, just before dinner.

DESSERTS (SWEETS)

To the British, the traditional word for dessert is "pudding," although it's also referred to as "sweets" these days. Sponge cake, cream, fruitcake, and meringue are key players.

Trifle is the best-known British concoction, consisting of sponge cake soaked in brandy or sherry (or orange juice for children), then covered with jam and/or fruit and custard cream. Whipped cream can sometimes put the final touch on this "light" treat.

The British version of custard is a smooth, yellow liquid. Cream tops most everything that custard does not. There's single cream for coffee. Double cream is really thick. Clotted cream is the consistency of whipped butter.

Fool is a dessert with sweetened pureed fruit (such as rhubarb, gooseberries, or black currants) mixed with cream or custard and chilled. Elderflower is a popular flavoring for sorbet.

Flapjacks here aren't pancakes, but are dense, sweet oatmeal cakes (a little like a cross between a granola bar and a brownie). They come with toppings such as toffee and chocolate.

Scones are tops, and many inns and restaurants have their secret recipes. Whether made with fruit or topped with clotted cream, scones take the cake.

BEVERAGES

Beer: The British take great pride in their beer. Many locals think that drinking beer cold and carbonated, as Americans do, ruins the taste. Most pubs will have **lagers** (cold, refreshing, American-style beer), **ales** (amber-colored, cellar-temperature beer), **bitters** (hop-flavored ale, perhaps the most typical British beer), and **stouts** (dark and somewhat bitter, like Guinness).

At pubs, long-handled pulls (or taps) are used to draw the traditional, rich-flavored "real ales" up from the cellar. These are the connoisseur's favorites and often come with fun names. Served straight from the brewer's cask at cellar temperature, real ales finish fermenting naturally and are not pasteurized or filtered, so they must be consumed within two or three days after the cask is tapped. Naturally carbonated, real ales have less gassiness and head; they vary from sweet to bitter, often with a hoppy or nutty flavor.

Short-handled pulls mean colder, fizzier, mass-produced, and less interesting keg beers. Mild beers are sweeter, with a creamy

PRACTICALITIES

malt flavoring. Irish cream ale is a smooth, sweet experience. Try the draft cider (sweet or dry)...carefully.

Order your beer at the bar and pay as you go, with no need to tip. An average beer costs about £4. Part of the experience is standing before a line of hand pulls, and wondering which beer to choose.

As dictated by British law, draft beer and cider are served by the pint (20-ounce imperial size) or the half-pint (9.6 ounces). In 2011, the government sanctioned an in-between serving size—the schooner, or two-thirds pint (it's become a popular size for higher-alcohol-content craft beers). A popular summer drink is a **shandy** (half beer and half British "lemonade," similar to 7-Up).

Whisky: While bar-hopping tourists generally think in terms of beer, many pubs are just as enthusiastic about serving whisky. If you are unfamiliar with whisky (what Americans call "Scotch" and the Irish call "whiskey"), it's a great conversation starter. Many pubs list dozens of whiskies and describe their taste profiles (peaty, smoky, woody, and so on).

A glass of basic whisky generally costs around £2.50. Let a local teach you how to drink it "neat," then add a little water. Make a friend, buy a few drams, and learn by drinking. Keep experimenting until you discover the right taste for you.

Consider going beyond single-malt whiskies. Blends can be surprisingly creative—even for someone who thinks they're knowledgeable about whisky—and non-whisky alternatives are pushing boundaries. Like microbrews, small-batch, innovative Scottish spirits are trendy right now. For example, you'll find gin that's aged in whisky casks, taking off the piney edge and infusing a bit of that distinctive whisky flavor.

Distilleries throughout Scotland offer tours, but you'll often only learn about that one type of whisky. At a good whisky shop, the knowledgeable staff offer guided tastings (for a fee and typically prearranged), explaining four or five whiskies to help you develop your palate. Some shops have several bottles open and will let you try a few wee drams to narrow down your options. If they're providing samples, they're hoping you'll buy a bottle at the end.

But the easiest and perhaps best option for sampling Scotland's national drink is to find a local pub with a passion for whisky that's filled with locals who share that passion.

For much more about whisky, see the "Whisky 101" sidebar.

Other Alcoholic Drinks: Many pubs also have a good selection of wines by the glass and a fully stocked bar for the gentleman's "G and T" (gin and tonic). **Pimm's** is a refreshing and fruity summer liqueur, traditionally popular during Wimbledon. It's an upper-class drink—a rough bloke might insult a pub by claiming it sells more Pimm's than beer.

Non-Alcoholic Drinks: Teetotalers can order from a wide variety of soft drinks—both the predictable American sodas and other more interesting bottled drinks, such as ginger beer (similar to ginger ale but with more bite), root beers, or other flavors (Fentimans brews some unusual options that are stocked in many pubs). The uniquely Scottish soft drink called Irn-Bru (pronounced "Iron Brew") is bright orange and tastes a little like bubblegum and ginger. Note that in Britain, "lemonade" is lemon-lime soda (like 7-Up).

Staying Connected

One of the most common questions I hear from travelers is, "How can I stay connected in Europe?" The short answer is: more easily and cheaply than you might think.

The simplest solution is to bring your own device—mobile phone, tablet, or laptop—and use it just as you would at home (following the money-saving tips below, such as getting an international plan or connecting to free Wi-Fi whenever possible). Another option is to buy a European SIM card for your US mobile phone. Or you can use European landlines and computers to connect. Each of these options is described next, and more details are at RickSteves.com/phoning. For a practical one-hour talk covering tech issues for travelers, see RickSteves.com/mobile-travel-skills.

USING A MOBILE PHONE IN EUROPE

Here are some budget tips and options.

Sign up for an international plan. To stay connected at a lower cost, sign up for an international service plan through your carrier. Most providers offer a simple bundle that includes calling, messaging, and data. Your normal plan may already include international coverage (T-Mobile's does).

Before your trip, call your provider or check online to confirm that your phone will work in Europe, and research your provider's international rates. Activate the plan a day or two before you leave, then remember to cancel it when your trip's over.

Use free Wi-Fi whenever possible. Unless you have an unlimited-data plan, you're best off saving most of your online tasks for Wi-Fi. You can access the internet, send texts, and even make voice calls over Wi-Fi.

Most accommodations in Europe offer free Wi-Fi, but some—especially expensive hotels—charge a fee. Many cafés (including Starbucks and McDonald's) have free hotspots for customers; look for signs offering it and ask for the Wi-Fi password when you buy something. You'll also often find Wi-Fi at TIs, city squares, major museums, public-transit hubs, airports, and aboard trains

PRACTICALITIES

Tips on Internet Security

Make sure that your device is running the latest versions of its operating system, security software, and apps. Next, ensure that your device and key programs (like email) are password-protected. On the road, use only secure, password-protected Wi-Fi hotspots. Ask the hotel or café staff for the specific name of their Wi-Fi network, and make sure you log on to that exact one.

If you must access your financial info online, use a banking app rather than accessing your account via a browser. A cellular connection is more secure than Wi-Fi. Avoid logging onto personal finance sites on a public computer.

Never share your credit-card number (or any other sensitive information) online unless you know that the site is secure. A secure site displays a little padlock icon, and the URL begins with *https* (instead of the usual *http*).

and buses. In Britain, another option is to sign up for Wi-Fi access through a company such as BT (one hour-£4, one day-£10, www. btwifi.co.uk) or The Cloud (free though sometimes slow, www. skywifi.cloud).

Minimize the use of your cellular network. The best way to make sure you're not accidentally burning through data is to put your device in "airplane" mode (which also disables phone calls and texts), turn your Wi-Fi back on, and connect to networks as needed. When you need to get online but can't find Wi-Fi, simply turn on your cellular network (or turn off airplane mode) just long enough for the task at hand.

Even with an international data plan, wait until you're on Wi-Fi to Skype, download apps, stream videos, or do other megabyte-greedy tasks. Using a navigation app such as Google Maps over a cellular network can take lots of data, so do this sparingly or offline.

Limit automatic updates. By default, your device constantly checks for a data connection and updates apps. It's smart to disable these features so your apps will only update when you're on Wi-Fi. Also change your device's email settings from "auto-retrieve" to "manual" (or from "push" to "fetch").

Use Wi-Fi calling and messaging apps. Skype, WhatsApp, FaceTime, and Google Hangouts are great for making free or low-cost calls or sending texts over Wi-Fi worldwide. Just log on to a Wi-Fi network, then connect with any of your friends or family members who use the same service. If you buy credit in advance, with some of these services you can call or text anywhere for just pennies.

Aye, There's a Wee Language Barrier

While the Scottish speak English, you sometimes might seriously doubt it. The distinct Scottish burr comes in various thicknesses (think actors Ewan McGregor and Sean Connery), and you'll hear a different (yet sometimes familiar) vocabulary: aye = yes, loch = lake, bonnie = beautiful. Accents aside, it's worth knowing that, besides English, Scotland has two official languages—Scottish Gaelic and Scots.

Scottish Gaelic is an old Celtic language that thrives only in the far-flung corners of the country—the Highlands and the Hebrides. But it is kept alive all over Scotland by those keen to remember its proud heritage. There are Gaelic schools, and you'll see signs listing both English and Gaelic spellings (*Edinburgh/Dùn Èideann*). One Gaelic-derived word we all know is whisky, from *uisge beatha* (water of life).

Scots—which is close to English—has been spoken for centuries but wasn't officially recognized by the UK government as a language until 1998—though some still consider it a dialect. Scots took a back seat to the Queen's English after the Act of Union in 1707, and a generation or two ago, schoolchildren from Scots-speaking families faced reprimands for saying "youse" to mean "you all." But today Scots is being taught to a new generation of kids.

Linguists who argue that Scots is technically an ancient Eng-

Some apps, such as Apple's iMessage, will use the cellular network for texts if Wi-Fi isn't available: To avoid this possibility, turn off the "Send as SMS" feature.

Buy a European SIM card. If you anticipate making a lot of local calls or need a local phone number, or if your provider's international data rates are expensive, consider buying a SIM card in Europe to replace the one in your (unlocked) US phone or tablet. SIM cards are sold at department-store electronics counters, some newsstands, and vending machines. If you need help setting it up, buy one at a mobile-phone shop (you may need to show your passport).

There are no roaming charges when using a European SIM card in other EU countries, though to be sure you get this "roam-like-at-home" pricing, buy your SIM card at a mobile-phone shop and ask if this feature is included.

lish dialect have clearly never heard a Scot read aloud the poetry of Robert Burns. Rabbie, as he's known, wrote in the unfiltered Scots of the 18th century's common people. Consider the opening line of his "Address to a Haggis": "Fair fa' your honest, sonsie face" (Good luck to you and your honest, plump face).

As you travel, you'll collect Scots words and come to relish the lovely lilt and colorful jargon. Aye, and ye likely ken (know) a few Scots words already. Listen in on this conversation at a pub in Scots between Angus and his mate Brodie:

Angus walks in and says, "Aright! Gae's a wee swally?" (Are you all right? Give me a sip of your drink.)

"So ye still on the buroo ar ye?" says Brodie. (Are you still getting unemployment?)

"Aye, fer noo." (Yes, for now.)

Their blether (talk) turns to the weather. Yesterday was "dreich" (lousy), today is "braw" (great), but tomorrow's going to be "pure Baltic" (freezing). Returning from the lavvy (bathroom), Angus brags that his football team Hibs is better than Brodie's Rangers.

"That's shite. Yer head's fulla mince," says Brodie. (S_____. You are full of nonsense.) "Yer bum's oot the windae." (Your rear end is out the window.)

Annoyed by their loud talking, the lads at the next table shout, "Haud yer wheesht!" (Shut up!)

At the end of the night, they all bid each other a hearty goodbye. "Bye bye fer noo. See ye efter."

For more Scots words and expressions, see the Scots-Yankee Vocabulary in the Appendix. To sample audio files of the various regional dialects around Scotland, visit AyeCan.com.

WITHOUT A MOBILE PHONE

It's less convenient but possible to travel in Europe without a mobile device. You can make calls from your hotel and check email or get online using public computers.

Most **hotels** charge a fee for placing calls—ask for rates before you dial. You can use a prepaid international phone card (usually available at newsstands, tobacco shops, and train stations) to call out from your hotel. Dial the toll-free access number, enter the card's PIN code, then dial the number.

If there's no phone in your **B&B** room, and you have an important, brief call to make, politely ask your hosts if you can use their personal phone. Use a cheap international phone card with a toll-free access number, or offer to pay your host for the call.

Public pay phones are hard to find in Britain, and they're expensive. To use one, you'll pay with a major credit card (minimum charge-£1.20) or coins (minimum charge-£0.60).

How to Dial

International Calls

Whether phoning from a US landline or mobile phone, or from a number in another European country, here's how to make an international call. I've used one of my recommended Edinburgh hotels as an example (tel. 0131/667-5806).

Initial Zero: Drop the initial zero from international phone numbers—except when calling Italy.

Mobile Tip: If using a mobile phone, the "+" sign can replace the international access code (for a "+" sign, press and hold "0").

US/Canada to Europe

Dial 011 (US/Canada international access code), country code (44 for Britain), and phone number.

▶ To call the Edinburgh hotel from home, dial 011-44-0131/667-5806.

Country to Country Within Europe

Dial 00 (Europe international access code), country code, and phone number.

▶ To call the Edinburgh hotel from Germany, dial 00-44-0131/667-5806.

Europe to the US/Canada

Dial 00, country code (1 for US/Canada), and phone number.

▶ To call from Europe to my office in Edmonds, Washington, dial 00-1-425-771-8303.

Domestic Calls

To call within Britain (including Scotland), from one British landline or mobile phone to another, simply dial the phone number, including the initial zero if there is one.

▶ To call the Edinburgh hotel from Glasgow or from London, dial 0131/667-5806.

Some hotels have **public computers** in their lobbies for guests to use; otherwise you may find them at public libraries (ask your hotelier or the TI for the nearest location). On a European keyboard, use the "Alt Gr" key to the right of the space bar to insert the extra symbol that appears on some keys. If you can't locate a special character (such as @), simply copy and paste it from a web page.

MAIL

You can mail one package per day to yourself worth up to $200 duty-free from Europe to the US (mark it "personal purchases"). If you're sending a gift to someone, mark it "unsolicited gift" (for details, visit www.cbp.gov, select "Travel," and search for "Know Before You Visit"). The British postal service works fine, but for

More Dialing Tips

Toll and Toll-Free Numbers: It's generally not possible to dial British toll or toll-free numbers from a US mobile or landline (although you can sometimes get through using Skype). Look for a direct-dial number instead.

More Phoning Help: See HowToCallAbroad.com.

European Country Codes		Ireland & N. Ireland	353 / 44
Austria	43	Italy	39
Belgium	32	Latvia	371
Bosnia-Herzegovina	387	Montenegro	382
Croatia	385	Morocco	212
Czech Republic	420	Netherlands	31
Denmark	45	Norway	47
Estonia	372	Poland	48
Finland	358	Portugal	351
France	33	Russia	7
Germany	49	Slovakia	421
Gibraltar	350	Slovenia	386
Great Britain	44	Spain	34
Greece	30	Sweden	46
Hungary	36	Switzerland	41
Iceland	354	Turkey	90

PRACTICALITIES

quick transatlantic delivery (in either direction), consider services such as DHL (www.dhl.com). For postcards, get stamps at the neighborhood post office, newsstands within fancy hotels, and some minimarts and card shops.

Transportation

Figuring out how to get around in Europe is one of your biggest trip decisions. **Cars** work well for two or more traveling together (especially families with small kids), those packing heavy, and those delving into the countryside. **Trains** and **buses** are best for solo travelers, blitz tourists, city-to-city travelers, and those who want to leave the driving to others. Smart travelers can use short-hop **flights** within Europe to creatively connect the dots on their itineraries. Just be aware of the potential downside of each option: A car is an expensive headache in any major city; with trains and buses you're at the mercy of a timetable; and flying entails a trek to and from a usually distant airport.

If your itinerary mixes cities and countryside, my advice is to connect cities by train (or bus) and to explore rural areas by rental car. Arrange to pick up your car in the last big city you'll visit, then use it to lace together small towns and explore the countryside. For more detailed information on transportation throughout Europe, see RickSteves.com/transportation.

TRAINS

Regular tickets on Britain's great train system (15,000 departures from 2,400 stations daily) are the most expensive per mile in all of Europe. For the greatest savings, book online in advance and leave after rush hour (after 9:30 weekdays).

Since Britain's railways have been privatized, a single train route can be operated by multiple companies. However, one website covers all train lines (www.nationalrail.co.uk), and another covers all bus and train routes (www.traveline.org.uk for information, not ticket sales). Another good resource, which also has schedules for trains throughout Europe, is German Rail's timetable (www.bahn.com).

As with airline tickets, British train tickets can come at many different prices for the same journey. A clerk at any station can figure out the cheapest fare for your trip.

While generally not required, reservations are free and can normally be made well in advance. They are an especially good idea for long journeys or for travel on Sundays or holidays. Make reservations at any train station, by phone, or online when you buy your ticket. With a point-to-point ticket, you can reserve as late as two hours before train time, but rail-pass holders should book seats at least 24 hours in advance (see below for more on rail passes). You must reserve in advance for Caledonian Sleeper overnight trains between London and Scotland (www.sleeper.scot).

Rail Passes

There are three Scotland-only passes: Spirit of Scotland (covers most trains in Scotland), Central Scotland (Edinburgh/Glasgow area), and Scottish Highlands (Glasgow and points north). For a Scotland-only itinerary, these probably won't save you money over point-to-point tickets (especially if you buy tickets in advance or use a discount Railcard—see "Buying Tickets," below). Kids pay half the adult rate on these passes. They can be purchased online or in staffed rail stations in Scotland.

Scotland's Public Transportation

Particularly if you travel between London and Scotland, consider the BritRail Pass (covers England, Scotland, and Wales). A rail pass offers hop-on flexibility and no need to lock in reservations, except for overnight sleeper cars.

Passes come in "consecutive day" and "flexi" versions, with price breaks for youths (under age 26), seniors (60 and up), off-season travelers, and groups of three or more. Most allow one child under 16 to travel free with a paying adult or senior. If you're exploring the backcountry with a BritRail pass, second class is a good choice since many of the smaller train lines don't even offer first-class cars.

BritRail passes cannot be purchased locally; buy your pass through an agent before leaving the US. Make sleeper reservations in advance; you can also make optional, free seat reservations (recommended for busy weekends) at staffed train stations.

If your travels are taking you from Britain to the Continent, the Eurail Global Pass covers trains on both sides of the English Channel, and Eurostar trains beneath it (with a paid seat reservation). It's generally cheaper to buy one pass for your whole trip than separate, single-country passes. Global passes also come in "consecutive day" and "flexi" versions, with price breaks for youths (under age 28) and seniors (60 and up). Up to two kids under 12 travel free with you on an adult-rate pass.

For more detailed advice on figuring out the smartest rail-pass options for your train trip, visit RickSteves.com/rail.

Buying Tickets

In Advance: The best fares go to those who book their trips well in advance of their journey. Savings can be significant. For an Edinburgh-Inverness round-trip (standard class), the peak "anytime" fare is about £62 (£52 for "off-peak"). An "advance" fare for the same ticket booked a couple of months out can cost as little as £25. If traveling longer distances, such as from Scotland to England, expect higher fares but greater advance discounts.

To book ahead, go in person to any station, look online at NationalRail.co.uk, or call 0345-748-4950 (from the US, dial 011-44-20-7278-5240, phone answered 24 hours) to find out the schedule and best fare for your journey; you'll then be referred to the appropriate vendor—depending on the particular rail company—to book your ticket. If you order online, be sure you know what you want; it's tough to reach a person who can change your online reservation. You'll pick up your ticket at the station, or you may be able to print it at home. (BritRail pass holders, however, cannot make online seat reservations.)

A company called **Megabus** (through their subsidiary Megatrain) sells some discounted train tickets well in advance on a few specific routes, though their focus is mainly on selling bus tickets (info tel. 0871-266-3333, www.megatrain.com).

Buying Train Tickets as You Travel: If you'd rather have the flexibility of booking tickets as you go, you can save a few pounds by buying a round-trip ticket, called a "return ticket" (a same-day round-trip, called a "day return," is particularly cheap for short excursions); buying before 18:00 the day before you depart; traveling

Rail Pass or Point-to-Point Tickets?

Will you be better off buying a rail pass or point-to-point tickets? It pays to know your options and choose what's best for your itinerary.

Rail Passes

A BritRail Pass lets you travel by train in Scotland, England, and Wales for two to eight days within a one-month period, 15 days within two months, or for continuous periods of up to one month.

Britain is also covered (along with most of Europe) by the classic Eurail Global Pass. Discounted rates are offered for children, youths, and seniors.

In addition, BritRail sells three different regional Scotland passes that are good for three to eight days of train travel within three, eight, or fifteen-day periods, sold online or at staffed rail stations in Scotland.

Rail passes are best purchased outside Europe (through travel agents or Rick Steves' Europe). For more on rail passes, including current prices, visit RickSteves.com/rail.

Point-to-Point Tickets

If you're taking just a couple of train rides, buying individual point-to-point train tickets may save you money over a pass. Use this map to add up approximate pay-as-you-go fares for your itinerary, and compare that to the price of a rail pass. Keep in mind that significant discounts on point-to-point tickets may be available with advance purchase.

Map shows approximate costs, in US dollars, for one-way, second-class tickets at off-peak rates.

after the morning rush hour (this usually means after 9:30 Mon-Fri); and going standard class instead of first class. Preview your options at NationalRail.co.uk.

Senior, Youth, Partner, and Family Deals: To get a third off the price of most point-to-point rail tickets, seniors can buy a Senior Railcard (ages 60 and up), younger travelers can buy a 16-25 Railcard (ages 16-25, or full-time students 26 and older), and two people traveling together can buy a Two Together Railcard (ages 16 and over). A Family and Friends Railcard gives adults about 33 percent off for most trips and 60 percent off for their kids age 5 to 15 (maximum 4 adults and 4 kids). Each Railcard costs £30; for non-UK citizens, it's best to purchase the pass at a staffed rail station in England, Scotland, or Wales as you need a UK delivery address to buy it online (pass also sold at some London airports, some passes require passport-type photo, passport needed for proof of age; see www.railcard.co.uk). These cards are valid for a year on almost all trains, including special runs such as the Heathrow Express, but are not valid on the Eurostar to Paris, Amsterdam, or Brussels.

BUSES

Although buses are about a third slower than trains, they're also a lot cheaper. And buses go many places that trains don't, including destinations in the Highlands and the islands. For details on bus connections in the Highlands—where buses are the most useful—see page 254.

Most long-haul domestic routes in Scotland are operated by **Scottish Citylink.** In peak season, it's worth booking your seat on popular routes at least a few days in advance (at the bus station or TI, online at www.citylink.co.uk, or by calling 0141/352-4444). At slower times, you can just hop on the bus and pay the driver. If you're taking lots of buses, consider Citylink's Explorer pass (£49/3 days in 5-day period, £74/5 days in 10-day period, £99/8 days in 16-day period).

Some regional routes are operated by Citylink's **Stagecoach** service (www.stagecoachbus.com). If a Stagecoach bus runs the same route as a Citylink one—such as between Glencoe and Fort William—it's likely cheaper (and maybe slower).

Longer-distance routes (especially those to England) are operated by **National Express** (tel. 0371/781-8181, www.nationalexpress.com) or **Megabus** (book far ahead for best discounts, www.megabus.com).

FERRIES

Ferries link the Scottish mainland to its many islands. For most west-coast routes, including the isles of Mull and Skye, you'll take a ferry run by Caledonian MacBrayne (tel. 01475/650-397,

www.calmac.co.uk). Ferries to Orkney are operated by North-Link (www.northlinkferries.co.uk) and Pentland Ferries (www.pentlandferries.co.uk);
Orkney Ferries runs the interisland routes (www.orkneyferries.co.uk).

Ferries can fill up in peak season—especially car spaces. During the summer, it's smart to reserve at least a day or two ahead (possibly more for popular routes). Check in at least 30 minutes ahead of your departure. Walk-on passengers don't need to reserve. Most car ferries have a café or cafeteria on board.

TAXIS AND RIDE-BOOKING SERVICES

Most British taxis are reliable and cheap. In many cities, two people can travel short distances by cab for little more than the cost of bus or subway tickets. If you like ride-booking services such as Uber, their apps usually work in Britain just like they do in the US: Request a car on your mobile phone (connected to Wi-Fi or data), and the fare is automatically charged to your credit card.

RENTING A CAR

It's cheaper to arrange most car rentals from the US, so research and compare rates before you go. Most of the major US rental agencies (including Avis, Budget, Enterprise, Hertz, and Thrifty) have offices throughout Europe. Also consider the two major Europe-based agencies, Europcar and Sixt. Consolidators such as Auto Europe (www.autoeurope.com—or the sometimes cheaper www.autoeurope.eu) compare rates at several companies to get you the best deal.

Wherever you book, always read the fine print. Check for add-on charges—such as one-way drop-off fees, airport surcharges, or mandatory insurance policies—that aren't included in the "total price."

Rental Costs and Considerations

Figure on paying roughly $250 for a one-week rental for a basic

British Radio

Local radio broadcasts can be a treat for drivers sightseeing in Britain. Many British radio stations broadcast nationwide; your car radio automatically detects the local frequency a station plays on and displays its name. The most prominent are the five BBC nationwide stations. These government-subsidized stations have no ads.

BBC Radio 1: Pop music, with youthful DJs spinning top 40 hits and interviewing big-name bands.

BBC Radio 2: The highest-rated station nationwide, aimed at a more mature audience, with adult contemporary, retro pop, and other "middle of the road" music.

BBC Radio 3: Mostly classical music, with some jazz and world music.

BBC Radio 4: All talk—current events, entertaining chat shows, special-interest topics such as cooking and gardening, and lots of radio plays.

compact car. Allow extra for supplemental insurance, fuel, tolls, and parking.

Manual vs. Automatic: Almost all rental cars in Europe are manual by default—and cars with a stick shift are generally cheaper. If you need an automatic, request one in advance. An automatic makes sense for most American drivers: With a manual transmission in Britain, you'll be sitting on the right side of the car and shifting with your left hand...while driving on the left side of the road. When selecting a car, don't be tempted by a larger model, as it won't be as maneuverable on narrow, winding roads or when squeezing into tight parking lots.

Age Restrictions: Rental companies in Britain require you to be at least 21 years old and to have held your license for one year. Drivers under the age of 25 may incur a young-driver surcharge, and some rental companies will not rent to anyone 75 or older.

Choosing Pick-up/Drop-off Locations: Always check the hours of the locations you choose: Many rental offices close from midday Saturday until Monday morning and, in smaller towns, at lunchtime. When selecting an office, plug the addresses into a mapping website to confirm the location. A downtown site is generally cheaper—and might seem more convenient than the airport. But pedestrianized and one-way streets can make navigation tricky when returning a car at a big-city office or urban train station. Wherever you select, get precise details on the location and allow ample time to find it.

Picking Up Your Car: Before driving off in your rental car, check it thoroughly and make sure any damage is noted on your

BBC Radio 5 Live: Sporting events as well as news and sports talk programs.

You'll encounter regional variations of BBC stations, such as BBC London, Radio York, BBC Scotland, and BBC Gaelic. At the top of the hour, many BBC stations broadcast the famous "pips" (indicating Greenwich Mean Time) and a short roundup of the day's news.

Beyond the BBC offerings, several private stations broadcast music and other content with "adverts" (commercials). Some are nationwide, including **XFM** (alternative rock), **Classic FM** (classical), **Absolute Radio** (pop), and **Capital FM** (pop).

Traffic Alerts: Ask your rental-car company about turning on automatic traffic alerts on the car radio (look for the letters *TA* or *TP* on the radio readout). When enabled, traffic reports for the area you are driving in will periodically interrupt programming.

rental agreement. Rental agencies in Europe tend to charge for even minor damage, so be sure to mark everything. Find out how your car's gearshift, lights, turn signals, wipers, radio, and fuel cap function, and know what kind of fuel the car takes (diesel vs. unleaded). When you return the car, make sure the agent verifies its condition with you. Some drivers take pictures of the returned vehicle as proof of its condition.

Be aware that Brits call it "hiring a car," and directional signs at airports and train stations will read *Car Hire.*

The AA: The services of Britain's Automobile Association are included with most rentals (www.theaa.com), but check for this when booking to be sure you understand its towing and emergency road-service benefits.

Car Insurance Options

When you rent a car in Europe, the price typically includes liability insurance, which covers harm to other cars or motorists—but not the rental car itself. To limit your financial risk in case of damage to the rental, choose one of these three options: Buy a Collision Damage Waiver (CDW) with a low or zero deductible from the car-rental company (roughly 30-40 percent extra), get coverage through your credit card (free, but more complicated), or get collision insurance as part of a larger travel-insurance policy.

Basic **CDW** costs $15-30 a day and typically comes with a $1,000-2,000 deductible, reducing but not eliminating your financial responsibility. When you reserve or pick up the car, you'll be offered the chance to "buy down" the deductible to zero (for an

PRACTICALITIES

additional $10-30/day; this is sometimes called "super CDW" or "zero-deductible coverage").

If you opt for **credit-card coverage,** you must decline all coverage offered by the car-rental company—which means they can place a hold on your card for up to the full value of the car. In case of damage, it can be time-consuming to resolve the charges. Before relying on this option, quiz your card company about how it works.

If you're already purchasing a **travel-insurance policy** for your trip, adding collision coverage can be an economical option. For example, Travel Guard (www.travelguard.com) sells affordable renter's collision insurance as an add-on to its other policies; it's valid everywhere in Europe except the Republic of Ireland, and some Italian car-rental companies refuse to honor it, as it doesn't cover you in case of theft.

For more on car-rental insurance, see RickSteves.com/cdw.

Navigation Options

If you'll be navigating using your phone or a GPS unit from home, remember to bring a car charger and device mount.

Your Mobile Phone: The mapping app on your phone works fine for navigating Europe's roads, but for real-time turn-by-turn directions and traffic updates, you'll need mobile data access. And driving all day can burn through a lot of very expensive data. The economical work-around is to use map apps that work offline. By downloading in advance from Google Maps, City Maps 2Go, Apple Maps, Here WeGo, or Navmii, you can still have turn-by-turn voice directions and maps that recalibrate even though they're offline.

You must download your maps before you go offline—and it's smart to select large regions. Then turn off your data connection so you're not charged for roaming. Call up the map, enter your destination, and you're on your way. Even if you don't have to pay extra for data roaming, this option is great for navigating in areas with poor connectivity.

GPS Devices: If you want the convenience of a dedicated GPS unit, known as a "satnav" in Britain, consider renting one with your car ($10-30/day). These units offer real-time turn-by-turn directions and traffic without the data requirements of an app. The unit may come loaded only with maps for its home country; if you need additional maps, ask.

A less-expensive option is to bring a GPS device from home. Be sure to buy and install the maps you'll need before your trip.

Paper Maps and Atlases: Even when navigating primarily with a mobile app or GPS, I always make it a point to have a paper map, ideally a big, detailed regional road map. It's invaluable for getting the big picture, understanding alternate routes, and filling

in if my phone runs out of juice. The free maps you get from your car-rental company usually don't have enough detail. It's smart to buy a better map before you go, or pick one up at a local gas station, bookshop, newsstand, or tourist shop.

Several good road atlases cover all of Britain. Ordnance Survey, Collins, AA, and Bartholomew editions are all available at tourist information offices, gas stations, and bookstores. The tourist-oriented Collins Touring maps do a good job of highlighting the many roadside attractions you might otherwise drive right past. Before you buy a map, look at it to be sure it has the level of detail you want.

DRIVING IN BRITAIN

Driving here is basically wonderful—once you remember to stay on the left and after you've mastered the roundabouts. Every year, however, I get a few notes from traveling readers advising me that, for them, trying to drive in Britain was a nerve-racking and regrettable mistake. If you want to get a little slack on the roads, drop by a gas station or auto shop and buy a green *P* (probationary driver with license) sign to put in your car window (don't get the red *L* sign, which means you're a learner driver without a license and thus prohibited from driving on motorways).

Many Yankee drivers find the hardest part isn't driving on the left, but steering from the right. Your instinct is to put yourself on the left side of your lane, which means you may spend your first day or two drifting into the left shoulder or curb. It

STOP AND LEARN THESE ROAD SIGNS

Speed Limit (mph) · Yield · No Passing · End of No Passing Zone · One Way · Intersection · Roundabout Ahead · Expressway · Danger · No Entry · Cars Prohibited · All Vehicles Prohibited · No Through Road · Restrictions No Longer Apply · Yield to Oncoming Traffic · No Stopping · Parking · No Parking · Road Narrows · Peace

helps to remember that the driver always stays close to the center line.

Road Rules: Be aware of Britain's rules of the road. Seat belts are mandatory for all, and kids under age 12 (or less than about 4.5 feet tall) must ride in an appropriate child-safety seat. It's illegal to use a mobile phone while driving—pull over or use a hands-free device. In Britain, you're not allowed to turn left on a red light unless a sign or signal specifically authorizes it, and on motorways it's illegal to pass drivers on the left. Ask your car-rental company about these rules, or check the "International Travel" section of the US State Department website (www.travel.state.gov, search for your country in the "Learn About Your Destination" box, then click "Travel and Transportation").

Speed Limits: Speed limits are in miles per hour: 30 mph in town, 70 mph on the motorways, and 60 or 70 mph elsewhere (though, as back home, many British drivers consider these limits advisory). The national sign for the maximum speed is a white circle with a black slash. Motorways have electronic speed limit signs; posted speeds can change depending on traffic or the weather. Follow them accordingly.

Note that road-surveillance cameras strictly enforce speed limits. Any driver (including foreigners renting cars) photographed speeding will get a nasty bill in the mail. (Cameras—in foreboding gray boxes—flash on rear license plates to respect the privacy of anyone sharing the front seat with someone he or she shouldn't.) Signs (an image of an old-fashioned camera) alert

you when you're entering a zone that may be monitored by these "camera cops." Heed them.

Roundabouts: Don't let a roundabout spook you. After all, you routinely merge into much faster traffic on American highways back home. Traffic flows clockwise, and cars already in the roundabout have the right-of-way; entering traffic yields (look to your right as you merge). You'll probably encounter "double-round-abouts"—figure-eights where you'll slingshot from one roundabout directly into another. Just go with the flow and track signs carefully. When approaching an especially complex roundabout, you'll first pass a diagram showing the layout and the various exits. And in many cases, the pavement is painted to indicate the lane you should be in for a particular road or town.

Freeways (Motorways): The shortest distance between any two points is usually the motorway (what we'd call a "freeway"). In Britain, the smaller the number, the bigger the road. For example, the M-8 is a freeway, while the B-8000 is a country road.

Motorway road signs can be confusing, too few, and too late. Miss a motorway exit and you can lose 30 minutes. Study your map before taking off. Know the cities you'll be lacing together, since road numbers are inconsistent. British road signs are never marked with compass directions (e.g., *A-9 North*); instead, you need to know what major town or city you're heading for *(A-9 Inverness)*. The driving directions in this book are intended to be used with a good map. Get a road atlas, easily purchased at gas stations in Britain, or download digital maps before your trip (see page 504).

Unless you're passing, always drive in the "slow" lane on mo-

PRACTICALITIES

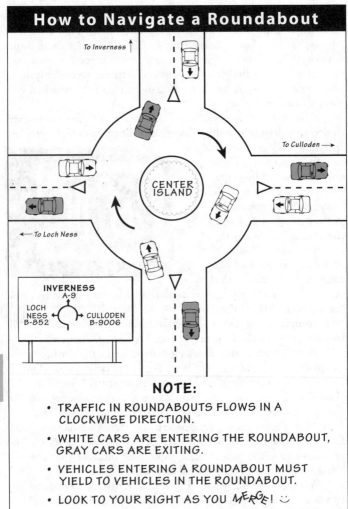

How to Navigate a Roundabout

NOTE:

- TRAFFIC IN ROUNDABOUTS FLOWS IN A CLOCKWISE DIRECTION.

- WHITE CARS ARE ENTERING THE ROUNDABOUT, GRAY CARS ARE EXITING.

- VEHICLES ENTERING A ROUNDABOUT MUST YIELD TO VEHICLES IN THE ROUNDABOUT.

- LOOK TO YOUR RIGHT AS YOU MERGE! ☺

torways (the lane farthest to the left). The British are very disciplined about this; ignoring this rule could get you a ticket (or into a road-rage incident). Remember to pass on the right, not the left.

Rest areas are called "services" and often have a number of useful amenities, such as restaurants, cafeterias, gas stations, shops, and motels.

Fuel: Gas (petrol) costs about $5.50 per gallon and is self-serve. Pump first and then pay. Diesel costs about the same. Diesel rental cars are common; make sure you know what kind of fuel your car takes before you fill up. Unleaded pumps are usually green.

Note that self-service gas pumps and automated toll booths and parking garages often accept only a chip-and-PIN credit card or cash. It might help if you know the PIN for your US credit and debit cards, but just in case a machine rejects them, be sure to carry sufficient cash. For more on chip and PIN, see page 461.

Driving in Cities: Whenever possible, avoid driving in cities. Most cities have modern ring roads to skirt the congestion. Follow signs to the parking lots outside the city core—most are a 5- to 10-minute walk to the center—and avoid what can be an unpleasant grid of one-way streets or roads that are only available to public transportation during the day.

Driving in Rural Areas: Outside the big cities and except for the motorways, British roads tend to be narrow. In towns, you may have to cross over the center line just to get past parked cars. Adjust your perceptions of personal space: It's not "my side of the road" or "your side of the road," it's just "the road"—and it's shared as a cooperative adventure. If the road's wide enough, traffic in both directions can pass parked cars simultaneously, but frequently you'll have to take turns—follow the locals' lead and drive defensively.

Narrow country lanes are often lined with stone walls or woody hedges—and no shoulders. Some are barely wide enough for one car (one-lane roads are often referred to as "single-track" roads). Go slowly, and if you encounter an oncoming car, look for the nearest pullout (or "passing place")—the driver who's closest to one is expected to use it, even if it means backing up to reach it. If another car pulls over and blinks its headlights, that means, "Go ahead; I'll wait to let you pass." British drivers—arguably some of the most courteous on the planet—are quick to offer a friendly wave to thank you for letting them pass (and they appreciate it if you reciprocate). Pull over frequently—to let faster locals pass and to check the map.

Parking: Pay attention to pavement markings to figure out where to park. One yellow line marked on the pavement means no parking Monday through Saturday during work hours. Double yellow lines mean no parking at any time. Broken yellow lines mean short stops are OK, but you should always look for explicit signs or ask a passerby. White lines mean you're free to park.

In towns, rather than look for street parking, I generally just pull into the most central and handy pay-and-display parking lot I can find. To pay and display, feed change into a machine, receive a timed ticket, and display it on the dashboard or stick it to the driver's-side window. Rates are reasonable by US standards, and locals love to share stickers that have time remaining. If you stand by the machine, someone on their way out with time left on their sticker will probably give it to you. Most machines in larger towns accept credit cards with a chip, but it's smart to keep coins handy for machines that don't.

In some municipalities, drivers will see signs for "disc zone" parking. This is free, time-limited parking. But to use it, you must obtain a clock parking disc from a shop and display it on the dashboard (set the clock to show your time of arrival). Return within the signed time limit to avoid being ticketed.

Some parking garages (a.k.a. car parks) are automated and record your license plate with a camera when you enter. The Brits call a license plate a "number plate" or just "vehicle registration." The payment machine will use these terms when you pay before exiting.

FLIGHTS

To compare flight costs and times, begin with an online travel search engine: Kayak is the top site for flights to and within Europe, easy-to-use Google Flights has price alerts, and Skyscanner includes many inexpensive flights within Europe. To avoid unpleasant surprises, before you book be sure to read the small print about refunds, changes, and the costs for "extras" such as reserving a seat, checking a bag, or printing a boarding pass.

Flights to Europe: Start looking for international flights about four to six months before your trip, especially for peak-season travel. Depending on your itinerary, it can be efficient and no more expensive to fly into one city and out of another. If your flight requires a connection in Europe, see my hints on navigating Europe's top hub airports at RickSteves.com/hub-airports.

Flights Within Europe: Flying between European cities is surprisingly affordable. Before buying a long-distance train or bus ticket, check the cost of a flight on one of Europe's airlines, whether a major carrier or a no-frills outfit like **EasyJet** or **Ryanair.** Well-known cheapo airlines that serve Scotland include **EasyJet** (www.easyjet.com), **Ryanair** (www.ryanair.com), **TUI Airways** (www.tui.co.uk), and **Flybe** (www.flybe.com).

Be aware that flying with a discount airline can have drawbacks, such as minimal customer service and time-consuming treks to secondary airports.

Flying to the US and Canada: Because security is extra tight for flights to the US, be sure to give yourself plenty of time at the airport. Charge your electronic devices before you board in case security checks require you to turn them on (see www.tsa.gov for the latest rules).

PRACTICALITIES

Resources from Rick Steves

Begin Your Trip at RickSteves.com

My mobile-friendly **website** is *the* place to explore Europe in preparation for your trip. You'll find thousands of fun articles, videos, and radio interviews; a wealth of money-saving tips for planning your dream trip; travel news dispatches; a video library of my travel talks; my travel blog; my latest guidebook updates (www.ricksteves.com/update); and my free Rick Steves Audio Europe app. You can also follow me on Facebook, Instagram, and Twitter.

Our **Travel Forum** is a well-groomed collection of message boards, where our travel-savvy community answers questions and shares their personal travel experiences—and our well-traveled staff chimes in when they can be helpful (www.ricksteves.com/forums).

Our **online Travel Store** offers bags and accessories that I've designed to help you travel smarter and lighter. These include my popular carry-on bags (which I live out of four months a year), money belts, totes, toiletries kits, adapters, guidebooks, and planning maps (www.ricksteves.com/shop).

Our website can also help you find the perfect **rail pass** for your itinerary and your budget, with easy, one-stop shopping for rail passes, seat reservations, and point-to-point tickets (www.ricksteves.com/rail).

Rick Steves' Tours, Guidebooks, TV Shows, and More

Small Group Tours: Want to travel with greater efficiency and less stress? We offer more than 40 itineraries reaching the best destinations in this book...and beyond. Each year about 30,000 travelers join us on about 1,000 Rick Steves bus tours. You'll enjoy great guides and a fun bunch of travel partners (with small groups of 24 to 28 travelers). You'll find European adventures to fit every vacation length. For all the details, and to get our tour catalog, visit www.ricksteves.com/tours or call us at 425/608-4217.

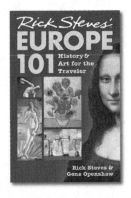

Books: *Rick Steves Scotland* is just one of many books in my series on European travel, which includes country and city guidebooks, Snapshots (excerpted chapters from bigger guides), Pocket guides (full-color little books on big cities), "Best Of" guidebooks (condensed, full-color country guides), and my budget-travel skills handbook, *Rick Steves Europe Through the Back Door*. A complete list of my titles—including phrase books, cruising guides, and travelogues on European art, history, and culture—appears near the end of this book.

TV Shows and Travel Talks: My public television series, *Rick Steves' Europe,* covers Europe from top to bottom with over 100 half-hour episodes—and we're working on new shows every year (watch full episodes at my website for free). My free online video library, Rick Steves Classroom Europe, offers a searchable database of short video clips on European history, culture, and geography (classroom.ricksteves.com). And to raise your travel I.Q., check out the video versions of our popular classes (covering most European countries as well as travel skills, packing smart, cruising, tech for travelers, European art, and travel as a political act—www.ricksteves.com/travel-talks.

Radio: My weekly public radio show, *Travel with Rick Steves,* features interviews with travel experts from around the world. It airs on 400 public radio stations across the US, or you can hear it as a podcast. A complete archive of programs is available at www.ricksteves.com/radio.

Audio Tours on My Free App: I've produced dozens of free, self-guided audio tours of the top sights in Europe. For those tours and other audio content, get my free **Rick Steves Audio Europe app,** an extensive online library organized by destination. For more on my app, see page 26.

APPENDIX

Holidays and Festivals

This list includes selected festivals in Scotland plus national holidays observed throughout Britain. Many sights and banks close on national holidays—keep this in mind when planning your itinerary. Before planning a trip around a festival, verify the dates with the festival website, the Visit Scotland website (www.visitscotland.com), or my "Upcoming Holidays and Festivals in Scotland" webpage (www.ricksteves.com/europe/scotland/festivals).

During July and August, book as far ahead as possible; Edinburgh is particularly jammed up in August during its festival season. Hotels also get booked up during Easter week; over the early May, spring, and summer Bank Holidays; and during Christmas, Boxing Day, and New Year's Day. On Christmas, virtually everything shuts down. Museums also generally close December 24 and 26.

Throughout the summer, communities small and large across Scotland host their annual Highland Games (like a combination track meet/county fair). These are a wonderful way to get in touch with local culture and traditions (see page 252).

Some Scottish towns have holiday festivals in late November and early December, with markets, music, and entertainment in the Christmas spirit.

Jan 1	New Year's Day (closures)
Jan 2	New Year's Holiday (closures)
Jan 25	Burns Night (poetry readings, haggis)
April	Easter Sunday-Monday: April 12-13, 2020; April 4-5, 2021
May	Early May Bank Holiday: May 4, 2020; May 3, 2021; Spring Bank Holiday: May 25, 2020; May 31, 2021
June	Edinburgh International Film Festival (www.edfilmfest.org.uk)
Mid-June	Royal Highland Show, Edinburgh (Scottish-flavored county fair, www.royalhighlandshow.org)
July	Edinburgh Jazz and Blues Festival (www.edinburghjazzfestival.com)
Early Aug	Summer Bank Holiday: August 3, 2020; August 2, 2021
Aug	Edinburgh Military Tattoo (massing of military bands, www.edintattoo.co.uk)
Aug	Edinburgh Fringe Festival (offbeat theater and comedy, www.edfringe.com)
Aug	Edinburgh International Festival (music, dance, shows, www.eif.co.uk)
Late Aug	Cowal Highland Gathering, west of Glasgow in Dunoon
Early Sept	Braemar Gathering, north of Pitlochry (first Sat)
Oct	Royal National Mòd (Gaelic cultural festival, www.ancomunn.co.uk)
Nov 5	Guy Fawkes Night (fireworks, bonfires, effigy-burning of 1605 traitor Guy Fawkes)
Nov 30	St. Andrew's Day (dancing and other cultural events); Bank Holiday
Dec 24-26	Christmas holidays
Dec 31-Jan 2	Hogmanay (music, street theater, carnival, www.hogmanay.net)

Books and Films

To learn more about Scotland past and present, check out a few of these books or films.

Nonfiction

Crowded with Genius (James Buchan, 2003). This account of Edinburgh's role in the Scottish Enlightenment details the city's transformation from squalid backwater to marvelous European capital.

Edinburgh: Picturesque Notes (Robert Louis Stevenson, 1879). One of the city's most famous residents takes readers on a tour of his hometown.

The Emperor's New Kilt (Jan-Andrew Henderson, 2000). Henderson deconstructs the myths surrounding the tartan-clad Scots.

The Guynd (Belinda Rathbone, 2005). The marriage of an American woman and a Scottish man endures through cultural gaps and household mishaps.

How the Scots Invented the Modern World (Arthur Herman, 2001). The author explains the disproportionately large influence the Scottish Enlightenment had on the rest of Europe.

The Life of Samuel Johnson (James Boswell, 1790). Scottish laird Boswell's portrait of his contemporary is so admired that it inspired the use of Boswell's name to mean a close and companionable observer (Sherlock Holmes, for instance, at times refers to Watson as "my Boswell").

Mary Queen of Scots (Antonia Fraser, 1969). The life and times of Mary Stuart, whose rocky tenure as queen of Scotland was as dramatic as it was tragic, finally ending when her cousin Queen Elizabeth I executed her for treason.

Scotland: The Autobiography: 2,000 Years of Scottish History by Those Who Saw It Happen (Rosemary Goring, 2007). Extracts from primary sources let a diverse cast of real-life characters, from Tacitus to Muriel Spark, tell the story of the nation.

Sea Room (Adam Nicolson, 2001). The owner of three tiny islands in the Hebrides contemplates their magical appeal and dramatic history.

A Traveller's History of Scotland (Andrew Fisher, revised 2009). Fisher probes Scotland's turbulent history, beginning with the Celts.

Fiction

For the classics of Scottish drama and fiction, read the "Big Three": Sir Walter Scott, Robert Louis Stevenson, and poet Robert Burns.

44 Scotland Street (Alexander McCall Smith, 2005). The colorful residents of an Edinburgh apartment house bring Scottish society to life.

Complete Poems and Songs of Robert Burns (Robert Burns, 2012, featuring work from 1774–1796). This collection showcases the work of a Scottish icon who wrote in the Scots language, including that New Year's classic "Auld Lang Syne."

The Cone Gatherers (Robin Jenkins, 1980). A staple of British secondary-school reading lists, this tragic novel about two brothers is set on a Scottish country estate during World War II.

Consider Phlebas (Iain M. Banks, 1987). In this first book in the popular *The Culture* science fiction series, Scottish author Banks describes a galactic war.

The Heart of Midlothian (Sir Walter Scott, 1818). This novel from one of Great Britain's most renowned authors showcases the life-and-death drama of lynchings and criminal justice in 1730s Scotland. Other great reads by Sir Walter include *Waverley* (1814), *Rob Roy* (1818), and *Ivanhoe* (1819).

Knots and Crosses (Ian Rankin, 1987). The Scottish writer's first Inspector Rebus mystery plumbs Edinburgh's seamy underbelly.

Lanark (Alasdair Gray, 1981). This eccentric, sprawling four-part novel set in Glasgow (and a fictional alt-Glasgow) tackles huge themes—capitalism, power, love—and earned Gray a reputation as a great Scottish writer.

Macbeth (William Shakespeare, 1606). Shakespeare's "Scottish Play" depicts a guilt-wracked general who assassinates the king to take the throne.

Outlander (Diana Gabaldon, 1991). This genre-defying series kicks off with the heroine time-traveling from the Scotland of 1945 to 1743. Later novels trace the Battle of Culloden, repression of Highland culture, and emigration to the Americas. A popular TV adaptation began airing in 2014.

The Prime of Miss Jean Brodie (Muriel Spark, 1961). The story of an unconventional young teacher who plays favorites with her students is a modern classic of Scottish literature. (The film adaptation from 1969 stars Maggie Smith.)

The Strange Case of Dr. Jekyll and Mr. Hyde (Robert Louis Stevenson, 1886). This famous Gothic yarn by a Scottish author chronicles a fearful case of transformation in London, exploring Victorian ideas about conflict between good and evil.

Sunset Song (Lewis Grassic Gibbon, 1932). Farm girl Chris Guthrie is rudely confronted by adolescence, modernity, and war in this lauded Scottish classic, the first book in the trilogy "A Scots Quair."

APPENDIX

Film and TV

The 39 Steps (1935). This Alfred Hitchcock classic about a London man wrongly accused of murder is set in Edinburgh, Glencoe, and other parts of the Scottish countryside.

The Angels' Share (2012). In this working-class comedy, a Glaswegian ne'er-do-well discovers he has a great nose for whisky.

Braveheart (1995). Mel Gibson stars in this Academy Award-winning adventure about the Scots overthrowing English rule in the 13th century.

Brigadoon (1954). In this classic musical, an American couple visiting Scotland discover a magical village.

Highlander (1986). An immortal swordsman remembers his life in 16th-century Scotland while preparing for a pivotal battle in the present day.

A History of Scotland (2010). This BBC series presented by Neil Oliver offers a succinct, lightly dramatized retelling of Scottish history.

Local Hero (1983). A businessman questions his decision to build an oil refinery in a small Scottish town once he gets a taste for country life.

Loch Ness (1996). A skeptical American scientist is sent to Scotland to investigate the existence of the Loch Ness monster.

Mary, Queen of Scots (2018). Saoirse Ronan stars in this portrayal of Mary upon her return to Scotland (from France) and her complicated relationship with cousin Elizabeth I. (A 1971 movie of the same name stars Vanessa Redgrave and Glenda Jackson.)

Monarch of the Glen (2000). Set on Loch Laggan, this TV series features stunning Highland scenery and the eccentric family of a modern-day laird.

Mrs. Brown (1997). A widowed Queen Victoria (Dame Judy Dench) forges a very close friendship with her Scottish servant, John Brown (Billy Connolly).

One Day (2011). Two University of Edinburgh students meet and fall in love on their graduation day, and their story continues to be told at each anniversary.

The Queen (2006). Helen Mirren expertly channels Elizabeth II at her Scottish Balmoral estate in the days after Princess Diana's death.

Rob Roy (1995). The Scottish rebel played by Liam Neeson struggles against feudal landlords in 18th-century Scotland.

Skyfall (2012). In this James Bond film, we learn that 007 grew up in the Scottish Highlands, with a climactic scene at his childhood home (filmed near Glencoe).

Stone of Destiny (2008). Glaswegian students sneak into Westminster Abbey to retrieve the Stone of Scone for Scotland. Ian

APPENDIX

Outlander Locations in Scotland

American novelist Diana Gabaldon's *Outlander* series spans continents and centuries, but the origin story—that of a Highlands laird and an English combat nurse caught up in the Jacobite rebellion—is grounded in Scotland. Much of the Starz television adaptation was filmed here. *Outlander* fans may enjoy seeing some of the following landmarks.

Outlander begins with Claire Randall on her honeymoon in 1945 **Inverness** (see page 350)—played on TV by **Falkland** village, near St. Andrews. Claire is mysteriously transported back in time to 1743 at **Craig na Dun,** a fictional stone circle inspired by **Clava Cairns** near Inverness (page 372). The TV version was filmed at **Dunalastair Estate,** between Pitlochry and Loch Rannoch.

Claire is rescued by the MacKenzie clan and tends to injured Highlander Jamie Fraser. They travel to the fictional **Castle Leoch,** seat of the Clan Mackenzie (the real-life Mackenzie home is Castle Leod, near Strathpeffer). Exterior scenes at Castle Leoch were filmed at **Doune Castle** near Stirling (page 209); the grounds—where Claire gathers herbs—were filmed in **Pollok County Park** (near Glasgow's Burrell Collection; page 173).

Claire meets the "witch" Geillis Duncan in fictional **Cranesmuir** village, but **Culross,** with its distinctive mercat cross (page 208) is a fine onscreen stand-in. The stone-and-thatched village where the MacKenzies collect rents was filmed at the **Highland Folk Museum** (page 391). Claire and Jamie visit the fictional Fraser family homestead, **Lallybroch** (on TV the deserted country estate of **Midhope Castle**—closed to the public).

In the books, Black Jack Randall's stout stone fortress is at **Fort William** (page 305); for TV those scenes were filmed at **Blackness Castle** on the Firth of Forth. Nearby, **Linlithgow Palace** is the filming location for the fictional **Wentworth Prison** (where Black Jack imprisons—and Claire rescues—Jamie), and **Aberdour Castle** plays the monastery where Jamie recovers. Scenes at **Ardsmuir Prison,** where Jamie is interned after the Battle of Culloden, were filmed at **Craigmillar Castle,** on the outskirts of Edinburgh. **Carfax Close,** where A. Malcolm has his print shop, is fictional—and played on TV by Edinburgh's very real **Tweeddale Court** and **Bakehouse Close.**

Many of the show's interior scenes are filmed at **Wardpark Studios,** a former factory converted into Scotland's first permanent film studio for *Outlander.* For more *Outlander* locations, see VisitScotland.com/outlander.

Hamilton, who led the 1950 raid in real life, has a bit part in the film (and co-wrote the script).

Trainspotting (1996). Ewan McGregor stars in this award-winning, wild, gritty picture about Edinburgh's drug scene in the 1980s. In *T2 Trainspotting* (2017), McGregor's character returns to Edinburgh 20 years later to reconnect with his buddies.

For Kids

Always Room for One More (Sorche Nic Leodhas, 1965). This Caldecott Medal-winning picture book presents a Scottish folktale with evocative illustrations.

Bagpipes, Beasties and Bogles (Tim Archbold, 2012). This whimsical story about spooky creatures and bagpipes serves up Scottish culture in a package perfect for young readers.

Brave (2012). This Disney flick follows an independent young Scottish princess as she fights to take control of her own fate.

Greyfriars Bobby (2005). Based on a true story, this family-friendly film is about a terrier in Edinburgh who became a local legend after refusing to leave his master's gravesite.

An Illustrated Treasury of Scottish Folk and Fairy Tales (Theresa Breslin, 2012). Kelpies, dragons, brownies, and other inhabitants of the Scottish Isles come to life in this lovely volume of traditional lore.

Kidnapped (Robert Louis Stevenson, 1886). This fantastic adventure story is based on events in 18th-century Scotland.

The Luck of the Loch Ness Monster (A. W. Flaherty, 2007). A picky American girl on a boat to Scotland throws her oatmeal out the porthole every morning, unwittingly feeding the Loch Ness monster that follows her.

Queen's Own Fool (Jane Yolen and Robert Harris, 2008). A historical novel for 10-and-ups based on the girl who was a jester in the court of Mary, Queen of Scots, the first of the "Stuart Quartet" books.

The Story of Scotland (Richard Brassey and Stewart Ross, 1999). This humorous, comic-book style history book will engage young travelers.

This Is Edinburgh (Miroslav Sasek, 1961, updated 2006). Vivid illustrations bring the Scottish capital to life in this classic picture book.

The Water Horse (2007). In this film based on a book of the same name, a young boy in 1940s Scotland discovers an egg, which later hatches into the fabled Loch Ness monster.

APPENDIX

Conversions and Climate

Numbers and Stumblers

- Some British people write a few of their numbers differently than we do: 1=1, 4=4, 7=7.
- In Europe, dates appear as day/month/year, so Christmas 2021 is 25/12/21.
- What Americans call the second floor of a building is the first floor in Scotland.
- On escalators and moving sidewalks, Scots keep the left "lane" open for passing. Keep to the right.
- To avoid the Scottish version of giving someone "the finger," don't hold up the first two fingers of your hand with your palm facing you. (It looks like a reversed victory sign.)

Metric Conversions

Scotland uses the metric system for nearly everything. Weight and volume are typically calculated in metric: A kilogram is 2.2 pounds, and one liter is about a quart (almost four to a gallon). Temperatures are generally given in Celsius, although some newspapers also list them in Fahrenheit.

1 foot = 0.3 meter	1 square yard = 0.8 square meter
1 yard = 0.9 meter	1 square mile = 2.6 square kilometers
1 mile = 1.6 kilometers	1 ounce = 28 grams
1 centimeter = 0.4 inch	1 quart = 0.95 liter
1 meter = 39.4 inches	1 kilogram = 2.2 pounds
1 kilometer = 0.62 mile	32°F = 0°C

Imperial Weights and Measures

Scotland hasn't completely gone metric. Driving distances and speed limits are measured in miles. Beer is sold as pints (though milk can be measured in pints or liters), and a person's weight is measured in stone (a 168-pound person weighs 12 stone).

1 stone = 14 pounds
1 Scottish pint = 1.2 US pints
1 schooner = 2/3 pint
1 imperial gallon = 1.2 US gallons or about 4.5 liters

Clothing Sizes

When shopping for clothing, use these US-to-UK comparisons as general guidelines (but note that no conversion is perfect).

Women: For pants and dresses, add 4 (US 10 = UK 14). For blouses and sweaters, add 2. For shoes, subtract 2½ (US size 8 = UK size 5½)

Men: For clothing, US and UK sizes are the same. For shoes, subtract about ½ (US size 9 = UK size 8½)

Children: Clothing is sized similarly to the US. UK kids' shoe sizes are about one size smaller (US size 6 = UK size 5).

Scotland's Climate

First line, average daily high; second line, average daily low; third line, average days without rain. For more detailed weather statistics for destinations in this book (and elsewhere), check www.wunderground.com.

J	F	M	A	M	J	J	A	S	O	N	D

EDINBURGH

42°	43°	46°	51°	56°	62°	65°	64°	60°	54°	48°	44°
34°	34°	36°	39°	43°	49°	52°	52°	49°	44°	39°	36°
14	13	16	16	17	15	14	15	14	14	13	13

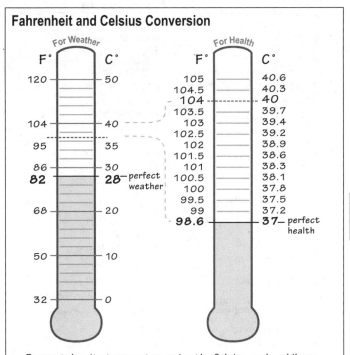

Fahrenheit and Celsius Conversion

Europe takes its temperature using the Celsius scale, while we opt for Fahrenheit. For a rough conversion from Celsius to Fahrenheit, double the number and add 30. For weather, remember that 28°C is 82°F—perfect. For health, 37°C is just right. At a launderette, 30°C is cold, 40°C is warm (usually the default setting), 60°C is hot, and 95°C is boiling. Your air-conditioner should be set at about 20°C.

APPENDIX

Packing Checklist

Whether you're traveling for five days or five weeks, you won't need more than this. Pack light to enjoy the sweet freedom of true mobility.

Clothing

- ☐ 5 shirts: long- & short-sleeve
- ☐ 2 pairs pants (or skirts/capris)
- ☐ 1 pair shorts
- ☐ 5 pairs underwear & socks
- ☐ 1 pair walking shoes
- ☐ Sweater or warm layer
- ☐ Rainproof jacket with hood
- ☐ Tie, scarf, belt, and/or hat
- ☐ Swimsuit
- ☐ Sleepwear/loungewear

Money

- ☐ Debit card(s)
- ☐ Credit card(s)
- ☐ Hard cash (US $100-200)
- ☐ Money belt

Documents

- ☐ Passport
- ☐ Tickets & confirmations: flights, hotels, trains, rail pass, car rental, sight entries
- ☐ Driver's license
- ☐ Student ID, hostel card, etc.
- ☐ Photocopies of important documents
- ☐ Insurance details
- ☐ Guidebooks & maps

Toiletries Kit

- ☐ Basics: soap, shampoo, toothbrush, toothpaste, floss, deodorant, sunscreen, brush/comb, etc.
- ☐ Medicines & vitamins
- ☐ First-aid kit
- ☐ Glasses/contacts/sunglasses
- ☐ Sewing kit
- ☐ Packet of tissues (for WC)
- ☐ Earplugs

Electronics

- ☐ Mobile phone
- ☐ Camera & related gear
- ☐ Tablet/ebook reader/laptop
- ☐ Headphones/earbuds
- ☐ Chargers & batteries
- ☐ Phone car charger & mount (or GPS device)
- ☐ Plug adapters

Miscellaneous

- ☐ Daypack
- ☐ Sealable plastic baggies
- ☐ Laundry supplies: soap, laundry bag, clothesline, spot remover
- ☐ Small umbrella
- ☐ Travel alarm/watch
- ☐ Notepad & pen
- ☐ Journal

Optional Extras

- ☐ Second pair of shoes (flip-flops, sandals, tennis shoes, boots)
- ☐ Travel hairdryer
- ☐ Picnic supplies
- ☐ Water bottle
- ☐ Fold-up tote bag
- ☐ Small flashlight
- ☐ Mini binoculars
- ☐ Small towel or washcloth
- ☐ Inflatable pillow/neck rest
- ☐ Tiny lock
- ☐ Address list (to mail postcards)
- ☐ Extra passport photos

APPENDIX

Scots-Yankee Vocabulary

Scotch is the peaty drink the bartender serves you, but his nationality is Scottish; you could also call him a Scot, and the language he speaks is Scots. Confused? Don't be. Let's dive in. Here are some Scots words that may be unfamiliar, and others that may come in handy.

auld: old

aye: yes

bairn, wean: baby, child

blether, blather: talk, gossip

bonnie: beautiful, handsome, good

braw, barrie: good, fine

bridie: savory meat pie (like a pasty)

ceilidh: "kay-lee," traditional celebration with dancing and singing

chippie: fish-and-chip shop, often with a vast array of deep-fried meals, from pizza to candy bars

close: alley leading to a court-yard or square

cludgie, lavvy, dunny: toilet

deugin: stubborn

dreich: lousy, dismal weather

drouthy: thirsty (for a strong drink)

gaun yersel!: You can do it! (words of encouragement)

haud yer wheesht: Shut up

ken: to know ("Ah dinnae ken"—I don't know)

kirk: church

lang: long

mince: ground meat, often in pies or with tatties—potatoes

nae: no (as in "nae bother"—you're welcome)

neeps and tatties: turnips and potatoes

peely-wally: pale, ill, unwell

pend: arched gateway

pump, air beige: fart

pure barrie: wonderful

rank: disgusting

reekin', pisht, blootered, para-lytic: drunk

scran: food

steamin': drunk

stramash: commotion

tattie scone: potato pancake

wee: small

wheesht!: shush!

wynd: narrow winding lane connecting major streets

Many Scots (and Gaelic) words relate to geography, and often turn up in place names:

aber-, inver-: confluence or mouth of a river

bal: town

ben: mountain

blair: clearing

brae: slope, hilltop

burn: creek. stream

crag, creag: cliff, crag, rock

drum: ridge

dun, dum: hill fort

eilean: island

fell: hill

firth: estuary

glen: narrow valley

innis, inch: island

kyle: strait

loch, lochan: lake, small lake

muir: moor

sea loch: inlet

strath: river valley

While Scotland has its own unique lexicon, Scottish people speak fluent English using many of the island-wide expressions that span Britain, from John O'Groats in the north of Scotland to Land's End at England's southern tip.

advert: advertisement

afters: dessert

anticlockwise: counterclockwise

aubergine: eggplant

bangers and mash: sausage and mashed potatoes

bap: small roll, roll sandwich

biro: ballpoint pen

biscuit: cookie

bloody: damn

bobby, rozzer: policeman ("the Bill" is more common)

Bob's your uncle: there you go, there you have it (with a shrug), naturally

boffin: nerd, geek

bollocks: all-purpose expletive (a figurative use of testicles)

bolshy: argumentative, aggressive

bonnet: car hood

boot: car trunk

braces: suspenders

bridle way: path for walkers, bikers, and horse riders

brilliant: cool, awesome

brolly: umbrella

bubble and squeak: cabbage and potatoes fried together

candy floss: cotton candy

caravan: trailer

car-boot sale: temporary flea market, often for charity

car park: parking lot

casualty, infirmary: emergency room

cat's eyes: road reflectors

cheap and cheerful: budget but adequate

cheap and nasty: cheap and bad quality

chemist: pharmacist

chips: French fries

chuffed: pleased

clearway: road where you can't stop

coach: long-distance bus

concession, concs: discounted admission

coronation chicken: curried chicken salad

cos: romaine lettuce

cot: baby crib

cotton buds: Q-tips

courgette: zucchini

crisps: potato chips

cuppa: cup of tea

dear: expensive

digestives: round graham cookies

dogsbody: menial worker, underappreciated staff

donkey's years: ages, long time

draughts: checkers

dual carriageway: divided highway (four lanes)

dummy: pacifier

elevenses: coffee-and-biscuits break before lunch

face flannel: washcloth

faggot: fried meatball

fancy: to like, to be attracted to (a person)

fiver: £5 bill

fizzy drink: pop or soda

flutter: a bet

football, footie: soccer

fortnight: two weeks (shortened from "fourteen nights")

fringe: hair bangs

Frogs: French people

fruit machine: slot machine

APPENDIX

full Monty: whole shebang, everything
gallery: balcony
gammon: ham; also an older person with right-wing views
gangway: aisle
ganja: marijuana
gaol: jail (same pronunciation)
gateau (or gateaux): cake
gear lever: stick shift
geezer: "dude"
goods wagon: freight truck
gormless: stupid
goujons: breaded and fried fish or chicken sticks
green fingers: green thumbs
half eight: 8:30 (not 7:30)
hard cheese: bad luck
hen night (or **hen do**): bachelor-ette party
homely: homey or cozy
hoover: vacuum cleaner
ice lolly: Popsicle
interval: intermission
ironmonger: hardware store
jacket potato: baked potato
jelly: Jell-O
jiggery-pokery: nonsense, shenanigans
Joe Bloggs: John Q. Public
jumble (sale): rummage sale
jumper: sweater
just a tick: just a second
kipper: smoked herring
knackered: exhausted (Cock-ney: cream crackered)
knickers: ladies' panties
knocking shop: brothel
ladybird: ladybug
lady fingers: flat, spongy cookie
lady's finger: okra
left luggage: baggage check
lemonade: lemon-lime soda
lemon squash: lemonade, not fizzy
let: rent

lift: elevator
loo: toilet or bathroom
lorry: truck
mack: mackintosh raincoat
mangetout: snow peas
marrow: summer squash
mate: buddy (boy or girl)
mean: stingy
mental: wild, memorable
moggie: cat
naff: tacky or trashy
nappy: diaper
natter: talk on and on
newsagent: corner store
nought: zero
noughts & crosses: tic-tac-toe
off-licence: liquor store
OTT: over the top, excessive
panto, pantomime: silly but fun play performed at Christmas
pants: (noun) underwear, briefs; (adj.) terrible, ridiculous
pear-shaped: messed up, gone wrong
petrol: gas
pillar box: mailbox
pissed (rude), **bevvied, wellied, popped up, merry, trollied, ratted, rat-arsed, pissed as a newt:** drunk
pitch: playing field
plaster: Band-Aid
plonk: cheap, bad wine
plonker: one who drinks bad wine (a mild insult)
prat: idiot
publican: pub owner
public school: private "prep" school (e.g., Eton)
pudding: dessert
pukka: first-class
pull, to be on the: on the prowl
punter: customer, especially in gambling
queue up: line up
quid: pound (£1)

randy: horny

rasher: slice of bacon

return ticket: round-trip

revising; doing revisions: studying for exams

rubber: eraser

rubbish: bad

satnav: satellite navigation, GPS

Scotch egg: hard-boiled egg wrapped in sausage meat and fried

self-catering: accommodation with kitchen

Sellotape: Scotch tape

services: freeway rest area

serviette: napkin

setee: couch

shag: intercourse (cruder than in the US)

shambolic: chaotic

shandy: lager and 7-Up

silencer: car muffler

single ticket: one-way ticket

single track: country road, often one lane

skip: Dumpster

sleeping policeman: speed bumps

smalls: underwear

snap: photo (snapshot)

snogging: kissing, necking, making out

sod: mildly offensive insult

sod it, sod off: screw it, screw off

sod's law: Murphy's law

soda: soda water (not pop)

soldiers: toast sticks for dipping

solicitor: lawyer

spanner: wrench

spend a penny: urinate

spotted dick: raisin cake with custard

stag night (or **stag do**): bachelor party

starkers: buck naked

starters: appetizers

state school: public school

sticking plaster: Band-Aid

sticky tape: Scotch tape

stone: 14 pounds (weight)

stroppy: bad-tempered

subway: underground walkway

surgical spirit: rubbing alcohol

suspenders: garters

swede: rutabaga

ta: thank you

take the mickey/take the piss: tease

tatty: worn out or tacky

taxi rank: taxi stand

tenner: £10 bill

tick: a check mark

tight as a fish's bum: cheapskate (watertight)

tin: can

tip: public dump

tipper lorry: dump truck

toad in the hole: sausage dipped in batter and fried

top hole: first rate

torch: flashlight

towel, press-on: panty liner

towpath: path along a river

trainers: sneakers

treacle: golden syrup

twee: quaint, cutesy

twitcher: bird-watcher

verge: grassy edge of road

verger: church official

wee (verb): urinate

Wellingtons, wellies: rubber boots

whacked: exhausted

whinge (rhymes with hinge): whine

wind up: tease, irritate

witter on: gab and gab

wonky: weird, askew

yob, chav, ned: hooligan

zebra crossing: crosswalk

zed: the letter Z

INDEX

INDEX

INDEX

MAP INDEX

Our website enhances this book and turns

Explore Europe

At ricksteves.com you can browse through thousands of articles, videos, photos and radio interviews, plus find a wealth of money-saving travel tips for planning your dream trip. And with our mobile-friendly website, you can easily access all this great travel information anywhere you go.

TV Shows

Preview the places you'll visit by watching entire half-hour episodes of *Rick Steves' Europe* (choose from all 100 shows) on-demand, for free.

your travel dreams into affordable reality

Radio Interviews

Enjoy ready access to Rick's vast library of radio interviews covering travel tips and cultural insights that relate specifically to your Europe travel plans.

Travel Forums

Learn, ask, share! Our online community of savvy travelers is a great resource for first-time travelers to Europe, as well as seasoned pros.

Travel News

Subscribe to our free Travel News e-newsletter, and get monthly updates from Rick on what's happening in Europe.

Classroom Europe

Check out our free resource for educators with 400+ short video clips from the *Rick Steves' Europe* TV show.

Rick's Free Travel App

Get your FREE **Rick Steves Audio Europe**™ app to enjoy…

- Dozens of self-guided tours of Europe's top museums, sights and historic walks
- Hundreds of tracks filled with cultural insights and sightseeing tips from Rick's radio interviews
- All organized into handy geographic playlists
- For Apple and Android

With Rick whispering in your ear, Europe gets even better.

Find out more at ricksteves.com

Gear up for your next adventure at ricksteves.com

Light Luggage

Pack light and right with Rick Steves' affordable, custom-designed rolling carry-on bags, backpacks, day packs and shoulder bags.

Accessories

From packing cubes to moneybelts and beyond, Rick has personally selected the travel goodies that will help your trip go smoother.

Shop at ricksteves.com

Experience maximum Europe

Save time and energy

This guidebook is your independent-travel toolkit. But for all it delivers, it's still up to you to devote the time and energy it takes to manage the preparation and logistics that are essential for a happy trip. If that's a hassle, there's a solution.

Rick Steves Tours

A Rick Steves tour takes you to Europe's most interesting places with great

with minimum stress

guides and small groups of 28 or less. We follow Rick's favorite itineraries, ride in comfy buses, stay in family-run hotels, and bring you intimately close to the Europe you've traveled so far to see. Most importantly, we take away the logistical headaches so you can focus on the fun.

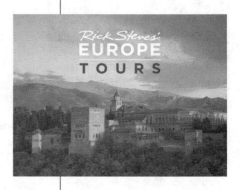

Join the fun

This year we'll take 33,000 free-spirited travelers—nearly half of them repeat customers—along with us on 50 different itineraries, from Athens to Istanbul. Is a Rick Steves tour the right fit for your travel dreams?

Find out at ricksteves.com, where you can also request Rick's latest tour catalog. Europe is best experienced with happy travel partners. We hope you can join us.

See our itineraries at ricksteves.com

BEST OF GUIDES

Full-color guides in an easy-to-scan format. Focused on top sights and experiences in the most popular European destinations

Best of England
Best of Europe
Best of France
Best of Germany
Best of Ireland
Best of Italy
Best of Scotland
Best of Spain

COMPREHENSIVE GUIDES

City, country, and regional guides printed on Bible-thin paper. Packed with detailed coverage for a multi-week trip exploring iconic sights and venturing off the beaten path

Amsterdam & the Netherlands
Barcelona
Belgium: Bruges, Brussels,
  Antwerp & Ghent
Berlin
Budapest
Croatia & Slovenia
Eastern Europe
England
Florence & Tuscany
France
Germany
Great Britain
Greece: Athens & the Peloponnese
Iceland
Ireland
Istanbul
Italy
London
Paris
Portugal
Prague & the Czech Republic
Provence & the French Riviera
Rome
Scandinavia
Scotland
Sicily
Spain
Switzerland
Venice
Vienna, Salzburg & Tirol

HE BEST OF ROME

, Italy's capital, is studded with
n remnants and floodlit-fountain
s. From the Vatican to the Colos-
with crazy traffic in between, Rome
erful, huge, and exhausting. The
the heat, and the weighty history

of the Eternal City where Caesars walked
can make tourists wilt. Recharge by taking siestas, gelato breaks, and after-dark
walks, strolling from one atmospheric
square to another in the refreshing evening air.

*Pantheon—which
dome until the
2,000 years old
over 1,500.*

*Athens in the Vat-
s the humanistic*

*diators fought
ther, entertaining*

ome ristorante

Rick Steves books are available from your favorite bookseller
Many guides are available as ebooks.

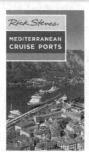

Credits

For help with this edition, Rick relied on. . .

RESEARCHERS
Ben Curtis

Ben is a native of the Pacific Northwest, but he's lived in the UK, Germany, Spain, Norway, Hungary, and a few other countries besides. He's worked as a professor of history and politics, a tour guide, and an advisor to the British government. These days, home is wherever he can go for a hike, listen to some Beethoven, and write.

Jessica Shaw

Jessica spent four years of her childhood living in Toulouse, France, begrudgingly dragged by her parents through countless museums across Europe. Little did she know, a childhood abroad would ignite her love of travel and inspire her career path. Jessica edits and researches guidebooks at Rick Steves' Europe, packing her free time with art projects and trips near and far with her partner, Felipe.

CONTRIBUTOR
Gene Openshaw

Gene has co-authored a dozen *Rick Steves* books, specializing in writing walks and tours of Europe's cities, museums, and cultural sights. He also contributes to Rick's public television series, produces tours for Rick Steves Audio Europe, and is a regular guest on Rick's public radio show. Outside of the travel world, Gene has co-authored *The Seattle Joke Book.* As a composer, Gene has written a full-length opera called *Matter,* a violin sonata, and dozens of songs. He lives near Seattle with his daughter, enjoys giving presentations on art and history, and roots for the Mariners in good times and bad.

ACKNOWLEDGMENTS

Thanks to Jennifer Hauseman for the original version of the Glasgow chapter and to Colin Mairs for his help in Glasgow and throughout this book.

PHOTO CREDITS

Front Cover: Inner Hebrides, Isle of Skye © Maurizio Rellini/SIME/ eStock Photo

Back Cover (left to right): © Shaiith/Dreamstime, © Craig Hastings/ Dreamstime, © Jim Ryce/Dreamstime

Title Page: © Dominic Arizona Bonuccelli

Public Domain via Wikimedia Commons: 7 (bottom), 69, 73, 92, 369, 432, 443

Additional Photography: Dominic Arizona Bonuccelli, Rich Earl, Jennifer Hauseman, Cameron Hewitt, David C. Hoerlein, Lauren Mills, Rhonda Pelikan, Jennifer Schutte, Rick Steves, Gretchen Strauch, Wikimedia Commons(PD-Art/PD-US), © Stephen C. Dickson cc BY-SA 4.0. Photos are used by permission and are the property of the original copyright owners.

Avalon Travel
Hachette Book Group
1700 Fourth Street
Berkeley, CA 94710

Text © 2020 by Rick Steves' Europe, Inc. All rights reserved.
Maps © 2020 by Rick Steves' Europe, Inc. All rights reserved.

Printed in Canada by Friesens.
Third Edition. First printing April 2020.

ISBN 978-1-64171-226-2

For the latest on Rick's talks, guidebooks, tours, public television series, and public radio
show, contact Rick Steves' Europe, 130 Fourth Avenue North, Edmonds, WA 98020,
425/771-8303, www.ricksteves.com, rick@ricksteves.com.

Hachette Book Group supports the right to free expression and the value of copyright. The
purpose of copyright is to encourage writers and artists to produce the creative works that
enrich our culture. The scanning, uploading, and distribution of this book without permission is a theft of the author's intellectual property. If you would like permission to use material from the book (other than for review purposes), please contact permissions@hbgusa.
com. Thank you for your support of the author's rights. The publisher is not responsible for
websites (or their content) that are not owned by the publisher.

Rick Steves' Europe
Managing Editor: Jennifer Madison Davis
Assistant Managing Editor: Cathy Lu
Special Publications Manager: Risa Laib
Editors: Glenn Eriksen, Julie Fanselow, Tom Griffin, Suzanne Kotz, Rosie Leutzinger,
  Jessica Shaw, Carrie Shepherd
Editorial & Production Assistant: Megan Simms
Editorial Intern: Bridgette Robertson
Researchers: Ben Curtis, Jessica Shaw
Contributor: Gene Openshaw
Graphic Content Director: Sandra Hundacker
Maps & Graphics: David C. Hoerlein, Lauren Mills, Mary Rostad
Digital Asset Coordinator: Orin Dubrow

Avalon Travel
Senior Editor and Series Manager: Maddy McPrasher
Editors: Jamie Andrade, Sierra Machado
Copy Editor: Maggie Ryan
Proofreader: Patrick Collins
Indexer: Stephen Callahan
Production & Typesetting: Lisi Baldwin, Rue Flaherty, Jane Musser
Cover Design: Kimberly Glyder Design
Maps & Graphics: Kat Bennett, Lohnes & Wright

*Although every effort was made to ensure that the information was correct at the time of going to
press, the author and publisher do not assume and hereby disclaim any liability to any party for any
loss or damage caused by errors, omissions, kilt malfunction, or any potential travel disruption due
to labor or financial difficulty, whether such errors or omissions result from negligence, accident, or
any other cause.*

COLOR MAPS

Scotland • Edinburgh • Glasgow

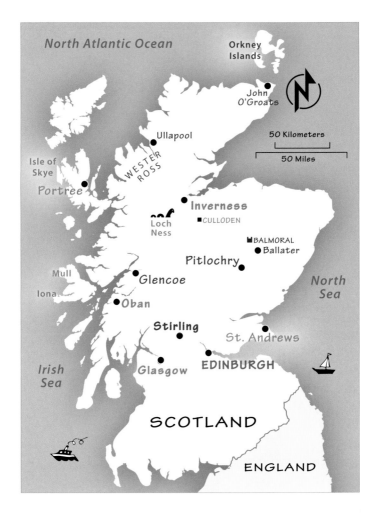

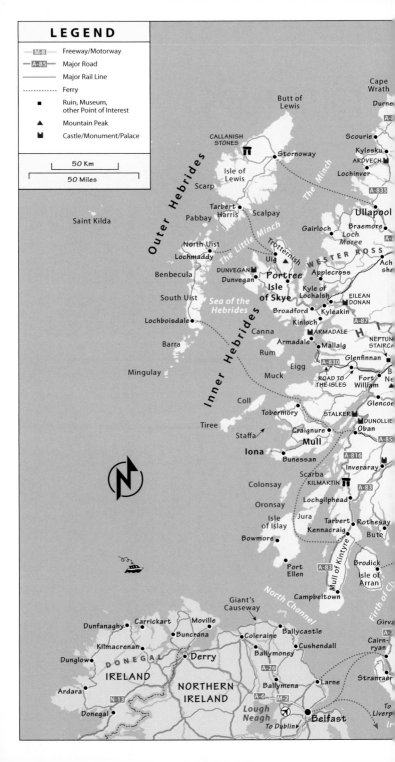

LEGEND

M-8	Freeway/Motorway
A-85	Major Road
	Major Rail Line
....	Ferry
■	Ruin, Museum, other Point of Interest
▲	Mountain Peak
⛫	Castle/Monument/Palace

50 Km

50 Miles

Cape Wrath

Durne

Butt of Lewis

Scourie

Kylesku

ARDVECH

Lochinver

CALLANISH STONES

Stornoway

Isle of Lewis

Scarp

A-835

Ullapool

Saint Kilda

Tarbert
Harris

Pabbay

Scalpay

Braemore
Loch Maree

Outer Hebrides

Gairloch

Trotternish

The Little Minch

WESTER ROSS

Ach
she

North Uist

Lochmaddy

Uig

DUNVEGAN

Dunvegan

Portree

Isle
of Skye

Applecross

Kyle of
Lochalsh

EILEAN
DONAN

Benbecula

South Uist

Sea of the
Hebrides

Broadford

Kyleakin

A-87

Lochboisdale

Kinloch

Canna

ARMADALE

NEPTUN
STAIRC

Armadale

Barra

Rum

Mallaig

A-830

Glenfinnan

B
Ne

Mingulay

Eigg

Muck

ROAD TO
THE ISLES

Fort
William

Inner Hebrides

Glencoe

Coll

Tiree

Tobermory

STALKER

DUNOLLIE

Oban

Staffa

Craignure

Mull

A-85

Iona

Bunessan

A-816

Inveraray

Colonsay

Scarba

KILMARTIN

A-83

Oronsay

Lochgilphead

Isle
of Islay

Jura

Tarbert

Rothesay

Bowmore

Kennacraig

Bute

Brodick

Isle of
Arran

Port
Ellen

A-83

Mull of Kintyre

Firth of Cl

Campbeltown

North Channel

Giant's
Causeway

Girva

Dunfanaghy

Carrickart

Moville

Ballycastle

A-7

Kilmacrenan

Buncrana

Coleraine

Cushendall

Cairn-
ryan

Dunglow

DONEGAL

Derry

Ballymoney

A-26

Stranraer

Ardara

IRELAND

NORTHERN
IRELAND

Ballymena

A-6   M-2

Larne

To
Liverp

Donegal

N-13

Lough
Neagh

Belfast

To Dublin

Ir

The Minch

Scotland

Orkney Islands

Mainland
Stromness • • Kirkwall
Orkney Islands

Pentland Firth

Scrabster
Thurso • • Gills
MEY
Halkirk
• John O'Groats

• Tongue
A-836

• Wick

A-9

• Kinbrace
A-99

• Helmsdale

• Lairg

Alness
A-9

• Brora
• Golspie
• Dornoch

Moray Firth

Orkney Islands
Westray   North Ronaldsay
Rousay   Sanday Island
SKARA BRAE 🏛   Stronsay Island
Mainland
Stromness • • Kirkwall
Scapa Flow
Hoy
South Ronaldsay
Scabster • • Gills • John O'Groats
Thurso •
Pentland Firth

• Fraserburgh

To Kirkwall, Orkney Islands & Lerwick, Shetland Islands

Elgin
A-96
Nairn
• Keith
■ CAWDOR
erness ✈
CULLODEN ■   • Huntly
A-82   *Spey* A-95
UHART   • Grantown   *Speyside*
■ Loch Ness   A-9
A-96
• Ellon

ort
ustus
• Aviemore   • Ballater   *Dee*   • Aberdeen
■ BALMORAL
• Dalwhinnie   Cairngorms National Park   • Stonehaven
DUNNOTTAR ■
C O T L A N D   A-90
BLAIR ■
• Pitlochry   Brechin •   • Montrose
Aberfeldy   GLAMIS ■ Forfar •
Loch Tay   A-9   Dunkeld •
• Kenmore   • Arbroath
• Killin   Dundee •
A-84   Perth •   Leuchars •   *North Sea*
Crieff •   • St. Andrews
M-90   **E A S T   N E U K**
e Trossachs   • Crail
DOUNE A-9   • Leslie   • Anstruther
ch   Culross •   *Firth of Forth*
ond   Stirling ■
Falkirk •   • Dunbar
yde   M-8   ✈ ⊗ **Edinburgh**
Glasgow ●   A-1
• Motherwell   • Eyemouth
East   A-7   Duns •
Kilbride   • Berwick-upon-Tweed
oon   • Kilmarnock   Coldstream •   Holy Island
y Prestwick   M-74   • Galashiels   • Wooler
yr   **B O R D E R S**   A-1
ybole   Hawick •   • Jedburgh   • Alnwick
• Moffat   A-68   • Amble
L O W L A N D S   **ENGLAND**
A-7
Newton   • Dumfries   • Tynemouth
Stewart   M-74   HADRIAN'S WALL   A-69   • Hexham   **Newcastle** ●
• Kirkcudbright   Carlisle •   • Brampton   • Sunderland
• Wigton   M-6   Durham •
• Whithorn   *Solway Firth*   Penrith •   A-1   • Hartlepool
Keswick •   To Manchester   To York
LAKE DIST.

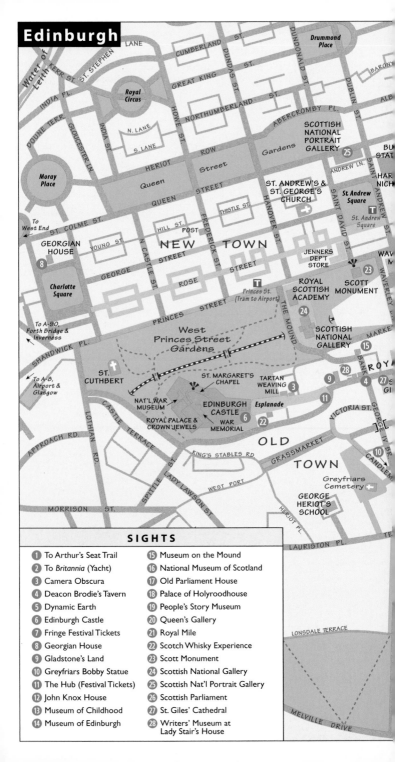

Edinburgh

SIGHTS

1. To Arthur's Seat Trail
2. To *Britannia* (Yacht)
3. Camera Obscura
4. Deacon Brodie's Tavern
5. Dynamic Earth
6. Edinburgh Castle
7. Fringe Festival Tickets
8. Georgian House
9. Gladstone's Land
10. Greyfriars Bobby Statue
11. The Hub (Festival Tickets)
12. John Knox House
13. Museum of Childhood
14. Museum of Edinburgh
15. Museum on the Mound
16. National Museum of Scotland
17. Old Parliament House
18. Palace of Holyroodhouse
19. People's Story Museum
20. Queen's Gallery
21. Royal Mile
22. Scotch Whisky Experience
23. Scott Monument
24. Scottish National Gallery
25. Scottish Nat'l Portrait Gallery
26. Scottish Parliament
27. St. Giles' Cathedral
28. Writers' Museum at Lady Stair's House

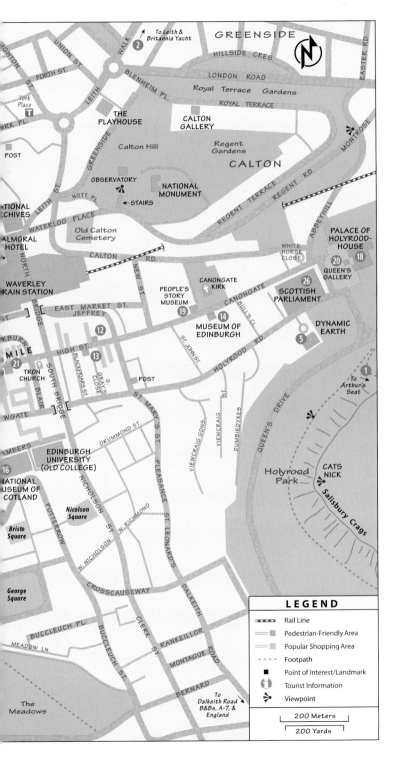

Glasgow

LEGEND

- ▪▪▪▪ Rail Line
- ▬▬ Pedestrian-Friendly Area
- ▬▬ Popular Shopping Area
- 🛈 Tourist Information

200 Meters
200 Yards

CEDAR ST.
N WOODSIDE RD.
ST. GEORGE'S RD.
WINDSOR TERRACE
N WOODSIDE RD.
MARYHILL RD.

SPEIR'S WHARF
CRAIGHILL RD.
GARSCUBE RD.
EDINGTON ST.
WINNI...

St George's Cross Ⓜ
N. CANAL
PAYNE...

ST. GEORGE'S RD.
W PRINCE'S ST.
GRANT ST.
ST. GEORGE'S RD.

M-8
PHOENIX RD.
M-8

ST. EWART ST.
MALLAIG...
YORK DUNDEE RD.
RENTON ST.
MILTON ST.

W GRAHAM ST.
Ⓜ Cowcaddens
COWCADDENS

19 TENEMENT HOUSE MUSEUM
BUCCLEUCH LN.
BUCCLEUCH ST.
DALHOUSIE LN.
HILL ST.
BARREL HILL ST.
GARNET ST.
REID BLDG.
SCOTT ST.
ROSE ST.
ROSE ST.

NAT'L PIPING CENTRE 12
McPHATER ST.

Glasgo Caledor Univers

FOOTBRIDGE
To 9
Ⓑ
RENFREW ST.
SAUCHIEHALL ST.
DALHOUSIE ST.
Ⓑ
COWCADDENS RD.
RENFREW ST.
Concert Square
Ⓟ
21

CHARING CROSS TRAIN STATION
ELMBANK ST.
NEWTON ST.
SCHOOL OF ART (CLOSED)
SAUCHIEHALL LN.
SAUCHIEHALL ST.
HOLLAND ST.
DOUGLAS ST.
11 MACKINTOSH AT THE WILLOW TEAROOMS
RENFREW LN.
SAUCHIEHALL ST.
W NILE ST.
BUCHAN
BUS STAT
KILLERMON
8 CONCE HALL

Ⓑ
BATH ST.
BATH LN.
W REGENT ST.
BATH ST.
BATH LN.
BATH ST.

M-8
Blythswood Square
W GEORGE ST.
W REGENT ST.
W GEORGE ST.
W GEORGE LN.
PITT ST.
BLYTHSWOOD ST.
DOUGLAS ST.
HOPE ST.
RENFIELD ST.
WEST NILE ST.
W REGENT ST.
W GEORGE ST.
BATH LN.
BATH ST.

1 Buchanan
Ⓜ
14 🛈
QUE STR TRA STA

ST. VINCENT LN.
ST. VINCENT ST.
CITIZEN LN.

CITY CENTRE
BOTHWELL ST.
BOTHWELL LN.
WATERLOO ST.
2
GORDON ST.
GOMA 7
17

CADOGAN ST.
HOLM ST.
THE LIGHTHOUSE
MURALS 10
BUCHANAN ST.
MITCHELL ST.
QUEEN ST.

To Loch Lomond & Oban
ARGYLE ST.
ARGYLE ST.
GLASGOW CENTRAL STATION
22
4
ARGYLE ST.

WASHINGTON ST.
McALPINE ST.
CARRICK ST.
BROWN ST.
YORK ST.
ROBERTSON ST.
JAMES WATT ST.
OSWALD ST.

To 16
BROOMIELAW
St Enoch
ST. ENOCH CENTER
HOWARD ST.
HOWARD ST.
FOX ST.
CLYDE ST.

M-8
River Clyde
TRADESTON PEDESTRIAN BRIDGE
KING GEORGE V BRIDGE
GLASGOW BRIDGE
Ⓟ

TRADESTON
To Airport
WEST ST.
CLYDE PL.
PAISLEY RD.
SUSPENSION BRIDGE
To 3

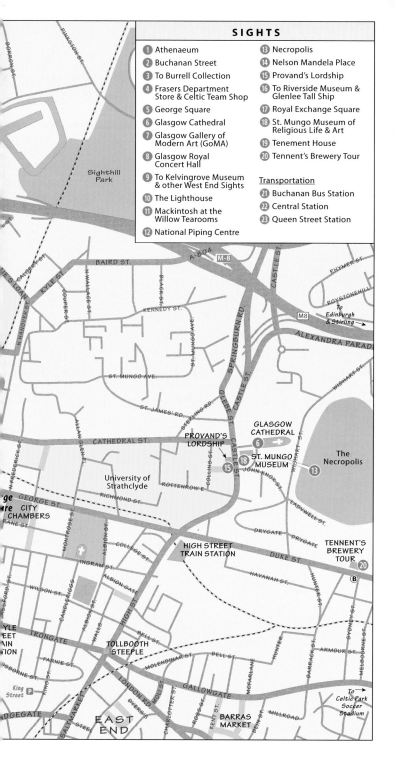

SIGHTS

1. Athenaeum
2. Buchanan Street
3. To Burrell Collection
4. Frasers Department Store & Celtic Team Shop
5. George Square
6. Glasgow Cathedral
7. Glasgow Gallery of Modern Art (GoMA)
8. Glasgow Royal Concert Hall
9. To Kelvingrove Museum & other West End Sights
10. The Lighthouse
11. Mackintosh at the Willow Tearooms
12. National Piping Centre

13. Necropolis
14. Nelson Mandela Place
15. Provand's Lordship
16. To Riverside Museum & Glenlee Tall Ship
17. Royal Exchange Square
18. St. Mungo Museum of Religious Life & Art
19. Tenement House
20. Tennent's Brewery Tour

Transportation
21. Buchanan Bus Station
22. Central Station
23. Queen Street Station

More for your trip!
Maximize the experience with Rick Steves as your guide

Guidebooks
Make side trips smooth and affordable with Rick's Britain and Ireland guides

Planning Maps
Use Rick's pre-trip planning tool for mapping out your itinerary

Rick's TV Shows
Preview your destinations with a variety of shows covering Scotland

Rick's Audio Europe™ App
Get a free self-guided audio tour for Edinburgh's top sights

Small Group Tours
Take a lively, low-stress Rick Steves tour through Scotland

For all the details, visit ricksteves.com